THE AMERICAN MARTIAL ARTS ALLIANCE

MARTIAL ARTS
MASTERS & PIONEERS
SERIES FINAL EDITION

Volume 3
SECOND EDITION

By

GRAND MASTER JESSIE BOWEN

Elite
PUBLICATIONS

2020 WHO'S REALLY WHO IN THE MARTIAL ARTS

i

THE AMERICAN MARTIAL ARTS ALLIANCE

MARTIAL ARTS MASTERS & PIONEERS

SPECIAL SERIES SECOND EDITION

FEATURING

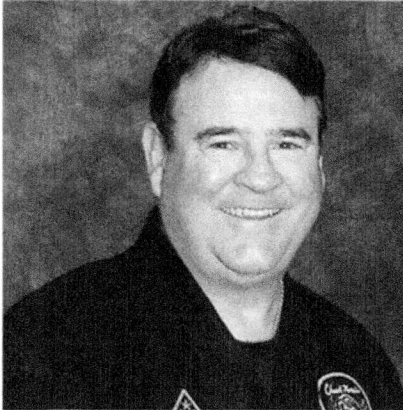
KEN GALLACHER

REGGIE COCHRAN

AARON NORRIS

AL FARRIS

JERRY SILVA

MICHAEL FARADAY

BERNIE FLEEMAN

TIM FOX

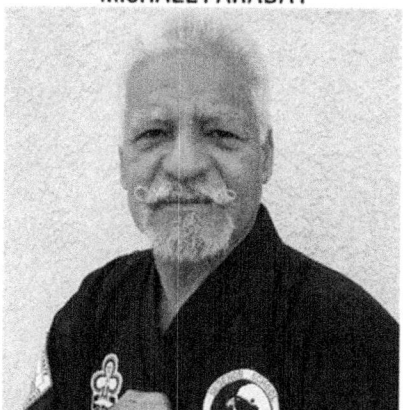
EUGENE SEDENO

2020 WHO'S REALLY WHO IN THE MARTIAL ARTS

Publisher: Elite Publications

First Printing of Vol. 3: June 2020

Second Edition of Vol. 3: November 2020

Language: English

Paperback ISBN-13: 9798565504002

Hardcover ISNB-13: 9781716419560

Library of Congress Control Number: 2020910382

Elite Publications, 1290 E Arlington Blvd, Greenville, NC 27858

http://www.whoswhointhemartialarts.com/

Ordering Information: Special discounts are available on quantity purchases by corporations, associations, educators, and others. For details, contact the publisher at the above address U.S. trade bookstores and wholesalers: Please contact Jessie Bowen.
Tel: (919) 618-8075 or email amaawhoswho@gmail.com.

THE AMERICAN MARTIAL ARTS ALLIANCE

MARTIAL ARTS MASTERS & PIONEERS

Publisher:

Elite Publications

1290 E. Arlington Blvd

Greenville, SC 27858

American Martial Arts Alliance

www.whoswhointhemartialarts.com

Editors:

Grand Master Jessie Bowen

Jessica C. Phillips

Christopher J. McLoughlin

Associate Editor:

Gwendolyn Bowen

Marketing Coordinator:

Jessica C. Phillips

Interior Design & Book Cover:

Krystal Harvey

Tiger Shark Media + Management

www.tigersharkmediausa.com

Contributors:

Joe Corley

Jeff Smith

Jim T. Chong

TABLE OF
CONTENTS

TABLE OF
CONTENTS

TABLE OF
CONTENTS

MARTIAL ARTS MASTERS & PIONEERS

Acknowledgements

I would like to express my greatest appreciation to Grand Master Chuck Norris, Grand Master Benny Urquidez, and the many other martial artists for entrusting their biographical information within the Martial Arts Masters and Pioneers Book.

I would also like to thank the subsequent individual's Joe Corley, Jeff Smith, Reggie Cohran, Arron Norris, and Carlo Silva for their expansive contributions of helping bring together this amazing group of martial artists.

Finally, to my caring, loving, and supportive wife, Gwendolyn Bowen, my deepest gratitude. Your encouragement, as we were faced with the many challenges, was much appreciated and noted.

Hanshi
Jessie Bowen

MARTIAL ARTS MASTERS & PIONEERS

Foreword

As this 2020 edition of Who's Who in the Martial Arts was being completed, we had a chance to spend a weekend with our friend of five decades, GM Chuck Norris. It was a momentous gathering of our predecessors in the martial arts, like Chuck, and our contemporaries, representing the first and second generation of American Martial Arts icons, tournament fighters, and champions in the United States.

Dedicated to the lifetime contributions of GM Norris, the subtitle for GM Jessie Bowen's book is "Giving Back for a Lifetime. "

At a celebration of life for our recently departed friend GM Skipper Mullins in Dallas, GM Norris shared his six decades of personal experiences with Skipper Mullins, who had been Chuck's formidable foe in the ring and a lifetime friend outside the ring.

GM Norris was a designated "honorary pallbearer" for Skipper, and he was told at graveside, "Chuck, just sit with your bride, Gena, and let these young guys do the heavy lifting." Chuck responded, staunchly, "No way. Skipper was my friend! "

These small gestures of friendship for those close to him and those he had never met have marked the life and legacy that is Chuck Norris.

Later in the day, as his wife and friends tried to shield him from his adoring fans, Chuck removed the COVID-19 protective mask from his face and stood with kids and adults alike, having his picture taken - giving back in a small way (big way to them) to fans he had never met and would likely never see again.

Chuck's friend Ted Gambordella pointed out that it was just last year in a fundraiser in Ft. Worth for Chuck's good friend GM J. Pat Burleson that Chuck stood for 4 1/2 hours with no break taking pictures with hundreds of people to raise funds for his friend J. Pat.

Chuck joined Jeff Smith on the cover of Fighter magazine with President George HW Bush, as they worked together in the President's Sports Fitness Council and Chuck's personal foundation, Karate Kicks Drugs Out of America, now known as Kickstart Kids.

In the past 30 years, Chuck has provided lessons, grants, and even college education for more than 100,000 kids who have been involved in the Kickstart program in his home state of Texas.

And so as Chuck has just celebrated his eighth decade on the planet, we know for sure that he has spent six of those decades sharing his enthusiasm, knowledge, stardom and wealth with those of us who were lucky enough to be in his circle of friends and with those whose needs he was able to supplement by giving of himself.

Thank you, Chuck Norris, first for your personal friendship and from all of us for being one of the really good guys that we all have been able to look up to for these many years.

-Jeff Smith & Joe Corley
PKA Worldwide

MARTIAL ARTS MASTERS & PIONEERS

WHY THE MARTIAL ARTS IN THE NEW ECONOMY IS PARAMOUNT

During this very historic year, we can notice that things have changed dramatically...especially since the "Lockdown". Arguably, this time period has been very significant in helping us all determine what is really most important. It's not about what we own or the external things, but about our internal mindset and how we approach and see things.

For some, the current events have been extremely traumatic. For others, this has been a time of self-reflection and discovery, At the same time, we have all been given time to determine the things that are most important to us. Some have discovered that it is about self-preservation while to others, it is about how they could best support those around them. Regardless of where we personally stand on the spectrum, it has been a time where we all are able to take a deeper inner journey as to what we are all about not just as an individual, but also as what we call "humanity".

Now more than ever, *the disciplines that are at the core of the martial artist paves the way to innovation.* Self-discovery is more significant than ever. As we read the stories that are captured in this book, we can all be inspired by the inspiration, discipline, heart, passion, focus, and other character qualities that the stories represent. This is not just another anthology or book of stories. This book is significant as it highlights some of those that are foundational to shaping what we know as the Martial Arts today starting with GM Chuck Norris and GM Benny "The Jet" Urquidez.

While we are able to appreciate all the wisdom and discipline that these specific stories represent, let's not forget that what we read in these pages are not to just educate, but also to help us be inspired and to rekindle, ignite, and/or feed ourselves with the passion to complete what we personally set out to accomplish in life. *It's not just about the people in this book but rather what we do within ourselves because of their story.* Arguably, the Martial Arts and Artists represent a significant cornerstone to the success and innovation of the future. Congratulations to those that have been featured and to you for having access to this wonderful resource.

Here is to an incredible new journey of self-discovery to live out our remaining days intentionally as we honor those stories captured in this book which serves as a significant milestone and historical reference to the foundation of the future.

"Never forget where you come from...and live to where you are destined to be."

-Jim T. Chong
Publicist, AMAAF
jtc.publicist@gmail.com
www.jimtchong.com

MARTIAL ARTS MASTERS & PIONEERS

Introduction to the Who's Who Series

The Martial Arts Masters & Pioneers book is not intended to be just another martial arts book. It is intended to be both inspirational and motivational as you discover martial artists whose lives have been changed through the study of an application of the principles taught in the martial arts.

For more than 1500 years, martial arts has played a key role in personal development training and through the pages of this book you will discover the journey of hundreds of martial artists sharing their journeys, describing how the martial arts has impacted their lives.

Grand Master Bowen's Martial Arts Masters & Pioneers Edition represents the shift we Americans have brought to the arts, by recognizing the accomplishments of the individuals who practiced and perfected their arts, as opposed to the glorification of the arts themselves. In reading about what the Martial Arts Masters & Pioneers Leaders here have done, one can only marvel at the magnitude of individual effort expended and sacrifices made, from the grassroots activities to global media and organizational results.

So, rather than debating which blocks or strikes or styles are more perfect, this work heralds the individual strengths of those who share the marital bond in America, whose legacies have impacted martial arts in America and thus, around the world.

No matter where you are in life, the martial arts offer a powerful tool to aid you physically, mentally and spiritually as your mind and body work better together. The study of the martial arts helps individuals look inside and find their purpose. Along the path, they discover how to let go of the negativity and the things that hold them back in life. Enjoy here the journeys of Masters & Pioneers.

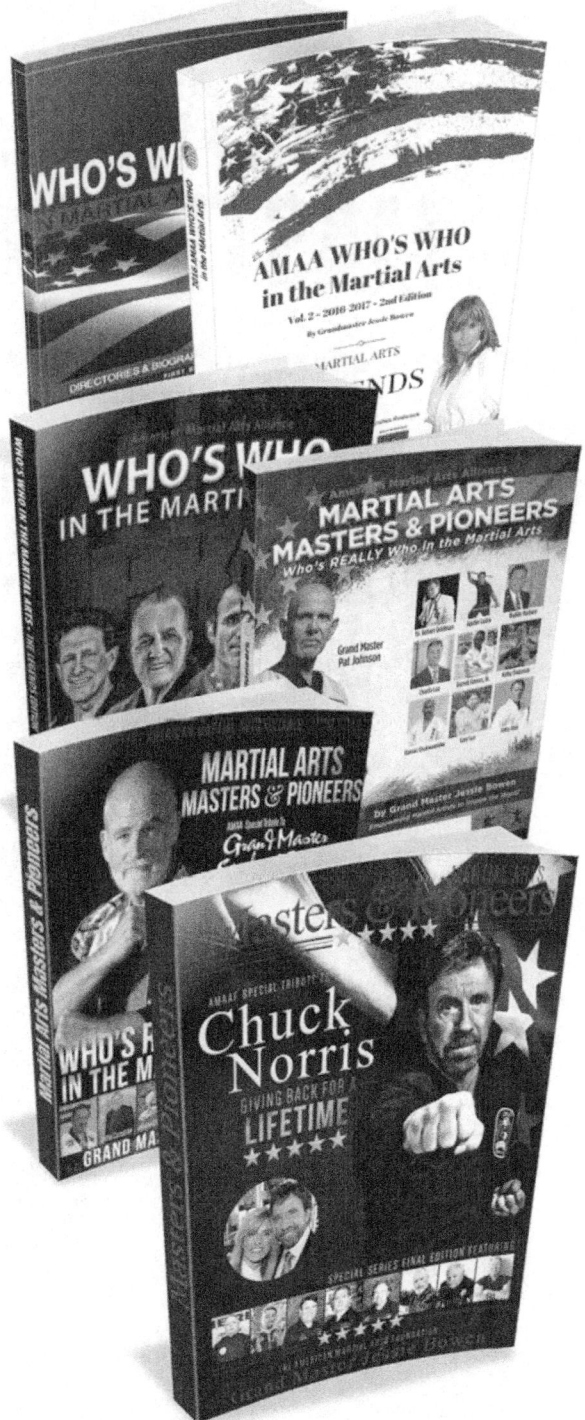

THE AMERICAN MARTIAL ARTS ALLIANCE

MARTIAL ARTS MASTERS & PIONEERS

HONORS

Chuck Norris

"GIVING BACK FOR A LIFETIME"

MARTIAL ARTS MASTERS & PIONEERS
HONORS
GRAND MASTER CHUCK NORRIS
GIVING BACK FOR A LIFETIME

And for those in the martial arts who have worked with him these past six decades, he is known to be a giving, inspirational leader who has positively affected many millions of lives, both directly and indirectly through his chosen fields of influence.

As this Who's Who Pioneers and Masters 2020 edition was being completed, Chuck and his wife Gena were at the Celebration of Life and Funeral Service for his friend of nearly six decades for two hours as he was being laid to rest. It was an assembly of the finest first and second generation American martial arts icons who had fought in the glory fighting era of Skipper Mullins and Chuck Norris.

Assigned the role of "honorary pallbearer" in the service program, the Mullins family said to Chuck "Sit here with Gena, and the young guys here will do the heavy lifting." Chuck's immediate response was, "No way. Skipper was my friend." These six words reflect the life attitude of Carlos Ray Norris, just two months after celebrating his 8th decade on the planet.

In the martial arts world, he is known by one name—Chuck.

In the film world, he is known as the nice guy who plays tough guys, and in real life is as tough as they come. And as nice.

The American Martial Arts Alliance proudly dedicates this 2020 edition to the life and career of Grand Master Norris and his incomparable impact on American Martial Arts for these past six decades.

Born Carlos Ray Norris in Ryan, Oklahoma on March 10, 1940, Chuck was the eldest of his two brothers. Chuck's brother Wieland Norris, born July 12, 1943 was KIA in Vietnam in 1970.

Aaron Norris, the youngest of the three, has done everything with Chuck from producing and directing their film and television projects to serving as Chairman for United Fighting Arts Federation. The Norris family relocated to Torrance, California when Chuck was 12 years old, and he was enrolled in high school there until he graduated in the class of 1958.

Chuck Norris joined the Air Force after graduation from high school and was stationed in Korea where he was an MP (Military Police) while in the service. Chuck became a voracious martial artist. He trained every night in Tang Soo Do and spent all day Saturday and Sunday training in judo (yudo in Korea). He left Korea as Black Belt in Tang Soo Do and a brown belt in judo.

After returning to his home in California, he worked for Northrop Aviation and taught Tang Soo

Do as a sideline. Just a couple of years later he had started teaching full time in his own martial arts school which not only flourished but also attracted a number of Hollywood's famous including Bob Barker from television and Steve McQueen from the movies.

TOURNAMENTS AND CHAMPIONSHIPS FOR A DECADE...

Now an international film and television star, Chuck started out as a tournament fighter. That endeavor lasted for a decade from 1964 through 1974, and it was a spectacular time for him. By 1966 he dominated the tournament scene and was almost unstoppable in competition. Fast, agile, powerful and relentless, he was in the first era of the thinking man's fighters winning over the best known fighters of the time from coast to coast.

His first major tournament victories began in 1966 with wins at both the National Karate Championships and also the All-Star Championships.

In 1967 the Norris name became well known when he won the World Middleweight Karate Championship and the All-American Karate Championship.

He set records with victories in the Ed Parker Internationals, World Professional Middleweight Karate Championship, All-American

Chuck and Joe Lewis (RIP) square off at Ed Parker's Internationals Championship in Long Beach

Championship, National Tournament of Champions, American Tang Soo Championship, and the North American Karate Championship, all in 1968.

Determined, handsome and polite, Norris won the admiration of his peers the hard way. Privately he was esteemed as a man who was respected and envied in the ring, who loved "his Mom's apple pie" and who loved to fight. And he did it well. He compiled a fight record of 65-5 with victories over all other champions of the day, and retired as undefeated Professional Full-Contact Middleweight Champion in 1974.

In his own words, Chuck tells us, "Whatever luck I

had, I made. I was never a natural athlete, but I paid my dues in sweat and concentration and took the time necessary to learn karate and become world champion."

Toward the end of his career as a fighter/competitor Chuck was a welcomed personality and friend to several of the country's major point and professional karate tournaments including one of the most prestigious events of the time, the Battle of Atlanta. Chuck attended many of the milestone events at the Battle of Atlanta, including the Professional Karate Association (PKA) events staged in Battle of Atlanta finals. Norris and company consisted of martial arts celebrities Pat Johnson, Bob Wall, Mike Stone, Tadashi

Chuck and Pat Johnson join Joe Corley on Finals Stage in the Georgia Dome for Battle of Atlanta Silver Anniversary

Yamashita, and Chuck's star fighter students including Darnell Garcia, Howard Jackson, Chip

Wright and John Natividad. And whether running a ring as Referee or Judge or merely watching a match, the fighters stepped up their game under Chuck's scrutiny.

ACTION IN FRONT OF THE CAMERAS...

Today we know that it was Steve McQueen, one of Norris' private students who became a close friend, who urged him to try acting, and he did. It began with an uncredited part in 1968 in The Wrecking Crew, an adventure movie starring Dean Martin, Elke Somer and Sharon Tate. But Norris wasn't alone in that film. Joe Lewis, Ed Parker, and Mike Stone were also very recognizable but uncredited as was Bruce Lee, a fight and stunt advisor.

Starring in some 200 episodes of Walker, Texas Ranger, people all over the world learned "the Eyes of the Ranger are Upon You!"

Now, over a half century later, the Chuck Norris

filmography is overwhelmingly impressive. He has a star on the Hollywood walk of fame, well-deserved for leading roles in more than 30 motion pictures and five made-for-television movies. But even with these credits, he is likely best known to the viewing audience for his near 200 consecutive leading appearances in "Walker, Texas Ranger" as the show's hero, Cordell Walker.

BUT NEVER REALLY RETIRED...

A ROUNDHOUSE KICK OF REFRESHMENT

Retired but by no means inactive, Chuck is married to Gena O'Kelly, is a father and grand-father, and lives on a ranch in Navasota, Texas. He and his wife both serve on the board of the National Council of Bible Curriculum in Public Schools.

He and Gena are Spokespersons for the Total Gym Fitness infomercials.

Chuck and Gena, while digging for an additional water source for cattle, discovered a huge aquifer on the Norris property, and now distribute a healthy drinking water, CForce Water. (CForce Bottling Co. is a certified woman-owned business founded in 2015 by Gena and Chuck Norris. Under CEO Gena Norris' leadership, CForce water is now available in dozens of states through thousands of retail locations. CForce is a full-service bottling facility that offers co-packing, raw bottle sales and branded product).

Chuck is also the author of five books.

He works for many charities, including the Funds for Kids, Veterans Administration National Salute to Hospitalized Veterans, the United Way, Make-a-Wish Foundation and KickStart, a nonprofit organization he created to help battle drugs and violence in schools.

He received "Veteran of the Year 2001" honor at the 6th Annual American Veteran Awards, visited US forces fighting in Iraq in November 2006, and he was made an honorary Marine in March 2007.

Chuck and his brother Aaron were made honorary Texas Rangers by Gov. Rick Perry on December 2, 2010 in Dallas, Texas.

He is a very vocal conservative Republican spokesperson and fundraiser, but has ruled out running for elected office himself, is a born again Christian, and an NRA member. In 2006 he won "The Jewish Humanitarian Man of the Year Award."

IN AND FOR THE MARTIAL ARTS...

In 2005 he founded the World Combat League, a full-contact, team-based martial arts competition.

He has founded the Chuck Norris System which he evolved from Chun Kuk Do ("The Universal Way") and American Tang Soo Do.

He has a 10th degree Black Belt in the United Fighting Arts Federation Chuck Norris System, and also an 8th degree black belt in Tae Kwon Do.

He has a 3rd degree black belt in Brazilian Jiu Jitsu (UFAF B JJ) under the Machado Brothers.

He holds a black belt in UFAF Krav Maga Force (KMF).

AND BEYOND ... KICKSTART KIDS

Thirty years ago as a martial artist and philanthropist Chuck stepped up to the line and took another fighting stance. It was in August of 1990 that he squared off and formed the Kick Drugs Out of America Foundation, and today it's known simply as Kickstart Kids. His goal was to provide a martial arts program that would instill in children all the character building traits that the martial arts could offer, and at no cost.

By 1992 Chuck, with the help of then-president George H.W. Bush, formally introduced the program to four schools in the Houston, Texas area. By 2003 and with the help of his wife Gena, the organization was formally renamed Kickstart Kids and is actively teaching character building through karate, empowering youth with core values including discipline and respect.

With the usual Norris tenacity, the program is a resounding success for Chuck and Gena. There are nearly 60 schools throughout Texas teaching almost 10,000 students, mostly in middle, junior and high schools. The not for profit organization is chaired by Chuck and Gena, and there are now more than 90 people on staff.

Chuck & Gena speak to the friends and family of Skipper Mullins at his Celebration of Life in Dallas

AND THE UNITED FIGHTING ARTS FEDERATION (UFAF) …

Chuck also put together the United Fighting Arts Federation (UFAF) in 1979 as the governing and sanctioning body for the Chuck Norris System. This is his personal development and fighting system evolved from Tang Soo Do and Chun Kuk Do. Since 2015, UFAF has provided technical standards for instruction and advancement in the system, and it also provides its students, instructors, and schools with Chuck Norris System rank certification, educational opportunities, special events, online community access, and other services.

Recently UFAF has expanded its scope to include other martial arts, specifically Brazilian Jiu Jitsu (USAF BJJ) and Krav Maga (KMF) in addition to the Chuck Norris System (CNS) and Chuck himself oversees UFAF's activities as Chairman, along with President Ken Gallacher and its board members, including brother Aaron, Reggie Cochran and others.

Chuck Norris is the most widely celebrated Martial Artist on the planet, and his legions of global fans raised their glasses in a collective toast as he has celebrated 8 glorious decades—Giving Back for a Lifetime.

MARTIAL ARTS MASTERS & PIONEERS
HONORS

GENA NORRIS
FIRST LADY OF UFAF AND A FORCE OF NATURE

Gena O'Kelley Norris is First Lady of UFAF and a Force of Nature.

It's a long-standing axiom— "Behind every great man is a great woman". And in the Norris family, we add "Behind every great woman is a great man!"

Partners in life. Gena and Chuck Norris are often quoted as saying their "better half" is their "best friend", "love of their life" and "great partner" in each and every thing they do, from organizing incredibly busy schedules, raising great twins together, building lives and futures for others via KickStart Kids and United Fighting Arts Federation (UFAF), TV series, film projects and so much more .

The subtitle of this 2020 edition of *Masters and Pioneers is Giving Back for a Lifetime*, and the words penned by Oyin Balogun for Amo Mamma described perfectly the synergy brought to the family Norris by Gena O'Kelley Norris: "Gena O'Kelley has lived a life of faith, strength, and partnership alongside her beloved husband, Chuck Norris. She continues to do so and embodies the 21st-century woman who has it all.

Gena addresses a group of Women CEOs discussing their CForce mission of giving back to their community

"While the wives of most Hollywood stars, who are not in the movie business may get shadowed by their husband's fame, Gena O'Kelley is not one of them. She might not be a big movie star, but the former model forged a path for herself that has brought her joy, contentment, and a sense of fulfillment."

In addition to all the incredible work above, Gena O'Kelley Norris, known to so many as The *First Lady of UFAF,* is also the CEO of CForce Bottling Company—the bottling and distribution of the Artesian Water that flows from deep in the earth on the Norris Ranch.

Add to that the philanthropic efforts that she and her generous partner are involved in, and Gena is indeed the embodiment of the successful 21st century entrepreneur.

Many THANKS TO YOU, Gena, from all of us, for all you have worked on with Chuck to provide to so many! Together—you two are indeed Forces of Nature!

God Bless!

THE AMERICAN MARTIAL ARTS ALLIANCE

MARTIAL ARTS
MASTERS & PIONEERS
HONORS

THE UNITED FIGHTING ARTS FEDERATION

...AND THEN IT BEGAN!

MARTIAL ARTS MASTERS & PIONEERS

HONORING THE UNITED FIGHTING ARTS FEDERATION (UFAF)

Formed originally in 1979, the United Fighting Arts Federation™ (UFAF), the Constitution for UFAF was ratified at its original meeting and printed first in 1980.

Now, 40 years later, UFAF is a worldwide martial arts membership organization with Grand Master Chuck Norris as Founder, Aaron Norris as Chairman and Ken Gallacher its President since 2008.

UFAF is the governing and sanctioning body for the Chuck Norris System (formerly Chun Kuk Do), UFAF Krav Maga Force, and UFAF Brazilian Jiu Jitsu, providing technical standards for instruction and advancement in the systems. Members of UFAF receive certification of their CNS, UFAF KMF, and UFAF BJJ rank/level from Mr. Norris himself! Aside from UFAF, the only other organization in the world where this happens is KICKSTART KIDS, UFAF's official charity, also founded by Mr. Norris.

President Ken Gallacher has recently announced that UFAF, as part of Grand Master Norris' long-term vision, is introducing the UFAF Affiliate Membership program. "In this new Affiliate Program, other styles can join the UFAF Family while retaining their independent styles. The objective is to include those whose organizations will bring their strengths to UFAF, and we will all operate according to the ethics and founding principles of UFAF".

UFAF BOARD OF DIRECTORS:

Chuck Norris: Founder and Chairman
Aaron Norris: Chief Executive Officer
Ken Gallacher: President
Ed Saenz: Director, Training and Advancement
Tip Potter: Director
Chip Wright: Vice President, Director, Tournament and Competition Development
John Presti: Director, Special Events
Tara Cox: Director Operations and Development; Treasurer
Reggie Cochran: Director Brazilian Jiu Jitsu (BJJ)
Stephen Hammersley: Director, UFAF Krav Maga Force (KMF)
David Rodriguez: Director, Latin American Affairs
Steve Nelson: Director of Master Development
Rick Prieto: Director of Training and Development
John Kurek: Director of Kickstart Kids Liaison
Mike Dillard: Director of Professional Development
Steve Giroux: Director of Professional Development

MARTIAL ARTS MASTERS & PIONEERS

HONORING THE UNITED FIGHTING ARTS FEDERATION (UFAF)

UFAF PROVIDES MANY SERVICES AND BENEFITS TO ITS MEMBER STUDENTS, INSTRUCTORS, AND SCHOOLS:

- UFAF KMF, UFAF BJJ and Chuck Norris System rank certification by UFAF and Chuck Norris!

- UFAF Affiliate School Program

- Annual membership card and membership premium

- Uniform patch (Chuck Norris System & UFAF BJJ) signifying membership and style identity

- Special events such as the annual UFAF International Training Conference (ITC) in Las Vegas

- News magazine published online, with "Extras" throughout the year -

- Educational opportunities, curriculums, and certifications

- Online community access

- Instructor training

- Business training for school owners

- Professional martial artist certification

- Access to a network of phenomenal martial artists

TO FIND A SCHOOL NEAR YOU, VISIT THE UFAF SCHOOL FINDER AT WWW.UFAF.ORG

THE AMERICAN MARTIAL ARTS ALLIANCE

MARTIAL ARTS
MASTERS & PIONEERS
HONORS

KICKSTART KIDS®

Character through Karate

GIVING BACK THROUGH KICKSTART KIDS

Chuck Norris' career as a martial artist was well known by the late 1980s. In the 60s and up through the 70s he had established himself as a world class competitor and champion karate fighter, he was a successful entrepreneur businessman operating a chain of karate studios primarily in California but with affiliated facilities throughout the country, and the camera loved him. His successes on the big screen as the hero and star in action motion pictures started in 1968, and his small screen appearances as celebrity guest, host, and commentator, not to mention his roles in popular television shows, kept his name and fame in the public eye. These were the times before the Walker, Texas Ranger days where he'll live on for a long, long time. Simply put, Chuck Norris was a success, but he wanted more. He set another goal for himself and started out to "pay it ahead" by simply giving back.

Chuck with President George HW Bush for early KickStart event

In the Fall of 1990 he founded a martial arts program for children and called it simply Kickstart Kids. The big name was and still is the Kick Drugs Out Of America Foundation. In the early days he funded it himself, and he still does. His idea was to provide a karate-based training program that would instill all the character-building traits that come from the martial arts disciplines, and at no cost to the young men and women who trained.

A short, fast two years later and with the help of his friend and then-president George H. W. Bush, the program was introduced in four junior- and high schools in Houston, Texas area. Taught by Black Belt instructors that he himself had mentored and trained, Chuck's program was a success and has grown steadily over the years. Today some of the instructors are themselves Black Belts who began their own training as a Kickstart Kid.

In 2003, and with the help and support of his best friend and wife, Gena O'Kelley Norris, the organization was formally renamed Kickstart Kids and is in action teaching character building through karate, empowering youth with core values including discipline and respect.

The two Norrises, Chuck and Gena, work with a staff of more than 90 people not including their Board of Directors Lloyd Ford, John G. Gibson, Bill Hickl, Brenda Love-Jones, Mike McSpadden, Kevin Mitchell, Keith Mosing, Laura True, and Special Advisor Mike Forshey.

GIVING BACK THROUGH KICKSTART KIDS

Today there are nearly 60 schools throughout Texas teaching almost 10,000 students, mostly in middle, junior and high schools. There are 62 active programs in session, and over 100,000 students have been impacted by the training. As a significant part of the Norris ethic, the organization was formed to develop self-esteem and focus in at-risk children as a tactic to keep them away from drug-related pressure by training them in martial arts. The daily classes include lessons focusing on eight specific character values from the unique Values Curriculum. These values include honesty, loyalty, courage, discipline, respect, dedication, kindness and responsibility

It is Chuck's vision that by shifting middle school and high school children's focus towards these positive and strengthening endeavors, the children will have the opportunity to build a better future for themselves.

Foundations thrive and grow based on philanthropic contributions, and Kickstart Kids is no exception. KickStart Kids has received great support from many generous supporters over the years and many different fundraisers have been staged to provide the successes for this incredible program.

Chuck's program teaches Honesty, Loyalty, Courage, Discipline, Respect, Dedication, Kindness and Responsibility

PLEASE VISIT
WWW.KICKSTARTKIDS.ORG

Chuck and Gena Norris with KickStart Kids in Patriot Uniforms

AARON NORRIS
AN INCREDIBLE, STALWART BROTHER-IN-ARMS

"We look so forward to sharing with the world at large the incredible influence that we martial artists have had on our society and the culture, and there are so many incredible stories to tell!"

Aaron Norris said "Whoa, the stories I can tell!" as he and Joe Corley started to catch up on the last 5 decades and the great successes of the Norris Brothers. Master Corley had always marveled at the love and affection of the brothers Norris and the incredible family built by and around them, from films and TV to UFAF, KickStart and beyond.

A Stephen Covey Seven Habits principle built on synergy is at the center of these successes. Many strong people working together can produce the best forms of synergy, and Aaron Norris, is and has been, one of the key linchpins.

Some background, important to know: Aaron Norris was a 17-year-old, 150-pound, all-state (California) standout linebacker. Linebacker. The college coaches said, "Put on more muscle and come back to see us!" For those that do not know, linebackers see things differently than other players and other people. Much differently.

This linebacker promptly enlisted in the Army in the Vietnam era, and a year later he was a solid 200 pound "linebacker", but was now vying for an even more challenging position as a "door gunner" on a Huey (helicopter), wanting to hang at the door with a 23 pound M-60 machine gun. "Sadly, they told me I didn't have the mechanical abilities for the job I wanted, so I was trained for other challenging jobs and extended my enlistment another year."

After Advanced Infantry Training, Aaron was specially chosen to train in the Army's Non-Commission Officers Academy. He was chosen because of his leadership abilities, and his rise in rank was fast. Aaron became a Sergeant E-5 in less than a year after joining the Army--and was only 18 years old.

His older brother Wieland had also joined the Army not long after Aaron, and Wieland ended up in Vietnam. Sadly, Wieland was killed in action saving his squad and was awarded the Silver Star for bravery.

Aaron's final year found him on the "Demilitarized Zone" (DMZ), a sergeant in Korea, responsible for a platoon, with bullets flying through the zone. His service period ended shortly thereafter.

Aaron returned to California to the world of film and television. He applied his Norris family values, linebacker attitude and champion martial arts determination that led to the successes an informed observer would expect. Just some of Aaron's feature film directorial credits include Braddock: Missing in Action III, Platoon Leader, Delta Force II, Hitman, Sidekicks, Hellbound, Top Dog and Forest Warrior. Aaron also directed the critically acclaimed two-hour pilot Sons of Thunder" for CBS which was so well received that the network placed an order for six additional episodes.

*Norris Warrior brothers, wearing the Tang Soo Do tops
and symbols proudly and representing the art so powerfully*

Before Aaron started directing films, he wrote and produced Silent Rage, Lone Wolf McQuade and Invasion: U.S.A. He then tried his hand at acting, starring in the HBO production Overkill. He executive-produced and co-wrote Logan's War: Bound by Honor, a Movie of the Week for the CBS television network. He also executive-produced two President's Man, part of CBS' Movies of the Week franchise.

A most important historic factoid. With his brother as Walker and Aaron as the "Show Runner / Executive Producer" starting the second season, Walker Texas Ranger became a Top Ten weekly program for CBS, almost unheard of for a weekend show when homes using television were traditionally way down. Walker ran for 9 seasons and 203 episodes!

And today? It is reported that 1,000,000,000 (one billion) people a day watch Walker, Texas Ranger all over the world! Aaron's website at AaronNorris.com overflows with credits, so many credits.

Aaron is the co-founder of the "ActionFest Film Festival". His partner, Bill Banowsky (CEO Magnolia Pictures), and Aaron have built a successful franchise in the film festival marketplace.

Aaron's fighting prowess got the attention of Black Belt Magazine, reporting another Norris was a top fighter!

Aaron and Ken Gallacher receive their 10th Degree Black Belt certificates from Chuck. They live now in the rare air of 10th Degrees

Aaron owned the film distribution company Tanglewood Entertainment for a number of years during which time he produced and oversaw worldwide distribution of more than a dozen feature films.

In his on-the-ground martial arts life, Aaron Norris taught in and managed Chuck Norris Studios in California. He then ventured east to Virginia Beach to teach in and manage the first Chuck Norris franchised school, a state-of-the-art facility that took martial arts instruction to the next level.

While there, Aaron expanded his competitive side and won the Four Seasons Championship in Las Vegas along with other impressive titles. He then ventured to the Battle of Atlanta in 1974, where the Tournament of Champions drew in fighters from everywhere. Aaron said this was one of his favorite competition stories and learning experiences. Aaron had used the 1973 tournament flyer as his "vision board", inserting his name in the slot that would be the Middleweight Champ in the eliminations in order to face the seeded champions. When he arrived and saw the size of the Middleweight division, he conferred right away with his brother.

Aaron said, "Carlos (Chuck) and I looked at the incredible lineup of talent, he looked at me and he said 'Lineup last Butch (Chuck called me Butch). Chuck told me this would give me a chance to watch all these people fight so I would know what to expect from them, giving me an advantage, since none of them had seen me fight. Long story short, I remember going through 12 bouts that day to win the Battle of Atlanta Middleweight Championship, giving me a slot against the 11 seeded champions. They teased me for "being so tired!" And even though I ended up losing to Fred Wren in the Tournament of Champions that day, everyone at the Battle of Atlanta knew I could fight AND could take shots from Fred Wren!". Joe Corley explained, "Everyone gained much respect for Aaron that day as 'not just another pretty face'!"

Aaron Norris is the CEO of UFAF's Board of Directors.

Fast forward to today, and you see martial artist Aaron Norris as the Chief Executive officer (CEO) of United Fighting Arts Federation, a 10th Degree Black Belt and a man still busy in Film and Television. "We are so proud of all our UFAF members and very excited about our new Affiliate Member program."

The Film/TV Producer/Director Aaron Norris has a mind exploding with exciting projects. "We look so forward to sharing with the world at large the incredible influence that we martial artists have had on our society and the culture, and there are so many incredible stories to tell!"

The Norris brother Aaron is equally moved by his activities in TAPS: Tragedy Assistance Program for Survivors helps the families who have lost loved ones in combat, something Aaron knows a lot about. "The Mission of TAPS is to provide comfort, care and resources to all those grieving the death of a military loved one.

Since 1994, TAPS has provided comfort and hope 24/7 through a national peer support network and connection to grief resources, all at no cost to surviving families and loved ones. I encourage all our fans to visit Taps.org to learn more and to assist", Aaron said.

Giving Back for a Lifetime. Thank you Aaron Norris. Thank you Chuck Norris. Thank you Gena Norris. Thank you to all the Norris related families for all you continue to do!

Visit AaronNorris.com for so much more…more films, video and great life adventures!

KEN GALLACHER
UFAF PRESIDENT

"We have all admired Grand Master Norris and have been inspired by him for all these years, and it is our pleasure to have helped him continue this fine tradition we all grew up in."

Years after seeing GM Norris flying, kicking and breaking, Master Gallacher himself breaks 4 boards with flying side kick!

As president of Chuck Norris' United Fighting Arts Federation, Ken Gallacher has nearly 5 decades of powerful memories in his martial arts segmented brain and mind. Now a 10th Degree Black Belt, a successful businessman with a great family and all the things that come with hard work, Ken reflects on his years with the most well-known martial artist on planet earth.

Imagine the 17 year old high school student watching Chuck Norris break boards so fast that the techniques are still a blur in Ken's mind, after which Chuck jumped over at least 4 people and smashed more boards with a flying side kick. It's often said that sometimes one event can lead to the change in your life, and this event was the start for Ken Gallacher. Now just 5.3 decades later, Ken has been the President of his role model's entire organization for 12 years.

After a brief stint in California with Jimmy Woo in Kung Fu, Ken was able to enroll in the Chuck Norris school of Dick Douglas School in Las Vegas in 1973. He was then lucky enough to have Chuck personally sit on his testing boards from his first white belt test all the way through 3rd degree.

Ken says, "I was a decent local competitor and I even tried my hand in some full contact bouts. My wife Marcia and I determined together that would not be the right career choice, so I focused on developing my insurance agency"—a good move that has served his family of 4 kids and 16 grandkids well. His eldest daughter Tara, now a board member for UFAF, began competition herself at age 6 and has been what Ken calls a powerful "Mighty Mite", now with 4 kids of her own. Marcia and Ken's 16 grand kids range in age from 8 – 24 and they have one 2-year-old great grandchild and have another "on the way".

Adversity and Opportunity: In his book Against All Odds, Chuck Norris described a 1987 accident experience where a drunk driver struck Ken Gallacher's parked van at 75 MPH on an expressway shoulder, launching Ken's body into the outside lane, where an astute driver was able to stop from running over him and saved him from others behind him dong the same. As he was recuperating from a fractured hip, bruised heart muscle, punctured spleen and lung, Grand Master Norris visited him in the hospital and invited him to a reorganization meeting the following weekend. It was there that Chuck appointed him Executive Vice President of UFAF. In 2008, Grand Master Norris promoted Ken to President of UFAF, as Aaron Norris became CEO of their United Fighting Arts Federation.

Ken has grown a beautiful Gallacher family at the same time he has helped to grow the global UFAF Family with GM Norris and the Board of Directors

"We have all admired Grand Master Norris and have been inspired by him for all these years", Ken said, "and it is our pleasure to have helped him continue this fine tradition we all grew up in. With his vision we have expanded our curriculum to include Brazilian jiu jitsu and Krav Maga to supplement our world champion karate legacy.

"In these coming years, we all look forward to expanding our UFAF Affiliate Member program", Ken said. "As a continuing part of GM Norris' long-term vision, UFAF will have the opportunity to influence many other styles and organizations through the incorporation of the strong foundational principles of UFAF".

As those who follow the principles of Stephen R. Covey and the Seven Habits of Highly Effective People would describe Ken Gallacher's mission and the vision of Gran Master Norris and UFAF: "Doing the Right Things, for the Right Reasons and with the Right Principles".

Master Chuck Norris, flanked by CEO Aaron Norris, Reggie Cochran, Rick Prieto, President Ken Gallacher and Chip Wright with all the dedicated members of the UFAF Board of Directors

The Iconic UFAF Logo now contains the new UFAF Affiliate mark, as other styles apply for membership in the United Fighting Arts Federation

REGGIE COCHRAN

Dr. Reggie Cochran, PhD, DCH (Doctor of Clinical Hypnotherapy) is a consultant and business partner with GM Norris and his wife Gena. Reggie is an internationally known Consultant, Coach, Speaker, Best Selling Author & Cross Disciplined Champion Martial Artist.

Reg has co-authored books with Bill Gates, Donald Trump, Brian Tracy, Dr. Wayne Dyer, Deepak Chopra, to name a few. The latest book he coauthored "Think and Grow Rich Today hit #1 Best Seller status on Amazon the first day it was released. This earned him the coveted Quilly Award and induction into the National Academy of Best Selling Authors.

His personal clients read like an international who's who directory filled with actors, entertainers, pro wrestlers, MMA champs, Gold & Platinum recording artist / musicians, top 1% entrepreneurs and business professionals.

Dr. Reg is an Independent Strategic Intervention Coach. Reggie received his Strategic Intervention Coach training from the prestigious Robbins-Madanes Center, founded by Tony Robbins and Cloe Madanes. Reg is also an Independent Certified Coach, Teacher and Speaker with The John Maxwell Team.

His coaching, speaking. and writing has earned him 3 EXPY awards. This keeps him in high demand as a keynote speaker and trainer for audiences ranging from youth to corporate events.

Reggie found discipline and direction in the martial arts after his father passed away. He feels fortunate to have been able to train with some very talented instructors, to train with others that challenged him to become better, and to get to know many people around the world, that have become close family, friends, mentors and role models to him.

His martial arts career has many facets. As a martial arts competitor he has won many state, national, international and World Champion titles. He opened his first martial arts studio in 1978 and has been blessed to have helped thousands of students over the decades. Now most of his time in the martial arts world is spent serving his martial arts brothers and sisters through the various Board positions he has.

Due to his father's suicide, today he is working on a complete online training series geared to help people recover from various types of surgeries, injuries, and PTSD. He is very passionate on this as his dad took his life due to PTSD from a severe war injury.

He's a long-time member of the United Fighting Arts Federation and has earned a 9th Degree Black Belt from his instructor, GM Chuck Norris. Reggie has served in various UFAF leadership positions since 1986. He is currently on the UFAF Board of Directors UFAF BJJ and special projects.

Sensei Reg is also a 10th degree Black Belt awarded by GM Pat Burleson, GM Ted Gambordello and recognized by the Professional Karate Association Board of Directors lead by GM Joe Corley, GM Jeff Smith & GM Bill Wallace. Today Reg also serves on the Board of Directors for the PKA.

Professor Reg earned a 2nd Degree Black Belt in Brazilian Jiu Jitsu from Professors Richard Norton, David Dunn, Chuck Norris & Rickson Gracie.

Sifu Reg also holds Master Instructor ranks in Kung Fu, Tai Chi and Qui Gong and is a Director for the International Chinese Boxing Association.

He is also a cofounding member of the International Federation of Mixed Martial Artist with Big John McCarthy and David Dunn. The IFMMA was one of the first organizations to offer a structured training and ranking program in MMA.

He is a multi-time martial arts Hall Of Fame member, Chuck Norris Man of The Year, recipient of the first Howard Jackson Memorial Award, The Sport Karate Museum Chuck Norris Natural Fighter award, Joe Lewis Eternal Warrior award and the UFAF Wieland Norris award.

Although Dr. Reg is very humbled and proud of his various martial arts accomplishments, titles and ranks, he also understands that with those things, comes much greater responsibility of serving others, not being served. He does not like to be called Master, Grand Master etc. as he still considers himself a work in progress and a life-long student.

As an instructor, his goals have always been to help each student become much better and successful than he has been. Most importantly he trains his students to take the discipline and focus they learn in the studio and apply to the rest of their personal and business lives.

Reggie will be the first to tell you that most of his accomplishments as a speaker, author and coach are partially due to the skills he learned from his martial arts instructors GM Chuck Norris, GM Richard Norton, GM Al Francis, GM Ted Gambordello & Professor David Dunn.

He also credits his success to every person he fought in the ring and trained in seminars with over the decades. Each match and each seminar reinforced and layered his determination, discipline and focus to be the best he can be in all areas of his life.

But first and foremost, he gives credit to God and his Lord and Savior Jesus Christ. Second to his wife Thresa Cochran who has stood by his side to support and encourage him. Thresa is also has Black Belts from GM Chuck Norris and GM Al Francis. And taught beside Reg over the years.

When asked what his highest titles are, his response is normally husband, father and grandpa. He continually strives to be a positive role model and influence to his family and friends. And to spread the good news of God's love, forgiveness and healing power through Jesus, with as many people as possible.

TARA COX

TRAINING INFORMATION

- Belt Ranks & Martial Arts Styles: 8th degree Black Belt, Chuck Norris System

- Instructors/Influencers: GM Chuck Norris

- Yrs. In the Martial Arts: 40+ years

- Yrs. Instructing: 24 years

- School Co-owner, Operator, and Instructor Legacy Martial Arts

PROFESSIONAL ORGANIZATIONS

- United Fighting Arts Federation (UFAF)

MAJOR ACHIEVEMENTS

- When I am not teaching or training I love to spend time with my family and watch our kids' activities. I'm happily married and have two children, two step children, one grandchild and another one on the way.

PERSONAL ACHIEVEMENTS

- 1980: present, active competitor in tournaments

- 1991: promoted to 1st degree Black Belt

- 1996: owner/operator of her own martial arts school

- 1998: awarded UFAF Female Competitor of the Year

- 2002: awarded Instructor of the Year

- 2003: inducted into the United States Martial Arts Hall of Fame

- 2006: my school awarded School of the Year

- 2008: and 2011 thru 2019 – World Champion in my kata division

- 2011: presented by GM Chuck Norris with the UFAF's most prestigious honor, the Wieland Norris Award (for GM Norris' brother who died in Vietnam)

- UFAF – Board of Directors

- UFAF – Director of Operations and Development

- UFAF – Chief Operating Officer of the UFAF corporation

KENNETH FJELD

" I am now in a position to influence other people like Grandmaster Norris influenced me.**"**

TRAINING INFORMATION

- Belt Ranks & Martial Arts Styles: Chuck Norris System - 5th Degree - Master rank, UFAF Krav Maga Force - Black Belt 1st Degree, Pambuan Arnis & Pambuan Tactical - Guro rank, Brazilian JiuJitsu - Purple Belt, Shotokan Karate Black belt

- Instructors/Influencers: Grandmaster Chuck Norris, Master Steve Nelson, Master Ed Saenz, Master Rick Prieto, Master Robert Sapp, Master Steve Hammersley, Master Howard Munding, Ama Guro Raffy Pambuan, Professor John Bernard Will, the late Master Tetsuhiko Asai, GM Samuel Scott

- Birthdate: December 10, 1974

- Birthplace/Growing Up: Norge, Drammen

- Yrs. In the Martial Arts: 34 years

- Yrs. Instructing: 32 years

- School owner, Manager, Instructor, UFAF School/UFAF Instructor

When I was a kid, I was a prosperous cross-country skier in Norway. However, at the age of 12, I got fatally ill. It got so bad that the doctors could not find a cure. I lost all my muscle power, and I was lying in bed for several months, fading away. I can still remember how my father had to carry me around.

While lying in bed, my uncle visited me one night and brought a couple of movies that he thought I could have an interest in watching. I was not allowed to see them by age restriction, but he put it in my VCR anyway. It was Lone Wolf McQuade and An Eye For An Eye with Grandmaster Chuck Norris.

Watching those movies made me wish that I could be as tough and strong as Grandmaster Norris. I promised myself that one day I would be able to do the same.

I asked my father to find the nearest Karate school. He answered first that the doctors had said I could never do any physical activity again in my life.

UNITED FIGHTING ARTS FEDERATION HONORS • 2020 MASTERS & PIONEERS

PROFESSIONAL ORGANIZATIONS

- United Fighting Arts Federation
- Pambuan Arnis
- Will/Machado BJJ Australasia
- Combat Kuntao

PERSONAL ACHIEVEMENTS

- 2016 BJJ Overall Champion - World Championship Las Vegas - UFAF
- Regional Chair of United Fighting Arts Federation Europe

MAJOR ACHIEVEMENTS

- I hold my Master's degree in the Chuck Norris System highest because Grandmaster Norris saved my life, and without him, I would not be able to do what I do today.

But after I convinced him, he found a Karate school, and I kept watching movies with Grandmaster Chuck Norris. GM Norris lit a fire in me that kept me alive when people wanted to give up and made me want to be stronger. I genuinely believe that he is the reason why I am still alive today. Not only that, but I have now been in the Martial Arts for 34 years, been an instructor for 32 years, and I have certified 46 Black Belts under me in Norway. Because of Grandmaster Norris's efforts, I can influence kids, youths, and adults all over Europe.

Grandmaster Norris is the sole reason I started in the Martial Arts, and today I proudly represent his art and organization in Europe.

Martial Arts has changed my life from desperate, helpless, and without hope to a life filled with fantastic people around me, friends all around the world, and abilities to do things that the doctors once said I could never do.

But most importantly, I am now in a position to influence other people like Grandmaster Norris influenced me, and that is the gift of life and the gift of Martial Arts.

STEPHEN HAMMERSLEY

"Simply put, after God and Family, Martial Arts is my Life!"

All my heroes growing up were martial artists, Chuck Norris, Bruce Lee, Tom Mclaughlin (Billy Jack) Joe Lewis, and I never missed an episode of Kung Fu, I always wanted to be the good guy who was on the right side of things that could take care of business when things got out of hand. I started training in martial arts in 1973 in Las Vegas, Nevada. I met a security guard, Master Oli Walker in the hotel where I was employed. Master Walker was a retired US Airmen and got his black belt in Yoshukai Karate while stationed in Japan. I fell in love with karate! I never missed a class. I trained for over a year and was about to test for my green belt (back then, there were only 4 belt ranks: white, green, brown & black) to my surprise! Master Walker informed me he was moving to California. Not only was I totally devastated that I was going to lose my Master, and friend, but now my green belt test was on hold. Master Walker explained to me that even though he was sure I was ready for my green belt in Yoshukai Karate, he also believed that he shouldn't belt test me, he explained to me that beginning another style of Karate with a color belt rank was not a good idea, and that I would be better off starting in a new style of karate from the beginning as a white belt, I was disappointed for sure, after almost two years of training, not testing and reaching my first belt goal, my master and friend was moving, I thought my life was over, I was crushed! That's when Master Walker informed me that he had made arrangements for me to meet some people he knew in the area and possibly could start my training over at their school. As a loyal student I

TRAINING INFORMATION

- Belt Ranks & Martial Arts Styles: 8th Degree Black Belt: (UFAF) United Fighting Arts Federation "The Chuck Norris System," 3rd Degree Black Belt: UFAF Krav Maga, 3rd Degree Black Belt: Krav Maga (PROTECT), 2nd Degree Black Belt: Krav Maga Force, 1st Degree Black Belt: Kuk Ki Won / Tae Kwon Do

- Instructors/Influencers: Master Ken Gallacher, Grand Master Chuck Norris, Grandmaster Dr. Itay Gil, Master Laurian Lapadatu, Grandmaster Polk S. Yun

- Birthdate: November 18, 1956

- Birthplace/Growing Up: Richmond, VA/Homestead, FL/ Las Vegas, NV

- Yrs. In the Martial Arts: 47 years

- Yrs. Instructing: 38 years

- School Owner, Manager & Instructor at American Martial Arts / Krav Maga Force Florida , UFAF School Instructor & Board of Directors

PROFESSIONAL ORGANIZATIONS

- International Director, "UFAF Krav Maga"

- International Director, "UFAF Affiliate Schools"

- Protect Security Solutions, Dr. Itay Gil

PROFESSIONAL ORGANIZATIONS

- Director (Florida) FIMA "Federation of Israeli Martial Arts"
- Paradigm Defense Concepts
- NRA

PERSONAL ACHIEVEMENTS

1996 Married the love of my Life: Erin Hammersley, we have five fantastic children, Shaunacy, Nathan, Portia, Kianna & Miles & eight beautiful grandchildren, Brodie, Grace, Luke, McKenna, Noah, Bradly, Grayson, & Madalana & one more on the way... God is great!

MAJOR ACHIEVEMENTS

- 1989-UFAF Fighting & Competition Team Member to travel & compete in the Soviet Union
- 1991-UFAF Man of the Year
- 1992-UFAF Professional Martial Arts Designation
- 1995-International Black Belt Hall of Fame "Instructor of the Year"
- 2000-Competitor of the Year, Weapons, Forms & Fighting
- 2005-Appointed UFAF International Board Member
- 2009-The Wieland Norris Award, awarded by Grandmaster Chuck Norris and Master Aaron Norris in remembrance of their beloved brother Wieland Norris, who served and fell in Vietnam.
- 2020-Appointed Director (Florida) FIMA "Federation of Israeli Martial Arts"

immediately said no sir! But I knew Master Walker had my best interest in mind, so I reluctantly agreed to meet these people and see what they were all about. A wise man once said, when one door closes, another opens. I didn't know at the time this meeting would literally change my life by meeting Grandmaster Chuck Norris, Master Ken Gallacher, Master Doug Ingram, & Master Dick Douglas, at this meeting I met my future, I met my mentors, and I met my destiny. Thus, I began my training in Tang Soo Do under Grandmaster Chuck Norris, we are now known as The "Chuck Norris" System, since that meeting I have never looked back, I have learned, studied, taught the martial arts ever since that day. In case you were wondering? I trained for another year, tested, and received my 8th blue belt, which means I was a white belt for almost three years. I tell this story to my students to remind them that the goal in martial arts is not the belt but the knowledge and that when we seek the knowledge, the belt will always follow.

Simply put, after God & Family, Martial Arts is my Life!

RICHARD PRIETO

"**Mr. Prieto has received many awards. Most notably the UFAF School of The Year, Hall of Fame, Weiland Norris Award, and the Most Inspirational.**"

TRAINING INFORMATION

- Belt Ranks & Martial Arts Styles: 9th Degree Black Belt, Chuck Norris System; 2nd Degree Black Belt with Itay Gil, Protect Israeli Security Solutions; Brazilian Jiu Jitsu Purple Belt with David Dunn

- Instructors/Influencers: Chuck Norris, Pat Johnson, Michael D. Echanis, Richard Norton and seminars with Itay Gil, David Dunn, Carlos Machado, Jean Jacques Machado, Benny Urquidez

- Birthdate: March 15, 1945

- Birthplace/Growing Up: Los Angeles, CA

- Yrs. In the Martial Arts: 52 years

- Yrs. Instructing: 51 years

- School Owner, Manager, Instructor & Founder

PROFESSIONAL ORGANIZATIONS

- United Fighting Arts Federation (UFAF), Board of Directors

- FIMA Representative for Texas with Ed Saenz

- US Air Force, Honorable Discharge

Mr. Richard Prieto, "Rick" to his friends, began his martial arts training in Sherman Oaks, California, in 1968. His first instructor was Pat Johnson, one of Chuck Norris' first black belts. He trained hard, putting in 10-12 hours a week. His first "claim-to-fame", he explains, was as a white belt competing in a tournament called the Four Seasons. The Four Seasons was hosted by Chuck Norris, Bruce Lee, Bob Wall, and Mike Stone. Rick, modestly recalls, "I took first place in sparring, twice, some three months apart and was presented with both trophies', on two different occasions, by Bruce Lee!"

Another exciting highlight of Rick's time "going through the ranks" was as a green belt. He was pictured on the cover of Black Belt Magazine, getting kicked by Jhoon Rhee. Pat Johnson was at the Black Belt Magazine offices and called Rick to ask if he could run down to the studio to pose for some pictures. He went down and posed with Jhoon Rhee and Ken Knudson, who was wondering what type of photos they should take so, Rick

PERSONAL ACHIEVEMENTS

- UFAF School of the Year
- UFAF Hall of Fame
- UFAF Weiland Norris Award
- UFAF Most Inspirational Best Martial Arts of the Woodlands, 6 consecutive years
- Best Business of the Woodlands, 2 years

MAJOR ACHIEVEMENTS

- Earned 1st Degree Black Belt in 1972
- Head Instructor for Mr. Norris at the Granada Hills, CA studio 1973 -1974
- Substitute Instructor for US Navy Seal Team while Mike Echanis was on
- Assignment (Echanis was head Instructor for Hand to Hand Combat for US Navy Seal Team)

suggested that Mr. Rhee put his foot in his stomach while Rick jumps up while he extended his Side Kick and it would look like he kicked me into the air. I guess Black Belt Magazine must have like it because it ended up on the cover for July 1970.

In 1972, Mr. Prieto received his first-degree black belt from Master Chuck Norris and became the Head Instructor for Mr. Norris's Granada Hills, CA karate studio. He also began helping Mr. Norris with various demonstrations, along with his brother, Aaron Norris. They did numerous demonstrations at places like the Pantages Theater, the Bob Barker Show and, the Martial Arts Expo at the LA Sports Arena. A memorable night was when they did a demonstration at the Grauman's Chinese Theater in Hollywood, CA, for the premiere of Bruce Lee's Enter The Dragon.

In 1974, Master Norris asked Mr. Prieto to move to Virginia and help open a new, "Chuck Norris Karate Studio" in Norfolk, VA. So, Rick packed up his belongings and, along with his good friend, Aaron Norris, opened this school and later another studio in Virginia Beach, VA. During this time, Rick and Aaron formalized the Chuck Norris teaching curriculum for what would become the Chuck Norris System of Karate and the United Fighting Arts Federation (Mr. Norris' Black Belt organization).

While teaching in Virginia, Mr. Prieto met Michael D. Echanis a, "Hwa Rang Do" martial artist who, at the time, was training the US Navy SEALs, in Hand-to Hand combat. Rick and several other instructors began training with Mr. Echanis but the only one he trusted to teach the SEALs in his place was Rick Prieto. When Echanis went out of town for eight weeks, he asked Rick to continue teaching the NAVY SEALs while he was away. Of this time, Mr. Prieto says, "The SEALs are a unique, fearless, tough, great bunch of guys. They showed me tremendous respect, and it was a privilege to teach them the martial arts."

In 1980 Mr. Prieto moved back to the San Fernando Valley and owned karate schools in Tarzana and Studio City, California, and, now, his "last school," "Karate of The Woodlands" in, The Woodlands, Texas.

For many years, Mr. Prieto was Chuck Norris' personal training partner along with his good friend, Howard Jackson. They trained for three and a

half hours a day, six days a week. (Over a thousand hours a year, for many years.) During these "work-out" periods many of the most famous martial artists in the world would show up and train with them, notably Richard Norton and Bob Wall, with an occasional visit from Charlie Sheen and Randy Travis

Mr. Prieto began his movie career in 1974, where he did a "fight scene" for the movie, "Black Belt Jones," starring Jim Kelly. His next exposure to the movies was in 1978, where he was an actor in the Chuck Norris movie, "A Force of One." He is also best remembered for his role as "Carlos" in Delta Force 2 where he had a memorable fight scene that ended when Mr. Norris kicked him into a statue of a warrior with an extended spear. The spear is going through his body and extending from his chest.

Rick is one of the nicest men you would want to meet and he plays such a good, "Bad Guy" in the movies and TV shows he has acted in. Watching his fight scenes, you may notice the incredible, natural precision with which he moves. The fight scenes he has done with Master Norris, in particular, are beautiful things to watch.

Rick has been in many movies and TV productions as an actor, stuntman and/or fight coordinator. Rick's movie and TV work credits can be seen on the IMBD website.

In 1990, Mr. Norris and President Bush 41 asked Rick to head up the Kick Drugs Out of America program, now called Kickstart, located in Houston, Texas. This program would teach the martial arts in various Junior High Schools in an attempt to instill discipline, integrity, and respect and lead the children away from joining gangs and doing drugs. These inner-city schools, which now include High Schools, are considered "high risk" because of the poverty and crime in their communities. Again, Rick packed-up, which included a wife and two children this time, and moved for Mr. Norris. The Houston Independent School District thought that the program would last only a few months. (This has been their experience in the past.) But the program is still going strong 30 years later and has advanced to dozens of schools, and is continuing to grow.

Mr. Prieto has received many awards. Most notably the UFAF School of The Year, Hall of Fame, Weiland Norris Award, and the Most Inspirational. For 6 years, his studio was named Best Martial Arts School of The Woodlands, Texas, and for two years, Best Business Of The Woodlands, TX.

Mr. Prieto is a 9th Degree Black Belt in the Chuck Norris System, a 2nd Degree Black Belt in Krav Maga, and a Purple Belt in Brazilian Jiu Jitsu, has been a member of the United Fighting Arts Federation, Board of Directors, for many years.

Recently, Mr. Prieto was asked again by Master Norris to update the Chuck Norris System of Karate's black belt requirements. The new testing requirements include a tremendous amount of "Stand-Up" and "Ground" combative elements. They hope to increase the abilities of the black belts further to protect themselves and others.

STEVE BERRY

> "The Martial Arts touches my life every day; how I think about the world around me, the people I encounter, and my response to them."

TRAINING INFORMATION

- Belt Ranks & Martial Arts Styles: USTF, ITF, Taekwondo, Blue Belt, Chuck Norris System Karate, 6th degree Black Belt, Chuck Norris System, Brazilian Jiu Jitsu, Blue Belt

- Instructors/Influencers: Mr. Jim Ford, Master Stan Martian, Master Charles Allen, Master Tip Potter, Professor David Dunn

- Birthdate: March 9, 1954

- Birthplace/Growing Up: Billings, MT/Washington DC/Casper, WY

- Yrs. In the Martial Arts: 50 years

- Yrs. Instructing: 26 years

- School Owner at Steve Berry's Martial Arts Academe, UFAF School Instructor & Board of Director Member

PROFESSIONAL ORGANIZATIONS

- Chuck Norris System Karate

I started training in a high school ROTC program that had a small Shotokan Karate program In 1970, I started training in Taekwondo in 1974, it was the USTF and ITF organization in Casper, Wyoming. I trained under Mr. Jim Ford and Mr. Stan Martin, now Master Stan Martin of the ITF. I received my blue belt in 1984 with the ITF.

In 1984 we moved to Tucson, Arizona, and I started training with Mr. Charles Allen under the UFAF organization, eventually earning my 1st degree black belt in 1988 #766 in Chun Kuk Do. I started my school, Steve Berry's School, Chun Kuk Do, in 1994. We now call our school Steve Berry's Martial Arts Academy.

In 1994 I became a member of the board of directors in region #5 under Master Tip Potter and the UFAF organization.

In 2019, Grand Master Chuck Norris promoted me to 6th degree black belt. I have also been training in Brazilian Jiu Jitsu and received my blue belt under Professor David Dunn in 2017.

I have competed in our annual ITC, Chuck Norris System World

PERSONAL ACHIEVEMENTS

- Married for 47 years
- 44 years, Centurylink Comm (Retired)
- Lifelong Martial artist
- Teaching Martial Arts for 25 years
- Three children, five grandchildren, four great-grandchildren

MAJOR ACHIEVEMENTS

- 6th Degree Black Belt, Chuck Norris System

Championships throughout the years, I have placed 2nd and 3rd place in forms or fighting 13 times since 2000, and this year due to Covid 19, we did a virtual competition, and I received 1st place in men's senior forms and 1st place executive men's weapon's forms.

The Martial Arts touches my life every day; how I think about the world around me, the people I encounter, and my response to them, my response to life itself is filtered through my Art. How I treat you, how I see you, how I react in every situation come through that filter. It's not something I have to think about. It's what I am.

CROSBY BROADWATER III

"This is not a job. It is a passion, a way of life & why I was put on this earth - to educate through the power of martial arts."

TRAINING INFORMATION

- Belt Ranks & Martial Arts Styles: The Chuck Norris System. Chun Kuk Do - 3rd Black Belt, UFAF Krav Maga Force - Black Belt

- Instructors/Influencers: Master Lindy Woods, Grand Master Chuck Norris

- Birthdate: October 5, 1988

- Birthplace/Growing Up: Augusta, GA

- Yrs. In the Martial Arts: 18 years

- Yrs. Instructing: 18 years

- School Owner, Manager & Instructor at UMAD Universal Martial Arts Dojos, UFAF School Instructor

PROFESSIONAL ORGANIZATIONS

- UFAF - United Fighting Arts Federation

- MAIA - Martial Arts Industry Association

- N.B.L. - National Blackbelt League

I got involved in martial arts to develop more confidence. Being a natural introvert, I was never very outspoken. This had other effects on my weight, focus, drive, goal setting, etc. When I first started, I realized this was the activity for me to achieve my goals and to become the person I was meant to be. Shortly after my start, I began instructor training to help with classes and never looked back. Starting in daycares began my teaching base and expanded to public schools, private schools, the U.S. Army, and national attention. The school I trained at closed in 2010, making me adapt to being self-motivated to accomplish my goals. After waiting eight years of no formal training, we founded our school, and now we are one of the leading schools in our style.

UMAD - Universal Martial Arts Dojos have been active in the CSRA since 2004. It is a UFAF (United Fighting Arts Federation) black belt school. The organization, established in 1979, and the Organization President, Grand Master Chuck Norris, has an active role in the organization and black belts. Sensei Crosby is the Chief instructor of Universal Martial Arts Dojos. He is a UFAF black belt and trained in martial arts for over half his life.

PERSONAL ACHIEVEMENTS

- 2019 3rd Degree Chuck Norris System Black Belt
- 2020 UFAF Krav Maga Force Black Belt

MAJOR ACHIEVEMENTS

- UFAF ITC World Champion - Kata & Fighting
- MA Success Magazine 2019 - School Showcase
- T.C.T. Regional Champion - Kata, Weapons & Fighting

This school aims to provide students the highest quality martial arts instruction in a safe and positive learning environment that people of all ages can enjoy. UMAD combines excellent student-instructor ratios within the state of an art, luxury training facility. Sensei Crosby is a Business Administration graduate and trained in Instructor Programming, representing more than seventeen years of research and development. He has made vast connections across the CSRA from daycares, public/ private schools, boys & girls club, the U.S. Army at Fort Gordon, business affiliates, and more. Sensei Crosby's reach has expanded with his connection to UFAF, with states across the U.S.A. & countries abroad.

UMAD is the 85th charter school of UFAF, that exclusively and currently teaches the Chuck Norris System (C.N.S.). UMAD combines C.N.S., Brazilian Jiu-Jitu, Krav Maga, Fitness, Youth Development, Life Skills, and more to bring the best possible martial arts experience. UMAD is a value-priced martial arts school, serving our community by providing several programs for various purposes, ranging from basic martial arts, self-protection, self-esteem, life skills, and more. UMAD plans to enhance its programs as it expands, developing new programs to ensure students have access to the different aspects of The Chuck Norris System and the Martial Arts.

Growing up today, youth and teens have outside pressures never imagined before. With social media, bullying, cliques, and other influences, this program teaches martial arts and relatable life skills. As terrorist threats to the United States have risen, self-protection has become more popular with people of all ages and backgrounds. We specialize in youth development- starting at three years old, traditional martial arts, contemporary martial arts, self-protection, group seminars, weapons, sport karate, and consulting.

Universal Martial Arts Dojos is also concerned with the personal development of each student. Individual attention is a feature of each class, allowing students to progress quickly and confidently toward their personal goals. Sensei Crosby takes his responsibility as a role model for youth seriously, teaching them the importance of discipline, integrity, loyalty, and respect.

Martial Arts has been one of the biggest and most influential aspects of my life. When I began my study, I was only interested in growing to my personal best, and achieving my Blackbelt. As time went on, however, I realized it was much more. The Chuck Norris System is the foundation for my further aspirations. Confidence was built, allowing me to know I had more potential than I realized. Before training, I never thought I could speak to a group of people, have my own business, or be a community activist. Now I do all that and much more daily while loving every minute. This is not a job. It is a passion, a way of life & why I was put on this earth - to educate through the power of martial arts.

Since opening UMAD we have taken off not only in our community but regionally & nationally. We are recognized as one of the best schools in our area even though we are one of the newest. This is because of our honesty, passion, professionalism, no pressure sales, focus on quality, and being true to our word. We are known highly by people in all walks of life, have several students who travel more than 30 minutes, and a few who come from hours away weekly to train. As I grow my skills and show my students what I am trying to create and aspire to, it gives them an extra push to be like Sensei.

As I continue my growth, I plan to obtain my Mastery and above, continue to win world titles, create Elite Blackbelts, become regional director & one day on the board of directors. I have very high aspirations to strive for but all possible; I will continue to trust God, believe in myself & my family, make this happen & make Grand Master Norris proud.

STEVE GIROUX

"The lessons I learned in competition were easily transferred into life. Facing up against someone in the ring takes guts and courage."

TRAINING INFORMATION

- Belt Ranks & Martial Arts Styles: Chuck Norris System -- 7th Degree Black Belt

- Instructors/Influencers: I have many

- Birthdate: May 30, 1976

- Birthplace/Growing Up: Waterbury, CT/Southington, CT

- Yrs. In the Martial Arts: 36 years

- Yrs. Instructing: 31 years

- School Owner at Giroux Bros Martial Arts

PROFESSIONAL ORGANIZATIONS

- United Fighting Arts Federation
- Martial Arts Industry Association

I started in the martial arts by following the footsteps of my older brother Jeff Giroux. He was really into martial arts and loved watching Bruce Lee and Chuck Norris movies. At first, my parents wouldn't let me join the school he was enrolled in to see my interest and seriousness. They enrolled me in a beginner course offered through our local YMCA. At the time I started, I was seven years old. After a short time, they knew I was into it and enrolled me at the same studio as my older brother.

Our studio was affiliated with the United Fighting Arts Federation, and in 1988 I earned my first-degree black belt at the age of 11. I loved training and working out, but after earning my 1st Degree, my eyes were opened to a whole new world of what I wanted to accomplish.

A couple of years later, I was invited to be a part of a team through UFAF to travel to Russia as a goodwill exchange. I was 13 at the time. During this trip, I watched Chip Wright fight and easily defeat everyone who entered the ring with him. It was at this point that I knew I wanted to pursue fighting and compete and travel the country.

PERSONAL ACHIEVEMENTS

- Author of "In the Black, Living the American Dream by Owning and Operating Your Own Small Business," Published 2016 by Archway Publishing

MAJOR ACHIEVEMENTS

- Grand Champion and Norris Cup recipient 1999, 2010, 2011
- Wieland Norris Award Recipient 2012
- UFAF Board of Directors member 2018

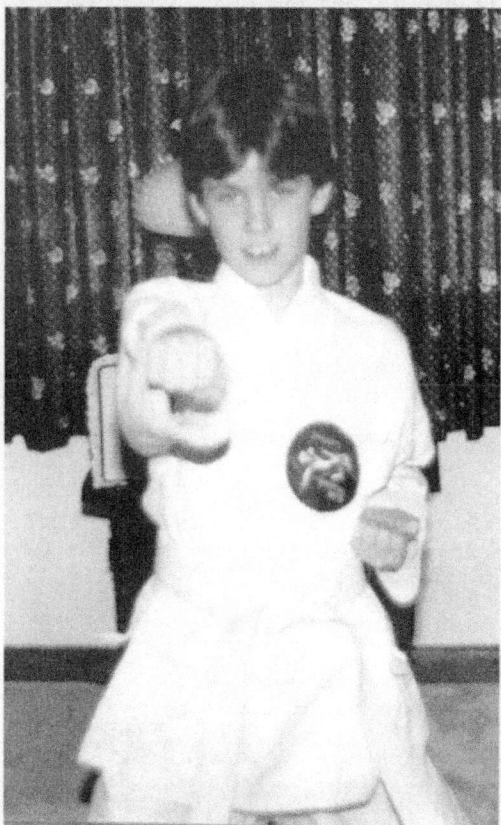

I continued training and earning rank in the United Fighting Arts Federation. At this point, a unique opportunity came up to purchase the studio from our instructor. My father Norm Giroux, an accountant, would run the behind the scenes while my brother Jeff (16) and I (13) ran the classes and handled enrollments. It was one of my younger years' best experiences, teaching me a great lesson in entrepreneurship that would ultimately lead me to my career as a multi-school owner.

I ran our studio, Champion Karate until I graduated high school. It was at that time that I decided to move to Boston to study business at Bentley College. I chose Bentley because it was a great business school, and knew some of the country's top fighters trained in the area. After bouncing around to a few studios, I found one that wasn't too close but was the one for me. I began studying fighting under John Payton, a member of the John Paul Mitchell National Karate Team in Quincy, Massachusetts.

Up until this point in my fighting career, I was primarily a kicker. John Payton was primarily a puncher, so it was perfect for me to learn and adapt a more versatile fighting style. When I would visit my hometown in CT, I would also train with Mike Conroy and his students in New Haven, CT. Between them and Chip Wright, I had some great tools to pursue a point fighting career.

Upon graduation from college, I decided to start a part-time studio with my brother Jeff. I wanted a school mainly so that I had a place to train and follow my dream of competing all over the country.

We named the studio Giroux Brothers Martial Arts. Both of us had jobs during the day but would go after work to teach lessons. A short time in, my brother met the girl of his dreams and decided to move back to CT, where they were both from. Having already established a brand, I decided to keep the school's name but operated it on my own from the very beginning. Giroux Brothers Martial Arts was established in January 1999.

I worked as an Accountant during the day and would teach at my studio at night and on the weekend. It was one of the hardest things I've ever done, mainly because I was only 22 with no money, no credit, and no time.

In 1999 I won the Grand Championship in Las Vegas at our annual United Fighting Arts Federation training conference. Shortly after winning, I began traveling and competing on the NASKA circuit. I fought against so many great competitors, including Raymond Daniels and Jadi Tention. I learned a lot from both of them, even though I could never pull off a win. I trained with Jadi many times over the years, who was another individual who helped me with my fighting skills.

I was determined to make my studio a success, and after many hard lessons was able to run it full time after about 3 years. I had many influencers in the business arena who helped my studio become professional and successful. Initially, Educational Funding Company and then I decided to hire some professional consultants -- first Eric and Pat Hensley and then Stephen Oliver. All of them helped me with turning my passion into my career.

I took a break from competition to grow and professionalize my studio when I was 25 and then decided to re-enter the competition arena when I was 33. I won the Grand Championship and Norris Cup at the 2010 and 2011 UFAF International Training Conference in Las Vegas. It was also at this point I became a sponsored member of Team Chun Kuk Do and traveled the NBL circuit for two years. At the age of 35, I decided it was time to retire from competition and focus on training my students to become the best they can be and pass along the experiences I had growing up.

Now, I'm going on 22 years with my first studio and recently started a second studio near my home. Our first studio is in the top 2 to 3 % of the industry, and the second one is starting to grow some legs even after experiencing a worldwide pandemic in the first year of operation.

I cannot imagine how different my life would be had I not started martial arts training as a kid. Even though many of the lessons I learned both in fighting and in business were hard, I wouldn't change a thing because the experiences have helped me become who I am today.

The lessons I learned in competition were easily transferred into life. Facing up against someone in the ring takes guts and courage. No one goes into a match knowing what the outcome will be, but hopefully, by putting in enough work will get you the results you desire. By taking the chance and winning is a great life lesson that you should always take the chance. You may get bruised along the way, but a winning attitude is a way of life.

My fighting has helped with me being successful in business too. It's the very same situation as facing an opponent. You need to do your homework, learn new things from those who have already achieved similar goals and milestones – practice, implement, repeat. If you lose – learn from it. When you win, do it again but even better.

When my brother and I took over the first studio, we hung a sign that read "A Winner Never Quits and A Quitter Never Wins." This quote is the way I live my life. It's always been hung through 5 different studios, including my new studio. I see it every single day, and as I continue to face obstacles in my own life, it's a constant reminder that the only way to lose at anything is to give up, and that is something I simply refuse to do regardless of the situation.

KENNETH HERRERA

"*After 50 plus years in the Martial Arts studying, training, competing, and teaching, I have been truly blessed and respect the legacy.*"

TRAINING INFORMATION

- Belt Ranks & Martial Arts Styles: Tang Soo Do - 9th Degree Black Belt, Superfoot System - 7th Degree Black Belt, Chuck Norris System - 5th Degree Black Belt, Joe Lewis Fighting System - 3rd Degree Black Belt, Shorin Ryu Karate - 1st Degree Black Belt, Doce Pares Stick Fighting - 2nd Degree Brown Belt

- Instructors/Influencers: Pat Johnson, Bill Wallace, Chuck Norris, Joe Lewis, Steve Smith, John Korab, Anthony Kleeman

- Birthdate: September 3, 1954

- Birthplace/Growing Up: Pasadena, CA

- Yrs. In the Martial Arts: 51 years

- Yrs. Instructing: 48 years

- School Owner & Instructor at World Survival Self Defense, UFAF School Instructor

PROFESSIONAL ORGANIZATIONS

- United Fighting Arts Federation
- Superfoot System
- Joe Lewis Fighting Systems

I got started in the Martial Arts out of fear. I played music and drums in a band at a young age at dances and events. For me, these were emotionally charged environments. Some big guy was high on drugs and alcohol at one event and wanted to beat me up for no reason. I was scared. I had never experienced that kind of fear before. Somehow, I was able to get out of that situation. It motivated me to want to learn how to protect myself. I got a Bruce Tegner Karate book and some Black Belt magazines and started practicing in my room like the Karate Kid. I wound up at the YMCA for a Shotokan program and met some guys that took me to Sherman Oaks Karate to begin my training journey with Chuck Norris. That was a life-changing experience for me.

Training with Chuck Norris brought out the best in me. He taught me so much about life and hard work. My training partner John Schumann and I traveled all over Southern California following Chuck Norris to where

PERSONAL ACHIEVEMENTS

- 1982 Driver in President Ronald Regan's motorcade
- 1991 Trained/Instructed at the FBI Training Center in Quantico, Virginia
- 1992 World Survival Self Defense Video with Bruce & Kris Jenner
- Television and Motion Picture Stunts
- Quartz Hill High School Hall of Fame
- Athena Award - California State Assembly
- Barcelona Martial Arts Instructor Award

MAJOR ACHIEVEMENTS

- 1986 "Instructor of the Year" United Fighting Arts Federation
- 1989 "Professional Martial Artist" designation - United Fighting Arts Federation
- 1991 Intersport USA Karate Team Co-Leader China Tour
- 1992 Intersport USA Karate Team Leader Russia Tour 1992
- 2019 United Fighting Arts Federation World Champion Black Belt Light Heavy Weight 60 + Sparring

he would be teaching that night. I met so many wonderful people and made lifelong friends that I remain close to today. Chuck Norris encouraged me to compete. So, I began competing in tournaments all through California and the Western United States. I met a girl in Albuquerque, New Mexico, at a tournament competing against one of our teammates. Cindi Peterson was a Top Ten competitor from Denver. We fell in love and got married. We traveled on the road around the United States, playing music, training, and competing. We settled down in 1978 to start a family, and I began teaching and training in other Martial Arts. In 1979 at our first Chuck Norris Black Belt Conference in Torrance, Bill "Superfoot" Wallace introduced his kicking style. This was another life-changing moment for me. Having Chuck Norris as an Instructor who encouraged you to train and learn from other people and styles was simply the best. He wanted you to find out what others were doing so you could plan to defend against it. Brilliant! The introductions he made for me to meet and learn from the best Martial Artists in the world is priceless! After 50 plus years in the Martial Arts studying, training, competing, and teaching, I have been truly blessed and respect the legacy. The most important thing that Chuck Norris taught me was the importance of faith and family. To continually be in a positive frame of mind to develop love, loyalty, and happiness. I am blessed to be married to Cindi for 46 years and have three wonderful children (Stephanie, Anthony, and Craig) and two Granddaughters (Sofia and Alivia).

HOWARD MUNDING

"My martial arts training and discipline have given me the mental focus and calm in dealing with stressful and dangerous situations..."

TRAINING INFORMATION

- Belt Ranks & Martial Arts Styles: 6th DAN Chuck Norris System, 2nd DAN Krav Maga Force, 1st DAN UFAF Krav Maga Force, ICCS Krav Maga Certified Instructor, Commando Krav Maga Certified Instructor, CDT Certified Defensive Tactics Instructor, Force Options Defensive Tactics Instructor

- Instructors/Influencers: Master Tip Potter

- Birthdate: December 16, 1960

- Birthplace/Growing Up: Toledo, OH

- Yrs. In the Martial Arts: 31 years

- Yrs. Instructing: 30 years

- School Owner & Instructor at Millennium Martial Arts LLC, UFAF School Instructor, UFAF Region 5 Regional Chairman & UFAF ITC Head of Security

I wanted to take karate as a little boy, but my parents could not afford it. I tried Judo at the YMCA and then went into wrestling, which became my passion. As an adult, when my boys wanted to take karate, I signed them up at a UFAF school in the area operated by Tip and Gretta Potter., It wasn't until one of my fellow firefighters was stabbed in 1989, on a medical call, that I decided to join. I knew that many bad people had more skills, and I needed to develop my skills for working as a firefighter on the streets. I began training in UFAF in 1989. I developed my skills and branched out into defensive tactics and Krav Maga to hone my street skills. In 2006, I conducted a research project on Violence Against Firefighters for the National Fire Academy. It was from this project that led to the development of a program called Street Smart EMS, a personal protection program for firefighters, paramedics, EMT's, nurses. This course has been presented across the country. In 2003, I purchased the school from the Potter's and continue to share my knowledge with people from all walks of life at the same school I started with in UFAF.

Studying martial arts impacted my life by refocusing my efforts not on myself but on others. In turn, it has helped me become a better husband,

PROFESSIONAL ORGANIZATIONS

- United Fighting Arts Federation

- Martial Arts Industry Association Elite Member

- Championship Martial Arts

- Israeli Contact Combat System (ICCS) Krav Maga

- Krav Maga Force

PERSONAL ACHIEVEMENTS

- USAF Veteran 1978– 1987 (Firefighter)
- One USAF Commendation Medal
- Three USAF Achievement Medals
- Two USAF Good Conduct Medals
- City of Peoria Fire Department (retired) 1988-2008
- Paramedic of the Year 2002
- Fire Chief City of El Mirage 2009 - 2014

MAJOR ACHIEVEMENTS

- Wieland Norris Award - 2001
- UFAF Instructor of the Year - 2018
- UFAF Krav Maga Force Chief Instructor (2016-2019)
- Certified 118 UFAF Krav Maga Instructors form 2016 -2019
- Former Editor of "The Octagon" the official publication of the United Fighting Arts Federation
- Created Street Smart EMS Personal Protection Program for First Responders

father, grandfather, and friend to those around me.

Martial arts has allowed me to grow as an individual and to help others achieve their goals. As an instructor and now a school owner, I have seen students grow and mature into productive members of society. I have black belts and students that have gone on to become police officers, firefighters, a pilot, nurses, a doctor, and honorably serving in all branches of the US Armed Forces. It has also allowed me to help women break through barriers and face their fears from domestic violence and sexual assaults.

My martial arts training and discipline have given me the mental focus and calm in dealing with stressful and dangerous situations during my 36 years in the fire department. By continuing to train and exercise martial arts training helped me recover from major heart surgery. I was back working at the fire station and teaching at the karate school in only eight weeks!

Martial Arts as a common language and brotherhood/sisterhood have allowed me the opportunity to build friendships literally around the world. It's an honor to teach and train across the United States and in Norway, Italy, France, Japan, and Mexico.

Martial Arts is indeed a way of life for both my family and me.

CHRISTIAN MOEN RØE

"Studying Martial Arts has led me to a deeper understanding in 'attention to details.'"

TRAINING INFORMATION

- Belt Ranks & Martial Arts Styles: 2nd Degree black belt Chuck Norris System, Karate, Four Striped blue belt Will/ Machado BJJ, Purple belt UFAF Krav Maga, Former MMA instructor

- Instructors/Influencers: Master Kenneth Fjeld

- Birthdate: April 3, 1979

- Birthplace/Growing Up: Drammen, Skotselv

- Yrs. In the Martial Arts: 8 years

- Yrs. Instructing: 6 years

- Instructor

PROFESSIONAL ORGANIZATIONS

- United Fighting Arts Federation
- Aesir Academy
- Will/ Machado BJJ Australasia

At the age of 33, I found out that it was time to start with something new, a fresh start, you might say. I had done some Aikido for six months but was searching for a Martial Art form with more kicks and punches, and at the same time, I wanted to get in better physical shape. My search took me to Master Kenneth Fjeld and Aesir Academy here in Norway. At his club, I started up with Chun Kuk Do (now Chuck Norris System) and Will/ Machado BJJ. Now the ball was rolling, and so was I. The love for these two Martial Arts and the excellent guidance of Master Fjeld, led me to where I am today.

Studying Martial Arts has led me to a deeper understanding in "attention to details." Taking notice of the smaller things that make up the big things, like how to break down technique into "bits" and teaching this way of thinking to students, has somewhat changed my way of thinking both in my job and on the mat.

PERSONAL ACHIEVEMENTS

Getting the white belt, I think, should be anyone's top personal achievement. This is where your story begins, and it is up to you to go as far as you can. For me, the most important personal achievement was filling the role as a BJJ and further on MMA instructor with the guidance of Master Fjeld. Getting the opportunity to make a difference in other people's progress and helping them reach their goals has been a major inspiration in my training. Reaching my goals and becoming the first Grand Champion in point fighting in Aesir Academy, getting recognition for achievements and hard work in BJJ in our club, training hard for black belt in CNS, I think would come second to seeing the students progress in their training.

MAJOR ACHIEVEMENTS

Family first. My major achievement is and will always be my family. They are pushing me towards new goals, accepting that training takes some of the family time, but they always stand behind me and share the ups and downs in my Martial Art training. Another significant achievement has been meeting some of the greatest people, both in students and some of the greatest names in Martial Arts; Master Kenneth Fjeld, Grand Master Chuck Norris, his wife Gena, and Prof. John Will.

MARTIAL ARTS MASTERS & PIONEERS

BENNY "THE JET" URQUIDEZ

For five decades, the legendary Benny "The Jet" Urquidez has been a moving force in martial arts. A six-time world champion in five weight class divisions, Urquidez pioneered full-contact fighting in the United States. Undefeated throughout his twenty-seven-year professional

fighting career, he catapulted to world prominence and ultimate dominance in the mid-1970s. Benny "The Jet" Urquidez became a world champion kickboxer in the same year full-contact karate was

introduced to the United States. He reigned over the sport throughout his entire career.

Benny's father was a professional boxer and his mother, a professional wrestler. He is the second youngest in a family of nine children. Benny and most of his siblings became boxers and black belts. Both Benny and his sister Lily went on to become champion fighters. By the age of five, Benny was competing in pee wee boxing, and at age seven began studying martial arts. His thirst for knowledge was insatiable. At fourteen, four years earlier than was generally permitted, he became the youngest martial artist to ever receive a black belt, earning the first of what would be nine black belts.

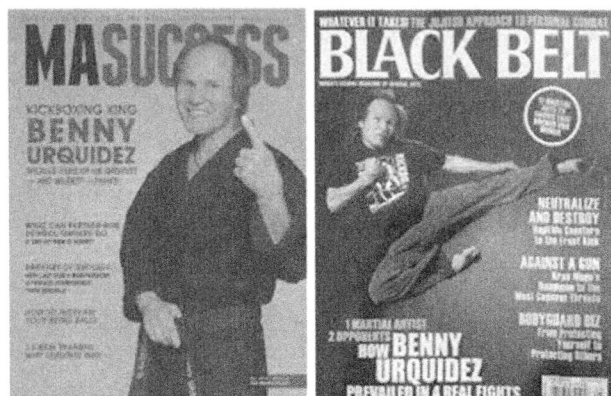

Benny immediately began competing in the adult black belt division. He won every major international tournament with his unique and extraordinary style of fighting and remained undefeated.

At that time, he began formulating a new style of martial arts termed free form martial arts. This was the genesis for the full contact karate now practiced in competition all over the world. It was then that he chose to pioneer the sport instead of becoming a pro boxer. In 1974, The Jet introduced what is known as full-contact karate or American

kickboxing to the United States. These practices were the foundation and inspiration for Sensei Benny's own original system of martial arts. Combining nine different styles, he created "Ukidokan" karate meaning a way of life, also referred to as internal training. Ukidokan bears the distinction of being the only new-age system recognized by the governing bodies of Japan as an official martial art. Urquidez's rare energy and force earned him the nickname The Jet after one of his peers witnessed the speed and accuracy of his

legendary and lethal jump-spinning-back-kick.

By 1977 The Jet had traveled the world and systematically defeated every world champion, winning the P.K.A. and W.K.A. world kickboxing championships, becoming a national hero in the process. After winning five world championships in four separate weight class divisions, The Jet retired in 1989 undefeated with an unprecedented title defense ring record of 62 wins, 57 knockouts, and 0 losses. In 1993, at the age of forty-two, The Jet came out of retirement to seal his legendary status, defeating 25-year-old Japanese world welterweight champion Yoshihisa Tagami and winning the world light-middleweight championship, bringing his record to 63 wins, 57 knockouts, and 0 losses. Unprecedented in ring history, Benny The Jet has achieved a feat never accomplished before or since He is the only fighter to have retained six world championships in five weight class divisions for twenty-four consecutive years.

In addition to his exceptional accomplishments in the ring, being an actor and a highly sought-after stunt and fight coordinator on film sets all over the world, Sensei Benny is and always has been a teacher. Teaching students of all levels, champion fighters and celebrities alike, he has written four instructional books, released eight instructional videos and countless online tutorials and classes. Visitors to bennythejet.com can find training tips, techniques, and teachings rooted in the Ukidokan system. Sensei Benny travels the world teaching seminars, classes, and personalized training. Having accomplished everything a fighter could dream of and more, Benny The Jet Urquidez is considered one of the greatest martial arts legends of all time. He remains not only the longest reigning champion ever in the history of modern martial arts but in all of professional sports.

MARTIAL ARTS
MASTERS & PIONEERS

HONOREES

ANTHONY ALBANESE

"Martial Arts has taught me to share my knowledge with others and help them achieve their goals."

TRAINING INFORMATION

- Belt Ranks & Martial Arts Styles: American Vadha Kempo Karate - 10th Degree Black Belt, Superfoot System - 5th Degree Black Belt, Joe Lewis Fighting System - 2nd Degree Black Belt, Goju - Junior Black Belt, CDT - Certified Tactical Master Instructor

- Instructors/Influencers: Grand Master John Salvaggio, Grand Master Bill Wallace, Grand Master Joe, Lewis, Grand Master Tom Patire

- Birthdate: May 9, 1960

- Birthplace/Growing Up: Staten Island , NY

- Yrs. In the Martial Arts: 51 years

- Yrs. Instructing: 40 years

- School owner, Instructor

The truth is I got started in the Martial Arts because I wanted to do the things that I saw Bruce Lee do on the Green Hornet, a TV series.

Since studying Martial Arts from childhood, it has taught me self-discipline, self-confidence and a strong appreciation for the talents of other people. I have learned never to give up and to stay the course. And most important, it has taught me to share my knowledge with others and help them achieve their goals, personal as well as in the Martial Arts. It has taught me humility and to respect my fellow man. It has helped me understand the brotherhood of the Martial Arts. I have met martial artists worldwide and have made so many amazing friends through the arts.

PROFESSIONAL ORGANIZATIONS

- PKA Worldwide
- Superfoot System
- Joe Lewis Fighting System

PERSONAL ACHIEVEMENTS

- Competed in the Mid-Western Championships
- Competed in the East Coast Championships
- Competed in Aaron Banks Tournaments in NYC
- Competed in S. Henry Cho National Championships in NYC
- Certified in Executive Protection
- MMA Conditioning Coach
- Certified Functional Strength Coach
- Trained Paul Holder, Bronze Winner of Senior World Judo Championships

MAJOR ACHIEVEMENTS

- Martial Arts University Grandmaster Hall of Honors
- Action Martial Arts Hall of Honors
- 10th Degree Black Belt Vadha Kempo

MIKE BIORN

"As an instructor, I strive to help others find that love of the martial arts."

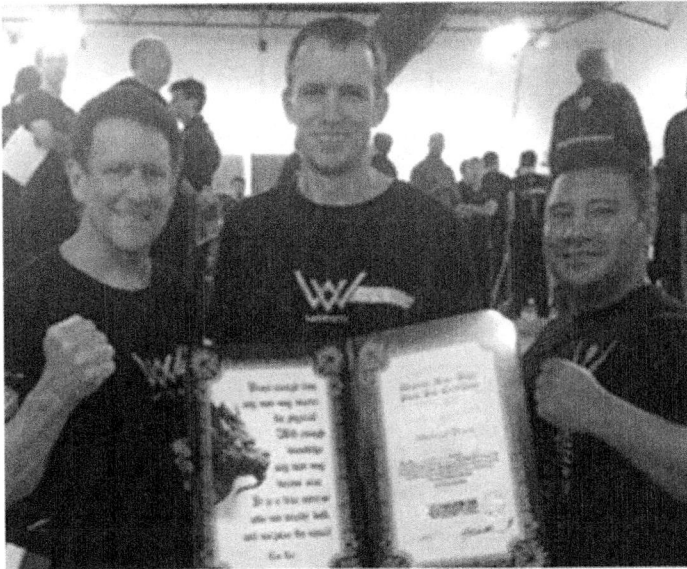

TRAINING INFORMATION

- Belt Ranks & Martial Arts Styles: Black Belt, Warrior Krav Maga and Ten-Chi Kenpo

- Instructors/Influencers: GM Joe Corley, Master Erick Alfaro; Yondan Richard Grandberry, Ryokudan Elliott Edwards

- Birthplace/Growing Up: Aberdeen, SD / Fairport, NY/ Cambridge, MA

- Yrs. In the Martial Arts: 21 years

- Yrs. Instructing: 6 years

- Instructor

PROFESSIONAL ORGANIZATIONS

- PKA Worldwide

After narrowly avoiding a fight my first month of college, I wanted to learn to defend myself. A couple new friends were interested too, so we checked out several options. Our favorite was Ten-Chi Kenpo karate because of the talented instructors, energized students and clear self-defense applications. We joined together and trained together religiously (often when we should have been studying our course work) for four years until we earned our black belts. During that time I learned to love the study of martial arts. The combined pursuit of physical, mental and spiritual improvement is rare in any other endeavor, but is a common thread throughout many martial arts. It builds character and friendships and capabilities all at once.

It has been more than thirty years since I took that first karate class. In that time I have moved frequently for the Navy, for jobs, for education and for family, but I have almost always been able to find new teachers, new friends and new skills to learn. I studied Kokushi-ryu jiu jitsu, Tai Chi Chuan, Tien Shan Pai, Cuong Nhu, F.I.G.H.T. Haganah, MMA, Gracie Barra BJJ and Muay Thai, sometimes earning belts of varying levels depending on how much carry-over there was from previous studies and how long before my next move. Sometimes I just studied as much as they would teach me and didn't worry about the belts.

Ten years ago was the last time I moved. After a year or so, my wife wisely told me, "You need to find a new karate school." When I took too long to get started, she researched a few and said, "This looks like a good one, I signed you up for an intro class."

PERSONAL ACHIEVEMENTS

- Black Belt, Warrior Krav Maga from GM Joe Corley and M Erick Alfaro
- Black Belt, Ten-Chi Kenpo from Yondan Richard Grandberry and Ryokudan Elliott Edwards.
- Married 20+ years; loving husband and proud parent
- Medical IT and Medical Sales Professional
- U.S. Navy Lieutenant
- Cum Laude Harvard University

She was right! I started studying Krav Maga at Atlanta Extreme Warrior and Joe Corley Karate. Grand Master Corley and other talented instructors had a lot to teach, and I studied eagerly. At first I wasn't worried about earning more belts as long as I kept learning, but GM Corley reminded me that testing and earning belts was part of the process to bring out the best in myself and my fellow students. I began to pursue the Warrior Krav Maga curriculum in earnest and eventually proudly earned my black belt. I taught Warrior Krav Maga for GM Corley for a few years, and I now teach for Precision Krav Maga, owned by another of GM Corley's students.

Over 30+ years, no exercise has held my attention like the pursuit of martial arts. You can't be lackadaisical while someone is trying to punch or kick you in the head! Focus and dedication are mandatory. You have to build from where you are and learn from your mistakes. You have to push yourself each day to be a little stronger, a little faster, a little smoother, a little better, a little more aware. On those days when you don't think you have it in you to push yourself, your instructors and classmates and friends are there to help pull you forward. No matter how bad (or good) the rest of my day has been, I have never regretted the classes I attended – only those I missed.

Now, as an instructor, I strive to help others find that love of the martial arts. The combined pursuit of physical, mental and spiritual improvement is rare these days. You can test your courage and patience and perseverance. You can fight with everything you've got, then (win or lose) finish with a solemn bow and a friendly handshake or bro-hug, knowing that everything that happens in class is supposed to make you better outside the class. It builds character and friendships and capabilities all at once.

IAN BLANCHARD

"Martial Arts has instilled discipline and focus in Ian's life. He has learned to work hard in order to attain his goals."

Ian was interested in karate when he was quite young. His mother, however, was worried about finding a good fit for Ian because he was diagnosed with significant ADHD and a language delay. Luckily, GM Joe Corley just happened to give a demonstration to Ian's second grade class while his mother was helping in the classroom. After talking with GM Corley, the family decided to enroll Ian. He began classes just after his 8th birthday. It was a fantastic fit for Ian. His parents and his karate instructors saw a giant leap for him with martial arts training. His focus and skills have improved significantly through the years. He is now an instructor at the studio, and he enjoys mentoring others in the lessons he has learned through American Karate.

Martial Arts has instilled discipline and focus in Ian's life. He has learned to work hard in order to attain his goals.

TRAINING INFORMATION

- Belt Ranks & Martial Arts Styles: 3rd Degree Black Belt, PKA American Karate
- Instructors/Influencers: GM Joe Corley
- Birthdate: August 2, 2003
- Birthplace/Growing Up: Marietta, GA
- Yrs. In the Martial Arts: 8.5 years
- Yrs. Instructing: 2 years
- Instructor, Member PKA Worldwide

PROFESSIONAL ORGANIZATIONS

- PKA Worldwide

PERSONAL ACHIEVEMENTS

- Member of the Symphony in GYSO

MAJOR ACHIEVEMENTS

- 3rd Degree Black Belt, American Karate

MEGAN BLANCHARD

"I have absolutely loved training with my children. It has been challenging, focusing and joyous for all of us!"

TRAINING INFORMATION

- Belt Ranks & Martial Arts Styles: 2nd Degree BlackBelt, PKA American Karate, 1st Degree Black Belt, PKA Kickboxing

- Instructors/Influencers: GM Joe Corley

- Birthdate: April 08, 1969

- Birthplace/Growing Up: Hoover, AL

- Yrs. In the Martial Arts: 8 years

- Yrs. Instructing: 2 years

- Instructor, Member PKA Worldwide

PROFESSIONAL ORGANIZATIONS

- PKA Worldwide

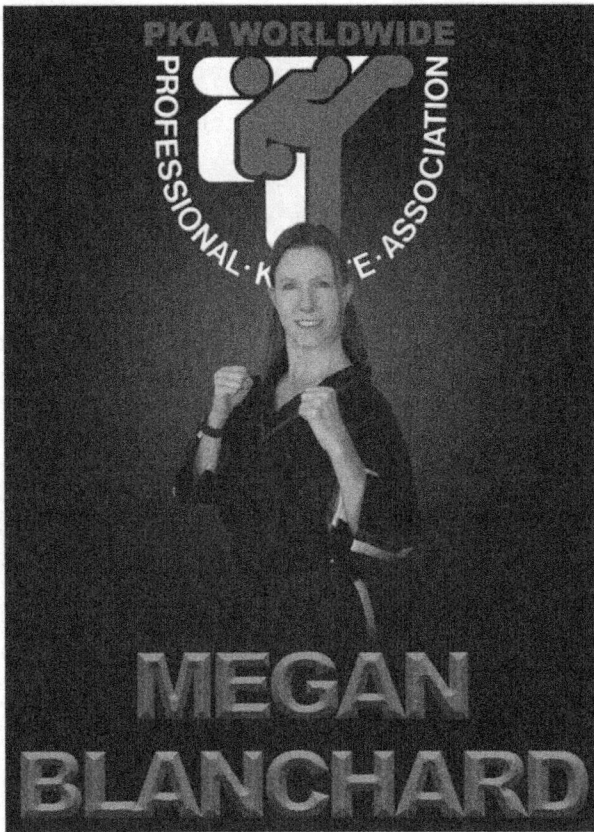

I fell into martial arts by accident. In 2011 two of my children began training at GM Corley's studio in Marietta, GA; my teen daughter enrolled in kickboxing and my 7-year old son started in karate. I would sit and watch the kids training, never thinking that I would join them. My daughter, Caitlyn, kept asking me to join her in class. The kickboxing instructor also kept encouraging me to try it, but I kept saying "no" to both of them. I really thought that I was 'too old' to pick up something new, especially martial arts.

Finally, after being a spectator for almost five months, I climbed into the hexagonal ring Master Corley had erected to learn kickboxing. I trained with my daughter for three years, and we earned our black belts in kickboxing together. That was a really powerful experience!

Soon after, Caitlyn left for college and I asked my son, who was a second degree black belt in karate by then if he would mind if I joined his class. He seemed excited about training with me, guiding me in something he had become quite good at, and so I began training in American Karate.

Because the kicks and punches in Master Corley's various classes are all the same, I already had a great sense of the basics, and I earned my

PERSONAL ACHIEVEMENTS

- Homeschooling my youngest, Ian, for 7 years

MAJOR ACHIEVEMENTS

- Black Belts in Kickboxing, American Karate and Warrior Xfit

second black belt, this one in American Karate, in 2017. At the same time, I was training in Master Bill Clark's Warrior X-Fit, and I recently earned my 2nd Degree Black Belt by achieving the desired results in 540 different workouts.

Today I'M in pursuit of my 3rd Degree Black Belt in karate and I'm training equally hard in Warrior Krav Maga as well. Now directing new and advanced students myself, I would never have believed 8 years ago that I would be leading classes in the studio.

I have absolutely loved training with my children. It has been challenging, focusing and joyous for all of us! Our family has wonderful memories training together. For me personally, the knowledge that with perseverance I could learn martial arts, gaining not only fitness but a high level of confidence as well is priceless. You are never too old, I have learned!

GM Joe Corley always introduces me to visitors to his studio as "The regular yet great Atlanta Mom who has already earned 3 Black Belts with us in Kickboxing, our American Karate Curriculum and in Warrior X-Fit, with over 700 daily wins in the fitness challenges of WXF, and she is now working hard towards her Black Belt with us in Warrior Krav Maga.

And her instructors, including Master Corley, her training partners and now her students will tell you as well, Megan Blanchard is a prime example of what martial arts are all about. She is a calm, collected, focused, dangerous fighting machine, and a humble, nurturing role model for all to see! "

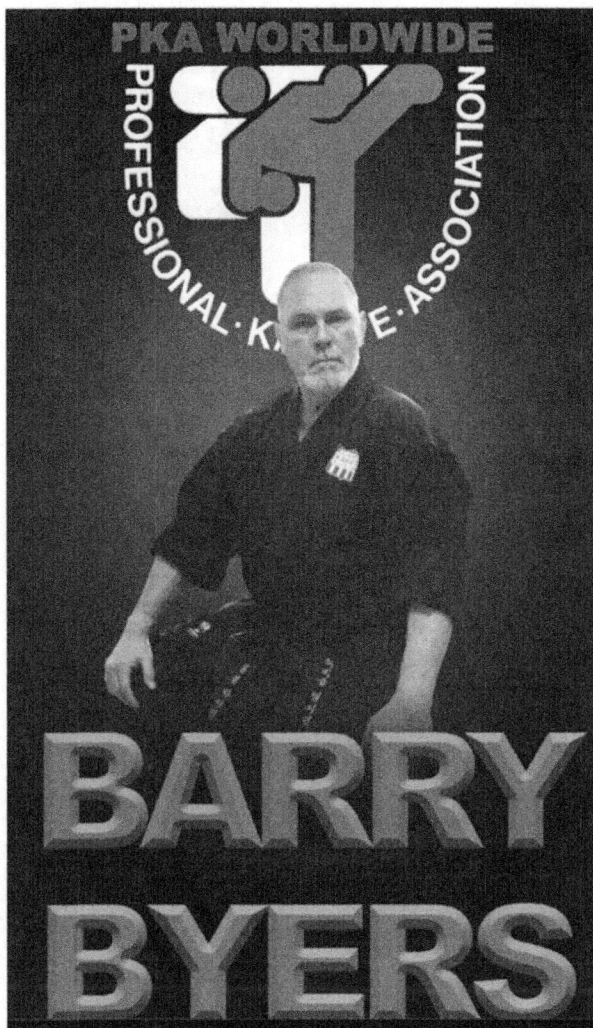

BARRY K. BYERS

"My whole life has been about a life in Martial Arts. It impacts everything..."

TRAINING INFORMATION

- Belt Ranks & Martial Arts Styles: 5th Degree Black Belt, Hapkido - Junior Instructor, Hung Gar - Kung Fu - Black Sash - Jo Gow Cup - Asst. Instructor, Chung Do Kwan - Asst. Instructor - Instructor - Master Instructor - 1978 to 2010, Full Contact Champion Kickboxing - Master Instructor, Twin Dragon Karate - Founder - Master Instructor

- Instructors/Influencers: GM Ray Heredia, Cal Farleys, GM Paul Sai, GM Travis Everett, GM Royce Young, GM James B Toney, GM Timothy Tieyah, GM Allen Steen, GM Jhoon Rhee, Colonel Penrod

- Birthdate: July 23, 1957

- Birthplace/Growing Up: Ft Worth, Tx

- Yrs. In the Martial Arts: 53 years

- Yrs. Instructing: 36 years

- School owner, Manager, Instructor: Founder of Twin Dragon Karate 1974; Instructor

PROFESSIONAL ORGANIZATIONS

- PKA - Lifetime Member
- WKA
- TKI

I began studying the martial arts for reasons of self-preservation, and discovered I had a passion for them at a very young age. I was intrigued by watching my instructors perform. Gangs had infected our Fort Worth, Texas neighborhood. After several attacks and beatings, at age nine my parents enrolled me in a karate class. It literally saved my life. I was never afraid again, and my journey as a lifetime student of martial arts began. I was a combat kid with military rifle and combat training starting before I was 10. Before I turned 12 I practiced scholastic fencing, wrestling and judo. Over the years I graduated to Black Sash Jo Gow Cup in Hung Gar Kung Fu. Learning and practicing daily skills is the medicine way.

My whole life has been about a life in Martial Arts. It impacts everything from creating pathways and closing doors, and fearless expressions were examined over and over again. Almost perfect: the decades of fighting is where repetition becomes instinctive reactions. I am fortunate to have this life.

PERSONAL ACHIEVEMENTS

- Found my Spiritual Higher Power
- Learned Fencing and Judo as a Military Cadet
- Founded a Karate club as freshman in high school
- Graduated as a Fellowship Christian Athlete
- Bible memory association honor team

MAJOR ACHIEVEMENTS

- Built a homestead for my family
- Built a substantial business worth millions
- Kept my children close to family
- Rode in the Rodeo at Cal Farleys Boys Ranch
- Got my first Black Belt as a junior - under 16
- Graduated High School, Texas Real Estate Certification
- Graduated Karate College
- Texas Undisputed Heavyweight Kickboxing Champion - Every bout but one ending in a first or second round knock-out. - 32 wins by KO – final record was 32-1- no draws
- One of the highlights in my fighting career was the opportunity to face Dennis "The Terminator" Alexio in Hawaii and another was to train with Bad Brad Hefton in Atlanta at the request of GM Joe Corley.
- Master Instructor Level - Professional Combat

MAJOR ACHIEVEMENTS

- Earned Five Black Belts; Master Instructor, Weapons Expert; Bare Knuckle Champion and Professional World Champion Kickboxer
- Earned a Black Belt under my Mentor GM Royce Young and family of Texas Karate Institute
- Texans Karate Club Team Champion and School of Heavyweights Black Belt Champion
- Fought the Worlds Undisputed Heavyweight Champion Dennis Alexio in a World Title Kickboxing Event

FRANK CALIGURI

"Martial Arts has helped me in all around life in general to give me a positive attitude and the confidence needed."

TRAINING INFORMATION

- Belt Ranks & Martial Arts Styles: 9th degree Black Belt, Shorin Ryu

- Instructors/Influencers: GM Robert Trias, GM Hidy Ochiai, GM Bruce Heilman, M Dan Kestner, Bobbi Snyder

- Birthdate: April 16, 1949

- Birthplace/Growing Up: New Kensington, PA

- Yrs. In the Martial Arts: 58 years

- Yrs. Instructing: 51 years

- School Owner, Instructor, Member PKA Worldwide

PROFESSIONAL ORGANIZATIONS

- Professional Karate Association (PKA)

- United States Association of Martial Artists (USAMA), State Representative, PA

- Karate Rating Association, (PKRA), Director

- International Karate Kobudo Federation (IKKF)

- Tournament Karate Association (TKA)

- United States Karate Do Kai (USKK)

- International Shuri-ryu Association (ISA)

As a kid, I was always interested in the Martial Arts. I would pick up a copy of Black Belt magazine and read it cover to cover. Finally, at the age of 12, an instructor moved into the area and started a small dojo. I signed up immediately.

Martial Arts has helped me in all around life in general to give me a positive attitude and the confidence needed.

PERSONAL ACHIEVEMENTS

- Rated in the Full Contact Karate Top 10 by Professional Karate Magazine,

- USKA Top 10 National Champion throughout the 70s and 80s,

- 1970 started the Academy of Martial Arts dojo

- 1975 founded the PA Karate Rating Association (PKRA)

- 1976 received the USKA Bushido Award

- 1986 promoted to Renshi by GM Robert Trias, 1st USKA Kobudo testing

MAJOR ACHIEVEMENTS

- Member of Hawkes International Society

- Tournament Promoter for 47 years

- Best Big Tournament Promoter by the PKC,

- Regional Director for USKA under GM Robert Trias until his death in 1989

- 1997 USK Alliance Hall of Fame inductee

- 1999 Alle-Kiski Hall of Fame

- 2001 World Champion Masters Kata Division, USK Alliance World Championships, New Orleans, LA

- Honoree with Bill Viola as the 1st promoters of MMA events in the USA with a display at the HJ Heinz Sports Museum in Pittsburgh, PA.

MAJOR ACHIEVEMENTS

- Western PA History Magazine feature story on Tough Guys - the book and Showtime movie, Frank Caliguri and Bill Viola

- Featured in the Godfathers of MMA-The Birth of an American Sport in Showtime documentary Tough Guys

TOURNAMENT DIRECTORS

FRANK, KELLI AND NANCY CALIGURI

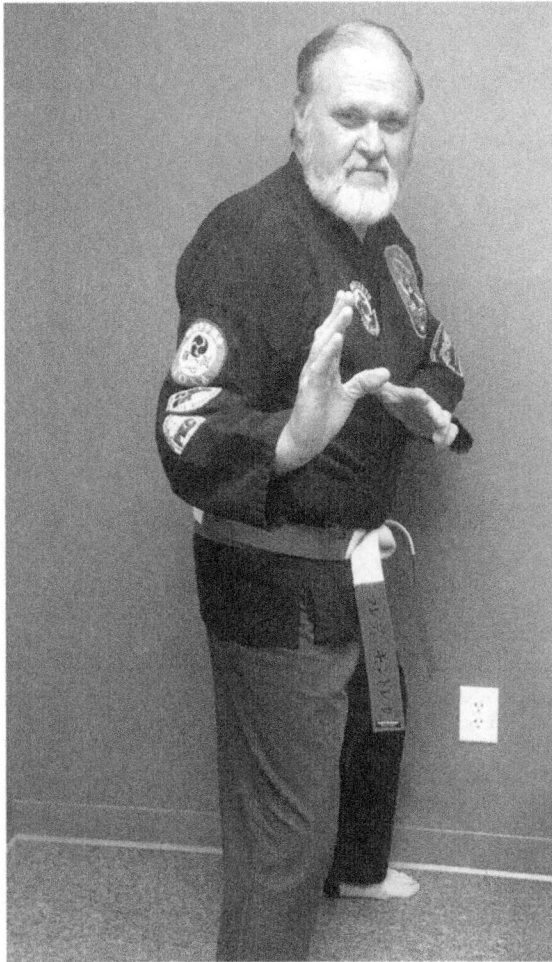

FREDDIE CANTRELL

"Training in martial arts has helped me overcome many obstacles in my life."

TRAINING INFORMATION

- Belt Ranks & Martial Arts Styles: Isshinryu Karate- Roku-Dan (6th degree)

- Instructors/Influencers: Master Harold Long, Master Robert Porterfield, Master Cas Cox, Master Glen Webb, Master Mike Clark, Master Don Roberts

- Birthdate: March 24, 1957

- Birthplace/Growing Up: White Pine & Pigeon Forge, TN

- Yrs. In the Martial Arts: 47 years

- Yrs. Instructing: 40+ years

- School owner, Manager, Instructor, Founder

PROFESSIONAL ORGANIZATIONS

- PKA Worldwide

- PKC Professional Karate Commission

- TOKA - Traditional Okinawan Karate Association

- IIKA- International Isshinryu Karate Association

- ICBA World Wide

I became interested in martial arts when I was in grade school. Bruce Lee was my inspiration for starting to train. At the age of sixteen when I started driving I traveled several days a week to Knoxville, Tennessee to train with Master Harold Long. Also, I was honored to have had the opportunity to train with Master Robert Porterfield, Master Cas Cox and I received my Shodan from Master Glen Webb. I continued training with Master Mike Clark until I opened my own dojo 21 years ago.

Training in martial arts has helped me overcome many obstacles in my life. I have the confidence to teach at seminars and I have entered competitions for 40+ years, and now, especially at my age I do well. I have probably trained hundreds if not thousands of students through the years including my wife and two children. Now retired, I enjoy training my students at my dojo that I have had for 21 years. Karate has been a way of life for me most of my life. In the 47 years I have been training I have never been inactive. If the dojo I was training at would close I would find another to train at.

PERSONAL ACHIEVEMENTS

- Receiving my Roku-Dan in August 2016

- Owning and opening my dojo for the last 21 years

- Training my wife and both of my children

MAJOR ACHIEVEMENTS

- Winning numerous world and national championships including:

- NBL World Breaking Championship 2005 and 2017

- WCMAO Creative Breaking champion 2003, 2004, 2005, and 2020

- TCT breaking championships 2008

- TKO Creative and Extreme Breaking championship 2019

- TOKA Dojo of the Year 20

- UMAHOF recipient

- History General - Sport Karate Museum

LIBBY CANTRELL

"I have the privilege to teach and work with young girls who are victims of rape, abuse and neglect..."

TRAINING INFORMATION

- Belt Ranks & Martial Arts Styles: Yondan, Isshinryu Karate (4th degree)

- Instructors/Influencers: Freddie Cantrell, Rokudan

- Birthdate: September 16, 1963

- Birthplace/Growing Up: Pigeon Forge, TN

- Yrs. In the Martial Arts: 28 years

- Yrs. Instructing: 20 years

- School owner, Instructor, Member PKA Worldwide, National Competition Team Coach

PROFESSIONAL ORGANIZATIONS

- PKA - Professional Karate Association
  PKC - Professional Karate Commission

- IIKA - International Isshinryu Karate Association
  TOKA - Traditional Okinawan Karate Association
  ICBA World Wide

I began my training at the age of 18 at the urging of my now husband after being the victim of an armed robbery in my home at the age of 17.

The Martial Arts are a way of life for me. In the beginning my biggest obstacle was gaining the confidence that I could defend myself in an emergency situation. Having been a victim, this is probably the hardest thing to achieve. Now, I have the privilege to teach and work with young girls who are victims of rape, abuse and neglect as well as women who have been abused by their husband, or are otherwise victims themselves. As I see them grow stronger and more confident I know this is what I was meant to do.

PERSONAL ACHIEVEMENTS

- I consider my greatest personal achievement is my children. Both adults now, they have grown into respectful hard working members of our community. When I began training in martial arts many years ago I never imagined that someday not only would I be an instructor, but I would co own with my husband our areas premier dojo, now in our 21st year of operation. As a woman I consider this a huge achievement and my goal is to train as many ladies, both young and old, in this sport that I treasure.

MAJOR ACHIEVEMENTS

- I am the Assistant to Mr. Don Willis, the Director of PKA Worldwide Associated Schools & Members

- Receiving my Shodan at the age of 39 - I consider this to be my greatest achievement in martial arts and continuing to go up in rank

- Teaching self-defense classes to ladies in the community, including training for handicapped and mobility challenged

- Numerous awards from the TOKA association, including Dojo of the Year and Outstanding Female

- Numerous nominations from the Isshinryu Hall of Fame and from the Isshinryu Nationals

- History General and Lady Black Belt award from the Sport Karate Museum

JOHN CHUNG

"Martial Arts has taught me to see, experience and live life positively and gratefully."

At a young age, I was interested in the Martial Arts. In Korea, I took Judo at my Middle School. In 1970, at the age of 12, I came to Washington, D.C and began my training in Tae Kwon Do with my Uncle, Founding Father of American Tae Kwon Do Grand Master Jhoon Rhee. Martial Arts has taught me to be a student for and of life. It has taught me the benefits of being a competitor and the joy of being the best individual that I choose to be.

The passion of Martial Arts has given me the opportunity to pay it forward by teaching since 1972. I have also been Blessed as a competitor, to be the Champion of the World, and to have traveled and enjoyed many Martial Artists and their cultures from various countries.

My philosophy: Learn Something, Get a Good workout and Have Fun! This has been my school motto and theme where students of all ages benefit.

Martial Arts has taught me to see, experience and live life positively and gratefully. I believe the president of 1st grade is just as important as a person as the president of a company. Everyone is treated with respect.

Always try your best, effort is the most important quality and seek joy in your goals and achievements.

TRAINING INFORMATION

- Martial Arts Title: World Forms & Fighting Champion
- Reston, VA
- Started Studying Martial Arts in 1970
- Instructing Martial Arts for 44 years and currently holds the rank of 9th Dan Black Belt studying martial arts styles: Tae Kwon Do

PERSONAL ACHIEVEMENTS:

- 1976, Graduated Wakefield High School, Arlington, Virginia
- 1984, Wake Forest University, B.S. in Business Administration, Winston-Salem, North Carolina

PERSONAL TIMELINE

- 1970: No Belt
- 1974: Black Belt
- 1977: PKA National Champion
- 1979: US Champion
- 1981: World Champion
- 1982: Black Belt Hall of Fame
- 1982: PKA Tournament Competitor of the Year
- 1983: World Champion
- 1984: Inductee Karate Hall of Fame
- 1985: World Champion
- 1989: Diamond Nationals Hall of Fame
- 1990: NASKA Hall of Fame
- 1990: Fighter International Hall of Fame
- 1993: World Martial Arts Hall of Fame
- 1996: Bluegrass Nationals Hall of Fame
- 1997: Founder of Sidekick International Competition Team
- 1998: Promoter of the Sidekick International Martial Arts Championship
- 1999: Promoter of the World Cup Finals Open Martial Arts Championship
- 2000: President of the World Cup Martial Arts Organization
- 2005: Ocean State Grand Nationals Hall of Fame
- 2006: World Mundo Federation Hall of Fame
- 2009: Universal Martial Arts Association International Hall of Fame
- 2012: All Pro Tae Kwon Do Martial Arts Hall of Fame
- 2013: New York Tournaments Martial Arts Hall of Fame

Seminars and training camps for Martial Artists of all styles and levels have brought me great opportunities to continually share my experiences as a student, competitor, instructor and business owner. Hosting tournaments and motivational speeches have been well received and appreciated by both Martial Artists and Non-Martial Artists.

In the years 1970-1987, I was fortunate to have competed in all major tournaments, National and Internationally, Winning World Championship titles since 1981. Most Recent Awards: 2014-Masters Hall of Fame, 2014-World Wide Tae Kwon Do Award, 2015 -AmeriKick Internationals Hall of Fame, 2016- Joe Lewis Eternal Warrior Award, And . . . 30 years of teaching Boot Camp for Martial Artists. Students from all over the world come to train together to improve, learn and experience world class training.

"People go to camps to meet a Champion. We come to John Chung's camp to become a Champion!"

HIGHLIGHTS:

"The best in the world! "King of Kata!" "World Forms & Fighting champion!" Any describe only one person.

Student of Grandmaster Jhoon Rhee, father of American Tae Kwon Do, John Chung.

John Chung, with his famous perfect side kick and techniques, has revolutionized the level of competition. Pioneer of musical forms and perfectionist of traditional forms, the King of Kata, John Chung, has brought the standard of excellence to the forefront.

World forms & fighting John Chung is passing down his experience and spreading his knowledge of martial arts, to students of Karate, Kung Fu and Tae Kwon Do. The best in the world, John Chung, excels as an instructor. The knowledge to understand and improve technically along with the edge to win in competition is currently given in worldwide seminars. All seminars vary from Tae Kwon Do history, traditional forms, musical forms, self-defense (applications of techniques) to necessary basics in stretching, strengthening, tournament & continuous sparring and open competition.

JOE CORLEY

"Martial Arts provided me with the opportunity to learn so many skills that apply to so many aspects of life."

HUMILITY OF A GRANDMASTER 10TH DEGREE CERTIFICATE:

One who has achieved the rank of GRAND MASTER in MARTIAL ARTS, in fact,

DOES NOT FEEL WORTHY...

Having BATTLED through the WARRIOR BLACK BELT RANKS OF 1ST, 2ND and 3RD DEGREE

And Having PROUDLY ADMINISTERED the TEACHER / INSTRUCTOR RANKS OF 4TH and 5th DEGREE

And Having SKILLFULLY & MASTERFULLY

EDUCATED THE INSTRUCTORS as a PROFESSOR 6th and 7th DEGREE and

Having CONSISTENTLY and DUTIFULLY GIVEN BACK TO THE MARTIAL ARTS COMMUNITY as 8TH and 9th DEGREE

The GRANDMASTER knows what he does not know; he knows how much there is left to learn.

At the same time, he embodies the sentiments in Master Educator Stephen R. Covey's 7 HABITS and his expression of HUMILITY: "Humility is the mother of all virtues. Courage is the father. Integrity the Child. Wisdom the Grandchild."

Having honorably carried out the BLACK BELT RESPONSIBILITIES above and having demonstrated exceptionally the virtues of

WISDOM, INTEGRITY, COURAGE and HUMILITY

THE PROFESSIONAL KARATE COMMISSION

DOES HEREBY BESTOW UPON

JOE CORLEY

THE GRAND MASTER RANK OF

10th DEGREE BLACK BELT

Atlanta's Joe Corley is still a black belt and sports entrepreneur with a mission, most recently honored for Lifetime Achievement in the 2019 Who's Who in Martial Arts and on the cover of the 2017 LEGENDS edition of the AMAA Who's Who in the Martial Arts 2017 edition. Now a Grand Master instructor with more than 5 decades experience in the martial arts, and the producer of PKA KARATE & KICKBOXING for television, Corley's life-long purpose for being has been to share with everyone the positive feelings of confidence, courage, intensity, focus, personal discipline and integrity engendered by good martial arts training and competition. He has done that through the promotion of the martial arts in his Atlanta chain of studios, through his Battle of Atlanta World Karate Championship and on television around the world.

Corley began his karate classes at age 16, earned his black belt at 19, opened his first studio at 19, won three US titles in the next three years, founded the Battle of Atlanta at age 23 and has fervently spread the word ever since. Joe has sought to share the most practical physical karate movements available and combine those real-life defensive techniques with modern American positive philosophy.

There are but a handful of men in the martial arts anywhere in the world who have accomplished so much for the furtherance of the martial arts philosophy and physical applications. As a fighter, Joe Corley won three United States Championships in point karate and went on to retire as the number one ranked Middle Weight contender in the world. Now a 10th degree Black Belt in American Karate, Mr. Corley and his Black Belts have taught more than 50,000 men, women and children in his chain of Atlanta studios.

As a Black Belt in Tang Soo Do, he opened Atlanta's first full time karate studio in 1967 while he was still competing and expanded the studios to become the most well-known martial arts chain in the Southeast.

In 1970, Joe Corley founded the BATTLE OF ATLANTA, one of the most prestigious open karate tournaments in the world. The Battle of Atlanta recently completed its Golden Anniversary and the GATHERING OF WORLD CHANGERS. The Battle, now owned and produced by Truth Entertainment, again hosted competitors from all over the world. In this same period, Art Heller joined Joe Corley, Sam Chapman, Bill McDoanald, Larry Reinhardt and Jack Motley in a meeting with Chuck Norris to kick off the South East karate Association (SEKA) from which so many great Southeast Champions emerged.

In 1975, Joe Corley challenged Bill "Superfoot" Wallace for his PKA World Middleweight Title in what became a historic fight before 12,000 fans in Atlanta's Omni. Wallace won the first of its kind 9 round bout. Master Corley would later be hired by CBS to cover Superfoot's future bouts because of his ability to articulate the inner workings of the sport and the techniques and strategies of the fighters.

Because of the great ratings at CBS, Master Corley also became the voice for American Karate and PKA KICKBOXING on other networks. He actually produced the programming and did commentary with long-term friends like Chuck Norris and the late Pat Morita (Mr. Miyagi) on NBC, CBS, ESPN, SHOWTIME, USA NETWORK, TURNER SPORTS, SPORTSCHANNEL AMERICA, PRIME NETWORK, SPORTSOUTH

and on international television syndication. As expert analyst and host for PKA KARATE World Championships on network, cable and pay per view, Mr. Corley became synonymous with the sport to the millions of fans who

Grand Master's Jeff Smith & Joe Corley receive their PKC 10th Degree Black Belts at Battle of Atlanta 2016

With events originating from such diverse locales as Canada, France, Belgium, South Africa, South America and the United Arab Emirates plus 50 cities in the United States, Joe Corley has educated 4 generations of sports fans.

Master Corley has been named Official Karate Magazine's Man of the Decade, was inducted into the prestigious Black Belt Magazine Hall of Fame and the International Tae Kwon Do Hall of Fame and has received more awards than anyone can count.

But the thing that continues to drive Joe Corley is the knowledge that he and his accomplished associates can use all their experiences to share with everyone around the world on television the great feelings of confidence, courage, discipline, honor and integrity that come from presenting the martial arts properly. His PKA WORLDWIDE KICKBOXING projects are the perfect vehicles to spread the messages of positive martial arts on a global scale.

"The unequalled success of the UFC, built on our previous successes, has set the stage for PKA Fighters to achieve the 'fame and fortune' the athletes of the UFC are now enjoying", he said.

Joe is in regular meetings with astute sports entrepreneurs in order to kick off the new project for 2020 and beyond. "We have the UFC's own research to indicate the timing is perfect for us now", he said. At the same time, he is building the grass roots for PKA WORLDWIDE Associated Schools and Members, bringing together the best martial artists from around the globe.

Mr. Corley's bride--Christina-- is his right arm and chief administrator in PKA WORLDWIDE. Mr. Corley's daughter, Christiana, 22, continues to be his lustrous link in this new millennium and his compelling force to make the martial arts world an even better place.

Master Corley's closest friends point to the PKC 10th Degree Grand Master certificate, saying the language of the certificate reflects the philosophy and humility they know to be the real Joe Corley (See above).

Master Corley is consulting with a number of martial artists to share his experience and wisdom and has been recruited to consult on other projects outside the martial arts. One such project is the introduction of a generation system destined to change the worlds of Solar, Wind Generation and Electric Vehicles.

"Martial arts provided me with the opportunity to learn so many skills that apply to so many aspects of life", he said. "I look forward to this 'next half' of my time on the planet applying the skills learned. I also fiercely love being a student, and I look forward to learning as much as I can in this last half. Learning brings me joy", he smiled.

"After 19 years as a 9th Degree Black Belt, I was so proud to earn my 10th Degree from the PKC and Grand Master Glenn Keeney in 2016. I was honored to have GM Pat Johnson, GM Allen Steen and GM Pat Burleson approve the PKC promotion. It was doubly sweet because lifelong friend Jeff Smith earned his that same day. These 5 men have all had such a great influence on my martial arts career in so many ways, and it was so very special to share the experience with all of them!"

JIM FLANAGAN

"...In many of my lectures I've spoken highly of the value of Martial Arts in everyday life."

TRAINING INFORMATION

- Belt Ranks & Martial Arts Styles: 2nd degree Black Belt Shito-Ryu

- Instructors/Influencers: Shihan Richard "Bulldog" Kelly, Kaicho Hanchi

- Birthdate: 1946

- Birthplace/Growing Up: Shreveport, LA/Kissimme, FL

- Yrs. In the Martial Arts: 42 years

PROFESSIONAL ORGANIZATIONS

- PKA Worldwide

- National Karate, Jiu Jitsu Weapons Union

- International Karate Kobedo Union

- Kita Kaze Bijutsu

As a former physical educator, I met Arthur Jones in March of 1971 at the famous Deland High School "Quonset hut" where he was testing his Nautilus prototypes. As the result of that first meeting, my career path changed dramatically when I became an early Nautilus customer in 1972 and the following year, with the opening of my own Nautilus Fitness Center in Orlando, Florida.

During the late 1970s thru the 1980s, I was operating my gym, Jim Flanagan's Nautilus Fitness Center, and working for Arthur Jones' Nautilus Sports/Medical Industries. I was instrumental in the launching of both of Mr. Jones' companies, Nautilus & MedX, on a global level and with the spread of High Intensity Training worldwide. My relationship with Arthur Jones and both of his successful companies spanned 36 years.

I learned that several members of my gym were studying martial arts from a local instructor named Richard "Bulldog" Kelly. In the Spring of 1978, I flew to Atlanta to address a Georgia Tech Football Clinic, and as I presented my airline ticket to the Delta gate agent, he asked if I was the owner of the Nautilus Fitness Center in Orlando. I responded "I am" and he introduced himself as Richard Kelly. That same year I became a student of Shihan Kelly. When I wasn't on the road for MedX, I trained under Shihan Kelly in the Shito-Ryu style of Karate, earning my second degree black belt in 1990. Our friendship began then and we remain

PERSONAL ACHIEVEMENTS

- Producer and promoter with GM Joe Corley of the PKA-Nautilus Full Contact Kickboxing ESPN live worldwide event

- Recognized in 1998 by the Florida Governor's Council on Physical Fitness for Florida Governor's Leadership Award for significant contributions and enduring commitment to fitness and sports in the community and the State of Florida

- Inducted in 2017 into the National Fitness Hall of Fame (NFHOF) for contributions to the Fitness Profession

- resident of Resistance Solutions, Inc.

- Consultant to Christner's Prime Steak & Lobster in Orlando, Florida

friends today. And since those days, in many of my lectures I've spoken highly of the value of martial arts in everyday life.

Later I was introduced to Joe Corley by Bill Clark of ATA fame, and as GM Corley's guest for the 1985 "Battle of Atlanta" I was seated with Chuck Norris and Pat Johnson. As a result of attending that event, I teamed up with Joe Corley and PKA, hosting a star-studded full-contact kickboxing event at the Nautilus television studios. This event with over 500 Nautilus attendees was broadcast live via ESPN worldwide.

The Nautilus Brand became strong in the Martial Arts World and, in fact, Bill Clark/ATA was ahead of the game because the majority of his schools were equipped with Nautilus machines.

In 1998 I was recognized by the Florida Governor's Council on Physical Fitness for Florida Governor's Leadership Award for significant contributions and enduring commitment to fitness & sports in the community and the State of Florida.

Then, in April of 2017, I had the great honor to be inducted into the National Fitness Hall of Fame (NFHOF) distinguished class of 2017 for my contributions to the Fitness Profession.

Currently, I'm the President of Resistance Solutions, Inc., and involved in fitness and business consulting projects worldwide and locally. I also consult on the operations side at Christner's Prime Steak & Lobster in Orlando, Florida. You can find me on FaceBook at "The-Real-Hit-Experience" and on his website www.TheRealHit.com.

TED GAMBORDELLA

"During the last 10 years I began to recognize the World's Greatest Martial Artists and started doing tribute videos, over 500 so far..."

TRAINING INFORMATION

- Belt Ranks & Martial Arts Styles: 10th Degree Juko Ryu Jiu Jitsu...Soke (Head of Family), 10th Degree Aiki Jitsu, 10th Degree Okinawan Karate, 8th Degree Tae Kwon Do, 8th Degree Weapons

- Instructors/Influencers: Bill Hawthorne, Soke Rod Sacharnoski, Soke Albert Church, Allen Steen, Royce Young, Keith Yates, James Toney, Vince Tamura, Carlos Machado

- Birthdate: February 22, 1948

- Birthplace/Growing Up: New Haven, CT / Alexandria, LA

- Yrs. In the Martial Arts: 57 years

- Yrs. Instructing: 57 years

- Instructor, Member of PKA Worldwide

PROFESSIONAL ORGANIZATIONS

- PKA Worldwide

My brothers used to beat me up so I started to learn to defend myself ... and they never beat me up again.

I started my Martial Arts journey in Alexandria, Louisiana in 1964 training under a man named Bill Hawthorne, in Shorindo Karate. This was during the Vietnam War, and the only people who knew martial arts were military people.

I earned my first Black Belt in 1968 in Okinawan Karate and during that time I met Soke Rod Sacharnoski, now famous for Combat Ki, at a class at LSU-A. I went there to beat him up since I had heard he was telling people how he could take full power punches and kicks and rather berating traditional karate. I soon changed my mind after I kicked him in the groin, smashed his ribs, and gave a vicious Shuto to the throat and the only thing that was hurt was my hand and foot. I became Soke's third Black Belt in America, and went to live with him in North Carolina where I meet one of his teachers, Soke Albert Church, a great man and teacher. Soke Church had a 100-year old scroll giving him his Sokeship.

I became a weapons black belt and 2nd degree Jiu Jitsu Black Belt under Soke Church. There were very few martial arts schools in Louisiana then, and only one was Karl Marx school in Alexandria. There were no jiu jitsu schools in existence in Louisiana, or in the South.

PERSONAL ACHIEVEMENTS

- 1st Black Belt 1968
- World Martial Arts Hall of Fame 1998
- Grandmaster Instructor of the Year 2000
- International Weapons Master Instructor of Year 2001
- Martial Arts Weapons Hall of Fame 2001
- World Head of Family Sokeship Council 1999
- Martial Art Legends Hall of Fame 2001
- Martial Arts Masters Hall of Fame 2002
- World Black Belt Hall of Fame 2003
- Personal Trainers Hall of Fame 2007
- Karate Masters Hall of Fame 2011
- Masters Hall of Fame 2014
- Joe Lewis Award from Joe Corley, 2017
- Patented Inventor

MAJOR ACHIEVEMENTS

- Author of 75 books and 42 DVDs 1st Jiu Jitsu Black Belt in Texas
- 1st weapons Black Belt in Texas, and Louisiana
- 1st Okinawan Karate Black Belt in Louisiana
- 1st to promote others to black belt in weapons and jiu jitsu in Texas and Louisiana
- 1st jiu jitsu team in Louisiana and Texas

I started the first Jiu Jitsu Club at LSU and was the first teacher to promote students to Black Belt in Jiu Jitsu, and weapons in the South. I started the first karate tournament at the college, the Southern Karate Championship.

At LSU I meet and trained with Dr. He Young Kimm, the great Hapikdo teacher and I was the first man to get a Doctorate from LSU in Martial Arts History.

I wrote my first book on the Martial Arts in 1975, The End of Injury, and traveled around the southern United States to work with colleges and professional teams to help prevent injuries in sports. I was endorsed by LSU, OU, OSU, Rice, Perdue, Alabama, Oral Roberts U, Louisiana College, The Houston Rockets, The New Orleans Jazz, and dozens of high schools.

During that time I developed my famous KI demonstrations. I would let the largest men hit me in the throat, groin, ribs, and solar plexus with no injury to me. I also became famous for knocking apples out of people mouths with nunchakus and bending a 12 inch razor sharp butcher knife on my neck.

I was promoted to 5th degree by Soke Sacharnoski, and moved to Texas in the 1980s. I had a martial arts school in Wichita Falls, Texas and came to Dallas to do a demo in Allen Steen's US Karate Open, and Pat Burleson's Texas Karate Championship. I was very successful with my demos and was the only man in the 25 years of Allen Steen's tournament to demonstrate for five years in a row. I also did demos at George Minshew's Karate Olympics and all the other major tournaments in Texas and Louisiana.

MAJOR ACHIEVEMENTS

- 1st Jiu Jitsu Black Belt at Louisiana State University

- Started first Jiu Jitsu club at LSU

- Produced 1st Karate Collegiate Championship tournament 1971

- 1st author of book on Hard KI (chi)

- 1st person to bend knife on neck in demonstration

- Wrote the 1st Complete Martial Arts Weapons manual in 1976, best-selling martial arts manual in history, still in print after 35 years

- Wrote 1st book on using martial arts techniques in sports to prevent injuries, improve performance and develop a winning attitude. Which was used and endorsed by University of Texas, OU, LSU, Oral Roberts, Louisiana College, Purdue, Rice University, Houston Rockets, New Orleans Jazz, dozens of high schools

- 1st Martial Arts black belt with a weekly TV show in America, 2 years on channel 11 DFW

- Voted "The Most Perfect Body in America 1980"

- Appeared on National TV 8 times with martial arts programs including Real People, Entertainment Tonight, Playboy Channel, Fox TV,

- Inside Edition, and dozens of local TV stations across Texas and Louisiana

- 1st Martial Arts Master to work with US Olympic committee training US Olympic athletes using martial arts techniques

I wrote my two most successful Martial Arts books during the 1980s, The 100 Deadliest Karate Moves, and The Complete Book of Karate Weapons. They sold 100,000+ copies and I began writing for Paladin Press who published eight more of my titles.

I produced the first digital martial arts books in 1986 at the start of the Internet. And then I produced the first digital Martial Arts CD, The Ultimate Martial Arts CD with 32 books, and five hours of video. And I had one of the first martial arts web pages, WWWIN.com. There was no streaming and only slow modems back then, so you could not do high quality online material.

I have been considered a fitness pioneer and operated some of the largest health clubs in Louisiana, and Texas for several years. I have been working out, eating right, and continually training for 45 years and look better today than I did 20 years ago.

I was inducted into the Personal Trainer Hall of Fame, and have appeared on National TV several times with my fitness books, martial arts, and motivational books.

I have written 75+ plus books on the Martial Arts and produced over 40 DVDs as well as 2,000 videos on You Tube.

During the last 10 years I began to recognize the world's greatest martial artists and started doing tribute videos, over 500 so far, and writing my book series The World's Greatest Martial Artists. I have done 19 volumes of the book now.

I wrote the End of Injury, the first book on using martial arts techniques in sports to prevent injuries, improve performance and develop a winning attitude. It was used and endorsed by University of Texas, OU, LSU, Oral Roberts, Louisiana College, Purdue, Rice University, Houston Rockets, New Orleans Jazz, and dozens of high schools.

MAJOR ACHIEVEMENTS

- 1st Jiu Jitsu demonstration at the Karate Olympics, US Karate Championship, Mardi Gras Nationals, Texas Karate Championships, Big D, (5 years in a row; no one had ever done more than three before), and dozens of other tournaments

- Featured in Black Belt Magazine, Inside Kung Fu, and Martial Arts Business cover story

- 1st American author of karate weapons manual
1st author to produce martial art book digitally in 1990
1st martial arts master author with Iphone application
1st martial arts master with Video's and DVD's
1st web site for martial arts books and videos 1990

- 1st martial arts author to sell digital books on Ebay

- Inventor with Patented products, Logo Glove and Vpower glove

- Started the Martial Arts Masters Hall of Fame 1992

- Started the first Martial Arts MLM "winners club" in 1982

- Invented the "Gambretta" the ultimate legal carry self-defense weapon

- TV Pilot Live2B100 in 2008

- Author of The World's Greatest Martial Artists...19 Volumes...honoring over 1,900 Great Martial Artists and counting

JOHN GRAHAM

" I owe all my personal success to the Martial Arts. **"**

TRAINING INFORMATION

- Belt Ranks & Martial Arts Styles: 8th Dan Joe Lewis Fighting System, 8th Dan Superfoot System, Shaolin Wushu 10th Dan, Wu Chu Chee Kim Thong 8th Dan

- Instructors/Influencers: Joe Lewis, Bill Wallace, Dato Chee Kim

- Birthdate: June 19, 1953

- Birthplace/Growing Up: Gulfport, MS / Mobile, AL

- Yrs. In the Martial Arts: 49 years

- Yrs. Instructing: 45 years

- School owner, Instructor

PROFESSIONAL ORGANIZATIONS

- PKA Worldwide

- Past President of International Wu Chu

- Board of Directors Superfoot System

I was a youth boxer at the age of 15 in Mobile, AL. I was stationed in Rota, Spain while in the US Marine Corps when I walked into a martial arts class and was totally sold. I knew I had found my path in life. It was love at first sight.

I had dropped out of high school in the 11th grade and joined the Marine Corps at 17 years old. I was floundering on where to direct my energy, but once I discovered the amazing benefits of martial arts, I learned to concentrate and focus. I went from a high school drop out to a person with many achievements including a Master's Degree. I owe all my personal success to the martial arts.

PERSONAL ACHIEVEMENTS

- AAU Chinese Martial Arts Region 3 Director
- Certificate of Completion: Special Weapons & Tactics (City of Mobile PD)
- Excellent Police Duty Award 1987
- Commander's Citation for Bravery (Mobile Police Dept.) 1988
- Mobile Police Department Service Ribbon (5, 10,15 and 20 year)
- Humanitarian Award (United Cerebral Palsy)
- Honorable Discharge (U.S. Marine Corps)
- Physical Fitness Award (U.S. Marine Corps)
- Am South Educational Excellence Award
- Certificate of Promotion to Sergeant in the United States Marine Corps
- Promoted to Lieutenant for the Mobile Police Department September 1996
- State of Alabama Proclamation by the Governor 1992
- Appointed Goodwill Ambassador, State of Alabama by Governor Fob James 1996
- State of Alabama Proclamation "National Martial Arts Day" October 7, 2002
- Mobile County Commission Resolution recognizing Gold Sash from China 2003
- Proclamation by Mobile AL Mayor Michael Dow, Organized and Implemented "National Random Acts of Kindness" for Youth May 1, 2003
- Alabama Resolution for Southern Nan Shaolin Team, August 31, 2000
- Mayor Sam Jones Award for Child Advocacy Center 2006

MAJOR ACHIEVEMENTS

- Master's Degree in Public Administration
- President of the Joe Lewis Superfoot System
- Vice President of the Joe Lewis Karate System

DR. RODNEY GRAHAM

"The Martial Arts have totally changed my self-image and self-esteem."

TRAINING INFORMATION

- Belt Ranks & Martial Arts Styles: 10th degree Black Belt, Wado-Ryu Karate-Do; 3rd degree Black Belt, Tae Kwon Do; 1st degree Black Belt, Tang Soo Do

- Instructors/Influencers: Grand Master Dr. Jim Thomas

- Birthdate: December 28, 1959

- Birthplace/Growing Up: Gauley Bridge, WV / Summerville, SC

- Yrs. In the Martial Arts: 47 years

- Yrs. Instructing: 25 years

- Instructor, Member PKA Worldwide

PROFESSIONAL ORGANIZATIONS

- Professional Karate Association (PKA)

- USA Karate Federation

- World Karate Federation

- World Tae Kwon Do Federation

- US Eastern Wado-Ryu Federation

- World Tang Soo Do General Federation

- US National Martial Arts Alliance

- USA Martial Arts Hall of Fame

- AAU Karate

- World Black Belt Bureau

- Christian Martial Arts Association, President

I was badly bullied, resulting in an ER visit, in middle school. In 1973-74, I began studying Shotokan. I later switched to Wado-Ryu Karate.

The Martial Arts have totally changed my self-image and self-esteem; they have given me tremendous confidence and a true sense of achievement.

PERSONAL ACHIEVEMENTS

- Seven college degrees including two Doctorals

- Three college certificates in addition to seven degrees

- Professional-class drummer, recorded, television and theatrical performances

- Notre Dame, Grand Canyon, and Charleston Southern Alumni Association

- Disney University College Program Graduate

- Induction into the Who's Who in the Martial Arts

MAJOR ACHIEVEMENTS

- Inducted in the National Hall of Fame four times

- Over twenty martial arts trophies

- Over forty martial arts medals, 12 on national level

- United States AAU District, SC State, Regional, and National Karate Champion

- Member of the kata team for the 2015 Guinness World Record holders

- Competitor Invitee, USA National Martial Arts Team, the World Cup, Cancun MX

- Ted Gambordella's "World's Greatest Martial Artists" listing

TIMOTHY HARRISON

"TM Martial Arts Academy focuses on teaching character development, self-defense skills, and developing strong leadership skills..."

TRAINING INFORMATION

- Belt Ranks & Martial Arts Styles: 7th degree Black Belt, Tae Kwon Do; 6th degree Black Belt, Combat Hapkido; 1st degree Black Belt, Joe Lewis Fighting System

- Instructors/Influencers: GM Pellegrini, GM Joe Lewis, GM Kyung Ho Park, GM Jeff Smith, GM Bill "Superfoot" Wallace

- Birthdate: May 14, 1965

- Birthplace/Growing Up: Naperville, IL

- Yrs. In the Martial Arts: 40 years

- Yrs. Instructing: 20 years

- School Owner, Manager, Instructor, Member PKA Worldwide

PROFESSIONAL ORGANIZATIONS

- PKA Worldwide

- International Combat Hapkido Federation

- Independent Tae Kwon Do Association

- Superfoot System

- Joe Lewis Fighting Systems

- Stephen Oliver's Martial Arts Wealth Mastery

- Hanminjok Hapkido Association World Kido Federation

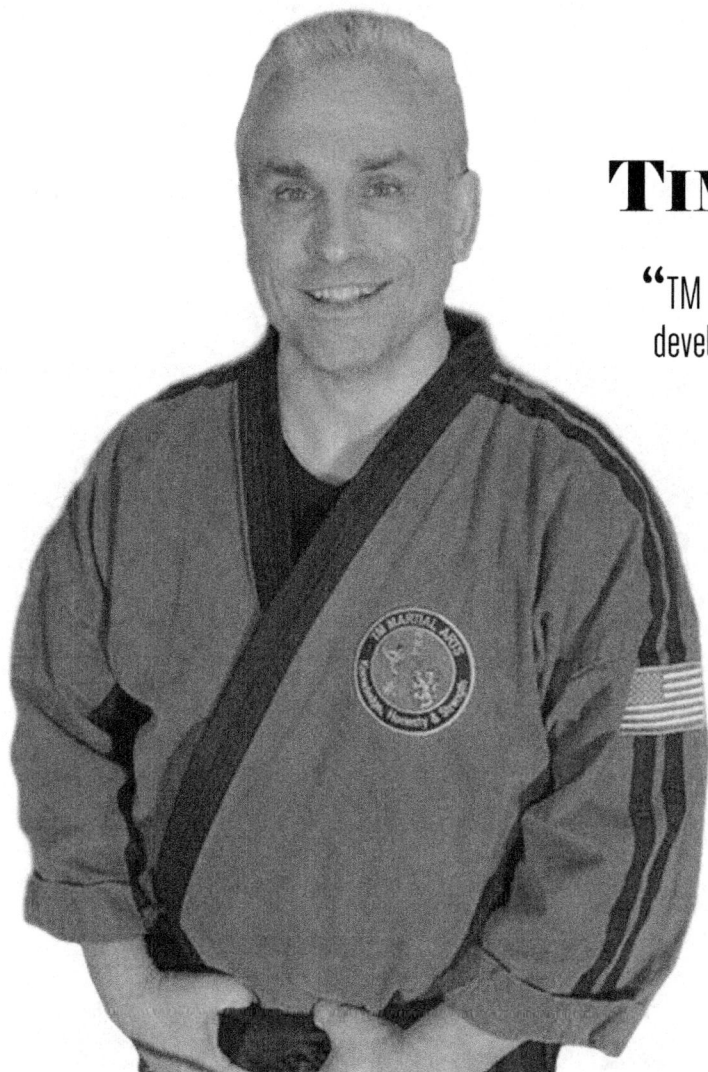

I started in the Martial Arts because my Dad thought it would be a good idea.

I started studying martial arts in 1972 at Tracy's Kenpo Karate in Downer Grove, Illinois. I studied there until approximately 1976. In the mid- to late 1980s I started in Tae Kwon Do and traditional Hapkido. In 1997 I attended Karate College at Radford, Virginia. While there, I was introduced to GM Joe Lewis, GM Bill "Superfoot" Wallace and many other well-known martial artists. I received my black belt from GM Joe Lewis in 2008. On February 3rd, 2003 I opened my school, TM Martial Arts Academy, teaching Tae Kwon Do, GM Pellegrini's Combat Hapkido, and various kickboxing and self-defense programs and seminars.

TM Martial Arts Academy focuses on teaching character development, self-defense skills, and developing strong leadership skills - even among

PERSONAL & MAJOR ACHIEVEMENTS

- Opened a school in 2003

- 7th degree Black Belt in Tae Kwon Do

- 6th degree Black Belt in Combat Hapkido

- 1st degree Black Belt in the Joe Lewis Fighting System

- Certified Instructor with the International Police Defensive Tactics Institute, the Military Combatives Association, and C.O.B.R.A self-defense

- Certified Instructor by the International Combat Hapkido Federation in Ground Survival and Anatomical Targeting Strategies

- Certified in Tactical Jeet Kune Do Principles by GM Joe Lewis

- Inducted in to the Action Martial Arts Hall of Fame in 2007 and 2011

- Budo International Magazine Outstanding Achievement Award

- 2006 Hapkido Instructor of the year by the USA Martial Arts Hall of Fame and by the World Head of Family Sokeship Council

- 2017 Who's Who Legends Award from the American Martial Arts Alliance

- 2019 Master of the year Combat Hapkido

the youngest students. My son Timothy is a small business owner and Marc is a police officer and a United States Marine. They all reside in the Chicago area.

EARNEST HART, JR.

"It was my devotion to self-discipline and self-control, learned through years of practicing Martial Arts, which helped me escape the dangerous streets of my childhood.**"**

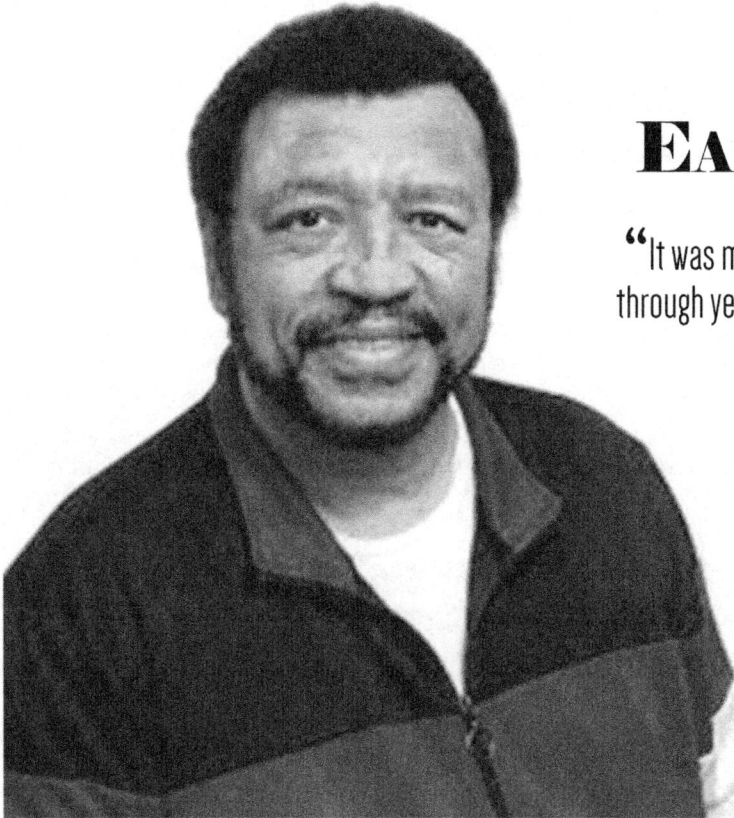

TRAINING INFORMATION

- Belt Ranks & Martial Arts Styles: Black Belt in 15 different martial art styles

- Birthdate: 1970

- Birthplace/Growing Up: St. Louis, MO

- Yrs. In the Martial Arts: 40+ years

- Yrs. Instructing: 40+ years

PROFESSIONAL ORGANIZATIONS

- Professional Karate Association (PKA)

I grew up in the St. Louis, Missouri housing projects; I lived with guns in my family's house and at an early age I learned to dive into a cast iron bathtub for protection when shooting started on the street. I was bullied by gangs until I mastered karate, boxing, judo and jiu jitsu and became a kickboxing champion who toured the world, appeared in Hollywood movies and consulted for famous actors and athletes.

It was my devotion to self-discipline and self-control, learned through years of practicing martial arts, which helped me escape the dangerous streets of my childhood. Today, I lead mentoring and training sessions at schools and civic organizations where we share non-violent methods to help at-risk kids develop self-confidence, self-respect and respect for others, enhance their personal safety, and avoid crime and drugs.

One of my approaches is to teach self-reliance, help kids build self-respect and avoid bullying, violence and abusive threats.

An important part of my program is to teach kids how to be safe, be aware, take responsibility for their personal safety and avoid dangerous situations when they feel vulnerable or threatened.

PERSONAL ACHIEVEMENTS

- World Champion Kickboxing title 4 times from the PKA

- Invited by the Emperor of Japan to teach the Imperial Guard self-defense tactics

- Worked with martial arts champion Chuck Norris, Ozzie Smith and other athletes

- Worked with actors George Clooney, Arnold Schwarzenegger and Willem Dafoe as a consultant and trainer

- Official martial arts trainer for 1999-2000 St. Louis Rams Super Bowl winners

- Movie Credits including Batman & Robin, Mortal Kombat, To Live and Die in L.A., Virtual Combat, Death Kick, and Karate Kid III

- Engaged by civic groups, businesses and families for personal safety training and mentoring

MENTORING SESSIONS & SEMINARS:

- Innovative Concept Academy at Blewett Middle School – City St. Louis

- Logos School – St. Louis County

- Premier Charter School - City of St. Louis

- Whitfield School – St. Louis County

- YMCA of Greater St. Louis Urban Core COVAM Program – City of St. Louis

Whether in the ghetto or the suburbs, kids who develop self-respect and self-confidence learn to respect others and build confidence in their own abilities; the benefit – they improve in school and in life.

PERSONAL ACHIEVEMENTS

PLAUDITS & COMPLIMENTS:

- "Earnest is totally dedicated to helping at-risk kids overcome personal challenges. He is one of the best-kept secrets in this area." - Elbert Harris, director of youth, teens and family activities for the YMCA of Greater St. Louis.

- "Earnest helps kids build self-confidence. We see a decrease in some of the negative behaviors we saw in the kids before Earnest got involved." - Kathy Boyd Fenger, Ph.D. head of school, Logos School.

- "Earnest has an informative, interactive style of presentation that engaged our kids and got the message across. He is a model of good character development." - Julie Leftridge, teacher-leader, Premier Charter School, St. Louis.

MARK HILL

"The study of Martial Arts gives me ability to be aware of my surroundings and act accordingly."

TRAINING INFORMATION

- Belt Ranks & Martial Arts Styles: 5th degree Black Belt, Goju-Ryu; Black Belt, Joe Corley PKA American Karate; Black Belt, Eddie Helm American Karate; Black Belt, Tae Kwon Do; Green Belt, Bando; Green Belt, Judo

- Instructors/Influencers: Durk Bryant

- Birthdate: December 4, 1962

- Birthplace/Growing Up: Chattanooga, TN

- Yrs. In the Martial Arts: 44 years

- Yrs. Instructing: 36 years

- Manager, Instructor, Member PKA Worldwide

PROFESSIONAL ORGANIZATIONS

- PKA Worldwide
- GTA Goju Soodo Traditional Association
- Member in Good-Standing in the State Bar Of Georgia
- Georgia Trial Lawyers Association

When I was ten years old in 1972, I watched Bruce Lee movies. I was always small for my age, and I wanted to be able to protect myself and not be bullied in any way. My mom enrolled in the Martial Art of Bando at the YMCA and I trained in that until 14 years old.

While in college, I ran my own Martial Arts Studio for 5 years until I moved from Chattanooga to Atlanta for law school. That's when I became an assistant instructor at the Joe Corley Karate Studios until about 2002. To this day I teach my own students and always continuing to strive to evolve and grow in the Martial Arts.

Due to my years of Martial Arts training, I never lack confidence in public. I have a feeling of knowing that I can properly defend my family

PERSONAL ACHIEVEMENTS

- Fighting Full-Contact in a ring before a lot of spectators - I did this at Ben Kiker's United Karate Studio in 1986. I won the fight

- Graduating from law school at the John Marshall School of Law - I passed the Bar in 1992 and started practicing Criminal Defense Law and Divorce Law

- Meeting my wife in 1998 on the freeway and marrying her in 2002 - we have 3 beautiful girls ages 24, 22 and 14

and those who cannot protect themselves if needed. The study of Martial Arts gives me ability to be aware of my surroundings and act accordingly. Martial Arts definitely gives me an edge while I am in the court room representing my clients; this is strategy and honor working together. I try daily to conduct myself as a warrior in the best interest of my fellow individuals. My family knows that when I pass to the next life, at my funeral I will be buried in my karate gyi to go to the next life as a warrior.

EZRA JOHNSON

❝Martial Arts helped me battle my insecurities, some of which I still have, but I can now better control it.❞

TRAINING INFORMATION

- Belt Ranks & Martial Arts Styles: Black Belt, Bill Wallace in the Superfoot System, Black Belt, Tae Kwon Do, Blue Belt, Royce Gracie at Jackson Academy of Martial Arts

- Instructors/Influencers: Bill Wallace

- Birthdate: June 3, 1996

- Birthplace/Growing Up: Ada, OK

- Yrs. In the Martial Arts: 12 years

- Yrs. Instructing: 6 years

- Instructor, Competitor

PROFESSIONAL ORGANIZATIONS

- Superfoot Joe Lewis Martial Arts Systems

As a child, my family was very poor to the point I would go to school with half shoes and starved. More often than not, I was bullied and grew with a bunch of insecurities. I had checked out a book at the local library called "Against All Odds," and the author who had a rough upbringing benefited greatly from martial arts, so I convinced my father to allow me to finally go.

When I was growing up, Martial arts helped me battle my insecurities, some of which I still have, but I can now better control it. Unfortunately, my first instructor was a fraud who bought rank and talked down on the legends and would discourage me from trying to seek them out to study. I ran across a kicking tape of Superfoot, and my teacher said I'd never be

PERSONAL ACHIEVEMENTS

- In competition, I achieved thirty-five 1st place, two 2nd and five 3rds.

MAJOR ACHIEVEMENTS

- I am so far, the first and only Black Belt under Bill Wallace in the state of Oklahoma, which has been a childhood dream.

able to kick high cause I was so big. I used the principles you are supposed to learn through martial arts and studied the tape every day for six months and went on a two-year tournament circuit without losing. This inspired me to keep goals and dreams, and that no matter how big the dream, small steps will still get you there. I use the tenets I gain from martial arts in all aspects of my life. Always trying to improve to be better than yesterday. My goal is to make the martial arts an ethic again instead of a watered-down business, I want to build "Higher caliber, martial artists".

JOSEPH KRAMER IV

> "I had originally started my Tae Kwon Do training with my son Perry and daughter Caroline in 2006, and we earned our 1st Degree Black Belts together in 2010."

TRAINING INFORMATION

- Belt Ranks & Martial Arts Styles: 2nd Degree Black Belt in Tae Kwon Do and Black Belt Candidate in Warrior Krav Maga

- Yrs. In the Martial Arts: 14 years

PROFESSIONAL ORGANIZATIONS

- PKA Worldwide

As a 2nd Degree ATA Black Belt in the Roswell suburb of Atlanta, I have had the pleasure of training with Joe Corley and his fine staff of instructors at Warrior Krav Maga and Precision Krav Maga since 2017. I am currently training for my Black Belt in Warrior Krav Maga with Senior Instructor Mike Biorn at Precision Krav Maga.

I had originally started my Tae Kwon Do training with my son Perry and daughter Caroline in 2006, and we earned our 1st Degree Black Belts together in 2010. I earned my 2nd Degree in 2012.

A graduate of the Citadel in 1992 with a BS in Business Administration, I then served 4 years as a US Navy Surface Warfare Officer from 1992-1996 on the USS Gallery FFG-26, a guided missile fast frigate.

I had the honor of earning my Eagle Scout status in 1987 and then from 2010-15 the pleasure of giving back as Assistant Scout Master

I certified as an NRA Shotgun Instructor in 2010 and recently provided some direction to Grand Master Corley and his family at one our favorite outdoor shooting ranges nearby. I am also an NRA Endowment member.

I am a Master Mason and a member of the American Legion Post in neighboring Alpharetta, Ga.

I started my own Communications Company in 2000, and we have just celebrated our 20-year anniversary.

PERSONAL ACHIEVEMENTS

- Graduate of The Citadel 1992 with a BS in Business Administration

- US Navy Surface Warfare Officer 1992-96 USS Gallery FFG-26

- Eagle Scout 1987

- Assistant Scout Master Troop 379 2010-15

- NRA Shotgun Instructor & NRA Endowment Member

- Master Mason, Roswell Masonic Lodge #165

- Member of the American Legion Post 201

- Founder and CEO Business Telecom Equipment, Inc. 2000-2020

CHRIS LANDINO

"As an Instructor I get the chance to help mold the lives of young people."

TRAINING INFORMATION

- Belt Ranks & Martial Arts Styles: 4th Dan Tae Kwon Do

- Instructors/Influencers: Rick Arnold, Benny Broadway, Sam Perez, Brian Beck

- Birthdate: September 11, 1979

- Birthplace/Growing Up: Gardnerville, NV

- Yrs. In the Martial Arts: 20 years

- Yrs. Instructing: 11 years

- Instructor

PROFESSIONAL ORGANIZATIONS

- PKA Worldwide
- World Black Belt Bureau
- AKATO
- United Taekwon-do Alliance

The Martial Arts have been an ever evolving journey for me. It started with wanting to learn to fight, to be able to protect myself. Growing up I was heavily influenced by friends of my father who were United States Marines who trained me in hand to hand combat. One of my best friends at the time was a Black Belt in the Ernie Reyes system and we would spar and train together. When I became an adult, a friend of mine began taking Tae Kwon Do because his children were taking it and he asked if I would go with him. I have not looked back since. I have trained in Kobudo, Krav Maga, Brazilian Jiu-Jitsu, Karate, and Judo as a supplement to my Tae Kwon Do training. I have had the great honor of training with some of the all-time greats from the original pioneers of Tae Kwon Do to the Texas Blood and Guts Legends.

At some point I realized that earning a Black Belt was achievable so that became my goal. As I achieve each new goal another is set and becomes my focus. Now that focus has spread to all facets of my life. I set and gain goals in my job and family life the same way.

PERSONAL ACHIEVEMENTS

- My Goals in competition were always to finish in the Top 3 in Region, and Top 5 in the state. I always wanted to win a true national championship. These are goals I set and have achieved. Outside of Martial Arts, I set my goals on becoming an ASE Certified Master Technician, and was able to achieve the Rank of Electrical Master for Chrysler and Master Technician for Fiat

MAJOR ACHIEVEMENTS

- 2008, 2009 - Top Regional Adult Heavyweight in AOK Texas Final Ranking 5th in Texas in Sparring

- 2008, 2009 - 3rd Place Finishes in Kata and Weapons

- 2008 AKATO Integrity Tenant Award Winner

- 2017, 2018 - United Taekwon-do Alliance National Champion in Sparring and Patterns

- 2019 - Karate for Christ Arkansas State Champion

- Over 100 Top 3 Finishes in tournaments

I am slower to anger and quick to find a solution. These were things that I was not naturally good at. Martial Arts has made me a better husband, father, and leader. As an Instructor I get the chance to help mold the lives of young people. What a great honor and responsibility. In the eyes of my son Leland, a Recommended Black Belt, I am the greatest Black Belt to ever live and that is a pretty good feeling too!

JIM MATTOCKS

"I have been able to protect myself and others through the knowledge gained in the Martial Arts."

TRAINING INFORMATION

- Belt Ranks & Martial Arts Styles: 2nd degree Black Belt, Tae Kwon Do, 10th Duan Chinese Kempo

- Instructors/Influencers: Master Cho, GM Michael Branden, GM Bill Packer, GM John Tsai

- Birthdate: June 19, 1956

- Birthplace/Growing Up: El Paso, TX / Bowie, MD

- Yrs. In the Martial Arts: 51 years

- Yrs. Instructing: 40 years

- School Owner, Manager, Instructor, Member PKA

PROFESSIONAL ORGANIZATIONS

- Professional Karate Association (PKA)

- Professional Karate Commission (PKC)

- USAMA

- AKA

- MATA

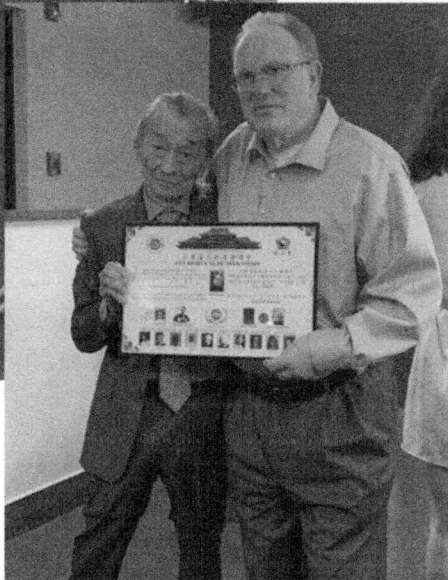

I was being bullied. I wanted to not stay that way so I got in the martial arts.

Studying the martial arts has taught me humility. It is not about you, but rather what you do for others. What do you give back? It has taught to me to manage my temper and to think before acting. I have been fortunate to be able to protect myself and others through the knowledge gained in the martial arts. I would not be the person I am today if it were not for those who had the patience and motivation provided to me.

PERSONAL ACHIEVEMENTS

- Vigil Honor--Order of the Arrow, BSA
- Medal of Honor, BSA
- Volunteer Firefighter and EMT
- Law Enforcement Instructor
- College Graduate

MAJOR ACHIEVEMENTS

- 10th Duan Martial Artist
- Eagle Scout

CHRIS MCLOUGHLIN

"…I'm proud of friendships made, martial skills learned, and promises kept…especially the ones to myself.."

TRAINING INFORMATION

- Martial Arts Title: Instructor
- Place of Birth / Growing Up: Atlanta, GA
- Started Studying Martial Arts in 1966
- Instructing Martial Arts for 54 years and currently holds the rank of 5th Degree Black Belt studying martial arts styles: American Karate
- Instructors: Grand Master Joe Corley

PROFESSIONAL ORGANIZATIONS

- J.S.T.A. (Justice System Training Association)
- Thor-Omega Group

It was an Atlanta weekend like any other in October 1966, except that I got in two fist fights, started neither and lost both. That was something I promised myself would never happen again. By mid-morning at work on Monday it was strongly suggested that I take some obviously well-earned time off until the mouse under my left eye went away and the shiner dimmed and was less noticeable. On Tuesday evening I showed up at the downtown YMCA and signed up for self-defense karate lessons, one hour a week for six weeks.

The classes were taught by Dae Shik Kim, a shoulder high Korean whose best friend in the karate world was Masutatsu Oyama, a Japanese Kyokushinkai legend, the man who fought bulls bare handed – and won. Mr. Kim subbed out his beginners to his brown belts, but he kept a watchful eye on the new guys, especially the ones who showed up with a black eye.

PERSONAL & MAJOR ACHIEVEMENTS

- Partner with Joe Corley, 1967, the first of a series of karate studios in Atlanta

- Co-founder with Joe Corley, 1970, The Battle of Atlanta

- Co-founder with Joe Corley, 1972, The Atlanta Pro-Am

- Co-director with Mike Foster and Joe Corley, 1972-74, Medalist Industries' Mike Foster Karate Camp

- Published by Official Karate, Black Belt, Karate Illustrated, Professional Karate, World Journal of Martial Arts, Fighter, Combat, Warriors, International Defense Review, Police Product News, Intersec, International Law Enforcement, Combat Handguns, SWAT, Law Enforcement Technology, and ten other open source firearms journals

- Centurion Group, 1999

- Joe Lewis Eternal Warrior Award, 2018

Six weeks, six hours and six lessons passed and I could stand bow-legged like I'd been riding a horse and throw a punch at the same time. I learned to do two types of front kick, escape from a side headlock, and break away from anyone who dared grab my wrist. But I couldn't fight a lick.

I asked Mr. Kim when some modicum of fighting skill would take hold, and he suggested I do another six-week enrollment at the Y and he invited me to join another six-week session on the other side of town. I did. Tuesdays and Thursdays, I trained, and it was during this time that I met Joe Corley, then a brown belt and Mr. Kim's most accomplished candidate for Black Belt.

It became clear to us that we wanted to host our own tournament in Atlanta, so we did. The ponderously named Southeast U.S. Open Karate Championship, sanctioned by the Southeast Karate Association, was attended by someof the most prominent karate fighters of the era, and so it was dubbed by BLACK BELT MAGAZINE "The Battle of Atlanta." The name stuck, and that was no surprise. We hosted a prestigious array of guests, officials, and competitors in the karate limelight. Joe Lewis was the first grand champion over a field of fighters and friends that has over time heralded Mitchell Bobrow, Joe Hayes, Ken Knudson, Thomas LaPuppet, Parker Shelton, J.T. Will, Jeff Smith, Bill Wallace, Glenn Keeney, Mike Stone, Pat Johnson, Chuck Norris, Howard Jackson, Bill Clark, Bob Wall, Jim Harrison, and Maung Gyi. The list rolls on predating today's full contact professional fighters and setting the standard for them. I lived in the time of these men, and in that time The Battle of Atlanta grew to be the biggest karate event of the era.

If ever there was a foundation, this was it. After The Battle, we launched another, smaller event, the Atlanta Pro-Am and this was a forerunner of the professional karate movement in the South. From these beginnings I worked as a director, administrator or executive committee member for S.E.K.A. (South East Karate Association and its Black Belt Examination Board), the P.K.A.

(Professional Karate Association and its Rules Committee), the P.K.C. (Professional Karate Commission), the S.E.P.K.C. (South East Professional Karate Commission), Jhoon Rhee's W.B.B.C. (World Black Belt Commission) and his W.P.K.C. (World Professional Karate Commission), and Martial Arts Productions, International.

As a licensed judge and ringside official, I worked world title PKA events in Atlanta, Charlotte, Dallas, Indianapolis, Las Vegas, New York, New Jersey, Rhode Island, Palm Beach, Jacksonville, Tampa, Washington, DC, and Paris, France and the US Virgin Islands. Similarly licensed, I've been ringside in an official capacity in Mosul, Iraq.

Being traveled led to writing some 200 articles in professional and sport karate magazines, and other martial disciplines journals have translated and published my work from American English into English, French, Spanish, German, and Chinese.

After the last Atlanta Pro-Am in 1977 I retired from our studio businesses and tournament operations, but, continued to work with private and corporate clients and instructor's groups including Kevin Parsons' JSTA (Justice System Training Association). Furthering my own martial arts interests I attended tours at Jeff Cooper's API (American Pistol Institute, affectionately known as "Gunsite"), Chuck Taylor's ASAA (American Small Arms Academy), and Gabe Suarez' Suarez International. These skill-training episodes were punctuated by ECM (Electronic Counter Measures) sessions with Spectra Research Group in New York, and

Gen. Mitchell L. WerBell, III's multi-faceted Cobray International in Powder Springs, Georgia

In terms of martial disciplines including small arms, personal security, protection and anti-kidnapping experience borne from American karate training, I've worked Cabo San Lucas to Cozumel, Mexico; the Cayman Islands; Cap Ferrat, Nice and Paris, France; Monaco and Monte Carlo; Zurich, Geneva and Lausanne, Switzerland; Turin, Italy; Cologne and Frankfurt Germany, London, England; New York City; Hong Kong, and Mosul, Iraq.

My sweat equity is in several martial disciplines including American, Korean, Japanese, and Kenpo karate, Brazilian jiu jitsu, aikido, judo, Escrima, PKA full contact and/or kick boxing, and the sweet science of American boxing. In terms of core rank, I hold claim to 5th Degree Black Belt in Joe Corley's American Karate. Apart from that I have been honored with Black Belt distinction in Atlas Jesse King's American Kick Boxing, Sam Chapman's American Karate, Jay T. Will's United Kenpo Karate Association, and Steve Fishman's International Association of TAI Martial Arts.

Now, more than a half-century after the 0-2 black eye episodes, I'm proud of friendships made, martial skills learned, and promises kept …especially the one to myself.

NIKOLAJ MCLEOD

"Nothing compares to being an instructor and making an impact on my student's lives."

TRAINING INFORMATION

- Belt Ranks & Martial Arts Styles: 6th degree Black Belt, American Sport Karate; 3rd degree Black Belt, Tae Kwon Do; 3rd degree Black Belt Shotokan; 2nd degree Black Belt Japanese Jujitsu

- Instructors/Influencers: John Hernandez, Jim McCleskey, Robert DeCeaser, DE Chambers, Scott Messina, Jeff Wolffe, Jae Chun

- Birthdate: August 07, 1982

- Birthplace/Growing Up: Houston, TX

- Yrs. In the Martial Arts: 30+ years

- Yrs. Instructing: 25+ years

- School Owner, Manager, Instructor, Member PKA Worldwide , Forever Student

PROFESSIONAL ORGANIZATIONS

- Professional Karate Association (PKA)

As a young child, I was very small, meek, and shy. Because of that, I was an easy target for bullies. Being in class at school there were never any issues; it was always on the bus ride to and from school that I was picked on the most. After the bullying didn't seem to end, my family decided that Karate lessons might be exactly what I need to boost my confidence, and to help me defend myself if I had to. But in reality, it was my begging that finally made them cave into letting me take classes. I had always been a fan of martial arts or anything related for as long as I can remember. I'm sure it had to do with the huge surge of martial arts films in the mainstream in the 80s that caught my eyes originally. But my best friend was in Karate, and he would always show me his belts, trophies, and new kata every time we would have sleepovers, so obviously I wanted to do classes with my best friend!

I began my martial arts training at the Dojo where my friend studied when I was seven years old, under Master John Hernandez (Shotokan). After training for a few years, during one of the classes each student was

PERSONAL ACHIEVEMENTS

- Texas State Champion in kata and sparring a few times
- Awards of recognition regarding working with youth

MAJOR ACHIEVEMENTS

- Three beautiful daughters: Madison, Makayla, and Rose. That's as major as it gets.

given one technique to "teach" the rest of the class (mine was the outside block), I knew that I wanted to teach Karate when I grew up. Needless to say, I was hooked!

Later when my first instructor's school closed, a Tae Kwon Do studio opened in its place. Living in a small town and with few options, I enrolled. I trained under Sensei Jim McCleskey and Master DE Chambers in the Fred Simon/Jhoon Rhee system. Switching styles opened my eyes to a whole new world of techniques and ideas, so I began cross train a lot at that point.

I was able to train under and with some of the best, in my opinion. Shihan Robert DeCeaser, Master Scott Messina, Master Jeff Wolffe, and GM Jae Chu I am currently focusing on my new Dojo, the Team Karate Academy, so I'm definitely not training like I should or under any specific instructor. But I'm sure that will change once business has settled down.

Martial Arts has made a huge impact on my life and I am very lucky to have found it at such a young age. No matter what personal achievements I have made, nothing compares to being an instructor and making an impact on my student's lives. For example, when you receive a note from a student telling you that you are the "best Sensei ever." Or a compliment from a parent about how their child attending classes has impacted their lives so much for the better. Even after I can no longer physically do a lot of the techniques I know, I will always have the knowledge and memories that I gained from the martial arts.

PAUL MILLHOLEN

> **"** Martial Arts have helped me deal with my challenges straight on in my daily life. **"**

TRAINING INFORMATION

- Belt Ranks & Martial Arts Styles: 4th degree Black Belt, Tae Kwon Do; 3rd degree Black Belt, Superfoot Systems; Brown Belt in Nihon Goshin Aikido

- Instructors/Influencers: Bill "Superfoot" Wallace, Terry Dow, Shihan Robert MacEwen, Soke Michael Depasquale Jr.

- Birthdate: January 14, 1983

- Birthplace/Growing Up: Washington / Willimantic CT

- Yrs. In the Martial Arts: 24 years

- Yrs. Instructing: 20 years

- School Owner, Instructor, Member PKA Worldwide

PROFESSIONAL ORGANIZATIONS

- PKA Worldwide
- Superfoot Systems
- Nihon Goshin Aikido
- International Federation of Jiu-Jitsuans

I got into martial arts because I went to a rough middle school and wanted to learn to defend myself.

Martial Arts have helped me deal with my challenges straight on in my daily life. One of my favorite aspects of the martial arts is sparring. In sparring you can't quit or run away. In life you can't just pack up and leave when times get tough. It also has helped me interact with people of all walks of life. I've taught in the rural parts of Vermont and Canada and to inner-city youth programs in the North end of Hartford. I love to teach and train with all types of styles and systems. I believe everyone can learn from each other to better the development of his or her skills.

PERSONAL ACHIEVEMENTS

- Passed a 100-man self-defense line including strikes, grabs, sticks and knife attacks under Shihan MacEwen

- Member of the 1999-2000 United States Tae Kwon Do Council demo team

- Taught martial art programs in over 10 public schools

- Taught classes and seminars for local community centers

- Taught classes and seminars for teen outreach programs

- Travel with Bill "Superfoot" Wallace assisting in seminars and belt testing

MAJOR ACHIEVEMENTS

- Honorary Black Belt and Instructor in IFOJJ awarded by Michael Depasquale, Jr

- Featured in instructional videos by Master Terry Dow

- Featured on the hit podcast Whistlekick Martial Arts radio with Jeremy Lesniak

- Operated and taught in my own school for ten years

KEITH NYLUND

"Martial Arts taught me respect, discipline, hard work, to never give up..."

TRAINING INFORMATION

- Belt Ranks & Martial Arts Styles: 3rd Degree Black Belt, Tokoshikan Bujutsu; 2nd Degree Black Belt, Kachido Aikijitsu; Brown Belt, Ko Sutemi Seiei Kan Karate Do; Panther School of Gung Fu - Red Sash

- Instructors/Influencers: Don Madden, Darrell Logan, Robert Cooper, Tom Manson, Herb Mowery, Scott Payne, Ed Shaffer, Tim Wolfe, Thomas Arthur

- Birthdate: October 9, 1972

- Birthplace/Growing Up: Portsmouth, OH

- Yrs. In the Martial Arts: 37 years

- Yrs. Instructing: a few years

- Instructor, Member PKA Worldwide

PROFESSIONAL ORGANIZATIONS

- PKA Worldwide

- Alliance

- World Sports Combat League

- United States Martial Arts Association

- Sembach Self Defense

- Tokoshi Martial Arts Federation

- International Martial Arts Combat Union

While I was growing up I watched Chuck Norris, Bruce Lee movies and Kung Fu Theater, I always wanted to be able to be like them in the fight department, but it wasn't until I got a butt kicking that I wanted to learn and took it seriously.

Well, the Martial Arts taught me respect, discipline, hard work, to never give up, to be positive, to stand up for what I believe in, to protect myself and my family and others who can't do it for themselves, and the list goes on. My outlook on life situations is better.

PERSONAL ACHIEVEMENTS

- I very seldom entered tournament competition which I regret, but I was more into just learning because I was in other sports as well

MAJOR ACHIEVEMENTS

- My induction into USA Martial Arts Hall of Fame, Action Martial Arts Magazine Hall of Honors, World Karate Union Hall of Fame

STEPHEN OLIVER

"I have taught well over 35,000 students, and graduated well over 3,500 Black Belts."

TRAINING INFORMATION

- Martial Arts Title: Grandmaster
- Golden, CO
- Started Studying Martial Arts in 1969
- Instructing Martial Arts for 32 years and currently holds the rank of 9th Degree Black Belt studying martial arts styles: Tae Kwon Do & Kickboxing
- Instructors: Jhoon Rhee & Jeff Smith

My career in the Martial Arts started when I was being picked on by a bullying next-door neighbor so I enrolled in a Jhoon Rhee Institute Branch Program in Tulsa, OK.

After studying for some time, I started teaching in Tulsa in 1974. Martial Arts has affected every area of my life, including my exclusive career path. I learned massive character development and focus. My Philosophy for the Martial Arts is "Martial Arts Without Philosophy Is Just Street Fighting." --Jhoon Rhee

I have taught well over 35,000 students, and graduated well over 3,500 Black Belts. The confidence and focus I learned through martial arts led to my National Merit Scholarship and full scholarship to college. I am an Honors Graduate of Georgetown University, MBA.

Classes: Operated Mile High Karate, now an international franchise operation.

PERSONAL ACHIEVEMENTS

- Founded Mile High Karate in 1983. Within 18 months the school grew to 1,500 students and 6 locations. Within 30 months it grew to six locations and 3,500 students.

- Promoted the Mile-High Karate Classic, a NASKA World Tour Event from 1989 to 1999.

- Founding member of the EFC Board of Directors 1985 to 2001.

- Founder Stephen Oliver's Martial Arts Business Coaching, now Stephen Oliver's Martial Arts Wealth Mastery.

MAJOR ACHIEVEMENTS

- Promoted the Mile-High Karate Classic, a NASKA World Tour event for 10 years.

- Served as Board Member, Executive Committee Member, and Sanctioning Director for NASKA for 10 years.

- Numerous Halls of Fame including EFC Hall of Fame, #1 Multi-School Operation

- Publisher of Martial Arts Professional Magazine

- CEO: - National Association of Professional Martial Artists

- Formerly on the Board of Directors and Member for Educational Funding CO

- Board of Directors, Sanctioning Director NASKA Branch Manager & Head Instructor Jhoon Rhee Institute

JOHN ORMSBY

"John Ormsby has been featured in Who's Who in Karate, Who's Who in American Martial Arts, and Masters, Founders and Leaders in American Martial Arts..."

John Ormsby has been involved in various martial arts going on six decades and is a Black Belt in Karate, Tae Kwon Do and Judo. He has been featured in Who's Who in Karate, Who's Who in American Martial Arts, and Masters, Founders and Leaders in American Martial Arts. He was the co-editor of Karate/Kickboxing magazine, associate editor of a national boxing magazine and a contributing columnist to various Karate and boxing publications. He has authored and published numerous martial arts books. He has served in various capacities with the martial art associations, SEKA, PKA, KICK, AAU and the Tampa Bay Boxing Commission. He has promoted numerous Karate tournaments, Full Contact/Kickboxing and professional boxing contests. He has trained or co-trained numerous Full Contact/Kickboxing World, North American, United States champions as well as state, regional and local champions and contenders. He also coached several international full contact/ Kickboxing teams. His students have won Karate tournaments all over the country including the prestigious Battle of Atlanta.

PROFESSIONAL KARATE ASSOCIATION HONORS · 2020 MASTERS & PIONEERS

He was first introduced to boxing at a very young age when his father gave him a set of boxing gloves that had belonged to an uncle, who was an up-and-coming pro boxer but was killed in a freak motorcycle accident. He jokes today that his dad forgot to tell him about "defense" as he was getting knocked around.

His first formal martial arts class was in a Judo class that was held at the high school gymnasium. The school [Southern Pines] was located next to the largest military reservation [Ft. Bragg] in the country. The school principle had arranged for the class and it was taught by a United States Army Special Forces drill instructor, Sgt. Lopez.

Later he and a friend drove over to the base, home of the 82nd Airborne, where they were allowed to join in a Karate class taught at the post boxing gym. Civilians normally were not allowed to participate in on-base activities but a little name dropping went a long way. The class was taught by a Shotokan Black Belt from Hawaii who was stationed at the base.

Upon arriving at his alma mater, University of North Carolina – Chapel Hill, he returned to Judo under the guidance of a Japanese exchange student, Hideka Kusama, and continued until Kusama completed his studies and returned to Japan.

Shortly after the Judo instructor returned home, another student started a Karate/self-defense class off campus. There wasn't a whole lot of real instruction as the new instructor seldom showed up for class and the class ended up being taught by the students that had previous martial arts experience.

After about six months, someone found out that there was a new chemistry exchange student from Korea who was supposedly some type of martial artist. After some searching, Yun Tae In, a 2nd Degree Black Belt in the Korean art of Chi Do Kwon Tae Soo Do, was located. The only problem, Yun didn't speak much English. However, a class was eventually formed. About a year later, Yun arranged for his friend, who was a 5th degree, to come to the US and enroll as a Tar Heel.

After graduating with a degree in accounting and economics, John moved to Charlotte, NC where he continued his training in Judo and Karate. In the 70's, he moved around from Florida, Ohio, Tennessee and Indiana.

In 1983, he made his best martial arts decision as he moved to Greenville, NC to join his former high school friend and Karate Hall-of-Famer, Bill McDonald. The two formed BEMJO Martial Arts that quickly became one of the most successful martial arts combinations in the country.

In 2005, after 28 years in the same location, the schools moved to new and smaller locations, and now operate more on a club concept than as a commercial enterprise, offering Karate/self-defense and boxing instruction. Sadly, Bill McDonald passed away in 2017, just prior to the Who's Who banquet in Washington DC.

John is the co-founder of Eastern North Carolina Sports Development, a non-profit which fosters the development of the Olympic sports of Judo, Tae Kwon Do and Boxing, and researches other amateur sports in attempt to ensure that their history is preserved. He also is a former inter-collegiate and senior billiard champion as well as former BCA [Billiard Congress of America] and ACS [American Cue Sports] instructor.

TED OSBORNE

"The Martial Arts have made me a better person inside and outside the dojo."

I liked to watch Bill Wallace fight on TV. This is how I was inspired to start training in the Martial Arts. Getting my Black Belt years ago was one of the highlights of my life. My major achievements within the Martial Arts has been teaching others. The Martial Arts have made me a better person inside and outside the dojo.

TRAINING INFORMATION

- Belt Ranks & Martial Arts Styles: Black Belt, Isshinryu Karate & Kung Fu
- Instructors/Influencers: Danny Romine and Freddie Cantrell
- Birthdate: March 08, 1960
- Birthplace/Growing Up: Virginia
- Yrs. In the Martial Arts: 40 years
- Yrs. Instructing: 28 years
- Instructor, Member PKA Worldwide

PROFESSIONAL ORGANIZATIONS

- PKA Worldwide
- Okinawan Karate Do Union
- International Chinese Boxing Association
- International Isshinryu Karate Association
- Traditional Okinawan Karate Association
- United States Karate Hall of Fame

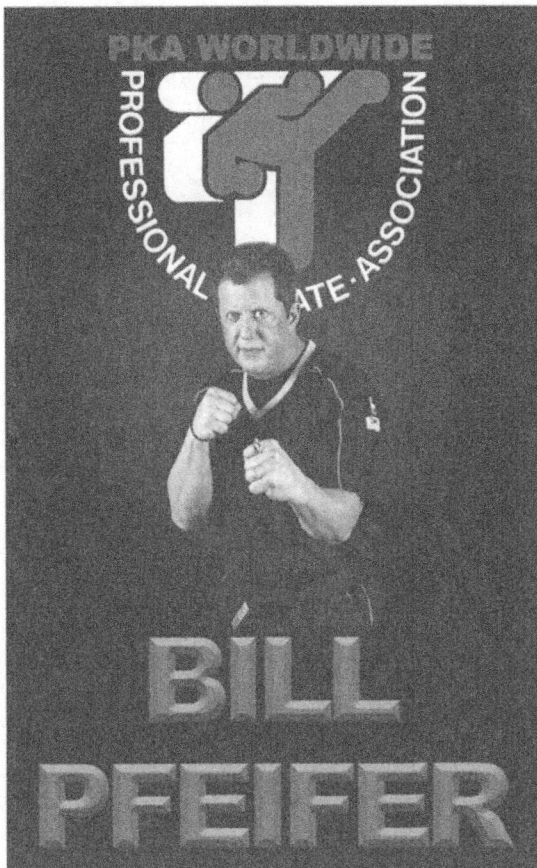

WILLIAM PFEIFER

"In particular, martial arts taught me to persevere in the face of adversity; to not let fear or pain get in the way..."

TRAINING INFORMATION

- Belt Ranks & Martial Arts Styles: Black Belt in Krav Maga and American Karate, Brown Belt in Yoshukai Karate, also trained in Pekiti Tirsia Kali, Armas Filomeno, Kempo, Akayama Jujitsu, and Kenjutsu

- Instructors/Influencers: GM Joe Corley, Mike Biorn, Erick Alfaro, Tommy McConnell, Apolo Ladra, Arnold Filomeno

- Birthdate: March 30, 1967

- Birthplace/Growing Up: Brunswick, GA / Anniston, AL

- Yrs. In the Martial Arts: 39 years

- Yrs. Instructing: 4 years

- Instructor, Member PKA Worldwide

PROFESSIONAL ORGANIZATIONS

- Professional Karate Association (PKA)

- Federation of Israeli Martial Arts

- World Kali Association

- Alabama State Bar Association

- Alabama Criminal Defense Lawyers Association

- American Bar Association

In high school, I became fascinated by martial arts movies as well as boxing. I spent months pestering my parents to let me take karate classes, but my mother was afraid it would cause me to start going around getting into fights. They attempted to placate me by buying me a heavy boxing bag and hanging it in the garage, and I spent many joyful hours pounding away on it. However, after a school bully picked a fight with me and I succeeded in showing him the error of his ways, my mother realized that learning how to fight was a good idea for boys. My father took me to try a class at a Yoshukai Karate school operated by Sensei Tommy McConnell, and then continued to take me there four nights a week until I had a driver's license and could drive myself.

Studying martial arts as a teenager instilled in me values and principles that have guided me throughout the years. In particular, martial arts taught me to persevere in the face of adversity; to not let fear or pain get in the way of pursuing goals; to maintain composure and control at all times; to focus on goals and take the steps to achieve them; and to never draw a weapon (literal or metaphorical) until the decision has been made to use it.

PROFESSIONAL ORGANIZATIONS

- National Trial Lawyers Association
- National Association of Criminal Defense Lawyers
- American Society of Legal Writers
- National Writers Union

PERSONAL ACHIEVEMENTS

- First recipient of the William Lunceford Award for Excellence in Philosophy at Samford University in 1985
- Pi Gamma Mu International Honor Society
- Farrah Law Society Scholarship at University of Alabama School of Law
- Member of John A. Campbell Moot Court Board at University of Alabama School of Law
- Editor of the Law and Psychology Review at University of Alabama School of Law
- Bench and Bar Legal Honor Society
- Admitted to the Alabama State Bar in 1993
- Past Master of Foley Masonic Lodge
- Chairman, Baldwin County Democratic Party (2000 - 2005)
- Former Member, Alabama State Democratic Executive Committee
- Published author of over 100 articles in a variety of publications, including magazines, newspapers, websites, books, and professional journals
- Instructor certifications in karate, kickboxing, Krav Maga, Kali, and fitness

And after deciding I was ready to retire from my career as a lawyer, martial arts provided me with a way to have a second career doing what I truly love by opening my own martial arts school.

MAJOR ACHIEVEMENTS

- Rated as an AV Preeminent Attorney by Martindale-Hubbell
- Avvo Attorney rating of 10.0 Superb
- Donald Springen Award, presented by Baldwin County Democratic Party
- Listed in Top 100 Trial Lawyers in Alabama by the National Trial Lawyers Association

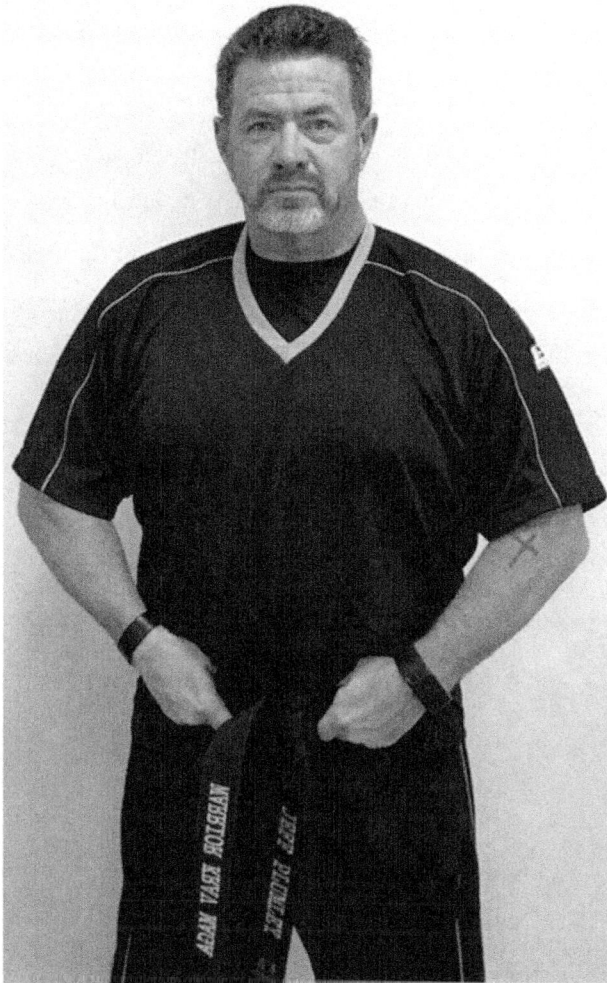

JEFF PLUMLEY

> "I now walk in peace knowing I can handle any situation that may be thrust upon me."

TRAINING INFORMATION

- Belt Ranks & Martial Arts Styles: Black Belt, Krav Maga; Green Belt, Tae Kwon Do; Brazilian Jiu Jitsu, White Belt; Freestyle and Greco Roman Wrestling

- Instructors/Influencers: GM Joe Corley, Mike Biorn, Chris York, Kenny Kim

- Birthdate: July 21, 1966

- Birthplace/Growing Up: Marion, OH / Columbia, SC

- Yrs. In the Martial Arts: 38 years

- Yrs. Instructing: 3 years

- Instructor, Member PKA Worldwide

PROFESSIONAL ORGANIZATIONS

- Licensed United States Customs House Broker

- PKA Worldwide

I always had an interest in martial arts and soaked up Kung Fu movies on cold Saturday afternoons in Ohio. My Father was a Force Recon Marine and all around great fighter who gave me my first lesson on how to defend myself if needed. From there I believe my parents simply saw a need for me to channel my energies and love of testing myself physically against larger opponents. After training further in high school under a Navy Seal friend I moved on to training in Tae Kwon Do in college at The Citadel, The Military College of South Carolina. After college I trained briefly in Jeet Kune Do.

While I continued to train on my own for the next 25 years, I did not take up formal training again until I met GM Joe Corley in 2015 and I began my latest journey in Martial Arts studying Krav Maga. At times I was taking group classes 7 times each week and managing private lessons from GM Corley. Without the guidance, mentoring and friendship of

PERSONAL ACHIEVEMENTS

- Who's Who in International Business

MAJOR ACHIEVEMENTS

- BSBA - The Citadel
- MBA - Winthrop University

GM Corley I would not hold my current rank of Black Belt. Of my most cherished achievements is that I am a "Joe Corley Black Belt."

In my day job I am executive in the International Logistics industry specializing in the global transport of liquid chemicals. My work takes me all over the world to various chemical plants, and they are rarely in nice areas. Before reigniting my martial arts training I was always extremely nervous to be at chemical plants in remote third world countries or on the docks after dark. I now walk in peace knowing I can handle any situation that may be thrust upon me.

KENNETH REBSTOCK

"My fellow students and Martial Arts friends are more than friends...they are family."

TRAINING INFORMATION

- Belt Ranks & Martial Arts Styles: Judo- Green Belt, American Karate- 5th Dan, American Taekwondo- 5th Dan, Shizen-Na Karate- 5th Dan

- Instructors/Influencers: Grandmaster Richard M. Morris, Lineage: Grandmaster Jhoon-Rhee, Grandmaster J. Pat Burleson, Grandmaster Richard M. Morris

- Birthdate: November 30, 1956

- Birthplace/Growing Up: Baltimore, MD / Jacksonville, IL

- Yrs. In the Martial Arts: 51 years

- Yrs. Instructing: 3 years

- Instructor

PROFESSIONAL ORGANIZATIONS

- International Council of Grandmasters

- American Martial Arts Alliance Instructor Charter Member

- American Karate Black Belt Association

- World Martial Arts Ranking System

- World's Martial Arts Congress For Education

- United States Judo Association

I began Judo in 1969 at the local YMCA because I was small and was picked on. I went on to wrestling and boxing in college. In 1979, after boxing, I switched to karate. I met GM Richard Morris in 1984 and have been with him ever since.

Martial Arts, Grandmaster Guy James, and Grandmaster Richard Morris basically saved my life. After my cancer returned as Stage 4 in 2012 it was recommended that I go on hospice care. I changed Doctors. I reunited with my friends Guy James and Richard Morris. Because of them, I got back into martial arts and I haven't looked back.

Through my cancer, I've been able to reach many other cancer patients encouraging them to stay active while receiving treatments using my martial arts and running as examples. With GM Richard Morris' blessing I started up the Cancer Warrior Martial Arts Program which started out only honoring kids with cancer or have beat cancer with their Cancer Warrior Black Belt and certificate signed and registered by GM Richard Morris and many, many other Black Belts. Soon I was honoring Martial Artists once a year at Gary Lee's National Sports Karate Museum Awards

PROFESSIONAL ORGANIZATIONS

- Dallas Guardian Angels
- Founder of Cancer Warrior Martial Arts Program
- Member of PKA Worldwide

PERSONAL ACHIEVEMENTS

- Married to Rosemary Rebstock for 41 years
- Children: Ben Rebstock, Tiffany Henderson, Brittany Kovach
- Grandchildren: Abby Rebstock, Alayna Rebstock, Rylee Henderson, Lexie Henderson, Blake Kovach, Blair Kovach
- Founder of International Cancer Warrior Martial Arts Program honoring kids and martial artists with their Cancer Warrior Black Belts for courage in fighting cancer (self-funded and blessed by GM Richard Morris)
- I have Stage 4 Colon Cancer and have received over 200 chemo treatments so far... 600 days on chemo since 2012

MAJOR ACHIEVEMENTS

- Graduated Southern Methodist University in 1979
- Lettered in Cross Country and Wrestling at Millikin University
- Lettered in Cross Country at SMU
- Southern Methodist University Lightweight Boxing Champion
- Qualified and Ran Boston Marathon Best Time 2:46
- Best Mile Time 4:19

honoring many Grandmasters, even my heroes GM J. Pat Burleson and GM Richard M. Morris! Hundreds have earned their Cancer Warrior Martial Arts Program Black Belts. It is international and no one that is nominated is ever turned down! I self-fund the program. You can see them all on the Facebook page Cancer Warrior Martial Arts Program. You can nominate someone by texting me at 817-689-2804. My fellow students, martial arts friends, and GM Richard Morris are more than friends...they are family.

MAJOR ACHIEVEMENTS

- 2018 and 2019 American Martial Arts Alliance Who's Who Award
- 2019 USA Martial Arts "Hall of Fame" Most Inspirational Martial Arts Man of the Year
- 2019 Masters Hall of Fame
- 2019 Martial Arts Hall of Fame
- 2020 Action Martial Arts Hall of Honors Humanitarian Award
- 2 Time Ambassador for the National Sports Karate Museum

MAJOR ACHIEVEMENTS

- Books, newscasts, magazines, and blogs featured in:
- Cure (A Cancer Magazine)
- Century Martial Arts Blog covering Cancer Warrior Martial Arts Program
- WFAA News Coverage of Cancer Warrior Martial Arts Program
- World's Greatest Martial Artists, The Fearsome 400 and The Sensational 600 by GM Ted Gambordella
- Top Texas Martial Artists by Ted Gambordella
- Cleburne Times Review - Kicking Cancer by Degrees by Matt Smith

KEN REBSTOCK

DANIEL RUSS

"I learned through life that sometimes you have to fight -for your life, your health, your freedom, your dignity. Better train."

TRAINING INFORMATION

- Belt Ranks & Martial Arts Styles: Second Degree Black Belt, Joe Corley American Karate; Kali and Silat

- Instructors/Influencers: Joe Corley, Jerry Rhome, Jim Korb, Larry Korb, Fred Degerberg, Danny Inosanto, Micheal Olajide, Sr.

- Birthdate: April 26, 1957

- Birthplace/Growing Up: Atlanta, GA/Dekalb County, GA

- Yrs. In the Martial Arts: 50+ years

PROFESSIONAL ORGANIZATIONS

- Professional Karate Association (PKA)

I was born at Georgia Baptist Hospital at 2:38 PM on Tuesday, April 16th 1957, Daniel Clay Russ; the fifth child and fourth son to Marvin Edward Russ, himself a child of refugees who emigrated from Russia to Scotland to South Carolina. My Mother, Irene Russ, was a Hungarian refugee who married Dad in Germany during the occupation. Dad was a ground crew chief in the 8th Air Force. Mom survived three concentration camps, two of which were Auschwitz, for 8 months and Ollendorf for 5 months. She saw the Russian Army shut down Auschwitz and the American Army shut down Ollendorf.

I grew up in Dekalb County Georgia and the greatest thing I ever did for myself was take Karate from Joe Corley. Joe Corley became the prime mover in a relatively new sport, Professional Karate. During this time, my brothers and I earned our Black Belts under Joe Corley. I was by accident and partly by luck, involved in this nascent sport. I trained with early champions like Jerry Rhome, and AAU national champions Jim Korb and Larry Korb. I was promoted to First-Degree Black Belt on August 25, 1974 and his Second degree on October 10th, 1982.

PERSONAL & MAJOR ACHIEVEMENTS

- First Creative Director for the US Air Force
- Launched the Nike Security Campaign
- Created TV spots for Texas candidate for governor Kinky Friedman, Fannie Mae, Virgin Atlantic, Cheerwine, GEICO and others
- Launched Cybercorp, a Charles Schwab software trading company; Bruce Lee is in the award-winning spots
- Stand-up comedian and shared the stage with Dave Chappelle, Bill Hicks, Ray Romano, Sam Kinison, and Brian Regan
- Nicknamed "Catfish" from playing blues and chromatic harmonica and played with The Fabulous Thunderbirds and David Kersh and recorded with Danny Levin, John Blondell and Ginger Leigh

After Atlanta I lived in Chicago for several years and made my martial arts home at the Degerberg Academy. There Fred Degerberg introduced me to Danny Inosanto, and I ended up studying under him for around 16 years, attending Kali seminars and introducing him to audiences in Richmond and Austin. In Chicago, I studied Kali and Silat as well as kickboxing.

I managed to put together 25 fights which included 7 boxing matches and 18 kickboxing matches. In the ensuing years, professional karate's growth exploded through gyms and dojos across Georgia, and there were numerous opportunities to fight including at Dobbins Air Force Base, the Savannah Civic Center, and many other venues in and around the country. Living in Wrigleyville in Chicago, I fought karate matches at karate tournaments in the Cicero area. And in New York I fought with teams out of Kingsway Boxing under Micheal Olajide, Sr. We often fought against the teams from Gleasons in Brooklyn, New York. One of my first fights was featured on CBS Sports Spectacular though it was nothing to brag about.

I grew up an Orthodox Jew in Dekalb County, Georgia, thus necessitating fighting and self-confidence skills. I attended a rabbinical parochial school called a Yeshiva, studied to be a rabbi, but that didn't take, and instead I became an ad guy. For seven years I worked at the famous Martin Agency in Richmond, Virginia under Harry Jacobs and Mike Hughes. I spent 13 years at GSDM under the tutelage of Guy Bommarito and Roy Spence. Then I spent three years as the Executive Creative Director at R&R Partners where I headed up What Happens Here Stays Here, a famous campaign for the Las Vegas Convention and Visitors Authority.

PROFESSIONAL KARATE ASSOCIATION HONORS • 2020 MASTERS & PIONEERS

My life spent in marketing reveals some personal milestones. I was the first ever creative director on the US Air Force account, and I served in this capacity for eight years. Militarily, accessions were down during an unpopular war with Iraq, yet our team filled Air Force rosters with little trouble.

I launched Wal*Mart's real people campaign and hired Academy award winning documentarian Albert Maysles to shoot it. I helped launch the Nike Security Campaign, numerous Fannie Mae marketing efforts, and created TV spots for Kinky Friedman running for Texas Governor, Fannie Mae, Virgin Atlantic, Cheerwine, GEICO and others. I helped launch Cybercorp, a Charles Schwab software trading company. Bruce Lee is in the award-winning spots.

I did stand-up comedy for 11 years and shared the stage with Dave Chappelle, Bill Hicks, Ray Romano, Sam Kinison, and Brian Regan. I got my nickname Catfish playing Blues and chromatic harmonica. I have played with The Fabulous Thunderbirds and Country star David Kersh, and I have recorded with Danny Levin, John Blondell and Ginger Leigh.

I wrote and published 28 science fiction and/or horror stories, and have written two screen plays which have placed in 16 screenplay/film contests. I speak fairly good French, a little Hebrew, and a little Yiddish, none of which come in handy in Texas.

Currently I am a Professor of Advertising at Indiana University in Bloomington, Indiana directing classes from Austin, Texas. I am enjoying seeding and entertaining the bright young minds of our next generation.

I learned through life that sometimes you have to fight -for your life, your health, your freedom, your dignity. Better train.

WALT SAPRONOV

"I've continued my martial arts practice, regularly working out to this day at American Karate schools such as Imperatori Karate and PKA Extreme Warriors."

TRAINING INFORMATION

- Belt Ranks & Martial Arts Styles: Black Belt in Shorin-Ryu, an Okinawan style
- Instructors/Influencers: Grand Master Shoshin Nagamine
- Yrs. In the Martial Arts: 54 years

PROFESSIONAL ORGANIZATIONS

- PKA Worldwide

I began my martial arts training in Shorin-Ryu, a classical Okinawan style of karate, while attending Ohio State University. It was to become a life-long pursuit. I began training in 1966 and earned my Black Belt under one of the first Americans to train in Okinawa directly under Grand Master Shoshin Nagamine, the founder of the Matsubayashi style of Shorin-Ryu. In 1970, he moved to Iowa City, Iowa to attend the University of Iowa. There, he established the Iowa City, Shorin-Ryu dojo, which was affiliated with the college. The dojo flourished and some of its students became Shorin-Ryu karate teachers in their own right.

After moving to Atlanta in the late 1970's, I joined the Joe Corley Karate Studio. Eventually, I changed (or adapted) my original Okinawan style to the American Karate style of karate, boxing and kickboxing. For many years thereafter I trained with other Professional Karate Association (PKA) fighters under the late Asa Gordon. I have competed in the Battle of Atlanta, the Vitali Gold Star, and other tournaments, and was a

sparring partner for then PKA Heavyweight Champion Jerry Rhome, Master Joe Corley and other professionals. For over half a century, I've continued my martial arts practice, regularly working out to this day at American Karate schools such as Imperatori Karate and PKA Extreme Warriors

In addition to my martial arts practice, I am a practicing attorney, concentrating on telecommunications law, transactions, regulation and finance. My law firm, Sapronov & Associates, P.C., has represented large institutional clients for over 35 years. Recently, the Firm has expanded its international practice to Moscow, Russia. Along with James (Jim) Thomas II, a fellow Black Belt "Who's Who" and well-known attorney who recently joined the Firm, we now represent Joe Corley and the new PKA, which is expanding its presence to professional martial arts venues both here in the U.S. and in Eastern Europe. For more information on the Firm, please visit www.wstelecomlaw.com.

I live in Atlanta with my wife, Susan. Our daughter, Sophia, a New York University (NYU) honors graduate in vocal performance, is a member of the Actors' Equity Association. As a professional actress she recently appearing in the Atlanta debut production of "Once" (https://www.horizontheatre.com/plays/once)

Inspired by our Faith, my family is actively involved in Christian Church work throughout the U.S.

DAVID SINOPOLI

"Through martial arts training I overcame self-esteem issues...and became stronger mentally and physically."

TRAINING INFORMATION

- Belt Ranks & Martial Arts Styles: 5th Dan, Sento Jiu Jitsu / MMA; 5th Dan ICAT (Integrated Combative Arts Training); 5th Dan, Joe Lewis Fighting Systems; 2nd Dan Superfoot Systems; 1st Dan American Kenpo; 1st Dan Tae Kwon Do; Brown Belt Judo; Purple Belt BJJ; Instructor level, SPEAR system

- Instructors/Influencers: Walt Lysak Jr., Walt Lysak, Rich Ryan, Joe Lewis, Bill Wallace, Kevin Sullivan, Byung Cho, Harry Chandler, Luigi Mondelli, Tony Blauer, Steve Giroux

- Birthdate: August 10, 1965

- Birthplace/Growing Up: Pittsfield, MA

- Yrs. In the Martial Arts: 46 years

- Yrs. Instructing: 15 years

- School Owner, Instructor, Member PKA Worldwide

PROFESSIONAL ORGANIZATIONS

- PKA Worldwide
- Joe Lewis Fighting Systems
- Superfoot Systems
- ICAT
- IFOJJ
- UFAF

I was over weight as a child and had bright red hair. I was picked on relentlessly in school to the point that I wanted to quit school altogether. I stayed home from school one day and watched a Chuck Norris movie and from that point my life changed. I was amazed at his confidence, skill level and the way he carried himself. So much so I started taking martial arts classes that following week. I started weight training and running to go along with it. As time progressed I would watch countless martial arts movies and train that much harder. While other children had famous athletes as their role models, mine were famous martial artists like Chuck Norris, Joe Lewis, Bill Wallace, Bruce Lee, Benny Urquidez,, Jeff Smith, Joe Corley and Don Wilson just to name a few. I bought every martial arts magazine on the market and watch the PKA matches on television. Martial Arts became a lifestyle for me, a passion that once started out as a way to defend myself from being bullied It became so much more.

I can honestly say that the martial arts has made me the man I am today, a better person, father, husband, friend and teacher. Through martial arts

PROFESSIONAL KARATE ASSOCIATION HONORS · 2020 MASTERS & PIONEERS

140

PROFESSIONAL ORGANIZATIONS

- Marine Corps League
- Disabled American Veterans
- Kore BJJ

PERSONAL ACHIEVEMENTS

- Student, Father, Teacher and Husband
- Doing a magazine cover with Joe Lewis and Walt Lysak
- Achieving my Black Belt from Joe Lewis
- Achieving my Black Belt from Bill Wallace
- Inducted twice into the United States Martial Arts Hall of Fame
- Inducted into the Action Martial Arts Hall of Fame
- Inducted to AMAA Hall of Fame 2019

MAJOR ACHIEVEMENTS

- Served my country as a United States Marine
- Full time firefighter, part time police officer
- Deputy Sheriff for 17 years
- Volunteered and spent a week at ground zero on 911

Through martial arts training I overcame self-esteem issues. I not only became stronger mentally and physically, but I found balance in my life. I went on to become a United States Marine, have a successful career in law enforcement and firefighting. I own and operate with my wife a gym and martial arts center. Martial Arts has been a blessing in my life.

WORLD CHAMPION

戦士・最強の9ノ

PKA KICKBOXING ASSOCIATION
WORLD CHAMPION

FIRST
PKA LIGHT HEAVYWEIGHT
WORLD CHAMPION

BLACK BELT
HALL OF FAME MEMBER

UNITED STATES KARATE
CHAMPION

THE LIVING LEGEND
JEFF SMITH

JEFF SMITH

"Jeff Smith is one of the, if not THE MOST, multi-talented martial artists of all time."

THE CURRICULUM VITAE OF GRAND MASTER JEFF SMITH:

- 1964- Jeff enrolled in a Tae Kwon Do class at Texas A&I University in Kingsville, TX

- 1966–Jeff competes in his 1st Karate Tournament in Houston, Texas.

- 1966-Jeff receives his 1st Degree Black Belt from GM Jhoon Rhee in Kingsville, Texas.

- 1970-Jeff moves to Washington DC to Teach at the Jhoon Rhee Institute for Grand Master Rhee and enlists his top protégés to join him in DC, building the basis

- 1970-1985 Served as Senior VP for GM Jhoon Rhee's Institute of TAE KWON Do, training and managing all of the Managers and Instructors for his 12 locations.

- 1969-74 Jeff won many of the Top National Point Tournaments including Joe Corely's Battle of Atlanta, Ed Parker's International Karate , Allen Steen's US Championships, Mike Anderson's Top 10   Nationals Bob Maxwell's Ocean City United States Pro-Am, Jim Miller's Mardi Gras Nationals George   Minshew's Houston Karate   Olympics, The Pan Am Championships in Baltimore, Md. and the North American Tae Kwon Do Championships inToronto, Canada to name a few.

Jeff Smith is one of the, if not THE MOST, multi-talented martial artists of all time. Champion, Innovator, Manager, Teacher, Coach, Mentor, Leader…and…and…and…

On June 17, 2016, Jeff Smith was awarded the rank of Grandmaster by the Professional Karate Commission with his 10th Degree Black Belt by Grand Masters Glenn Keeney and Allen Steen with the additional signatures and approval of Pat Johnson and J Pat Burleson.

One of the most popular and highly respected martial artists in the world, Grandmaster Jeff Smith has influenced millions of Martial Artists around the world, both directly and indirectly.

Voted by his Top Ten peers as the Number One Point Fighter in the Nation in 1974 by Professional Karate Magazine, Jeff went on immediately to win the very first PKA World Light Heavyweight Kickboxing Championship title on ABC's Wide World of Entertainment.

All the while, he was training the next generation of International Champions, coaching them to World Titles, as he managed and taught the instructional staff of the Jhoon Rhee Institute schools in Washington DC. As articulate as he is dangerous, Grandmaster Smith has appeared before the camera as a multi-talented point fighter and PKA World Champion Kickboxer and as an expert analyst for the next generations.

THE CURRICULUM VITAE OF GRAND MASTER JEFF SMITH:

- 1973-74 Jeff was ranked the number 1-point fighter in the USA in by Professional Karate Magazine.

- 1973-2016 Jeff has been on the cover of every major martial arts publication and was selected by Washingtonian Magazine as one of Washington's top athletes.

- 1974- Jeff is the first recipient of the Bruce Lee Award (selected by Mrs. Bruce Lee and Professional Karate Magazine) and listed is listed in the first Who's Who of Martial Arts.

- 1974-80-Jeff is recognized worldwide as the seven-time PKA "World Light Heavy Weight Karate Champion."

- 1975- 50 million worldwide viewers observed Jeff's title defense against Don King's heavy weight fighter Kareem Allah as the co-main event of the Ali vs. Frazier III World Boxing Title Fight, known as the "Thrilla in Manila."

- 1980-90 Jeff was coach of the WAKO World Champion United States Karate Team winning consecutive World Titles in all those 10 years.

- 1989-1993-Jeff performed at the White House for President Bush in the "Kick Drugs Out of Your Life" campaign and again with his students in California for President Bush in his "Drug Abuse is Life Abuse" program. Jeff conducted seminars in public schools all over the USA for the "Just Say No to Drugs" campaign.

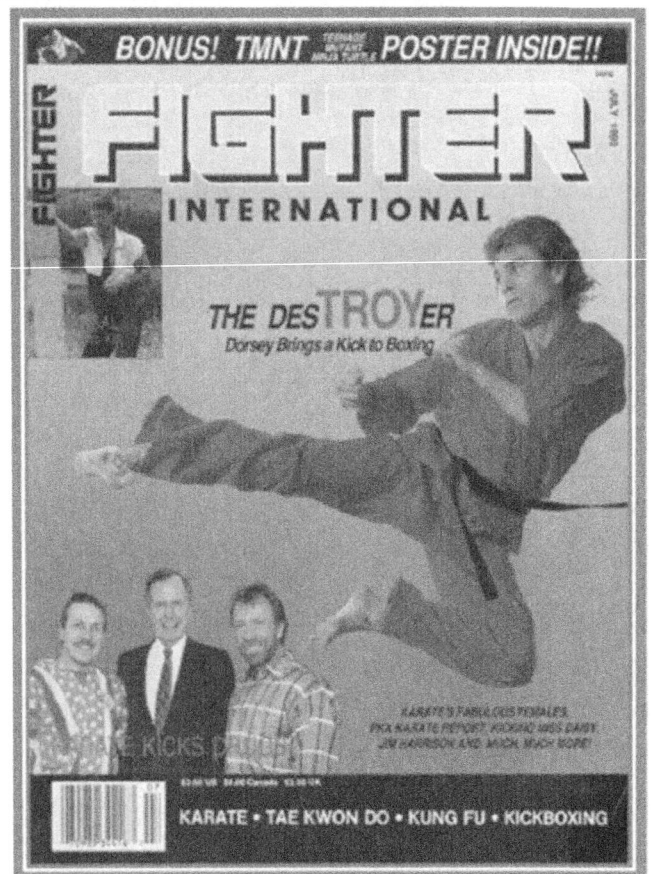

THE CURRICULUM VITAE OF GRAND MASTER JEFF SMITH:

- 1974-1985 Jeff appears on ABC's "Wide World of Entertainment," "The Champions" TV series, and does Expert Commentary on Showtime, ESPN and Pay-Per-View events

- 1990-92 Jeff performed for Arnold Schwarzenegger on the White House lawn with his students for the "Great American Workout" for the President's Council on Physical Fitness.

- 2000-2016 Jeff is inducted into the Tae Kwon Do Hall of Fame, Black Belt Magazine Hall of Fame, NASKA Hall of Fame, Action Magazine's Martial Arts Hall of Fame, The Battle of Atlanta's Centurion Hall of Fame Award, and with Chuck Norris, is the first recipient of the of the Joe Lewis Eternal Warrior Award.

- 2005-Present Jeff is the National Director of Mile High Karate Franchises and Martial Arts Wealth Mastery Consultant with GM Stephen Oliver. Jeff owns and operates his own Mile High Karate School in Sterling, VA.

- He also travels globally, officiating at National and International tournaments. He conducts both Business and Training seminars for Martial Arts schools all over the world.

Contact GM Smith for Seminars and Appearances at:
GMJeffSmith@gmail.com

JOHN THERIEN

"Hanshi Therien created the World Kobudo Federation to fulfill his vision of what a world-wide organization should be."

MAJOR ACHIEVEMENTS

- Title of Hanshi (Leader of Leaders)
- 9th Degree Black Belt
- Man of the Decade 1980's – PKA (Professional Karate Association)
- 1982: PKA Promoter of the Year
- 1996: Inducted into the CJA Hall of Fame
- 1997: Inducted into the WKF Hall of Fame
- Canadian Government Award for achievement in Jiu-Jitsu
- Golden Belt Award for being a pioneer of Jiu-Jitsu in Canada
- Golden Belt Award for being a pioneer of Kickboxing in Canada
- Ranked #1 Jiu-Jitsu instructor in Canada by his peers
- Manager of 23-time world Kickboxing Champion, Jean-Yves Thériault
- May 2010: Canadian Blackbelt Martial Arts Hall of Fame
- 2007-2014: President of the Vanier Merchants Association
- Member of the Board of Canadian Blackbelt Hall of Fame
- Recipient of the city of Ottawa Community Builder

With more than 50 years of martial arts experience, Hanshi Therien created the WKF to fulfill his vision of what a world-wide organization should be. Based in Ottawa, Canada, he organizes many of the WKF events and travels around the world giving seminars and promoting the positive values of the martial arts.

He also founded Therien Jiu-Jitsu & Kickboxing in 1968, one of Canada's largest and most successful group of Martial Arts schools. He has certified and graduated over a thousand Black Belts and is the head instructor for more than 3000 active students in the Can-Ryu system.

Aside from the activities and responsibilities of the Therien Jiu Jitsu & Kickboxing organization, Hanshi followed his vision of bringing the world of Martial Arts together, and has organized training camps, conventions and recognitions all over the world.

DALIA VITKUS

"I continue to pursue my passions in the Martial Arts and in making the world a better, safer place..."

TRAINING INFORMATION

- Belt Ranks & Martial Arts Styles: Tae Kwon Do (3rd Degree Black Belt)

- Instructors/Influencers: GM Bill Wallace, Sr. GM Edward B. Sell, GM Brenda Sell, Rob Davidson

- Birthdate: September 11, 1962

- Birthplace/Growing Up: Chicago, IL

- Yrs. In the Martial Arts: 14 years

- Yrs. Instructing: 10+ years

- School owner, Manager, Instructor

PROFESSIONAL ORGANIZATIONS

- Member PKA Worldwide
- Member USCDKA

I was born in Chicago and grew up in a rough neighborhood where challenging situations were a way of life. I'm no stranger to the haunts of having been bullied and dealing with aggressive gang mentality. I found Tae Kwon Do a way to achieve inner peace with physical self-defense as a bonus!

My teaching now focuses on SELF defense for life: Strength, Encouragement, Learning and Fitness. This incorporates strengthening balance, coordination and fitness for a healthy mind, body and spirit; thereby reducing stress and promoting inner peace. My passions include self-defense for women, working with youth and adults of all ages and family Tae Kwon Do.

In fact, having participated for many years, as a board member with a non-profit organization that strives to empower youth by teaching bullying prevention and suicide prevention strategies, such tactics play an important role, and I incorporate learned programs and awareness as a way of life.

PERSONAL ACHIEVEMENTS

- PROFESSIONAL ORGANIZATIONS: Berrien County Juvenile Center, Adjunct Professor with Colorado Technical University Online, Lithuanian Sea Scout Organization

MAJOR ACHIEVEMENTS

- Gave birth to and raised two sons and a daughter
- Achieved Officer rank in the Lithuanian Sea Scout Organization
- Achieved 3rd Degree Black Belt in Tae Kwon Do and the Superfoot System
- Owns and operates the New Wave Kicks Martial Art and Kickboxing School
- Inducted into the Alliance Black Belt Hall of Fame
- Master's Degree in Criminal Justice

I am dedicated to bullying prevention, building self-esteem and positive growth with the youth and adults of today.

Studying Martial Arts has not only helped me to grow positively in mind, body and spirit, as I continue to grow in confidence and value, but they continue to enrich my life. I continue to pursue my passions in the Martial Arts and in making the world a better, safer place by sharing what I know and always striving to learn more.

BILL "SUPERFOOT" WALLACE

"SUPERFOOT: A Martial Arts Legacy of ALL TIME!"

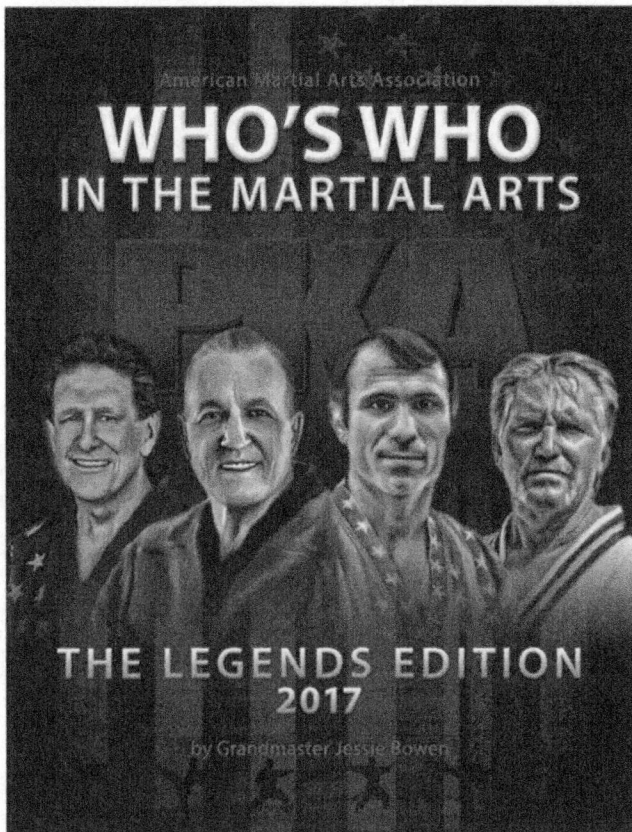

The entire world knows him as SUPERFOOT! He was featured on the Cover of Who's Who Legends 2017 with his brother in arms original world light heavyweight champion Jeff Smith and friends Joe Corley and Bill Clark. Five + decades after he started martial arts, Bill Wallace is a Grand Master Instructor and one of the global martial arts world's most influential personalities.

Grand Master Wallace was born in Portland, Indiana, and trained in wrestling during his high school years. He began his study of Judo in 1966 and was forced to discontinue his Judo related activities because of an injury he suffered to his right knee during practice. He then began to study Shorin-ryu Karate under Michael Gneck in February 1967, while serving in the U.S. Air Force.

Wallace was a prolific point fighter, and he won tournaments all over North America and fought on the US teams competing internationally. An injury to his right knee forced him to abandon kicking with that leg and he perfected kicking with the left leg. Clocked at nearly 60 miles an hour, he was perennially ranked as the premiere kicker in the country and among the top 10 fighters by all ratings services.

In September, 1974 the Professional Karate Association (PKA) emerged and held the world's first Full Contact Karate Championship in the LA Sports Arena. Bill Wallace was chosen to represent the Untied States and emerged as the world's first Full Contact Middleweight Champion on ABC's Wide World of Entertainment.

Honing in on his incredible speed and accuracy, he was nicknamed Superfoot, a moniker that became synonymous with Bill Wallace the world over. Superfoot's first title defense was against Atlanta's Joe Corley at the 1975 Battle of Atlanta, where he captured his first defense win in 9 rounds. As a result of his incredible reputation, CBS signed Wallace for quarterly live title defenses, and in 1977 they also signed Joe Corley to be the expert commentator for the Superfoot bouts. Superfoot would continue winning and would retire live on CBS in 1980, one of the few fighters who stayed retired and remained undefeated at 23-0.

The PKA promoted the sport of full-contact karate on NBC, CBS and ESPN. PKA Full-contact karate differed from Muay Thai style kickboxing in that leg kicks were allowed in kickboxing and forbidden in full-contact karate. Wallace, the epitome of high kicking, joined Joe Corley on ESPN for the Defense and Fitness Tips of the Week, where Wallace showed world-class athletes from golf, basketball, baseball, football and track the proper ways to use the sponsor's Power Stretch machine to improve their athletic performance and prevent injuries. Wallace and Corley together inspired thousands of viewers to join karate schools through their series.

In 1990 Bill Wallace (166 lbs) fought one last exhibition kickboxing/ karate match with friend Joe Lewis (198 lbs) on pay per view. Both Wallace and Lewis were refused a boxing license because of their age. The exhibition ended with one judge in favor for Wallace, another in favor for Lewis, and the third judge scored the bout a tie, ending the exhibition in a draw.

Wallace has taught karate, judo, wrestling and weight lifting at Memphis State University. The author of a college textbook about karate and kinesiology, he continues to teach seminars across the United States and abroad.

He was the arch nemesis of long-time friend Chuck Norris in A Force of One. His other film credits include Kill Point, with Cameron Mitchell, Continental Divide and Neighbors, with John Belushi; The Protector, with Jackie Chan; Los Bravos with Hector Echavarria; A Prayer for the Dying, with Mickey Rourke; Ninja Turf; and Sword of Heaven.

Wallace was the play-by-play commentator for the inaugural Ultimate Fighting Championship pay-per-view event in 1993 alongside fellow kickboxer Kathy Long and NFL Hall of Famer Jim Brown.

Wallace administers an organization of karate schools under his "Superfoot" system, all members of the PKA WORLDWIDE Associated Schools.

He was elected to Black Belt Magazine's Hall of Fame in 1973 as "Tournament Karate Fighter of the Year" and again in 1978 as "Man of the Year", has appeared on magazine covers the world over and still today is one of the most sought after instructors in the world.

SUPERFOOT: a Martial Arts Legacy for All Time!

DON WARRENER

"I still thank my instructors for the royal beatings I received at the end of their fists and feet..."

TRAINING INFORMATION

- Belt Ranks & Martial Arts Styles: Shodan, Canadian Karate

- Instructors/Influencers: Benny Allen, Wally Slocki, Teddy Martin

- Birthdate: 1960-ish

- Birthplace/Growing Up: Canada

- Yrs. In the Martial Arts: 54 years

- School Owner, Manager, Instructor, Martial Arts Author, Member PKA Worldwide

My martial arts career began on March 15, 1966 in Hamilton, Ontario in Canada. My teacher in Canadian Karate was Benny Allen who trained the best of the best fighters in Canada including Wally Slocki and Teddy Martin. I still thank them for the royal beatings I received at the end of their fists and feet. I was promoted to Shodan two years to the day after I started.

In 1973 my teacher then introduced me to Richard Kim and I soon became his student. Over my years in the martial arts I also received instruction from Morio Higaonna, Gogen "The Cat" Yamaguchi, Joe Lewis, Frank Lee, Dr. Dom Lopez, and Wally Jay to name but a few.

In 1977 I started one of Canada's most successful magazines, "The Voice of the Martial Arts."

PROFESSIONAL KARATE ASSOCIATION HONORS • 2020 MASTERS & PIONEERS

In 1980 I started a publishing company, Masters Publishing, and it's still going strong today.

In 1985 I restored one of the most significant historical buildings with over 20,000 square feet as a martial arts school. This structure, the Hamilton Custom House, was previously owned and built by Queen Victoria at a cost of over $1 million dollars. I've also received certificates honoring me from the federal government for my efforts.

That done, I then started to establish the largest chain of schools in Canada and have over 33 schools opened with 103 franchises sold and an enrollment of over 9000 students.

In 1998 I made a radical jump and relocated to sunny Los Angeles, California. There I started a video production company, Rising Sun Productions, and today the library has over 1800 titles available in it. My publishing company now has more than 123 titles, and I personally have written over 23 books on martial arts.

CARL WHITAKER

"My martial arts journey has taught me respect for others, and to stand up for those who cannot stand up for themselves."

TRAINING INFORMATION

- Belt Ranks & Martial Arts Styles: 7th Dan, American Tae Kwon Do / American Karate

- Instructors/Influencers: Bob Beasley, Jim Choate, Troy Dorsey

- Birthdate: April 17, 1965

- Birthplace/Growing Up: Dallas & Quinland, TX

- Yrs. In the Martial Arts: 45 years

- Yrs. Instructing: 41 years

- School Owner, Manager, Instructor, PKA Worldwide Member

PROFESSIONAL ORGANIZATIONS

- Professional Karate Association (PKA)

- Museum of Sport Karate

At the age of eight I watched the movie "Billy Jack" directed by Tom Laughlin. In the movie, Billy Jack stood for what was right. He was confident and helped others. He knew how to defend himself with his hands and feet. I wanted to be like him.

Martial Arts has developed inspiration and discipline in my life since the age of ten. Where I was shy, I became confident. Where I was weak, I learned to be strong. I realized not only do you need balance to kick, but balance in life, as well. In learning to fight comes responsibility. All the sweat and hard work in becoming a black belt was just the beginning. Giving back and teaching others what I have learned has been a true joy.

PERSONAL ACHIEVEMENTS

- By the age of 16, I opened my first dojo, The Karate School, and helped promote others in the Dallas / Ft. Worth area. I have been instructing for 4 decades and have had the pleasure of teaching men, women, and children from all backgrounds, including those with special needs, and the blind.

- I have held self-defense training seminars for women from the Dallas / Ft. Worth area, including The Women's League of Dallas, Nexus Women's Center, and many other organizations.

MAJOR ACHIEVEMENTS

- 1982 A.O.K. Black Belt Rookie of the Year

- 1983 & 1985 member, WAKO. US World Champion Karate Team, London, England and Munich, Germany

- Member of Texas Team in Mexico City, and Acapulco

- Inductee, USA Martial Arts Hall of Fame

- Inductee, Universal Martial Arts Hall of Fame

- Inductee, Masters Hall of Fame

Some tournament competition wins include:

- US Karate Championships

- Oklahoma Nationals

- Ft. Worth Pro Am

- Texas State Karate Championships

- Galveston Hurricane Nationals

- Karate Olympics in Houston, TX

My martial arts journey has taught me respect for others, and to stand up for those who cannot stand up for themselves. Through karate, I've had the opportunity to travel across the world making many lifelong friends, teaching and giving back what was given to me.

DON WILLIS

"The Martial Arts have made it possible to achieve a great many good things in my life..."

TRAINING INFORMATION

- Belt Ranks & Martial Arts Styles: 6th Dan American Karate, 7th Dan World Martial Arts & Kobudo Association

- Instructors/Influencers: Curtis Herrington, Andy Horne, I.J. Kim

- Birthdate: March 8, 1943

- Birthplace/Growing Up: Canton, OH

- Yrs. In the Martial Arts: 60 years

- Yrs. Instructing: 40+ years

- School owner, Manager, Instructor, Founder and member of PKA Worldwide Board of Directors

PROFESSIONAL ORGANIZATIONS

- PKA Worldwide

- PKC Professional Karate Commission

I was a smaller person when young and that made me an easy target for bullies. I was picked on quite a bit, and I did not have a lot of self-esteem. I joined the military in 1960 when I was just 17 and I loved the hand to hand combat. I worked out with anyone I could for my three years in the service. When I was discharged in 1963 it was impossible to find a school, but was able to find a few guys that knew "a little."

The Martial Arts have made it possible to achieve a great many good things in my life, and to overcome many obstacles. I have the idea that is due to the never quit mindset that is prevalent in the martial arts. As to myself, I have emphysema and I attribute my training in breath control and my never quit attitude to be able to keep going.

PERSONAL ACHIEVEMENTS

- Police Training Sargent - Canal Fulton, OH

- Nominated for Ohio Governor's Cup - National Competitor all divisions
  Presidential Sports Award from Richard Nixon

- Founder of the Don Willis American Karate System

- Opened the first Martial Arts school in Ft. Lauderdale, FL 1970

- Operated Martial Arts schools in Florida and Ohio

- Founded Don Willis International

MAJOR ACHIEVEMENTS

- Member, the Professional Karate Association Executive Committee

- As Chairman of the Professional Karate Association's Reps and Officials Committee, I have personally trained well over 1000 PKA Officials worldwide.

- In 1983 was the only person ever to be awarded both Professional Karate Association Man of the Year and Professional Karate Association Official of the Year.

- On behalf of the PKA, I've traveled as far from home as Nice, France and Anchorage, Alaska, and I've represented the association in almost all of our CONUS states.

- I am the original United States Director of Operations for the Professional Karate Commission and I have work alongside GM Glenn Keeney in building that organization's recognition in the Martial Arts.

MAJOR ACHIEVEMENTS

- Being presented with a Joe Lewis Eternal Warrior Award has been the highlight of my martial arts career.

- Most important, I have now teamed with GM Joe Corley to the grow PKA WORLDWIDE. I consider my long time friendships with GM Glenn Keeney and GM Joe Corley as a major achievement. These two have done more than I can say to build the Martial Arts.

DON "THE DRAGON" WILSON

"'The Dragon' is successful in the film for the same reasons his ring career was so powerful. He focuses on continuous improvement—now as an actor--and he projects integrity, warmth, and likeability."

Don "the Dragon" Wilson's humble beginnings started in Cocoa Beach, Florida, where he was born and raised in the shadow of Cape Canaveral, where his father worked as an engineer for NASA. Don was an honors student at high school, and his quest was to follow in his father's footsteps. He attended the Coast Guard Academy, where he studied engineering, and wanted to become a military officer, but a lesson from his older brother, Jim, who had already been studying kung-fu, changed his life forever.

Don had also been a great athlete in high school, captaining both the football team and the basketball team, where he was the team MVP in both sports. And do it was that he couldn't understand why at a solid 205 pounds, he could not outfight his smaller 155 lb. brother. Don was soon competing in karate competitions, known as point fighting.

Don was studying the dragon style (pai lum) of kung-fu, however he did not feel fulfilled with this style, and he wanted to prove that kung-fu practitioners could really fight. He discovered the world of kickboxing, where he became a student of the game, and started his professional kickboxing

career in 1974, training and fighting out of his brother Jim's dojo. By 1978 his ring performances had attracted sponsorship from an investment group, and by 1979 he was the PKA U.S. middleweight champion.

At that point, Don had been working on his techniques with PKA world champion, Bill "Superfoot" Wallace. This training became the genesis of Don's legendary kicking skills. He was able to use every kind of kick "invented", including the jumping and spinning variety, and could deliver double and triple kicks from each leg.

And in this time frame, the PKA's Joe Corley had arranged for Don to be the main event fighter on the PKA's first ever event on a new fledgling sports network—ESPN—during its very first week on the air, where Don faced Jimmy Horseley in Orlando. The center referee was Bill Clark. Naturally, Don won that now historic first ESPN title bout.

At that time, Don was considered the heir apparent to the PKA world title vacated by the retirement of Bill "Superfoot" Wallace. However, the PKA advocated a policy dictating that all contenders had to fight exclusively in the PKA, and Don felt that it was not to his advantage to be exclusive. Don decided he would fight under any sanction, against any fighter, to prove his abilities.

In 1980, Don won the WKA Light-Heavyweight World Championship, his first World title. Later in 1980, he won his second World title, the STAR Light-Heavyweight Championship. In 1982, he won the WKO World Light-Heavyweight title. In 1983, Don won the KICK World Light-Heavyweight title, and later in the year added the WKA World Cruiserweight title. He also was named Official Karate magazine's Fighter of the Year.

In 1984, Don won Super Light-Heavyweight World titles in both the WKA and STAR organizations, along with Official Karate, and Black Belt magazine's Halls of Fame, and culminated with STAR Career Champion – The Highest rated Kickboxer of all time. By the time Don hung up the gloves, he had won 2 more World titles under the sanctions of ISKA, and the PKO. What made Don "The Dragon" the greatest champion is the fact that he won 11 World Titles, in 3 different weight classes under 6 different sanctioning organizations. He was world champion for 11 straight years, defeating 12 other world champions, 12 number-one contenders and 15 National champions on four continents.

Don thoroughly dominated kickboxing as the undisputed world champion, fighting anyone, under any rules, and he defeated the best champions in their own hometowns, while they were in their prime. Don's impressive career record consists of 71 wins, 47 by knockout, and 6 by kick-knockout, and he was also the first kung-fu practitioner to become a World Kickboxing champion. In 1996, Don was named the Greatest Competitor of All Time by Kickside magazine-Europe.

As Don's phenomenal kickboxing career was winding down, he came to Hollywood at the suggestion of his friend and fellow martial artist, Chuck Norris. After hooking up with agent Ray Cavaleri (who is still his agent), Don got a national commercial, and a stint on the soap opera "General Hospital". Shortly thereafter came a fateful audition with the legendary filmmaker Roger Corman, who had discovered such talents as William Shatner, Jack Nicholson, and Robert DeNiro. Corman was so impressed with Don's kickboxing career and his natural charm, that he immediately signed him to a non-exclusive seven movie contract, and Don starred in the huge hit, "Bloodfist". Since Don was still fighting, Corman actually once insured Don's face for $10 million with Lloyd's of London.

The tremendous success of "Bloodfist" urged Corman to produce a sequel, and that success led to eight different versions of "Bloodfist". Don had discovered his niche of producing (yes, he has co-produced all but the first 4 films) and starring in exciting action films where he can showcase his incredible kicking skills, his keen sense of humor, and his undeniable charisma.

"Bloodfist III" earned rave reviews in Variety magazine, and the next project was "Ring of Fire", for which Don added the screen credit of producer for the first time. The success of "Ring of Fire" led to sequels for that film, which led to his next important film "Red Sun Rising". Don has been continually producing hit films that are exciting and fun to watch, but more importantly make a profit, which seems to be happening less and less these days. He also appeared in one of the hugely popular Batman films, with a small role in Batman Forever. Don is also not afraid to stretch out as an actor, having taken a break from the action genre, by starring in and co-producing a horror film called Night Hunter, in which his character becomes a vampire hunter after witnessing his parents being killed by vampires as a youngster.

Don has established himself as a hard-working Hollywood action star, having starred in 29 films since his film career began in 1989. He has had as many as 5 films released within a 14-month period. His most recent effort is an intense Sci-Fi Action film called The Last Sentine", which he considers one of his best, and has two other name co-stars in Katee Sackhoff, and Bokeem Woodbine.

"The Dragon" is successful in the film for the same reasons his ring career was so powerful. He focuses on continuous improvement—now as an actor--and he projects integrity, warmth, and likeability.

Roger Corman, who has discovered some of the greatest talent in the history of the film business, told Don that he would be a star the first time they met. Don "The Dragon" Wilson's star is definitely on the rise–as he proved recently when one of his movies premiered during Primetime in the U.S. on NBC Universal's Sci-Fi Channel.

DJ YATES

"The impression and impact the arts have made on me are enormous..."

TRAINING INFORMATION

- Belt Ranks & Martial Arts Styles: Okinawan Shorin-ryu Matsumura, Rokudan 6th Dan Renshi

- Instructors/Influencers: Hanshi Tomasada Kuda, Kyoshi Doug Yates (Father)

- Birthdate: April 9, 1981

- Birthplace/Growing Up: Xenia, OH

- Yrs. In the Martial Arts: 36 years

- Yrs. Instructing: 24 years

- Instructor, Member of PKA Worldwide

PROFESSIONAL ORGANIZATIONS

- Okinawan Matsumra Shorin-Ryu karate

- Kobudo Association

I started training in the Martial Arts under the direction of my father, Doug Yates at the age of 3 (1983) . Martial Arts have granted me the privilege to travel around the world, learning, and training with the best of the best. The impression and impact the arts have made on me are enormous, and it has allowed me to give back to others to teaching and seminars.

PERSONAL ACHIEVEMENTS

- United States National Karate Team from 1994-2013

- (USANKF, PKC, AKJU, USMAA)

- Countries Attended: Canada, Mexico, Dominican Republic, Argentina, Switzerland, Germany, Hungary, England, Ireland

MAJOR ACHIEVEMENTS

- USANKF All-american

- International and National Karate Champion.

- International medal count:

- 13 gold, 2 Silver, one bronze

- Honored by the United States Congress and House of Representatives.

- Honored by the Ohio Senate

- USA Martial Arts Hall of Fame Alumni

- Trained at USA Olympic Center

- Teaches seminars around the United States

DOUG YATES

"The teaching of others and being part of their goals and dreams humbled me..."

TRAINING INFORMATION

- Belt Ranks & Martial Arts Styles: 8th degree Black Belt, Okinawa Shorin Ryu

- Instructors/Influencers: Kuda, Tomasada, Sensei Okinawa Shorin Ryu Matsumura, Kenpo Karate Kobudo Association

- Birthdate: June 6, 1957

- Birthplace/Growing Up: Maysville, KY / Xenia, OH

- Yrs. In the Martial Arts: 47 years

- Yrs. Instructing: 44 years

- School owner, Manager, Instructor, Member of PKA Worldwide

PROFESSIONAL ORGANIZATIONS

- Professional Karate Association (PKA)

- Okinawa Shorin Ryu

- Matsumura Kenpo Karate Kobudo Association

- Askari Ki Karate Kobudo Federation

I was a baseball player and wanted to train during the off season to stay in shape; karate seemed to be the way to do it.

As a young kid growing up I found myself in trouble at school. In 7th grade I failed and had a large number of after school detentions left to serve. I was called to the office and the Assistant Principal, Mr. Stacy, said he understood that my grades were bad yet my grades in Gym was straight As. I said, "Well, I like gym." So he made a deal. He would erase all my detentions if I played sports, but if I got in trouble I would get all my detentions back to serve. I agreed. The following year I played sports and never got into trouble again.

Fast forward to the 1994 Goodwill Games in St Petersburg, Russia as I walked around Kiev Stadium during the Closing Ceremonies in front of 85,000 people on Worldwide TV. I thought of Mr. Stacy. He gave me a break.

PERSONAL ACHIEVEMENTS

- President and Co-Founder of the Miami Valley Tournament Association (MVTA)

- President of the AKARI KI KARATE KOBUDO FEDERATION

- 1996 Inducted in World Karate Union "Hall of Fame

- 2001 Inducted in United States Martial Arts Hall of Fame

- 2006 Inducted in the United States Alliance Hall of Fame

- 2008 Inducted in the OHIO PKC Hall of Fame

MAJOR ACHIEVEMENTS

- 1980 Karate Illustrated National Ratings. #1 Weapons and #7 Fighting

- Professional Karate Association (PKA) Full Contact Karate Fighter

- 1981-1985 PKA World Ranked Honorable Mention, Middleweight Division.

- 1981 PKA Ohio State Light Heavyweight Champion

- PKA fight record, 16 wins (12 by KO), 9 losses

- PKA Trainer of the Year – Sport Karate, twice nominated

- 1994 USAKF TEAM USA, Team Member, Goodwill Games St Petersburg, Russia

- Gold Medal Winner and walked during Closing Ceremonies on Worldwide TV before front of 85,000 people

- 1994 USAKF TEAM USA IJJF Team Member, World Jujitsu Championship in Bologna, Italy

- 1995 AJKU TEAM AMERICA, won Gold, Silver and Bronze medals, Irish Cup Dublin, Ireland

Sports lead me to karate and I've achieved many honors and recognition that I would had never received if I had not gotten that break from Mr. Stacy. Karate, the ESPN Fights, the teaching of others and being part of their goals and dreams humbled me and I thank God for allowing me to find my first karate teacher Sensei Dale Holzbauer.

DOUG YATES
WINNER - KNOCK OUT
1:39 2ND ROUND

THE AMERICAN MARTIAL ARTS ALLIANCE

MARTIAL ARTS
MASTERS & PIONEERS

PKA
WORLDWIDE
HONOREES

BRAZIL

FÁBIO AMADOR BUENO

Fábio Bueno knows well the meaning of the word fight. At 54, he is one of the longest-running publishers of martial books and magazines in the Brazilian market. There are more than 2 million copies distributed in newsstands and bookstores in the country.

He started his editorial career in the 1990s, when he worked in a studio that served some of the country's publishers, such as Escala, producing magazines about ecotourism, computer science, sport fishing, etc.

But by the end of this decade, then-editor-in-chief Fabio Kataoka, Karate's black belt, identified the absence of martial arts titles on the newsstands, and because Bueno had affinity with the subject and practiced Full Contact and Taekwondo, he entrusted him with the mission of creating a magazine. Thus was born, in 1998, Inside Kumite, by the publishing house Millennium, with 30 thousand copies, distributed bimonthly throughout Brazil.

The title only remained active for one year and had six editions. Kataoka and Bueno launched a new magazine, this time by another publisher, totally restructured and with an emphasis on traditional martial arts. It was Fighter Magazine's turn to break into the print scene. The magazine was a great success and lasted over six years and 21 issues, all with 30,000 copies.

With Fighter, the editor has gained notoriety and respect from teachers and masters. After her, he produced the Shaolin Gong Fu, Self Defense Collection, Martial Arts Collection, launched by Editora Online in Brazil and Europe. This series was so successful that it sold out quickly, to the point of being reprinted and redistributed.

In mid-2000, as a contributor to Escala, he made several books. In 2009, after so many years working in São Paulo for major publishers, he identified that the time had come to open his own office. The decision was supported by his wife, Elaine Ferreira, who had just left the management of a bank and took over the company.

Bueno Editora was founded in the city of Santos, aiming to be a reference in the production of books and magazines of martial arts in Brazil and in design services, marketing advisory and press.

Master, one of the first bets, conceptualized itself as the only magazine in Brazil that addresses the main modalities. Still in 2009, the director dared to launch an unpublished book of biographies: Great Masters of Martial Arts in Brazil. Today, the work is a national reference and has been circulated in more than 20 countries through its participants. Over 11 editions, there were thousands of featured biographies.

He is an Honorary Doctor in Martial Arts from Erich Fromm World University / USA and in 2019 received important awards such as the MMDC Medals, awarded by the Veterans Society of 32, and the Jiu Jitsu Sports Merit Award.

He is also 4th honorary degree in Taekwondo Martial and Honorary President of the Brazilian Confederation of Taekwondo Martial. He was recently honored with the Commendation of Martial Merit by the Brazilian Confederation of Karate-Do Goju Ryu.

GRANDMASTER ROBERTO CANEIRO

Born on the 13th day of March 1965, in the city of Cruz Alta, State of Rio Grande do Sul, Brazil, the Grand Master Roberto Nochang Carneiro, still as a teenager, already had his own academy reaching hundreds of students. His strong connection with Argentina and Europe made him one of the precursors of Full Contact, Tang Soo Do and Hapkido in Southern Brazil. His skills as a martial manager gave him the opportunity that in 1988, by designation of Grand Master Haeng Ung Lee [in memoriam] was appointed Vice President for Brazil of the Songahm Taekwondo Federation, implanting in Brazil, which is one of the most organized martial arts today. He remained until 1995, when he then followed his path as a martial leader in then created ASAMCO Style of Martial Art, which already existed as an organization since 1987.

Throughout his life, he had the opportunity to constitute a respectable educational, military and martial curriculum, being awarded hundreds of certificates of recognition and more than 80 military, civic and cultural medals. He had the honor of participating on several occasions in the Book of the Great Masters of Brazil, authored by Grand Master José Augusto Maciel Torres and Fábio Amador Bueno. It appeared in the book Libro de Oro de La Etica Marcial - Volume I of the World Combat Union, written by the notorious Grand Master and writer José Manuel Mosquera Castelo, who also invited him to participate in a book on War Refugees; one of the most geopolitical themes today complexes. Possessing a differentiated organizational capacity and deep systemic knowledge, he helped organize many styles of martial arts and their federations around the world. He formed more than 700 black belts throughout his martial teaching, where the vast majority of them stood out in academic studies, being doctors, masters, eminent scientists and outstanding military personnel.

He was one of the founders of the Military Melee Combat at the Military Academy of Agulhas Negras - AMAN, a military higher education institution in charge of training the combatant officers of the Brazilian

Army, where he served for 8 years. He received from the American President Bill Clinton the titles of Traveling Ambassador and Capitol Citation. In 2016, he was honored by Ms. Helena Nancy Paniágua, president of the Escuelas Hermanas International Peace Program, as National Outstanding Coordinator and in 2017 she entered the Hall of Fame and Award the Best of this organization. In the years of 2017, 2018 and 2019, he was awarded the Sports Merit of the Legislative Assembly of the State of São Paulo.

He is currently President of the World ASAMCO Federation, Major General Special Force HC Supreme Commander Latin America of ICTC / BUCU / ABC and belongs to the Staff of ISKA Latino Americana, among others. The international respect achieved by the ASAMCO Style of Martial Art has led many international martial authorities and organizations to publicize our activities as allied ambassadors in more than 100 countries. Grand Master Roberto Nochang Carneiro is a criminal expert, has a degree in Public Security, a postgraduate degree in Public Security and Doctor Honoris Causa in martial arts from Erich Fromm University, as well as other commendations from some of the most prestigious academic arts institutions martial arts in the world, such as Indonesia's INPROFITS; Baptist University of India and Akhlaaqul Karimah Science of Jakarta Indonesia, and other similar titles.

Grand Master Roberto Nochang Carneiro has a tradition of preparing special and military forces, receiving honorary titles from Special Forces from the most respected military and police institutions in the world. In his honor, his disciples created an institution called Mr. Carneiro's Black Belt Club for civic, philanthropic and humanitarian activities. Respectable gurus and spiritual leaders of modern martial arts recognize him as a guru, spiritual leader and mentor, a fact that allows him to use the term of Supreme Guru ASAMCO and has reached the 10th Dan. Grand Master Roberto Nochang Carneiro wants to leave his legacy for the martial arts as a diplomat, educator, spiritual leader and martial philosopher.

GRAND MASTER ANTONIO DIAS

Grand Master Antonio Carlos Dias is 58 years old. Born in Rio de Janeiro, Brazil. He's 9th dan black belt of Kickboxing by ISKA, and 7th dan of Taekwondo by the World Taekwondo Interstyle League and National Taekwondo League. By the age of 4, he started his life in the Martial Arts, beginning with Judo. Two years later, he made a brief passage through Capoeira until he finally got to Taekwondo, at 8 years old. More than a decade passed before he traveled to the United States for a swimming exchange program in Tallahassee, where he had his first contact with Kickboxing.

Antonio returned to Brazil in 1981, initiating his first Kickboxing class, where he finds himself today. He not only graduated more than 200 black belts, but also won several titles in his career; 4 World Titles in Forms and Point Fight, in addition to 5 Pan-American, 5 South-American, 14 Brazilians and 15 state championships.

According to the Grand Master, his biggest pride and accomplishment inside the Martial Arts was seeing his daughter follow her own footsteps, becoming a great champion and master in the Martial Arts.

"My philosophy has always been to mold people of good character first, and then to form a black belt, thus ensuring the honorable continuity of my legacy," says Grand Master Antonio Dias.

PROFESSIONAL KARATE ASSOCIATION BRAZIL HONORS · 2020 MASTERS & PIONEERS

FABIO GOULART

The Brazilian Master made history by becoming the first Brazilian to win a gold medal at a Taekwondo Pan American Championship in Puerto Rico (1990).

But it did not stop there. The following year, at the event's edition in Havana, Cuba, he reached the highest place on the podium, becoming also the first Brazilian to reach this mark.

He is a two-time Brazilian champion, winner of the National Selectives (1989, 1990, 1991 and 1992), and the Brazilian Cup and the Winnipeg Pan American Games Selective (1999). For many years, he was the captain of the Brazilian team of Taekwondo.

The Santos native served as a professor of Rhythmic Gymnastics, Gymnastics and General Gymnastics at his hometown´s Faculty of Physical Education of Unimonte, from 1998 to 2006.

In 1987, he founded the Academia Fábio Goulart de Taekwondo (AFG) in Santos. With persistence, credibility and confidence, it has surpassed the 5,000 students mark and continues to form many masters and champions.

In the 90's, he developed the "Adote um Fera" project, which took over 200 athletes abroad and resulted in the achievement of numerous medals (over 400).

In addition to building a brilliant career as an athlete, he excelled as a teacher and coach. He led the junior Brazilian team in various competitions, being the coordinator from 2001 to 2009, and served as director of Taekwondo of Santos Futebol Clube (establishing a partnership from 2001 to 2018) and becoming four-time Brazilian interclub champion.

He served as CBTKD's technical director in 2009 and contributed to the expansion of the sport in Brazil and worldwide. His career records important passages in various countries, especially in Portugal and the United States.

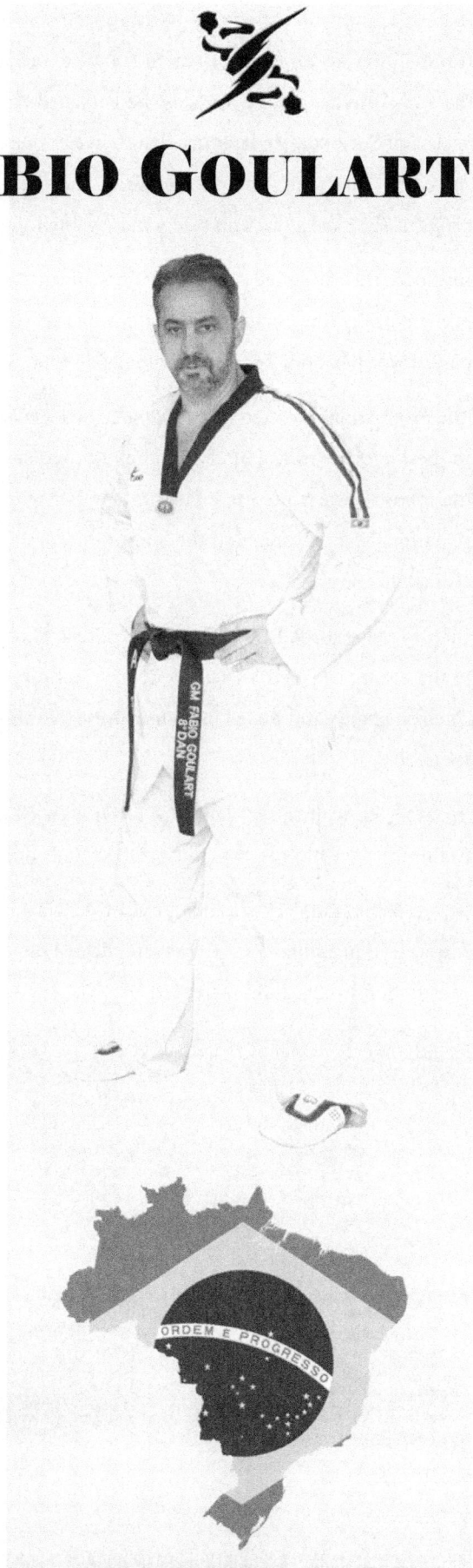

In 1994, he innovated by writing the book "Taekwondo: Basic Competition Techniques". Then, in 2007, he was one of the conductors of the Pan American flame. In 2009, he launched the book "Taekwondo: In Search of Success". He later decided to live in the US, where he stayed for six years. He's since returned to Brazil, where he has several ongoing projects, such as lectures on career management for athletes.

In 2016, he accepted the invitation of director Halder Gomes to participate in the movie "The Shaolin of the Wilderness", in which he played wrestler Toni Tora Pleura alongside great national stars.

The production attracted more than 620,000 viewers and won two awards for best comedy movie of 2016. The performance was highly praised, and the following year he was invited to another work by the same director, this time, "Parças", starring the humorists Tom Cavalcante, Whinderson Nunes and Tirulipa.

In 2018, he recorded Cine Holliúdy for Rede Globo, in which he gave life to the character Quebra Quengo. The series broke all audience records on Tuesday nights and Rede Globo has already confirmed the second season for 2020.

In 2018, he won the 8th dan (CBTKD) with GM Yong Min Kim as his examiner, for whom he has much respect and admiration.

Master Fábio Goulart is a member of CBTKD and WTF, has a degree in Physical Education, a postgraduate degree in Sports Training and a Master of Business Administration.

SILVIO LEE

The fascination with martial arts, in particular, with the star Bruce Lee, led Silvio Antônio Fragoso Filho to start training Jeet Kune Do in September 1986, self-taught, through books, in the city of Alegre, Espírito Santo.

He was such a fan of the martial artist that he was soon called Silvio Lee, a nickname he still carries today.

In 1988, he was assisted by one of the great Wing Chun masters in Brazil, Luiz Carlos Soté. "In my view, he is the best teacher. An undeniably honest human being, for whom I have much respect and admire", he praises.

Over the years, from contact with other masters, he practiced new styles, including San Da, Tai Chi, Chin-na, Ninjutsu, Aikido, Northern Shaolin, Savate, Boxing, Shuai Jiao, Wrestling, Jiu Jitsu, Kali Silat and Full Combat Krav Maga. In 1999, Master Silvio Lee took another big step in his journey by idealizing the Kajeetsu, which matures with the evolution of martial arts. In it, he is 10th dan.

In 2015, the art was the subject of many media platforms for being very effective and useful in real situations. According to reports from police officers and other servers, the system transmits security and trust. Kajeetsu is based on years of training in various martial arts. It has the influence of Mixed Martial Arts (MMA), but with a detail: the student receives graduation according to his dedication.

In general, the drills feature tougher and more efficient techniques, but with easy adaptation and evolution against the opponent, thus maintaining their originality in the simplicity and efficiency of Jeet Kune Do's ideology and concepts. The first belt to conquer is white, followed by red, blue, purple, brown and finally black.

It is basically subdivided into three areas: B, T and S. The first refers to Boxer and consists of Boxing, Sanda, Wing Chun, Krav Maga, Kali Silat and Chin Na. The second comprises Transition, with Wrestling, Sambo

and Shuai Jiao as references, and lastly, there is the Solo area, formed by Jiu Jitsu, Wrestling and No Gui. Kajeetsu also uses weapons like Karambit, Filipino Rods and so on.

Silvio Lee is a Bachelor in Nursing, Creator and 10th dan in Kajeetsu, Master in Wing Chun, 3rd dan in Full Kombat Krav Maga, teacher of San Da and Tai Chi, Jiu Jitsu blue belt, very experienced in Jeet Kune Do, with more than 30 years of practice, and has decades of practice as a trainer in the area of public and private military security.

He is also the creator of the TNT System - Temporary Neutralization Techniques / SCOP System - Police Operational Combat, was a teacher qualified for three years by the Espírito Santo Military Police (Police Self Defense) and worked as a penitentiary inspector for six years.

MASTER LUCIANO MARTINS

Master Luciano Martins, Editor of the magazine KICKBOXING BRAZIL NEWS, and 6th Dan in Kickboxing and President of the Federacao Paulista de Traditional Kickboxing. He was a coach at the Selecao Santista de Kickboxing and at the Brazilian Kickboxing at CBKB / WAKO, and was a Brazilian champion, South American Freestyle Kickboxing and Kickboxing.

Master Luciano Martins was responsible for Beach Kickboxing PKA in the city of Santos, São Paulo and one of the greatest supporters of Kickboxing PKA for the state of São Paulo. Master Luciano was responsible for one of the seminars that brought Grandmasters Bill Wallace and Joe Corley to Brazil, this was the first seminar in Brazil held in Santos with a participation of 70 Masters and black belts.

He started in the martial arts training Judo. After leaving a test to be a professional in football, he saw a sign with the name Full Contact where he entered the academy and fell in love with the sport, becoming a champion of the city of Santos, then champion of São Paulo and Brazilian, even competing in Argentina for the South American Kickboxing title. A title he holds today. His cartel is of 33 fights and only 4 defeats. His last fight was on May 1, 2017. He participates as a guest in several ceremonies of the Book of the Great Masters of Brazil. He is one of the biggest highlights currently in Brazil for PKA and Kickboxing in Brazil.

MASTER JOSENILTON NASCIMENTO

In 1974, Master Nascimento started to practice Martial Arts (Taekwondo) with the first Master 6th Dan from Korea, Mr. Nam Wong Kim, who in 1978 went to the USA. Followed by Master Joon-Ho Kim, also 6th Dan of the noble art introduced in Brazil in the 70s. They both were the two pioneers of this sport in this nation. Master Nascimento received his black belt 1st Dan on November 6, 1976, one of two of the first black belts in São Paulo.

He was the Brazilian Champion of Taekwondo in 1980, standing out among several fighters as the best in Brazil and the State of São Paulo for several times. In 1980, he went to the United States to participate in the Miami International Open Championship where he was the international champion in his category.

In 1982, he began to practice a sport developed in the United States called Full Contact Kickboxing. He disputed for the South American Title of the category heavyweight and was the South American Champion of Full Contact Kickboxing, competing against the South American long time champion, Paraguayan Miguel Angel Saenz. He had several title defenses with the South American Belt of Full Contact Kickboxing with various fighters from South America. Such as Paraguay, Chile, Argentina, and others. His boxing trainer was Boxing Olympic Medal champion in México, Servilho de Oliveira in the Pirelli club in Santo André City.

Since then, there have been several disputes over the South American Belt of ASAKF, ABRAFUCON and ISKA South American. He was prepared to fight for world title belt against North American Dennis Alexio, but the fight never happened, then he resolved to start his own work on 05/05/1986 in the Guarda Civil of Santo André as self-defense instructor of the Guarda Civil Municipal, remaining in the Municipal Office of Santo André until 1997.

In the same year of 1997, he started his studies at the University of São Paulo, where he finished his undergraduate Degree in Law, obtaining a

law degree, followed by his Graduate Degree at University of Gama Filho of Rio de Janeiro- RJ, where he also received a postgraduate degree in Civil Law. Due to a personal and family decision, he decided to stop fighting Full Contact Kickboxing in 1997.

He returned to martial arts, especially Taekwondo and Kickboxing, a couple years later to keep it alive. He helped to bring to Brazil, World Kickboxing Champion Bill "Superfoot" Wallace and Joe Corley, protagonists of great world fights, in an event produced by the great friend Grandmaster Carlos Roberto Silva, ISKA Director of PKA for Latin America, which also honors us with its presence, and which has the honor of receiving it in its residence, at a very special moment.

He is affiliated with PKA and CBKBT, for which he does legal work, assisting fighters and entities from all over the country. He's an advocate in the areas of family, business and sport law, linked always to Martial Arts. He is also a lecturer talking about very important topics for practitioners, instructors, and teachers.

Master Josenilton Nascimento is a renowned lawyer from the City of Sao Bernardo do Campo in São Paulo capital. Master Josenilton Nascimento was South American Champion, full contact, and one of the pioneers in Brazil of this sport. He is also a Taekwondo master at MUSA International and is now one of the leaders of this organization in Brazil and also a master at PKA, responsible for Bill Wallace's seminar in Brazil, also in the state of Sao Paulo.

Master Josenilton Nascimento, better known in Kickboxing as Master Nilton Nascimento, was one of the biggest names in the sport in the 70s, 80s and 90s, arriving and being the biggest highlight of Brazil in combat in Latin America, along with Luiz Augusto Alvarenga and Sergio Batarelli. Master Nilton graduated from University of Gama Filho and UNIBAN SBC.

Titles:

- 7 times South American Champion (Kickboxing)

- Brazilian Champion (TKD)

- American Full Contact Champion (Kickboxing) Professional - 32 fights Full Contact professionals in Paraguay, Chile, Argentina, Venezuela and Brazil.

- Made 8 disputes for the South American belt Full Contact by AAKFC, ISKA, and PKA.

- He was 8 times South American Full Contact Champion by several International Organizations.

Master Nilton Nascimento, a precursor of Kickboxing and Taekwondo in the State of São Paulo, along with Master Jose Belarmino o (Beloca) and other friends from the 1970s. Starting in 1978, he participated in the Miami USA open Championship. In 1980, he became Vice World Champion. In Taekwondo, he stood out in 1978 as a competitor of the sport in several championships in Sao Paulo and several other states in Brazil, contributing to the development of this sport in Brazil with the team of Master Kim-Nam Wong, who was recently arrived from Korea as 6th Dan Taekwondo Master.

Master Nilton Nascimento is one of the greatest exponents of kickboxing in Brazil and has the recognition of several organizations including PKA. He did a great seminar in Sao Bernardo with Bill Wallace in 2019.

GRANDMASTER LAÉCIO NUNES OLIVEIRA

Born in Itanhém, Bahia State Brazil, on June 9, 1970. Grandmaster Laécio Nunes started in Martial Arts on February 10, 1986, in the city of Vitória, Espirito Santo State, Brazil, training Kung Fu Shaolin, with Master Sebastião Nogueira da Gama.

Even though he liked it, his passion is Kickboxing, which in January 1988, he started to train Full Contact, as it was called at the time and currently named Kickboxing. He had the privilege to start with the person who introduced Kickboxing to the State of Espírito Santo on August 31, 1981.

Grandmaster Nilson Ferreira de Souza, Black Belt 9th Dan, who is his coach to this day. He became a Black Belt on September 14, 1992 and founded the Vitória Fighter Academy on the same date, having formed 65 black belts. His Rank in Kickboxing thru international Organizations:

- Black Belt 5th Dan Wako International

- Black Belt 6th Dan ISKA International

- Black Belt 7th Dan IKTA International

- Black Belt 8th Dan PKA International (Being the only Black Belt in the country 8th Dan, recognized and having a diploma signed by the father of Kickboxing, GM Bill Wallace, GM Don Willis, and the President of PKA, GM Joe Corley

Leadership Positions in International Organizations:

- IKTA (International Kick Tai Boxing Association)- Director in Brazil.

- PKA (Professional Karate Association)- Director in Brazil.

- ISKA Kickboxing Director in the State of Espírito Santo.

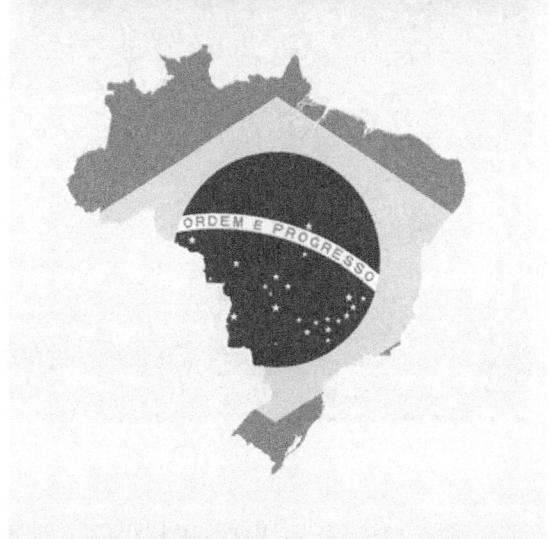

Titles as a professional athlete:

• Penta World Champion in 4 different categories

I. 64,500 (World Prof)

II. 66,800 (CNKB)

III. 70,000 (IKTA)

IV. 73,000 (IKTA)

• Intercontinental Champion by IKTA and WAKO

Grandmaster Laécio Nunes is still undefeated in 51 fights, since June 28, 2002 when he became a professional athlete, when he won the Brazilian professional title.

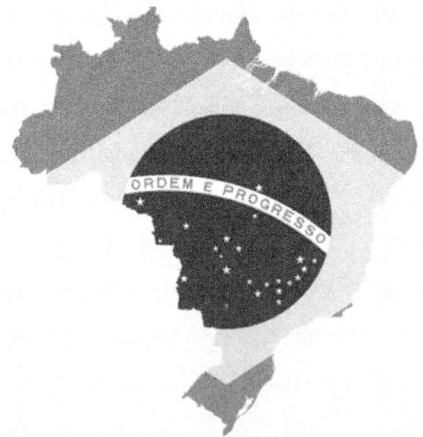

MASTER SANDRO RAMOS

Born on August 2, 1973, Master Sandro is the best fighter of Paraiba State and the First Brazilian to fight internationally in the Caribbean Island Trinidad & Tobago for the ISKA Pan-American Title. He is the Paraiba State Northeast and Brazilian Champion in his category and was chosen to represent Brazil in the Brazil versus Trinidad & Tobago Challenge. His best performance in Brazil was at the event, Duel of Titans, where he became solo champion of that spectacle.

Master Sandro is also the founder of the ASKIVA, Valentina Kickboxing Association. It is the best Kickboxing Association of the Northeast of Brazil, where lots of champions came from. He also runs a social project where poor and street kids are saved from a dark future in drugs and gangs. This program has more than 20 years and has the support of the Paraiba State Government and City Hall. This project was an inspiration for many other projects in Brazil and today is an example of success on rescue kids for drugs and gangs inspired by Chuck Norris Kick Drugs from America.

The ASKIVA was founded on July 4, 2005 and has more than 200 students and about 15 black belts, the best in Paraiba State in competitions in the Northeast region of Brazil. Master Sandro Ramos is a Student of Grandmaster Carlos Silva, the Founder of Kickboxing in Paraiba State and representative of PKA for Latin America. He is preparing a golden team to participate in future PKA events in Brazil and looking forward to promoting PKA in the whole Northeast region.

Master Sandro Ramos has a record of 21 professional fights winning 11 by knock-out and 2 losses. He is a 4th Degree Black belt in Kickboxing with 26 years of experience and dedication to this sport and helping the needy to succeed in life through his social project in one of the poorest parts of Brazil. He is a big example of citizenship and dedication to noble causes. And a big fan of Bill Wallace, Joe Corley and Joe Lewis.

MASAHIRO SHINZATO

Master Masahiro is the eldest son of Yoshihide Shinzato (in memoriam) who was responsible for having trained him in Karate and spreading the Shorin-ryu style in South America.

A fan of martial arts for years, he was always at his father's side and closely followed the growth of the sport in Brazil. HIs martial resume includes the titles of three-time Karate champion in the adult absolute kata category, champion of team shiai kumite, runner-up in the 8th Brazilian Tournament of Shorin-ryu, among others.

He appeared in several courses and updating seminars with the main names of the sport, such as Katsuya Miyahira, Masatoshi Nakayama, Takeshi Oishi, Katsuyoshi Kanei, Juichi Sagahara, Mitjo Buyo, Koji Tkamatsu and Taketo Okuda.

Mestre Masahiro Shinzato presided over the São Paulo Federation of Karate three times (1992, 1994, and 1997). In 2008, due to the death of his father, he assumed the presidency of the Shinshukan School. Currently, the organization he chairs is among the most respective of Karate in Brazil. The School is based on the principles of Dojo-Kun and Budo, and is in full development both nationally and internationally.

Sensei Masahiro is focused on technical standardization, adoption of inclusive actions and the organization of events and seminars with the presence of global personalities. It also disseminates the Shorin-ryu Shinshukan style and also Kobudo in Brazil.

The organization promotes various social projects and aims to contribute to a more just society, offering in addition to physical, mental and spiritual health, self-esteem, concentration and support for children who live at the mercy of violence.

GRANDMASTER CARLOS ROBERTO SILVA

Grandmaster Carlos Roberto Silva was born in João Pessoa, Paraíba, and is a Brazilian kickboxer. At the present time, he holds the presidency of the Brazilian Confederation of Traditional Kickboxing.

At the age of 12, he began his studies in the martial arts, practicing Judo and Shotokan Karate. Later he was introduced to Muay Thai by professor Carlos Nunes. He met Shihan Pericles Damiski Veiga and started in the Shorin-ryu style of then Master Moritoshi Nakaema.

After Master Alfredo Apicella of the World Association of Kickboxing Organizations (WAKO) handed him the black belt, he assumed the Presidency of the Hammerhilt Kickboxing Association of Paraíba.

Grandmaster Silva created the Federation of Kickboxing of the State of Paraíba, making this federation one of the first of the sport in the country, that later changed its name to Federation of Kickboxing Full Contact of the State of Paraíba.

In 1990 he founded the Brazilian Confederation of Traditional Kickboxing, known as CBKBT. Since then, CBKBT's mission has been to teach American Kickboxing (traditional).

He holds the title in 10th dan of Kickboxing, 9th dan in Karate Shorin-ryu, 5th dan in Hapkido, kru in Muay Thai and 1st dan in Taekwondo (Kukkiwon) and Shotokan Karate. He also dedicated time to the study of Ninjutsu.

Grandmaster has been featured on the cover of Fight Magazine in Brazil and also had work published by Kumite Magazine, among others.

In 2019, Grandmaster Silva introduced PKA Worldwide to South America. PKA is the organization which created professional martial arts for television in the United States in 1974, revealing the first World Champions: Bill Superfoot Wallace, Jeff Smith, Joe Lewis (RIP) and Isaias Duenas.

Grandmaster Silva brought to Brazil Grandmasters Bill Wallace and Joe Corley for a series of 3 Seminars, 2 in São Paulo and one in Vitória, Espirito Santo State, all 3 events were successful and made a good impression of PKA on all Black belts who participated.

In São Paulo, during the first event, Grandmasters Bill Wallace and Joe Corley had the opportunity to be interviewed by the local and national broadcast and also meet the most prestigious masters in Sao Paulo of all Martial Arts in the country. The event also had the support of the ASAMCO of Grandmaster Roberto Nochang, who brought all his Black belts who helped in the organization, security and production of the seminar.

During the second event, produced by Master Josenilton Nascimento in Sao Bernardo do Campo, the team ASAMCO also helped and supported. Most of the Masters who participated were from the Book of Brazil Greatest Masters of Martial Arts, which was going to be held after the seminar on the House of Representatives of the state of Sao Paulo.

After the seminar, Grandmaster Carlos Silva brought to São Paulo City to the House of Representatives of the state both Grandmasters Bill Wallace and Joe Corley and there they were honored by about 950 Head of Styles, Grandmasters, Masters, instructors and fighters from the whole country, gathered for these honorable occasions, that happens yearly in Brazil. They, both Grandmasters, were happy to be there and enjoying this historical day for the martial arts in Brazil. The Book Edition of November 2019 was the first to include the two continents North and South America and the US presence with PKA really was a mark, a turning point for the history of Kickboxing and Combat Sports in Brazil.

The next day in Vitória, Espirito Santo State, the last event took place and there the local and national broadcast also made their presence closing the first visit of Grandmaster Bill Wallace and Joe Corley to Brazil. Grandmaster Laércio Nunes also did his and his students black belt examination, and finally they all returned to the US.

These great seminars in Brazil opened the door for PKA to grow in Brazil and Latin America. The sky's the limit for this organization and we expect great things as the result of the successful PKA trip to that country.

GRANDMASTER MARCOS STARLING

At the young age of fifteen years old, Marcos Starling started training Karate and Japanese Ju-Jitsu in Belo Horizonte, Minas Gerais with Master Senador. Soon after starting his martial arts journey, he switched to training the Korean martial art of Taekwondo. With intense dedication, he was able to open a studio called Tigre Taekwondo Clube before he even graduated for his 1st Dan Black Belt in Taekwondo. As a color belt, he taught classes in his studio with the blessing and watchful eye of Master Jong Chang Pyun. Starling's school was located in João Monlevade, MG, and still operates to this day.

In 1979, Starling was the 46th Black Belt to receive his 1st Dan by the Brazilian Association of Taekwondo (ABT) through Master Jong Chang Pyun and Grand Master Sang Min Cho. In the same year, he also became a National Champion and started teaching self-defense to the military division of the Police quarters in his city. He was recognized and respected by several municipal schools for his teaching in Taekwondo and general physical education. Because of his hard work and dedication in enriching his town, he was presented with a medal of honor from the mayor of the city Joao Monlevade and the region of Vale do Aco.

In 1980, Starling was named Athlete of the Year by the State Press Association of Minas Gerais. With the support of his wife, Daisy with whom he has been married since 1980, he moved to the United States in January 1984. Once he moved, he started teaching classes at the YMCA in Pasadena, Texas. Soon after his arrival, he started teaching tactical defense to the National Guard of Texas.

The following year he moved with his family to the state of Massachusetts. Once arriving, he started teaching Taekwondo at a local fitness academy. About a year later, he opened his own studio in Framingham, Massachusetts. He taught there for over 18 years and graduated numerous black belts. He trained, developed, and coached over a dozen students into becoming National Champions in the United States, including his two daughters. His students and two daughters dominated the Taekwondo tournament scene for many years earning multiple medals, awards, and college grants for their talent and dedication within the sport.

In 1990, he organized the first American Taekwondo Team to compete in Brazil with the support of Grandmaster Yong Min Kim. Two years later, he was elected as Vice president of the Massachusetts Taekwondo Association. In the following years, he was the Director of the Exhibition Committee, the Massachusetts State Team Coach, an International Referee, and the General Secretary of the Massachusetts State Taekwondo Association. Within the 1990's he also arranged one of the biggest, most successful and well-organized state tournaments of the time. At the opening ceremony of the Pan American Taekwondo Competition in Boston, Massachusetts, Starling unofficially matched the world record with a breaking demonstration. He broke five baseball bats; two bats individually, one with bare hand strike, the other was swung at his shin by a baseball player and then striking three Louisville Slugger bats tied together with his tibia bone using a kick. The breaking demonstration was presented in the presence of the PATU President, the Secretary-General of Kukkiwon, and members of the World Taekwondo Federation board and the Korean Tiger Team.

In a solemn ceremony held in the city of Lawrence, Massachusetts, he was proclaimed a prominent Honorary Citizen and Honorary Sergeant by the Chief of Police and was recognized by Senator Edward M. Kennedy and Governor William F. Weld. By conducting research with several Grand Masters, Starling deepened his knowledge and discovered secrets of martial arts history that are still considered 'classified' by guru martial art educators.

Through his years of training and interest, Starling graduated and studied other martial arts, such as Krav Maga and Police Defensive Tactics, as well as creating his own Personal Tactical Defense System, based on reality "Survival Combat." Today he teaches seminars in what is called "Hoshinsull-Survival Combat" in many studios in the United States and Brazil. Grand Master Marcos Antonio Starling is also the author of the book "Survival Combat", published in Brazil, in which he discusses how to deliver a correct punch and the effects of adrenaline with self-defense. Currently, GM Marcos Starling offers a Martial Art Taekwondo course in which he explains/interprets in-depth details of practical everyday uses for basic and advanced hand techniques, kicking techniques, and deeper understanding of why certain stances are used for a stronger 'base'. In this course, he teaches the control of "Ki" and the energy circulation of the body via meridians, and how to strike pressure points. Grand Master Starling also offers courses and lectures on how to survive real hand combat on the streets for self-defense against a knife or gun.

THE AMERICAN MARTIAL ARTS ALLIANCE

MARTIAL ARTS
MASTERS & PIONEERS

HONORING
THE MARTIAL ARTS

Schools
OF THE YEAR

FLAHERTY'S KENPO KARATE ASSOCIATION

Since 1991, when I began Flaherty's Kenpo Karate Association (FKKA), I have concentrated on implementing safe martial arts training programs and classes for children, teens and adults. As a business owner, teaching students and marketing the martial arts to people from all walks of life, I've noticed that people have a difficult time choosing a martial arts school or style that best fits their needs. Martial arts prospects often ask me, "Which martial arts school is the best?"

My ongoing answer: "Whichever one you put your heart, mind, body, and soul into."

We try to be that kind of school at Flaherty's Kenpo Karate by offering quality self-defense lessons in a safe environment with good communication, and a high level of ethics. We not only encourage skill development; we encourage good student behavior. We have high expectations for our students and consistently provide words of encouragement, along with step-by-step explanations and demonstrations of the day's objective. As each student masters the learning objectives, ample opportunities are offered by the instructors for students to demonstrate their proficiency levels. In addition, instructors continuously review prior lessons in order to ensure that students do not lose the ability to recall previous learning objectives.

In addition to creating martial artists, we also work to build leaders. Instructors are encouraged to act in a way that shows others how to act. We teach that leaders must LEAD BY EXAMPLE, that by walking your talk, you become a person that others will want to follow. When leaders say one thing, but do another, they erode trust. Trust is a critical element of productive leadership. Positive leaders do the work, practice, know the school's material of study well, respect the chain of command, listen to the team, take responsibility, and remember that their actions and words will have a direct impact on morale. A true leader is a person who knows the way, goes the way, and shows the way by taking responsibility for the team; who will inspire class attendees and spectators with his or her martial arts skills and knowledge.

We offer the information in this article to help or assist our brothers and sisters in the martial arts business industry. We believe it is important to have a well-established martial arts business that is always kept clean, bright, inviting, organized, and air-conditioned. We have matted floors, punching and kicking bags, and mirrors for martial arts performance viewing. Our lobby, which is open to parents, guests, and students, is adorned with motivational wall photos of karate action pictures, plaques of awards, and trophies, and weapons on display. The lobby has clean seating and an open viewing area, offering a first public impression that the academy is clean, busy, exciting, and successful.

On the walls throughout the training areas there are many awards and accomplishments that attest to the FKKA's long and distinguished martial arts history, newspaper articles, and pictures of our students, parents, and many FKKA instructors, in a way that warms the hearts and minds of most on-lookers.

To keep the excitement going, it's good business to have a class schedule in place with an excellent martial arts system for learning, teaching, and promoting. According to one of our karate parents (a 7th grade math and science teacher), "The FKKA curriculum and instruction is detailed, comprehensive, and embraces different modalities of learning. Student engagement is paramount, and the instructors equip all students with the necessary skills, strategies, routines, and knowledge in order to perform at, or above, their established belt levels."

FKKA has an open-door policy for communication. Many instructors from other martial arts businesses have dropped by the academy to have a look, offer their respect, hang out for a while, or just to talk about martial arts history.

With the ups and downs of our society, Flaherty's Kenpo Karate owners are always willing to change and adapt to individual needs as warranted. Safety, organization, and quality of service are the most important values in our martial arts academy. During all crisis situations, the FKKA will make safe and well thought out adjustments and modifications while still assuring that legal, safe, and high-quality ethical standards are met and practiced. Any time people are faced with a crisis situation, our hearts and prayers go out to everyone involved.

Please, stay warm, safe and prosperous!

-Grandmaster Randall Flaherty
Flaherty's Kenpo Karate Association

MARTIAL ARTS MASTERS & PIONEERS
HONORS

RISING STORM TRAINING ACADEMY

When first starting the Martial Arts, the idea was to prove myself in the dojo. Training strong five days a week became so routine I showed up on holidays, not realizing they would be closed.

I remember being asked to test for my Yellow Belt and refusing. Just enjoying the practice and not in it for the belts. I was content with my White belt and refused the Yellow Belt exam a second time. However, the third approach from Shihan was not an option. He explained to me how, when new students come in wearing a white belt and are just learning the basics, they will be intimidated and uncertain by looking at me wearing the same belt for so long. I accepted that yellow belt. Then shortly after, more and more rank. It became an experience more significant than myself.

After assisting in classes, I realized that students were gravitating to my particular approach in instruction. This propelled me forward into teaching students. That is when Rising Storm started to take form.

MARTIAL ARTS MASTERS & PIONEERS
HONORS

Rising Storm Training Academy opened in 2011. In nine years, we have grown into 3 locations, and 10 satellite programs. Our school's philosophy is "Building Character Through Martial Arts."

Now I'm in that same position as the instructor 20 years ago, with blackbelt leaders, an incredible staff, and the patience to keep moving forward.

Nathan Porter
Rising Storm Training Academy

THE AMERICAN MARTIAL ARTS ALLIANCE

MARTIAL ARTS MASTERS & PIONEERS

50 Years
IN THE MARTIAL ARTS

ANTHONY ARNETT

"Having accountability to my instructors and my students has made me the man I am today."

TRAINING INFORMATION

- Belt Ranks & Martial Arts Styles: Traditional Wing Chun Kung Fu

- Instructors/Influencers: Grandmaster William Cheung

- Birthplace/Growing Up: Baltimore, MD / Jacksonville, FL

- Yrs. In the Martial Arts: 52 years

- Yrs. Instructing: 42 years

Growing up in the city of Baltimore Maryland, there were a lot of obstacles for young black men to achieve a good education and livelihood. My uncle Richard Brooks was a military man who started me in the Martial Arts training at the age of 5yrs old.

Because of the early exposure to the arts, I was able to deal with most adversities that confronted me on a daily basis, as I matured into a teenager and adult I had the confidence and internal strengths of my teachings to overcome life demanding challenges. The self-discipline led me in the right directions and away from the bad choices that came my way, I eventfully became an instructor and shared my martial arts skills and life experiences with others, and I have made significant positive changes in the lives of everyone that I taught.

As a National Tournament Competitor, I have won more than 4,000 awards, cash prizes, trophies, medals, and certificates thus far in my competition career. With more than 37 years on the competition circuits (Fighting, Forms, and Weapons), I still compete locally and nationally. I owe all my success and winnings to my instructor, mentor, and Kung-Fu father 8th Generation Grandmaster William Cheung.

PERSONAL & MAJOR ACHIEVEMENTS

- 1974-1976: Competed in Points Tournaments in Baltimore, MD and Washington, D.C.

- 1977: Became Division Champion on several local circuits and began competing nationally on the "Professional Karate Association" (P.K.A.) circuit.

- 1982: East Coast Grand Champion and ranked 8th in the Nation on three Tournament Circuits.

- 1983: Met Grandmaster William Cheung in Chicago, IL and accepted as one of Grandmaster Cheung's Disciples.

- 1983: Began competing in Tournaments using Wing Chun Kung-Fu. As an honor to my teacher Grandmaster William Cheung, opened the first Wing Chun School in Baltimore, MD.

PERSONAL & MAJOR ACHIEVEMENTS

- 1984: First place Heavy Weight Champion and Runner-up for Grand Champion in "Ziggs Hard Contact Tournament" the first "hard contact" Tournament in Alexandria, VA.

- 1985: Competed in Hard and Full Contact Tournaments in Maryland and Virginia.

- 1986: Opened first Traditional Wing Chun School in Waynesboro, GA.

- 1987: Opened second Traditional Wing Chun School in Augusta, GA.

- 1988: Begin competing local and state tournaments throughout Georgia.

- 1989: Grand Champion in Fighting and Forms category in Georgia.

- 1990: Opened first Traditional Wing Chun School in Florida.

- 1991: Grand Champion in Continuous Fighting Format Tournaments in Florida.

- 1992: Undefeated as Continuous Fighting Format Grand Champion Title and Division Champion in Point Tournament.

- 1992: Grand Champion of the "North FL Open Martial Arts C.S.F." in continuous Fighting, Forms, and Weapons.

- 1993: Undefeated as Grand Champion in continuous Fighting and Division Champion in Point Tournament. "Cheung Style Sport Kung-Fu" was dedicated to Grandmaster William Cheung. Participated in the "Night of Legends" All Star Champions, Jacksonville, FL.

I can't begin to express my gratefulness to all of my instructors and my students, because of having accountability to them both has made me the man I am today; to be a trustworthy leader in my community, a productive citizen in the construction industries, and a role model to future generations of martial artists.

PERSONAL & MAJOR ACHIEVEMENTS

- 1994: Created "The Fighting Dragons" team and traveled throughout FL and GA competing in Point Team Fighting Competition. "Night Of Legends" All Star Fighters, Won Grand champion Men's Fighting Heavy Weight.

- 1995: Coached Full-Contact fighters for competition on the "International Sport Kickboxing Association" (I.S.K.A.) Circuit. Retained Division Champion in Points Title in Georgia. Travelled with Grandmaster William Cheung to California.

- 1996: Accompanied Grandmaster William Cheung on California tour and featured in MA Training Magazine.

- 1996: Coached 6 full contact fighters to victory in the "Memorial Day Massacre" fight in Jacksonville, FL. Completed a 3 volume video series on "Cheung Style Sport Kung-Fu" starring Grandmaster William Cheung and Master Arnett. Retained Division Champion Points Title in Georgia.

- 1997: Division Champion in Forms, Weapons, and Fighting in Georgia. Retained Division Champion in Point Fighting in Georgia.

- 1998: Opened first private lesson studio exclusively for one-on-one sessions in Jacksonville, FL. Retained Division Champion Points Title in GA for Forms, Weapons, and Fighting.

PERSONAL & MAJOR ACHIEVEMENTS

- 1999: Retained Division Champion Title on the Tri-State Circuit. Established the Certificate Course Program (C.C.P.) through Private Lessons. Promoted Tournament training seminars and camps.

- 2000: Awarded "Provisional Master Grade Level-5" by Grandmaster William Cheung. Division Champion in Fighting and Forms in the North FL Martial Arts Association. Division Champion in Fighting, Forms, and Weapons in the "National Karate & Kung-Fu Union" (N.K.K.U). Awarded the overall Grand Champion in the "National Martial Arts League" for Forms and Weapons Demonstration. Awarded the "Most Competitors" Award.

- 2001: Awarded "National Karate & Kung-Fu Union" (N.K.K.U.) Ultimate Grand Champion in Forms, Weapons, and Fighting in the Masters Division.
Grand Champion in the "North FL Martial Arts Association".
"Southern Sport Karate Open" Grand Champion in Men's Black Belt for Fighting.
New chapter of Cheung Style Sport Kung-Fu opened in Hilton Head, SC.

- 2001: Began the sport of Olympic Style Fencing under Mr. Raul Toro at the Jacksonville Fencing Club. Participated and placed 3rd in Fencing Competition in Gainesville, FL. Placed 1st in Inner School Fencing Tournament.

PERSONAL & MAJOR ACHIEVEMENTS

- 2002: Awarded the North Florida Martial Arts Association Fighting and Forms Division Champion (Masters Division). Open 3rd Chapter "Cheung Style Kung-Fu Academy of Orange Park, FL. Continued Certificate Course Program (C.C.P.) to develop instructors.

- 2003: Awarded "NFMAA" Fighting and Forms Division Champion.

- 20-year Celebration as a student of Grandmaster William Cheung. Honored as the "Founder of Cheung Style Sport Kung-Fu" (10 years).

- Invented new self-defense weapon called the "Arn-Knot". Four state summer tour promoting The "Arn-Knot".
Featured in Jacksonville weekly publication Folio Weekly article called "Fight Club".

- 2004: North FL Martial Arts Association (NFMAA) Division Champion in Fighting and Forms. Gallops Karate Tournament Grand Champion in Fighting Masters Division. Gainesville Challenge (Gainesville, FL) Grand Champion in Fighting Masters Division. Universal Hall of Fame winner for Kung-Fu Artist of the Year. Orlando Universal Martial Arts Competition 1st place winner in Fighting Masters Division. Opened new Traditional Wing Chun School on Chester Avenue (Jacksonville, FL).

PERSONAL & MAJOR ACHIEVEMENTS

- 2005: "Bethel Champion of Champions" Grand Champion for Fighting. "Gainesville Challenge" 1st place winner for Fighting Masters Division. "Gallops Karate Tournament" 1st place winner for Fighting Masters Division. "North Florida Martial Arts Association" (NFMAA) Division Champion for Fighting and Forms. Became the Official Martial Arts Instructor for NFL Football Team Jacksonville Jaguars.

- 2006: Appeared in Black Belt Magazine with Grandmaster William Cheung. Appeared on Inside Kung Fu Magazine May 2006 front cover with Jackie Chan. Featured in Inside Kung Fu Magazine article "Cheung Style for Tournaments. Retained Division Champion for "NKKU", NFMAA", "Gainesville Challenge", and "Gallops Karate Tournament".

- 2007: "Gallops Karate Tournament" Grand Champion. Successfully coached 3 students for MMA Competition in Jacksonville, FL.

- 2008: "National Karate & Kung-Fu Union" (N.K.K.U.) Grand Champion and Gold medal winner. "NFMAA" 1st place winner in Masters Fighting Division. "Gainesville Challenge" 1st place winner in Masters Fighting Division. "Gallops Karate Tournament" Grand Champion. "Bethel Champion of Champions" Grand Champion for Fighting.

- 2009: "National Karate & Kung-Fu Union" (N.K.K.U.) Grand Champion and Gold medal winner in Masters Division. "Gallops Karate Tournament" 1st place winner for Fighting Masters Division.

PERSONAL & MAJOR ACHIEVEMENTS

- 2010: "Clash of the Titans" Tournament 2nd place winner Men's Black Belt Fighting. "Clash of the Titans" Tournament 1st place winner Men's Black Belt Weapons. "National Karate & Kung-Fu Union" (N.K.K.U.) Gold medal winner in Fighting for Masters Division. "Gallops Karate Tournament" 1st place winner for Fighting and Forms Masters Division.

- 2011: Opened Sport Kung Kung-Fu Academy of Jacksonville under President of the Global Traditional Wing Chun Kung-Fu Association, Grandmaster William Cheung. Participated in foster camp program, "Camp for Champions". National Karate & Kung-Fu Union (N.K.K.U.) Grand Champion in Fighting Masters Division and Gold Medal winner in Forms.

- 2012: Gainesville Challenge, Gainesville, FL – 1st Place Fighting, 1st Place Forms. Low Country Classic, South Carolina – 2nd Place Sparring, 1st Place and Grand Champion Forms, 1st Place Weapons. Gallops Karate Tournament – 1st Place Forms, 2nd Place Fighting National Karate & Kung Fu Union (N.K.K.U.) Savannah, GA – 1st Place Sparring, 1st Place Form. Interviewed and Premiered on University of North Florida's Inside Jacksonville "Self Defense" Segment. Featured on UNF's Inside Jacksonville for Self-Defense segment. Workshop and demonstrations at Emmett Reed Cultural Center for Foster Care Teens & Self Awareness Program Guest Speaker during Black Expo Demonstration – Relax It's Okay to Be Single. Personally, invited by Grandmaster William Cheung to be guest instructor at HQ in Melbourne, Australia for 3 months as Head Instructor and recertified for Master Level. Received 1-hour private lessons from Grandmaster for 3 months.

- 2013: Gallops Karate Tournament, Tallahassee, FL – Masters Division 1st Fighting, 1st Place Forms. Opened new school in Brierwood Shopping Center. Offered Fencing classes through JFC at Brierwood location. National Karate & Kung Fu Union (N.K.K.U.), Savannah, GA – Master Division 1st Place Weapons, 1st Place Forms, 1st Place Fighting, 2nd Place. Grand Champion Fighting Received Honorary mention in the historical returning of the TWC back to the Shaolin Temple. My name is listed among other Masters of TWC. Inscribed on the monument placed in the inner court of the Shaolin Temple. Opened second private lesson studio dedicated to teaching the Traditional Wing Chun through one-on-one sessions and semi-private sessions.

- 2014: Gallops Karate Tournament, Tallahassee, FL – Masters Division 1st Place Fighting, 1st Place Forms, 1st Place Weapons Demonstration. Gainesville Challenge, Gainesville, FL - 1st Place Masters Division Sparring, 1st Place Masters Division Weapons, 1st Place Masters Division Forms. National Karate & Kung Fu Union (N.K.K.U.), Savannah – GA – Masters Division 1st Place Weapons, 1st Place Forms, 1st Place Fighting.

PERSONAL & MAJOR ACHIEVEMENTS

- 2015: Taught Summer Martial Arts Program for Valor Academy Boys School – Jacksonville, FL. Interactive Martial Arts Demonstration for NAS Jacksonville Multi-Cultural Awareness. Gallops Karate Tournament, Tallahassee, FL – Masters Division 1st Place Fighting, 1st Place Forms, 1st Place Weapons Demonstration. Gainesville Challenge, Gainesville, FL - 1st Place Masters Division Sparring, 1st Place Masters Division Weapons, 1st Place Masters Division Forms. National Karate & Kung Fu Union (N.K.K.U.), Savannah – GA – Masters Division 1st Place Weapons, 1st Place Forms, 1st Place Fighting.

- 2016: Gainesville Challenge, Gainesville, FL - 1st Place Masters Division Sparring, 1st Place Masters Division Weapons, 1st Place Masters Division Forms. National Karate & Kung Fu Union (N.K.K.U.), Savannah – GA – Grandmasters Division 1st Place Weapons, 1st Place Forms, 1st Place Fighting.

- 2017: Gainesville Challenge, Gainesville, FL - 1st Place Masters Division Sparring, 1st Place Masters Division Weapons, 1st Place Masters Division Forms. National Karate & Kung Fu Union (N.K.K.U.), Savannah – GA – Grandmasters Division 1st Place Weapons, 1st Place Forms, 1st Place Fighting.

- 2018: Master Anthony Arnett has the honored of being inducted into the Hall of Fame with "The American Martial Arts Alliance" in the "Martial Arts Masters & Pioneers" by Grand Master Jessie Bowen.

PERSONAL & MAJOR ACHIEVEMENTS

- 2018: Continued competition in the "36th Annual US Capitol Classics China Open" August 3rd & 4th, 2018 held at the "Gaylord Resort National Harbor Maryland", Competing in the Master Sparring Division placing 1st Place, Competing Master Weapons Division Placing 3rd Place, competing in the Master Forms Division Placing 3rd Place.

- 2019: Continued competition in the "38th Annual Tournament of the "Gainesville Challenge" held by Grand Master Keith Teller, competing in the Master Sparring placing 1st Place, competing in the Master Weapons Division placing 1st Place, competing in the Master Forms placing 2nd Place.

- 2019 Conducted several Free Women Empowerment Workshops hosted by "The Defenders" held at the AWCT and held at The Philippian Community Church and give-away a Free Self Defense Weapon, these workshops are intended women from 13yrs. Old and up in the Jacksonville Florida Duval County.

- 2019 Competed in the National Karate and Kungfu Union tournament NKKU held in Savannah GA., winning 1st place Master Weapon Division, 1st. place Master Forms Division, 1st. place Master Men Sparring Division.

- 2019 Appointed East Coast Represented for The Global Wing Chun Kungfu Association GWCKFA, under the president Grandmaster William Cheung of the Australia Headquarters.

- 2020 Inducted into The Hall of Fame AMAA Legends, Martial Arts Masters & Pioneers, as a Martial Arts Ambassador of The Year 2020.

- 2020 Inducted into Wikipedia, https://en.wikipedia.org/wiki/Anthony_Arnett?wprov=sfti1

Its A Great Day Lets Play

Sportkungfu.com

LAWRENCE ARTHUR

"Each step was first a dream, a goal, all part of a journey, into tomorrow's dreams."

TRAINING INFORMATION

- Instructors/Influencers: Don Mike Davis, h G.T. Massie, Walter Chen, Joe Gutowski
- Yrs. In the Martial Arts: 52 years

PERSONAL & MAJOR ACHIEVEMENTS

- 1969 Started training to fight "Full Contact Karate" (before there was kickboxing)
- 1972 Received 1st Degree Black Belt through the American Taekwondo Association (ATA).
- 1976 Opened first school, the American Taekwondo Academy in Lynchburg, VA
- 1976 Began competing extensively on the East Coast in Black Belt forms, weapons and fighting
- 1976 Began hosting the Top Ten Nationals Karate Championships
- 1976-78 Won 3 out of 4 professional full contact karate matches.
- 1976 Received 1st Degree Black Belt from the National Institute of Martial Arts (NIMA) in a Korean style, Tang Soo Do, Tom Palitini
- 1976 Founded and Documented the American Freestyle Karate System

Not unlike many other great masters and innovators of the art of karate, Grand Master   Lawrence Arthur has conceptualized and painstakingly developed "The American Freestyle Karate System". In 1976, after almost a decade of experience and dedicated devotion to the study of martial arts, Master Arthur originated "American Freestyle Karate". Master Arthur's formidable background in the martial arts included the study of Tae Kwon Do, Tang Soo Do, Karate, Kobudo, Judo, Aikido, Bando, American Boxing and Kickboxing. Taking the best techniques from each of these highly respected art forms, he incorporated them into a unique system which allowed for growth and improvement. This concept was very much different than that taught by traditional martial arts philosophies.

To further his skills and knowledge, Master Arthur began training in full contact karate and kickboxing. Through years of competition and painful experiences, he discovered techniques that were very effective and those which were totally ineffective. Refinement and added   techniques have proven over the years to be successful. This system has produced many world champion point, full contact and forms champions for years.

The Black Belt instructors and Masters of American Freestyle Karate are

PERSONAL & MAJOR ACHIEVEMENTS

- 1978 Received 2nd Degree Black Belt from American Martial Arts Association under Jan Wellendorf (AMAA)

- 1982 Invented and Patented new karate safety equipment, "DURA" Gloves, Boots and Shin Guards. Patent # 4,361,912

- 1982 Article in the 1982 edition of "Who's Who in Martial Arts"

- 1983 Won "Chuck Norris Free for a Day" nationwide contest by Orion Pictures for enrolling the most new students in one month.

- 1986 Established the Super Kicks Karate license program.

- 1986 Founded the American Freestyle Karate Association (AFKA)

- 1986 Licensed first Super Kicks school in Pawtucket, Rhode Island to Grand Master James Perlini.

- 1992 Produced 26 Public Access TV shows, "The Dynamics of American Freestyle Karate". Documenting the AFKA system.

- 1992 Founded the AFKA tournament circuit and promoted the AFKA National Finals.

- 1994 Qualified as a member of the DKT Force One National Karate Team.

- 1995 Won the WKO World Championships, Heavy Weight Fighting Division, held in Port of Spain, Trinidad

- 1995 Named "Top 200 Schools" by Martial Arts Business Magazine Andrew Wood

- 1996 Named "Top 200 Schools" by Martial Arts Business Magazine

- 1997 Named "Top 200 Schools" by Martial Arts Business Magazine

dedicated to the pursuit of excellence in the art. Master Arthur's training methods, motivation, philosophy of instruction, and inspiration have been instilled in his instructors. Master Arthur personally trains each of his Black Belt instructors and teaches them the importance of their task as martial arts instructors.

American Freestyle Karate is like the world we live in. It will continually change in order to adapt itself to new environs, circumstances, technology, and situations. The system will remain on the cutting edge of martial arts instruction and from time to time will lead the way, as history marches on.

PERSONAL & MAJOR ACHIEVEMENTS

- 1998 Founded and coached Team AFKA National Competition Team

- 2000 Named National Black Belt League (NBL) Arbitrator of the Year

- 2001 Began expansion of the Super Kicks Academies, opened 2nd and 3rd locations

- 2001 Founded the yearly AFKA Hall of Fame

- 2001 Received title of Grand Master from AFKA Master's Council.

- 2002 Opened fourth Academy

- 2002 Named NBL "Man of the Year"

- 2003 Named NBL "Arbitrator of the Year"

- 2003 Awarded 10th Degree Black Belt through the AMAA, by O'Sensei Jan Wellendorf and Hanshi Jessie Bowen

- 2004 Honored as a "Sport Karate Living Legend" by Professor Gary Lee

- 2005 Documented the AFKA Certified Instructor Training Program (CIT)

- 2006 Documented the AFKA Master Instructor Training Program

- 2007 Continued to grow AFKA to 7 Academies, 1,600 members in 5 cities, 3 states.

- 2008 Founded the Independent Black Belt Association, IBBA, a sister organization to the AFKA

- 2010 Grew AFKA to 12 locations

- 2011 Founded the Black Belt Success Systems consulting firm to train martial arts instructors on proper business practices

PERSONAL & MAJOR ACHIEVEMENTS

- 2015 Feature Article as a Legend in the 2015 "Who's Who in Martial Arts".

- 2016 Published 40th Year Anniversary "AFKA BLACK BELT CURRICULUM MANUAL"

- 2016 Feature Article in 2016 "Who's Who in Martial Arts".

- 2017 Will be featured on cover of Martial Arts Success Magazine and to be featured on cover of Tae Kwon Do Times

— SPECIAL INVITATION —

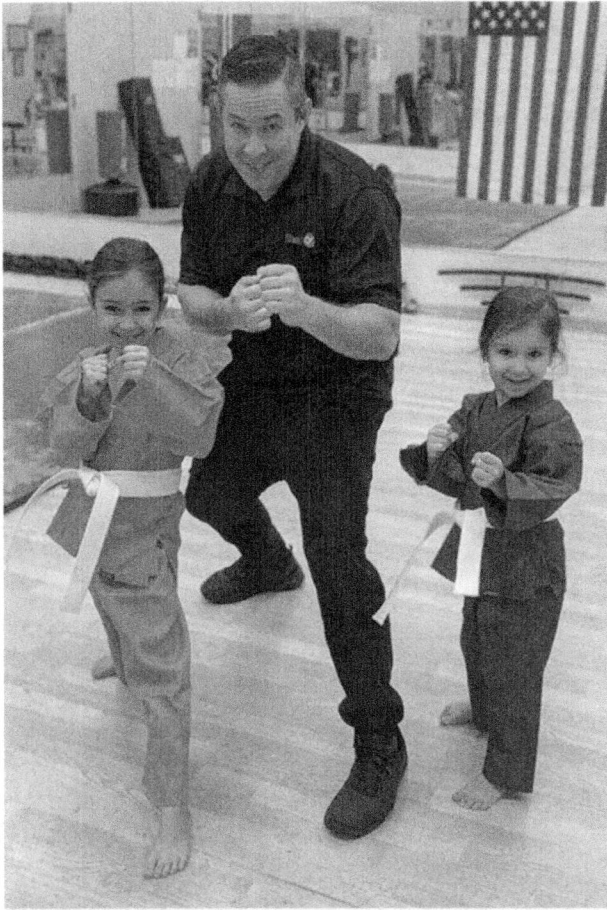

F.D. NICK BRAAKSMA

"...GM Jhoon Rhee asked me and reminded me to always lead by example..."

TRAINING INFORMATION

- Belt Ranks & Martial Arts Styles: Teaching certificates and black belts in Judo, Shotokan, Tae Kwon Do, Muay Thai Kickboxing, Shinkyokushin Karate, Russian Sambo

- Instructors/Influencers: Hanshi Hub Alken, Master Bill Osterholt, John, Howard and Phillip Chung, Dr. Charles Richman and Rick Heatley, GM Jhoon Goo Rhee, Master Sarshar, Yoon Lee, GM Jeff Smith, my fight coach Master Danny Boccagno, Bruce Jones, Scott Anderson, Mario Yamasaki, Leo Dalla, Mike Koss, Shihan Roony Boye, Sergio Velásquez, Kancho Henry Oh, Shihan Roger Alken, Master Mike Balwin, World Champions John de Ling and G. Hasham

- Birthdate: December 16, 1961

- Birthplace/Growing Up: The Hague - The Netherlands, Dutch Guyana/Surinam Aruba, WI

- Yrs. In the Martial Arts: 53 years

- Yrs. Instructing: 38 years

- School Owner and Instructor at Shogun Martial Arts - Kime Ryu Dojo at Fitness CF of Saint Cloud, FL

My father Henk E. Braaksma, a WW2 veteran in the Dutch Resistance, enrolled me at age 5 in my 1st Judo class with Grand Master Joseph Lee. At age 16, I met Steve Palmberg who introduced me to the late Grand Master Hub Alken who coached us both to the Dutch Karate Nationals in 1981. After that I was hooked for life.

My martial arts training became my lifestyle and allowed me to travel the world during my 4 decades of competition. My endeavors prepared me to become a national coach, a tenacious competitor and Security & Tactical trainer.

Staying anchored to my principles was my father's wish and GM Jhoon Rhee asked me and reminded me to always lead by example. I'm keeping my promise no matter how hard it is, to my parents, my teachers, senseis, sabamnims, mentors but most of all to my students. They are the ones who help shape me to be the man and teacher I've become... thank you all!

PROFESSIONAL ORGANIZATIONS

- Dutch Guyana/Surinam Judo & Jiujitsu Federation
- Dutch Judo Federation - JBN
- Dutch Karate Federation - KBN
- Jhoon Rhee Institute of TaeKwon Do
- Professional Karate League - PKL Region 10 top 5
- N. American Sport Karate As. - NASKA Region 10 Top 10
- World Champion Jeff Smith Karate - Head Instructor
- Gold's Gym of Alexandria, VA - Manager for Pleasant Lewis
- Rhodhana Security Aruba - MOD/ Manager of Training
- F.I.M.A.C. Sijou van der Spek - NL
- Aruba Muay Thai Kickboxing - Dojo Roony Boye
- Shinkyokushin Boye/Aruba - World Karate Organisation
- International Olympic Committee Aruba National Coach
- Shogun MMA/Kime Ryu Mobile, AL - Derick Payne
- Shogun MMA/Kime Ryu Aruba - Gesterkamp/Koolman
- American Martial Arts Alliance 2016 - Hall of Fame

PERSONAL ACHIEVEMENTS

- Wake Forest University class of 1985
- Aruba National director with AmeriSciences
- International Olympic Committee - National Trainer

A special thank you goes out to all my students, sponsors and those who fought and represented our dojo in the ring or in the cage; win or lose, Shogun MMA - Kime Ryu Dojo's good name is held high because of you!

Ossu,

Nick San

PERSONAL ACHIEVEMENTS

- Aruba Karate Federation - AKB National Coordinator
- PE School teacher for I.D.E.F.R.E Aruba
- Juvenile inmate PE counselor for K.I.A. Aruba
- Thai-Bo Cardio Master Instructor for the Dutch M.T.K.A.
- North American Kyokushin Organisation Grappling Coach
- Shinkyokushin Aruba National Team
- National Kendo Official Aruba - Dojo Sergio Velásquez
- 2016 Who's Who in the Martial Arts - GM Jessie Bowen

MAJOR ACHIEVEMENTS

- 1968 National Surinam Junior Team
- 1981 Southern Dutch Karate Champion
- 1981 Dutch Karate Federation National Contender
- 1983 Jhoon Rhee Nationals Team Champion
- 1989 PKL Region 10 rated top 5 Contender
- 1996 NASKA Region 10 Middleweight Contender
- 1996 U.S. Sambo Nationals Silver Medalist
- 1999 MMA bout vs Muay Thai WC John de Ling (Draw)
- 2001 WADO World Championships Silver Medalist
- 2005 Shinkyokushin World Cup Qualifier Finalist
- 2013 Battle of Atlanta - Finalist
- 2017 Battle at the Beach Wheeles Karate - Finalist

BOBBY BRIGGS

> "Martial Arts taught me perseverance and overcoming whatever challenging obstacle I faced."

"I grew up in the mountains of Western, NC, as a poor farm kid. Both of my parents worked multiple jobs to make ends meet. My grandparents (Cherokee Grandfather and Irish Grandmother), raised my sister and I until our teenage years so our parents could work, sometimes multiple jobs, as well as, work on the farm. As a young kid, I was interested in sports and boxing. And I was a "huge" Bruce Lee fan. It was recommended to me to take Martial Arts to help with my coordination. I couldn't have been happier as a kid. But unfortunately, my family could not afford to pay for classes all the time. So, when I couldn't go because of no money, my friends that took Martial Arts classes would teach me what they learned in class, and we would practice together. I would go to class when I could afford to pay for it. I used hand-me-down Gi's and equipment and, more often than not, practiced in sweat pants and a t-shirt. I did whatever it took to get to, and be able to, take classes and continue learning Martial Arts, including walking to class in all kinds of weather. I played sports in school, worked on our farm, and worked for neighbors until I was old enough to get a job, all because I wanted to take Karate so badly. I did this until I graduated High School, and soon after I joined the military. I've never stopped studying Martial Arts since I was a young boy."

Soke Bobby S. Briggs was born May 24, 1962, in Spruce Pine, NC, and he is the oldest of two children to the late Albert Briggs and Mrs. Ruth Doane. Soke Briggs graduated high school at Mountain Heritage High School in Burnsville, NC. Soke Briggs enlisted in the US Army after high school and later transferred over to the

TRAINING INFORMATION

- Belt Ranks & Martial Arts Styles: Kidokime-ryu Karate-Do, 10th Deg, Okinawa-te, 9th Deg, Shotokan, 1st Deg, Shito-ryu, 1st Deg

- Hapkido, 1st Deg, Tae Kwon Do, 1st Deg, American Goju-ryu, 1st Deg, American Kick Boxing (instructor)

- Instructors/Influencers: Hanshi James White, JuDan

- Birthdate: May 24, 1962

- Birthplace/Growing Up: Spruce Pine, NC / Yancey County, NC

- Yrs. In the Martial Arts: 50+ years

- Yrs. Instructing: 40+ years

- School owner, Kidokime-ryu Karate-do of Charlotte, NC , Manager, Instructor

PERSONAL ACHIEVEMENTS

- Numerous military and civilian police awards and decorations.

- Won/placed in hundreds of sport karate competitions all over the world, resulting in receiving hundreds of trophies and awards.

PROFESSIONAL ORGANIZATIONS

- National Universal Karate Association (N.U.K.A.)

US Air Force, where he attended both the Community College of the Air Force as well as Eastern Kentucky University. Soke Briggs studied Criminal Justice, Police Sciences, Criminal and Child Psychology before earning his degree. Soke Briggs is married to Sensei Mary Beth Briggs, and they have four children; Michael Brown of Lynchburg Va, Nycole Fitt of Atlanta Ga, JoAnna Brown of Moneta Va, and Daniel Briggs of Charlotte NC. Soke and Sensei Briggs have four Grandkids; Nathaniel and Cassandra of Atlanta Ga, Penelope of Lynchburg Va, and Jenna of Moneta Va. Soke Briggs is a retired military combat veteran with 24 yrs of service. He then moved to Charlotte, NC, and went to work with the Charlotte-Mecklenburg Police Department (CMPD), where he retired there in Jan 2018 as a Traffic Officer with CMPD. He has received numerous military awards and medals in both the military as well as a North Carolina Police Officer.

Soke Briggs started his Martial Arts training as a young kid in the late 60s and early 70s in Western NC and continued his Martial Arts training throughout his military career. Soke Briggs has Multiple Black Belts in different styles, such as Shotokan, Shito-ryu, Okinawan Karate-do (Okinawa-te), American Karate-do, Hapkido, and Tae Kwon Do. Soke Briggs has studied well over 30 different styles during his life, but more in-depth in Japanese/Okinawan and American Martial Arts. Soke Briggs has studied, taught, and competed all across the United States in NC, SC, GA, FL, VA, TN, KY, TX, NY, MT, CA, NV, AK, and HI, and overseas in Japan, Okinawa, Philippines, Thailand, Central and South America, and Iraq. Soke Briggs has competed in both sport Karate and full-contact kick-boxing. He has won hundreds of trophies, awards, and competitions over his life, in many different categories, all across the world. Soke Briggs is also a Military Combatives Instructor, where he taught hand-to-hand combat tactics, and has taught Defensive Tactics at various Police Academies and schools. Soke Briggs also teaches Rape Prevention/Self-Defense Classes to various church organizations, corporations, social clubs and organizations, and various other types of women's groups. Soke Briggs over-sees Kidokime-ryu Karate-do and Instructors as the Head Instructor of this style/system of the Martial Arts. Soke Briggs now trains others and judges at these events. Soke Briggs has dedicated most of his life to the study of the Martial Arts during his 51+ yrs in the Arts. Soke Briggs was

MAJOR ACHIEVEMENTS

- Promoted to 10th degree Grand Master August 4, 2018.

- Inducted into the Martial Arts Legends Hall of Fame as the 2019 Karate Grandmaster of the Year in Mt. Laurel, NJ October 26, 2019

- Inducted into the Action Martial Arts Hall of Honors /Hall of Heroes 2020 for Outstanding Achievements in the Martial Arts as a Grandmaster in Atlantic City, NJ. January 25, 2020.

- Soke Briggs is the sole founder of Kidokime-ryu Karate-do system of Japanese-American Karate. He tirelessly obtained certification of this system through his own time, efforts and money.

inducted into the Martial Arts Legends Hall of Fame as the 2019 Karate Grandmaster of the Year in Mt. Laurel, NJ. He was also inducted into the Action Martial Arts Hall of Honors /Hall of Heroes 2020 for Outstanding Achievements in the Martial Arts as a Grandmaster in Atlantic City, NJ.

"More than anything else, Martial Arts taught me perseverance, overcoming whatever challenging obstacle I faced. I used my martial arts both during my military career for military schools and as a combat veteran and through my civilian police career in all situations on the streets of Charlotte, NC.

Martial Arts has also reinforced what my late father taught to me while growing up in the mountains of Western NC: Hard work always pays off, never give up, whatever you do in life...be the best at it. And the rules of our house; Love, Discipline, Respect, Courtesy, Loyalty, Honesty, Integrity, and the Courage to stand up for what is right!"

MAX CARDOZA

"Through Martial Arts, I learned to be confident but not arrogant."

TRAINING INFORMATION

- Belt Ranks & Martial Arts Styles: Shotokan Japanese Karate 1st Dan, American Karate 1st - 10th Dan

- Instructors/Influencers: Shotokan Master Don Shaw, American GM J. Pat Burleson, American GM Billy Bramer

- Birthdate: March 15, 1946

- Birthplace/Growing Up: Bronx, NY / Ville Platte, LA / Fort Worth, TX

- Yrs. In the Martial Arts: 50 years

- Yrs. Instructing: 52 years

- Instructor

PROFESSIONAL ORGANIZATIONS

- MKHAF
- USAHOF
- UNKHOF

When I started, I was a shy and a standoff-ish person. I learned to speak in public, which I was terrified to do. I learned a tremendous amount of confidence. I also learned that a small man, being me at the time, 5'4" and about 120 lbs, could not only overcome but beat larger people. I was blessed with blazing speed, which enabled me to out maneuver most large opponents.

I, along with my son, teach for GM Billy Smith. We instruct for no compensation. The greatest part of giving back is to see the young students progress. It's just that much fun now.

I found myself surrounded by some of the greatest martial arts practitioners ever. I fought in the late 60s & 70s. In Texas, it was known as the blood & guts era. A mouthpiece, cup, gi was all we had; no protective gear. As I mentioned earlier, I learned to be confident but not arrogant. I learned something from every class I took and later every class I taught.

PERSONAL ACHIEVEMENTS

- Started a Design Business in 1969. Today my firm employs 9 full time salesmen

- I placed in more than 50 tournaments for kumite & kata

MAJOR ACHIEVEMENTS

- 2014 Master Karate Hall of Fame

- 2014 USA Karate Hall of Fame

- 2018 Universal Karate Hall of Fame

ENRICO CHIN

> "For me, Martial Arts is not something you do; it is something you are. I am a Martial Artist."

I began training in martial arts at a very young age, studying various styles of the art. Training with Master Yamanaka, I attained the Black belt level in both Kempo Karate as well as Ju Jitsu, before being introduced to Choy Le Fut Kung Fu. It is upon meeting my instructor Master Mo Chow, that my study in Kung Fu began. So, with the support of my family, I ate, drank, and slept, Kung Fu. While my friends were out at parties, dates, and movies, I ran miles barefoot in the snow. After many years of serious training, I attained the Sifu level, under the instruction of Master Mo Chow.

I opened my first club in 1979, "Future Dragons Kung Fu," seeing the preservation of the art through the instruction of children I taught.

My reputation for traditional and quality teaching and preservation of the culture multiplied, necessitating a more massive club. Some of my first students still train with me privately to this day.

My journey in Kung Fu has enabled me to have many memorable experiences, such as the invitation to teach a seminar in Norway with Grand Master Yamanaka and Professor Morris. I also had the opportunity to work on several movies and T.V. series, including "Kung Fu The Legend Continues" with David Carridine. I have worked in and choreographed one of the fight scenes in the T.V. series Aderlaide.

I had a role in the commercial trailer for Raiders of the Lost Ark, produced by Blockbuster. Other movie roles were Golden

TRAINING INFORMATION

- Belt Ranks & Martial Arts Styles: Choy Lay Fut Kung Fu Red Sash, 5th Degree Black Belt Kempo Karate, Black Belt Jujitsu

- Instructors/Influencers: Master Mo Chow, Soke Ron Yamanaka and Professor Morris

- Birthdate: March 10, 1957

- Birthplace/Growing Up: Jamaica/ Canada/Florida

- Yrs. In the Martial Arts: 58 years

- Yrs. Instructing: 41 years

- Instructor

PROFESSIONAL ORGANIZATIONS

- Choy Lee Fut General Assembly of Guangdong Province China

PERSONAL ACHIEVEMENTS

- The opportunity to preserve this beautiful art through the gift of teaching new generations. Perhaps the greatest was participating in a training session at my own son's Martial Arts School. I could not have been prouder.

MAJOR ACHIEVEMENTS

- Chairman of Choy Lee Fut General Assembly of Guangdong Province China as the US Overseas Advisor Choy Lee Fut Kung Fu

- 1994 Elvis Stojko trained in my school, working with myself and one of my students on choreography, incorporating some martial arts moves into his figure skating routine to balance hard/ soft. This was the year he won the Gold Medal

Golden Phoenix with Kung Fu brother Jalal Merhi.

For me, Martial Arts is not something you do; it is something you are. I am a Martial Artist. I fell in love with Martial Arts at an early age while watching Kung Fu movies and began to train. I wanted to be one of those strong protectors. So, I trained, I studied, and I trained some more, until as they say, "I got HARD." I feel the Arts has molded me into the role of a teacher/protector. It has given me confidence; the strong should always protect the weak; this is Ying/Yang, the perfect balance of the weak/strong. Kung Fu is a true balance of hard and soft it teaches us to flow.

JOE CICCONE

"The Martial Arts has taught me to be resilient in my approach to impact the students on a personal level."

TRAINING INFORMATION

- Belt Ranks & Martial Arts Styles: Sil-lum Kung-Fu (3rd Degree Black Belt), Wing Chun (Choy Le Fut Advanced Student), Jiu Jitsu (Purple Belt), Taekwondo, Tang Soo Do (1st Dan), Hapkido

- Instructors/Influencers: Si gong Tai Chueng Sau, Master Duncan Leong, Master Soo Wong Lee, Master Jung Bai Lee, Master Harold Hankins, Master Gary Daniels

- Birthdate: November 20, 1955

- Birthplace/Growing Up: Norfolk & Virginia Beach, VA

- Yrs. In the Martial Arts: 53 years

- Yrs. Instructing: 49 years

- School owner (Yee Chi Kwan Fighting Academy), Instructor, Founder of Yee Chi Kwan

PROFESSIONAL ORGANIZATIONS

- International Federation of Martial Arts

- EUSAIMAA,

- International Martial Arts Association

- American Martial Arts Alliance Black Belt Membership

Growing up I was in a private school until 5th grade when I started public school. That was an eye opener. In private school we were like family but when it came to public school that's when the bullying started. I was chubby and dressed conservative wearing wingtip shoes, an Insurance man's briefcase with Vitalis in my hair. I was begging for a beat down and I didn't even know it. There was one big kid who didn't like my face because he was always talking about smashing it in. Every day after class he would beat me down to the ground until finally one day my Mother walked into my bedroom when I was changing and saw the bruises all over my body. I had to come clean about the bullying and my Mother put a stop to it. A teacher was fired over it because he allowed it to go on. Back in the early sixties nobody ever did anything about bullying they never thought it was a big deal.

PERSONAL ACHIEVEMENTS

- Taught self-defense for TRIS Tidewater Rape Information Services

- Was an advocate for Women's self-defense and training

- Taught Police hand to hand defense, defense against weapons

- I was the 1st one in the state of Virginia to teach and recognize nunchaku as a weapon and get them passed into law

- Helped develop side handle batons modeled after the tonfa

- Taught Special Forces specialized training

- Taught Government Agencies specialized training

MAJOR ACHIEVEMENTS

- Founder and developer of my own style: Yee Chi Kwan

- Competed in full contact free style and won the world championship in 1975. When it was disbanded in 1978, I was undefeated

- Inducted into the Who's who of the Martial Arts Elite in 1988

- Inducted into the Who's Who of the Martial Arts in Karate International in 1992

- Inducted into the Who's Who in the Martial Arts of Masters and Pioneers in 2019

- Inducted into the Who's Who in the Martial Arts as Ambassador of the year in Martial Arts Legends and Pioneers in 2020

- Author of "Not Your Average Joe's Journey To Faith," in 2016. I have done radio show interviews and have spoken at many venues about my book and faith as a Christian Speaker

My Father got me involved in working out, wrestling, boxing and Martial Arts. It was through the Martial Arts that I learned confidence and self-esteem. I became very proficient in fighting and was able to protect myself and others. I would not tolerate bullying against anyone and was quick to come to their defense. As I continued throughout school, I had many opportunities to face my fears and to become an overcomer. It was through the discipline of the Martial Arts and being fortunate enough to have great Teachers in each style I studied that impacted my life. I sit back and reminisce over 52 years and realize how fortunate and blessed I've been. The wisdom I have attained through the Martial Arts and my faith in God has changed the direction of my life for the better. I can only hope to continue on the path set before me, to give to others the knowledge and faith that I have learned.

The Martial Arts has impacted my life in many ways. It has given me confidence in myself when I was being bullied as a young child. It has strengthened my body as well as my mind, and gave me a purpose at times when I felt like I was defeated. Through the many styles I have learned it was so interesting how different they were yet how inner woven they could be. How accepting over the years, they have become and were more tolerant to other styles. In the early years it was always a power struggle on which style was the best. There would be a student that excelled in these different styles and so when they would win, they would claim their style to be superior to the others. They couldn't grasp it was the individual and not so much the training in the Art they represented. I know through my studies I have learned to take whatever works from everything I have been taught and apply it to what is useful. When I teach, I recognize not everyone's the same, so I can specialize training that will work for each unique individual. The Martial Arts has taught me to be resilient in my approach to impact the students on a personal level. When I promote, I use the different ways of stimulating my students' achievements whether it's rewarding with belts, patches, sashes or certificates. As long as they feel a sense of accomplishment they will strive in their learning. I have learned this through the many teachers and how their style differs from the others. Over the years I have attained wisdom and knowledge and a proper way of treating people like we need to be treated. If we put people first, we will be able to teach more effectively because people know whether or not you care. If they know you care it will touch them to care about others and they will be better students, teachers and individuals in the Martial Arts and in life. Studying the Martial Arts has truly impacted my life as well as my students and the people I have come into contact with. I hope people's lives are changed and touched for the best by being a small part of a life that I have tried to live as an example.

JAMES COOK

"The rank means nothing, the knowledge means everything..."

TRAINING INFORMATION

- Belt Ranks & Martial Arts Styles: Kodakan Judo-3rd kyu, Shotokan-4th Kyu, Goju-4th Kyu, Bak Mie Pai Gung Fu -4th Level, Ishinryu, O Do Gwan Tae Kwon Do-3rd Dan, Northern Praying Mantis-8th Level "8th Dan"

- Instructors/Influencers: Bob Howard, Clifford Yates, John Custer, Wally Cowper, Tiger Division (VIETNAM) 66-67, Ku Muc Whe, Do Hak Soo - Chun Gwon Ho - Jung Ho Ming

- Birthdate: March 11, 1947

- Birthplace/Growing Up: Cleveland, OH

- Yrs. In the Martial Arts: 63 years

- Yrs. Instructing: 55 years

- Instructor

PROFESSIONAL ORGANIZATIONS

- USKA
- PKA
- AMERICAN BLACK BELT ASSOC.
- SOUTHWEST KARATE ASSOC.
- CHAN MOO KWON WORLD ASSOC.
- UNITED STATES ASSOC, OF MARTIAL ARTS
- WORLD CHINESE MARTIAL ARTS FED.

Growing up in Cleveland Ohio back in the 50's was not an easy task. We had a coal & wood burning pot-bellied stove in the middle of the kitchen, and a pump on the sink.

We were poor, but it was a good thing that we didn't know it. As a kid, I looked like Steve Urkle with the glasses with tape hanging on my nose and the high-water pants with suspenders and penny loafers. I was the target for bullies in elementary school and junior high. One day I was watching an old "Ozzie & Harriet" episode and Ricky Nelson was getting bullied in school and decided to take karate from a gentleman named Ed Parker.

That was the first time that I viewed martial arts. At that time, I was 10, and we lived around the corner from Corey Recreation Center where I used to take magic classes. One day the instructor didn't show up, so I wandered around the center for the first time.

It was then I passed a room that was full of people wearing pajamas with different color belts on. I watched for a moment and realized that it was judo, and a way for me to learn how to defend myself.

At first, I was just another clumsy kid with 3 legs, but under the instruction of Mr. Bob Howard, I slowly turned into a swan. I finally made

PERSONAL ACHIEVEMENTS

- CLEVELAND MARTIAL ARTS HALL OF FAME
- PENNSYLVANIA KARATE LIFETIME ACHIEVEMENT AWARD
- WHO'S WHO LEGEND AWARD
- JOE LEWIS ETERNAL WARRIOR AWARD
- PKA WARRIOR AWARD
- KARATE HALL OF FAME AWARD CAL.
- NATIONAL MARTIAL ARTS HALL OF FAME AWARD
- MASTERS HALL OF FAME LIFETIME ACHIEVEMENT AWARDS
- SPORT KARATE MUSEUM DRAGON IMAGE FIGHTING AWARD
- USA MARTIAL ARTS LEGEND AWARD

MAJOR ACHIEVEMENTS

- 1981 - Martial Arts Hall Of Fame Inductee
- 1980 - Karate Hall Of Fame Inductee
- 1977 - Top 10 Fighter in the U.S.; Official Karate Magazine
- 1977 - Top 3 World Weapons Expert.; Official Karate Magazine
- TOP TOURNAMENT ACHIEVEMENTS
- 1996 - Top fighter & form competitor Knoxville Pro Am
- 1980 - International Grand Champion; Venezuela
- International Weapons Champion; Venezuela

it to the green belt and was proud.

One day after class, I walked out without my shoes. As I returned to get them, I looked in and Mr. Howard and his brother were kicking and punching and it was confusing because in Judo, there are no kicks or punches. "This was karate". In those days, you could not take karate before the age of 18. Bob got around it by making me a mascot.

As I remember, Bob took me to my first tournament where I watched Bill Hayes, Russell Benefield, Joe Pennywell, and the great Zenpo Shimabuku. This was back in the day when you fought with only tape on you first, and the technique had to be within 2 inches from the target to be called a point. The control of these fighters was amazing. I watched with amazement as Master Shimabuku countered his attackers with the most fantastic jump spin trust kick that was perfectly timed. After the tournament, I ran to the dressing room to ask him about the kick. He spoke no English, so I motioned, attempting to do the kick.

He positioned me, gently grabbed me by my collar and belt and lifted me up in the air turning, and sitting me back down again. I never forgot that, and the technique became one of my trademarks.

MAJOR ACHIEVEMENTS

- International Forms Champion; Venezuela

- 1979 - International Middleweight Champion; Venezuela

- International Weapons Champion; Venezuela

- International Forms Champion; Venezuela

- 1978 - Battle of Atlanta Middleweight Champion

- Battle of Atlanta Weapons Champion

- Battle of Atlanta Forms Champion

- 1977 - United States Karate Association Grand Champion; Pittsburgh Pa.

I trained with Bob in Shotokan for a year and a half when he left. I found that two of his advanced had studied Isshinryu, and started training with Henry Story and Jake Lacey.

They had both studied under a marine named Clifford Yates who would visit and train all 3 of us. Clifford eventually returned to the marines and once again, I was in search of an instructor. It made no difference to the system, I just wanted to learn. While in gym class one day in junior high, I found myself off in a corner practicing kata when one of my classmates walked over and asked me about my training. James Yee and his brother and sister's family owned a Chinese restaurant down the street from the high school.

As it turned out, his father was a Kung-Fu disciple who would train the family at night when they closed. The system was Bak Mei Pai. "White Eyebrow". It was my first venture into art that was more like dance. So graceful and deceiving.

Upon graduation from high school in 1965, I joined the army where I found myself in Qhinhon Vietnam training with "Tiger Division " (Korean army) Hq and earning my 1st Dan, I later started the first Army karate team at Ft. Bragg and worked with Ron McNair of the shuttle disaster. I went on to become an instructor for the military in both Germany and Korea. I left the military in 1975 and returned to Cleveland where I opened my first school. Over the years, I've trained over 9,000 students and fighters to include "Billy Blanks".

I went back into the army in 1983 and finally retired in 2007. With over a thousand competitions under my belt, along with winning the internationals in Venezuela in 1980, I feel like I am just reaching my peak at 72 years of age.

James Cook was born in 1947, the oldest of 4 brothers and sisters in Cleveland Ohio. As a child, he was very awkward and shy. He possessed an imagination that was beyond his years.

He grew up in a very poor and rough part of Cleveland where sometimes he and his playmate sometimes find bodies in the alley next to the house. Both his step-father and grandfather were musicians which later contributed to him becoming a songwriter in Nashville Tennessee as well as an accomplished guitarist.

When his parents couldn't afford toys, he would construct his own for himself as well as his siblings. He would take notebook paper and teach himself to draw, which later he would become an art major.

Because of his small build, he was constantly bullied by those around him. It was in the 50's that he discovered martial arts at a local recreation center.

Under the tutelage of Bob Howard, a 62-year journey in martial arts would begin. Mr. Howard was a very patient man that one day called James, a 3-legged duck because he was so clumsy. This stuck in his mind and lit a fire that would push him even harder. It was years later that he would receive the ultimate compliment, when Mr. Howard came to him and said, "You have traveled further and flown higher than I ever did" and asked him to train his son.

From the streets of Cleveland, Ohio through the jungles of Vietnam, the hills of Germany and the mountains of South Korea, this young man chased his dreams of reaching for the ultimate reality of being the best that he could be. Over the years, he had the honor of befriending such greats as Robert Trias, Ed Parker, Mike Stone, Billy Blanks, Joe Corley and so many more.

He often tells his followers, "You don't learn martial arts, you study martial arts". His promotion to first degree black belt came in Phu Bai South Vietnam while training with the famed "Tiger Division" Korean Army. He recalls being handed his belt and looking down at it and thinking, this is merely a piece of cotton that means I have now begun to study. He later went on to become the first black actor in Korean movies.

Today, as an 8th Dan with over 1,000 competitions behind him, including winning the "World Internationals" in Venezuela as well as the United States Karate Association Grand Nationals in 1977, he has touched the stars. He has gone from being a poor child in Cleveland to becoming a musician, comedian, Artist, Guitar maker (Luthier) and more than all, a true martial artist.

The rank means nothing, the knowledge means everything.

It is said, "In order to know your enemy, you must first know yourself.

Today, all that knows this man, knows that he knows himself.

JOHN COX

"Martial Arts is what has molded me and defined me as a person."

My interest in the martial arts started when I was 8-9 years old. Watching tv wrestling was as close to the Asian arts I knew of. I was given a karate magazine when I was close to 10, and there was an article about karate vs boxing. Even at that age, I read the article and was fascinated and hooked. But not hooked on an Asian style, just Karate, Kung Fu and Judo.

One of my school friends was into kung fu, some sort of tiger style, and we played around with it. I got my hands on a Bruce Tegner judo book and studied every picture religiously. Another school mate saw me with my book after school and told me about a guy who taught Kung Fu, Wing Chun to be exact. Fast forward, begging my mom, she finally met with him and "they" agreed to let me study. Wow, how hard it was, physically, mentally, time wise. But I was hooked for life. That was 50 years ago.

Originally, I wanted to be tough like the tv wrestlers, I got beat up a lot by my brother back then. After my first sash test, I started getting the bigger picture. I loved the discipline and challenges. But not the hard work that came later. But I found I was good at it, had a good memory for it, and surprisingly exceptional understanding of it. I moved up quickly, but not in rank. My Sifu wouldn't allow a kid to become a black belt. Something today I agree with.

From the early beginning of TV wrestling, a Karate magazine, to the Brue Tegner Judo book that I still have today, it has been a tremendous journey. A journey that starts over everyday. Surprisingly the journey hasn't gotten easier.

TRAINING INFORMATION

- Belt Ranks & Martial Arts Styles: 9th Degree Black Shou Chin Na, 3rd Black Tracy Kenpo, 3rd Black Kenpo JuJitsu, 2nd Black (advanced red sash) Shou Wing Chun, Black Belt instructor (Menkyosho Kiden) Iaido, Shodan (Red Sash) Shou Tai Chi.

- Instructors/Influencers: Sifu Micheal Green, Shihan Garrison Hall, GM Al Tracy, Soke Oshiro Mizune, Hamiko Nishimoto

- Birthdate: September 16, 1960

- Birthplace/Growing Up: Greenville, SC

- Yrs. In the Martial Arts: 50 years

- Yrs. Instructing: 45 years

- School Owner, Instructor

PERSONAL ACHIEVEMENTS

- 30-year career firefighter, retired as Captain over Training Academy

- International accredited fire instructor I II

- State licensed residential builder and home inspector

- Traveled to Japan / China twice

- N.R.A. firearms instructor

- America in Defense flight crew instructor

PROFESSIONAL ORGANIZATIONS

- United States Martial Artist Association

- International Martial Arts Society

- International Board of Black Belts/ World Black Belt Council

- International Combat M.A. Unions Association

Oh sure, the techniques have, but not the physicality – in the beginning, 50 years ago, I was so small it was hard to do. Today, I've grown 50 years older, so yes, the physicality is just as hard, but in a different way. Harder for the body to react at my age. But the desire, drive, and interest is as intense as it was when I started. I'll study the arts as long as I live, and I have learned to appreciate every and all styles, for all have something to offer. My joy comes from learning something new every day. No matter how fresh or tired, I study. I live by a saying Steven Segal says, "When you don't have anything left, show me what you got". And that mantra was instilled in me by my Sifu 50 years ago, it just wasn't presented in that way. It was a little more physical if you get my drift.

From my beginning in Wing Chun (equivalent to 2nd black belt), I transitioned into a Family style of Chin Na (to which I inherited that system) – 9th degree. 23 years ago, I started in Tracy Kenpo (3rd degree black belt) to which I now incorporate both systems into my art. Along with Kenpo, I have a third dan in Kenpo JuJitsu. I also hold black belt ranks in Tetsu Ishi Nagari Mizo Ryu Iaido and Shou Tai Chi (sash equivalent).

How did I get started in the martial arts you ask? The "how" I guess was a book. But the "why" is the most important question. To mold yourself into a better human being through discipline, life goals, self-discovery and improvement, tolerance, and a lifelong enjoyment of helping teach, mold, others so they can perpetuate these things to others they know. So, the cycle can continue and life continues. But I think more importantly, at least to me, is to never forget the past masters, their sacrifices, and their betterment of the world we live in. To that, I thank all who have come before me and all that come after me. Wow, the why...in the beginning those TV wrestlers were bad men.

My time in Martial Arts has been a true blessing. From day one, it's been an ongoing journey in discovery - discovering the potentials in every student, knowing my instructors/colleagues, and finding myself. It has also been about knowing what I could do, what I thought I couldn't do but did, and what I could pass on to others. Throughout the last 50 years, it's been a challenge, to say the least: early days old school training, one kick, one punch, one block for months.

MAJOR ACHIEVEMENTS

- Action Martial Arts Magazine H.O.F inductee 3 times
- London International M.A. H.O.F. inductee
- Universal M.A. Association H.O.F inductee
- Action M.A. Radio H.O.F inductee
- Black Warrior M.A. H.O.F inductee

Hours of footwork, days I preferred to play with friends or fishing. Throughout all the injuries and surgeries, was it worth it? Oh my, yes! It's what has molded me and defined me as a person.

I am the inheritor of the Chin Na system I teach; a single-family system passed down from family members until none left. Being taught old school like it was in early 20th century China was hard, maybe too hard for today's students, but it has worked for me. And I wouldn't change one thing during my tenure in the martial arts. The people I've met and the friends I'm blessed to know is something that can't be bought.

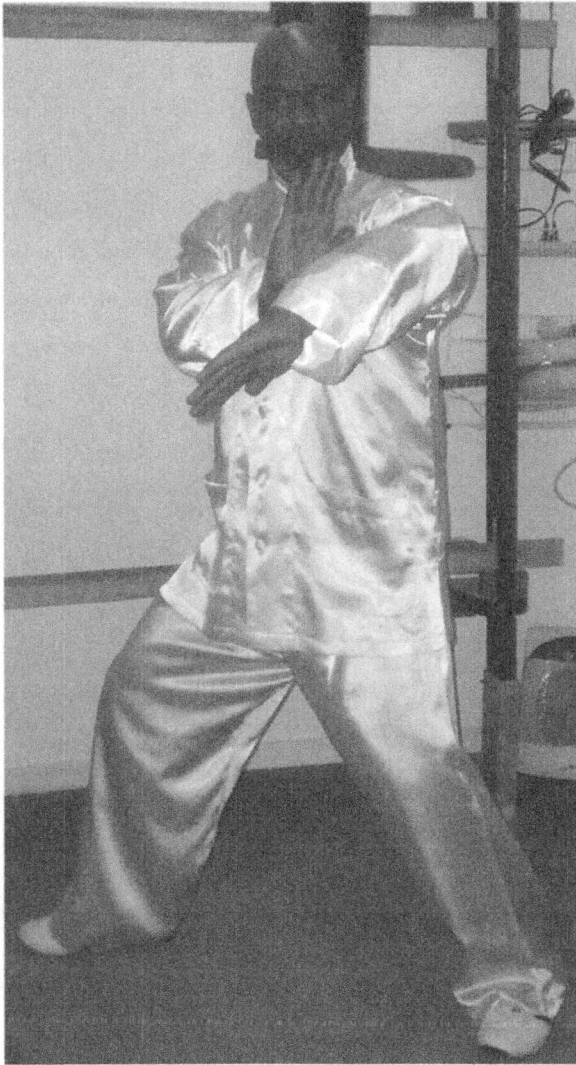

JAMES DARBY

"Martial Arts has allowed me to grow into a self-motivated, disciplined, self-starting person."

As a Teen in the '70's, EVERYBODY WAS KUNG FU FIGHTING!!! With the arrival of Bruce Lee's movies and boundless energy to burn --- It's what we all did in our various neighborhoods for friendly competition. It kept us busy since we did it every single day after school and on weekends. It was something POSITIVE to do for physical fitness and kept us out of trouble and out of the House. (We played outdoors back then)! There were other youth in close neighborhoods who trained various styles, including Karate, Kung Fu, Wrestling, and even Boxing. We met and traveled to meet each other for matches that lasted for hours. There was NEVER any hatred or ill will toward one another . . . only all-out battles that always ended in friendly handshakes and promises to get them back NEXT TIME if there was a defeat on that day. What a time it was!!!

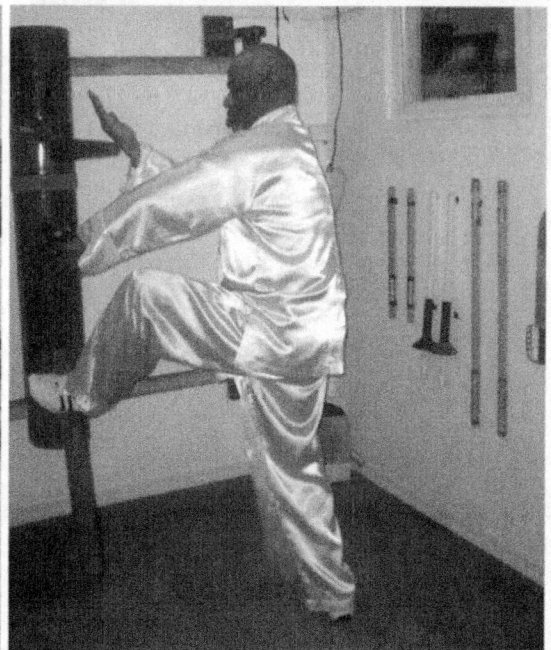

TRAINING INFORMATION

- Belt Ranks & Martial Arts Styles: Jeet Kun Do, Shotokan Karate, Traditional Wing Chun Kung Fu

- Instructors/Influencers: Sifu Nathaniel Singletary, Sensei James Little, Master John Clayton

- Birthdate: April 24, 1956

- Birthplace/Growing Up: Baltimore, MD

- Yrs. In the Martial Arts: 50 years

- Yrs. Instructing: 28 years

- School Owner, Darby Wing Chun Academy, Manager, Instructor

PROFESSIONAL ORGANIZATIONS

- Global Wing Chun Kung Fu Assoc

- Arnett Sport Kung-Fu Assoc

PERSONAL ACHIEVEMENTS

- 2015 "SIFU of The Year" Award from The United Fellowship of Martial Artists Assoc

- 2014 Certificate of Ordination as Deacon from "My Father's House" from The Baltimore Deacon's Counsel

- 2012 Local Resident Instructor at The Johns Hopkins University Kung Fu Club on Campus in Baltimore

- 2010 Founder and Chief Instructor of The "Kicking it For Christ" Kung Fu Ministry at that same Church

- 1992 Founder and Chief Instructor of The Darby Wing Chun Academy

An early introduction to Martial Arts has allowed me to grow into a self-motivated, disciplined, self-starting person. Each style has impacted me differently. My exposure to the Art of Jeet- Kun- Do as a teen gave me a taste of diversity, as well as a sense of being versatile. It allowed me to become more open-minded and to not "settle," - but instead, become willing to adapt to changing situations in combat as well as life situations. Thanks to N. Singletary (a childhood friend), the camaraderie was a lesson well taught and applied every day. Sensei Little was more of a mentor to me while showing me the art of treating people with respect, giving your ALL to whatever endeavors you undertook, and dedicating yourself to family life. That style taught me tenacity, focus, and goal setting.

When Wing Chun came into my life, I began to understand the simplicity, as well as the complexity, and the true principles of being a BETTER person, and a complete teacher. I also learned how important it was to become more diligent in fine-tuning each aspect of what I learned and practiced day by day. I try to pass those very principles on to my students, as I want them to improve on who they are, and how they represent themselves inside and outside of the Kwoon.

MAJOR ACHIEVEMENTS

- 42 Yrs. of Marriage to Wife Vanessa Darby (Soulmate)!

- Father of 3 GREAT Children who keep Him Grounded and Proud!

- Grandfather of 6 Grandchildren worthy of Spoiling Rotten!

- Great Grandfather of 1 Grandson!

RAYOT DIFATE

"I encourage my older karate comrades to put themselves out there and continue to participate when possible."

Hachidan Rayot Difate was born in 1941 in Yonkers, New York. He entered the army in 1960 and volunteered for the 101st Airborne Division. Upon being sent to Korea for a period of 3 years, he began the study of Judo. Upon being honorably discharged in 1963, he returned to White Plains, New York to continue his studies in Kyokushin Karate. In 1965, he joined the Yonkers Police Department while continuing his martial arts training. After a one year of intense training program, under Sensei Shigeru Oyama, Rayot became the 1st Black Belt student to be promoted in the US, in 1967, in the style of Kyokushin Karate Do.

In 1976, during an undercover operation with the Yonkers Police Department, Rayot sustained life threatening injuries, forcing his retirement from the Police Department, due to permanent disabilities followed by years of multiple surgeries. As part of his personal physical and mental rehabilitation, he returned to the dojo with a modified training program. In 1998, he was promoted to the rank of Shihan.

TRAINING INFORMATION

- Belt Ranks & Martial Arts Styles: World Oyama Karate, 8th Dan

- Instructors/Influencers: Shigeru Oyama (Deceased)

- Birthplace/Growing Up: Yonkers, NY/West Harrison, NY

- Yrs. In the Martial Arts: 60 years

- Yrs. Instructing: 55 years

PERSONAL ACHIEVEMENTS

- As of the age of 70 years old: Started and completed 100 tournaments through Age 75 years old, in both   national and international competitions. Continues to be one, if not, the oldest Tri-state competitor in New York, New Jersey, and Connecticut. Continues to both train and compete on a regular basis.

PROFESSIONAL ORGANIZATIONS

- Yonkers Police Department (Retired 1978)

- Veterans of Foreign War, Post 4037

- American Federation of Martial Arts

- New Breed Life Martial Arts Association

- Eastern USA International Martial Arts Association

- Bushiken Karate

From 1998 to present, Rayot has taught at the White Plains Dojo, under the direction of Shoshu Oyama. Shihan has spent the past 58 years in both the study and instruction of martial arts. On September 10, 2014, after 55 years of training with World Oyama Karate, Shihan Rayot was awarded promotion to 8th Degree Black Belt. He has also been inducted into the American Federation of Martial Arts Hall of Fame, as Diamond Lifetime Achievements in 2013, Ambassador of Goodwill to the Martial Arts in 2014, International Instructor of the Year in 2014, and The New Breed Life Arts Education Association in Harlem, in 2015.

Hachidan has participated and given seminars in the US, Canada, Panama, Haiti, and the Dominican Republic. Upon turning the age of 70, Hachidan decided that his "Bucket List" would consist of competing in 100 tournaments, over the next 5 years. In July of 2017, upon turning 76 years old, he completed this goal. He continues to participate in tournaments in the Tri-State area, displaying his form and techniques in Kata, Weapons, and Self-Defense. He takes great pride in his trophies and medals surrounding his family room. He enjoys membership with the Harrison, New York Veterans of Foreign War.

He continues to be a source of inspiration to other martial artists, wherever he goes, as the oldest competitor, doing what he truly finds both motivating and rewarding. In 2008, at the invitation of Shihan John Turnball, he was accepted into the American Federation of Martial Arts. In 2014, he was conferred the rank of Black Belt 7th Dan. Also, in 2014, he was awarded the rank of 8th Dan by both Shugeru Oyama and the American Federation of Martial Arts. In 2015, he was conferred with the rank of 10th Dan by Grand Master Lamarr Thornton of NBLA. In 2017, he was inducted into the Eastern USA International Martial Arts Association. Presently, Hachidan is a member of Bushiken Karate.

On June 30th 2019, Grandmaster Rayot Difate competed in Hue, Vietnam in a 3-day martial arts tournament sponsored by NGHIA Dung Karate-Do Mo Rong.

This was the first time in 60 years that this Asian tournament was open to Americans. Grandmaster traveled with a party of five, to be only one of two Americans competing.

MAJOR ACHIEVEMENTS

- Completion of 100 tournaments between the age of 70 and 75, in both national and international Karate tournaments

- Membership in the Harrison, New York, Veterans of Foreign War, Post 4037

- Honorary discharge from the US Army in 1963

- Honorary Retirement from the Yonkers Police Department in 1978

- One, if not the oldest, competitor in the Tri-State Martial Arts Tournaments

- Achievement of 10th Dan in Martial Arts

- 9th Dan presented by Adolfo Ennever, Hanshi/Soke of the American Federation of martial arts on December 3, 2018.

- 9th Dan, by Eastern USA International Arts Association, under Grandmaster John Kanzler, Soke, on November 10, 2018.

- 10th Dan, presented by Grandmaster Lamar Thornton, under New Breed Life Association, October 10, 2015.

Grandmaster took third place in Kata and 5th place in weapons. There were 800 competitors over the entire three-day event. He competed in the 50-year and older Masters division, in which he had the honor of being the oldest competitor at the age of 78. Besides representing the USA, were other Asian countries with Australia and Canada. He continues to teach, train, and compete. He encourages his older karate comrades to put themselves out there and continue to participate when possible.

ERNEST DUKES, JR.

"Martial Arts allowed me to raise my kids properly, keep a successful marriage, and learn how to treat everyone equally."

TRAINING INFORMATION

- Belt Ranks & Martial Arts Styles: Shorin Ryu Traditional Okinawan Hanshi (10th Dan Black Belt), Itosu Ryu Karate (1st Dan Black Belt), Judo (Blue Belt), Cella Funk Kung-fu (Green Belt), Tae Kwan Do (Yellow Belt)

- Instructors/Influencers: Soke Ryusho Sakagami

- Birthdate: October 14, 1958

- Birthplace/Growing Up: Miami, FL

- Yrs. In the Martial Arts: 50 years

- Yrs. Instructing: 41years

- School Owner at Dukes Martial Arts Academy

PROFESSIONAL ORGANIZATIONS

- Kuro Bushi Martial Arts Organization

I got started in the Martial Arts because I wanted to improve my mental stamina, enhance social skills, self-defense skills, better coordination, flexibility, and confidence. I also wanted to be a world champion. I watched a marathon of action movies during an extended weekend and it seemed like a decent idea to try out martial arts as a way to get fitter.

Luckily, my teacher was a cool guy who taught me a lot more than I expected. I did have a hard time catching up with the fitness level of the other students, but it was worth it.

Martial Arts allowed me to raise my kids properly, keep a successful marriage, and learn how to treat everyone equally. It also kept me out of trouble.

PERSONAL ACHIEVEMENTS

- Teaching Karate Classes
- Promoting (13) Tournaments
- Hosting (4) KBMA Hall of Honors Awards Banquets
- Becoming a physically healthier person

MAJOR ACHIEVEMENTS

- Won the 1999 NBL Grand Championship - Traditional Weapons
- Won the 2001 NBL Grand Championship – Traditional Forms
- Won the 2001 NBL Grand Championship- Adult Mans BB Sparring
- Living legends Sports Karate Competitor – AKANA 2003 Silver Tomoe
- Inducted into: American Martial Arts Alliance Hall of Fame - 2006 Grand Master of the Year
- Battle of Atlanta Hall of Fame - 2007 35+ years of Devotion to the Martial Arts
- Universal Martial Arts Association Hall of Fame – 2007 Regional Instructor of the Year
- World Martial Arts Magazine Hall of Fame – 2008 State Promoter of the Year
- Action Martial Arts Hall of Honors – 2009 Exemplary Dedication to the M.A. 37+ Years
- The Kuroshi-Do Hall of Fame – 2010 SOKE of the Year

ROBERT DUNN

TRAINING INFORMATION

- Belt Ranks & Martial Arts Styles: Tae Kwon Do (9th Degree Black Belt)

- Instructors/Influencers: Grand Master Kong Young II

- Birthplace/Growing Up: Chester, PA

- Yrs. In the Martial Arts: 57 years

- Yrs. Instructing: 54 years

PROFESSIONAL ORGANIZATIONS

- International Juntong Tae Kwon-Do Federation

PERSONAL & MAJOR ACHIEVEMENTS

- Grandmaster Robert Dunn started his Martial Arts training in 1962, where Grandmaster Parker Shelton once owned a School in North Carolina.

- In 1969, Grandmaster Robert Dunn was introduced to Grandmaster Kong Young Il a Pioneer in the Art of Taekwon-Do and started his training in Taekwon-Do under the direction of Grandmaster Kong Young Il.

- In 1970, Grandmaster Robert Dunn opened his first Taekwon-Do school

- In 1977, Grandmaster Robert Dunn met Grandmaster Ahn Eung Choon and started training under him.

- In 1987, Grandmaster Ahn Eung Choon certified Grandmaster Robert Dunn as an International Judge.

- In 1988, Grandmaster Robert Dunn was inducted into the International Karate Hall of Fame by Dan Soward, the president of the International Karate Hall of Fame in Las Vegas, Nevada.

- 1989, Grandmaster Robert Dunn was contracted to teach the Art of Taekwon-Do to Peruvian troops in Lima, Peru.

- Grandmaster Robert Dunn competed in Regional and National level tournaments during the late 1960's and early 1970's.

PERSONAL & MAJOR ACHIEVEMENTS

- Grandmaster Robert Dunn has competed with and trained and received seminars from many of the pioneers in the Martial Arts.

- 2009, on February 21st Grandmaster Robert Dunn was promoted to Grandmaster 9th. Dan Black Belt by Grandmaster Eung Choon Ahn in Macon, Georgia

- 2013, Grandmaster Robert Dunn was inducted into the Black Belt Karate Hall of Fame by Jeff Helaney the president of the Black Belt Hall of Fame in Omaha, Nebraska

- 2013, Grandmaster Robert Dunn establishes a European International Headquarters in the United Kingdom.

PERSONAL & MAJOR ACHIEVEMENTS

- 2013, Grandmaster Robert Dunn establishes a Caribbean International Headquarters in Cabo Rojo, Puerto Rico.

- 2014, Grandmaster Robert Dunn establishes a Israeli International Headquarters in Hoshmonaim, Israel.

- 2014, Grandmaster Robert Dunn has now established International JTF schools in a number of countries around the world

- 2014, Grandmaster Robert Dunn is Recognized by the Black Belt Hall of Fame and Awarded the Pioneer & Legends Award from Grandmaster Jeff Helaney.

- 2017, Grandmaster Robert Dunn is Inducted into the Official Taekwon-Do Hall of Fame and Recognized as a Pioneer of Taekwon-Do in the New York City Ceremony.

- 2018, Grandmaster Robert Dunn travels to Southeast Asia to train Black Belts in the Philippines and train with Grandmaster Kong Young Il in Vietnam.

- 2018, Grandmaster Robert Dunn is appointed as Secretary General of the Young Brothers Taekwon-Do International (YBTI) by Grandmaster Kong Young IL - International Headquarters in Kuala Lumpur, Malaysia.

- 2018, Grandmaster Robert Dunn was inducted into the 2018 "Who's Who" in Martial Arts in a ceremony in Washington, DC.

- 2019, Grandmaster Robert Dunn was selected to be inducted into the "The Book of Grandmasters", sanctioned by the United States National Grandmasters Federation.

PERSONAL & MAJOR ACHIEVEMENTS

- 2019, Grandmaster Robert Dunn was Honored in the 2019 "Who's Who" in Martial Arts in a ceremony in Las Vegas, Nevada.

- 2019, Grandmaster Robert Dunn attends the Taekwon-Do Hall of Fame Ceremonies in Bangkok, Thailand with 4 of his students that have become Grandmasters for their Induction.

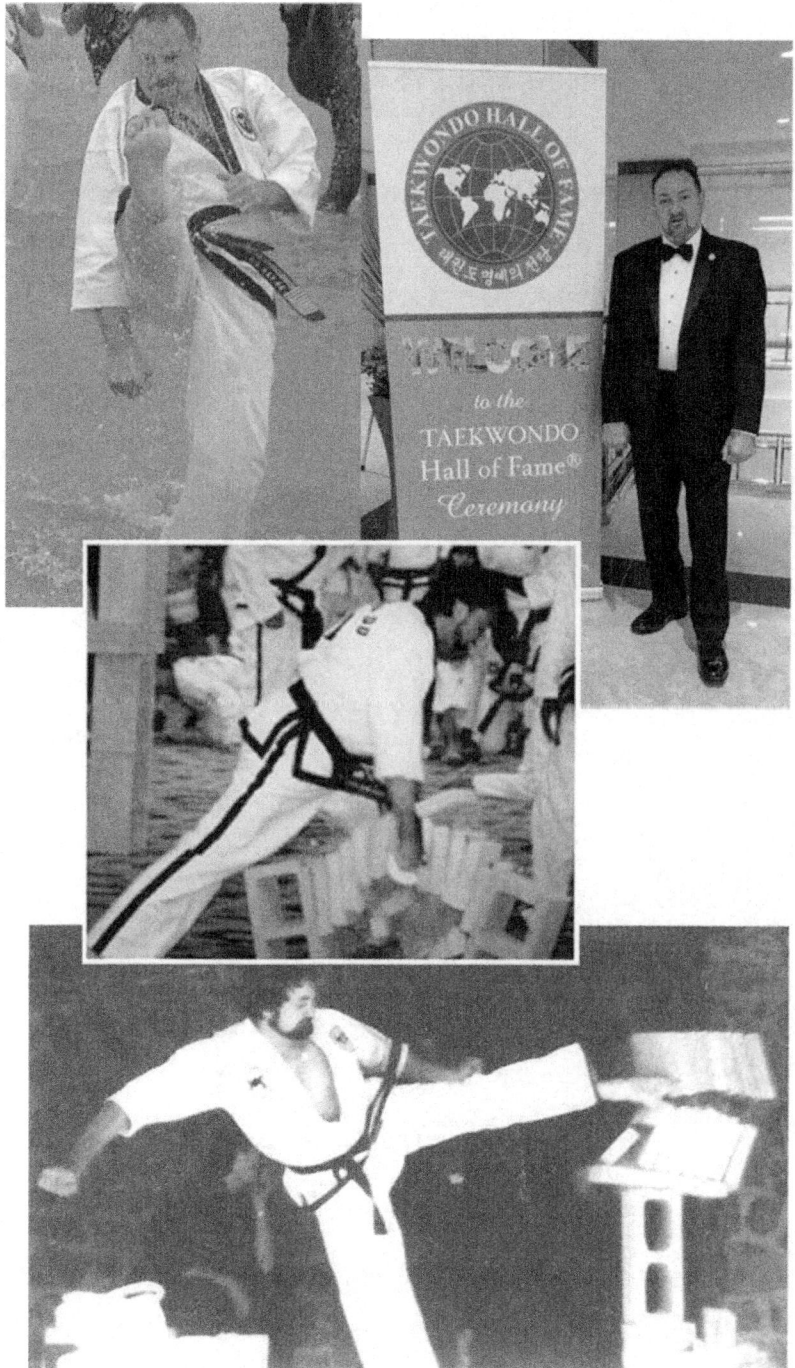

DOUG EMERSON

"Practical application is the heart of a Karate training regimen. If you cannot apply the skills, then they are worthless."

I began my martial arts training in 1968 at the age of 15. Like many others, I began my karate training as a means of self-defense. I had no idea what to expect when I went to my first class. The beginner class overlapped with the advanced class by 30 minutes. During that time, we were taught self-defense techniques for several types of attack. That was my initial impetus for training. I soon learned that there was no end to the study of martial arts and self-defense was just the beginning. I saw that Karate could give me more than self-defense. I saw it as a good workout and more interesting than other sports I played. Moreover, I saw Karate training as a way of life and that it could have applications in anything I wanted to do. I learned that I could use my karate skills in almost anything and the principles I

TRAINING INFORMATION

- Belt Ranks & Martial Arts Styles: American Karate, AKBBA Black Belt, 9th Degree
- Instructors/Influencers: Grand Master J. Pat Burleson, Grand Master Chuck Loven
- Birthdate: September 1952
- Birthplace/Growing Up: Texas
- Yrs. In the Martial Arts: 51 years
- Yrs. Instructing: 50 years
- Manager & Instructor

PROFESSIONAL ORGANIZATIONS

- American Karate Black Belt Association
- World Martial Arts Ranking Association
- State Bar of Texas

learned could be applied to help achieve my goals. I saw that the path to excellence was not easy, required hard work and dedication. I set a goal to reach my fullest potential and attained a black belt. It was not an easy path and I faced mental, emotional, and physical hurdles along the way. I was promoted to 1st degree black belt on 1/31/ 71.

The way that Karate has impacted my life is immeasurable. My experiences in the Karate school defined me in a way that I carried throughout my life. As I stated above, I began my Karate training at a very young age. I found myself in a Karate school and I knew that I belonged there. As I progressed through the ranks, I learned to set a goal and achieve it. I was proud to be promoted, but the belt was secondary. It was more important to exceed the expectations of a given rank. I was my own worst critic and my primary goal was the pursuit of excellence.

I learned to have pride and confidence in who I was and my ability. I trained and fought before safety gear was introduced by GM Jhoon Rhee. We fought bare knuckles and feet. Techniques were to be controlled, but it didn't always work that way. Competition was tough and classes were no different. To attain rank, we were expected to strive for excellence and exhibit a strong and focused attitude.

I used my karate skills in everything. That means I learned to assess a problem or opponent, strategize and plan an efficient solution and execute a plan of attack. I learned to persevere and never give up. These skills served me throughout my life. I lived as a blackbelt every day. The principles and skills I learned helped me overcome obstacles I encountered as a U.S. Marine. It helped me progress in the workforce, in competition, and academics. I graduated from UNLV and California Western School of Law by applying the lessons of the martial arts. There are many other examples where I applied the lessons of the martial arts.

In sum, hard training and high standards are imperative. Practical application is the heart of a Karate training regimen. If you cannot apply the skills, then they are worthless.

Beginning my Karate training was the best thing I have ever done. I am thankful I trained in the era I did. I am thankful for the training and guidance I received. Lastly, my eternal gratitude and respects to my primary instructors GM Chuck Loven and GM J. Pat Burleson.

PERSONAL ACHIEVEMENTS

- Promoted to the Rank of Black Belt - 1971
- United States Marine Corps 1971 - 1974 (veteran)
- Chief Instructor at Professional Karate Studios in Las. Vegas, Nevada
- Ranked in the top ten Black Belt competitors on the West Coast region-1977
- Assisted in the production of Las Vegas television special "Karate: Fact or Fantasy?"
- Graduated from UNLV, BA Criminal Justice -1985
- Graduated from California Western School of Law, JD degree -1987
- Admitted to State Bar of Texas - 1988
- Inducted U.S.A. Martial Arts Hall of Fame- 8/8/15
- Inducted Masters Hall of Fame- 6/4/16
- Inducted International Black Belt Hall of Fame- 9/30/17
- Promoted to 9th degree Black Belt by GM J. Pat Burleson- 12/19/15
- Instructor at The Karate University (present)
- President/ Chief Justice of Phi Alpha Delta legal fraternity, California Western chapter-1986
- Included in Who's Who of American Law Students- 1987

MAJOR ACHIEVEMENTS

- Promoted to the Rank of Black Belt- 1971
- United States Marine Corps 1971 - 1974 (veteran)
- Represented the USMC at the United States Karate Championships -1972
- Chief Instructor at Professional Karate Studios in Las. Vegas, Nevada
- Ranked in the top ten Black Belt competitors on the West Coast region-1977
- Assisted in the production of Las Vegas television special "Karate: Fact or Fantasy?"
- Graduated from UNLV, BA Criminal Justice -1985
- Graduated from California Western School of Law, JD degree- 1987
- Admitted to State Bar of Texas-1988
- Inducted U.S.A. Martial Arts Hall of Fame- 8/8/15
- Inducted Masters Hall of Fame -6/4/16
- Inducted International Black Belt Hall of Fame- 9/30/17
- Promoted to 9th degree Black Belt by GM J. Pat Burleson - 12/19/15
- Instructor at The Karate University (present)

BERNIE FLEEMAN

> "Watching kids and adults experience Martial Arts for the first time spreads joy to my heart."

When I was 4 years old, my father taught me Slap Fighting to improve my reflexes and coordination. I was the youngest and therefore the smallest in the family. It was a precious and important time spent with my dad. When I was 5, my parents divorced, and soon I found myself with an alcoholic stepfather who created an abusive environment at home. As a result, I was determined to become the family peacemaker. It was also in my nature to protect kids from bullies at school. I desperately wanted to learn defensive fighting, which began my martial arts journey.

When I was 12, I prevented a rape in Long Beach, CA, and the teenage victim told the police that she was sure I saved her life. When I became a Karate instructor, I felt I achieved the role of peacemaker that I desired. I was intent on learning any and

TRAINING INFORMATION

- Belt Ranks & Martial Arts Styles: 10th Dan Kenpo, Black Belt Joe Lewis Fighting Systems, 9th Dan UCHU Do, Shotokan

- Instructors/Influencers: Kazuo Kuriyama, Robert Halliburton, Joe Lewis, Al Tracy, Bruce Lee, Gene LeBell, Robert Koga

- Birthdate: February 12, 1952

- Birthplace/Growing Up: San Pedro, CA/American Samoa/Las Vegas, NV

- Yrs. In the Martial Arts: 63 years

- Yrs. Instructing: 53 years

- Instructor

PROFESSIONAL ORGANIZATIONS

- Bakersfield Police Department Retirees

- Joe Lewis Fighting Systems

- International Martial Arts Council

- American Martial Arts Alliance Who's Who

- Sports Karate Museum

- Dylan Vargas Mixed Martial Arts Academy

PERSONAL ACHIEVEMENTS

- (1984) World (International) Police Olympic/Law Enforcement Champion Gold Medalist

- (1984) Gold Medalist Champion by invitation Nevada Police Olympics, Freestyle (Light Weight 165 lbs. or less)

- (1985-86) Multiple Championships in California Police Olympics - Freestyle Fighter Super Lightweight (145 lbs. or less) Division

everything I could about fighting skills and quickly realized I wanted to be one of the best. At 14, when I began competing, I discovered that my opponents and competitors could become personal friends. This camaraderie motivated me to further my Martial Arts study, particularly within other disciplines. I was even more motivated to continue my journey.

"Over the years I have opened or helped open numerous Martial Arts Studios. Watching kids and adults experience Martial Arts for the first time spreads joy to my heart."

I have met and created friendships with champions from various cultures. These include people from many walks of life such as Martial Arts, First Responders, the military, sports and entertainment, law enforcement, politicians, and the like from all over the world.

After my introduction to Martial Arts, my family moved to American Samoa which was my first interaction with a different culture. As a child, my Samoan friends taught me several warring arts. Sailors and soldiers from various countries landed on the beaches of Samoa to practice their Martial Arts and often included me in their training. My interest in Martial Arts was the glue that overcame language barriers and cultural differences.

When I returned to the states, my formal training in Martial Arts continued to allow me to create friendships with students from all over the world. In the late 1960s, I began to teach beginners at the Way of Japan in Fresno, CA, which opened more doors for me, and allowed me to meet others with similar backgrounds and interests. Charity events, Martial Arts tournaments, police academies, schools, and many other activities in this arena have opened doors to positive aspects of life, for which I am eternally grateful. The Marital Arts has been a major part of my life and was the catalyst for me to reach my goal of becoming a peacemaker.

PERSONAL ACHIEVEMENTS

- (1988) Instrumental in bringing the California Police Olympics to Bakersfield, CA which was a huge success

- Consultant to and an extra in the TV Movie Night Partners

- Bakersfield, CA accomplishments: Teams/squads: Bomb Squad Member, Defensive Tactics Advisor, SWAT Team/Anti Sniper, Metro/Undercover Drug Enforcement Team, Presidential Candidate Protection Team, Lincoln High Crime Area Enforcement Team, K-9 Team/ Agitator, DUI Enforcement, Recruit and Reserve Trainer, Alliance on family violence (Battered Women's Shelter) Trainer-Liaison, High Crime area Footbeat

- 10th Degree Black Belt in Tracy's Chinese Kenpo (Yudanshakai)

- 2005-2008 Director of Enforcement – Town of Pahrump, NV: Program Developer, Tactics Instructor, Manager-Supervisor, Director of Fall Festival Security and Personal Protection for Entertainers

- 1973-present Schools/Clubs owned: (1) Torrance, CA, (1) Las Vegas, NV, (1) Tonopah, NV, (2) Bakersfield, CA, (1) Pahrump, NV

- Learned to interact with celebrities of all kinds through performing protection details. Examples include: Muhammad Ali, Jimmy Conners, Chris Evert, Tom Jones, Frank Sinatra, Sammy Davis, Jr, The Osmonds, Elvis Presley, and others

MAJOR ACHIEVEMENTS

- 1978 – Chosen Deputy of the year for distinguished service and valor for Nye County Sheriff Department: Commendation for delivery of a child, Crystal Heart Nominee for saving the life of a Catholic Priest, Father John Geary who suffered a cardiac arrest

- 1985 – Award for effective gang and drug enforcement in high-crime area

- 1991 – Certification of Appreciation from M.A.D.D. (Mothers Against Drunk Drivers)

- 2007 – Inducted as a Charter Member of the Kenpo Hall of Fame – Gathering of the Eagles

- 2008 – Created and taught a system for street survival tactics called ALERT (Attitude for Life Effective Response Training)

- 2008 – Established Fleeman's Fight Federation to teach individuals and groups in the art of self-defense with the slogan "The Polite Animal."

- 2011 – Inducted into the International Martial Arts Council (IMAC) Hall of Fame

- 2011 – Kenpo Lifetime achievement award (Yudanshakai)

- 2015 – IMAC Lifetime achievement award

- 30+ years as a police officer or enforcement officer in Boulder City Police Department, Nye County Sheriff Department, Bakersfield Police Department, and Town of Pahrump, Nevada.

- Former Senior Patrol Street Advisor and Bomb Squad member with Bakersfield Police Department

- Sport Karate Museum—Dragon Image-Joe Lewis Memorial Natural Fighter Award, The History General Award , First Responder - American Hero Award

JEFFREY HELANEY

"Martial arts has inspired me to take the time to get to know those around me and to live my life with intention and positivity."

My father, Wallace G. Helaney, studied martial arts in WWII while in the US Navy. His passion for martial arts carried through my childhood and beyond. In 1969 I was first introduced to martial arts at the Omaha Karate and Judo school in Benson, Nebraska, under the tutelage of GM S.K. Shin (d). I first began taking classes at the urging of my father Wallace G. Helaney (d), who had been a personal friend of GM Shin. What started as a few trial classes quickly grew into what would become a lifelong passion.

What I learned from the journey is there is so much more to martial arts than the physical aspects. It has helped me grow as a person and created a desire to help others. It has been part of my life for almost as long as I can remember.

TRAINING INFORMATION

- Belt Ranks & Martial Arts Styles: 9th Degree Black Belt - Traditional TaeKwon-Do, 5th Degree Black Belt – Hapkido, 5th Degree Black Belt - Sports Karate (ACS), 2nd Degree Black Belt - Poekoelan/ Pent Jak Silat

- Instructors/Influencers: Grandmaster Robert Dunn, Grandmaster Troy Trudeau, GM S.K Shin (d), GM H.U. Lee (d), GM E. Sell (d), GM D. Meyer(d), SM S. Johnson, Master F. VanAkeren, GM S.K. Shin(d), GM J. Pelligrini, GM D. Meyer(d), SM S. Johnson, GM Emeric "Sonny" Scarsella (d), Dr. N. Gerassimakis, GM S.K. Shin (d)

- Birthdate: February 14, 1964

- Birthplace/Growing Up: Omaha, NE

- Yrs. In the Martial Arts: 51 years

- Yrs. Instructing: 38 years

- School Owner, Manager, Instructor

PROFESSIONAL ORGANIZATIONS

- United States Kido Federation (President)

- International Jun Tong Tae Kwon-Do Federation (Advisor to the Board)

- World TaeSool Association/ International PaSaRyu Tae Kwon - Do Federation (Board of Directors)

- World Organization of Martial Arts Athletes (Regional Director)

- Police Self-Defense Institute (International Advisory Board)

I spent the spring and summer of my adult life doing things that most people could not imagine. I saw the best and worst in people. I was tested in ways that are hard to describe and have memories that both haunt and comfort me. I can honestly say that it helped me know myself and what I can endure. Through some of those toughest days, the things I learned through my study of martial arts gave me tools to move forward even when I wanted to give up.

It has taught me that every one of us has a story. It is written in the decisions we make, the lives we lead, the scars we carry, and the people whose lives we impact. Most of us hope that our lives have meaning and that the things we do will have a lasting impression on those whose paths we have crossed.

Martial Arts has introduced me to some of my best friends, taught me that respect is both hard-earned and easily lost, that everyone has a story to tell, that everyone's journey is different, and that how we choose to treat others when "no one" is watching is a reflection of who we are at our core. It has helped me overcome pain, adversity, and gave me the strength to walk away from bad decisions. It is hard not to find a segment of my life that Martial Arts has not impacted in some form. It has inspired me to take the time to get to know those around me and to live my life with intention and positivity.

Last but not least, Martial Arts has allowed me to share my passion with my wife, Michele Helaney, and my daughter, Paige Helaney. This gift has allowed me to spend my life doing what I love, but being able to live it every day with my family.

PERSONAL ACHIEVEMENTS

- International Sport Science Association, PFT #371114
- State of Nebraska Licensed Massage Therapist – License #3474
- Institute of Korean Natural Health, Doctor of Science Oriental Medicine
- American Alternative Medical Association – Board Certification #66402412
- Training Center for the Academy of Traditional Chinese Medicine – Medboo, OM/Acupuncture Certificates A-G
- North American Hombu Hakko-Ryu Jujitsu Federation – KoKoDo Shiatsu Basic Certification
- American Massage Therapy Association – Professional Member
- American Association of Acupuncture and Oriental Medicine – Professional Member
- Assistant Chief of Police (Retired)
- International Association of Chiefs of Police (IACP) Retired Member

MAJOR ACHIEVEMENTS

- 2019 - Who's Who in Martial Arts Legends Award
- 2005 – Budo Magazine's Hall of Fame: Grand Master of the Year – Tae Kwon-Do
- 2004 – Ohio Department of Education: Partnering in Progress Award
- 2004 – Professional Karate Commission's Ohio Black Belt Hall of Fame: Inductee
- 2004 – Ne-De-U-Kan-Tae Federation: Outstanding Contributions to the Martial Arts

MAJOR ACHIEVEMENTS

- 2003 – World Wide Martial Arts Hall of Fame: Master Instructor of the Year Award
- 2003 – World Martial Arts Hall of Fame: Induction Award, honorary title and degree Professor of Martial Arts (Ph.D./MA) awarded, and appointment to the Hall of Fame Board
- 2002 – North American Black Belt Hall of Fame: Most Distinguished Martial Artist of the Year
- 2002 – Action Martial Arts Magazine: Outstanding Contributions to the Martial Arts and 2002/2003 Trading Card
- 2002 – World Wide Martial Arts Hall of Fame: Outstanding Organization of the Year for Kick Drugs Out of Alliance Program
- 2001 – World Wide Martial Arts Hall of Fame: Master Instructor of the Year
- 2001 – Team Power Master's Hall of Fame: Inspiration Award
- 2001 – North American Black Belt Hall of Fame: Outstanding Contributions to the Martial Arts
- 2001 – Alliance Board of Education: Commendation for Excellence in Education
- 2001 – National Exchange Club, Alliance Chapter: Police Officer of the Year, Service to Youth
- 2000 – USA Karate Federation and US Jujitsu Federation Hall of Fame: Sadaki Nakabayashi Award for Community Service
- 1998 – United Martial Artists Association Black Belt Hall of Fame: Outstanding Contributions to the Martial Arts
- Contributor multiple periodical TaeKwon-Do Times, Budo Magazine, Grandmaster, etc.
- Contributor (book) Dim Mak by Vincent Lyn
- Contributor (video) Dim Mak with Vincent Lyn
- Producer, Director, Host (television show - 13 Episodes) Just for Kicks: Martial Arts for Everyone
- Producer, Director (television show - 13 Episodes) Focus on Fit Producer, Director, Host (television special) Omaha National Martial Arts Championship
- Host (television special) Alliance Drug Free Open Martial Arts Tournament
- Appearance (television show – 2 Episodes) To Serve and Protect: The Real Story
- Appearance (television show – 1 Episode) America's Dumbest Criminals

GUY JAMES

"The martial arts have given me self-confidence from skill development and a mindset to achieve, win, and overcome obstacles."

TRAINING INFORMATION

- Belt Ranks & Martial Arts Styles: American Karate, 9th Degree Black Belt

- Instructors/Influencers: Master Shelbron Barnes, Grand Master Pat Burleson, Grand Master Richard Morris

- Birthdate: September 14, 1955

- Birthplace/Growing Up: Cleburne, TX

- Yrs. In the Martial Arts: 58 years

- Yrs. Instructing: 27 years

- Retired School Owner

PROFESSIONAL ORGANIZATIONS

- World Martial Arts Ranking Association

PERSONAL ACHIEVEMENTS

- Branch President and Board Member, First State Bank of Rio Vista, Texas

- Senior V. President of Community Bank

- Currently, Senior V. President of Lending for Pinnacle Bank

- As a professional musician, wrote and performed "Black Belt Dream for the National Sport Karate Museum

In 2020, I am blessed from a lifetime of the great friends I have made through martial arts and the great lessons from mentors, peers, and students involved in learning and teaching and sharing.

I believe that the opportunity to learn, grow, and improve exists right now. In the summer of 2020, and at the age of 65, I adopted a practice followed by my instructor's instructor, the great Grand Master Jhoon Rhee, and I do 1000 pushups daily added to my daily training. The discipline I follow is never to miss a day, the Good Lord willing. I am a Christian martial artist, and I give credit to health and happiness to my Lord and Savior, Jesus Christ. and daily count my blessings and like to encourage other Christian martial art leaders to share the gospel with their circle of influence.

MAJOR ACHIEVEMENTS

- 1993 Sport Karate International World Champion
- 1994 National Black Belt League Title
- 1998 Texas National Tour Heavy Wt. Champion
- 2001 Pioneer Presenter at George Minshew's/Zulfi Ahmed World Masters Symposium
- 2012 Dragon Image fighting Award from Sport Karate Museum
- 2013 Inducted into the USA Martial Arts Hall of Fame
- 2015 Joe Lewis Fighting Award for Sport Karate Museum
- 2015 History General Award
- 2015 guest speaker, Legends Roast and Sport Karate Gathering
- 2016- present, a performer at Legends Roast/Sport Karate Museum
- 2017 History General of the Year Award
- 2017 Inducted in Who's Who in the Martial Arts Hall of Fame- Legends Award
- 2018 AMAA Eagle Award
- 2019 Promoted to 9th Degree Black Belt by Grandmaster Pat Burleson
- 2020 Action Martial Arts Hall of Honors- Esteemed Modern Warrior

I started my martial arts training as a child in 1962, studying Judo, and in 1965 began training in Korean Karate/ Taekwon-Do as taught by Allen Steen and the Texas Karate Institute. In my youth, I was fascinated by the martial arts for self-defense and develop confidence and an ability to learn that transcended even beyond martial arts. After earning my 1st Dan training under Shelbron Barnes, I furthered my training through Pat Burleson and was promoted to advanced degrees under GM Pat Burleson and GM Richard Morris. My primary arts are American Karate and Taekwon-do, and I have cross-trained in Jiu-Jitsu.

Mainly, I have gleaned a system and approach to learning, starting from martial arts, that expands to all areas of learning. This particularly led to a philosophy for me, which GM Pat Burleson gave me a name for my philosophy, "TaeSabaki." I have embraced the mind, body, and spirit training as a way of life. In my uniques skill set as a professional businessman, clinical hypnotherapist, and martial artist, I have used this philosophy to train martial artists, financial professionals, sports players, musicians, and others in numerous endeavors.

As a speaker and presenter, I bring martial arts philosophy and training as a great way of development training. Currently, I help numerous people with direct service as a commercial lender in the banking industry, which I have served for 45 years.

Formerly, I was the owner/operator of "James Karate" in Johnson County, Texas, and have trained sport karate champions. Also, I conducted self-defense and martial arts workshops and seminars with GM Pat Burleson and was a trainer and a pioneer presenter at the Masters World Symposium.

I still do civic and group presentations.

The martial arts have given me self-confidence from skill development and a mindset to achieve, win, and overcome obstacles. They have provided me a discipline and philosophy, providing me a life-long endeavor and pursuit producing health, wealth, and mental well-being. I have enjoyed sharing my knowledge with others to enhance their lives.

RODNEY KAUFFMAN

"Martial Arts has given me confidence to believe in myself, always to do my best and never give up."

TRAINING INFORMATION

- Belt Ranks & Martial Arts Styles: NE--DU-U-KON-TAE Karate Kung Fu; 9th Dan Black Belt, Tae Kwon Do; 8th Dan Black Belt, Bladed Weapons, Escrima, Kali; Instructor certification, Ch'Uang Chuan Pai Chinese Boxing; 9th Level Black Sash, Shao Lin Kung Fu Lung Fa, Chinese Kempo and Kick Boxing; two years training

- Instructors/Influencers: GM Yeen Lee Chong , Chen My Chow, Master Mike Brown, GM David M. Grago Sr., GM Frank Morris Jr., Marty Boyd, Master Nick Desantze, Master Al Fuzzy, GM Jeffrey Helaney, GM Troy Trudeau

- Birthdate: October 3, 1959

- Birthplace/Growing Up: Canton, OH

- Yrs. In the Martial Arts: 54 years

- Yrs. Instructing: 43 years

- School owner (Kaufman Self Defense Academy), Instructor

PROFESSIONAL ORGANIZATIONS

- American Karate Black Belt Association, Chin Sook Hage Kwan.

- Don Willis International

- United States Kido Federation

- World Tae Sool Association

I started martial arts because a couple of my friends were taking Kung Fu and the other one was taking Tae Kwon Do. They were older than I was but I would go to class with them any time I got a chance. I was really amazed at all the things they could do with kicks, punches, weapons, self-defense and forms (katas). They would show me moves and I would practice what they showed me! My parents knew I was very interested and decided to put me in class! Our instructor was very strict and very traditional. When we would go to tournaments, I would be so mesmerized by all the events and respect that was shown by all the competitors, judges and instructors. As well as the knowledge of all the black belts and masters which made me want to learn and train even harder. I loved to watch Kung Fu movies with Bruce Lee and Chuck Norris. My parents were very strict and I always had to do extra chores and help neighbors and relatives to make money to pay for my classes, uniforms, weapons, and equipment.

Martial Arts has helped me in all aspects of my life. As a parent, employee, employer, and citizen. Not just in my martial arts career, but in my construction business, law enforcement career, and professional career. It has given me confidence to believe in myself, always to do my

PROFESSIONAL ORGANIZATIONS

- International Martial Arts Council
- CH'UANG CHUN PAI- Wing Pai Federation International
- United States Police Defensive Tactics Association National Youth Gang Task Force
- Associated Special Investigators and Police International
- United Artist Association
- Philippines Karate Union
- Ohio Peace Officers Training Council
- PKA World Wide Association
- Tang Soo Do Karate Association
- GO- KAU Self Defense Association

PERSONAL ACHIEVEMENTS

- To become a respected student, martial artist, instructor, citizen, tournament promoter, law enforcement training officer, and most of all humble. To become someone that can make a difference in young children and fellow martial artist life and all my peers can say that Mr. Kauffman is a true martial artist and friend!!

MAJOR ACHIEVEMENTS

- Many time local, state, national and international competitor
- 1992 Promoted to Captain for the Associated Special Investigators and Police International
- 1998 Karate Kickboxing Hall of Fame Law Enforcement Training Officer/ Instructor of the year

treat everyone with respect, and always, no matter what decision you make in life, always be able to look in the mirror and be ok with what you see and how you can live with your decision!

MAJOR ACHIEVEMENTS

- 2005 Kick Drugs Out of Alliance Outstanding Service Award
- 2003 USA Martial Arts Hall of Fame Legend / Landmark Award
- 2004 United States Martial Arts Hall of Fame Instructor of the year
- 2009 World Head of Sokeship Council International Hall of Fame Instructor Of the year
- 2013 United States Kido Federation Hall of Fame Diamond Lifetime Achievement
- 2017 United States Martial Arts Hall of Fame Pioneer Award

PHILIP LEE

"Martial Arts made me do a complete turn-around to become better at everything!"

TRAINING INFORMATION

- Belt Ranks & Martial Arts Styles: Grand Master - Art of Fluid Adaption, Tae kwon Do - 7th Dan, Hapkido - 2nd Dan, PaSaRyu - 3rd Dan, Kenpo - 1st Dan, Shotokan - Brown Belt, Tang Soo Do - Blue Belt, Hungar Kung Fu - Blue Sash, Muy Thai - 3 years training, Krav Maga - 6 years

- Instructors/Influencers: My Dad, H.P. Lee, Dan Smith, Stan Wigginton, Kang Rhee, Dale Hertzfield, Skip Beard, Benny Green, Bob Kendall, H.Tillman, Ken Eubanks

- Birthdate: September 11, 1952

- Birthplace/Growing Up: Selmer & Michie, TN

- Yrs. In the Martial Arts: 59 years

- Yrs. Instructing: 50 years

- School owner

PROFESSIONAL ORGANIZATIONS

- PKA

- World Black Belt Bureau

- Black Belt Schools International

- The Alliance

- US Head of Family Martial Arts Association

- Rskc

- NASKA

- SEKAA

My dad had to protect himself one day and I saw him apply his martial arts skills to a group of three men and it was over in a few seconds. I wanted to be like him. That is what got me into Martial Arts. He trained me until he passed away and left me at the age of 9 with my interest at an all-time high. I continued to study the art.

I was quiet and shy when I was a kid. My interest in any type of martial arts grew to wanting to have more and more training. I started training in my first official school when I was seventeen. Before that, I was training with my cousin in the backyard. When I got into an official school, my personality started to get stronger. I began to go to the front of the class. I made more noise than anyone else. I was chosen to be the assistant instructor. I was getting more and more confident. In college, I began to do public speaking. The confidence I gained was awesome. I began to compete in tournaments. At one point, I was on stage performing kata in front of five thousand people.

PERSONAL ACHIEVEMENTS

- 1974- I graduated college and opened my first business.

- 1976- I got married and produced two amazing sons.

- 1974-1989- I kept my business going for 15 years.

- 1996- I met a very independent woman who became my wife of 22 years. She is my friend and business partner. We raised her daughter and have 2 grandkids. I am very lucky to have such a great group of family to be around. So, thanks to my wife Rhonda; my two sons, Chris and Jesse; my daughter, Lauren and my three grandkids, Ally, Lilly, and Raelyn.

MAJOR ACHIEVEMENTS

- 1973- I opened my first commercial karate studio.

- 1978- I owned 4 commercial schools.

- 1990- My first year promoting an open karate tournament,

- 2000- I was awarded 5 Star Diamond with United Professionals

- 2007- Martial Artist of the Year/ Alliance,

- 2009- Instructor of the Year/ Alliance,

- 2009- I received my Doctorate in Martial Arts Science,

- 2010- US Martial Arts Hall of Fame/Tae Kwon Do Master,

- 2012- I received my 10th Dan/ Grandmaster/Soke ,

- 2018- I became a member of Black Belt Schools International

So, how has it made an impact? I went from being a shy kid to performing in front of five thousand people. It made me do a complete turn-around to become better at everything!

MAJOR ACHIEVEMENTS

- 2019- Joined PKA

- 2019- I got inducted into the Martial Arts Masters & Pioneers Book

- 2020- Became a lifetime member of PKA Worldwide

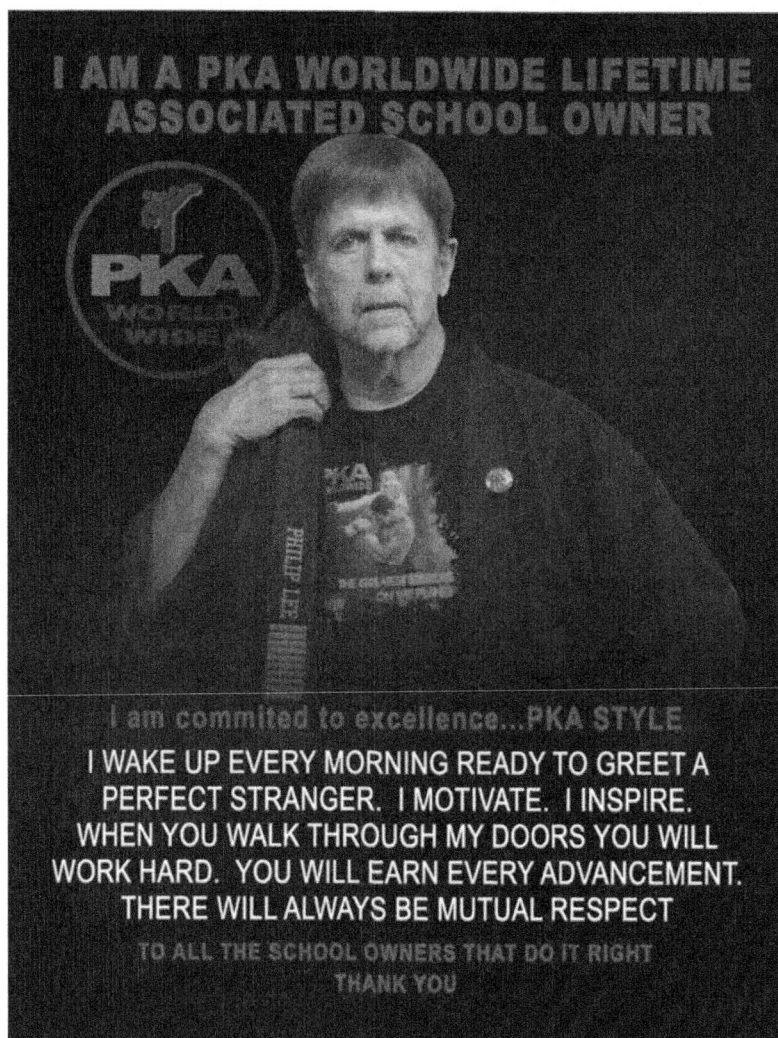

I AM A PKA WORLDWIDE LIFETIME ASSOCIATED SCHOOL OWNER

I am commited to excellence...PKA STYLE

I WAKE UP EVERY MORNING READY TO GREET A PERFECT STRANGER. I MOTIVATE. I INSPIRE. WHEN YOU WALK THROUGH MY DOORS YOU WILL WORK HARD. YOU WILL EARN EVERY ADVANCEMENT. THERE WILL ALWAYS BE MUTUAL RESPECT

TO ALL THE SCHOOL OWNERS THAT DO IT RIGHT
THANK YOU

SIJO JOE MARTIN

"My journey through Martial Arts made it possible for me to be motivated by many true Masters of Martial Arts..."

Martial Arts was recommended to me by a close friend. Martial Arts teaches one to be yourself in a world where everyone is doing their best to influence you to be what they deem best. It requires living as a warrior, embracing courage, integrity, confidence, tenacity and risk. My journey through Martial Arts made it possible for me to be motivated by many true Masters of Martial Arts to acquire, assimilate and live as a warrior the unique individual that is the TRUE ME.

PROFESSIONAL ORGANIZATIONS

- Healing Tao USA Instructor's Association
- Universal Healing Tao Thailand Instructors Association
- International Black Belt Association, Lebanon
- Worldwide Association for Chinese Internal Martial Arts
- American Chinese Chi Gong Acupressure Association
- Co-founder of World Wushu Tui Shou Society
- Founder of Center for Holistic Instruction, LLC

TRAINING INFORMATION

- Belt Ranks & Martial Arts Styles: Goju-Ryu/Isshin-ryu Karate (1st degree Brown), Li Ka Kung Fu (Choy Ka, Kam Ka Hong Ka) 2nd Start Black Sash (4th degree black belt), Hong Chun Kung Fu (4th Degree Black Sash), Chun Li Kung Fu (4th Degree Black Sash), Sil Lum Fa Kung Fu (4th Degree Black Sash), Old Yang Style Tai Chi Chuan, Sifu - No ranking system, Certified Tai Chi Chuan Instructor from Universal Healing Tao, Thailand - No ranking system, Head founder, Sijo - Esoma Kung Fu Grandmaster 6th degree (Only 5 working ranks in this system)

- Instructors/Influencers: Bob Alexander, (student of Don Nagle), Alfredo Sui (top student of Li Kum San - Lima Peru), Harry Shupla, (step father of Roy Jerry Hobbs), George Phipps, John Stover (student of Albert Church), Todd Qian, (Student and son of Qian Timing), Mantak Chia (student of Taoist hermit Yi Eng know as `One Cloud`), All of the above to develop Esoma Kung Fu, George Xu (USA), Volker Jung (Germany), John Farris (USA), Lui Bao Yu (China), Zhao Ya Jun (China)

- Birthdate: January 13, 1950

- Birthplace/Growing Up: York, SC / Gastonia, NC

- Yrs. In the Martial Arts: 56 years

- Yrs. Instructing: 53 years

- School owner, Manager, Instructor

PERSONAL ACHIEVEMENTS

- Husband, Father, Grandfather, Great-grandfather
- Survived fighting a "bear".
- Healing Arts related Acupuncture system, qi energy manipulation and economical mobility
- Graduate of The Therapeutic Massage Training Institute
- Developer of Esomassage and Tai Chi Massage (Using the principles of Tai Chi and the hand-striking position of Kung Fu for healing
- Certified Charka Technician by the World Institute of Technologies for Healing, A.I.S.B.L.
- Recognition from the Tree of Light Institute, Inc. for the Body System's Approach to Natural Healing
- Touch for Health I – IV – Certified by the International Kinesiology College (IKC)
- Professional Kinesiology Practice (PKP) Level I
- Reiki
- Founder of the Center for Holistic Instruction, LLC

MAJOR ACHIEVEMENTS

- Recognized by Shaolin Kempo Karate Society, International as Head founder of Esoma Kung Fu 1985
- Grand Master of the Year 2004 by World Head of Family Sokeship Council International
- Developer of Esoma Kung Fu
- Developer of PowerPlus Martial Art Secrets
- Developer of Tai Chi for the Living Room
- Legends of Carolina Martial Arts 2018
- At 69 years of age, on no pharmaceutical medications, no surgeries, never been hospitalized.

GM VIC MOORE

"Martial Arts helped me develop into a better person and gave me more discipline."

TRAINING INFORMATION

- Belt Ranks & Martial Arts Styles: 10th Degree Black Belt
- Instructors/Influencers: Ron Williams, Bill Demetri, Robert Trias, Mhung gi
- Birthdate: August 23, 1943
- Birthplace/Growing Up: Indianapolis, IN/ Cincinnati, OH
- Yrs. In the Martial Arts: 70 years
- Yrs. Instructing: 60 years
- School owner, Instructor

PROFESSIONAL ORGANIZATIONS

- United States Karate Association
- Traditional World Karate Association
- Black Dragon Fighting Association

I watched the Ku Klux Klan ban black folks and I wanted to be able to protect myself. Martial Arts looked like a lot of fun. Hard work, but a lot of fun. I wanted to be a world champion.

The Martial Arts helped me develop into a better person and gave me more discipline. It made me have more determination. I succeeded in football, track, and national championship teams. I ran the winning touchdown in an all-state championship, and also ran in a championship. I was on a gymnastics team that went all state. We had three teams that won state championships: football, track and gymnastics.

PERSONAL ACHIEVEMENTS

- 1965- Beat Mike Foster and became the first grand national champion in the world. Mike Foster was undefeated, USKA Grand national in Miami FL.

- 1967- Defeated Bruce Lee in a match of speed at the internationals in California

- 1968- Defeated Joe Lewis to become the first world pro champion

MAJOR ACHIEVEMENTS

- 1966- Defeated the all Hawaiian champion for the world championship

- 1967- Defeated Chuck Norris at the internationals in California.

- 1969- Defeated Jim Kelley at the team championships. Also defeated my idol, Mike Stone who was undefeated with 91 straight victories, for the light heavyweight champion of the world

- 1970- Defeated Superfoot Bill Wallace for the USKA World Championship in San Antonio Texas

- 1975- first person to train a chimpanzee to do karate and went to tournaments

1967

Vic Moore and Chuck Norris, Two Top Champions Vic defeated Chuck Norris at Ed Parker's International Tournament in California.

PAUL ORTINO

"The martial arts has been a blessing to me and I want to share the traditions with all who want to learn."

TRAINING INFORMATION

- Belt Ranks & Martial Arts Styles: Hanshi,9th Degree Black Belt Okinawa Kenpo Karate Karate (GM Seikichi Odo,GM Richard Gonzalez), 9th degree black belt (GM Robert Dunn Taekwondo), 6th Dan Hawaii Karate Ko-danshakai(GM Bobby Lowe,GM James Miyaji), 3rd Degree Black Belt Red Dragon Karate (GM Al Smith), 3rd Degree Black Belt Shotokan Karate, 3rd Degree Black Belt Chi lin Chuan Fa

- Instructors/Influencers: GM Seikichi Odo Okinawa Kenpo Karate (10th Dan), GM Robert Dunn Tackwondo (9th Dan), GM Al Smith Red Dragon Karate (10th Dan)

- Birthdate: July 13, 1954

- Birthplace/Growing Up: Philadelphia PA / HI, FL, NC / Las Vegas, NV

- Yrs. In the Martial Arts: 51 years

- Yrs. Instructing: 45 years

- President and Chief Instructor (Okinawa Kenpo Karate Dharma-Ryu Dojo)

I began my Martial Arts study when I was 13 in Judo because I wasn't that big and was getting into fights a lot with what we now call bullies. Wanting to be able to defend myself, I pleaded with my parents to let me take martial arts. I then started taking karate in Reading, PA and never stopped.

Everywhere I moved I signed up for Karate, Taekwondo or Kung Fu. The funny thing was that the better I got the less fights I was getting into. Having Senseis such as Robert Dunn (Taekwondo), Al Smith (Red Dragon), Charlie Lewchalermwong (Shotokan) and finally Richard Gonzalez and Seikichi Odo (Okinawa Kenpo) I was taught the principles of Karate as well. I realized that it was better to walk away from a fight not because I was afraid of getting hurt but because I really didn't want to hurt someone else. The Martial Arts taught me to be humble, respectful and to refrain from violent behavior.

PROFESSIONAL ORGANIZATIONS

- Ryu Kyu Hon Kenpo Kobujutsu Association (BOD)
- American Martial Arts Alliance
- Hawaii Karate Kondanshakai (original member)
- Hawaii Karate Congress (former President)
- Seishinkai Karate Union (former Shibucho to Hawaii- GM Robert Burgermeister, Kaicho)
- Pennsylvania Black Belt Society
- Florida Black Belt Association

PERSONAL ACHIEVEMENTS

- Won Triple Crown -1st place kata, weapons, kumite (GM James Miyaji tournament/Waipahu HI)
- Rated in the top 10 kata, weapons and kumite in the Hawaii Karate Congress annual ratings
- Represented USA at GM Ken Funakoshi's Annual tournament San Jose CA Kumite division
- Made 4 DVDs of the Okinawa Kenpo System as taught by GM Seikichi Odo
- Martial Arts Representative for the "Strike Back Training System"
- Co-founded Florida Academy of Judo-Karate with Master Don Rosenthal 1978

In the beginning I just wanted to protect myself but after I started training, I realized there was so much more to karate than meets the eye. It became a way of life. I no longer wanted to fight other people and was able to walk away feeling confident about myself. From the moment I entered the dojo of GM George Dillman back in the late 60's I wanted to become a Black Belt. Even before I became a Black Belt, I was an assistant instructor.

I wanted to help others get their self-confidence back and be able to protect themselves. I believed that every man, woman and child should learn to protect themselves and my wife Daisy, my daughters Cheryl, Sherry Anne and Shanelle all became Black Belts and helped me teach in Hawaii. My son Angelo is working his way to being a Black Belt one day. The family that trains together stays together.

Now I travel throughout the United States to do seminars on self-defense and karate. The martial arts has been a blessing to me and I want to share the traditions with all who want to learn.

MAJOR ACHIEVEMENTS

- Former President of the Hawaii Karate Congress
- Karate Commissioner for the Aloha State Games (1990-2003)
- Taught all branches of the US Military in Hawaii for 26 years
- Promoted to 9th Degree Black Belt, Hanshi June 10th 2010
- Co-founded the UNC-Greensboro Karate Club under the direction of Master Charlie Lewchalermwong 1972
- 2019- awarded " The History General Award" by Professor Gary Lee and the Sport Karate Museum

JERRY OTTO

> "If I am an Ambassador of anything, it is to teach the ethnic children in my communities..."

My interest in martial arts began in Taiwan as a teenager in 1965 when my step-father was stationed in Taiwan. I studied a local style of Chinese Kung Fu in a small village on Yamingshan Mountain, outside of Taipei. After returning to the United States in 1973, I began formal training in the art of Korean Tai-Kwon Do. The next year I undertook studies in two other styles, Okinawan Shorin-Ryu and Chinese Kempo at the Red Dragon Karate Dojo, Easton Pennsylvania. In 1978, I was promoted to 1st Degree Black Belt and credit Grandmaster Paul Ortino, now 9th Degree Grand Master of Okinawan Kenpo Karate Dharma-Ryu Dojo in Las Vegas, as being most instrumental, in my early years of development. Through the years, I trained with great martial artists like GM Ed Hartzell and GM Nimr Hassan. I became a student of the renown, GM Tadashi Yamashita, in the early '90s and have continued with his teachings in Okinawa Shorin-Ryu.

If I am an Ambassador of anything, it is to teach the ethnic children in my communities, the skills to handle the ugly hatred and racism in our world today. It is not if it will happen; it is when it will happen. It is my mission

TRAINING INFORMATION

- Belt Ranks & Martial Arts Styles: Grand Master of Shen Dragon Karate Dojo, Hanshi Dan, Okinawa Kempo, 4th Dan, Chi Ling Pai, 4th Dan, Krav Maga Instruction

- Instructors/Influencers: Grand Master Tadashi Yamashita

- Birthdate: August 2, 1950

- Birthplace/Growing Up: Baltimore, MD / Taiwan / Germany

- Yrs. In the Martial Arts: 52years

- Yrs. Instructing: 42 years

- School owner, Manager, Instructor, St. Thomas, US Virgin Islands

PROFESSIONAL ORGANIZATIONS

- United Taekwondo Association

- Martial Arts Association (Gary Alexander, Founder)

- United Karate Kung Fu Association, (Lou Cassamassa, Founder)

- Oriental Defensive Arts Association, (Master Condi)

PROFESSIONAL ORGANIZATIONS

- West Virginia Chinese Martial Arts Association, (Master Denis Decker)

- East Coast International Kosho-Shorie Association, (Master Nimr Hassan)

- U.S. Tang Sho Dau Chinese Martial Arts Federation (Master Steve L. Martin)

- Yamashita International Martial Arts Association, (Hanshi Tadashi Yamashita)

- Okinawa Kenpo Karate Kobudo Dharma-Ryu Dojo. (Grand Master Paul Ortino)

- Kenpo Jujutsu Ryu Kosho Kenpo Ryu Schools and Temples (Grand Master Edward Hartzell)

- Victory Martial Arts International Council – Lifetime Member (Grand Master Jason Victory)

- American Martial Art Alliance – Charter Member (Grandmaster Jessie Bowen)

- Action Martial Arts Magazine – Hall of Honors- Alan Goldberg

PERSONAL ACHIEVEMENTS

- AMAA Who's Who in the Martial Arts, "Hall of Fame" Legends Award 2017

- Nominated to the World Head of Family Sokeship Council 2017

- Action Karate Magazine "Hall of Honors" Golden Lifetime Achievement Award - 2018

- Joe Lewis "Eternal Warrior Award" "Battle of Atlanta 50th Anniversary" 2018

in life, to teach these children the necessary skill sets to prepare physically (fighting skills), mentally (focus), emotionally (remaining calm), and spiritually (inner peace) for when they encounter this unfortunate situation. Our training program is beyond preparing for a "Bully." We prepare them with social and intellectual skills, self-confidence, and self-respect, which are the two main ingredients to survive racist slurs or innuendos. We prepare our children with the skills that will be with them for the rest of their lives.

I am a world traveler who has lived and worked in many countries, cultures, and ethnic communities. This diversity has opened my eyes to humanity, love, compassion, and a deep understanding of how we are all connected as one people, sharing the world as our home. While traveling and living among these beautiful people, I have had the privilege of sharing my martial arts, with thousands of people, from almost every race and religion, on this planet. But, the one thing I have found that united me within these cultures is my martial arts. I have trained notables like Chief Hillary Frederick (RIP) of the Caribe Tribe, in Dominica, to protecting His Holiness, the Dalia Lama, at the Buddhist Learning Temple, in Washington, NJ. I have had the privilege of training under the renowned Grand Master Tadashi Yamashita and with lifelong friends like Grand Master Paul Ortino and Grand Master Ed Hartzell. My training has always been hard, vigorous, and dedicated to the one common goal, to perfect my skills and to teach the true meaning of the Martial Arts. I hope my efforts enlightened and fulfilled the needs of the many.

PERSONAL ACHIEVEMENTS

- AMAA "Eagle Alumni Award" Who's Who in the Martial Arts – 2018
- Action Karate Magazine "Hall of Honors" Esteem Martial Artist Award - 2019
- AMAA Charter Member – Shen Dragon Karate Dojo – 2018 – 2019 - 2020
- AMAA Advisory Board Member – 2018 - 2019
- Martial Arts School of the Year Award, Shen Dragon Karate Dojo, Who's Really Who, Martial Arts Masters & Pioneers, AMAA – 2019
- AMAAF "Ambassador of the Year" for the Caribbean Island Region - 2020

MAJOR ACHIEVEMENTS

- Founded Shen Dragon Karate Dojo, 1981
- Teacher of the Year USKKA 1986
- National Competitor of the Year USKKA 1987
- Ranked 3rd Senior Blackbelt Forms in U.S. & Canada PKL & NASKA 1987
- Ranked 1st in U.S. & Canada in Men's Senior Blackbelt Forms NASKA 1988
- Ranked 1st in U.S. & Canada in Men's Senior Blackbelt Weapons NASKA 1988
- Ranked 1st in U.S. & Canada in Men's Senior Blackbelt Forms PKL 1988
- Ranked 1st in U.S. & Canada in Men's Senior Blackbelt Weapons PKL 1988

MAJOR ACHIEVEMENTS

- PKL "Hall of Fame" "Senior Competitor of the Year PKL 1988
- Undefeated Two Division Champion Forms & Weapons
- Ranked 1st in U.S. & Canada in Men's Senior Blackbelt Forms PKL 1989
- Ranked 1st in U.S. & Canada in Men's Senior Blackbelt Weapons PKL 1989
- Executive Committee Players Commissioner PKL 1990-91

Doug Pierre

"I would truly recommend any discipline to anyone who is seeking a better life for themselves without fear or self-imposed restrictions..."

TRAINING INFORMATION

- Belt Ranks & Martial Arts Styles: Atillo Balintawak Saavedra Eskrima – Inheritor, Modern Arnis - 8th Dan, Soul Goju - 8th Dan, Chen Wei Gun Tai Chi - Certified Sifu, Yahming Esoteric Blade Art - Full Instructor, Universal Tae Kwon Do - 3rd Dan, Amok International Blade Fighters Guild – Instructor, Myama Ryu Jujitsu (Comb. Jujitsu/judo/aikido) - 2nd Brown, Yan Ja Pei - Muay Thai, Dragon Society International - Pressure Point Student

- Instructors/Influencers: GM Remy Presas, GM Crespulo Atillo, GM Chen Wei Gun, GM Inocencio Glaraga, GM Judah Maccabe, GM Anthony Powell, GM Tom Sotis, GM Otis Harris, GM Carter Wong, GM Tom Muncy/Rick Moneymaker

- Birthdate: August 28, 1947

- Birthplace/Growing Up: Harlem & South Bronx, NY

- Yrs. In the Martial Arts: 50 years

- Yrs. Instructing: 40 years

- School owner (Village Mixed Martial Arts Institute), Manager, Instructor

Until the age of 10, I lived in Harlem, New York. I had a great deal of adventure growing up. It was my inquisitive nature that got me in trouble. I went to a Catholic school until the 5th grade. For those unfamiliar, my hands were made tough in school from the beatings measured out by the nuns.

It wasn't until the 6th grade in a public school that the fighting and the need to know how took hold. So much so I was shipped off to a Catholic boy's home, and there I was surrounded by hundreds of boys from everywhere. There I played every sport, learned a variety of trades, and academics were highly emphasized. My favorite was learning boxing from one of the Jesuit brothers in charge of our cottage.

After two years back home, we moved to the South Bronx, and the boxing came in handy. I would have to fight because of my academic mindset

PROFESSIONAL ORGANIZATIONS

- International Modern Arnis Federation
- World Balintawak Arnis/Eskrima Association
- Yahming Kali/Eskrima/Arnis Blade esoteric Arts Association
- Guangdong Wu Shu Federation
- European Sin Moo Hapkido
- W.U.K.O. (World Union of Karatedo Organization
- Amok Blade Fighters Guild
- MAGIC (Martial Arts Grandmasters International
- NBLA (New Breed life Arts Association)
- U.S. BUDO KAI KAN

PERSONAL ACHIEVEMENTS

- 2x International Gold medalist
- 6x International Silver medalist
- 7x National Gold medalist
- 5x National Silver medalist
- Being the oldest living full contact stick fighter
- Produced 3 beautiful children
- Traveled to more than 20 countries
- Wrote a book not published yet. Coming soon
- Started a new business

from the boy's home. I played HS football, but when I started college, I was exposed to Judo that the seed of this journey began, I was 23. I played with this for a short time. I watched a national geographic program about Karate. I watched men in white pajamas breaking wood, stone, chopping the heads off bottles, catching live swords with their bare hands. I wanted to do and learn from that moment.

I moved to the Lower Eastside of Manhattan, which was known for its fierce martial arts fighters, schools, biker gangs, thugs, drug dealers, community activists, an integrated mix of cultures, and creativity. I threw myself into the art head first, and it has been a never-ending journey of self-discovery, from friends from around the world. I appeared in books, magazines, movies, training world champions, became a pillar in my community, and owned my school in New York City. None of this would have happened had I not studied martial arts and had the privilege of studying and learning from some great martial arts masters and people.

MAJOR ACHIEVEMENTS

- President R.A.I.N. a consortium of homesteaders on the lower East Side (600 members)
- President F.L.O.W. (Freer Living Our Way) H.D.F.C.
- Taking over a drug infested building from drug dealers to owning it
- Owning my martial arts school in New York
- Going to India to be in a movie (Johnny 2005)
- Traveling to several countries teaching and studying
- Being featured in several books, magazine and newspaper articles
- Creating "FORCE 12" an all Women's program of self-offense
- Appearing at the APOLLO in New York to perform Arnis for the first time with other Martial Artists
- Appearing on ABC News day time show teaching and demonstrating Arnis in Penn Station N. Y.

If my life hadn't taken this winding turn, I would have missed so much. I stay in the martial arts for two great opportunities, one to help others. The other, more importantly, to continue to grow and develop as a person. Only then can I contribute to society. There is a vast amount of knowledge gained by the study of Martial Arts. It goes beyond the basic physical things like forms training (kata's) and self-defense techniques that may never be used because most martial artists don't live in violent neighbors, or they avoid these kinds of confrontations. It is the other things for me that fascinate me to no end. It entails nutrition, pressure point science study, biology, math, politics that affect your daily life and your students, anatomy, psychology, physics, healing, plants, animals, your relationship with the planet and to the universe. I could never get bored with martial arts; there is too much to master, especially being YOURSELF.

My reason is very clear; Martial Arts have enriched my life significantly. I would recommend this practice to anyone. As for me, I will be a white belt forever. Knowledge is something to pursue from the cradle to the grave and beyond. I see life as a railroad track that we ride via a train (our body mind and spirit). Along this ride, there are stops where we get off to learn things that prepare us to continue the journey. Too often many people get off a stop, and unfortunately, they stay there and never get back on the train of life. It would explain why people are so rigged in their thoughts. My advice to all is to get back on the train of life and live without fear.

How has studying the martial arts impacted my life? Where do I begin? Before the serious study of Martial Arts, I was shy and an introvert. I didn't want to upset anyone or offend them, so I took a lot of verbal and sometimes physical abuse, so I stayed to myself a lot growing up in Harlem.

The first five years were spent in Catholic school. The 6th year I attended public school, then a Catholic boy's home. My mother insisted on getting a better education but growing up in the hood, that was not the priority, so I fought. I've always been mischievous with an inquisitive mind that also got me into trouble.

Being sent to a boy's home changed my direction. I learned to live with other people, mechanical skills, technical skills, and academic skills.

I participated in all types of sports. Through the study of Martial Arts, I have learned that none of these matters if you are not in control of your life. Most people go along with whatever is fed to them through various methods and means, but as a faithful follower of the way, you gain perseverance, humility, courage, selfless in the service of others. You learn loyalty and the development of a serious fighting spirit. I have learned and gained so much from my study of Martial Arts that I really believe I would never have accomplished all that I have done if not for my studies.

I would truly recommend any discipline to anyone who is seeking a better life for themselves without fear or self-imposed restrictions. The benefits received will amaze you.

Finally, to all my brothers in the art, all too often, we only become interested in the fight scenes. What is interesting and extremely important is the philosophy of what makes a good person and student principal that all too often are missing in our society and culture. These are the tenants that I pattern my life and live by. With that said, keep studying and training from the cradle to the grave.

GRAND MASTER
DOUG PIERRE

JOHN PREVATT

"Studying the Martial Arts has taught me over the years to be humble, care about other people and to be very patient when instructing!"

TRAINING INFORMATION

- Belt Ranks & Martial Arts Styles: American Karate (9th Degree), ATA Tae Kwon Do (4th Degree)

- Instructors/Influencers: GM Soon Ho Lee ATA, GM Young Sun Seo ATA, GM Bill Clark ATA, GM Many Aggrella

- Birthdate: July 31, 1944

- Birthplace/Growing Up: Jacksonville & St. Augustine, FL

- Yrs. In the Martial Arts: 54 years

- Yrs. Instructing: 45 years

- School owner (John Prevatt Karate, John Prevatt Martial Arts USA)

PROFESSIONAL ORGANIZATIONS

- Naska Fame FBBA

In junior college I was introduced to Larry Rhineheart, a Kung Fu Instructor who taught me how to specialize in Take Downs (spinning techniques including back fist) and groin kicks which were legal at that time. I moved to Milwaukee and joined the ATA where I achieved my Black Belt.

Then I opened a martial arts studio in Merritt Island Florida under ATA and expanded into Melbourne, Fl with active testing over 250 students.

I relocated to Tampa, Fl and eventually opened 7 studios where I franchised them out to my Black Belts and they are still open. I presently operate one studio and am considering franchising this one!!

Studying the Martial Arts has taught me over the years to be humble, care about other people and to be very patient when instructing!

I also have a great respect for children and their accomplishments while watching them excel from level to level. In addition, my own life grew as a result of teaching martial arts!

PERSONAL ACHIEVEMENTS

- Ranked # 5 Lightweight Division PKA - Diamond National Winner 1992

- Naska Fighting Champion 1992, 1996 - FBBA and FAME State Champion – 2-time winner New England Championship

- 10-time US Open winner - Empire Nationals

- 2-time Champion - Blue Grass National

- 4-time Champion Capital Classic

- 2-time Champion -Denver Mile High Champion

- Battle Of Atlanta 3 times Champion

- National Karate Competition Champion 1996

MAJOR ACHIEVEMENTS

- Received Lifetime Achievement Award (2001)

- Inducted into The World Karate Union HOF (1996) Inducted into International HOF (1998, 2006, 2007) Inducted into Cosmopolitan HOF (1989, 2002, 2005, 2006) President of Tae Won Do AAU

- Inducted into Universal Martial Arts HOF (2002)

- Inducted into the Outstanding Contribution (2003) Awarded Union Martial Magazines (2005 & 2006) Inducted Alan Goldberg The Action Martial Arts HOF (2006 & 2020)

- Inducted into Preservation of Martial Arts (2006) Ambassador to Martial Arts (2006 & 2007)

MAJOR ACHIEVEMENTS

- Honored In The World of Family Sokeship Council (2006 & 2007)

- 45 years of Martial Arts Award

- Received Highest Honor Shogun Award

- Award to Undefeated US Open Champion

- USA Martial Arts HOF Pioneer Award (2016)

- Lifetime Achievement Award (2019)

SID RAYFORD

"My life has been positively impacted by knowing that I have made a difference in the lives of so many others..."

I began training to keep up with my two older brothers who were practicing punches, kicks, blocks, and forms at the house all of the time. They were also athletes. I had seen team sports, but this was different and it was the most beautiful thing that I had ever seen. They began teaching me at home. In the early 70's, a man began to teach Shito-Ryu Karate in the recreation center of our small town. We joined that dojo and this was my first training in an actual dojo. I have been training ever since.

Studying the martial arts has caused me to meet and become good friends with some of the most extraordinary people in the world. I have met famous martial arts movie stars and attended functions wherein I was honored along with celebrities because we had martial arts in common.

The greatest impact that martial arts has had on my life is the opportunity to serve people by teaching them what I have learned. Doing so has created wonderful and lasting relationships with people that would otherwise not exist. I have had the honor and pleasure of helping people to better themselves through the learning of martial arts, which has created opportunities for them as well. Children that I taught many years

TRAINING INFORMATION

- Belt Ranks & Martial Arts Styles: Shito-Ryu Karate-1st Dan, Matsubayashi Shorin-Ryu-2nd Dan, Kobayashi Shorin-Ryu Karate-9th Dan, Okinawan Kobudo-9th Dan

- Instructors/Influencers: Hanshi Sid Campbell (deceased)

- Birthdate: November 9, 1962

- Birthplace/Growing Up: Hanford & Avenal, CA

- Yrs. In the Martial Arts: 50 years

- Yrs. Instructing: 30 years

- School owner (Rayford Shorin-Ryu Karate & Kobudo of Merced, California)

PROFESSIONAL ORGANIZATIONS

- Vice-President of the World Okinawan Shorin-Ryu Karate & Kobudo Association (WOSKKA)

- President of the American Teachers Association of the Martial Arts (ATAMA)

- Board Member of the World Registry of Black Belts Organizations and Federations (WRBBOF)

PERSONAL ACHIEVEMENTS

- Numerous athletic, scholastic, and music awards throughout high school

- Drum major in band for junior and senior years of high school. Lettered in Football, Basketball, Baseball, and Track and Field all four years of high school

- Participant in Football and Track and Field in College

- Recipient of the Bank of America Music Award upon graduation from high school

MAJOR ACHIEVEMENTS

- Pioneer of Kobayashi Shorin-Ryu to Merced County in Central California

- The only person to have been given a Shihan License from Shorin-Ryu pioneer Hanshi Sid Campbell

- Masters Hall of Fame induction in New Port Beach in 2003 for Lifetime Achievement

- WRBBOF Hall of Fame induction in 2013

- World Masters of Martial Arts Hall of Fame induction in 2018

ago have returned to me as an adult to tell me of the positive difference that training with me has made in their lives.

My life has been positively impacted by knowing that I have made a difference in the lives of so many others; and that some of them have escaped a life of gang membership and crime by developing a sense of self-worth, self-respect, and respect for others while training in my dojo. There has been no greater joy than to make such differences in the lives of those who really had no other chance to succeed in life.

NINDO RYU LEGENDS

忍道流古武術

Kyoshi
Joseph P. Rebelo
Nindo Ryu Kobujutsu

JOSEPH REBELO

"I have studied over 60 styles/systems of martial arts in my career, earning rank in over 22 of them."

TRAINING INFORMATION

- Belt Ranks & Martial Arts Styles: Currently holds the ranks studying several martial arts styles

- Instructors/Influencers: Kenpo: Fred "Ed" E. Hosmer, Tony Cogliandro, Doreen Direnzo [Formerly Cogliandro], Joe Palanzo, Frank Trejo, Ed Parker. Nindo Ryu: Carlos Febres. Kung Fu:Shao Choy Hung Kung Fu-Robert Smith, Wu Tan (Praying Mantis, Tai Chi, Pa Kua,Weaponry) Ed Jata {Jason Tsou Lineage} Kajukenpo Pai Lum :Bill Gregory. Tae Kwon Do/ Tai Chuan Tao: John Gabriel. TAI: David German . Filipino Martial Arts: Remy Presas [Modern Arnis] Rene Navarro {Arnis Lanada, Arnis Abanico Lapunti]

- Birthplace/Growing Up: New Bedford, MA

- Yrs. In the Martial Arts: 52 years

- Yrs. Instructing: 42 years

PROFESSIONAL ORGANIZATIONS

- Member of the Kenpo "Yudanshakai" (Black Belt Society) by GGM Al Tracy

- World Combat Arts Federation-Massachusetts Representative

I stared in the martial arts in 1968, my dad and I were doing Father-Son horseplay and he hit me with a karate chop! Instead of crying, I asked, "What was That?' He said Karate! He then showed me 2 books he had on the subject and told me he was studying with Dave Shuster at the "House of Oyama" dojo in New Bedford. At the time there were no children or women allowed. So he would teach me various aspects of the Kyokushin system.

In 1974, I started training at one of the first United Studios of Self Defense, founded by Fred Villari, under the instruction of Fred E. Hosmer [known as Ed], I got up to my blue belt when the studio when through instructor changes before closing. I found a kung fu studio locally where I met Leo Lacerte. I would later meet John Gabriel at European Health Spa and would train with him for years in the Tai Chuan Tao system. I met Sensei Jack Leonardo of the New Bedford Aikikai and trained with him in Aiki Ken and Aiki Jo. I met Shirfu Edward Jata of the Wu Tang/Wu Tan kung fu tradition from Master Jason Tsou at SMU [Southeastern Massachusetts University]. I reconnected with Jim Gagnon, Assistant Instructor at USSD and completed my Kenpo training, Having him teach at Mr. Lacerte's studio & testing for Black Belt in January of 1983.

PROFESSIONAL ORGANIZATIONS

- Kempo International-USA Vice President & Massachusetts Representative

- United Martial Arts Alliance International-Member & Technical Advisor

- Coalition of Ancestral Martial Arts International -Member & Massachusetts Representative

- Kempo Jutsu International-Member and board member *Member of Society of Ancient Warriors

- Member Lo Lum Combat Arts Society

- Kokusai Nihon Bugei Rengokai-Board Member & Nihon Kempo division Kancho

MAJOR ACHIEVEMENTS

- 1989 KRANE Top Ten is soft style black belt forms

- 1989 PKL Top Ten in black belt forms region 12

- First black belt to place in New England performing Ed Parker Kenpo Forms

- Honored by New Bedford City Council for martial arts career

- Honored by Mayor Fred Kaliz for "Tai Chi Day" in New Bedford

- Action Martial Arts Hall of Honors member "Outstanding contributions to the Martial Arts"

- World Martial Arts Federation Hall of Fame "Historian of the Year"

- Budo International Magazine Hall of Fame

- Kenpo Hall of Fame [2007] Kenpo Hall of Fame-Lifetime Achievement award

- International Kenpo Council of Grandmasters Hall of Fame

Mr. Lacerte contacted Ed Parker in that year and I joined the IKKA and worked with Mr. Parker and others in his art. After Mr. Parkers death, I met with David German and studied his system of TAI in it's various incarnations, being listed at the official historian for the style.

I have studied over 60 styles/systems of martial arts in my career, earning rank in over 22 of them. I was born with a photographic memory and a 162 IQ. I am an exception to the rule. I hold rank in Chinese, Okinawan, Japanese, Korean, Filipino and American Martial Arts. I never thought I would be a grandmaster or master or any of the ranks/titles I now hold. I just wanted to learn. I say "Titles are the shields of the weak, Actions are the swords of the strong!"

PERSONAL ACHIEVEMENTS

Joseph P. Rebelo II is the Senior Instructor of Rebelo's Kenpo Karate (which includes the NINDORYU FUDOSHIN KOBUKAI and the WU TANG DRAGON MASTER KUNG FU ACADEMY - Wu Tang Lung Si Gung Kung Fu Kwoon). He has been involved in and at the Martial Arts for over 49 years and will celebrate his 50th year in the arts on October 3, 2018. As an instructor, Mr. Rebelo has taught for almost half a century in Southeastern Massachusetts area. He has been the owner/operator of 5 commercial studios. In the past, he has taught countless students at the New Bedford YMCA & YWCA, The North End Youth Agency, The Faunce Corner Racquetball Club, The New Bedford Boys & Girls Club, as well as outreach classes at various locations. He has been a self defense instructor for the New Bedford Auxiliary Police and the New Bedford Chapter of the Guardian Angels. He has instructed civic groups such as the Southeastern business woman's group on his "Everyday Gestures that will save your life" lecture for practical self defense. He has taught group and private lessons throughout his tenure, Now focusing on long-distance advanced students as well as local individuals. He is considered by many as a "Walking encyclopedia of Martial arts". As a tournament competitor, Mr. Rebelo was in the top ten for both KRANE (Karate Referees Association of New England) & PKL (Professional Karate League) in 1989. Where He was listed in "Karate Illustrated" magazine and was the first top ten rated competitor performing Mr. Parker's Forms in tournaments in New England. He has also promoted/produced 4 open tournaments in the New Bedford area. A noted martial arts historian,

CURRENT RANKS & STYLES

- 9th Degree BLACK BELT (Master of the art) in Ed Parker's American Kenpo Karate (AKWA certified)

- 9th Degree BLACK BELT in David German's T.A.I.(Transitional Action Incorporated)(Kempo International certified)

- 9th Degree Black Belt in Chinese Hawaiian Kenpo (Pesare/Cerio Lineage) IKGC Certified

- 7th Degree BLACK BELT (SHICHIDAN) in Nindo Ryu Iaijutsu

- 6th Degree BLACK BELT (ROKUDAN) in Nindo Ryu Goshin Jujutsu

- 6th Degree (ROKUDAN) in Okinawan Kempo

- 5th Degree BLACK BELT (GODAN) in Karazenpo Goshinjutsu (Past MA. Co-Vice Pres)

- 5th Degree BLACK BELT (GODAN) in Chuan Fa/Kempo (Bill Gregory's Kajukenpo-Pai Lum)[Sigung]

- 5th Degree BLACK BELT (GODAN) in Nindo Ryu Atemido

- 4th Degree BLACK BELT (YODAN) in Nindo Ryu Gendai Ninjutsu [Taijutsu]

- 1st Degree Black Belt in Feliciano "Kimo" Fereira's Kempo Jutsu Kai

- 1st Degree BLACK BELT (YEEDAN) in Tai Chuan Tao

- 1st Degree BLACK BELT in Tae Kwon Do

- 5TH Degree BLACK BELT (GODAN) in George Elmer's American Chinese Kenpo Karate [Technical Advisor]

- 1st Degree BLACK BELT (SHODAN) in Mark Shuey's Canemasters Curriculum

Mr Rebelo is frequently asked for information on various arts and has been quoted in texts as well as on the internet as a valued resource on martial arts history. He has been inducted into 5 Halls of fame as a historian. He has one of the largest martial arts book, magazine and video collections in the United States. He has also been a featured TV announcer for the Ocean State Grand Nationals and the Junior National Karate Championships & cohosted "Championship Kickboxing" in the Rhode Island area. Later, He created Television programs: "Martial Arts Today TV", "Self Defense & You" and the self titled "Rebelo's Kenpo Karate". Presently, He has produced over a dozen instructional DVDs on the diverse arts in which he holds rank. He is the Master of Ceremonies for Alan Goldberg's Action Martial Arts Mega Weekend Trade Show at the Tropicana in Atlantic City,NJ. Presently, He has a Youtube Channel with over 150 videos on various martial arts and extended episodes of his TV shows.

CURRENT RANKS & STYLES:

- 10th Degree/Level (Duan/Toan) BLACK BELT/SASH (Hei-Se)Shao Choy Hung Kung Fu [Chin Na-5 Animal Style-Chuan Fa][Inheiritor of style]

- SHIR FU (INSTRUCTOR) in Northern Shaolin Praying Mantis [LIU HO {SIX HARMONY}, CHI SHING {SEVEN STAR} & BA FA OR BA BU {EIGHT STEP} KUNG FU/KUO SHU/WU SHU (6TH LEVEL -White Dragon Kung Fu association certified)

- SHIR FU in Tai Chi Chuan (Wu's Short 24, Yang's Long 108, and Chen's Short 24 Forms

- INSTRUCTOR in American-Filipino Arnis-Escrima-Kali Training System

DANIEL ROSS

"Martial Arts has allowed me to meet and train with some of the best martial artists in the world."

TRAINING INFORMATION

- Belt Ranks & Martial Arts Styles: Taekwondo 9th Dan; Chinese Kempo 7th Dan; Brazillian Jujitsu Brown Belt

- Instructors/Influencers: Grandmaster Yong Chin Pak, Grandmaster Angelito Barongan, Grandmaster Renner Gracie

- Birthdate: January 25, 1963

- Birthplace/Growing Up: Prairie City & Des Moines, IA

- Yrs. In the Martial Arts: 51 years

- Yrs. Instructing: 35 years

- School owner (Retired), Manager, Instructor

PERSONAL ACHIEVEMENTS

- Speaker at Pulmonary Arterial Hypertension Conference

- Governors Citation of Excellence

I was born January 25th, 1963 in Des Moines, Iowa. My family had lived in the small farming community of Prairie City, Iowa for the first six years of my life and then when my father got a new job, we ended up moving to the city of Des Moines. Unfortunately, it was a bad area we ended up moving into. Gangs, drugs, neighborhood bullies, and break-ins were common. So, my oldest brother took myself and my other brothers to the local YMCA to start studying self-defense under The Kim's Academy banner. This would begin my 49-year journey in the martial arts.

As time went by Kim's Academy stopped teaching at the YMCA and opened a series of stand-alone dojos. Most of my other brothers stopped going, but I had a friend in school whose mom would drive myself and him to the local dojo to continue training. My belt advancement in Taekwondo was a slow but a steady process. In 1976, my brother Bill was taking wrestling lessons at Iowa State University and decided to have me transfer my study of Taekwondo there under Grandmaster Yong Chin Pak. Training under Grandmaster Pak was more regimental and the training was more focused. As well as advancing in my belt levels, I also started to compete in local and regional tournaments.

MAJOR ACHIEVEMENTS

- Three USA Martial Arts Hall of Fame
- Action Martial Arts Magazines Hall of Fame
- Munich Hall of Honours
- Masters of Karate/Kungfu Hall of Fame
- Who's Who in The Martial Arts
- Instructor of a 30-day training course for the Hillsborough County Sheriff's Office in 2016
- Teaching women's self-defense classes at colleges across the country every summer since 2014

I was able to compete almost every weekend and started to follow the careers of such greats in martial arts as Cynthia Rothrock, Kathy Long, Karen Shepard, Don Wilson, Chuck Norris, Benny Urquidez, and Bill Wallace. My Taekwondo training was rigorous, and I had advanced to my 3rd Dan level.

The summer of 1981, after I graduated from Des Moines East High School, I left Iowa to attend college in California. While there, I decided to once again turn to the martial arts for a source of exercise and protection. As I asked people at school where I should go, the Gracie name seemed to be the one that stuck out, so I decided to attend classes and check it out for myself. Thus, began my journey with the legendary Gracie family in Brazilian Jujitsu. I learned to adapt my size to defend against all sizes and styles of attackers.

I was a student of the Gracie family for four years when I returned to Des Moines, Iowa and back to my roots. I once again took up Taekwondo. I started working at Montgomery Wards and met a gentleman there who himself was an accomplished martial artist and decided to workout with him at his West Des Moines dojo. This was the beginning of my training in Chinese Kempo under Grandmaster Angelito "Bobby" Barongan. Under Grandmaster Barongan, I was able to train with other masters such as Hanshi Carl De Los Reyes, Master Danny Mulane, Sensei Roger Zoffi, Hanshi Frank Raymond, Master Jim Perkins, and so many others. This helped me to develop a wide range of skills to use not just for tournaments but also for self-defense.

Martial Arts has given me focus and helped me to find a release for anger and stress as well as allowing me to help others such as special needs children, elderly, handicapped, and at-risk youth. It also has allowed me to meet and train with some of the best martial artists in the world and discuss philosophy and history of martial arts.

WESLEY RUIZ

"Everything I have learned through Martial Arts I have been able to incorporate into my everyday living."

TRAINING INFORMATION

- Belt Ranks & Martial Arts Styles: Black Belts: Dirty Karate, Chikara RU, Combat Kiru-Do, TaekwonDo, Molum Combat Arts, Kempo Jitsu, Caceres System of Urban Combat Chikara Ryu, Blue Belt: Shaolin Kempo United Martial Arts, Katago Ketsugo Karate, Apprentice Instructor PFS/JKD, Phase I instructor PFS/JKD, Apprentice Instructor in Kali, CCDW Instructor, KY

- Instructors/Influencers: Grandmaster Joe Torres, Master Joe Perry, Grandmaster Ellis Caceres, Grandmaster Tim White, Master Maurice Pierce, Grandmaster Len Kirshbaum, Master Michael Vanbeek, Master Paul Vunak, Guro Melegritos

- Birthdate: September 8, 1953

- Birthplace/Growing Up: Bronx, NY/Puerto Rico

- Yrs. In the Martial Arts: 54 years

- Yrs. Instructing: 50 years

- Instructor, Student

In 1966, my big brother, Rocky came from school one day and started kicking and punching and I asked him, what is that? And he said, that is karate! Ever since, I fell in love with Martial Arts. I am the Co-Founder of Dirty Karate (1971), Founder of Chikara-Ru (1986), Co-Founder Kiru-Do (1997), and Founder of Combat Kiru-Do (2009). I started Martial Arts in 1966 at the age of 13. I started Healing Arts in 1973 at the age of 20. I have trained in Shotokan, Kiokushinkai, Goju Ryu, Shaolin Kempo, Contemporary Jeet Kune Do, TaeKwon-Do, Shaolin, Sil Lum, Aikido, Kempo Jitsu and Ninjutsu. I am a Certified Reiki Master, Shiatsu/Acupressure Practitioner, Quantum Touch and Spiritual Healing.

The Martial Arts is my way of life. Everything I have learned I have been able to, in one way or another, incorporate in my everyday living.

PROFESSIONAL ORGANIZATIONS

- Black Dragon Fighting Society
- The Eastern USA International Martial Arts Association
- Progressive Fighting Systems

PROFESSIONAL ORGANIZATIONS

- Molum Combat Arts Association and Honor Society

- The International Alliance of Martial Arts Schools (L.A.O.M.A.S.)

- The International Nindo Ryu Fellowship

- Koga Ryu International Fellowship

- Borinquen Jujutsu Society

- International Original TaeKwon Do Association

PERSONAL ACHIEVEMENTS

- Four time Martial Arts Hall of Fame Inductee

- Received my Sokeship from the EUSAIMAA in November 2017

MAJOR ACHIEVEMENTS

- 10th Dan Black Belt from Cobra Martial Arts Association on February 27, 2018

ALLEN SARAC

"Martial arts has given me a skill that I can go anywhere in the world with the knowledge in my mind and teach to anyone."

I started in the Martial Arts in late 1960 because of the bullying and being a child with the lack of confidence, walking to and from school in one of the not so great neighborhoods of Akron Ohio was a scary part of my childhood.

At the age of nine, my parents signed me up at a local karate studio. It was very appealing to me because I could compete against myself and not be part of a team that was most of the time the last to be picked for, so martial arts gave me the confidence to excel and then as I gain the confidence I became part of a team in other sports.

Martial Arts has impacted my life by first teaching me to set goals. Then it gave me the confidence to do or try anything that I ever

TRAINING INFORMATION

- Belt Ranks & Martial Arts Styles: Song Moo Kwan TKD 8th Degree Black Belt, Judo 1st Degree Black Belt, Wing Chun Kung Fu 1st Degree Black Sash

- Instructors/Influencers: Grand Master Il Joo Kim (1969-1970), Grand Master Bob Chaney (1970-2016), Master Frank Morris Jr (1975-1980)

- Birthdate: March 24, 1961

- Birthplace/Growing Up: Akron/Canton, OH

- Yrs. In the Martial Arts: 51 years

- Yrs. Instructing: 42 years

- School owner, Instructor

PROFESSIONAL ORGANIZATIONS

- WTF
- ASMK
- WSMK
- AAU

PERSONAL ACHIEVEMENTS

- 8th Degree Black Belt & Grandmaster in Song Moo Kwan – Tae Kwon Do

- Over 51 years of experience in Song Moo Kwan – Tae Kwon Do

- 5 years training in Olympic Judo

- 5 years training in Wing Chung Kung Fu

- 12 years body-guard service to celebrities

- Weapons Certified Instructor

- N.R.A. Weapons certified

- 1992 Inductee to the International Karate Hall of Fame

- 1989 Former World Champion (Oslo, Norway)

- Idaho, Pennsylvania, and Ohio State Championships

- East Coast Grand Champion

- 4 Time National AAU Champion

imagined doing, and it gave me the confidence to teach children and see them turn into disciplined mature, and honorable adults. Martial arts has given me a skill that I can go anywhere in the world with the knowledge in my mind and teach Martial Arts to anyone.

MAJOR ACHIEVEMENTS

- Founder of the non-profit organization "Get High On Kicks, Not Drugs!"

- Founding member of LV Community Gang Task Force

- Recipient of the Congressional Certificate of Congratulations for non-profit work and community service.

- Senatorial Recognition from United States Senator John Ensign for community involvement.

- Proclamation from the Mayor of Henderson and Boulder City proclaiming June 27 as "Get High On Kicks Not Drugs Day.

- Recipient of the "The Jefferson Award" in 2001 by the American Institute for Public Experience.

- Masters & Pioneers book Inductee 2019

- President of Arbecy Global Foundation (teaching Martial Arts to children that are blind, deaf or autistic)

EUGENE SEDENO

"I owe all my successes in life to my teachers, who taught me never to quit, to think, analyze, and to be happy."

TRAINING INFORMATION

- Belt Ranks & Martial Arts Styles: San (3rd) DAN, Shidou-in in Okinawa Kobudo, Go (5th) DAN Kenpo Karate, IKKA, Ku (9th) DAN, Grand Master in SHAOLIN KENPO, Ku (9th) DAN, Senior Grand Master in KAJUKENBO, Ju (10th) Dan, Professor in CHINESE KEMPO, Shihan, Master of KOSHO SHOREI KENPO

- Instructors/Influencers: Shihan Mikio Nishiuchi of Kochi, Japan, SGM Edmund Parker, SGM Rick Alemany and GGM Ralph Castro, Professor Walter Godin and Sijo Adriana Emperado, Professor Walter Godin and Professor William Kwai Sun Chow, Professor James Masayoshi Mitose

- Birthdate: August 31, 1952

- Birthplace/Growing Up: Honolulu, HI / Kalihi, and Waianae HI

- Yrs. In the Martial Arts: 58 years

- Yrs. Instructing: 51years

- School Owner & Instructor at Sedeno School of Self Defense

As a young boy, I was always interested in combat arts. Growing up in Hawaii, I was surrounded by it. Philippine stick fighting, Judo, boxing, Aikido, Karate, and of course, Kenpo was to be found everywhere.

I started boxing and Judo with Mr. Raymond Yee at the age of ten in Kalihi Valley, Oahu. At the age of 12, when I moved to Kaimuki, I started in Kajukenbo with Professor Walter Leo Niakala Godin, a black belt of Sijo Emperado.

I stayed with him and his assistant Mr. Tony Cambra until we moved to Waianae in 1967. In Waianae, I started training with Mr. John Makepa and Brother Abe Kamahoahoa, students of Professor William Kwai Sun Chow. While in high school, I met Professor Rick Alemany in Waianae. I have been teaching with and for him ever since.

I received his first Black belt from Grand Master Brother Abe Kamahoahoa in Waianae, Hawaii, in 1970. I also received a Black Belt from Professor Walter L. N. Godin with an extra certificate from his school at the Palama Settlement.

PROFESSIONAL ORGANIZATIONS

- American Teachers Association of Martial Arts
- Kajukenbo Self Defense Institute
- Kajukenbo Ohana Association
- International Shaolin Kenpo Association
- Okinawa Kobudo Association, USA
- Sei Kosho Shorei Kai

PERSONAL ACHIEVEMENTS

In 1980, I won the Chinese Martial Arts Association's and the International Kung Fu Association's Competitor of the Year Awards. My last major win, prior to retiring from competition, was at the 1984 International Karate Championships, where I took first place in the Masters/ Instructor Division in Kenpo Kata.

MAJOR ACHIEVEMENTS

- 2019 Portugal, Hall of Fame, Platinum Lifetime Achievement Award
- 2008 Masters Hall of Fame, Platinum Life Achievement Award
- 2007 Charter Member of Kenpo International Hall of Fame
- 2002 Masters Hall of Fame, Golden Life Achievement Award
- 1999 Recognized at Kenpo's Historic International Gathering of Eagles for contributions to the art
- 1993 Inducted into the World Martial Arts Hall of Fame as INSTRUCTOR OF THE YEAR
- 1987 Recognized in Who's Who in American Martial Arts

In 1980, I won the Chinese Martial Arts Association's and the International Kung Fu Association's Competitor of the Year Awards. My last major win, before retiring from competition, was at the 1984 International Karate Championships, where I took first place in the Masters/Instructor Division in Kenpo Kata. I was also a private student of Edmund K. Parker and was promoted by him on November 20, 1980, to the rank of 5th degree Black Belt.

On May 7, 1999, the Great Grand Master Ralph Castro promoted me to the rank of 7th degree Black Belt with the title of Professor in the International Shaolin Kenpo Association.

On August 18, 2005, I was promoted to the rank of 9th degree Black Belt, with the title of Grand Master, in Shaolin Kenpo by Senior Grand Master Rick Alemany.

On June 17, 1996, I was promoted by the International Okinawa Kobudo Association, the USA, to the rank of Sandan by Shihan Mikio Nishiuchi of Kochi, Japan.

On June 12, 2007, I was promoted to 9th degree Red Belt with Silver Trim and with the title of Grand Master by Sijo Adriano D. Emperado in the Kajukenbo system.

I was also the last person promoted by Great Grand Master James Masayoshi Mitose, before his death twelve days later, to the rank of Master on March 15, 1981.

On November 5, 2019, I was promoted to 10th degree Black Belt in Godin's Kula Ona Kupale Chinese Kempo by Professor John Hackleman and in the presents of Professor Walter L. N. Godin's daughter Delilah.

I have been teaching since 1969 and currently instructs at Sedeño's School of Self Defense in Albuquerque, NM.

MAJOR ACHIEVEMENTS

- 1984 Recognized in Knights of Heaven - Brotherhood of Martial Arts

- 1983 Recognized in Who's Who in Karate

- 1981 Recognized in James M. Mitoses book "What is True Self-Defense"

- 1980 Won the Chinese Martial Arts Association's and the International Kung Fu Association's COMPETITOR OF THE YEAR awards

I have gained so much from my training. Starting in elementary school, my grades improved, my ability to analyze math problems increased, and my overall outlook on learning improved. This followed me all the way to my master's degree.

I have met so many interesting people and got to visit and teach all over the world; I love sharing what I have learned and watching the faces of students as they progress.

I was very fortunate to have been born in Hawaii and growing up with teachers who are legends. Because of them, I have been able to defend myself and my family and, more importantly, stay healthy and happy.

I owe all my successes in life to my teachers, who taught me never to quit, to think, analyze, and to be happy.

The HeadKnocker

GRANDMASTER
Mark Shuey Sr

CANE MASTER

MARK SHUEY

"The success of The Warrior Cane project has encouraged instructors to teach all over the United States."

TRAINING INFORMATION

- Martial Arts Title: Grand Master
- Studied Tang Soo Do, Tae Kwon Do, and Hapkido
- Teaching for 38 years
- Started studying Martial Arts in 1970

PROFESSIONAL ORGANIZATIONS

- USMA Hall of Fame
- World Head of Family Sokeship Hall of Fame

I am humbled to have been included in articles in the media, like the article by Jennifer Levitz in the Saturday July 12, 2008 edition of The Wall Street Journal entitled "Everybody Is 'Cane Fu' Fighting At Senior Centers, So Watch Out (Older People Get Healthful Exercise And Learn to Wield a Ready Deterrent)". To be interviewed on major television sports and entertainment programs (PBS, NBC, ABC, FOX) helped to bring Mark's system of cane self-defense to the attention of the world at large.

In addition to Cane Fu, I created several other systems for the use of the cane: The American Cane System (a traditional martial arts curriculum with ranking), Cane Chi for Health and Exercise, Cane-Ja for street self-defense and the Silver Dragons for those over 50.

The Warrior Cane Project was created by Thomas Forman and Mark is a partner in this organization as an instructor conducting

PERSONAL ACHIEVEMENTS

- Formed the Cane Masters International Association for students of the cane and to certify instructors for his system

- Recognized in article by Jennifer Levitz in the Saturday July 12, 2008 edition of The Wall Street Journal

- Interviewed on major television sports and entertainment programs (PBS, NBC, ABC, FOX)

MAJOR ACHIEVEMENTS

- 1970 Started Martial Arts in the Chuck Norris System of Tang Soo Do

- 1978 Received 1st degree Black Belt

- 1979 Started teaching; Master's Certification with USNKA (United States National Karate Assoc.), ATAMA (American Teacher's Assoc. of the Martial Arts), USMA (United States Martial Arts Association), and the Independent Karate School Association.

- 1994 Competitor of the year in with the National Coalition of Martial Artists.

- 1997 Rated #2 in overall points in the Pacific Rim Tour Tournament circuit.

- Rated #1 in traditional weapons and katas in M.A.R.R.S for his age division and number #2 in overall points.

- 1998 Unified World Martial Arts Federation 1st place Forms katas, traditional weapons, kumite and won overall Grand Champion in both traditional weapons and forms.

sessions at multiple Armed Forces bases and across the country. Its purpose has been to assist wounded veterans help with rehabilitation, providing them with combat canes and training sessions for free. The success of this project has encouraged instructors to teach all over the United States and train Wounded Warriors to become Combat Cane Instructors.

MAJOR ACHIEVEMENTS

- Grand Champion in Kata's Golden State Karate Assoc. (GSKA) as well as first place in the traditional senior weapons and open weapons, kata and kumite.

- National title in traditional senior weapons in IMAC,

- Competitor of the Year by IKSA.

- Inducted into the Martial Arts Masters, Pioneers, and Legends Hall of Fame as a "Master Instructor"

- 1999 Promoted to 7th degree by the USMA and ICHF

- NASKA'S World and National, Masters Traditional Weapons Title, IMAC'S National title

- 2000 Defended his World Champion title for NASKA and won top honors in the World for the KRANE Ratings.

- Inducted into the USMA Hall of Fame, as well as the prestigious World Head of Family Sokeship Hall of Fame.

- Formed the Cane Masters International Association for students of the cane and to certify instructors for his system.

- Recognized as a Grand Master by the World Head of Family Sokeship for the creation of the CMIA.

- 2001 Defended his National and World titles on the NASKA tournament circuit (again in 2002)

- Inducted into the Action Martial Arts Hall of Fame, International Association of Karate, Kobudo, Puerto Rico Hall of Fame and USMA.

- Appointed to the Board of the World Head of Family Sokeship.

- 2003 Inducted into the Black Belt Magazine Hall of Fame as "Weapons Instructor of the Year".

- 2008 Created Cane-Fu cane self-defense and exercise system for seniors and the physically challenged

GM IRVING SOTO

"Seeing my students become successful in life through the study of Martial Arts practice and training is fulfilling."

TRAINING INFORMATION

- Belt Ranks & Martial Arts Styles: Atemi Jujitsu Waza, Aiki Jujitsu (10th Degree Black Belt Founder System)

- Instructors/Influencers: O-sensei Tashioshi, Charlie Sparrow, Rudy Jones, Dr. Moses Powell, Saigon Ellis Evans, Daniyal McEaddy, Ronald Duncan, Aaron Banks, John Denora, Siegfried Boedeker, Rev. Dr. Donald Miskel

- Birthdate: March 7, 1954

- Birthplace/Growing Up: Bronx & Brooklyn, NY

- Yrs. In the Martial Arts: 64 years

- Yrs. Instructing: 56 years

- School owner, Instructor, Founder of Atemi Jujitsu Waza, Aiki Jujitsu

PROFESSIONAL ORGANIZATIONS

- Sport Karate Museum Dragon Image Fighting Award

- Samurai Ju jitsu Association international /All-Japan Sabukan Martial Arts & Way Association

- Daito-Ryu Aiki Ju- jitsu Director Association of the United States of America)

- USA Martial Arts Hall of Fame Alliance all systems

- International Martial Arts Hall of fame GGMRHF

I was born in the Bronx and started training in the martial arts of Jujitsu (1956) at the tender age of 2- years old. I grew up in Brooklyn, NY, a neighborhood known as Brownsville East NY. Economically, my family was very poor.

My mother had very little money to spend on any activity, but she managed to enroll me in martial arts classes held in the back of a laundromat. Once I stepped into the martial arts school, I discovered it was going to be a way of life for me.

One of my first teachers in martial arts that I trained with was O-sensei Tashioshi, who was Japanese. He taught me the application of Jujitsu. I received my black belt at the age of 11-years-old.

PROFESSIONAL ORGANIZATIONS

- WOMA World Organization Of Martial Arts
- USA Warlord Martial Arts magazine
- Sekai - Day Han Martial Arts Federation
- US International Grandmasters Soke Union Worldwide
- Black Dragon Fighting society BDMFS
- Oriental World of Self-Defense Show at Madison Square Garden / Gm Aaron Banks 1960 -PRESENT
- World Professional Martial Arts Organization Gm Aaron Banks
- The Hitokui Tora Martial Arts Federation / Dr. Dan R. McEaddy
- International Martial Arts Olympic Committee Martial Arts Olympic I.M.A.O.C 01/09/2009
- America's Finest international Martial Arts Federation
- United States Head Of Family Martial Arts Association International Supreme Elite Warrior Council
- World Organizer of Martial Arts
- USA & Japan Atemi International Ju jitsu Federation

Tashioshi invited me to attend an international martial arts tournament held in Tokyo Japan Many years ago. I was amazed by what I saw that day. O-sensei Tashioshi moved back to Japan in early 1968. I continued my thirst and quest for martial arts knowledge of Jujitsu.

I furthered my instructions with a group of masters in the neighborhoods from where I grew up in Brooklyn, New York. (1973). I was invited by the Japanese association to compete in an open championship tournament held in Japan, upon winning the Kumite. I got the opportunity to travel overseas to obtain martial arts knowledge. Throughout the years, I continue to train within the United States with other masters in martial arts.

Soke Grandmaster Irving Soto is a winner of numerous championships and the last person to be taught Atemi, Aiki jujitsu waza. He has been studying and teaching the martial arts of Atemi jujitsu waza for the last 57 years.

Soke Soto has traveled all over the world to demonstrate his Techniques and been teaching the military arm forces like the army. Soke Soto has been in numerous commercials, and tv shows such as MTV, NBC, Phil Donahue Show Live TV, Inside Edition, New York, Newsday, Barbra Sang live TV network show, The Aaron Banks live martial arts show, and the Oriental world of self-defense Show at Madison Square Garden Production. Soke Soto has been inducted into the Aaron Banks martial arts Hall of fame.

Soke Soto has appeared in GM Aaron Bank live tv show in martial arts for 47 times. He's also appeared on the live Hong Kong Television by Raymond Chow, and on sports TV ESPN Sports Martial Arts Channel, the list goes on. Soke Irving Soto is an author of five books. He has been honored by former Mayor of San Diego Susan Golding and by Mayor of Hollywood Johnny Grant.

Soke Grandmaster Irving Soto is a member of the law enforcement community. He has taught special operations overseas and the United States and the federal police, New York Sheriffs' Federal Correctional Facilities and NYPD tactical defense for DEA, FBI, the US Treasury,

PERSONAL ACHIEVEMENTS

Soke Grandmaster Irving Soto is a winner of numerous championships and the last person to be taught Atemi, Aiki jujitsu waza. He has been studying and teaching the martial arts of Atemi jujitsu waza for the last 57 years.

Soke Soto has traveled all over the world to demonstrate his Techniques and been teaching the military arm forces like the army. Soke Soto has been in numerous commercials, and tv shows such as MTV, NBC, Phil Donahue Show Live TV, Inside Edition, New York, Newsday, Barbra Sang live TV network show, The Aaron Banks live martial arts show, and the Oriental world of self-defense Show at Madison Square Garden Production. Soke Soto has been inducted into the Aaron Banks martial arts Hall of fame.

Soke Soto has appeared in GM Aaron Bank live tv show in martial arts for 47 times. He's also appeared on the live Hong Kong Television by Raymond Chow, and on sports TV ESPN Sports Martial Arts Channel, the list goes on. Soke Irving Soto is an author of five books. He has been honored by former Mayor of San Diego Susan Golding and by Mayor of Hollywood Johnny Grant.

Soke Grandmaster Irving Soto is a member of the law enforcement community. He has taught special operations overseas and the United States and the federal police, New York Sheriffs' Federal Correctional Facilities and NYPD tactical defense for DEA, FBI, the US Treasury, teams for the Navy, as well as teaching for the DOD police academy and the department in Aberdeen Maryland.

teams for the Navy, as well as teaching for the DOD police academy and the department in Aberdeen Maryland.

Soke Soto has received accolades from former Mayor Susan Golding of San Diego, CA, former Mayor Dinkins of New York City and Mayor of Hollywood CA Johnny Grant, Brigadier General, US Army Commanding Rodger A. Nadeau, US Army Aberdeen Proving Grounds. Colonel US Army Deputy Installation Commander John T Wright for his hard work in teaching the US armed force 2002- 2016. Irving Soto is still teaching, training, and working with the military to the present day.

"As a coach in the martial arts, it's been a great fulfillment to teach martial arts science in rural neighborhoods and communities around the countryside to young men, women, kids of all ages and from all walks of life.

Seeing my students become successful in life through the study of Martial Arts practice and training is fulfilling. I enjoy working within the local neighborhood, helping men and women build a sense of awareness and confidence in their abilities in everyday life. I've owned my martial arts business for over 47 years and grateful to make a difference and positive influence in the community. "

PERSONAL ACHIEVEMENTS

Soke Soto has received accolades from former Mayor Susan Golding of San Diego, CA, former Mayor Dinkins of New York City and Mayor of Hollywood CA Johnny Grant, Brigadier General, US Army Commanding Rodger A. Nadeau, US Army Aberdeen Proving Grounds. Colonel US Army Deputy Installation Commander John T Wright for his hard work in teaching the US armed force 2002- 2016. Irving Soto is still teaching, training, and working with the military to the present day.

DARYL STEWART

"Being introduced to the Martial Arts was probably one of the best things that ever happened to me or possibly to anyone else."

TRAINING INFORMATION

- Belt Ranks & Martial Arts Styles: 10th Dan Black Belt, Tang-So-Do, Isshinryu, Japanese styles, Korean Tae-Kwon-Do, Kung-Fu, 4th Dan in Iss-Hogai Jujitsu, 1st Dan Black Belt in Modern Arnis, 1st Dan Black Belt in Kobuko

- Instructors/Influencers: Master David Yeaman

- Birthdate: July 7, 1948

- Birthplace/Growing Up: Nixon, TX

- Yrs. In the Martial Arts: 57 years

- Yrs. Instructing: 54 years

- School owner, Manager, Instructor, Promoter

PROFESSIONAL ORGANIZATIONS

- Professional Karate Association "Lifetime Member 2020"

- Universal Martial Arts Hall of Fame "Vice President"

- Masters Hall of Fame Alumni

- Ambassador and History General for the Museum of Sport Karate for over 23 Years

- Arbitrator for the "Texas National Tour Circuit" 1997

- Arbitrator and Judge for the National Black Belt league for the last 23 years for "The Great State of Texas"

Grandmaster Daryl K. "Bigfoot" Stewart was introduced to karate by his friend Buddy Raines. They were out surfing and that day, the surf was really going off with waves crashing on to the beach. Buddy said Daryl, "Come go with me." GM Stewart said "Buddy, look at the surf, it's really good." Buddy replied, "Hey you will like it, it's about fighting." So off they went. Later, GM Stewart was introduced to a gentleman by the name of David Yeaman. He was actually introduced to karate in 1962 in Amarillo, Texas but was only there for a couple of weeks. So other than that, GM Stewart really doesn't count that in his inventory of martial arts. He says his journey in the arts started in Galveston, Texas. It turned out that he would continue to be his instructor for most of his career. He is still doing it today and has been for over 50 plus years.

PROFESSIONAL ORGANIZATIONS

- Judge- Amateur Organization of Karate
- Judge- Texas Karate Organization
- Judge- The United States Karate Association
- Remy Presas (IMAF) International Modern Arnis Federation
- Texas Martial Arts Hall of Fame

PERSONAL ACHIEVEMENTS

- Studying the martial arts has given GM Stewart confidence and the ability to focus on one self and others. To spread the knowledge that he has received throughout his career from other great people and the martial arts. To help them give back to our kids and adults, and our future generations. To help them prepare for their lives and help prepare other people in their pursuit of life. He always likes to say that martial arts is good for the Mind, Body, and Soul. To show them the way through knowledge of martial arts and to help keep them off the streets and out of trouble. To give them guidance and positive influences in their pursuit of happiness to keep the minds and body in shape and to give off a positive attitude. To always be helpful to others in the martial arts and the community.

Daryl was very young when he started studying Judo and Karate. He believes that the martial arts played a major role in his life. The martial arts gave him a solid framework of discipline and self-confidence as he was growing up. He associated with like-minded people that had direction and helped him to stay out of trouble. While surfing and studying the martial arts, he had a framework to stay in excellent shape. At this time, he was surfing in contests for major surfing companies and traveling all over to surf in competitions in the surfing community and also at the same time entered into Karate Tournaments. He was going to school, working, training, and enjoying the life of a kid. Not knowing at the time, he was setting the path that his life would be headed down into the future.

The martial arts gave GM Stewart confidence that he could take care of himself and his mother. He and his mother lived in Galveston, Texas at the time. With his mother working long hours to support them, and single, he wanted a way to help watch over his mother. At this point, he was having a hard time with his school work and trying to make ends meet. With the guidance of his dear mother, and that of his Martial Arts instructor, Mr. David Yeaman, he moved up through the ranks in karate and judo. He was pretty much always a natural in sports so he took to karate naturally.

MAJOR ACHIEVEMENTS

- Coach and fighter for the United States Navy Seabees Fighting Team 1972-1975

- Induction into "The Universal Martial Arts Hall of Fame" in 2000 Houston, Texas

- Induction into "United State Hall of Fame" 2001 Oklahoma City, Oklahoma

- Induction into the "Action Martial Arts Magazine Hall of Fame" in 2001-2002 Atlantic City, New Jersey

- Induction into the "World Christian Martial Arts Hall of Fame" 2001 Newark, New Jersey

Being introduced to the Martial Arts was probably one of the best things that ever happened to GM Stewart or possibly to anyone else. Through the training and discipline of the Martial Arts, he has tried his best to always be kind and friendly to everyone that he meets. To show kindness and help to any one that may require his help or that may need some guidance. To be supportive of everyone and encourage others to do the same. He does his best to help the younger generation with their lives and encourage them to strive to be a better person, to reach out in life and embrace it with zest to reach their goals. In life, if you can envision it, you can reach it if you believe in yourself. And to teach them some life skills in the Martial Arts to work on themselves to go through the belt system to prepare their minds, body and soul and achieve their goals as they go through the ranks.

The Martial Arts gave him a path to help him throughout his life to reach his goals that he has wanted to achieve. He has met many interesting people throughout his life. The Martial Arts has been the key. He has been around the world a couple of times in the Military and saw and done things a lot of people may never have the opportunity to do. He thanks God for taking care of him along the way in his travels. He always strives to be a better person every day.

MAJOR ACHIEVEMENTS

- Became Vice President of "Universal Martial Arts Hall of Fame" 2002

- Induction into the "International Black Belt Honor Hall of Fame" 2003

- Induction into the "Keeper of the Torch Hall of Fame" 2004 Florida

- Induction into the "Master Hall of Fame" in Costa Mesa, California 2012

- "International Black Belt Hall of Fame" 2016

- Semi-Pro Surfer Featured in a recent movie "Broken Waves" a documentary of Surfing Culture on Gulf Coast by Lauryn Le Clere's productions. Galveston, Texas 2017

- "Professional Karate Association" 2019 now a lifetime member as 2020

- Remy Presas International Modern Arnis Federation

- Texas Martial Arts Hall of Fame

CRAIG TERRY

"Martial Arts has helped me understand my strengths and limitations better."

TRAINING INFORMATION

- Belt Ranks & Martial Arts Styles: 2nd Dan-Danny Lane Fighting System, 2nd Dan-Goju Ryu, Brown Belt-Shotokan
- Instructors/Influencers: GM Danny Lane, Master Dane Emmel, Master Chuck Anderson
- Birthdate: June 6, 1952
- Birthplace/Growing Up: Idaho / Utah
- Yrs. In the Martial Arts: 50+ years
- Yrs. Instructing: 35+ years
- School owner, Instructor

PROFESSIONAL ORGANIZATIONS

- WMAF (World Martial Arts Federation) Member
- SIMAF (Superfoot International MA Federation) Lifetime Member
- USKA (United States Karate Assoc.) Lifetime Member
- AAKF (All American Karate Federation) Lifetime Member
- UBBA (Utah Black Belt Assoc.) Lifetime Member

Every day I would pass this karate school - riding my bicycle delivering newspapers in the 60's while in Jr. High. I would stop and watch the classes and became enthralled with it all - never seeing it before but hearing about it. I, too, wanted to do all that punching, kicking, spinning, grabbing, throwing, etc., etc. I forged my parents' signature and started taking classes off and on as I could afford it for a couple of years without my parents knowing - because they wouldn't have allowed it since Karate in the '60s had a bad reputation according to a lot of people. I started Karate all over in the '70s since my passion was still there. I met Master Emmel at a YMCA, and he offered to privately train me in Goju Ryu - consequently receiving my Black Belts under him.

Martial Arts became a 'Way of Life' for me. It has helped me understand my strengths & limitations better - both physically and mentally. It has taught me always to respect others - regardless of their abilities, race, or gender. Practicing Martial Arts has given me many opportunities over the decades to humble myself because there's always someone out there more intelligent, better trained & skilled than myself.

PERSONAL ACHIEVEMENTS

- A career highlight was having a 3 round exhibition fight with Bill 'Superfoot' Wallace.

- AAU Certified Referee / Judge (Amateur Athletic Union)- Fighting, Forms & Weapons

- USKA Certified Referee / Judge (United States Karate Federation)- Fighting, Forms & Weapons

- Private Instructor to Academy Cadets / Salt Lake City Police

- Co-Established & Instructed @ Salt Lake Community College - Physical Education Karate Classes

MAJOR ACHIEVEMENTS

- 2020 Hall of Fame (Ambassador of The Year / Martial Arts) American Martial Arts Alliance

- 2020 Martial Arts Masters & Pioneers Book inclusion (World Edition) American Martial Arts Alliance

- 2020 Hall of Honors (Esteem Martial Artist) Action Martial Arts Magazine

- 2019 Hall of Fame (Instructor of The Year - Goju Ryu) Legends of The Martial Arts

- 2019 World's Greatest Martial Artists Book (Volume 2) GM Ted Gambordella

- 2019 Martial Arts Masters & Pioneers Book inclusion (Who's Really Who) American Martial Arts Alliance

- 2019 Masters of the Martial Arts Award Ceremony

- 2018 Hall of Fame (Who's Who Legends Award) American Martial Arts Association

MAJOR ACHIEVEMENTS

- 2018 Hall of Honors (Goodwill Ambassador/ Martial Arts) Action Martial Arts Magazine

- 2018 Masters of the Martial Arts Award Ceremony

- 2017 Hall of Honors (Outstanding Achievements / Martial Arts) Action Martial Arts Magazine

PROF. DANIEL TORRES

"Studying the Martial Arts impacts my life by improving wellness and makes a positive impact on emotional health."

TRAINING INFORMATION

- Belt Ranks & Martial Arts Styles: Vee Jitsu Jujitsu System, DanTor Ryu Jujitsu 9th dan Kudan, DanTor Ryu Jujitsu & MMA 10th Dan Judan

- Instructors/Influencers: Grandmaster Robert J. Copper, Grandmaster Jose A. Velez, Grandmaster Florendo M. Visitacion, Hanshi Carlos H. Montalvo

- Birthdate: February 12, 1959

- Birthplace/Growing Up: Brooklyn, NY / Williamsburg

- Yrs. In the Martial Arts: 51 years

- Yrs. Instructing: 43 years

- School owner (DanTor Ryu Jujitsu & MMA) Instructor

PROFESSIONAL ORGANIZATIONS

- Life member of the International Ronin Martial Arts Federation

- Ronin Red Belt Society

- Ronin Mixed Martial Arts International (MMA)

- Certified Instructor for the Ronin Police Defensive Tactics Association

- Prof. Torres has appeared in Action Martial Arts Magazines Collectors Cards 1998, 1999 and the year 2000

It started back in 1969 just attending intermediate school 318, Eugenio María de Hostos, in Williamsburg Brooklyn. Back then, they had gangs called the Spanish Kings and the Justice of Brooklyn. The Spanish Kings were guys & girls mostly looking to recruit young kids to join their group. I the son of a Pentecostal Minister/ Preacher was confronted by one of the gang leaders to join the group and I said to them many times "no". So, I knew that one day I will have to fight one of them. So, I started to prepare myself with my friend Sammy Caraballo. We were watching movies like Billy Jack, Green Hornet, and all of Bruce Lee movies. We started to go to Saint Peter and Paul Catholic Church community center where there was a brown belt instructor named Nelson teaching classes of martial art, and we started to attend. Six months later, the instructor went to the military and we never heard from him again.

I met with Sensei Robert J. Cooper who was a physical education teacher in Williamsburg Brooklyn, and he said he was teaching jujitsu at the

PERSONAL ACHIEVEMENTS

- One of my personal achievements is that I am the only one in the United States that works for a Boxing Commission or Athletic Commission that holds the rank of a 10th degree black belt in jujitsu and licensed as a Professional MMA Judge and Referee Professional Kickboxing Judge and Professional Boxing Judge.

- Personal bodyguard for many high-profile celebrities and politicians.

MAJOR ACHIEVEMENTS

- One of my major achievements and fulfillment was to obtain respect in the martial arts as a Hall of Fame and attained the rank of 10 Dan in Jujitsu.

- Self-accomplishment

Tompkins Community Center, located at 303 Vernon Ave. Brooklyn, NY 11206 in the Bedford-Stuyvesant Community. I started to attend class three times a week and when I became a yellow belt in Jujitsu., one day after school, I was approached by the same group of guys and was asked again to join the gang and my response to them was no. They started to follow me to my home. When I got to my block, I was approached again, but this time they wanted to fight and I did not hesitate. I remember throwing the first punch and kick then we went to the ground between two parked cars fighting. I remember there were a lot of people watching us fight. My sister Felicita "Chicky" Torres heard that her baby brother was fighting, so she came down with a stick and started to swing at them and from then on, I got the respect from the gang leaders. But I remember him telling me this is not over. That's when I decided I will continue my martial arts study especially in jujitsu. 50 + years later, I'm still in the art.

Professor Daniel Torres is a 9th Dan/ Kudan Master Instructor under the Vee Jitsu System and 10th Dan Judan under the International Ronin Martial Arts Federation.

Prof. Daniel Torres currently works for the State of Florida Boxing Commission and licensed as a Professional Mix Martial Arts Judge/ Referee, Professional Kickboxing Judge, Professional Boxing Judge.

Studying the Martial Arts impacts my life by improving wellness and makes a positive impact on emotional health. Self-esteem and self - confidence increase as well as decreasing stress and tension.

The American Martial Arts Alliance
Making A Real Difference In The Martial Arts

Action Martial Arts Magazine Hall Honors Martial Arts
Organization of the Year

Martial Artists, Groups, Schools, and Organizations – All Styles Welcome

The American Martial Arts Alliance has been committed to the growth of the martial arts since 2002. we continue to build and grow the martial arts through the great Masters and Grand Masters who are affiliated with the American Martial Arts Alliance. the foundation of this program is built on knowledge and the continuous growth of the martial arts as we build structures to support the teaching and continued development of martial artists.

Through the American Martial Arts Alliance, our members have the opportunity to be a part of our continuing education program supporting martial arts business management. Our members have the opportunity to be apart of the online Institution tour audio courses, books, video, and audio training lessons. Plus our members have an opportunity to participate in a weekly conference call with GM Jesse Bowen and other success teachers with decades of experience and Leadership training to support business and personal success. **Visit our website www.whoswhointhemartialarts.com or call 919-618-8075**

Black Belt Memberships

THE AMERICAN MARTIAL ARTS ALLIANCE BLACK BELT MEMBERSHIP
Please fill out your billing information below.
Membership includes:
- Framed AMAA Black Belt Member Certificate
- AMAA Membership Card & Patch
- 30-DAY Mentor eCoaching
- Access to Our Online Business Degree Program and Other Online Courses Discount.
- Press Release Template
- FREE Elite Listing on the International Who's Who Directory
- Monthly Newsletter
- Online Blog

All black belt membership applicants must be 18 yrs of age.

Instructor/Owner Memberships

THE AMERICAN MARTIAL ARTS ALLIANCE SCHOOL OWNER MEMBERSHIP
Please fill out your billing information below.
Membership includes:
- Framed AMAA Black Belt Member Certificate
- AMAA Membership Card & Patch
- 90-day Online Coaching & Mentorship (Business and School Management)
- Access to Our Online Business Degree Program and Other Online Courses
- Press Release Template
- FREE 60-DAY CLICK 4 COURSE
- FREE Elite Listing on the International Who's Who Directory
- Monthly Newsletter
- Online Blog

All black belt membership applicants must be 18 yrs of age.

Charter School Memberships

THE AMERICAN MARTIAL ARTS ALLIANCE CHARTER SCHOOL MEMBERSHIP
Please fill out your billing information below.
Membership includes:
- Framed AMAA Black Belt Member Certificate
- AMAA Membership Card & Patch
- 1 year Online Coaching & Mentorship (Business and School Management)
- 10 Members FREE
- Access to Our Online Business Degree Program and Other Online Courses
- Press Release Template
- FREE 60-DAY CLICK 4 COURSE
- FREE Elite Listing on the International Who's Who Directory
- Monthly Newsletter
- Online Blog

All black belt membership applicants must be 18 yrs of age.

THE AMERICAN MARTIAL ARTS ALLIANCE

MARTIAL ARTS
MASTERS & PIONEERS

Ambassadors
IN THE MARTIAL ARTS

Ambassadors
GRAND MASTERS

DANA ABBOTT

"Not even the stark, bone-chilling wooden floor of the aging creaking dojo on this cold winter morn could break my direct concentration."

TRAINING INFORMATION

- Belt Ranks & Martial Arts Styles: 7th Dan studying martial arts styles: Japanese Swordsmanship Kenjutsu

- Instructors/Influencers: Abe Shinobu, Shizawa Kunio, Nakamura Taizaburo, Tanabe Tetsundo, Tabuchi Mitsunobu

- Currently Resides: Japan / USA

- Yrs. In the Martial Arts: 42 years

- Yrs. Instructing: 22 years

HONORS & AWARDS

- Black Belt Magazine Hall of Fame
- Golden Shuto Award
- Elite Black Belt Hall of Fame
- Martial Arts History Museum
- Budo Spirit Award
- Master of the Year
- Master of the Sword Award
- Zenith Award
- Contributions to the Martial Arts
- Lifetime Achievement Award
- Kenjutsu Master of the Sword
- Grandmaster Achievement Award
- Hall of Masters Certificate of Recognition
- AMAA Who's Who in the Martial Arts

Over the years, I have been asked these very prevalent questions, "What was it like learning Kenjutsu from the great sword masters in Japan for all those years?" Others asked, "Can you give me a few pointers on how to master a technique?" Some even wanted to discover the essence of swordsmanship and asked, "What do you mentally think about during practice?

For years, I approached these questions by cutting through the mysteries of swordsmanship, explaining all the various nuances, subtleties, and fine details involving sword technique. These questions were usually followed up by demonstrating steadfast proficient techniques gained through decades of my cutting and sparring experience.

Most of those questions asked could and can be answered by identifying physical techniques, movements, and transitions. Understanding the mental aspects of Japanese swordsmanship is extremely challenging to identify with. Therefore, I have given you mental images shown below, which I hope will offer you a much better insight into the mindset of any student of Japanese swordsmanship.

Not even the stark, bone-chilling wooden floor of the aging creaking dojo on this cold winter morn could break my direct concentration. Arising

PERSONAL ACHIEVEMENTS

- Shihan Dana Abbott's expertise is in Kenjutsu, known as Japanese swordsmanship, where he studied in Japan for 15 years during the Showa era. Upon arrival in Japan, he enrolled in Nihon Taiiku Daigaku, Japan's esteemed Martial Arts University, where he learned Kendo and all its applications. All his training and certification was through the Japanese Department of Education and Recreation. Shihan Abbott 7th dan has written and published five books, designed a US Patent, and created a completely new niche in the martial arts industry. He has conducted seminars in over 30 countries and holds the esteemed rank of Shihan, which he obtained at the Hombu dojo in Yokohama, Japan.

from a deeply focused meditation of what might have been minutes or hours, I feel purified and centered. Simple indeed - but this task has become mine.

I bow long and deep with my weapon resting at my side. Then in a deliberate manner, raise my sword in front of me, once again bowing long and deep. Then, with a sense of finality, holster the weapon in my hakama as I have always been instructed to do.

In my Seiza position on the chilled floor, I slowly lean forward with my hands positioned to draw my sword. The moment my hands move from my side, my left hand grasps the scabbard as my right hand grasps the handle. It was at this point when I became one with my weapon in both mind and spirit.

At the speed of light, my right leg surges forward, and my drawn sword whistles upward, deftly hunting for its mark. Anyone observing at this point knows that only a disciplined student of the sword could have harnessed the mind and body necessary for that. The second cut is even more devastating. First upward, parting the cold air of the dojo with sonic-boom speed. Then downward, with a simple, severing accuracy.

Following centuries' old tradition, I then ritually return my sword into my sheath. I again bow with the happiness of knowing I am in harmony once again.

RONNIE ARMSTRONG

"The discipline of the martial arts has given me the courage to stand up for what I believe in..."

TRAINING INFORMATION

- Belt Ranks & Martial Arts Styles: American Karate, 9th degree Black Belt, Kodokan Judo - 5th degree Black Belt, U.S.J.A. JuJitsu - 4th degree Black Belt, Sil-lum Choylay -fut Wing-chung Hung-gar Kung Fu - 2nd Degree Red Sash

- Instructors/Influencers: Grand Master Samuel Barger, Andrew S. Holt III, Sifu James Frazier

- Birthdate: July 5, 1956

- Birthplace/Growing Up: Durham & Hillsborough, NC

- Yrs. In the Martial Arts: 47 years

- Yrs. Instructing: 44 years

- School owner, Instructor, Manager, Director of Non-Profit Organization Kiai, Inc. - Provide Free Karate Classes to children

PROFESSIONAL ORGANIZATIONS

- United States Judo Association, Life Member

- United States Martial Arts Association, Life Member

- American Martial Arts Association, Life Member

- Kiai, Inc. President

- International Martial Arts Federation, Associate Member

I started in martial arts in 1972, three years after the death of my father. My mother wanted me to be mentored by outstanding men in the community so she allowed me to participate in Kodokan Judo at the Y.M.C.A. in Durham, N.C. under Sensei Andrew S. Holt, III. Sensei Holt was her employer and friend. I was in need of guidance and support to get through my adolescent years. Sensei Holt encouraged me to compete in Judo Tournaments which taught me to face challenges in my life. Sensei Holt has served as a lifelong friend and role model.

The lifelong relationships I have developed over the past 47 years in Martial Arts has created the most impact on my life. My Martial Arts instructors provided examples to assist me to become an outstanding Christian Martial Artist. They taught me to face life in a very positive outlook and the belief that all challenges can be met and won. My personal philosophy has been taken from many of the martial arts. The discipline of the martial arts has given me the courage to stand up for what I believe in and to serve others

PERSONAL ACHIEVEMENTS

- 1976 Became the 1st Black Belt of the Durham Judo Club

- 1976 Certified Instructor of Sillum Choylay-fut Wing-chung and Hung-gar Kung-fu

- 1977 Regional Junior Olympic Champion and participated in the AAU Junior National Championship

- 1978 State of North Carolina Senior Judo Champion

- 1979 All Star in Judo for the North Carolina AAU

- 1992 Head Coach and Sensei of Alamance Judo and JuJitsu Club

- 2004 Certified Master Instructor by the American Martial Arts Association

- 2004 National Judo Rank Examiner by the United States Judo Association

- 2004 JuJitsu Rank Examiner by the United States Judo Association

MAJOR ACHIEVEMENTS

- 1975-1979 Assistant Sensei of Durham Judo Club under Sensei Andrew S. Holt, III

- 1979-1983 Assistant Sensei of Burlington Judo Club under Sensei Morris Blanchard

- 1990- Present, Assistant Sensei of American Karate and Barger Martial Discipline Systems

- 1992- Present, Head Coach and Sensei of Alamance Judo and JuJitsu Club

- 1993- Present, Vice President of Kiai, Inc., Superkid Karate Program

DAVID BROCK

"I've trained and been coached by some of the greatest..."

TRAINING INFORMATION

- Belt Ranks & Martial Arts Styles: Kenpo Karate, 8th Degree Black Belt

- Instructors/Influencers: SM Bob White (1st Black Belt student)

- Birthdate: January 4, 1953

- Birthplace/Growing Up: Pensacola, FL

- Yrs. In the Martial Arts: 50 years

- Yrs. Instructing: 45 years

- Instructor—was asked to join PKA by Mike Anderson & Bill Wallace but was a studio owner and had to decline at the time

PROFESSIONAL ORGANIZATIONS

- Extreme Fighters World Championships, President/CEO

MAJOR ACHIEVEMENTS

- Becoming a Born Again Christian 23 years ago, nothing is more significant than that — well, beating #1 lightweight fighter Benny "The Jet" Urquidez in the semi-finals of Long Beach International's 1974 might be considered major to me

- 82 lightweight finals, 82 wins

My friends talked me into joining Martial Arts at 17 years old. I'm currently an 8th degree black belt in Kenpo Karate. I'm honored to have stayed with it. I've trained and been coached by some of the greatest such as Chuck Norris, Mike Stone and my instructor, Bob White.

PERSONAL ACHIEVEMENTS

- 8-time International's fighting champion

- 5-times Las Vegas Nationals Grand Champion

- #1 rated lightweight tournament fighter in California 1975-76

- Honored to be in Legends of Who's Who in Martial Arts Book - nominated by World Champion Jeff Smith

- Inducted into Kenpo Karate Hall of Fame 2018

- Received Joe Lewis fighting award 2019

MICHAEL P. FARADAY

"Our students are the future of the next generations to come in the Martial Sciences, and in this I find great joy..."

I began my interests in the arts at the very young age of 10; when I used to love for Saturday afternoons to come so I could watch the Kung-Fu theater. Then when I turned 12, I officially was introduced into the arts of Martial Science & began my training due to a relative, who wishes to remain unknown, who was in the Armed Forces for our great country as a ranger in the 101st Airborne Division.

When I 1st began my training in the Martial Arts, it was to better myself in esteem, physical endurance, & discover the culture of the orient. As I became older, I referred to what I did as Martial Science & it became a way of life to me. I then took all my knowledge from the teaching of many legendary instructors' through the years and developed my own system for which I call

TRAINING INFORMATION

- Belt Ranks & Martial Arts Styles: 8th Dan, Pi Lum Kung-Fu, Goju Ryu, The Vallari System, Ken Sho Ryu Kenpo, American Kenpo, Shotokan, Chinese Goju, Taikyokuken Ken Sho Ryu

- Instructors/Influencers: Shidoshi Glenn Perry, Shidoshi Ron "The Black Dragon" Van Clief, Sifu Ruben Rodrigues, Sensei Carl Paglione, Sensei John Giaquianto, Hanshi Alan D' Allessandro, sensei Chuck Tarr, & Hanshi Wayne Mello.

- Birthdate: May 12, 1970

- Birthplace/Growing Up: Southbridge, MA/Webster, MA

- Yrs. In the Martial Arts: 38 years

- Yrs. Instructing: 21 years

- School Owner, QuickSilver the Silver Dragon, Inc., Instructor

PROFESSIONAL ORGANIZATIONS

- N.E.K.A

- I.P.P.O.N.E.

- N.A.S.K.A.

- K.R.A.N.E.

- W. O. M. M. A.

- Team America,

- Chuck Norris; Kick Drugs out of America

- A.M.A.A.

PERSONAL ACHIEVEMENTS

- Recruited onto Team America in 1999 for which I traveled all over the World representing our great country of the United States of America against 26 different countries in competition until 2005.

Taikyokuken Ken Sho Ryu. Using the philosophies of the foundations to this discipline as well as Chinese Goju. I enjoy passing this knowledge to my students so that we will be remembered through them, & our teaching can be carried forward with their philosophies attached to ours; for our students are the future of the next generations to come in the Martial Sciences, and in this I find great joy for it reflects through the wisdom of my teacher's to me, and then to my students.

PERSONAL ACHIEVEMENTS

- Consecutively winning six World games in Australia, Ireland, Honolulu HI, Mexico, & Mainland U.S.A. During this time, I earned a total of 26 medals for our country. In total; 4 Gold, 13 Silver, & 9 Bronze. I also won the Nationals, taking home 1 Silver & 2 Bronze medals in 2000.

- In all my competitive years on the I.P.P.O.N.E., N.A.S.K.A., & K.R.A.N.E. circuits, my total wins were 46 with 1 loss, & 1 D.Q. I became a 6-time state champion in my home state of Massachusetts being named # 1 in Weapons, # 1 in Kata, & # 3 in fighting. (1998 - 2005).

- 2009 produced DVD entitled: Katas & Bunki.

- 2010 produced my 2nd entitled: Tribute to the Orient, & 3rd entitled: The Art of Defense. All available by: Thrutheyears.com.

- 2012 did my 1st live radio talk show on the MMA Subway in Los Angeles CA.

- 2019 the live radio show with A.M.A.I.

- I am a veteran letter carrier for the U.S.P.S. 31 years.

- Husband to Tammy Faraday and Father to Mason Faraday.

MAJOR ACHIEVEMENTS

- 2010 inducted into the Martial Science Hall of Fame by; Ron Van Clief.

- 2010 - 2020 inducted into the Action Martial Arts Magazine Hall of Fame 9 times by Sifu Alan Goldberg. (Excellence in the teaching of Martial Arts, Exemplary contributions as an Ambassador of Goodwill in the arts, Esteemed modern warrior award, & Outstanding contributions to the arts as a Grandmaster.)

- 2012 inducted into the World Head of Family Sokeship Council by G.M. Frank Sanchez for Master Instructor of the Year.

- 2012 inducted into the American Temple Training Union by G.M. Anthony Elam as an American Master.

- 2018 inducted into the London Halls of Fame by G.M. Gary Wasniewski, receiving the Humanitarian Award.

- 2018 Filmed in a seminar documentary with G.M. Gary Wasniewski in London. (Spirit of Karate)

- 2019 inducted into the Kung-Fu & Karate hall of Fame by Sifu Cliff Kupper.

- 2019 inducted into the American Martial Arts Alliance by G.M. Jessie Bowen as Who's who Legend Award.

- 2019 inducted into the Legends Hall of Fame by G.M. Cynthia Rothrock for Legendary Silver Pioneer.

- 2020 inducted into the Kung-Fu & Karate Hall of Fame by Sifu Cliff Kupper as an American Master.

- 2020 - 2021 Filmed in the documentary film by Sifu Cliff Kupper entitled "Martialist Two: The Decline & Rebirth of Martial Arts."

- 2009 - 2020 have 26 different books published & available on Barnes & Noble & Amazon. Out of these 26 only 12 are about Martial Science & all the others are fictional, true life, poems, & quotes.

RANDALL FLAHERTY

"Don't give up. Keep going, and one day your accomplishments will positively impact many lives."

TRAINING INFORMATION

- Belt Ranks & Martial Arts Styles: 10th Degree Black Belt (Kenpo Grandmaster)

- Instructors/Influencers: Angel Martial, Bruce Crary

- Birthdate: March 27, 1964

- Birthplace/Growing Up: KY, San Francisco & San Jose, CA

- Yrs. In the Martial Arts: 41 years

- Yrs. Instructing: 38 years

- School owner (Flaherty's Kenpo Karate Association), Instructor, Manager

PROFESSIONAL ORGANIZATIONS

- Owner of Flaherty's Kenpo Karate Association (FKKA)

- Licensed Manager with the California State Athletic Commission's Office (CSAC)

- Original USA Martial Arts Hall of Fame/Inductee

- American Martial Arts Alliance (AMAA)/Inductee

Back in 1972, my father, Robert Flaherty, introduced me to Kenpo Karate. I remember sitting on my father's knee, outside our Kentucky country home, listening to army stories about Dad's Asian friend. As the story goes, back in about 1951, Robert was observing his friend being harassed by a GI for several minutes. My father recounted, "Before I could blink an eye, my Asian friend reached into the big GI's rib cage with incredible hand-speed, and popped it out using his finger-tips (Kenpo Karate in action)." Stories like this one motivated me to learn.

I want to start by taking you on a journey back to my humble beginnings in a little white house in the country, in the great state of Kentucky. My father, Robert Flaherty, verbally planted in me mental pictures of excellent martial arts practitioners who possessed skills of incredible accuracy, hand speed, and power, and others who were skillful at breaking bricks, or as my father put it, "the individuals who were able to walk through walls." Needless to say the stories of human speed development, and the stories of crashing through walls with extraordinary human power, and the descriptions of precision fighting techniques planted the seeds for learning and developing such skills in my young, eight-year-old brain. I suppose you could say that Dad created a "superhero image" of incredible martial artists who possessed excellent skills, especially in his stories of

PERSONAL ACHIEVEMENTS

- Celebrating 41 years in the Martial Arts (1979 to 2020)
- Achieving 10th Degree Black Belt (Grandmaster) rank
- Promoted over 100 Black Belt graduating members

MAJOR ACHIEVEMENTS

- 1984, I received my 1st Degree Black Belt at the International Martial Arts Academy located in San Jose, CA
- 1991, I earned a place on the International Kenpo Karate Association (IKKA) Family Tree as a 4th Degree Black Belt
- 2004, Flaherty's Kenpo Karate Association (FKKA) joined the Better Business Bureau and received an A + rating. In addition, I received "Master of the Year" from the U.S.A. Martial Arts Hall of Fame. (Presented by Dr. Jim Thomas)
- 2005, I received a National Leadership Award, Honorary Chairman, and Businessman of the Year from Congress, Washington D.C
- 2006, I received the Congressional Order of Merit, Washington D.C. and the "Pioneer Award" from the U.S.A. Martial Arts Hall of Fame
- 2008, I received the "Silver Life Award" from the U.S.A. Martial Arts Hall of Fame
- 2011, I received a "Distinguished Service to California Award" from the State Capital. In addition, Flaherty's Kenpo Karate was voted #1 for the "Best Martial Arts Studio" of San Joaquin County

Kenpo Karate in action.

Growing up, the life lessons I learned, whether consciously or subconsciously, came from participating in school sports, attending inspirational church services, and listening to my father's glowing stories about old school martial arts. I vividly remember how those stories extolled the power of martial artists, but at the same time stressed the need to remain humble. A couple of Robert Flaherty's humbling quotes to me included, "Son, it doesn't matter how big (good) you get; there is always someone else better," and, "Wherever there are two or three that are known, there is always one who is unknown." The last quote was always followed by: "Train hard, in case you ever meet the unknown!"

In 1979 in Kentucky, before moving to California, I joined my first official karate studio called the "DOJO." At least the word "DOJO" was written with big letters on the top of the building that was formerly a clothing store. At the DOJO, led by a father and son team, I learned fighting concepts such as the "slip roundhouse kick."

In 1980, after moving from Kentucky to California, I joined Kenpo, Karate, Kung fu, and Judo classes at the International Martial Arts Academy, located in San Jose, California. I received both group and private lessons directly under the tutelage of the Academy's Chief Instructor and Owner, Angel Martial.

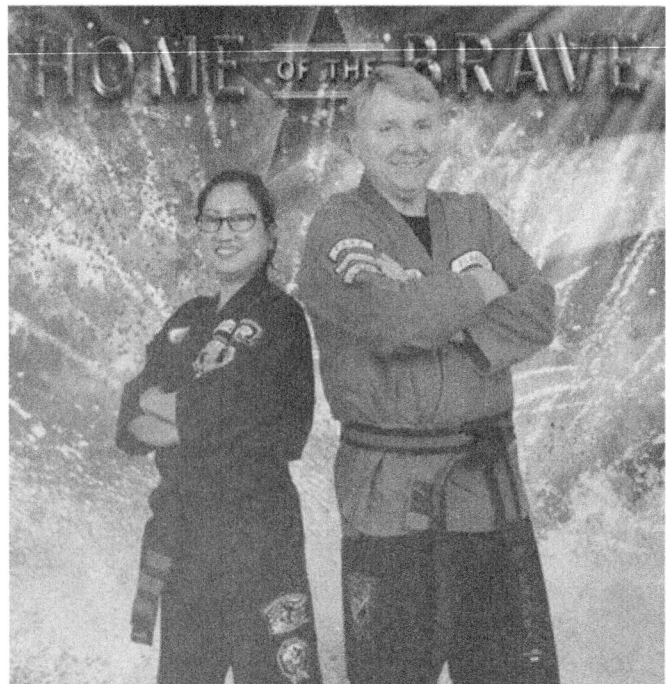

MAJOR ACHIEVEMENTS

- 2012, I earned, from the years of degree promotions, dedication and commitment, the FKKA 10th Degree Black Belt. In addition, I received the "Kenpo Grandmaster of the Year" award from the U.S.A. Martial Arts Hall of Fame

- 2013, Flaherty's Kenpo Karate Association received the "Best of Stockton Award." (Presented by the Stockton Award Program. According to the program management, nationwide, only 1 in 70 (1.4%) 2013 Award recipients qualified as two-time winners.)

- 2016, I celebrated 25 years in business (martial arts)

- 2017, I received the "Grandmaster of the Year" award from the U.S.A. Martial Arts Hall of Fame, along with, a beautiful three Samurai Sword Set with stand, and Tonfa Set

- 2019, I received crystal & plaque awards for "Best in Martial Arts Training for Eight Consecutive Years" by the Business Hall of Fame (Presented by: Stockton Award Program)

- 2019, inducted into the American Martial Arts Alliance (AMAA) Masters & Pioneers Autobiography Program

- 2019, my martial arts academy, Flaherty's Kenpo Karate Association, was voted #1 for "Best in Martial Arts Training"

- December 2019, my students and Black Belt Instructors presented me with a monumental "Award of Excellence" for a lifetime of inspiration, motivation, and outstanding teaching

In 1982, Bruce Crary, a former student of the legendary kickboxing champion, Joe Lewis, presented me with the tournament nickname "Bullet" (Sparring Division), and I received the international martial arts title as "Junior Instructor."

In 1984, Dan Ancheta, a "Brotherhood of Arnis" founder, welcomed me into his stick fighting and martial arts family as an insider. Over the years, I have enjoyed teaching, training, and developing in the fine art of Arnis (i.e., sword, stick, and dagger fighting).

In 1986, I studied "Aikido" from Instructor Bart (no last name given) who received his training from the Old Man's Aikido in the Philippines (Bart knew his instructor as "Old Man's Aikido"). Also, I was featured in local newspapers and a Spanish television commercial with my lifelong martial arts friend and martial arts brother, Ricardo Chaverri.

In 1987, I studied Wushu Kung fu directly under the tutelage of Master Jin Sun Ding. Master Ding became recognized throughout the martial arts industry, along with the "Wushu Institute." According to the Master, "If you lose a competition, then you are not recognized within the Wushu Institute." My Wushu Master Instructor never lost a competition.

In 1988, I trained at the Jet Center in Los Angeles, California, under the instruction of top kickboxing champion fighters, legends, and movie actors, such as Bill "Superfoot" Wallace and Benny "The Jet" Urquidez. I couldn't make the trip from San Jose to Los Angeles often, but when I was able to make the trip, I enjoyed my time training and learning kickboxing skills, boxing movements, and working out in the weight room with lots of sweat, exercise, fellowship, and much more.

In 1991, I opened my first martial arts school (D.B.A.: Flaherty's Kenpo Karate).

In 1994, I instructed a "Women's Week" program, in self-defense, at San Jose State University (Over 50 ladies were in attendance).

In 1996, I opened another martial arts business and was featured in local Bay Area magazines and newspapers. In addition, over the years of earning Degree promotions, I received my 6th Degree Black Belt from the International Martial Arts Academy's Owner, Angel Martial.

In 2000, I opened another martial arts business, while at the same time, developing after school karate programs for elementary-age students. The newly founded, low cost after school children's program, "The Young Karate Masters Program," became very successful for seven consecutive years within the Alum Rock School District.

In 2007, I opened another martial arts business, while continuing the process of developing effective and efficient FKKA self-defense programs for all participants to enjoy.

In 2012, my wife, Mariana, and I modeled karate uniforms for the Tiger Claw Magazine. In addition, I became reunited with my kickboxing instructor, Bill "Superfoot" Wallace, during the U.S.A. Martial Arts Hall of Fame banquet in Los Angeles, CA. Bill Wallace agreed to offer "Super" training classes at my academy. On September 22, of this year, all attendees, along with a news reporter, had an absolute blast during the super-workout day.

In 2017, I developed and released "Flaherty's Kenpo Karate Association's Student/Instructor Code of Conduct." (The "CODE" pages could prove useful for any martial arts business.)

The year of 2019 was an incredible year for the FKKA and me! It was an honor to have Dr. Jim Thomas, Founder and President of the U.S.A. Martial Arts Hall of Fame, instruct a training day seminar at the FKKA. Meeting and being inducted into Grand Master Jessie Bowen's American Martial Arts Alliance/Institute was incredible. Getting selected as one of five martial artists to represent the entire state of California as an inducted member of the American Martial Arts Alliance, Who's Really Who in the Martial Arts, being selected as one of the authors of the 2019 & 2020 Masters and Pioneers Autobiography books, and being recommended and accepted for induction into the 2020 Action Martial Arts Magazine Hall of Honors (Induction Category: Distinguished Renowned Martial Artists Award) were but a few additional humbling highlights.

I want to take this opportunity to thank everyone mentioned in my brief 2020 autobiography, especially to my Black Belt teachers, training coaches, and family members who, over the years, have offered me excellent leadership advice and training. And, as always, my ongoing advice to anyone beginning in martial arts is: "Don't give up. Keep going, and one day your accomplishments will positively impact many lives, especially your own."

PHILIPPE FLOCH

"A Master should not teach false techniques. They must be realistic and applicable to everyday life."

TRAINING INFORMATION

- Belt Ranks & Martial Arts Styles: MODERN COMBAT FLOCH SYSTEM: 10th Dan, JIU-JITSU: 10th Dan, JIU-JITSU GOSHIN-RYU: 10th Dan, COMBAT JIU-JITSU: 9th Dan, JIU-JITSU KOBUDO: 8th Dan, KRAV MAGA: 6th Dan, KARATE: 5th Dan

- Instructors/Influencers: Soke Krzysztof Kondratowicz, Soke Keido Yamaue

- Birthdate: November 26, 1957

- Birthplace/Growing Up: Brest, France

- Yrs. In the Martial Arts: 47 years

- Yrs. Instructing: 40 years

- School owner [Budokan Brest Karate-do, I.M.C.F. (INTERNATIONAL MODERN COMBAT FEDERATION), F.K.M. (France Krav Maga)], Instructor

PROFESSIONAL ORGANIZATIONS

- Philippe Floch Tygrys Security

As an adolescent, I practiced many sports at school, and in clubs and competitions: football, gymnastics, athletics. I also practiced in leisure, boxing (sport from my paternal grandfather side), and Breton wrestling (art learned from my maternal grandfather). I was drawn to combat sports.

When Bruce Lee's first film hit theaters, I went to see it. It left me transcended coming out of the cinema. I wanted to do kung fu. So, I started my martial path with kung fu, then I joined a karate club at 15 years old.

Every month, I used to buy the magazine "karateka" later to be called "karate." I was fond of the articles upon great champions such as Dominique Valéra, Bill Wallace, Benny Urquidez, and so many others. But what I loved the most were the interviews with the Japanese masters.

MAJOR ACHIEVEMENTS

- 1988: Police shooting monitor
- 1990: Police sports instructor, Sniper
- 1991: Trainer in intervention security techniques
- 1993: Federal karate instructor
- 1994: trainer in gestures and professional techniques intervention
- 1996: Founder and professor of Budokan Brest Karate-Do, Monitor in physical and professional activities, State certificate of karate teacher
- 1997: Technical advisor, coach and coach of the regional karate team Police, Police tonfa monitor
- 2000: Krav Maga instructor
- 2004: Consultant in self-defense and intervention techniques for the Polish Ministry of the Interior
- 2006 : Founder, President and Technical Director of the I.M.C.F. (International Modern Combat Federation), designer of the "Modern Combat Philippe Floch System" and the "Modern Combat Pro", Founder, President and technical director of F.K.M. (France Krav Maga), First State-certified Krav Maga teacher in France, member of the Krav Maga technical commission at the French Karate Federation
- 2007: Police telescopic baton instructor
- 2008: Gold medal for youth and sports
- 2012: 10th Dan modern combat
- 2013: Soke, Modern Combat, by GM Masashi Yokoyama (International Martial arts of Culture Federation), Anti-terrorist instructor

I enjoyed the anecdotes, the words of wisdom, the teaching, and the meaning of Budo.

Reading this advice of masters, I decided for myself from that time that I wanted to follow this path. Several masters of karate, Japanese and from Okinawa, have guided me throughout my acquisition of this martial art.

I also liked the TV series "Kung Fu," with David Carradine, broadcast in France from 1974 and "Walker, Texas Rangers," with Chuck Norris, later. The competition started for me quite young with satisfactory results. But it was above all the essence of Budo that fascinated me. So, I decided, when I was 17, to dedicate my life to the study of martial arts.

What I loved above all in the practice of Budo was its nobility and respect for nature. Winning competition is not the point. I especially liked to improve myself. The spirit of self-defense is for me more than anything.

At 20, I replaced my teacher when he was away. I systematically added, in my karate lessons, self-defense techniques that I had learned from the police academy. In my place, I was the first to teach self-defense in the 1980s since judo and karate clubs did not teach self-defense. The spirit of justice and defense is what attracted me to the highest point and still does.

In my place, I was the first to teach self-defense in the 1980s since Judo and Karate clubs did not teach self-defense. The spirit of justice and defense is what attracted me to the highest point and still does.

PERSONAL ACHIEVEMENTS

I was born in Brest (France) in 1957 and I attended secondary school until the end of high school where I obtained my baccalaureate in 1975. From the age of 9, during all my schooltime, I practiced gymnastics and athletics and practiced club football for 8 years. In these three sports, I achieved good results in the regional level. At the same time, I practiced boxing and kung fu in private rooms.

Then I stopped football at the age of 15 to devote myself exclusively to the practice of karate.

In the 1980s, I was a regional finalist for karate kata championships several times. In 1976, during my military service, I became France vice-champion of Karate in kumite.

MAJOR ACHIEVEMENTS

- 2016: 10th Dan (Daishoji Imperial temple)
- International recognitions
- 2017: (World Head of Family Sokeship Council) Master Instructor of the Year Award
- 2019: (World Head of Family Sokeship Council) Grandmaster Member of the Year Award and Seminar Award: Floch Modern Combat
- 2020: (Action Martial Arts Hall of Honors) Distinguished Renowned Martial Artist Award

PERSONAL ACHIEVEMENTS

In 1977, I joined the Police Academy where I mainly developed in sport and self-defense. I also discovered a new discipline, police shooting, which I immediately joined. With a lot of work, I obtained the title of national major of my promotion and also that of national major in shooting and self-defense.

This promotion allowed me to choose my assignment, Brest, city of my birth.

My whole life, then, was settled between my professional development in the police and the improvement of my martial art, which at the time was only karate.

In 1982, I was assigned to an anti-crime brigade, working by night. For 7 years, I was confronted with various situations, most of them were very dangerous. Practicing combat sports helped me, with some skill.

In 1988, I became the gunsmith of my police station. I was then responsible for the training for such as (sport, self-defense, combat sports, tonfa, telescopic baton, intervention techniques, shooting, armaments, driving for specialized services).

In 1996, I bought a room to build my dojo. 10 years later, I created two federations (modern combat and Krav Maga).

When I started studying martial arts at the age of 15, I never stopped training, learning, witnessing master, and expert scenes. I have followed numerous instructor training courses in several fields. Qualifications obtained allowed me to have a certain notoriety in the world of martial arts but also the field of professional activities (armed forces, police, customs, gendarmerie, firefighters). For this reason, I was invited to several European countries to develop my methods and demonstrate the benefits of my martial art, the "Philippe Floch modern combat system."

I bought a dojo, which allowed me to study freely, without constraints, to develop myself and to teach fairly the arts of defense. A master should not teach false techniques. They must be realistic and applicable to everyday life.

Knowledge of martial arts also allowed me to flourish in my police profession for 30 years since I became an instructor for self-defense, combat sports, shooting, telescopic baton, tonfa, and techniques of intervention. This knowledge has allowed me the opportunity to travel, make interesting connections, and, most importantly, develop a complete personal defense system accessible to all.

Several books, authored by me, are currently under study, but the lack of time has not yet allowed me to finalize their writings. It will be my next task.

JEFF N. JONES

" I am most grateful for the students who still drive miles to come and see me and seek my knowledge of the Arts, which I am proud to pass on... "

TRAINING INFORMATION

- Belt Ranks & Martial Arts Styles: Grand Master - Kenpo Karate, Black belt- ITF Tae Kwon Do, Black belt - Joe Lewis System, Wing Chun Kung Fu, Boxing Arnis

- Instructors/Influencers: Tim Teausant, Jerry Wolles, Joe Lewis, Larry Morgan, Paul Boyer, Al Tracy

- Birthdate: June 5, 1958

- Birthplace/Growing Up: Portland, OR

- Yrs. In the Martial Arts: 47 years

- Yrs. Instructing: 44 years

- Instructor

PROFESSIONAL ORGANIZATIONS

- Society of Kenpo Studies - Pacific Northwest

- USA Martial Arts

- American Martial Arts Alliance

After initially not wanting to study the martial arts, I started to feel like this was something that I could really enjoy and do for many years. Even to this day, I enjoy the activity and the purpose that martial arts gives me. After making and winning a bet with my dad (earning a B in math class), I started in Tae Kwon Do, eventually earning my black belt. About the time that I was receiving it, I found a Joe Lewis school teaching the 26 Principles. There I met one of Joe's blackbelts and his sparring partner, Tim Teausant. Tim and I hit it off and I started taking Kenpo lessons from him. He was not only my instructor but became a close friend and Godfather to my daughters. Mr. Teausant also taught the Tracy's Kenpo System as he was also one of their original black belts. Learning the Tracy's Kenpo System and Joe Lewis' 26 principles became almost a full-time job for me and I loved every minute of it.

PERSONAL ACHIEVEMENTS

- Promoted to Master rank - 1999 - by Tim Teausant and Al Tracy
- Promoted to Grand Master rank - 2013 - by Tim Teausant
- Named Grand Master of the year - 2015, USA Martial Arts Hall of Fame

MAJOR ACHIEVEMENTS

- Kenpo International Hall of Fame in Chicago IL - 2009 by Al Tracy
- USA Martial Arts Hall of Fame - 2014 by Jim Thomas
- Inducted into the Who's Really Who in the Martial Arts - 2019 by Jessie Bowen & my students

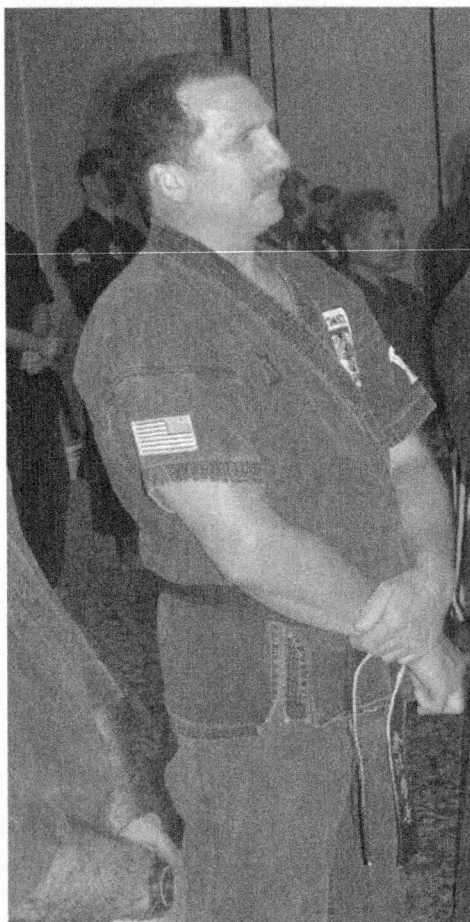

Although I've been fortunate to receive high rank and many awards during my time in the martial arts, I am most grateful for the students who still drive miles to come and see me and seek my knowledge of the arts which I am proud to pass on.

Teaching my daughter and young grandchildren has become the highlight of my week. In addition to my principle instructors, I am also grateful to the many men and women who have stepped in to share with me what they've learned through their training over the years.

The martial arts impacted my life in many ways. Once I started competing as a Tae Kwon Do brown belt, I remember the exhilaration of training like an athlete and being a part of something bigger than myself. Being a part of a large martial arts competition was something I never would have dreamt as a high school kid in SE Portland just a few years earlier. This led to a strong foundation in not only karate basics but the ability to push through injuries and fatigue that has stayed with me to this day. When I started in Kenpo with Joe Lewis and Tim Teausant, I knew that Kenpo would be the martial art that would stay with me throughout the rest of my life. Not only has martial arts enriched my life physically but also mentally. Working with others, training them the way I was trained, has not only helped them physically but has helped me reach my potential as a well-rounded person. I've found I'm much more patient and understanding when others are struggling. Working with underprivileged children has taught me patience and empathy. While they may be part of a gang in the neighborhood, they are all one 'gang' in my class. Everyone works with everyone as rivalries, school issues and family problems are left at the door.

CHRIS KESTERSON

"Knowledge is the true power in martial arts and having the ability to always learn is crucial."

TRAINING INFORMATION

- Belt Ranks & Martial Arts Styles: Kestese (8th Dan), Karate, TKD, Judo, BJJ, Boxing
- Instructors/Influencers: Howard Pittenger (current)
- Birthplace/Growing Up: Knoxville, TN
- Yrs. In the Martial Arts: 44 years
- Yrs. Instructing: 31 years
- Instructor

PROFESSIONAL ORGANIZATIONS

- USMA
- USMAA
- WBBB
- MAMWF
- IBJJF
- CAC Leadership
- Shekinah Masonic Lodge
- Moose Lodge
- Tennessee Sheriff's Asso.
- ICMAF
- SKKA
- American Legion
- AZA
- POI

My father got my brother and I started at an early age. I began my journey as many did with the available arts at the time in my location. Isshinryu was my first discipline followed several years later by Taekwondo. I enjoyed the athletic qualities of both arts. As I aged, the more I was able to travel and other arts became available, I was hungry to try each I encountered and over the past 40 plus years it has been an amazing journey.

Martial arts has made me a better Father, Husband, and Friend through self-control and actions. My earliest experiences with martial arts was that of defense. Like many young martial artists from my era, I was influenced by the actors and fighters that I watched on TV and in the movies. Some of my earliest memories revolve around my larger than life heroes, like Chuck Norris, Bruce Lee, Bill 'Superfoot' Wallace, and Benny "The Jet" Urqiudez. As I aged and broadened my knowledge of the arts, my main focus was beyond the defense aspect and more into the philosophy of the arts.

PERSONAL ACHIEVEMENTS

- IMDB listed actor
- Tennessee Firearms and Defense Instructor
- HOF entries for Martial Arts
- Who's Who in the Martial Arts
- SPF World Record Holder

MAJOR ACHIEVEMENTS

- Recognized for my contributions to Martial Arts through several organizations

I have learned that no matter how many years you dedicate to your art, no matter how many degrees you earn, and no matter how many disciplines you study to improve your craft and art we should all hunger for more knowledge...we should all be that anxious, eager and hungry white belt we began as. Knowledge is the true power in martial arts and having the ability to always learn is crucial. My life, my base and my core values are heavily influenced and shaped by my 40 plus years in the martial arts.

MIKIE ROWE MOORE

"Mikie was one of the first 10 women to be nominated for Nations Top 10 Karate Women."

TRAINING INFORMATION

- Belt Ranks & Martial Arts Styles: Karate
- Instructors/Influencers: Nancy Miller
- Yrs. In the Martial Arts: 52 years
- Yrs. Instructing: 51 years

PROFESSIONAL ORGANIZATIONS

- AKANA (American Karate Academy National Association)

After seeing Bruce Lee as Kato, Mikie wanted to learn Karate. In 1968, Mikie started karate with her first instructor, Nancy Miller. Nancy A Charles Gaylord (Black Belt) was the first women to be promoted to 1st Degree Black Belt in Kajukenbo-Kempo.

On March 3, 1973, Mikie received her 1st Degree Black Belt at the Northern California Referees Associations End of The Year Banquet, where she was the only female member. Grand Master Gaylord removed his belt and promoted Mikie with it. He said he wanted no one to ever question her rank or that she earned the right to wear a Black Belt.

Mikie was instrumental in forming women divisions in California tournaments. She asked Al Reyes Sr. to have a division for women in all weight classes, sizes & belts at his tournament.

She also promised that if no one showed up, she would pay for the trophies. The following month karate history was made. California tournaments continued to add women divisions from then on. Mikie continued to be a champion for Women's & Children's divisions, making them more conducive for women and children to compete in.

In 1969, Mikie opened a karate school in Orinda California where she and her Black Belt husband taught Karate. In 1972, she opened a Women's

PERSONAL & MAJOR ACHIEVEMENTS

- 1973: Earned 1st Degree Black Belt
- Champion for Women's Divisions in Karate
- 1969: Opened first Karate School
- 1973-75: Exercise show on San Pablo Channel 6
- 1977: First Place Lightweight Black Belt, Women's Division, Ed Parkins International
- 1973: Received Mike Stone Gold Fist Award
- One of first 10 women nominated for Nation's Top 10 Karate Women
- One of first 5 women rated in Karate Illustrated
- Inductee, Kenpo International Hall of Fame
- Inductee, Cleveland Martial Arts Hall of Fame
- Kumite Classic Bushedo Award Recipient
- First Woman inducted into Cleveland Actions Magazine
- Hall of Honors Lifetime Achievement Award
- Joe Lewis Eternal Warrior Award Recipient
- 1970s-80s: Martial Arts advisor in film industry

Figure Salon and Karate School in El Sobrante California 25 miles from the Orinda School.

She became a familiar face on Local TVs San Pablo Channel 6. Mikie had her own exercise show in 1973-1975 where she famously incorporated Self Defense into the exercise format.

Mikie and her students did demonstrations for the City of Richmond, California 4th of July Celebration for over 20,000 people in 1975 & 1976.

Mikie competed in most of the major tournaments where she won or placed. In 1977 she won first place at Ed Parkers International lightweight black belt in the women's division. She bowed out to her student and teammate who had won the heavyweight black belt Women's Grand Champion. This was the first year that there was a Grand Champion black belt women's competition. Mikie's 2 women black belt teams took first and second place and her white belt team earned a first place.

In 1973, Mikie received the coveted Mike Stone's Gold Fist Award for Outstanding Competitor, 1971-1973, which was the only year the Golden Fist was awarded.

Mikie was one of the first 10 women to be nominated for Nations Top 10 Karate Women, the first from Northern California. She also was one of the first top 5 to be rated in Karate Illustrated. She remained in top 10 and top 5 until she retired from competition in 1977. She has been inducted into Kenpo International Hall of Fame, Cleveland Martial Arts Hall of Fame, and received the Kumite Classic Bushedo award. Additionally, she was the first woman to be inducted in Cleveland Actions magazine. Amongst others, she received Hall of Honors Lifetime achievement award and the Joe Lewis Eternal Warrior Award. In the Bay area during the 1970's and 80's, Mikie was a consultant on movie sets as a martial arts advisor and she also was on national talk shows where she promoted her "Common-Sense" Self Defense.

Mikie, age 75, is still training and teaching seminars all over the country. She has been a member of AKANA (American Karate Academy National Association) since 2014. Mikie also promoted The Sport Karate Museum all over the country as well.

Recently, she entered a tournament after being inactive in competition since 1977 and took third place. When asked why she decided to complete, Mikie replied, "I teach how to fight in competition so I needed to see if what I am teaching still worked!" In reality, Mikie just likes to mix it up!

STEVE NEMETZ

> "It is a privilege to pass on the knowledge I have gained over the last 42 years..."

In 1978, I walked by Chay's Karate and Tae-Kwon-Do Center in Green Bay, Wisconsin, looked in the window and saw a friend of mine in there. I signed up and have been with the Martial Arts ever since. Sensei Paul Harris was the instructor there and he started his own Karate School called, Harris Karate Academy. I went with him when he opened his own school. Sensei Harris wanted to add more hand techniques to the curriculum that we were teaching, so we started training with the Soaring Eagles Boxing club out of Oneida Wisconsin. Sensei Harris also wanted to add weapons and other styles of the Martial Arts for the advanced belts, so he added Filipino Eskrima, Okinawan Kobudo, and Shorin Ryu to the curriculum training under Kyoshi Neil Stolsmark of Waukesha, Wisconsin.

TRAINING INFORMATION

- Belt Ranks & Martial Arts Styles: American Karate, 8th Degree Black Belt

- Instructors/Influencers: Sensei Paul Harris

- Birthplace/Growing Up: Rantoul, IL/ Green Bay, WI

- Yrs. In the Martial Arts: 42 years

- School Owner, Harris Karate Academy - Plumer Karate America Green Bay-Senior Instructor

PERSONAL ACHIEVEMENTS

- Received my 8th Degree Black Belt in American Karate

- Wisconsin State Heavyweight Black Belt Champion in AAU Continuous Sparring in 1981 - 1983

- Wisconsin State Heavyweight Black Belt Fighting Belt Champion – 1987, 1988

- Won 50+ Black Belt Fighting Grand Championships in Midwest and National tournaments

- Fought Full Contact Karate

- Taught self-defense classes at Boys and Girls clubs helping troubled teens

- Taught self-defense classes in high schools and local Domestic Abuse and Crisis Centers

- Instructor Certified in Reactionary Knife and Pressure Point applications

- Instructor Certified in Eskrima

- Practiced Okinawan Kobudo, Shorin Ryu Karate, Boxing, Jiu Jitsu

Sensei Paul Harris died in January 2010, but Harris Karate Academy stayed open until January 2016. In April 2016, a group of us wanted to continue Sensei Harris' legacy and teachings through Plumer Karate America Green Bay. It is a privilege to pass on the knowledge I have gained over the last 42 years, and to see how our students grow in confidence and gain self-esteem in themselves.

MAJOR ACHIEVEMENTS

- Inductee, Elite Black Belt Hall of Fame

- Inductee, United States Martial Arts Hall of Fame

- Inductee, USA Martial Arts Hall of Fame

- Inductee, Legends of the Martial Arts Hall of Fame

- Inductee, Action Martial Arts Magazine Hall of Honors 4 times

- Inductee, Expo 11 Masters of the Martial Arts Hall of Fame

- Inductee, Tournament of Champions Hall of Fame

- Inductee, Who's Who in the Martial Arts Hall of fame

- Inductee, Masters Hall of Fame

DAVID RIVERA

" Grand Master Rivera's philosophy is that Martial Arts is a way of life. "

TRAINING INFORMATION

- Belt Ranks & Martial Arts Styles: 10th Dan, Vee Jitsu Ryu Jiu Jitsu Te and 9th Dan, Chung Do Kwan Tae Kwon Do, Chung Do Kwan Tae Kwon Do, Vee Jitsu Te Jiu Jitsu, Angola Capoeira, Arnis (Arnis Lanada: Cinco Tero System)

- Instructors/Influencers: Grand Master Robert J. Cooper, the late Supreme Grand Master Florendo Visitacion, the late Grand Master Duk Sung Son, Grand Master Joao Grande

- Birthdate: February 15, 1970

- Birthplace/Growing Up: Brooklyn, NY

- Yrs. In the Martial Arts: 46 years

- Yrs. Instructing: 31 years

- Head instructor at the Frederick County YMCA

PROFESSIONAL ORGANIZATIONS

- International Martial Arts Academy, LLC

- International Martial Arts Institute (Brooklyn, NY)

- American Martial Arts Foundation (AMAAF)

Grand Master David Rivera is a 10th Dan Black Belt who began his Martial Art training at the Thompkins Community Center in Brooklyn, New York, in 1974. He trained under Grand Master Robert J. Cooper, and his father, Grand Master Michael Medina, both of whom were taught by the late Supreme Grand Master Florendo Visitacion. After many years of hard training, Grand Master Cooper promoted Grand Master Rivera in the arts of Vee Jitsu Ryu Jiu-Jitsu Te and Chung Do Kwan Tae Kwon Do. Subsequently, Grand Master Rivera was introduced and continued training under the late Supreme Grand Master Florendo Visitacion (VJJ), the late Grand Master Duk sung Son (TKD), and Grand Master Joao Grande (Capoeira Angola). All of these outstanding men influenced Grand Master David Rivera's Martial Arts career. From the late 1970s to the early parts of the 1980s, Grand Master Rivera met many phenomenal Martial Artists who competed in Open Tournaments hosted by the late Great Grand Master Aaron Bank at Madison Square Garden. In 1989, Grand Master David Rivera began teaching Vee Jitsu Ryu, and Chung Do Kwan Tae Kwon Do at St. Hyacinth College in Massachusetts. An affiliate to UMASS. Upon graduating and returning to Brooklyn, Grand Master Rivera opened a Martial Art School, Most Holy Trinity Martial Arts Club,

in Brooklyn, NY, under the direction of Grand Master Robert J. Cooper. In 1995, as a result of the knowledge gained from his teachers and hard work, Grand Master Rivera was selected by J.H. Park to train on the U.S. Olympic Tae Kwon Do National Team—one of Grand Master Rivera's proudest moments. Over the years, Grand Master Rivera produced many Quality Black Belts and in 1997 was featured in Soke Michael Depasquale's International Black Belt Karate Magazine.

PERSONAL ACHIEVEMENTS

Grand Master Rivera has been awarded several honors due to his dedication and talent in the Martial Arts: Master of The Year from the Notre Dame Martial Arts School, Certificate of Achievement from Dr. Moses Powell, Plaque of Achievement from the Holy Trinity Martial Arts Club, Cosmopolitan Florida Hall of Fame inductee as Master of the Year (2007), World Professional Martial Arts Hall of Fame Inductee at Madison Square Garden as Most Dedicated Martial Artist of all Time by Great Grand Master Aaron Banks (2009), Action Martial Arts Magazine Hall of Honors as Outstanding Achievements in the Martial Arts (2015), Action Martial Arts Magazine Hall of Honors as Ambassador (2017), bestowed Honorary Recognition/Achievement/Doctorate from Boricua College in the Department of Human Services for contributions, the pursuit of higher learning, and acquisition of knowledge in the Martial Arts as a 10th Degree Black Belt on December 15th, 2018, and Action Martial Arts Magazine Hall of Honors as Esteemed Martial Artist and included in the Who's Who amongst Martial Artist in the world (2019) Directory. These were huge milestones and honors. In addition, Grand Master Rivera was inducted into the Legends and Pioneers of the Martial Arts Hall of Honors and included in the Who's Really Who Legends and Pioneers Book in June of 2019 held in Las Vegas. In July 2019, Grand Master Rivera was also inducted into the 20th Anniversary Masters Hall of Fame in Costa Mesa, CA for Martial Arts excellence and on October 25 -27, 2019, Grand Master Rivera was inducted into the Legends of the Martial Arts Hall of Fame in Mount Laurel, NJ and in June 2020, Grand Master Rivera will be presented by the American Martial Arts Alliance as Ambassador of the year.

MAJOR ACHIEVEMENTS

Throughout his career, Grand Master Rivera has taught, and participated in numerous demonstrations throughout the United States including participation as part of a seminar team, which conducted seminars and promotions in Tae Kwon Do, Vee Jitsu, and Capoeira Angola at Notre Dame University South Bend, Indiana (1995-present); seminars in Tae Kwon Do and Vee Jitsu at Indiana University Indianapolis, Indiana; seminars in Vee Jitsu and Capoeira Angola at "Kick-Connection Martial Art School" in Pasadena, Maryland (2002, 2003, and 2004); promotions and Maryland International Martial Art Tournaments hosted by Master Apolo Ladra as a referee and coach; and by invitation of Hanshi Daryl King to conduct Vee Jitsu seminars at the Sanuces Ryu Jiu Jitsu School in Upper Marlboro, Maryland (2004-present); and by invitation of Grand Master Daryl King to conduct Vee Jitsu seminars at the Sanuces Ryu Jiu Jitsu School in Capitol Heights,, Maryland (2004-present); Taught at the Mushin Combat School of Survival Sanuces Ryu in Rockville and Silver Springs, MD (2016-2018); by invitation of Masters Chonfa and Victor Rivera to conduct a Vee Jitsu seminar to Tae Kwon Do and Hapkido students in Puerto Rico (2002 and 2007); by invitation of Holton Arm board of directors to demonstrate Capoeira Angola (2008) and serve on faculty as the head martial art instructor; by invitation of Grand Master Sayfullaah Al-Amriykiy to present at the Preserving the Legacy of Dr. Moses Powell held January 13, 2018 in Philadelphia, PA; by invitation of the YMCA of Frederick County to conduct a Self Defense Seminar to promote public safety to teenagers and adults (February 2019); and by invitation from the Thurmont School of Self Defense to conduct a seminar on Vee Jitsu (March 2019).

MAJOR ACHIEVEMENTS

In addition to providing training through seminars, and his own programs, Grand Master Rivera has shown his commitment to sharing the Arts and works of charity by providing Martial Arts training to those unable to afford training throughout New York and Maryland. These programs include teaching at the "Y" on 92nd St, NYC, New York (1997), the Boy's Club of America in NYC, New York (1999), the Beacon's Program (a program for the underprivileged, 2000 whereby children were able to learn the tenets of Martial Arts and several styles), and presently teaches at the YMCA of Frederick County, MD. Grand Master David Rivera not only taught adults, but also children with various physical and learning challenges such as, Autism, severe attention deficit disorder (ADD), attention deficit hyperactivity disorder (ADHD), dyslexia, and blindness.

Upon moving to Maryland in 2002, Grand Master Rivera taught Vee Jitsu Ryu, Chung Do Kwan Tae Kwon Do, Arnis (Cinco Tero System), and Capoeira Angola drawing students of all ages and founded the International Martial Arts Academy, LLC at Docksiders Gymnastics. Upon moving to the Potomac area of Maryland, Grand Master Rivera relocated IMAA to Holton Arms until finally residing in Frederick County at the YMCA of Frederick County, MD. Grand Master Rivera has been teaching at the YMCA in Frederick, which is one of the oldest YMCAs in the United States, since August of 2017 to children and adults. In January 2019, Grandmaster Rivera was featured in the YMCA Newsletter and video presentation which promoted the YMCA's Mission Statement. As a result, The YMCA has put their Organization Trademark logo behind Grand Master Rivera. This was a huge accomplishment since the core values of the YMCA were featured in connection with Grand Master Rivera's Martial Art philosophy. Here is the link to the video: https://www.youtube.com/watch?v=LzCrRYmtECY&feature=youtu.be

For years, Grand Master Rivera has been involved and active in Martial Arts. Grand Master Rivera's philosophy is that Martial Arts is a way of life. It is through the Martial Arts that we gain self-respect, caring, and responsibility that leads the way to integrity, positive motivation, good attitude, and achievement not only in Martial Arts but in everything we do. It is through these Tenets that Grand Master Rivera develops individuals in the community and fosters a safe environment. The greatest achievement in Grandmaster Rivera's life is to be able to give back to the Martial Arts in the form of teaching, whereby individuals form a positive society.

LONNIE WALKER

"For me, it is not about rank; it is the knowledge gained."

TRAINING INFORMATION

- Belt Ranks & Martial Arts Styles: 9th Degree Black Belt Tae Kwon Do, Tang Soo Do American Kenpo, Tai Chi

- Instructors/Influencers: Master Jun S Kim (RIP), Master Benny Scott (RIP), Master Steve Amaro, Master Steve Cooper, Sifu Tyson Kern

- Birthdate: January 22, 1948

- Birthplace/Growing Up: Las Vegas, NV

- Yrs. In the Martial Arts: 48 years

- Yrs. Instructing: 42 years

- Instructor

PROFESSIONAL ORGANIZATIONS

- AMAA
- DAV
- VIETNAM VETERANS OF AMERICA
- THE ORDER OF THE PURPLE HEART

The main reason I started the study of Martial Arts was to help with my anger and depression issues. When I got out of the Army and Vietnam, I was suffering from PTSD and didn't know it. My weight was out of control, and I was angry. I began studying Tae Kwon Do to get exercise. I had prayed for a way to get my life in control. God answered my prayers with the Martial Arts. Martial Arts became a way of life for me.

PERSONAL ACHIEVEMENTS

- I have been competing in Martial Arts tournaments since 1974. I have competed in major tournaments and minor tournaments. I never saw a match I wouldn't go to. I have competed in the NASKA, NBL, AKO, TPA, USKA, and IMAC and a lot other I have forgotten. I haven't always won first place, but I know I have the most 2nd and 3rd places in the USA.

MAJOR ACHIEVEMENTS

- The biggest and most significant thing I have ever done was accepting Jesus Christ as my Lord and Savior.

- I was inducted in the Who's Really Who Legends and Pioneers, the Master's Hall of Fame, and the Rocky DiRico's International Black Belt Hall of Fame.

Martial Arts changed my life for the better. I went from bitter and angry to healthy and wise. Like I said before the Martial Arts is a way of life, not a fad. For me, it is not about rank; it is the knowledge gained. Martial Arts is much like life, a long journey with lots to learn along the way.

JOHNNY WARREN

"Martial Arts is the biggest part of who I am and what I have become; a leader and a teacher."

Not a typical bullied kid, but growing up as a small child with very aggressive manner due to being born in a war-torn country at that time (Vietnam) to an American soldier and a Vietnamese mother. I was always looked at as the odd kid and the enemy because of my father who was an American soldier fighting in Vietnam and because I would never back down from a fight. My Vietnamese uncle started training me so I could protect myself and have a venue to release my aggression. Even when I was younger, I always wanted to fight and become a fighter. At that time, that was what the Martial Arts was for me. After years of training and fighting, it was much more.

Johnny Warren began his martial arts journey at the age of 4 years old in Vietnam. His mother is a Vietnamese native, and his father

TRAINING INFORMATION

- Belt Ranks & Martial Arts Styles: WarKwanDo (8th Dan/Hachidan) "GM", KiDoKwan (8th Dan/Hachidan) "GM", Vovinam (2nd Dan/Nidan), Kongo-Do (1st Dan/Shodan), Kyokushin (1stDan/Shodan), Okinawan Shorin-ryu (1stDan/Shodan)

- Instructors/Influencers: Nguyen Van Tuoi, Akira Hachirou, Harold Diamond, Chuck Daily, Larry Shepard, Conrado P. Alvarado, John Westerterp

- Birthdate: March 2, 1969

- Birthplace/Growing Up: Saigon Vietnam/ Panama City Beach, FL/ San Francisco, CA

- Yrs. In the Martial Arts: 48 years

- Yrs. Instructing: 26 years

- School Owner, WarKwanDo, Instructor, Manager

PROFESSIONAL ORGANIZATIONS

- WarKwanDo
- KiDoKwan
- Kongo-Do
- PKA WORLDWIDE
- American Martial Arts Alliance

PERSONAL ACHIEVEMENTS

- Grand-Master/Director/President of KiDoKwan System and promoted to 8th Dan/Hachidan before the passing of his first instructor- Nguyen Van Tuoi. Owner/Director/President/Grand Master of WarKwando system, which continues to grow. With his students taking it to another level on both the sport aspect and Martial Arts community.

- Raising two boys as a single parent and passing the Martial Arts to them

is an American soldier. Johnny's mother enrolled him in martial arts due to his aggressive nature and interest in the martial arts from a young age. After moving to the USA, he continued his training under different instructors and systems. At an early age, he was always trying to better himself as a fighter and a martial artist. On the advice of his uncle, Johnny enrolled in a boxing gym to better his hand techniques, as well as continue his martial arts training. Johnny met Larry Shepard at a point karate tournament. Larry Shepard noticed that Johnny, at 14, was fighting and winning in the adult divisions. Larry encouraged him to get into kickboxing. After watching kickboxing on TV, he was interested in getting into the ring as a fighter. Johnny began to train with Larry and after just three months of kickboxing training he had his first amateur fight in kickboxing; he was now hooked.

Johnny moved to FL and kept up his fighting going from the then PKA and moving to ISKA. After taking a few fights in Colorado, he turned pro under the ISKA banner, winning local and minor titles and championships in ISKA. Johnny then decided to move onto another organization due to lack of matches he could get under ISKA. But during his time under the ISKA organization, he fought and beat fighters such as Felipe Garcia (former world ISKA, PKA champion), Rick and Randy Ford, James Chavez, Francisco Landin, and many more. Johnny decided to change to international rules that allow leg kicks, where he could get more fights.

Johnny won fights and world titles under IKBF, IKBO, IKBA, beating fighters like Byron Robinson, Mariano Liano, Somrak Yudathag, Defino Perez, Geraldo Navaro.

Johnny's titles include:

1) IKBO World Jr. Lightweight Champ

2) IKBA World Lightweight Champ

3) ISKA US Regional Featherweight Champ

4) ISKA Colorado State Bantamweight champion

5) IKBF North American Bantamweight Champ

MAJOR ACHIEVEMENTS

- IKBO World Jr. Lightweight Champion
- IKBA World Lightweight Champion
- ISKA US
- Regional Featherweight Champ
- ISKA Colorado State Bantamweight Champion
- IKBF North American Bantamweight Champion
- Colorado State Point/Kata Grand Champion

Johnny was known and still is known for his flashy, fast, powerful kicks. Some of his peers such as Steve Shepard, Curtis Bush, Harold Diamond, Chuck Daly, and John Westerterp have stated that Johnny may be one of the greatest kickers ever. With 30 KO's in his pro record, his kicks were the significant amount of them, 19 by kicks.

After retiring from kickboxing with a record of 38 wins-4 losses-1 draw-30 KO's in 2001 (due to eye injuries), Johnny started to blend all the things he picked up to incorporate into his system called WarKwanDo.

Having over 40+ years in the Martial Arts/Combat System world, Johnny currently teaches and trains his two sons and has free classes for inner-city kids in kickboxing and WarKwanDo system in San Francisco CA. Johnny's love for the Martial Arts has always pushed him to better not only his art of WarKwanDo, but the Martial Arts in general and to pass along his knowledge to future martial artist and fighters. He does a few seminars a year for free to help spread the Martial Arts.

"Martial Arts gave me a chance to not only fight and become a world champion, but is the biggest part of who I am and what I have become; a leader and a teacher. It will always be in my life."

TIMOTHY J. WHITE

"Martial arts taught me to overcome some of my fears, and not to let my 2000-pound ego override my good judgment."

TRAINING INFORMATION

- Belt Ranks & Martial Arts Styles: Molum Pai Kung Fu Sijo Inherited through the death of Sijo Tak Chueng Wong, Molum Combat Arts Systems (10th Dan), Keisatsu Jujutsu (9th Dan)

- Instructors/Influencers: GM Wes Ruiz, GM Dan Onan, Sijo Tak Chueng Wong, Sifu William

- Birthdate: August 22,

- Birthplace/Growing Up: Milwaukee, WI/Indianapolis, IN

- Yrs. In the Martial Arts: 47 years

- Yrs. Instructing: 45 years

- School owner (Molum Combat Arts)

PROFESSIONAL ORGANIZATIONS

- American Martial Arts Alliance (AMAA)

- Professional Karate Commission (PKC)

- Professional Karate Association (PKA)

- Cobra Martial Arts Association (United Kingdom) (CMAA)

- Eastern United States International Martial Arts Association (EUSIMAA)

- MLCAA/Kiru-Do Association

- MLCAA Honor Society Founder

I started Martial Arts while stationed in Darmstadt, Germany, while serving in the US Army. I wanted to enhance my combat skills and enhance my self-defense skills, as well. I was so motivated through the training that I continued. It also helps me in my professional career as a law enforcement officer.

Since I started in the martial arts in 1972, there are many landmarks that impact how I see and do martial arts. In the beginning, it was mostly about self-defense and physical fitness. As I grew in martial arts through different instructors, I began to get insight as to learning and teaching. Two of my teachers had no experience in law enforcement. However, in 1976 Hanshi Dan Onan was a Defensive Tactics Instructor for the Indiana Department of Corrections. He had some great concepts for law enforcement, and I liked them and continued studying with Sijo Wong at the same time.

It has impacted how I think of Martial Arts as a whole and not a single system. For example, A Martial Arts system in itself doesn't make the person work; the person makes that martial arts system **work for them**.

PERSONAL ACHIEVEMENTS

- Co-Author of Cell Extractions for Jail and Prisons, published 2004

- Author Straight Baton, using the ASP model, published 1995

- Published articles on the ASP Baton in Karate International Magazine

- Inherited the Molum Pai Kung Fu Systems

- Chosen for the 2019 Who's Who for the Action Martial Arts Magazine Mega Event

- Public Safety Institutes National Trainer Certification for Physical force and Defensive Tactics

- ASP Baton Certification

- Chosen as the Chief Defensive Tactics Instructor for Police Corps Indiana 2000 to 2005

- Defensive Tactics Instructor Johnson County Jail 1996 to 2004

- CERT Team Leader Johnson County CERT Team 2011 to 2014

MAJOR ACHIEVEMENTS

- Selected for 2017, 2018 and 2019 Who's Who in Martial Arts

- Top Ten Competitor in the PKC and 2004 Regional Champion

- Producing PKC Region #2 Champions in the Youth Divisions

- Letters of Commendation from Army Commanders for teaching Self Defense

- 2013 Tactical Instructor of the Year EUSAIMAA

- 2015 Action Martial Arts Hall of Honors

- 2018 Lifetime Achievement Award EUSIMAA

It is a choice. Rank is a matter of Achievement and not of character.

Sports Martial Arts taught many little things that impacted my life; like in the ring, all Black Belt are on equal ground, and rank has no part in it. Sports Martial Arts also taught me the fundamental fairness in all aspects of training. That in itself and impacted many things in my career as well.

Martial arts taught me to overcome some of my fears, and not to let my 2000-pound ego override my good judgment.

MAJOR ACHIEVEMENTS

- 2017 Grandmaster of the Year EUSIMAA

- 2003 PKC Humanitarian Award

- Participation in the PKC Legends Demonstrations at the PKC International Tournament

- 2019 Action Martial Arts Hall of Honors

- Numerous Military Awards to include the Meritorious Service Medal, the Indiana Distinguished Service Medal and many others

- State Guard Association of the United States Distinguished Service Award and Meritorious Service awards as well

Ambassadors
MASTERS

JENNIFER BRANCH

"It's my goal to teach and instill the martial arts philosophy in every student I meet."

TRAINING INFORMATION

- Belt Ranks & Martial Arts Styles: Taekwondo - 7th Dan, Shorin Ryu
- Instructors/Influencers: Grandmaster Roy Kurban
- Birthdate: October 13, 1965
- Birthplace/Growing Up: Dallas & Arlington, TX
- Yrs. In the Martial Arts: 46 years
- Yrs. Instructing: 25+ years
- Chief Instructor

PROFESSIONAL ORGANIZATIONS

- American Karate Black Belt Association
- Chin Sook Hage Kwan - currently serving as Secretary to the High Dan Board
- The United States Traditional Taekwondo Society - under GM. Roy Kurban and GM. Won Chik Park

I started Martial Arts at the age of 9. I was a kid of the 1970's and grew up watching Bruce Lee on TV. I found a local school and met my real-life hero and instructor, Roy Kurban in 1974. And the rest is history.

Martial Arts has been a part of my life for as long as I can remember. It has simply shaped every phase of my life. The traditional principles of martial arts: courtesy, integrity, self-control, perseverance and indomitable spirit became my guiding philosophy throughout life. These tenets continue to influence all my endeavors. The process of being a student, competitor, and eventually becoming a teacher has been the most important work in my life.

Training, learning and teaching the philosophy of traditional martial arts continues to bring tremendous purpose and fulfillment to my life. I especially enjoy working with young students and watching their growth in all aspects of their lives. In fact, I believe so much in what the martial arts can do for young people that I founded the non-profit "Team Zen Champions for Life, 501(c)3". This non-profit aspires to teach character development and community leadership through martial arts.

PERSONAL ACHIEVEMENTS

- 1980-84 - Student instructor under the guidance of Grandmaster Roy Kurban

- 1984-87 – Arlington Country Day, Private School for 1st-6th grades

- 1984-87- Arlington Girls Club and various recreation centers throughout Arlington, Texas

- 1987-90- Conducted private lessons at Four Seasons Health Club

- 1990 – Founded the martial art program at Los Colinas Sports Club, Irving, Texas

- 1991 – Founded the martial art program at GTE World Headquarters, Irving, Texas

- 2004 – Founded the Austin Black Belt Academy

- 2015 – Founded Team Zen-Champions for Life; 501c Non-Profit for Youth Development through Martial Arts

MAJOR ACHIEVEMENTS

- 1974 - Began Taekwondo training under Grandmaster Roy Kurban at the American Black Belt Academy in Arlington, Texas.

- 1975-2010 – Competed in local, national, and international events

- 1981 - Top 5 Jr. Fighter in Texas, A.O.K.

- 1982 - Top 10 Jr. Competitor, Official Karate Yearbook

- 1984-87 - Top 3 Adult Competitor, A.O.K., Forms and Fighting

- 1986-87 - Regionally Ranked Forms and Fighting, Karate Illustrated Magazine

Each student I work with inspires me every day to be a better person. It's my goal to teach and instill the martial arts philosophy in every student I meet, with the hope of motivating each to live their dreams.

MAJOR ACHIEVEMENTS

- 1987 - Competed on Ft. Worth Team in Black Belt team Challenge; International Kickboxing Council

- 1990-95 - Top 5 Competitor, Traditional Karate League, Eagle Award Winner

- 1996 - Texas State TKD Championships, Gold & Silver Medalist

- 1996 - US National TKD Championships, US Olympic Training Center, Silver Medalist in Forms

- 1996 - Awarded 5th Dan Master Certificate under the aegis of Grandmaster Roy Kurban and Grandmaster Won Chik Park

- 2008 - Battle of Atlanta, 1st Fighting and 2nd Forms

- 2009 - Awarded 6th Dan under Grandmaster Kurban and Grandmaster Won Chik Park, USTKD Grandmaster Society 2010 - USAT TKD US National Qualifier, Sport Poomsae, Gold Medalist

- 2014 - 42nd Annual US Karate Championships, Texas Legends Team Match

- 2014 - Awarded 7th Dan under GM Roy Kurban and GM Won Chik Park, USTKD GM Society and American Karate Black Belt Association Chin Sook Hage Kwan

RICHARD LEE BROWN

"Martial arts always been the one special constant that only I could appreciate."

TRAINING INFORMATION

- Belt Ranks & Martial Arts Styles: Universal Karate Do (8th Degree Black Belt), Tang Soo Do and Kuk Sool Won (Black Belts)

- Instructors/Influencers: Hanshi James E. White, Sensei Rogers Reece, Master In Joo Suh, Master Nick Flores

- Birthdate: October 26, 1961

- Birthplace/Growing Up: Lancaster, SC

- Yrs. In the Martial Arts: 43 years

- Yrs. Instructing: 38 years

- School owner, Manager & Instructor at Universal Karate Studio HQ

PROFESSIONAL ORGANIZATIONS

- National Universal Karate Association

The Chief Master Instructor of Universal Karate Studios is Master Richard L. Brown. He earned the 8th Degree Black Belt with over 42 years of experience in a martial arts system called Universal Karate Do. He began martial arts training in 1977 in Lancaster, S.C. under Hanshi James E. White, 10th Dan, and Grand Master of Universal Karate Do. After enlisting in the U.S. Air Force in 1981, Shihan Brown was stationed in Ramstein AB, Germany, where he began teaching Universal Karate Do. During that time, he also studied the fundamentals of Tang Soo Do with Sensei Rogers Reece, a student of Hwan Kee of Korea. He began his black belt competition career in Germany with many successes that followed him back to the United States. After relocating to San Antonio, TX. Master Brown continued being a formidable opponent for competitors all over the country and Mexico, Canada, Guatemala in Traditional forms, weapons, and point sparring. While still working for the Air Force, he developed a successful martial school that developed several skilled black belts who still own and operate their schools today. To further develop his

PERSONAL ACHIEVEMENTS

- Family first
- Throughout the 1980s, 90s, and the 2000s, he was a nationally top-ranked competitor winning many championships in Forms, sparring, and weapons categories
- Completed 33 years of service Retired Air Force veteran
- Earned a Master's Degree in Organizational Management
- Bachelor's Degree from Wayland Baptist University
- Occupational Education Associates Degree from Wayland Baptist University
- Management Associates Degree from Palo Alto College
- Kinesiology Associates Degree from Community College of the Air Force
- Education and Training Management

MAJOR ACHIEVEMENTS

- World Karate Union Hall of Fame - June 1998 Promoter of 29th Invitational Tournament of Champions 2019 and all years before
- Shihan of Universal Karate Do as appointed by Hanshi James E. White
- Facilitated numerous Seminars National and International National Black Belt League Tournaments

training, Master Brown became proficient in Kuk Sool Won's art under the study of Master In Joo Suh, earning a Black Belt in that system. Continuing to grow, he later began his training with Master Nick Flores of George West, Tx. to further study Okinawan Kempo, which is one of the root systems of Universal Karate Do. Through many years of training under Hanshi James E. White of Universal Karate Do, Master Brown had worked his way to mastery of the system. He found himself training in Okinawa, Japan, where he could touch the root of Karate. Through these many years of Martial Arts training and teaching, he presently owns 2 dojos in San Antonio, Texas, where he teaches Karate, Kobudo, Jujitsu, and Tai Chi. Though his life has been dedicated to Martial Arts, Master Brown shares a wealth of academia with a Master's Degree in Organizational Management, Bachelor of Science and Occupational Education, Associates of Applied Science in Management, Wayland Baptist University. Associate of Applied Science in Education and Training, Community College of the Air Force and Associates of Applied Science in Kinesiology degree, Palo Alto College. Also, Master Brown retired as a Master Seargent in the USAF Reserves after serving 33 years active duty and reserve in support of Desert Storm, Desert Shield, and Iraqi Freedom campaigns. He shares the philosophy of dedication, honor, obedience, and loyalty with his students believes in the AF credo, "Excellence in all we do." With his wealth of martial arts experience, Master Brown was honored with SHIHAN's rank and wore a red and white belt known as Renshi to signify professorship in Karate do. Our martial arts system is a comprehensive training program founded in 1975 and comprises traditional Korean and Japanese martial arts. Master Brown also holds Black Belt ranks in Tang Soo Do and Kuk Sool Won. Throughout the 1980s, 90s, and the 2000s, he was a nationally top-ranked competitor winning many championships in Forms, sparring, and weapons categories. As a mentor, he is stern, caring, and a great leader who ensures that all UKS staff are well trained.

Studying martial arts has influenced my life since the day I started. It has given me confidence and mental concentration to achieve great things throughout my life. It has always been the one special constant that only I could appreciate. When times were hard, during peacetime and wartime in the Air Force, Karate fed my spirit. When a relationship wasn't going right, it was there to lift me. It has indeed been a way of life, and I enjoy sharing it with anyone who wants to learn. I share this gift with my family because I pray they all develop the confidence to pursue their life dreams and aspirations as I have. I've allowed martial arts to carry me worldwide training, studying, and competing to make me always try to be better. I desire to continue sharing the many lessons I've learned with as many people as possible in hopes that they will enjoy the experience.

MICHAEL T. BUTLER

"I've had the opportunity to know and train with some of the greatest Martial Artists in the world."

TRAINING INFORMATION

- Belt Ranks & Martial Arts Styles: Tang Soo Do (1st Red Belt), American Taekwondo (5th Degree Black Belt)

- Instructors/Influencers: Master Gene Pack, Grandmaster James Stevens

- Birthplace/Growing Up: North Massapequa, Long Island, NY

- Yrs. In the Martial Arts: 38 years

- Yrs. Instructing: 20 years

- Instructor

It started with my older son and I. We would sit on Saturday and watch Kung Fu movies in the early 70's and late 80's. After watching them, he said to me, "Wow Dad, I'd really like to learn karate and self-defense." A friend of mine was in martial arts. He was a kung fu black belt. I spoke with him and he told me where I could meet his master. I met Sifu Wallace Gupp. He was a man about my size. I spoke with him and watched what he did. He was very flexible. I wasn't and thought that wasn't going to work for me. My friend told me to find something that fits my body. In 1981, I was driving and saw a sign on a building that said "Chuck Norris". I knew who he was. I watched him on tv in the seventies. I went in and met the head instructor, Ed Young. He was a direct descendent of Chuck Norris; he received his black belt from chuck Norris. I told my son and we started training.

PERSONAL ACHIEVEMENTS

- Personal Achievements:
- Raising two great sons
- Being married to a great wife
- Making rank of Master 5th Degree Black Belt

MAJOR ACHIEVEMENTS

- 1984- AOK Competitor of the Year
- 1984- Astro world shows with grandmaster Gary Lee
- 1986 & 1987- Chuck Norris system national forms champion
- 1993- Achieved the rank of 3rd degree black belt under Grandmaster Jimmy Gato Tabares
- 2010- Achieved the rank of 4th° black belt for my work with master Jean Pack and Grandmaster James Stevens
- 2014- Inducted into the United States Martial Arts Hall of Fame
- 2016- Received the Ambassador and the first ever Steve Marz Natural Fighter Award from the National Sport Karate Museum
- 2017- Achieved the level of Master 5th degree black belt
- 2018- Inducted into the Universal Martial Arts Hall of Fame

Since I started training, it has helped me look at many things in a different light. It helped me focus better at work and appreciate my family more. When I started to teach, it was a great feeling to be able to help other people to improve their own self-discipline and confidence. I saw how the martial arts teaching helped young teens struggling in school improve their grades and their attitude. I gained this sense of what was going on around me and I would walk away when I felt there was going to be trouble. On the job they would say to me they were amazed how calm I would always be and they felt it was due to my martial arts training. I watched how martial arts helped my youngest son gain self-confidence and discipline. It has always amazed me how different martial arts styles come together and share their ideas and thoughts. It would be nice to see the rest of the world come together in the same way. I've had the opportunity to know and train with some of the greatest martial artists in the world. Being a martial artist is a way of life with honesty and integrity.

ART CAMACHO

Award winning, Film Director/Fight choreographer Art Camacho has a varied and eclectic background in the martial arts. He's been training for over 25 years and has Black Sash in the art of Wun Hop Kuen Do (5th degree) under the Grand Master Eric lee. He has also trained in Kung Fu San Soo, Bruce Lee's Jeet Kune Do, Japanese Karate, Filipino Kali, Kickboxing, martial arts weapons, was an amateur boxer and most recently started training in Wing Chun Kung fu under renowned Master Samuel Kwok. Camacho came from a very humble background in a barrio in East Los Angeles born to Immigrant parents. He was always getting into trouble as a kid and that lead to him having a run in with rival gang bangers who beat him to a pulp. He ended up with eleven stitches over his right eye and bruises and cuts all over. After a few weeks of rehab, he began his Martial arts journey. At first it was to exact revenge and to release all that bottled up anger he had inside. That was soon to change. Camacho soon discovered the one person whose influence would be felt the rest of his life: Bruce Lee. "I remember sitting in an old downtown theater, three quarters of the way empty and watching my first Bruce Lee movie "The Chinese Connection". I sat there mesmerized by what was happening on that screen. After the movie was over I walked out of that theater transformed". Camacho began to change his focus from wanting to beat people up to wanting to really understand the martial arts. He trained in various styles and trained beneath many Masters until he finally ended up with martial arts legend Sifu Eric Lee where he found his home in the art of Wun Hop Kuen Do. Sifu Al Dacascos' Wun Hop Kuen Do, was the right fit for Camacho, with its explosive and effective fighting techniques.

Having dropped out of high school at 16 he went back and earned his G.E.D. He then began working at a Spanish Language Advertising agency whereby he went onto garner praise and awards for outstanding contributions as a Spanish language Commercial Director in the entertainment industry.

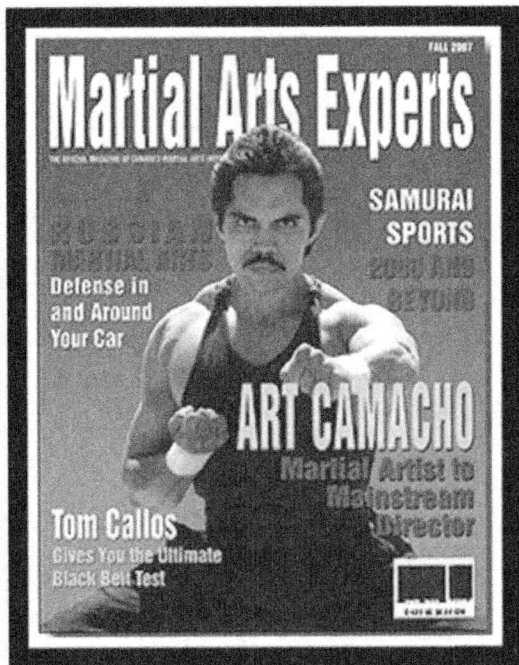

His film career began as an actor working in local theater productions and bit parts on television shows. He then landed leads in a few independent feature films. From there he was given the opportunity to choreograph fight scenes in various films. This soon led him to Direct Action films. Camacho became world renowned as a Premier fight choreographer and independent action film director and was dubbed "The Fight Master" by the leading martial arts publications. He has worked with such icons of the martial arts action genre such as Dolph Lundgren, Randy Couture, Lo Meng, Hwang Jang Lee, Don "The Dragon" Wilson, Gary Daniels, Cynthia Rothrock, Steven Seagal, Olivier Gruner, Richard Norton, Lorenzo Lamas, Quentin "Rampage" Jackson, WWE"s Goldberg, Bob Wall, John Saxon, James Lew, Ron Yuan, and many, many others.

In between his film work, Camacho became in demand as a martial arts action trainer because of his background in both martial arts and cinematic fight action.

Some of the people he's trained through the years have included WWE wrestling champions, UFC champions, Actors and actresses and super models. He developed a method that combines actual well-rounded training in the martial arts with execution for, and awareness of camera." Real martial arts in all practicality has be modified for films or it would look real boring and short, be it Krav Maga, MMA, boxing, Karate etc.

"Film action much like acting has to feel organic. In order to make it as exciting as possible the person has to develop a foundation and execute it cinematically."

In addition to his directing and fight choreography career, Camacho teaches a few select private students in his unique method of martial arts and screen fighting.

Art Camacho is also an author, having authored a very candid and personal auto-biography: "Art Camacho, A filmmakers Journey", detailing his journey in martial arts, life and movies.

Art Camacho has been inducted into 8 martial arts Halls of fames including USA Martial arts Hall of Fame, Legends of the Martial arts Hall of fame, Masters Hall of Fame, the Golden State Karate Association Black Belt Hall of Fame, and the Hall of honors. Camacho has also graced the covers of many international martial arts magazines and books and has been featured in "Black Belt magazine", "Inside Kung Fu", "Karate International", "Cinturon Negro", "Masters and Styles, "Secrets of the Masters", "Martial Arts Illustrated", "Who's Who in Entertainment" "Encyclopedia of Martial Arts" Canada's "Martial arts experts". L.A.'s largest Spanish Language Newspaper "La Opinion" has done several stories on Camacho He was also featured on "Hola Los Angeles", "Cinemax" Mexico's channel 12, "Despierta America" and "Control". Camacho was also featured on Latin Nation and he was the first recipient of the "The Outstanding Director of the Year" award from the Action on film, film festival 2005/2006, The Golden and Bronze halo awards from the Hollywood motion picture counsel. Camacho was also recipient of an award from the World Martial arts Association that was presented to him on behalf of Alan Horn (Walt Disney Studios Chairman) and Michael Klausman (President of CBS studios). He was also honored by Grand Master Byong Yu and Grand Master Chuck Norris with the "Night of the Stars" award at CBS studios. The Martial arts history museum honored him with an Official "Art Camacho" Day and the prestigious "Funakoshi" award for his outstanding influence and contributions to the martial arts.

KEN DAUGHERTY

> "Martial arts has had a lifelong impact. Not only the martial side but the art (Do) as well."

TRAINING INFORMATION

- Belt Ranks & Martial Arts Styles: Traditional ITF Taekwon-Do - 6th Dan (VI Degree Black Belt), Studied/trained in various other disciplines (American Taekwon-Do - 5th Dan, Boxing, Kickboxing, Krav Maga, Jujitsu, et cetera)

- Instructors/Influencers: Grandmaster Orlando Vega

- Birthdate: May 17, 1971

- Birthplace/Growing Up: Omaha, NE / Spanish Fort & Mobile, AL

- Yrs. In the Martial Arts: 35 years

- Yrs. Instructing: 25 years

- Manager, Instructor, Business Owner

PROFESSIONAL ORGANIZATIONS

- International Taekwon-Do Federation - The Americas

- International Taekwon-Do Federation - ITF HQ Korea

- Oriental Sports Center

I was a very skinny, small, and short child. I was bullied frequently. I enjoyed watching many martial arts movies (Bruce Lee, Chuck Norris, Ninja movies, etc.) and when I was getting bullied at a young age, I knew it would help me in order to protect myself.

Martial arts has had a lifelong impact. Not only the martial side but the art (Do) as well. It teaches humility, compassion, respect and honor. We should never forget our roots or those who have made a difference in our lives. The most important person that walks into the room is the beginner student who has a love of martial arts. Without them, our art dies and the legacy of what we teach disappears.

It always comes full circle when I'm somewhere in public and a student from years ago (who is now grown) that I taught as a child comes up to me and tells me how I changed their lives. That's what it's all about! Making a positive difference in someone's life that's more important than your own.

PERSONAL ACHIEVEMENTS

- Ken Daugherty has placed and/or won at several tournaments Nationally, Internationally and in Open tournaments.

- Coming back from major knee surgery on two different occasions. (Perseverance to the art of Taekwon-Do)

- Being promoted to 6th Degree (VI Dan) Black Belt at the PanAm Games in front of many International Grandmasters and Masters in an Old School outdoor test

- Certified International Instructor (in front of Pioneer GM Park Jong Soo)

- Certified International Umpire Class A

MAJOR ACHIEVEMENTS

- Became the Secretary General for the ITF The Americas Organization

- Became the State Representative for the ITF HQ Korea for Alabama.

- Influential in helping to achieve a merger between two different International Taekwon-Do Federations, a first in the world to promote unity between the various ITF organizations

JENNIFER FRASER

"Having sign language will give better communication in the Martial Arts world."

TRAINING INFORMATION

- Belt Ranks & Martial Arts Styles: Kickboxing- Black Belt 3rd Degree, AMAAD Karate- Black Belt 5th Degree
- Instructors/Influencers: Neil Ehrlich, Wilson Jerome
- Birthdate: October 30, 1967
- Birthplace/Growing Up: Los Angeles & Redding, CA
- Yrs. In the Martial Arts: 28 years
- Yrs. Instructing: 20 years
- Instructor

PROFESSIONAL ORGANIZATIONS

- JAKI Martial Arts and Self Defense

I started training at Master Neil Ehrlich's American Karate Institute to learn kickboxing and karate. There were several deaf students who wanted me to join and Neil knew sign language and helped to communicate in martial arts. We all became friends and became passionate in martial arts and boxing.

Martial Arts impacted my life for many years and gave great achievement to help other deaf and hard of hearing children and adults to become martial arts leaders. They can be involved in many tournaments to build their confidence and skills. Having sign language will give better communication in the martial arts world. It is a very rewarding experience.

PERSONAL ACHIEVEMENTS

- Received three college degrees and currently enrolled in Computer Security Management at Strayer University in second Masters Degree

- Currently working as a Quality Assurance Analyst with GCE/ Department of Defense contractor in Northern Virginia

- Certified in security+

- Beside my work, I have a son and one granddaughter

- I am a proud granny

MAJOR ACHIEVEMENTS

- Received many tournament awards in sparring: 1st and 2nd places from 1995 to 2015. World Championship Deaflympics in Rome, Italy and won silver medal in forms and bronze in sparring in the year of 2002. Invitational games for the deaf in Taipei, Taiwan, I won silver in sparring in the year of 2008. Martial Arts Magazine Hall of Honor Inductee in 2010. America Martial Arts Association for the Deaf Vice President and Director from 2001-2008. Ran two tournaments of AMAAD 2007 and JAKI Karate 2012. Executive Producer and actress in Martial Arts Kids, 2014. Kung Fu and Expo Masters of Martial Arts Award Ceremony since 2017.

'JENNIFER R. FRASER-TAYLOR'

WILLIAM FRIEND

"Martial Arts keeps me healthy mentally and physically. My school and my students are like my family."

TRAINING INFORMATION

- Belt Ranks & Martial Arts Styles: 5th Dan Shuri-ryu, 3rd Dan Shotokan

- Instructors/Influencers: Grandmaster Vic Moore

- Birthdate: March 10, 1980

- Birthplace/Growing Up: Madison, KY

- Yrs. In the Martial Arts: 34 years

- Yrs. Instructing: 22 years

- School owner

PROFESSIONAL ORGANIZATIONS

- Traditional World Karate Association

- American Martial Arts Alliance

Movies and television were a huge reason I started studying the martial arts. A lot of shows were about martial arts: Chuck Norris, Cynthia Rothrock, and Bruce Lee.

Martial Arts keeps me healthy mentally and physically. My school and my students are like my family.

PERSONAL ACHIEVEMENTS

- Continuing to practice martial arts and continuing to learn is an accomplishment

MAJOR ACHIEVEMENTS

- Running two schools for over two years now

Goldman hook kicks Auld

MICHAEL GOLDMAN

"I was convinced that Sport Karate competition was what I wanted to do after watching fighters like Bill Wallace, Mike Warren, John Natividad, Howard Jackson and many other superstars compete..."

With a flashy fighting style, an almost uncanny kicking ability, a pair of fast hands and a refined sense of timing that put him in the winners bracket more times than not, Goldman was pegged with the nickname "Hotdog" by peer Super-Lightweight black belt fighters in the south.

After watching the films "Billy Jack" and "Enter the Dragon", Goldman became hooked on the Martial Arts, and in 1973 he signed up for karate lessons in Columbia, SC. with instructors Howard Vanderbeck and Tom Jorge.

He says he was convinced that Sport Karate competition was what he wanted to do after watching fighters like Bill Wallace, Mike Warren, John Natividad, Howard Jackson and many other superstars compete during his first trip to a major karate tournament (The Battle of Atlanta) as a blue belt.

He first began to flourish as a competitor under the guidance of instructor

ACHIEVEMENTS & RECOGNITIONS

- Consistently rated Top 10 in either the National or World Sport Karate Rankings throughout his sport fighting career from 1977 until 2001 and rated #1 at various times in each of the following divisions:

*   18-29 Super lightweight Black Belt Fighting

*   30-39 Lightweight Black Belt Fighting

*   40-49 Lightweight Black Belt Fighting

- 77-78 South East Karate Association Super-Lightweight Black Belt Top Fighter of the Year

- 1998 USA National Champion

- 1998 KRANE AAA Warrior Sword Lifetime Achievement Award

- 2000 NASKA World Champion

- 2004 Living Legend of Sport Karate Award

- 2012 Museum of Sport Karate - Keith Vitali Natural Fighter Award

- 2013 Inducted into the South Carolina Black Belt Hall of Fame

- 2016 Sport Karate Museum - Dragon Image Fighting Award

- 2016 presented with the honorary title "Native Texan Black Belt" by the AKBBA

- 2016 Elite Battle of Atlanta / PKA Warrior and International Martial Arts Ambassador

- 2018 presented with the Joe Lewis Eternal Warrior Award

Bruce Brutschy and then under Black Belt Hall of Fame Fighter Keith Vitali at the University of South Carolina in the mid 70's.

Goldman received his Black Belt in Tae Kwon Do from Vitali in 1976 and together with team-mates Richard Jackson, John Orck, Steve Vitali, Tony Bell and many others started competing and constantly winning Open Karate Tournaments throughout the Southeast USA.

After Vitali moved to Atlanta to work with the legendary Joe Corley, Goldman continued his training with a man he refers to as "the smartest fighter God ever created," Mike Genova.

Under Genova's guidance, Goldman continued to win and consistently climbed in the Karate Illustrated ratings. At one point he even held the #1 position over instructors Vitali, Genova and Brutschy (an honor that to this day Goldman calls a "terrible mistake" by the voters).

During that time he was named the 77-78 South East Karate Association (SEKA) Super-lightweight Black Belt "Top Fighter of the Year", and when the World Journal of Martial Arts became the first magazine to officially recognize the world's top sport karate fighters they ranked him the 7th best light-weight black belt in the world (even though he competed in the super-lightweight division which was not included in the rankings as a separate division).

He has competed and won tournaments sponsored by virtually every major sanctioning sport karate organization, including the PKA, PKC, ISKA, NBL, WKF, USKA, KRANE and NASKA.

ACHIEVEMENTS & RECOGNITIONS

In 2000 he decided to fight seriously for 1 year (or as seriously as a full-time executive producer could while doing shows and events all around the country) managing to win the NASKA 40-49 Lightweight Black Belt World Championship in the process. Finishing 1st, 2nd or 3rd in every major open karate tournament held on the NASKA world tour (and some that weren't) including...

- The USA Nationals
- The World Series of Martial Arts
- The Empire State Nationals @ Madison Square Gardens
- The Compete Nationals
- The Southern American Karate Championships
- The New England Open
- The Cactus Classic
- The Bluegrass Nationals
- The US Capitol Classic
- The US Open & International Sport Karate Association World Championships
- The Battle of Atlanta
- The Diamond Nationals

Goldman was eventually bitten by the music bug and put karate tournaments on the back burner to compete in dance contests. He went on to host a television show called DANCE on an NBC affiliate before deciding that DJ'ing and the entertainment business was his future because (in his words) "there was no money in sport karate and it wasn't part of the Olympics at the time".

In 1989, Goldman went to work for the Walt Disney Company in Orlando but continued competing on the FAME circuit where tournaments always seemed to come down to, he and James Sisco fighting for the 1st place trophy. That rivalry is reminiscent of the legendary one between Keith Vitali and Bobby Tucker.

In his professional career outside the Sport Karate world (as a Production Manager and Executive Producer) he has been involved in numerous high profile productions including The Academy of Television Arts & Sciences Hall of Fame Induction Ceremonies and Superbowl XXIX Half-Time Show for Disney, The Red Bull Air Race and (3) AMA / Redbull Supermoto Championship races, The Sports Broadcasting Hall of Fame Ceremonies in New York (2021 will be his 14th time as Producer of that prestigious event), The AA International Meetings for 50,000+ attendees from 90+ nations (2 times) - 2020 would have been his 3rd time producing the stadium event if not for the COVID-19 outbreak, the Hyperloop Pod Competition for Space X and the BSA Jamboree w/ guest speaker President Donald Trump).

He has worked with countless performers, actors and sports superstars including Lady Gaga, Kesha, Academy Award Winner Shirley MacLaine, Tony Bennett, Garth Brooks, Trisha Yearwood, Michael Jackson, Smashmouth, Shaquille O'Neal, Charles Barkley, Dana Carvey, Joe DiMaggio, Yogi Berra, Miami Sound Machine, Loverboy, Lionel Richie, Leann Rimes, The Beach Boys, Jason Alexander, Jay Leno, Destiny's Child, Akon, Pitbull, Cyndi Lauper and many, many more.

Still an avid lover of Sport Karate competition Goldman continued to stay active even after officially "retiring" occasionally jumping into the ring whenever it suited him.

KAREN EDEN HERDMAN

"Writer, Speaker, Teacher ...The Master of Inspiration."

TRAINING INFORMATION

- Belt Ranks & Martial Arts Styles: Tang Soo Do (6th Degree Black Belt)

Karen Eden is a 6th degree martial arts master in the traditional Korean art of Tang Soo Do. She is one of only a handful of women certified to teach anti-terrorist tactical maneuvers by the U.S Department of Homeland Security. In addition, Karen is a former East Coast tournament winner and world champion competitor (TSD.) She was inducted into the Sport Karate Museum in Houston Texas in 2017.

Known as "The Master of Inspiration," for her philosophical writing style, Karen has written for and appeared in every major martial arts magazine in the country and around the world, including six magazine covers of her own.

Karen currently has 4 books out and writes two monthly karate columns (Taekwondo Times Magazine, Martial Arts Success Magazine / Century Martial Arts.) She also has two martial art product lines available through Century Martial Arts, both which have successfully sold around the world (I Am a Martial Artist; They Call Me Master…the book, apparel and gift items.)

Master Karen has appeared in two major Hollywood productions, including stunt work in Van Damme's "Sudden Death," and a feature role in "Sworn to Justice" with Cynthia Rothrock, as seen on Showtime.

MAJOR ACHIEVEMENTS

- 2012-the Mayor of Denver City and County, honored Master Karen with her own day, establishing June the 16th as officially "Karen Eden Herdman Day," for her work with less fortunate youth in the city, state and across the globe.

- 2015-Inducted into the Battle of Columbus Hall of Honors for Literary Contributions, Columbus, OH.

- 2017-The Office of the President of the United States presented Karen with The Presidents Lifetime Achievement Award for her lifelong commitment to building a stronger nation through community volunteer service.

- 2017-First female martial arts "Professor" (in its 30-year history) at "Karate College," Radford University, VA

- 2017-Inducted into the Sport Karate Museum for Editorial Contributions, Houston, TX.

- 2018-First female presented with the Bill "Superfoot" Wallace Service Award

- 2018-First female martial arts master inducted into the Korean Masters Hall of Fame for Literary Contributions, Atlanta, GA.

In addition, Karen is a broadcast journalist and has worked as a reporter and news desk anchor for NBC, FOX and PBS affiliates. She has also appeared on CNN and reported for FOX National and Animal Planet.

Master Karen currently teaches street youth and former gang-members in the under-privileged areas of Denver Colorado. In 2000, Master Karen joined The Salvation Army in starting the largest inner-city martial arts program in the world. Instructors volunteer their time at their local Salvation Army corps, and the program is funded by the organization. She started "The Blood and Fire Federation" which still currently oversee inner-city programs in the U.S., Africa, Canada and Eastern Europe. Her "Dojo Disciple / Darling" line was launched to support students who can't otherwise afford a uniform to train in. Hundreds of martial artists have purchased her t-shirts to help pay for a less-fortunate student's belt and uniform. Karen is also working to bring martial arts training into the tribal lands and reservations of our Native American youth.

MAJOR ACHIEVEMENTS

- Gran, Hawaiian Kosho Ryu Kenpo Jiu-Jitsu
- International Black Belt Hall of Fame
- Top Weapons in Texas, 1980
- Top Ten Fighters in Texas, 1979-1999
- Rated by Karate Illustrated Magazine, rated National
- Who's Who in Karate, 1982
- 3rd Degree Black Belt Test, 1982, Lama Nationals, Chicago IL
- Creator Six Flags Amusement Park Shows, Gary Lee's Texas Karate All-Stars,
- 1984-1994, {5,000 shows}
- Texas State B.A.S.S Federation Champion, 1987
- Filmed SIDEKICKS the movie, 1990
- Gold Medalist USAKF Nationals, Dallas, Texas, 1992
- Won five {5} National NBL TITLES, Atlantic City, NJ, 1992
- Sabaki Ryu Challenge 3rd Place Kumite, Honolulu, Hawaii, 1992
- National Black Belt League World Champion, Breaking, New Orleans, USA, 1993
- Man, of the Year, Bushshiban 1993
- BIG BASS TOURNAMENT, Sam Rayburn, Jasper, Texas, 2nd Place, 3,200.00 winnings, earned a 3rd round seed into the Classic Championship 1993, Yeah Baby!!!!
- Texas NBL Arbitrator
- Star of Hollywood Stunt Show, Astroworld, Six Flags, Houston, Texas, USA, 1993
- Creator 'KIDS EXPO" Astrodome, Houston Texas.1993-1996

GARY LEE

TRAINING INFORMATION

- Belt Ranks & Martial Arts Styles: 9th Degree Black Belt, Okinawa Karate
- Birthdate: 1954
- Birthplace/Growing Up: Honolulu, HI

MAJOR ACHIEVEMENTS

- Golden Greek Top Texas Overall Winner, AOK RATINGS, 1997, 1998
- Nominated Black Belt Magazine "Player of the Year", 1997
- Texas Sport Karate Player, MVP
- Opened World Championship Karate Studios, 1998
- Created the Living Legends Celebrity Roast; 1999 - present.
- To date Professor Lee has celebrated 15 American Pioneers in Sport Karate.
- Staff Writer for WORLD BLACKBELT, 1999
- Created Tales OF the Old Sensei for World Black Belt, monthly column
- Master of Ceremonies, Martial Art History Museum, Las Vegas, Nevada, 1999
- Director Michael Matsuda says 'Gary Lee is the voice of Karate, Black Belt Magazine
- Director of Junior World Black Belt Kids Club
- Produced and Directed Living Legends, 'the Tim Kirby Celebrity Roast, Houston, Texas, USA, 2000
- Kumite International Black Belt Hall of Fame Award and Scholarship given in Professor Gary Lee's name for $1,000.00, Pittsburg, Pa, 2000
- Creator of BLACK BELT TV, A online network for Martial Artist and Martial arts Exclusive personal interviews with the stars of martial arts.

WESLEY LEE

"You need to open your eyes, ears, and heart to see what defeat can give to you."

TRAINING INFORMATION

- Belt Ranks & Martial Arts Styles: Taekwon-Do (5th Dan)
- Instructors/Influencers: Grand Master Harry Payne
- Birthdate: October 26, 1973
- Birthplace/Growing Up: Fox River Grove, IL
- Yrs. In the Martial Arts: 17 years
- Yrs. Instructing: 15 years
- School owner, Manager, Instructor

PROFESSIONAL ORGANIZATIONS

- IJTF (Treasurer)
- JTF-USA (National Director)
- KMATA (Founder and President)

I grew up in the Midwest in a small town with no martial art schools. I took wrestling starting in elementary through high school but never took striking or traditional martial arts. It was not until I was in my late 20s that I was invited by a coworker to try class at a school he had opened. At first, I thought it would be a waste of time. Hearing the class was Taekwon-Do did not interest me at first. I only had in mind what I had seen at 'McDojos', but I tried a class to be respectful.

I was instantly hooked on the style of Taekwon-Do Master Payne taught. It was a traditional Korean combat style, not flashy, but effective. It was the style taught to the Korean ROK soldiers. Everything that Master Payne taught had a purpose and not just 'because that is how we do it'.

At first, I saw it as a great way to complement my grappling by adding a solid striking game. I started doing tournaments only 4 months into training. In the beginning it was tournaments that drove me to get in shape, to improve my technique, to train every chance I got.

This quickly changed from wanting to learn how to punch and kick to how to improve myself: physically, mentally, emotionally, and spiritually. Finally, I went from being a student, to being an instructor, and now school owner and active in running the IJTF. Taekwon-Do went from just a striking art to who I am.

PERSONAL ACHIEVEMENTS

- Competed and won many tournaments both purely Taekwon-Do and open styles

- Helping to bring about a tournament community in Tucson AZ by getting location schools, of different styles, to start competing together

MAJOR ACHIEVEMENTS

- Opened Vail Taekwon-Do Academy in 2014

- Appointed to Regional Director of IJTF in 2015

- Appointed to IJTF Administration as IT Director in 2016

- Appointed to Umpire and Tournament Director of the JTF-USA in 2017

- Appointed to IJTF Treasurer in 2017

- Appointed to JTF-USA National Directory in 2017

- Inducted into the US Kido Federation Black Belt Hall of Fame 2017 for Outstanding Instructor of the Year

- Inducted in to AMAA Martial Arts Masters & Pioneers in the Black Belt section 2019

- Founded Korean Martial Arts Tournament Association in 2020

Taekwon-Do started as a desire to learn how to strike, and it turned into a way of life. I learned that I could overcome adversity with practice and perseverance. I learned that there are times you will be beaten, but it is in those times that you can learn the most. You need to open your eyes, ears, and heart to see what the defeat can give to you.

That applies to tournaments and life in general. The skills I learned to overcome losing a match applies to my work and family life. There are times we fail to do the right thing, but if we practice and persevere, we can overcome anything and succeed.

LOUIS MARKSTROM

"We must always remember that we are Martial Artists and that we must hold ourselves to a high standard."

TRAINING INFORMATION

- Belt Ranks & Martial Arts Styles: Running Fist Kung -Fu, Title: Sibak, Rank: 7th Dan

- Instructors/Influencers: Josi James Robinson

- Birthdate: November 28, 1970

- Birthplace/Growing Up: Englewood, NJ/Long Island, NY/ Sydney, Australia

- Yrs. In the Martial Arts: 41 years

- Yrs. Instructing: 36 years

- School owner & Instructor at Running Fist Australia

PROFESSIONAL ORGANIZATIONS

- World Warrior Alliance - Lifetime Member

- Pun Wha Nae Jir Gi American Kung-fu Federation (Lifetime Membership Commenced December 15, 1987)

I began martial arts training at age 9. I had a friend who was bullied, and he asked myself and two others if we wanted to join a martial arts class with him. Forty-one years later, I am so glad that I did. In that very first class, there was something that was just right about it. Just doing basic stances, I knew I had found something that was meant for me.

As the head instructor for Running Fist Australia, I've had the privilege of establishing the Running Fist Kung-fu branch of Australia. My martial arts journey began at the age of 9 in 1979. I first trained in an American Eclectic Style of martial arts and earned my rank of Shodan in 1986. In 1984, I began training in Running Fist Kung-fu under Josi James Robinson. I was awarded the title of Sibak in 2017, hold the rank of 7th Dan and am a member of the Running Fist Council. I am honored and humbled to be the "elder" of the Running Fist Sifu's and to help guide their journey, and to honor the memory and legacy of my teacher, Josi James Robinson, who passed in 2019.

Over the years, I have trained in many arts, including Shotokan, Judo, Jiu-Jitsu, Aikido, Tang Soo do, boxing and kickboxing.

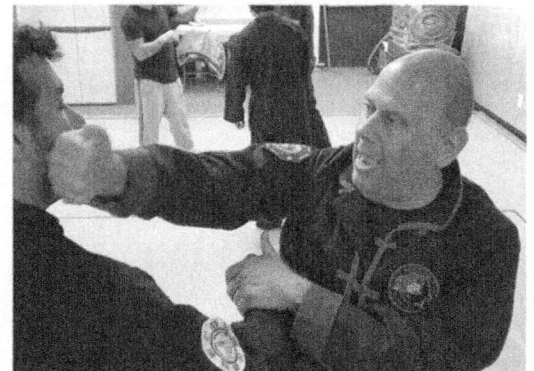

PERSONAL ACHIEVEMENTS

- Founder and CEO of Results Group International
- Honors Graduate Stern School of Business at New York University
- Stern School of Business Hall of Fame
- NYU Entrepreneurship Hall of Fame
- Association of Collegiate Entrepreneurs Hall of Fame
- Published over 50 articles on driving business and organizational performance
- Book Co-author: Unleashing the Power of IT: Bringing People, Business and Technology Together
- Book Author: Results: Creating High-Performance Organizations, Teams, and Individuals
- Numerous Keynote Speaking Engagements

MAJOR ACHIEVEMENTS

- Awarded Title of Sibak: 2017
- Promoted to 7th Dan: 2017
- Teacher at World Warrior Alliance Summit (2017, 2018, 2019)
- American Federation of Martial Arts (AFMA) Hall of Fame, November 19, 2004
- AFMA Silver Life Time Achievement Award, November 19, 2004
- AFMA Elite Silver Warrior Lifetime Achievement Award, May 5, 2007
- Action Martial Arts Magazine Hall of Fame
- Action Martial Arts Magazine Silver Lifetime Achievement Award
- Who's Who in The Martial Arts "The Legends Edition" (2017)

My belief and philosophy of martial arts is that it is a way of life that develops individuals as complete human beings, and to do this, both the "martial" and the "art" must be present. As martial arts on the "martial" side, we must be able to utilize and apply our techniques to defend ourselves, our loved ones, and those who need defending. On the "art" side, we must strive to improve ourselves mentally, emotionally, and spiritually. We must strive to develop our students and ourselves as human beings, to develop character, integrity, discipline, focus, respect, and determination, and to then bring these qualities out to be successful in all areas of life. We must always remember that we are martial artists and that we must hold ourselves to a high standard. One of our precepts is that "through developing the depth of your mind, the strength of your body, and the vastness of your spirit, you can accomplish anything." It is this belief that I want to instill in all those who I have the opportunity to teach, train, or work with in any way.

The characteristics, attitudes, and habits I developed as a martial artist have served as the foundation for the successes I have achieved in other areas of my life. I'm the founder and CEO of Results Group International and have worked with over 40,000 people in various organizations to develop high performing organizations, teams, and individuals. I'm a graduate of the Stern School of Business at New York University. In addition to my martial arts Hall of Fame inductions, I have been inducted in the Stern School of Business Hall of Fame, the NYU Entrepreneurship Hall of Fame, and the Association of Collegiate Entrepreneurs Hall of Fame.

KAMAKAZE MCMILLAN

"I keep my cup empty so I am always learning until the day I die."

TRAINING INFORMATION

- Belt Ranks & Martial Arts Styles: Jiu Jitsu (7th Dan)
- Instructors/Influencers: Great Grandmaster Charles Elmore
- Birthplace/Growing Up: Brooklyn, NY
- Yrs. In the Martial Arts: 48 years
- Yrs. Instructing: 32 years

PROFESSIONAL ORGANIZATIONS

- Ring 8 Boxing
- Tomiki Aikido

I started training in the arts 1972 because at that time, there were a lot of gangs in Brooklyn, New York and I got into a lot of street fights. Back then, you had to know people in other neighborhoods in order to go there or you might have to fight your way out. My mother said that if I kept fighting like I was, then I would not live to be 18 years old.

I had good skills, but wanted to be better, so I saw my brother was training he had good skills so I decided to get like that and better. I started training with a gentleman named Arron for couple of years, but then I started looking for more than just karate. I wanted something similar to Bruce Lee's well-rounded style of arts. That's when I found Great Grandmaster Elmore. My uncle and cousins were training with him and I didn't want them to know, so I got a place for us to train. Master Elmore gave me permission to train in other systems to be even more well-rounded. That's when I started with E.P. System with Grandmaster Bouncey. He got me fighting in tournaments, which was great. I also started training with Master Sabu, boxed out of Bed-Sty Gym, trained under Grandmaster Rudy, Jiu Jitsu under Leon Knight, trained in the

PERSONAL ACHIEVEMENTS

- Fought in Point System in the 80s and 90s
- Amateur Boxer in the 70s
- Played Semi-pro Football for 17 years
- Pro tryout in 1986
- Orthopedic medical assistant
- Pro Boxing Trainer, Judge and Timekeeper
- Karate coach for AAU
- All Pro Cornerback playing Semi-pro Football

MAJOR ACHIEVEMENTS

- Award for Empire State Games boxing coach
- Award for amateur boxing
- Master martial arts award
- Athletic Trainer Award from boys/girls high school
- Awards for fighting in Martial Arts tournaments
- Press Conference Martial Arts Hall of Fame
- Action Martial Arts Hall of Fame

with Grandmaster Bouncey. He got me fighting in tournaments, which was great. I also started training with Master Sabu, boxed out of Bed-Sty Gym, trained under Grandmaster Rudy, Jiu Jitsu under Leon Knight, trained in the Princeekata E.P. System, Judo and Tomiki Aikido under Sensei Watanabe, and I also trained Hagumdo Korean Sword under Master Mike Simmons, P.T.K. Stck System under A.K. and Brazilian Jiu Jitsu under Juaco.

The martial arts made me a better person and more humble also. Martial artists have to understand that it's about the system, not the person. Professor Shelley is one of two elders still alive who is my Elmore Ryu teacher. My respect, discipline, honor, and loyalty comes from my family, but most of all, the arts. My art is used to protect family and not to show how skilled I am. I do demonstrations a couple times a year and seminars if asked. I keep my cup empty so I am always learning until the day I die. I shall live my life in peace and harmony with my fellow man.

HAMILTON PERKINS

"The leadership qualities that I've learned through the martial arts has allowed me to positively influence others..."

I was initially influenced by the fantastic athleticism that was displayed in martial arts movies. As a teenager, I was influenced by the technical precision and business aspects of karate by Jan Wellendorf and Dale Brooks' AMAA-Karate International Organization. I am thankful as an adult, for the lifelong benefits that are made possible through the continued study of Karate-Do. I attribute my success in every area of life, to the tremendous level of desire, dedication, and determination that I've gained through 40 plus years of martial arts training.

Martial arts has greatly enhanced my ability to remain humble during accomplishments and achievements and increased my ability to remain dignified, dedicated, and determined during temporary setbacks. To me, martial arts is a parallel to all areas of life. My goal is to inspire others to succeed through the utilization of good character, self-discipline, positive mindset, and positive focus. The leadership qualities that I've learned through the martial arts has allowed me to positively influence others as a High School Teacher and Coach, Public Speaker, Martial Arts Instructor, and as a servant of the community.

TRAINING INFORMATION

- Belt Ranks & Martial Arts Styles: 7th Degree Black – Japanese Karate, 4th Degree-Okinawan Karate, 3rd Degree-Korean Tae Kwon Do, 2nd Degree-American Karate

- Instructors/Influencers: Irvin Shelton, Larry Isaac, Greg McDonald, Yong Kim, Bill Osterholt, Jan Wellendorf

- Yrs. In the Martial Arts: 44 years

- Yrs. Instructing: 40 years

- School owner (Mid Eastern Karate Association)

PROFESSIONAL ORGANIZATIONS

- Mid Eastern Karate Association
- AAU

PERSONAL ACHIEVEMENTS

- Kyoshi
- Menkyo-Kaiden
- PKL National Black Belt Hall of Fame
- Numerous Instructor of the Year Awards
- Numerous Competitor of the Year Awards
- Ranked in Fighting, Forms, and Weapons – PKL
- Instructor of World Champion – Sue Brazelton
- Featured in Several Martial Arts Magazines
- Clinic and Seminar Conductor
- High School Sociology and Psychology Teacher
- High School Basketball Coach – Over 475 wins
- Keynote Public Speaker
- For Martial Artists – I've conducted Kata, Kumite, and Kobudo Clinics. I have also conducted Seminars on Bunkai and Oyo
- For the Community – I've been a Keynote Speaker at Educational and Civic Events. I've also conducted Self-Defense and Safety Awareness Courses for Business and Professional Groups

MAJOR ACHIEVEMENTS

- Battle of Baltimore – 2nd Fighting, 2nd Kata, 3rd Weapons
- New York Nationals – 2nd Kata, 3rd Fighting, 3rd Weapons
- Coors Silver Bullet Nationals – 2nd Fighting, 3rd Kata
- California Nationals – 3rd Fighting, 3rd Kata
- Dixieland Nationals – 1st Kata
- Jhoon Rhee Nationals – (Chung) 2nd Fighting

I've learned confidence, courage, discipline, honor, integrity, etc. These critical "Pillars of Character" have been greatly emphasized during my training and my martial arts research, and I do my best to live by them daily.

MAJOR ACHIEVEMENTS

- Boston Summer Open – 3rd Kata
- Niagra Nationals – 2nd Kata
- Top Ten Fall Nationals (L. Arthur) – 1st Fighting, 1st kata, 3rd Weapons
- Battle of Atlanta
- US Open
- Capital Classics
- Ocean State Nationals
- Bluegrass Nationals
- Kyoshi
- Menkyo-Kaiden
- PKL National Black Belt Hall of Fame
- Numerous Instructor of the Year Awards
- Numerous Competitor of the Year Awards
- Ranked Competitor – Fighting, Forms and Weapons
- Kyoshi Award
- Menkyo-Kaiden Award
- PKL National Black Belt Hall of Fame
- Chief Instructor
- Conducted Seminar and Clinics
- Self Defense and Safety Awareness Courses
- Promoter of Alamance Nationals and Alamance Open Tournaments

JOHN PERRY

"Martial Arts has always been a part of me from the start of my childhood at an early age."

TRAINING INFORMATION

- Belt Ranks & Martial Arts Styles: Jidokwan Tae Kwon Do 5th Dan, Tomiki Aikido 4th Dan, Yang Tai Chi Chuan, Shaolin Five Animal Kung Fu 2nd Dan, Kenpo Karate 2nd Dan

- Instructors/Influencers: Herb McGuire, Don Madden, Mike Stanhope

- Birthdate: August 31, 1969

- Birthplace/Growing Up: Chillicothe / Jackson, OH

- Yrs. In the Martial Arts: 47 years

- Yrs. Instructing: 31 years

- School owner, Manager, Instructor

PROFESSIONAL ORGANIZATIONS

- American Jidokwan
- American Martial Arts Alliance
- AKJU Ko Sutemi Seiei Kan
- Eastern U.S.A. International Martial Arts Association
- Tian Dao Jian Kang Heaven Way Health

Master John Perry started his martial arts training in 1973. This year, 2020, marks his 47th year in his martial arts career. Over his lifetime in martial arts, he has trained in the arts of Hapkido, Eagle Claw Kung Fu, Wing Chun, and earned instructor titles and black belts in Yang Style Tai Chi Chuan, Shaolin Five Animal Kung Fu 2nd Dan, Kenpo Karate 2nd Dan, Jidokwan Tae Kwon Do 5th Dan, and Tomiki Aikido 4th Dan.

He graduated from the American Institute of Alternative Medicine in 2016 with a Masters Level Degree in Acupuncture and Traditional Chinese Medicine. Master John Perry is the owner, manager, and instructor for Heaven Way Health / Tian Dao Jian Kang. He travels promoting Martial Arts for self-defense and health. He also teaches and promotes healing through alternative methods such as prayer, massage, Tai Chi Chuan, qigong, meditation, acupuncture, and nutrition.

PERSONAL ACHIEVEMENTS

- Master's Degree in Acupuncture and Traditional Chinese Medicine 2016

MAJOR ACHIEVEMENTS

- Eastern U.S.A. 27th Annual Black Belt Hall of Fame Induction 2014
- 2014 Silver Anniversary Achievement
- 2015 Martial Arts Dedication
- 2016 Master Black Belt of the Year
- 2017 Extraordinary Martial Arts Loyalty
- 2018 Continual Commitment to the Martial Arts
- 2019 5 Year Honor Award - Outstanding Service and Contribution to Improving Global Martial Arts
- Action Martial Arts Magazine Hall of Honors Induction 2019
- 2019 Esteemed Modern Warrior Award
- 2019 Esteemed Martial Arts Community Growth and Support
- 2020 Esteemed Martial Arts
- American Martial Arts Alliance
- 2020 Martial Arts Ambassador of the Year

The many years of studying have allowed Master Perry to travel and meet some of the greatest martial artists, healers, and teachers in the world. He enjoys learning, teaching, and visiting others to exchange knowledge. He states, "My training has taken the people who were my martial art heroes, and has turned them into colleagues, friends, brothers, and sisters. I hope to continue to make lifetime friendships. Life is about love and enjoying the time with those in our lives. I thank God for the life of learning and the path that He chose for me along the way."

Master John Perry would like to honor the ones who made him who he is today. I would like to say, "Thank you to God, family, friends, Grandmasters, Masters, and Teachers. "The foundation of my spirit is a gift from God that has come from all of you. You have forged me into something I could have never been alone. I am honored to have you in my life, and to be a part of your lives. May the world be flooded with love, kindness, joy, peace, and righteousness to unite us together in harmony."

How has studying the Martial Arts made an Impact on my life? This is a question that has caused great reflection for me. The memories come rushing back as I ponder the question. Martial Arts has always been a part of me from the start of my childhood at an early age. I can't imagine where I would be without traveling the path that was given to me. Would I still have been a good person? What career would I have followed? Who would be in my life? I am glad that I chose the path I am on. I have so many great relationships with friends and family members from studying and teaching martial arts. These are treasures that I wouldn't want to live without.

With a lifelong path of martial arts, I am grateful for what it has given me. Studying Martial Arts has defined me as a person. The greatest impact on my life is that I have made lifelong friends from all over the world, and continue to do so at every gathering. I have had the opportunity to learn from others, and share the knowledge that I have obtained. I have learned not only martial techniques, but arts of healing, meditation, life lessons, and experience from the masters who were my heroes as I was growing up. It was through their wisdom, love, compassion, and teaching that the martial arts have made me who I am today.

CYNTHIA ROTHROCK

Cynthia Rothrock is one of the greatest martial arts/action film stars in the world, Few other performers can match her presence and energy on the silver screen. She is the undisputed "Queen of Martial Arts films". Cynthia Rothrock is not only a great action star, but also an incredibly accomplished martial artist. She holds 5 Black Belts in various Far Eastern martial disciplines. These Arts include; Tang Soo Do (Korean), Tae Kwon Do (Korean), Eagle Claw (Chinese), Wu Shu (contemporary Chinese), and Northern Shaolin (classical Chinese).

When she was a 13-year-old growing up in Scranton, Pennsylvania, she started taking lessons at her parents best friends private gym. Little did she know at the time that this casual   interest would lead to a full-time professional career. Her natural abilities were quickly recognized by her martial arts teachers and they encouraged her to enter open karate competition, By the time she had earned her first Black Belt she was well on her way to becoming a martial arts champion. By 1982 Cynthia was one of the premier Kata (forms) and weapon competitors in the United States. Competing in divisions that were not segregated by male-female categories, she literally captured every title in both open and closed karate competition.

From 1981-1985 she was the undefeated World Karate Champion in both forms and weapon competition. Establishing a legacy of wins and accumulating hundreds of trophies for her martial arts prowess; a feat that is unparalleled even to this day! She is a consummate performer with such Chinese weapons as the Chinese Double Broad Swords, Staff, Chinese Nine-section Steel Whip Chain, Chinese Iron Fan, and an assortment of Okinawan Kobudo and Japanese Bugei Weapons.

As a Forms and Weapon Champion, Cynthia Rothrock has traveled the world performing the intricacies of her martial arts arsenal. With precision flare and panache she has demonstrated before hundreds of thousands of spectators across the globe.

Her "action-packed" self-defense and fight scenario performances garnered her the reputation as a consummate professional in the World of Martial Arts.

This international exposure soon propelled her to martial arts celebrity status and within a mere period of less than two years Cynthia became a household name in martial arts circles. In addition to being featured on the cover of virtually every martial arts magazine in the world, Cynthia has been featured in over 300 stories and articles in national and international publications. Some of these magazines include Black Belt Magazine (United States), Inside Kung-Fu (United States), Martial Arts Training (United States), Martial Arts Stars (United States), Inside Karate (United States), Sensei (Spanish-Argentina), Australian Fighting Arts, China Sports (Beijing, China), Budo (Brazil), Combat Sport (Spanish-Brazil), Combat Magazine (England), Sushido (French), Kung-Fu Wu Shu (French), Karate Budo Journal (Germany), Australian Tae Kwon Do, The Fighters (England), Martial Arts Illustrated (England), Michael De Pasquale Jr.'s Karate International (United States), Budo Karate (Japan), Banzai International (Italy), Czarny Pas (Poland),   Cinturon Negro (Spain), Ninja Weapons (United States), El Budoka (Spain), Kicksider (Germany),   Impact Magazine (Germany), Karate Illustrated (United States), Ninja Weapons (United States), El Budoka (Spain), Kicksider (Germany),   Impact Magazine (Germany), Karate Illustrated (United States), The Swedish Fighter's International (Sweden), Master (United States), Kung-Fu Illustrated (United States), The Fighter (Thailand), Masters Series (United States), The Martial Arts Gazette (United States), Karate Profiles (United States), Sport Karate International (United States), The World of Martial Arts (United States), The Dojo (United States), and hundreds of   National and International newspapers.

Cynthia Rothrock is also one of the very select individuals to be inducted into the Black Belt Hall of Fame and Inside Kung-Fu Hall of Fame. Inclusions in such renowned organizations as the Martial Arts Gallery of Fame, MARTIAL ARTS, Traditions, History, People, The Martial Arts Sourcebook, and dozens of other historical reference books of martial significance.

Cinematically, Cynthia burst onto the scene like a stick of dynamite after "starring" in a Kentucky Fried Chicken commercial in the early 1980s. Soon there after Producers and Directors recognized her martial arts skills and her career began a steady climb upward. Cynthia's first full length motion picture was Yes Madam also starring Michelle Yeoh. The movie turned out to be a hit and broke all box office records in Hong Kong. Cynthia and Michelle were launched and on their way to becoming two of the most successful female action stars in the world.

Putting it briefly, when Cynthia was invited to Hong Kong to appear in motion pictures, she didn't know what to expect. She thought they were going to do period pieces where she would have to wear tight pigtails and traditional Chinese costuming. To her surprise she soon thereafter discovered that she would be starring in Chinese action films set in modern times with contemporary themes.

As a result Cynthia Rothrock spent five years in Hong Kong starring in Asian produced motion pictures. In that time she had starred with kung-fu greats Samo Hung and Yuen Biao.

She was even offered a role opposite of Jackie Chan in Armour of Gods, but Jackie got injured so the company instead put her in Righting Wrongs with super star Yuen Biao. During that Asian tenure she, unbeknownst to her, has set a record of becoming the very first non-Chinese westerner to carry an action movie single-handedly in Hong Kong. In fact, she left Hong Kong as one of the most celebrated action stars in Hong Kong's cinematic history! Cynthia Rothrock's movie career "shooting schedule" has taken her to some of the most exotic locations on the planet. Paradoxically, she has also endured some of the worse climatic conditions that anyone in the motion picture could ever anticipate – all in the name of making "action-adventure" motion pictures.

Publicity has followed Cynthia Rothrock through every stage of her illustrious career. She is the "media darling" of virtually every reporter, writer, and martial arts magazine in the world. They know that she draws readers by the thousands to their publication. In fact, her "image" and "career" is perhaps followed more closely (by martial arts enthusiast) than any other "martial arts" actors except Chuck Norris or Jackie Chan.

ERIC STEVENS, SR.

"I will always train in Martial Arts because it saved my life..."

TRAINING INFORMATION

- Belt Ranks & Martial Arts Styles: Taekwondo (6th Degree Black Belt), Judo (Black Belt), Aikido (Black Belt)

- Instructors/Influencers: Johnny Abrahams, Thomas Miller, Robert Clark, Robert Moses, Richard Carr, Kent Hamilton, Larry Taylor

- Birthdate: May 22, 1964

- Birthplace/Growing Up: Stints Mary's Camden County, GA

- Yrs. In the Martial Arts: 41 years

- Yrs. Instructing: 25 years

- School owner (Independent Martial Arts Alliance), Instructor, Manager

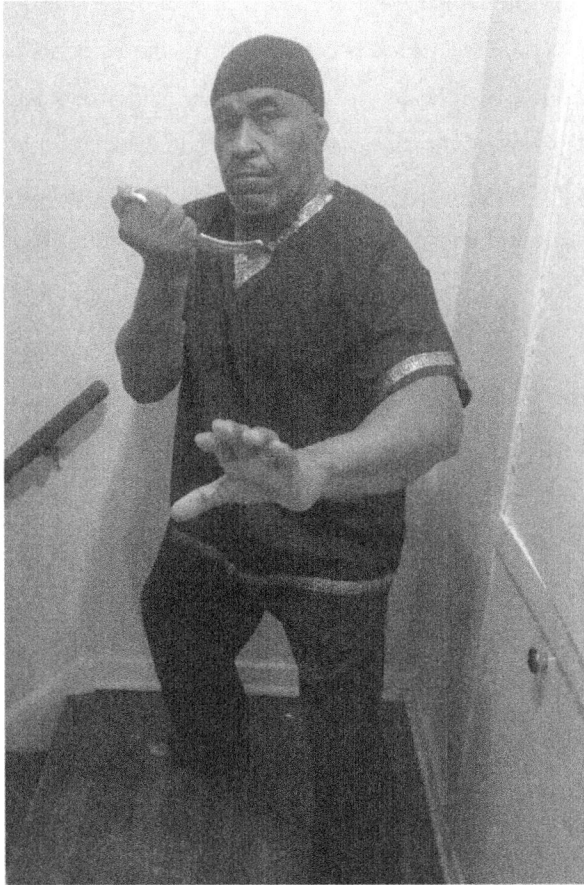

My parents divorced when I was young, and in 1971, I went to live with my grandparents. In 1978, I went to live with my mother in Savannah, GA. Shortly after that, in 1979, at 15 years of age, my mother, 13-year old brother, two-year-old sister, and I moved to Dover, Delaware. Being a country boy, moving to a big city, I did not want to attend a new high school where I would be tested about my accent and told I would not amount to anything. Being bullied back then and coming from a divorced family did not help at all. I started rebuilding and doing things I was not supposed to be doing.

I had to find something to keep me occupied, and I heard that they were doing TKD classes on the college campus. I went to check it out, and that's when I met my first instructor, Mr. Jonny Abraham's Ove American Sports TKD. I asked how much the class cost, and he said $25 a month. I went home to ask my mother and learned we could not afford it. I went back the next day and told him we could not afford the class. The coach talked to my mother after learning how many children she cared for gifted me the class for four years until I received my black belt status.

PERSONAL ACHIEVEMENTS

- AFA CT 2008 Nationals Connecticut Shoreline
- 2010 Karate Championships AFA Ct. Ratings
- Kata Form Fighting Weapons Spirit Award
- 1995 Kingsland GA Tuff Man Contest Winner
- AFA CT Ratings 8th Place Divisional
- Kata Form Fighting Spirit Award 1990 / 1998 Florida Championship

MAJOR ACHIEVEMENTS

- Certified Amateur Boxing Coach, State of Connecticut

I am genuinely blessed. We moved back to where I continued my TKD training and 6 months later, I got married in Connecticut and met my Judo and Aikido Instructor. After training together for several years, we merged our styles to create the COMBAT HIPKIDO Fighting System.

Martial Arts impacted my life by helping me become a better person, deal with situations as a young teenager, and as an adult, giving me confidence when I did not have it. Before being able to hold my head up high and feeling like a better person than I did before feeling good when someone can come to you for advice dealing with the martial arts system's there is no better feeling than that for many years before the martial arts I tried to fit in. Still, I couldn't fit in, but I started training people starting viewing me and started looking at me and a different way because of martial arts I'm evolved with people now than I ever been before of the art it a great feeling when you teach kids women and men and all come to you asking questions on techniques. I never was the smartest person in school. I will always train in martial arts because it saved my life. Sometimes I take time off to rest, but I will never quit. It's my destiny and the only thing that keeps me going other than my family.

ANDRÉ STEWART

> "Studying Martial Arts has not only shaped the way I look at others but also the way I see myself."

I began as a student in the Martial Arts at the age of six to obtain an activity that would assist in my physical defense because I lived in an area with an excessive amount of violent crimes. By the time I was 12, Martial Arts was more than just an activity, but it had become a genuine part of who I am today.

I feel that over the years of studying Martial Arts in different states and different countries, it has not only shaped the way I look at others but also the way I see myself. It has also brought me so much understanding of my walk with Jesus Christ. The greatest lesson has been learning the importance of sharing my life experiences with those I come in contact with being a valuable member of the community. Being confident in who I am

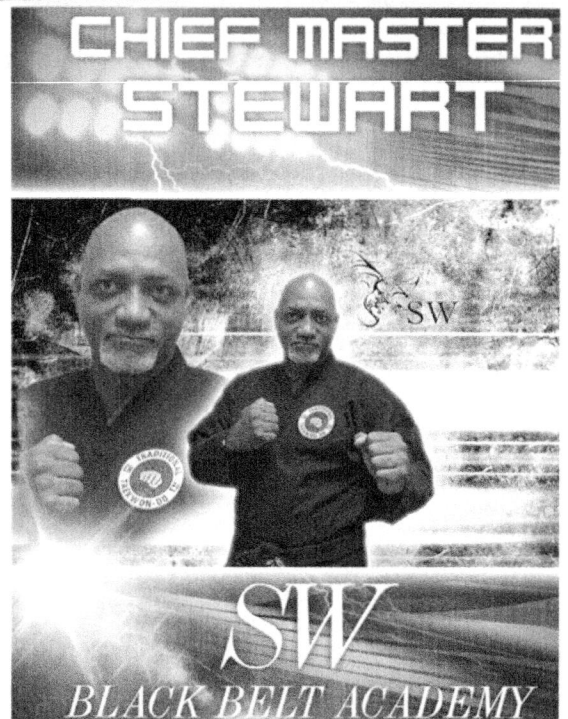

CHIEF MASTER STEWART

SW

BLACK BELT ACADEMY

TRAINING INFORMATION

- Belt Ranks & Martial Arts Styles: 7th Dan in Jun Tong Taekwon-Do, 6th Dan in Kenpo & Hapkido, 3rd Dan in Shotokan Karate, 2nd Dan in Midori Yama Budokai Karate.

- Instructors/Influencers: Grand Master Robert Dunn

- Birthdate: May 5, 1966

- Birthplace/Growing Up: New Orleans, LA

- Yrs. In the Martial Arts: 47 years

- Yrs. Instructing: 35 years

- School owner, Manager, Instructor

PROFESSIONAL ORGANIZATIONS

- The Freedom House Kingdom Of God

- Jun Tong Tackwon-Do Federation

- American Martial Arts Alliance Institute

- Midori Yama Budokai (MYB)

- Fort Bragg TKD & Karate

PERSONAL ACHIEVEMENTS

- Born Again In The Lord our Savior Jesus Christ

- Learning German

- Walking after major bilateral leg surgeries after being told I would not walk correctly again.

has made me a better instructor and student in every aspect of my life. I understand people on such a deeper level and always seek the good in them over the bad. Martial Arts is who I am. It makes me a better person in all walks of my life, with God, with my kids, with my students - a whole person.

MAJOR ACHIEVEMENTS

- Earning My 7th Dan Under Grand Master Dunn

- Bachelor of Arts Degree In Business Management

- Opening and Managing My Own Martial Arts School (SW Black Belt Academy)

- Induction into the Black Belt Hall Of Fame

- Competing in Europe and Winning Nation Titles

- Head Instructor for Law Enforcement Commands in Self-Defense while stationed in Germany at which time, I trained over 400 Law Enforcement soldiers from 2003 to 2007

- Shortly after joining the U.S. Army I was invited to join the Fort Bragg All Army & TKD team to train and compete on a National level

- Head instructor to teach private classes on hand-to-hand combat for my brigade from 2008-2009

BILL VIOLA, JR.

"Martial arts consumes me. I am a lifelong 'Martial Wayist' blessed to teach my children Gabby and William the 'way.'"

TRAINING INFORMATION

- Belt Ranks & Martial Arts Styles: Shotokan - 6th Dan, Kobudo, Kickboxing, Japanese JuJutsu

- Instructors/Influencers: Grandmaster Bill Viola, Sr.

- Birthdate: April 9, 1977

- Birthplace/Growing Up: Pittsburgh, PA

- Yrs. In the Martial Arts: 41 years

- Yrs. Instructing: 27 years

- School owner & Instructor at Allegheny Shotokan "Viola" Karate Dojo

PROFESSIONAL ORGANIZATIONS

- Screen Actors Guild - SAG

- American Federation of Television and Radio - AFTRA

- USA National Karate Federation - USANKF

- USA Karate Federation - USAKF

- Police Athletic League - PAL

- North American Sport Karate Association NASKA

Viola Jr. began his career following in his father's footsteps. Viola recalls, "I was kicking before I could walk and began formal lessons at 3-years-old. The dojo was actually my daycare." He experienced the "Golden Era" of MMA firsthand as his father, Bill Sr., was credited as the co-creator of the sport (a decade before the UFC) by the Heinz History Center, in conjunction with the Smithsonian Institute. He jokes, "Growing up with a martial arts master as a father, you do what Sensei Says!"

"Martial arts consumes me. I am a lifelong 'Martial Wayist' blessed to teach my children Gabby and William the "way." I know they will continue our family legacy. The confidence and work ethic karate has instilled in me has given me the tools to succeed. I am a black belt in life."

MAJOR ACHIEVEMENTS

- Amazon #1 Bestselling Author - Tough Guys

- Producer Showtime film - Tough Guys

As a youth, Viola was one of the most consistent and well-rounded competitors in the country, recognized as a USAKF Jr. Olympic champion and 1993 Overall Sport Karate International Champion. He was the most successful sport karate champion in Pennsylvania Karate Rating Association of his era, winning an unprecedented 8-consecutive black belt overall state titles (1992-1999). As an open and traditional competitor, Viola excelled in multiple circuits, including NBL, NASKA, AAU, and USAKF. He competed across North America as a member of the X-Caliber and Metro All-Star national travel teams. He was the most successful Pennsylvania State Karate Champion of the era. He was recognized as a multiple USA Karate All-American Athlete and National Champion. Viola was the only adult black belt triple gold medalist (Kata, 65 Kilo Kumite, Kobudo) at the 1997 USAKF National Championships in Akron, Ohio.

As a Junior at the University of Pittsburgh, he was recognized by Arnold Schwarzenegger as a World Champion at The Arnold Sports Festival, Columbus, Ohio, in 1998. In 1999, he sustained a cervical neck injury in an automobile accident followed by surgery on his esophagus that ended his competitive aspirations.

Viola has won numerous national and international titles and was inducted into the National Black Belt League Hall of Fame in 2003 (Houston, Texas). He was also inducted into the National Federation of Martial Arts Hall of Fame, Kumite International Hall of Fame, and the Pennsylvania Karate Rating Association Hall of Fame. In 2004, he was honored at

PERSONAL ACHIEVEMENTS

Bill Viola, Jr. graduated Summa Cum Laude from the University of Pittsburgh in 1999 with a bachelor's degree in Political Science. Viola Jr. moved to Hollywood, California, to gain hands-on experience in the entertainment industry. Subsequently, he was accepted into the Screen Actors Guild and American Federation of Television and Radio and established his own company, Kumite Classic Entertainment (KCE). He gained notoriety from his role in the Britney Spears video Stronger (2000) and was able to network and build relationships with leading directors and producers.

His company's signature event, the self-titled "Kumite Classic," is regarded as the largest karate event in Pittsburgh and the media has dubbed it the mecca for martial arts in Western Pennsylvania. KCE also produced the annual Pittsburgh Fitness Expo, recognized as the largest and most established multi-sport convention in Western Pennsylvania, attracting sports and entertainment icons such as Lynn Swann, Franco Harris, Antonio Brown, Ice-T, and Royce Gracie over the years. Viola has served as a consultant, referee, and event coordinator for some of the largest martial arts events in the world. In 2017 he brokered a partnership with Century Martial Arts and WAKO to produce the North American Open in Las Vegas, Nevada, in conjunction with UFC Fight Week.

In 2011, Viola began a research project to document the origins of MMA in America. His work was honored with a permanent exhibit installed at the Western PA Sports Museum and Senator John Heinz History Center. The display is located next to the Franco Harris "Immaculate Reception."

MAJOR ACHIEVEMENTS

The Sport Karate Living Legends Banquet with the Lifetime Achievement Award, Lynchburg, Va.

- Recognized as World Champion by Arnold Schwarzenegger -1998

- Triple Gold Medalist USA Karate Jr. Olympics

- USA National Champion, Junior athlete 1987-1994

- Member of the USA Karate National Team

- 4x USA Karate Federation National Champion (1995-1998)

- 4x USAKF All-American Athlete (1995-1998)

- Creator Sensei Says ® Life Skills Curriculum

- 2003: Inducted into National Black Belt League The Martial Arts Hall of Fame, 2003

- 2005: Recipient of The Lifetime Achievement Award, Sport Karate Museum

- 2011: The Willie Stargell "MVP Award" for community service

- 2016: Pittsburgh Magazine's 40 under 40 recipient.

- 2017: "Whos Who in the Martial Arts" (Legend of American Karate recipient)

Bill is the head coach of "Team Kumite," an all-star travel team representing Pittsburgh on an international level. Most recently, his protégé Xander Eddy won the Pan American Championships in Cancun, Mexico. Eddy became the youngest American in history to win Gold and was honored by the Pennsylvania Governor Tom Wolf and WTAE featured athlete. The team is slated to visit Tokyo, Japan, in the Summer of 2021 for the Olympic Games.

PERSONAL ACHIEVEMENTS

Viola is a Sport Karate History Generals and recipient of the Sport Karate Museum's "Lifetime Achievement" and awarded the Champion Associations Willie Stargell M.V.P. Award (2011) for community service. He was honored with his students with the "Positive Athlete" award and featured on KDKA's Hines Ward Show.

Bill Viola Jr. is a bestselling author, film producer, and creator of CommonSensei® life skills book series. He is currently President of Kumite Classic Entertainment based in Pittsburgh, Pennsylvania.

THIEN VO

"I continue to live my life through Martial Arts. A good mentor or instructor can set a good path for their children, kids, and students."

TRAINING INFORMATION

- Belt Ranks & Martial Arts Styles: Taekwondo - 7th Dan Black, Tang Soo Do - 5th Dan Black

- Instructors/Influencers: Grandmaster Saejin "Jack" Hwang", Master Trinh Manh Chu, Grandmaster Jim Hammons, Grandmaster Brooks Matsuda, Grandmaster Micheal Shintaku

- Birthdate: June 22, 1972

- Birthplace/Growing Up: Saigon, Vietnam/Fort Smith, AR

- Yrs. In the Martial Arts: 36 years

- Yrs. Instructing: 10+ years

- School owner & Instructor at Refuge Martial Arts Academy

PROFESSIONAL ORGANIZATIONS

- Hwa Rang World Tang Soo Do Federation

- Western Pacific Tang Soo Do Association

- World Dang Soo Do Union

- United Taekwondo Alliance

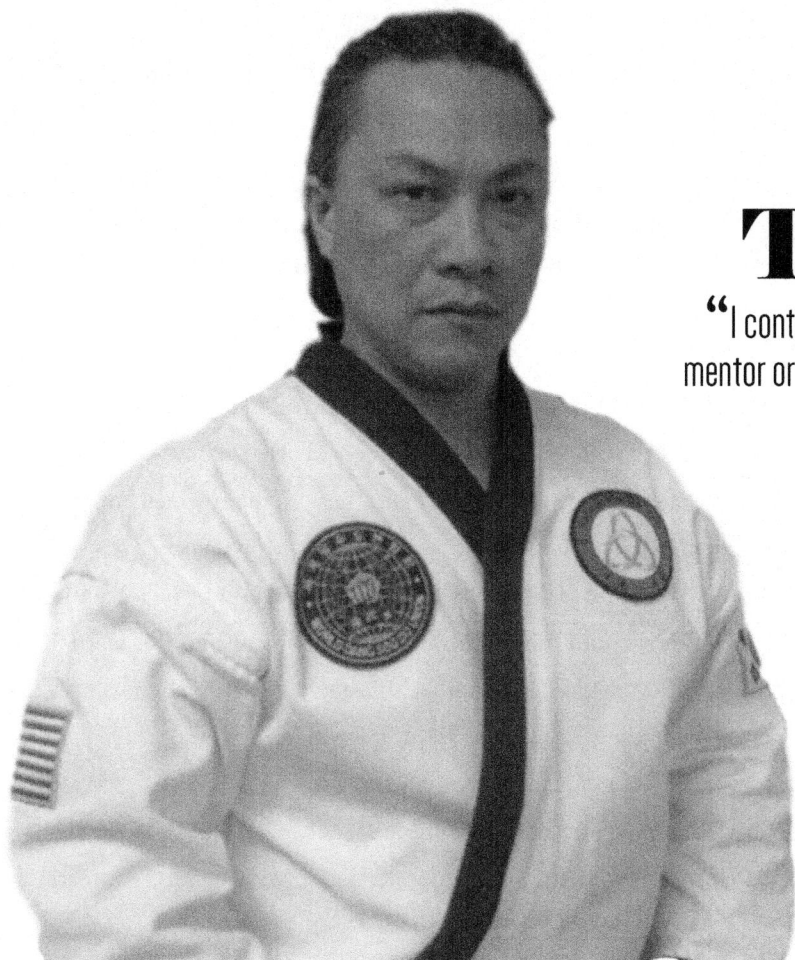

From that starting point of my childhood life – 8 years old, I barked or began this unknown journey, the art of Tae Kwon Do – Way of the Kick and Punch. The year was 1984. I was enrolled in the first intro-class conducted by Mr. Jimmy Hammons, now Master Jim Hammons. At first, it was confusing for me. The first class wasn't what I witnessed my uncle doing, so I said to Mr. Hammons, "I wanted to do what my uncle was doing- jumping, yelling, breaking." He instructed me to drop and give him 50 pushups. I just looked at him? Uh, my first day of class???

Since I began this journey, I have gained very little knowledge, but that doesn't mean that I will give up. I have realized that wisdom comes not just from the accumulation of knowledge but also life application. The art of Tae Kwon Do has come to mean more to me than I could imagine. Martial arts means more to me than I can ever imagine. I enjoy the physical activities that are involved, but the philosophy behind understanding what it means. Martial Arts have a combination of movements of Japan's Karate and the circular movements of Chinese art.

PERSONAL ACHIEVEMENTS

- March 1992 – 2nd Place Open Forms
- March 1993 – 1st Place Open Forms
- March 1994 – 3rd Place Open Forms, 3rd Dan and above
- March 1995 – 2nd Place Open Forms, 3rd Dan and above
- March 1996 – 3rd Place Open Forms, 3rd Dan and above 2nd Place Sparring
- April 1997 - 3rd Place Open Forms 3rd Dan and above, 3rd Place Sparring
- April 1998 - 2nd Place Sparring
- April 2000 - 1st Place Open Forms, 3rd Dan and above, 2nd Place Sparring
- April 2001 - 1st Place Open Forms, 3rd Dan and above
- April 2002 - 1st Place Open Forms, 3rd Dan and above, 2nd Place Sparring
- April 2003- 1st Place Open Forms, 3rd Dan and above, 2nd Place Sparring
- 28th - 35th / 37th - 39th Annual All-American Taekwondo, Karate Championship presented by Grandmaster Jack Hwang, Oklahoma City, Oklahoma
- May 2012 - 2nd Place Traditional Forms, 1st Place Power Break
- May 2014 - 1st Place Traditional Forms, 2nd Place Sparring 10th - 11th Annual Battle of LA Presented by Grandmaster Ho Sik Pak, Granada Hills, California
- July 2018 – 3rd Place Masters Fight, West Coast Regional Championship Presented by WPTSDA / WDU

It creates a beautiful flow of motion that is inspiring to strength, grace, balance, coordination, speed, reaction, flexibility, endurance, and cardiovascular conditioning when performed with mental focus and spiritual expression. Mentally, Tae Kwon do means perseverance, the pursuit of my personal development of a positive mental attitude, self-control, clarity of thoughts. I have found that my mind must be connected to what my body is doing and not only be connected to what my body is doing but be focused. Spiritually, this art encourages peace and contentment. It is important to appreciate each present moment and experience it to its fullest. The pursuit of goals is great and necessary, but not at the expense of what is here and now. I cannot focus on what is behind me or too far ahead without missing what is right in front of me. I have valued my life and the things that surround and revolve around me. My uncle introduced me to "meditation." He taught me how martial arts and meditation could help relax the mind and body. After learning a few breathing techniques, I have taken an interest in meditation. It has helped me in many ways that I couldn't imagine. I have a strong desire to remain calm within, no matter what is coming at me or in front of me. Meditation has helped me with stress, slowing my pulse, controlling my breathing, and overcoming various physical and mental obstacles.

As time passes and training, I appreciate every belt level I have accomplished and believe each step toward my advanced belt "Black Belt – First Degree." I have succeeded as much as I failed, but it has been full of a valuable lesson in my life. As I progress in my journey, I learned patience by being given opportunities where I needed it. That is also the way I have been developing self-discipline and control. I say to myself, why am I the only one being challenged? Or what is that; that I am doing to deserve this. But I thought again; everyone goes through hoops, ropes, and rings. Everyone has different challenges in their life. No one is getting something or anything for free. So, from then on, I wanted to advance with the ranks. I have to do it the old way, "earn it.

Martial arts code: Courtesy, Integrity, Perseverance, Self-Control, and Indomitable Spirit. I strongly believe that without these codes, there would not be any victory. At first, it wasn't easy to live life by these codes. I would have to channel it, absorb it, and act upon it in my daily life. I would ask myself how these codes could be implemented in my everyday

PERSONAL ACHIEVEMENTS

- October 2018 – 3rd Place Master Forms, 2nd Place Masters Fight Gold Team Fight East Coast

MAJOR ACHIEVEMENTS

- June 1997 – 1999 Recognition Award, Arkansas Invitation Taekwondo Championship presented by Guldi's Taekwondo

- May 2012 – HWTSDF 10th Annual Battle of LA Recognition Award Present by Grandmaster Ho Sik Pak

- June 2013 – HWTSDF Region 5, Recognition Award Presented by Master Daniel Delenela

- December 2013 – 2014 Advantage Martial Arts, Appreciation Award Presented by Master Jim Hammons

- May 2014 – HWTSDF Meritorious Commendation Award Present by Grandmaster Ho Sik Pak

- May 2015 – Battle of Columbus and Bruce Lee Legends / Martial Arts Hall of Honor Inaugural Award Honorees - Master Spirit / Tang Soo Do Master Indomitable

life and activities. Well, I thought the achievement of black belt would provoke a feeling of pride in myself, but I found that the closer I am to my goals, the more I am humbled by discovering things I need to improve myself. Unlike when I began this journey, I now have peace and confidence that I can own up to the challenges in front of me. Life is a never-ending learning process.

I had an opportunity to learn more from a Korean Grandmaster "Jack Sae Jin Hwang" about Korea and many different martial arts styles that come from Korea. Some of the most important things I have learned are mental strengths. I now measure my success against my past as a child, teenager, and adult. I envision myself as a 5th Dan as a whole person by my own mistakes, success, my past performance, "achieved or failed" rather than "against" others.

Martial arts have helped me manage my emotions and aggression from my teen years to adulthood. Martial arts is often used to help me to avoid confrontation and illnesses. But to regain my sense of control and empowerment.

I continue to live my life through Martial Arts. A good mentor or instructor can set a good path for their children, kids, and students. I strongly believe that martial arts are good for children. It can reduce anger, violence, and delinquency.

I know that I'm not perfect. My life has its ups and downs. I try to follow the codes of Tae Kwon Do and Tang Soo Do. For me, instructing / teaching kids, teenagers, adults, I have to maintain discipline. No matter how frustrated I become. Always be humble to my students. There's an old golden rule "treat others as you want others to treat you. My family and students are my energy.

MICHAEL JAI WHITE

"Martial Arts was the therapy I needed and provided the confidence I needed to prosper in my life."

TRAINING INFORMATION

- Martial arts title: Sensei
- City/State: Sherman Oaks, CA
- Started studying martial arts in 1972
- Teaching for 30 years and currently ranked as Yodan, studying martial arts styles: Kyokushin, Goja Ryu, Shotokan, TKD, Kobudo, Tang Soo Do, Superfoot Systems
- Instructors: Shigeru Oyama, Bill Wallace, Matty Mellisi, Rex Lee, Anthony Marquez, Jerry Kleinman, Eric Chen, Joe Lewis, Hosu Wang

Sensei White holds eight different Black Belts. He is a martial arts champion, film star, and many believe he is one of the most dynamic martial arts film stars to grace the big screen. He is a husband to Gillian White, father to six children, grandfather to 4 grandchildren, and a great grandfather to one great-granddaughter.

He started his training in 1972. Like most Martial Artists in the 70's, he was influenced by the prowess of Bruce Lee, and Martial Arts became a mainstay in his life. As of 2013, he had achieved his 8th black belt. His styles of study include Kyokushin, Shotokan, Goju, Tae Kwon Do, Kobudo, Seido, Tang Soo Do, and the Superfoot System. In 2015, he was presented his 9th Degree from a board of high- ranking instructors from the east coast.

Sensei White has trained several years with Benny Urquidez as well as Byong Yu. Eddie Bravo and Rigan Machado have been his Brazillian Jiu Jitsu instructors for the past six years. He's also trained with such greats as

Shigeru Oyama, Bill Wallace, Joe Lewis, Matty Mellisi, Rex Lee, Anthony Marquez, Jerry Kleinman, Eric Chen, and Hosu Wang.

As a competitor, he has won many tournaments as a fighter as well as a forms competitor. He competed in hundreds of tournaments in the 80's and 90's. He said, "There are almost too many to name given their various style distinctions and affiliations. Being that I only considered PKA and WKA the only legitimate worldwide fighting entities at that time, and I held none of those titles, I never bothered to claim any coveted titles other than regional and national point system tournaments which were free to name their tournaments any glorious title they wished."

In the movie SPAWN, he was the first African American to portray a superhero. As a writer, producer, actor, and director, he has created movies like Blood And Bone, Black Dynamite, Falcon Rising, Never Back Down 2 and #3, and No Surrender--a love letter to traditional martial arts. As an international star of many martial art films, he is one of the few Americans currently representing martial arts in film on a worldwide platform today.

As of publication, Sensei White has several movies coming out. He is also the host of the newest MMA Reality-based TV show called Last Fighter Standing. He is helping to blaze a trail to find the world's best Martial Arts fighters and bring them international recognition.

"Martial Arts have saved my life, literally and figuratively," Sensei White said. "I came into the arts as an insecure youngster searching for armor to protect me from the hardness of life, and I emerged as a peaceful warrior who viewed life as a series of obstacles to be easily overcome by my efforts. I was hyperactive and extremely aggressive. The physical and mental outlet the martial arts provided for me was a life-saving receptacle for my surplus angst. It was the therapy I needed and provided the confidence I needed to prosper in my life." He continued. "Every aspect of my life has been enhanced through Martial Arts. The discipline achieved is the very thing needed in every aspect of success. I was on my own since the age of 14, living in the harsh inner-city where my only role models were Martial Artists who adhered to a life of vigorous training, self-denial, and virtuous living. I was as far from where I sit now as I could possibly be and could barely see past a five-block radius.

Only through the furnace of karate training could I achieve the self-realization that I was meant to break from the restraints of my community and venture toward my destiny. Only through the lesson that, 'in life, as in belt levels, the obstacles are overcome through consistent work and discipline. I am a successful husband and father because of these very tenets.'

As an actor, Michael Jai White has 83 acting credits, according to IMDB. He has four credits as Producer, four as Director, and three for stunts.

"In my opinion, Michael Jai's fight scenes are consistently the best martial arts scenes on film," PKA president Joe Corley said. "The techniques are clean, 'old school' martial arts, shot well, edited well, and easy to understand. I'd have to guess that Michael Jai insists on that clarity in those action scenes."

Sensei White has been inducted into several Halls of Fame, including Alan Goldberg's Action Martial Arts Hall Of Fame as well as the late Arron Banks Hall of Fame about a decade ago. In 2014, Michael Jai earned the prestigious Black Belt Magazine Man of the Year award.

In 2019, he was proud to be given the title of "Black Dragon" by Grandmaster Ron Van Clief. Sensei White plans to resurrect a new movie honoring that title in the near future.

Ambassadors
BLACK BELTS

RAYMOND BELLAMY

"Martial Arts has provided me the opportunity to grow spiritually and naturally."

TRAINING INFORMATION

- Belt Ranks & Martial Arts Styles: Karate, Tai Chi, Taekwondo, Tangsoodo

- Instructors/Influencers: Master John Fagliarone

- Birthdate: January 2, 1968

- Birthplace/Growing Up: Brooklyn, NY

- Yrs. In the Martial Arts: 27 years

- Yrs. Instructing: 8 years

- Instructor

PROFESSIONAL ORGANIZATIONS

- AAU

- WKU

- Wesleyan Church feeding the homeless

- Sembach Self Defense Gathering

- The Black Belt Gathering / TBBG

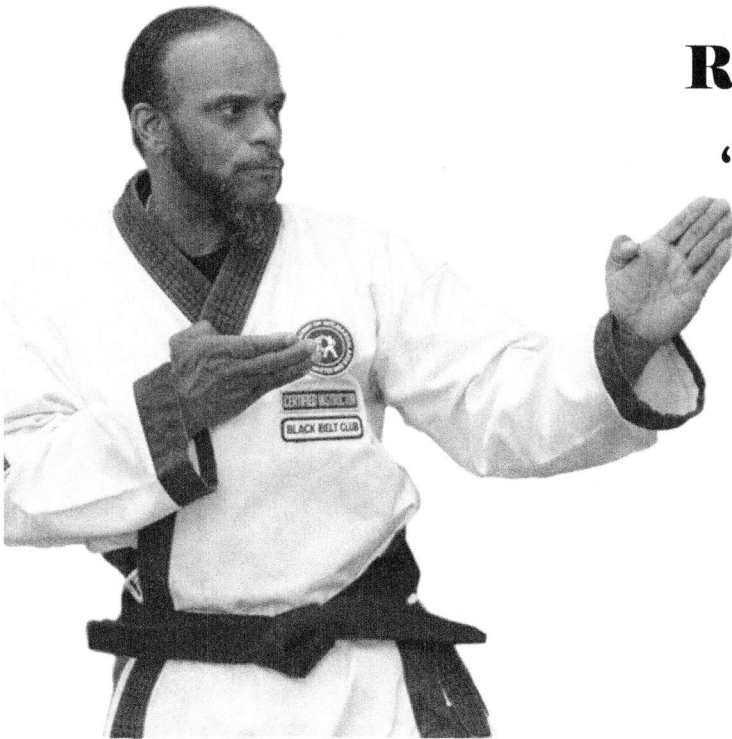

I have always been fascinated by the spirit of martial arts growing up. I watched martial artists exhibit strength, endurance, spiritual growth, and develop a brotherhood and sisterhood that cannot be found anywhere else.

Studying martial arts has provided me the opportunity to grow (reach one -teach one); growing spiritually and naturally. Studying martial arts has opened many doors that have afforded me the opportunities such as playing small roles in upcoming movies, as well as connecting with the young and old which has always been a passion of mine.

PERSONAL ACHIEVEMENTS

- H.U. Gourmet Services Rookie Of The Year
- Cary Cardinals Assistant Football Coaches Awards and Trophies
- Hampton Cavaliers Football and Basketball Coaches Awards
- Hollywood Certificate by Action Movie Director and Movie Star Art Camacho
- 2001 Hampton Cavaliers City Champions
- 2002 Intermediate Head Coach Hampton Cavaliers Basketball Runner - Up Championship
- Double - Goal Coach 1, 2, & 3 Certificates

MAJOR ACHIEVEMENTS

- The Philadelphia Historic Martial Arts Society Hall Of Honor
- Vita Saana & Bitma Awards, The Legend Of The Martial Arts
- Blacks In The Martial Arts, Bitma Awards
- Masters Of The Martial Arts Award
- L.P.S.D.A.W. Awards
- Action Martial Arts Magazine Hall Of Honors
- Senbach Self Defense Certificate
- Who's Who Legends Awards
- 2 Martial Arts Championship Belts
- 1 Board Breaking Championship Belt
- TBBG SAGE COUNSEL MEMBER

KENNETH DAY

"To this day, Tae Kwon Do has been an important part of my life and has made me the person that I am today."

TRAINING INFORMATION

- Belt Ranks & Martial Arts Styles: Tae Kwon Do (3rd Degree Black Belt)

- Instructors/Influencers: Grand Master Myuang Hak Kang, Grand Master Jhoon Rhee, Master Cleanzo Vollin, Master Instructor Andre Yamakawa (deceased), Grand Master John Chung, Grand Master Dongju Lee, Master Apollo Ladra, Grand Master Michael Coles

- Birthplace/Growing Up: Washington DC / Arlington, VA

- Yrs. In the Martial Arts: 46 years

- Yrs. Instructing: 13 years

PERSONAL ACHIEVEMENTS

- I am a twenty-six-year cancer survivor.

- I worked thirty-two years with Giant Food and retired.

- I have been with Anne Arundel County Public Schools for fourteen years, the last four of which has been a promotion to Senior Facility Engineer and am responsible for the operation and maintenance of a middle school, including supervising seven employees.

- I have advanced in Tae Kwon Do from white belt to black belt and been an instructor for 13 years.

I come from a family of twelve children living in a two-bedroom house. My mother died when I was fourteen years old. In 1974 I took my first Tae Kwon Do class under Grand Master Myuang Hak Kang located in Arlington, VA and the Grand Master is still teaching classes today.

I studied Tae Kwon Do in 1976 with Grand Master Jhoon Rhee and trained with Jangs Tae Kwon Do from 1976 to 1981. My training continued in Maryland with Grand Master Lee at the Lee Karate studio and Grand Master Apolo at the Apolo East Coast Tae Kwon Do School.

I was diagnosed with cancer in 1992. I endured radiation and chemotherapy treatment from 1992 to 1998, including two reoccurrences of the cancer.

To this day, Tae Kwon Don has been an important part of my life and has made me the person that I am today. At present I am the Chief Instructor for Performance Martial Art in Bowie, MD. I strive to be fair, compassionate and loyal in everything that I do and that is how I live my life. I have mentored other cancer patients and young martial arts students, instilling them with determination and the spirit to never give up, whether in athletics or health related situations.

BARRY HARBIN

"Martial Arts over the years has taught me so many life lessons. Most of which deal with Self Confidence, Self-Control, Focus, and Character."

TRAINING INFORMATION

- Belt Ranks & Martial Arts Styles: Yoshukai 1st Dan, American Freestyle 2nd & 3th Dan, American Karate Academies National Association 4th Dan, AKANA Advance Instructor and title of Tashi

- Instructors/Influencers: Rod Lowery

- Birthdate: October 30, 1961

- Birthplace/Growing Up: Albertville, AL

- Yrs. In the Martial Arts: 42 years

- Yrs. Instructing: 12 years

- Instructor

PROFESSIONAL ORGANIZATIONS

- Yoshukai World Association
- American Freestyle karate
- American Karate Academies National Association
- National Sport Karate Museum

I began my Karate career in 1978 at the age of 16. At that time, I was a teenager with big dreams to play football. But as a teenager, only 5'7 and 120 pounds soaking wet, you quickly learned that you are not going to make the team, and the coach told me that he wished that his other players had my heart and determination to play the game as I did. Since I was way too short and underweight and had no musical talent, I couldn't be in the band. So, I ended up feeling like I was a misfit and would never be able to do anything that would amount to anything. I was just an oddball teenager.

Then I met a man by the name of Rod Lowery, and he said, "Why don't you come to try karate?" I told him, "Look at me. I'm 5'7 and 120 pounds. Do you really think I'll be good at karate?" He looked me square in the eyes and said, "Size does not matter if you have the will and the determination." So, I thought to myself, why not? At least he's given me a chance. Shortly after training a few months, he told me it was time to test, and I received my first yellow belt on April 4, 1978. From then on, I was hooked. I continued training and competing, and on October 2, 1983, I received my 1st-degree black belt.

PERSONAL ACHIEVEMENTS

- 1st Dan 10/02/1983
- 2nd Dan 10/13/1984
- 3th Dan 07/19/1986
- 4th Dan 06/09/1990

MAJOR ACHIEVEMENTS

- 1981 Full contact champion in light weight for North Alabama
- 1998 Boy scouts woodbadge award while working with a local scout group
- 2005 Letter of Accommodation from Alabama State Defense Force 1st infantry brigade for help with hurricane Katrina victims
- 2009 Alabama Rescuer of the year award
- 2017 IKF-Albertville Karate Yoshukai True Karate person award
- 2018 Inducted in to the American Martial Arts Alliance Hall of Fame

On that day, Mr. Lowery walked up to me and asked me if I feel like a misfit now. I told him "no Sir" and thanked him for all he's done for me over these years. He had taken a young boy who had lost all his confidence and helped him to gain it back with determination and the ability always to keep an open mind.

Shortly after that, I got married to my wife Lee Ann, and we had two children, Anthony and Aimee. At that time, I thought due to my job, I would have to hang up my belt because of traveling for long periods of time, but while in Georgia, I was able to train at American Freestyle Karate to reach the rank 4th Dan. Then my job has me traveling to different places around the country only for a few months at a time. Somehow, I managed to find a dojo that would let me train temporarily.

Now that I look back on it, I thought maybe it was a blessing that I got to train with many great people like Francis Fong, Chuck Valentine, and others. The knowledge, experience, and wisdom of these men I received have carried me through tough times and good times. But I have never forgotten what Mr. Lowery taught me so many years ago-- always to keep an open mind. A black belt is just the beginning of learning and always give back what karate has given you.

Today, I am a member of the American Karate Academy National Association with Hanshi Jerry Piddington, a great man with lots of wisdom and knowledge that I hope to learn. To give back to my students as they start their never-ending journey into this world, we call martial arts.

I currently train at IKF Karate Albertville with a long-time friend Rachel Camp.

Martial Arts has been a significant part of my life since I was 16 years old. Martial Arts over the years has taught me so many life lessons. Most of which deal with Self Confidence, Self-Control, Focus, and Character.

1st: Self-confidence- Martial arts has taught me to always believe in myself and to know I can face the challenges that life throws at me and to do anything I set my mind to do.

2nd: Self Control- It has taught me always to try to keep a cool head and not to lose my temper and to remember that there are always two sides to a story. When we are faced with those moments that test our patience and

and when anger and frustration take over, take a deep breath and let it go.

3th: Focus- Always focus on the job at hand, whether it's doing your job, marriage, or on your sparring partner.

4th: Character- Always treat people with respect and courtesy no matter their race, gender, or religion because Martial Arts is a way of life.

KENNETH HILL JR.

"The principles that I learned in martial arts have been essential in every aspect of my life."

TRAINING INFORMATION

- Belt Ranks & Martial Arts Styles: U.S. Hapkido - 4th Dan, U.S. Tae Kwon Do - 4th Dan, International Tang Soo Do - 2nd Dan, American Freestyle Hapkido - 2nd Dan, World Tang Soo Do Federation - 1st Dan

- Instructors/Influencers: Grandmaster David Brodecki, Grandmaster William Kinicki, Grandmaster Gerald Mingin, Master Ronald Pettie, Master Christopher Rydbom, Sa Bu Nihm Tobie Warren

- Birthdate: September 14, 1964

- Birthplace/Growing Up: Riverside, NJ/Cinnaminson, NJ

- Yrs. In the Martial Arts: 47 years

- Yrs. Instructing: 21 years

- School owner & Instructor at U. S. Hapkido Alliance, LLC

PROFESSIONAL ORGANIZATIONS

- World Hapkido Alliance

- American Martial Arts Alliance Institute

- PKA Worldwide

- North American Federation of Martial Arts

- Cinnaminson Fire Department

- CMT Athlete

- John Maxwell

- Toastmasters International

I went to the drive-in movie with my family to see "Enter the Dragon" starring Bruce Lee. Once I saw that film, which is my favorite movie of all time, I didn't want to do anything else.

I started at the age of nine, and I've been blessed to have studied and trained for more than 47 years. I was a small kid who was bullied and wasn't very athletic. Later in life, I was diagnosed with a hereditary neuropathy called Charcot Marie Tooth disease.

Even though I was told that I would be confined to a wheelchair by the age of 35, God's grace and martial arts have given me the focus and perseverance to defy my doctors' diagnosis.

I've been an instructor at a martial arts school for special needs children and adults for almost eight years, and soon I'll continue our journey as an owner of a new school. It has been a blessing to teach every student, and I

PERSONAL ACHIEVEMENTS

- Achieving my 4th Dan in U.S. Hapkido and Tae Kwon Do
- One million miles accident-free fleet
- 13-year volunteer firefighter

MAJOR ACHIEVEMENTS

- Dragon Fire Martial Arts Kung Fu and Karate Expo 13/Masters of Martial Arts Hall of Fame Award - April 2019
- American Martial Arts Alliance Institute/Who's Who in the Martial Arts Hall of Honors - June 2019
- Legends of Martial Arts Hall of Fame/Global Korea Martial Arts Federation - Golden Lifetime of Achievements (40 years) - October 2019
- Action Martial Arts Magazine Hall of Honors/Outstanding Achievements in Martial Arts - January 2020
- Dragon Fire Martial Arts Kung Fu and Karate Expo 14/Masters of Martial Arts Hall of Fame Award - August 2020

I hope to inspire them the way that they have inspired me.

To go from a kid who had a difficult time walking to a six-time Hall of Fame martial artist is a blessing that only God could provide! I'm truly grateful and humbled. Just Breathe...

The principles that I learned in martial arts have been essential in every aspect of my life. Focus, discipline, perseverance, and indomitable spirit are just a few elements that I've used.

My self-esteem was low from being bullied, and I was very shy. I was often "overlooked" because of my small size and lack of athleticism. I didn't participate in many activities with my peers because I didn't have much confidence in my abilities. Martial arts changed all of that! As my strength and ability increased, my confidence increased. As my confidence grew, I focused on "what I can do" and eliminated what I couldn't do.

Over time, I would challenge myself to try new things and focus on doing my very best and not necessarily being first. When I established that approach, I was able to achieve greater heights than I anticipated.

I emphasize two things from martial arts every day that have been essential in my growth as a martial artist and a person.

1) Always Remain a Student, and

2) Just Breathe

RAYMOND JAMES

"Through Martial Arts, I find purpose in life, overcome challenges, give back to my community and really just understand how impactful it can truly be to the development of any and every individual."

Martial Arts classes were initially a place for me to express my energies in a constructive manner. At the time I was getting into a lot of trouble at school – I didn't have control or discipline. My mother was concerned that if I didn't find an outlet for my energetic / curious behavior it might hinder my growth as an individual. At the time we lived in a very impoverished area of Rockland County called Spring Valley; which at the time we resided in one of the most dangerous parts, "THE HILL" a very, very distant cousin from Beverly Hills. Let's just say it was normal to see drug dealers, violence and random acts of ignorance at that time. So, my mom really saved me from the environment by placing me in a cultured environment from a very young age. I learned very early that you could be amongst the worst and still grow in a very different way.

Martial Arts has helped me to organize my ideas, thoughts and visions, if you will, as an artist, slow the very busy/hectic world, discover how to achieve/unlock balance within myself and others. It's allowed me to meet people from all walks of life and become friends/family with them. It's allowed me to see the world, experience other cultures, compete with some of the most talented people in sport and art, appreciate what this world has to offer and teach others how to do the same. Martial Arts diffuses violence, inspires, uplifts, transforms minds, bodies and spirits, makes a difference and promotes well-being.

TRAINING INFORMATION

- Belt Ranks & Martial Arts Styles: Belt Ranks & Martial Arts Styles:
Tang Soo Do (4th Degree), WTF Tae Kwon Do (3rd Degree), ITF Tae Kwon Do (3rd Degree), Western Boxing (Since 1998), Wrestling (Since 1997), Muay Thai (Since 2000) Senior Instructor, Tai Chi (Since 1995, Capoeira (Azul) Ninjitsu- (Shodan), Akijujitsu (Since 2016, Yoshisutni (Since 2016)
Wing Chun-Kung Fu (Si Fan Duan), Judo (Black Belt), BJJ (Black Belt), MMA

- Instructors/Influencers: Grand Master Anthony Richards, Grand Master Charles Lundi, Grand Master Alan Bernard, Grand Master B.M Kim, Grand Master Jung Chu Lee, Grand Master Joon P. Choi, Master Kru Phil Nurse, Grand Master Guerrido, Sifu KarlRomain, Sensei Thomas A. Renner, Grand Master Alan Goldberg, Grand Master Cynthia Rothrock, Sifu Samuel Kwok, Grand Master Dr. Robert Goldman

- Birthdate: June 6, 1982

- Birthplace/Growing Up: Jamaica West Indies / Rockland County NY

- Yrs. In the Martial Arts: 32 years

- Yrs. Instructing: 19 years

- School owner, Manager, Instructor , Coach

PROFESSIONAL ORGANIZATIONS

- Kukkiwon
- Action Martial Arts Hall of Honors Inductee

PERSONAL ACHIEVEMENTS

- Jamaican Tae Kwon Do National Team Member
- Action Martial Arts Hall of Honors Inductee
- 4x Good Will Games Champion
- Cover & Tear Sheets featuring Martial Arts
- Men's Health
- Details
- Muscle & Fitness
- Muscular Development
- Flex
- GQ
- Getty Images Editorial & Creative Contributor
- 6th Year Series Producer for NYC TV: Shows scope featuring Art, Culture & Travel
- Business Owner
- Mixed Media Professional
- Actor - Stage & Screen
- Model- Print & Runway
- Writer Author & Editor
- Creative Director - For several companies
- NYC 6th year Series Producer (Cable TV & Streamed Internationally)
- Creative Director / 2nd Shooter & Stunt Choreographer at PAJARITO Productions
- Getty Images & Shutter Stock Global Contributor
- Creative Director & Cinematographer For:
- Beauty Bar by Camila Mello; Philanthropy, Academy & Lifestyle
- Vitruvius Productions Lead Cinematographer

Through it, I persevere through adversity, be aware of the energies around me and within me, master my train of thought, become a better producer, cinematographer, writer, actor, stuntman, choreographer, director, athlete, human being. Through it, I find purpose in life, overcome challenges, give back to my community and really just understand how impactful Martial Arts can truly be to the development of any and every individual.

MAJOR ACHIEVEMENTS

- New York State Champ (several times)
- US OPEN Champ (several times)
- Global Campaign for Isopure Company that allowed me to share my story about Martial Arts and how it changed my life. I appeared on the cover a couple dozen magazines around the world and there were 3 versions of the commercial that played around the world including time square in NYC. (https://www.youtube.com/watch?v=tfzwsuoMn5k)
- *I was almost the first person to make it to the Olympics for Jamaica*

MARVIN KING

"The study and practice of Martial Arts defines how I manage wellness, stay fit, teach, and live."

TRAINING INFORMATION

- Belt Ranks & Martial Arts Styles: Tae Kwon Do, Traditional Shuai-Chiao (Black Belt), Ch'ang style T'ai-chi-ch'uan and Hsing Jing [Ch'ang's "essence of Hsing-I"] (Black Belt), Brown Belt: Shaolin Do Kung Fu (Brown Belt), Hung Fut Southern Shaolin Kung Fu (Black Sash), Krav Maga, Target Focus Training (TFT), Korean Sulsa, Ju-Jitsu

- Instructors/Influencers: Grandmaster Ch'ang Tung-Sheng, Master Chi-Hsiu Daniel Weng, Grandmaster Sin Kwan, The Grandmaster Tai Yim, Master Tim Larkin, Pavel Tsatsouline, Master David Dance, Master Marc Nance

- Birthdate: March 20, 1960

- Birthplace/Growing Up: Cleveland, OH

- Yrs. In the Martial Arts: 45 years

- Yrs. Instructing: 20 years

- School owner, Manager Instructor

PROFESSIONAL ORGANIZATIONS

- Professional and Leadership

- Project Management Institute (PMI)

- Project Management Professional (PMP)-2012 to present.

- Project Management Institute (PMI), Agile Certified Practitioner (PMI-ACP) 2020

My martial arts journey started as an adolescent at a time in the 60s when martial art schools were very traditional, tough, and gritty. As a new student in my very first Karate class I was paired with a bigger student who choked me out by applying too much neck pressure during a basic choke escape drill. That first experience was painful and nearly caused me to quit. But I didn't. I quickly learned during those early days in the dojo that to earn a black belt, you need discipline, patience, and courage. I remember falling a lot, picking myself up, and pushing my physical limits as my Sensei drilled us in the art of kicking, punching, sparring, and self-defense. With discipline and hard work, I eventually earned a green belt in Tae Kwon Do, but because the school was far from home and expensive, I stopped training there. Being removed from the dojo was disappointing, but unbeknownst to me then, that transition would be what ignited my great love, commitment, and journey in the martial arts. It also reminded me of what my parents taught about not settling for the status quo and to keep moving forward.

PERSONAL ACHIEVEMENTS

- 2 Time Marine Corp Marathon Finisher
- 1 Time Philadelphia Marathon Finisher
- 3 Time Army 10-miler finisher
- 3 Time Annapolis 10-miler finisher
- 2 Time Cherry Blossom 10-miler finisher

MAJOR ACHIEVEMENTS

- First Black Belt from the late Grandmaster Ch'ang Tung-Sheng and Master Chi-Hsiu Daniel Weng- 1982
- Member of the first-generation USA Shuai-Chiao Black Belts. (3 years teaching)
- 2019 Inductee into the American Martial Arts Alliance (AMAA) Who's Who Legends Hall of Honors.
- Featured in the 2019 Martial Arts Masters and Pioneers Autobiography Book.
- 2020 Action Martial Arts Hall of Honors Inductee and received the (40-Year Martial Arts Golden Lifetime Contributions Award.
- Featured in the 2020 Action Martial Arts Hall of Honors World History Book.
- Third degree Brown Belt in Shaolin Do Kung fu where I learned the Qigong breathing meditations under Grandmaster Sin Kwan The.
- Black Sash in Southern Hung- Fut Kung fu system under 8th Generation Grandmaster Tai Yim. (13 years teaching)

My turning point was when I realized that being a martial artist was not about a school or a system but of practice, discipline, consistency, perseverance, and patience!

Curious to know more, I researched books and literature and accumulated and absorbed everything on the subject. I learned about strength training, kinesiology, bodybuilding, philosophy, meditation, and diet, among others. Bruce Lee's movies also inspired me. I appreciated the variety of martial art systems and was humbled to know that each system offered an abundance of knowledge, tradition, and history.

By age 12, I transformed my body by consuming healthier foods and adding weight training and meditation to my martial arts practice. During the 70's I took Karate classes in gyms and auditoriums and trained with accomplished Tae Kwon Do Black Belts. In 1980 I joined the International Shuai-Chiao Academy in Cleveland, Ohio, with Master Chi-Hsiu Daniel Weng Ph.D. Master Weng would often host his teacher Grandmaster Ch'ang Tung-Sheng (aka The Flying Butterfly) when he visited from Taiwan. I was humbled after witnessing the power, balance, and grace of these Masters and was excited to learn Chinese Kung Fu finally. Shuai-Chiao training included the Ch'ang style T'ai-chi-ch'uan and Hsing Jing (Ch'ang's "essence of Hsing-Yi"). I stayed with Shuai-Chiao, practiced hard every day, and was honored to earn my first Black Belt from the late Grandmaster in 1982. I successfully competed in many Shuai-Chiao and Karate tournaments in the years following my training and was appreciative when tournament rules were changed to accommodate more fighting styles.

MAJOR ACHIEVEMENTS

- World Kung Fu (WKF) National Forms and Weapons Grand Championship - 1995

- National Council of Strength and Fitness (NCSF) Certified Professional Trainer (CPT) - 1999 to present.

- Russian Kettlebell Challenge (RKC) Level 1 Certification - 2006 to present with Kettlebell and strength expert Pavel Tsatsouline.

- Russian Kettlebell Challenge (RKC) Level 2 Certification - 2009

Today I'm more focused on the simplicity of Reality-Based Self Protection, Qigong, and the development of functional strength that can only be achieved from Hardstyle Kettlebell exercises. Under the guidance of Kettlebell and strength expert Pavel Tsatsouline, I earned the Level 1 and Level 2 Russian Kettlebell Challenge (RKC) Certifications. I was fascinated and awestruck with how quickly the Kettlebell 1-Arm Swing and Turkish Get Up (TGU) improved the martial artist fighting endurance and power. I immediately implemented the RKC strong man philosophy and training methods to my martial arts practice with immediate positive results. Hard Style Kettlebell Swings teach the Martial artist how to generate explosive hip power while relaxing the arms and anchoring the feet. Like Yin / Yang, the TGU (Yin) develops the elusive soft elements of strength, while the Kettlebell Swing (Yang) accentuates the martial artist's ability to generate explosive power.

In 2014, I created the Bowie Kettlebell Club (BKC), a strength and holistic wellness-based school that teaches and trains the student to be functionally fit at any age by using Kettlebells, Qigong, and Martial Arts. Self-protection classes at the BKC focus on understanding what real violence is and the simple tools anyone can use to protect themselves. No previous training or martial arts prerequisites are required for this class. The BKC "Loaded Yoga Program" is a creative blend of Kettlebells and Qigong exercises that, when done in a specific pattern, will add a unique strength element to the Yoga and Qigong students' regular practice.

I'm humbled by this opportunity to serve others and live by the straightforward philosophy, "You don't have to please anyone! You only have to be the best you can be!" So, "Find a path, stay humble, and always march forward, courageously!"

The study and practice of Martial Arts defined how I manage wellness, stay fit, teach, and live. The discipline and optimistic worldview instilled through martial arts practice helped me manage life's obstacles. These obstacles usually disguised as truths are designed to distract, steal dreams, and keep you from reaching your full potential and purpose. Author Stephen Pressfield in the book "War of Art," describes these obstacles as "Resistance." I learned that being a martial artist was not about a school or a system but of discipline, practice, consistency, perseverance, and patience. I learned through martial arts practice that I embody the martial arts.

JOHN LOMBARDO

"The study of Martial Arts has instilled in me a belief in the greater good."

TRAINING INFORMATION

- Belt Ranks & Martial Arts Styles: Bushi Ban International - 4th Dan, Sensei, Isshinryu Karate - Brown Belt, Shotokan Karate - Brown Belt, Ninpo Taijitsu - Brown Belt, Yammani Ryu Kobudo - Green Belt, United States Chanbarra Association – Instructor, American Judo System - Instructor

- Instructors/Influencers: Grand Master Zulfi Ahmed, Senior Master Hassan Saiyid, Hanshi Kiyoshi Nishime, Shihan Dan Abbott, Grand Master Dr. Maung Gyi, Grand Master Masayuki Ward, Sensei Jimmy Pedro, Anshu Stephen K. Hayes, Shidoshi Jean-Pierre Seibel, Master Dennis Bootle

- Birthdate: October 3, 1966

- Birthplace/Growing Up: Bayside, NY

- Yrs. In the Martial Arts: 42 years

- Yrs. Instructing: 13 years

- School owner, Manager Instructor, Student

My journey in the Martial Arts began back in 1978 when I attended my first Martial Arts class at the urging of my very best childhood friends. We were going to be the next Martial Arts superstars.

At that time, I had no idea of what I was getting into. I spent 4 years at that dojo studying Isshinryu Karate under Sensei (now Master) Dennis Bootle. After a brief break in training, I began training in the art of Shotokan Karate under various instructors while serving in the United States Air Force as an Information Systems Specialist. After my military service, I continued to practice my martial arts skills and searched for a new home. I began training at NY Budo in the mid 1990's under Shidoshi Jean-Pierre Seibel. NY Budo was part of the Bujinkan Dojo of Soke Masaaki Hatsumi under the oversight of An-Shu Stephen K. Hayes. As part of that organization I had the honor and privilege on several occasions of training with An-Shu Stephen K. Hayes. Career and family caused me to take a break from formal training for a while but I continued

PROFESSIONAL ORGANIZATIONS

- Bushi Ban International
- United States Chanbarra Association
- Yammani Ryu Kobudo
- American Judo System
- American Martial Arts Alliance - AMAA
- Masters Hall of Fame
- Black Horse for Heroes

PERSONAL ACHIEVEMENTS

- 4th Dan, Sensei - Bushi Ban International
- Regional Director - Bushi Ban International
- Director, Information Technology - UBS AG

MAJOR ACHIEVEMENTS

- Black Belt of the Year - Bushi Ban International - 2012
- Masters Hall of Fame - Outstanding Contribution - 2012
- American Martial Arts Alliance - Legends Award - 2019

to hone my skills and live by the warrior codes and martial principles that were taught to me over the years.

In April 2004 while seeking out an instructor for my son Vincent, I met then Sensei, now Senior Master Hassan Saiyid of Bushi Ban Connecticut. I was immediately taken in by his openness and warmth, needless to say I enrolled both of us in Bushi Ban that very day, and just like that day in 1978, I had no idea what I was getting myself into. As part of the Bushi Ban family I have had the privilege of meeting and training not only with Senior Master Hassan but with so many amazing martial artists, most notably Great Grand Master Dr. Maung Gyi, Great Grand Master Masayuki Ward, and Grand Master Zulfi Ahmed (Founder, Bushi Ban International).

I was awarded my Bushi Ban Black belt on March 24, 2006 and honored with the award of 4th DAN and Sensei title on August 8, 2015.

Through the generosity of GM Zulfi and SM Hassan, I have been able to train in numerous systems and achieve ranking and certifications from Shihan Kiyoshi Nishime, Shihan Dana Abbott, and Master Jimmy Pedro. My personal weapons of choice are the Katana, and Tanto. In addition to those, I enjoy the Bo, Sai, Tonfa, and Kali Stick.

In October of 2010, I became the Director of Bushi Ban Southbury and with the guidance of Senior Master Hassan and assistance of Sensei Joe Guarente we began to broaden the influence of Bushi Ban on the east coast.

In January of 2018 after the relocation of SM Hassan to Texas the year before, I assumed the reigns of Bushi Ban Seymour and took on the role of Regional Director for Bushi Ban International in Connecticut.

These past 16 years as part of the Bushi Ban Family have taken me to places I had never thought of going and opened my eyes to all that there is yet to achieve.

…and the journey continues.

TOBY MILROY

> **"** The discipline, focus and 'indomitable spirit' you develop in your martial arts training are an amazingly powerful force when you apply them to ANY aspect of your life. **"**

TRAINING INFORMATION

- Belt Ranks & Martial Arts Styles: TaeKwonDo (5th Dan), TangSooDo (5th Dan)

- Instructors/Influencers: Master David Schmidt, Master Jason Farnsworth

- Birthdate: October 18, 1973

- Birthplace/Growing Up: Dubuque, IA

- Yrs. In the Martial Arts: 39 years

- Yrs. Instructing: 23 years

- Executive Vice President - AMS, President and Editor in Chief - Martial Arts World News Magazine

My fascination with the Martial Arts started when I was very young.

The media in the late 70's was my original inspiration for studying martial arts. I first saw a snippet of Enter the Dragon in 1978. I still remember being in awe of the Super Hero like speed and skill I saw in those few stolen minutes of the film. Then I became a somewhat ravenous seeker and consumer of all things martial arts. "Kung Fu" re-runs on television, Black Belt and Karate Illustrated Magazine, and even some early Chuck Norris movies solidified my passion and resolve to study the martial arts.

I was fortunate enough that a family friend was a part time martial arts instructor at a local collage, and he agreed to work with me once a week. After a few months, my enthusiasm for training had only grown, and I was finally able to convince my Mother to enroll me in the local "real" full time Karate School.

At that time, it was NOT standard practice to accept student as young as I was, but the school made an exception and allowed me to attend classes. The 'full time' structured training at the Dubuque Karate Club, under

PERSONAL ACHIEVEMENTS

- Successful Multi School Operator
- Author – Coaching Children to Succeed in Life
- Author – The Path to Leadership
- 2007 - Chief Operating Officer - NAPMA (National Association of Professional Martial Artists
- 2007 - Chief Operating Officer – Martial Arts Professional Magazine
- 2015 - Executive Vice President - AMS (Amerinational Management Services)
- 2015 - President and Editor in Chief - Martial Arts World News Magazine
- Helped Thousands of Martial Arts School Owners Create More Successful Schools

Master David Schmidt was a LIFE changer for me.

I was already passionate about martial arts, but this experience lit a fire in me that has helped me create a level of success in the martial arts, in the martial arts business, and in my life that I never would have thought possible.

The Martial Arts has given me a "core" set of skills that has created an amazing life and career for me. It has imbued me with the sense of self-confidence and focus of will that has allowed me to accomplish goals that most people think are impossible to reach.

When I first opened a Martial Arts school, I was a good Martial Artist, and I wanted to pass on the arts that I loved so much, but I was clueless about running a successful school. I was missing a LOT of martial arts business fundamentals.

I pretty quickly realized that running successful martial arts schools requires a COMPLETELY new set of skills that I'd never really learned as a martial arts student, BUT I also realized that IF you apply the same PRINCIPLES you master while studying the martial arts, you can easily acquire the new skills you need, and implement them to create amazing businesses and make a substantial positive impact on your students and your community.

The discipline, focus and "indomitable spirit" you develop in your martial arts training are an amazingly powerful force when you apply them to ANY aspect of your life. Not only do these principles empower you to be successful in a martial arts school, but in ANY career path, profession or avocation you might want to pursue.

It's been the greatest honor of my life to help so many martial arts students and school owners reach their goals and impact more of the world with the positive values of the martial arts.

JOHN MORGART, JR.

" John Morgart, Jr. has all the qualities of a true martial artist and is revered by many martial artists around the world . "

TRAINING INFORMATION

- Belt Ranks & Martial Arts Styles: 4th Degree Black Belt in Tang Soo Do, Studying Chun Kuk Do/ United Fighting Arts Federation, Krav Maga, Tae Kwon Do, Judo & Jujitsu, Hapkido, Wei Son Do Martial Arts (Founder)

- Instructors/Influencers: Grandmaster Chuck Norris, Sensei Steve Brown, Grandmaster Chun Sik Kim, Master Joe Goss Sr., Master Patrick Leach, Master John Nigro, Master Jack Pistella, Grandmaster Robert Zang, David Kahn

- Birthdate: June 22, 1993

- Birthplace/Growing Up: Allegheny County & Irwin, PA

- Yrs. In the Martial Arts: 16 years

- Yrs. Instructing: 12 years

- School owner, Manager, Instructor

John Morgart Jr's dad, John Morgart Sr., wanted him to take martial arts when he was 7 years old so he would know how to defend himself. At the time, John Morgart Jr. was too scared and intimidated to take martial arts. At the age of 11, he was watching Jackie Chan and Bruce Lee movies and got inspired. He then went to his dad and asked him if he could take martial arts. His dad said "yes" and enrolled him at the International Tang Soo Do Federation at the Headquarters in Monroeville, Pennsylvania on July 9, 2004. Thus, started his career in martial arts.

Mr. Morgart's journey in martial arts and in life has been extraordinary. In some ways, he is a typical martial arts practitioner, but his journey is far from usual. The motivation and determination that he possesses is incredible. Looking at his personal and major accomplishments. From being nominated for martial artist of the year award to being an actor in theatre plays without any formal acting classes. He has all the qualities of a true martial artist and is revered by many martial artists around the world. He became a notable practitioner in martial arts and now a martial arts legend next to some of the greatest martial artists in history.

PERSONAL ACHIEVEMENTS

- Uploaded over 200 Videos to Karate55210 YouTube Channel
- Inducted into the National Society of Leadership and Success, 2020
- Broke Two Boards of Plywood with a Palm Strike, 2019
- Had a meeting with Pittsburgh's Governor Tom Wolf, 2019
- Bakes and sells baked goods at Maddy's Bakery
- Helped Vendors set up their tents at the Latrobe, Keystone, Murrysville, Downtown Irwin and Mt. Pleasant Farmers Markets
- Works in the IT department at the Westmoreland County Courthouse
- On the Occupational Advisory Committee at Westmoreland Career & Technology Center
- Actor in Theatre Plays (2014 – 2017):
- "Ruthless" The Musical Comedy by Marvin Laird at the Greensburg Civic Theatre (School Girl, Newscaster, Judge and Father)
- "The American Trailer Park Musical" by Betsy Kelso at the Ligonier Theatre (Cameraman, Dancer, Mailman, Club Announcer, Kidnapper, Bartender and Cowboy)
- "Rumors" by Neil Simon at the Greensburg Civic Theatre (Officer Welch)
- "Lend Me A Tenor" by Ken Ludwig at the Ligonier Theatre (Bellhop)
- "The Underpants" by Steve Martin at the Ligonier Theatre (Scientist)

MAJOR ACHIEVEMENTS

2020 Arnold Schwarzenegger's Battle of Columbus Martial Arts Tournament

- Gold Medal - 1 vs 1 Self Defense
- Gold Medal - 1 vs Multiple Attackers
- Gold Medal - Forms Competition
- Silver Medal - Weapon Forms
- Silver Medal - 10 Board Power Break

Inducted into the Action Martial Arts Magazine Hall of Honors for Outstanding Dedication in the Martial Arts, 2019

2019 Arnold Schwarzenegger's Battle of Columbus Martial Arts Tournament

- Silver Medal - Forms & Sparring
- Gold Medal - Weapon Forms
- Referee & Judge (TKD & TSD)
- Sparring Coach

2018 Arnold Schwarzenegger's Battle of Columbus Martial Arts Tournament

- Silver Medal - Forms Competition
- Referee & Judge (TKD & TSD)

PERSONAL ACHIEVEMENTS

- University of Phoenix Student Speaker Award, Pittsburgh Campus, 2015

- Graduated from University of Phoenix majoring in Bachelor of Science in Information Technology with a concentration in Information Systems Security, September 2015

- Graduated from Central Westmoreland Career & Technology Center, 2011

- Voted Most Original in Class of 2011, Yough Senior High School

- Graduated from Yough Senior High School, 2011

- He was One of Eight students honored for fundraising for charity at Central Westmoreland Career & Technology Center

- Nominated for Pennsylvania's Trib Total Media Outstanding Young Citizen Award, 2011

- Director's List, Central Westmoreland Career & Technology Center, Special Honor and Recognition Award, 2011

- Karate Demonstration at Yough Senior High School's Talent Show, 2010

- Inducted into the National Technical Honor Society, Central Westmoreland Career & Technology Center, 2009 – 2010

- 1st Place Web Design Local Competition, Central Westmoreland Career & Technology Center, 2008

- Yough Intermediate Middle School Cougar of the Month Award, 2006 – 2007

- Who's Who Among Outstanding Middle School Students Award, 2006 – 2007

MAJOR ACHIEVEMENTS

- Inducted into the American Martial Arts Alliance Legends Hall of Fame, 2018

- Nominated for Greatmats Martial Arts Instructor of the Year Award, 2018

- Pittsburgh City Paper wrote an article about John titled Pittsburgh-area Martial Artist creates new karate style, 2018

- Silver Medal for Weapon Forms and Forms at Pittsburgh's Open Martial Arts Tournament, 2018

- Karate demonstration at the 5th Annual Mental Health Awareness Event for Westmoreland County Behavioral Health / Developmental Services, 2018

- Founder of Wei Son Do Martial Arts, 2018

- 43rd Annual Technical Advisory Committee Standardized Training and Skills Seminar Certificate of Achievement in the International Tang Soo Do Federation, May 2017

- Featured in the Tae Kwon Do Times Magazine, September 2015 issue

- Became a Notable Practitioner of Tang Soo Do alongside Chuck Norris, Aaron Norris, Cynthia Rothrock, Ho Sik Pak, Pat E. Johnson, Michael Jai White, Chloe Bruce, Billy Blanks, Hwang Kee, Jack Pistella and other notable practitioners of Tang Soo Do

- Nominated for Martial Artist of the Year Award at C.S. Kim Karate

- Karate Demonstration at Monroeville Convention Center, 2012

- 3rd place in sparring at the ITF 12th World Championship Tournament in 2012

- Picture in the Trib newspaper for performing in a karate demonstration for Relay for Life at Gateway Middle School

- 3rd place in sparring at the National All Martial Arts Championship Tournament in 2008, 2010, 2011 and 2012

- 1st place in Forms at the National All Martial Arts Championship Tournament in 2008

- Participated in Kick-a-Thons to help raise money for the Muscular Dystrophy Association

STEPHAN MORRIS

"Without the "fighting spirit" of the Martial Arts, I doubt, very much, I would have had the strength to go on."

TRAINING INFORMATION

- Belt Ranks & Martial Arts Styles: 1st Dan World Tang Soo Do, 1st Dan WTF Tae Kwon Do, Red Belt ITF Tae Kwon Do, 3rd Dan Danny Lane's World Martial Arts Federation (WMAF), GM Larry Tatum's American Kenpo Program

- Instructors/Influencers: Master James Harlan, Master Paul Mimidis, Master David Cooper, Master Luis Meja, Grandmaster Danny Lane, Grandmaster Larry Tatum

- Birthdate: March 21, 1963

- Birthplace/Growing Up: Ephrata, PA

- Yrs. In the Martial Arts: 43 years

- Yrs. Instructing: 5-10 years

- Instructor, Promoter

PROFESSIONAL ORGANIZATIONS

- International Superfoot Martial Arts Federation, President

- Grandmaster Larry Tatum's Kenpo Karate Association

- IKKF (International Kenpo Karate Federation)

- Board Member - "Social Media Consultant" of the Action Martial Arts Hall of Honors

I believe when I was about 12 or 13, I started hearing about Bruce Lee and the mysterious nature of his art. I was also attracted to the mysterious and beautiful artwork of the orient. I attended some Bruce Lee movies at local theaters and was "amazed" by his abilities; I would get so excited when he began to fight. I started collecting magazines like Black Belt and Fighting Stars and anything with Bruce Lee or Chuck Norris. An Associate Pastor at our church was a Sensei in Wado Ryu Karate, so I began attending karate lessons. I loved the sense of fellowship and wearing a Gi with fancy patches. It was difficult for me to attend class due to worsening agoraphobic condition and I'd often get sick from the strenuous workouts. I quickly discovered I loved to spar and kick targets and really felt like I belonged in a dojo. Chuck Norris movies became a personal favorite or mine; now I had a real "hero" to look up to. I heard other great names like Bill Wallace, Kathy Long, Don Wilson, and Benny Urquidez who also became heroes and fueled my passion for this "mysterious" art and its ancient history. I also was drawn to the diversity, so many styles and weapons; I was thrilled learning the nunchuk's.

PERSONAL ACHIEVEMENTS

- B.S. Psychology
- CNE Novell Engineering
- MCSA Microsoft Systems Administrator
- Network Helpdesk Analyst for 6 yrs in 2 corporations.
- Network Technician and Engineer: 6 + yrs.
- Monitor of Sex Offenders Unit 1 yr.
- CNA 1 yr.
- Monitor Group home 2 yrs.
- Made almost a full recovery from severe agoraphobia with the help of my wife (Deb), who passed away in 2004.

MAJOR ACHIEVEMENTS

- My #1 achievement in martial arts would have to be, becoming the #1 in the world martial arts promoter on social media (Facebook) with 25 groups and 20 pages, representing 21 celebrities in the arts. I continue to add to this list as I think of new groups or pages. I also earned 10 international martial arts awards in the last 5 years.
- I believe the 5 yrs. I trained for my first black belt in WTSDA. I gave it everything I had and was known for my exceptional kicking abilities. I had to deal with a lot during this period, including a stressful job and a "sick" wife. I was almost 2nd Dan but my "soul mate" passed away in 2004, which devastated my life.
- Creator and administrator of over 26 Facebook Groups and 23 Facebook Pages

I believe I was drawn to "heroes" and when Bruce Lee and Chuck Norris began appearing on the "silver screen", I had real heroes with amazing abilities. I was "hooked" for life!

Without the "fighting spirit" of the martial arts, after my wife committed suicide in 2004, I doubt, very much, I would have had the strength to go on. I probably wouldn't be here anymore. The "fighting spirit" has helped me endure despite a lot of pain. The desire to want to study martial arts formally in a dojo also was a big factor in my overcoming agoraphobia. I still battle with sadness and depression of losing the only person I considered my "soul mate". My Christian faith has been a positive force in giving me the hope of seeing my wife again and hope is all I need.

DAISY ORTINO

"The dojo is our happy home. As we always say, the family that trains together stays together."

TRAINING INFORMATION

- Belt Ranks & Martial Arts Styles: Sandan in Okinawa Kenpo Karate and RHKKA
- Instructors/Influencers: Hanshi Paul Ortino Jr.
- Birthdate: December 16, 1967
- Birthplace/Growing Up: Philippines and Hawaii
- Yrs. In the Martial Arts: 23 years
- Yrs. Instructing: 10 years
- Instructor

PROFESSIONAL ORGANIZATIONS

- Okinawa Kenpo Karate Dharma-Ryu Dojo
- Ryukyu Hon Kenpo Kobujutsu Association
- Hawaii Karate Congress

I was only 29 years old when I lost my first husband. He left me with three beautiful daughters. I wanted my daughters to grow up knowing how to defend themselves. My priority goal was for my daughters to grow up strong and not be bullied at school. I was bullied when I first came to Hawaii from the Philippines when I was 14 years old. I couldn't really speak English then. I saw this Thailander girl being bullied at school and she did a spinning hook kick on this bully. I was so impressed. No one bullied her again. When I met Paul Ortino, he became our Sensei in 1996. We loved karate, weapons and all the friends we were making. The other martial arts students became family to us. The dojo became our home. We trained with Sensei Paul (now my husband) for over 12 years. We had karate in the brain. All my girls became black belts and also graduated in college with honors.

The Martial Arts has impacted my life in so many ways. Since I began training in 1996, my health has improved. I used to have severe asthma when I was growing up and heart palpitations.

PERSONAL ACHIEVEMENTS

- Achieved 3rd Degree Black Belt in Okinawa Kenpo Karate as taught by Grandmaster Seikichi Odo

- Assistant Commissioner to the Aloha State Games in Hawaii 1990 until 2003

- Assistant Instructor to the Okinawa Kenpo Karate Dojos in Hawaii 1999 until 2006

- Assistant Instructor to the Okinawa Kenpo Karate dojo in Naples FL 2006

MAJOR ACHIEVEMENTS

- A top competitor in Hawaii Karate Congress tournaments and rated in Kumite, Kata and Kobudo for many years

- Helped to run all the Aloha State Games Karate tournaments as well as all the annual tournaments put on by the Okinawa Kenpo Karate Dharma-Ryu Dojos in Hawaii

- Taught Karate for the military and their dependents in Hawaii from 1999 until 2006

- Asked to become the female representative for the Strike Back Training System

Working out and training made my body stronger. My girls and I were happier and healthier. Cheryl, Sherry Anne and Shanelle were more focused in school and more confident. They always did homework first and then trained with us. All three of my daughters as well as myself became black belts and assisted teaching Sensei Paul in all of his dojos. Sensei Paul and I got married in May 1998. We had the best time of our lives while training. We developed a stronger bond together. The dojo was our happy home. As we always say, the family that trains together stays together.

WILLIAM PUGH

> "My whole essence of my being is about the martial spirit and the warrior path."

TRAINING INFORMATION

- Belt Ranks & Martial Arts Styles: Ryu kyu hon Kenpo Kobujustu, Okinawan Kenpo Karate Kobujustu, 1st Dan Shodan
- Instructors/Influencers: GM Seikichi Odo, Hanshi John Snyder, Kyoshi Joe Angelisanti
- Birthplace/Growing Up: Reading, PA
- Yrs. In the Martial Arts: 39 years
- Yrs. Instructing: 24 years
- School owner (Open Call Martial Arts), Manager, Instructor, Martial Arts Actor (SAG AFTRA)

PROFESSIONAL ORGANIZATIONS

- SAG AFTRA
- WKU World Karate Union Board of Directors
- Okinawan White Crane Fed
- White Crane United Federation of Martial Artist- Dr. John Lee
- Universal Martial Arts Assoc
- Ryukyu Hon Kenpo Kobujust
- Okinawa Kenpo Karate Kobusdo
- Philadelphia Hall of Fame Assoc

My Uncle Joe Angelisanti got me into Martial Arts. I started in his basement with him teaching me. Then he took me into his dojo where he taught and introduced me to a guy named Grandmaster Seikichi Odo. I said to him I wanna be like Yoda Sensei because he looks like the Star Wars character, Yoda. So, from that moment till today, I have trained every day. Him, Joe Angelisanti and Hanshi John Snyder have been my guiding force in my training in Okinawa Kenpo Kobudo.

I was a little punk kid in the urban City of Reading, getting picked on and beat up. I always wanted to be like my uncle who is a Vietnam veteran of Marine Corp. I wanted to be like him and a karate master. Throughout all my studies and teaching karate and kobudo, I found it is a way of life for me. It's in my blood and in my soul. I could write a book about the journey of my time in karate.

I saw Sensei Odo, so short in stature and little, throw and manipulate big guys. I was like, "Wow! He is little. If he can do that then I can do that too cause I'm a little guy." Then through the years, training transformed me

- International Circle of Masters
- 3rd degree Scottish Rite Mason
- 3rd degree Blue Lodge Master Mason Scottish Rite Side

into a true warrior. I became a Marine and still follow the ways of Okinawa Kenpo Kobudo.

Martial Arts has impacted every part of my life. My whole essence of my being is about the martial spirit and the warrior path. As a Marine, Martial Artist, and a Mason, I guide my journey to always better myself and help others along the journey. The dojo is my sanctuary. Helping others and being a guiding light to my students and others in my community helps me deal with the demons that come along with being and walking that warrior's path.

Helping others and my students is who I am. Fighting and teaching those who can't defend or speak up or fight for themselves is what we as warriors are entrusted to do. Along the path of my personal journey, doors have opened in the movie industry and my career. The Martial Arts has helped me raise my kids by myself. It helped me deal with stress of life and dealing with others' stress and weakness. So, I do not fall prey to drugs, alcohol, and other things that can destroy the very fabric of my life's journey and end it before my time is supposed to. There's so much I can say that has impacted my life, but I will say this: instead of me writing about the impact, look at my life and see the impact it has for me and others.

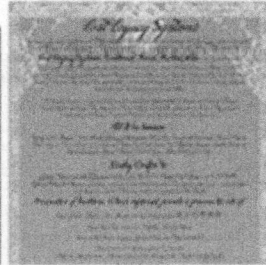

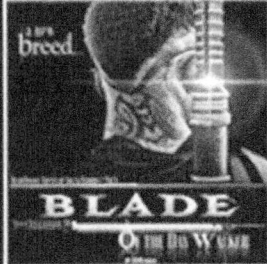

404

THE AMERICAN MARTIAL ARTS ALLIANCE

MARTIAL ARTS
MASTERS & PIONEERS

Pioneers
IN THE MARTIAL ARTS

Pioneers
GRAND MASTERS

TYRONE BULLOCK

"I am so grateful to my Master and past teachers who made me who I am today."

TRAINING INFORMATION

- Belt Ranks & Martial Arts Styles: Southern Shaolin Kung-Fu, 9th Degree Black Belt
- Instructors/Influencers: Master Feng
- Birthdate: December 3, 1967
- Birthplace/Growing Up: Newark, NJ
- Yrs. In the Martial Arts: 49 years
- Yrs. Instructing: 35 years
- School owner (Shaolin Dragon School of Kung-Fu), Instructor

PROFESSIONAL ORGANIZATIONS

- Gospel Martial Arts Union (Member)
- Black Dragon Fighting Society (Member)
- Dragon Entertainment (Owner)

I was put into Martial Arts at the age of 2 1/2. My mother wanted me to study the art from the fear that I would join a gang because of the environment we lived in.

Studying Martial Arts has impacted my life a great deal. From becoming a humble person, learning to heal from within, touching so many lives in a positive way, and helping raise youth and seeing them become leaders. I cannot express the joy and gratitude I felt because I played a role in these people's lives. I've helped train our military, Guardian Angel's, Churches, Recreation Centers, Safety Awareness, and was a role model to my children. Martial Arts has been a phenomenal journey. I am now teaching stunts and fight choreography for film. Many Blessings. I am so grateful to my Master and past teachers who made me who I am today.

PERSONAL ACHIEVEMENTS

- Taught over 10, 000 students

- Helped aid many families with my After School and Summer Camp programs

MAJOR ACHIEVEMENTS

- I am a Hall of Fame Inductee for being a founder for a combative system known as the Beckwith System. I provided the U.S. Military with strategic and tactical benefits, triangular thought, concepts as they relate to warfare, close range fighting, to get in and take out your opponent as quickly as possible.

AARON CARDOZA

> **"**I do believe without martial arts; I would not have had the confidence to pursue better opportunities in life.**"**

TRAINING INFORMATION

- Belt Ranks & Martial Arts Styles: Shotokan, Aikido, American Karate (9th Dan)

- Instructors/Influencers: Maxie Cardoza, David McMurry, Richard Morris, Pat Burleson, Billy Brammer, Billy Smith, Thaine McVean, George Harrison

- Birthdate: December 19, 1969

- Birthplace/Growing Up: Fort Worth, TX

- Yrs. In the Martial Arts: 44 years

- Yrs. Instructing: 31 years

- School owner (Southwest Martial Arts), Instructor

PROFESSIONAL ORGANIZATIONS

- AKBBA
- AOK
- NTKA
- MKHAF

I grew up in Fort Worth, Texas, and had an excellent role model to look up to, my father. He was my first martial arts trainer. He was a martial artist in the late '60s through recent times. I grew up in a very happy and loving family. I was in and out of martial arts from a young age and didn't fully commit to training until I was 13 and started taking martial arts seriously. I was a very outgoing person and very easy to get along with. I believe martial arts help me with respect and confidence at a younger age.

The main reason I started in karate as a serious sport was because two class bullies chased me home after I got off the bus, both had bats to beat me. I was lucky to make it home and closed the door. From that point on, I spoke with my father about getting me into karate classes. I started taking lessons with GM Richard Morris.

PERSONAL ACHIEVEMENTS

- I spent my time working on sparring and forms from age 13 to 33 and placed as one of the top competitors in the U.S. during my time. I transitioned into teaching after father time caught up with me. More than anything, I loved all the people in martial arts; they were like family. I have way too many trophies to count, but that is not the point! It was always about the people and memories. Lastly, it was about passing on what I know to others. The older instructors are disappearing, and the knowledge needs to be passed on to others so that they can teach others as well, or it will disappear altogether.

MAJOR ACHIEVEMENTS

- 2016 Master Karate Hall of Fame
- 2014 USA Karate Hall of Fame
- 2018 Universal Karate Hall of Fame

I achieved the rank of 1st Dan under Richard Morris in 1989 and 2nd Dan in 1991. I received my 3rd Dan under Maxie Cardoza in 1993. I received my 4th Dan in 1995 under Billy Brammer. I received my 5th, 6th, and 7th under Billy Brammer: 5th 1999, 6th 2000, 7th 2001. I received my 8th Dan under Maxie Cardoza: 8th Dan 2013. I received my 9th Dan Under Billy Smith & Richard Morris: 9th Dan 02/24/2018.

I do believe without martial arts; I would not have had the confidence to pursue better opportunities in life. I believe in being able to protect yourself and your family. Martial Arts has also made me a better person and a better husband to my family. This sport kept me out of trouble and taught me respect for myself and others. I can't begin to thank all the instructors that helped me out in my life. I believe wisdom is passed down to those who continue in the service to others.

DR. T.R. CRIMI

"Martial Arts is my Life..."

TRAINING INFORMATION

- Belt Ranks & Martial Arts Styles: Kenpo Karate - Dojo Shodan, Danzan Ryu Jujutsu - Shodan through Kudan, Hikari Ryuza Jujutsu - Judan

- Instructors/Influencers: Professor Francis Merlin "Bud" Estes

- Birthdate: January 30, 1950

- Birthplace/Growing Up: Long Beach, CA

- Yrs. In the Martial Arts: 64 years

- Yrs. Instructing: 51years

- School Owner, Manager & Instructor at Hikari Ryuza Do Kan

PROFESSIONAL ORGANIZATIONS

- CEO - Hikari Ryuza Bujutsu International

- Past CEO/President of ATAMA (American Teachers Association of the Martial Arts) and current BOD Advisor to the President

- Executive Board Member of WOSKKA (World Okinawan Shorin-Ryu Karate & Kobudo Association)

- Past Chair of Healing Arts Division - Advisor BOD at WHFSC (World Head of Family Sokeship Council)

- International Director at International Kenpo Jiujitsu Organization

Sr. Grandmaster Crimi's Martial beginnings arose in the '50s in Filipino Arnis arts, which transmuted into years of Judo. His first Dojo Black Belt was earned after 5 years in Karate. At this point, a major shift occurred, and his Karate instructor, knowing he could not provide the training that Sr Grandmaster sought, gave his blessing as he ventured out to find his teacher. This quest took him through instructors of various Martial Arts styles, including Aikido, Hapkido, Kung Fu, and other Korean and Chinese arts, and yet each time he knew that he had not found "the one." This is not to say that we do not encounter many teachings along our way in life, since principally, every person or thing holds a lesson for our growth; yet, as far as finding a lifetime mentor goes, we believe that you only get one.

The first day Sr. Grandmaster met Great Grandmaster Estes he realized this was the teacher he had diligently sought. After the seminar was over, he took off his black belt in Karate and asked to become a student. "No" was the answer he received. As you can imagine, this rejection was heartbreaking. It wasn't a real "no," though. If he wanted to become a private student of GGm Estes's, he would have to earn the privilege by first getting his Black Belt in Jujutsu. So, twelve months later, he was knocking on GGm Estes's front door. "Remember me?"

As a private student, Sr. Grandmaster traveled to Chico from Reno and, in later years, Grass Valley to gain the wise teachings of his master. Some of

PROFESSIONAL ORGANIZATIONS

- Platinum Member & Advisor at O -Hana 8
- Board Member at Worlds Martial Arts Masters Association
- Certified DOJ POST D.T. Instructor for Law-Enforcement

PERSONAL ACHIEVEMENTS

Senior Grandmaster Crimi has been passionately immersed in Martial Arts for over 60 years. He holds the rank of Kudan (9th degree Black Belt) in Danzan Ryu Jujutsu. He is the Shodai (Founder) and a Judan (10th degree Black Belt) in Hikari Ryuza Bujutsu®, which incorporates Danzan Ryu Jujutsu, Karate, and Senkotiros Arnis. Senior Grandmaster Crimi has been teaching Martial Arts to students of all ages at the Hikari Ryuza Center® for over 43 years.

In addition to adult and children's classes, for the last 43 years Senior Grandmaster Crimi has volunteered his time as a DT (Defensive Tactics) instructor - Training Northern California law enforcement through his POST (Peace Officer Standards and Training) certified defensive tactics course and offering free classes to volunteer and retired deputies for 20 years. Out of a passion for furthering women's empowerment, he developed a comprehensive women's self-defense course, Hikari Ryuza Fujin Goshin No Maki®, which has trained over 1,000 women in the Northern California.

his classes consisted of shoveling turkey manure in Chico's baking 120-degree weather. GGm Estes would bring him out a glass of lemonade and a tuna sandwich on white bread for lunch, which he would gratefully accept and then get straight back to stinking and sweating. Other classes were held on the lake in a fishing boat, doing, you guessed it, fishing. This was his least favorite thing to do, but it didn't matter because every minute with his teacher was golden, and there was always a lesson. Then there were the 6-hour classes of throwing Hane Koshi, drenching 3 gi's in sweat, tiring out 3 to 4 different uke's, only to get "your pinky toe was in the wrong place on that last technique" from his teacher. Or the time when he arrived for his private class, and they drove past the Dojo, eventually parking in the back alley of a mysterious building, walking in, having an apron thrown at him, and told to put it on. He served the homeless in a soup-line for 16 hours that day. The lesson: "always give back to your community."

There are too many stories to share; just know that the bond between Sr Grandmaster and his teacher was unparalleled by any other relationship. What can you give back to someone who teaches you how to live? Teaches you how to love? This is the mark that a real teacher leaves upon your soul.

He realized the only way he could remotely attempt to repay his teacher was to give back to others what was given to him. When he received his Sandan, GGm Estes whispered in his ear "welcome aboard, how does it feel to be a servant of mankind for the rest of your life?" At this point, he was given the title "Sensei."

When he was a Nidan he was given permission to open his Dojo. Of course, his Dojo had to be sponsored for the first year, and GGm Estes volunteered for that, knowing that his dutiful student would uphold the virtues of Black Belt without disappointment. After all, SGm had already been in Martial Arts for 19 years and was anxiously awaiting authorization to start his school. Gaining permission to open a dojo was not an entitlement. He worked faithfully and patiently under his teacher's guidance to earn the privilege, but he undertook it with the utmost seriousness once permission was granted.

MAJOR ACHIEVEMENTS

- Founded Hikari Ryuza Bujutsu/ Hikari Ryuza Do Kan in 1977
- O.M.D. (Doctor of Oriental Medicine)
- Raising 40 people to Black Belt
- Meritorious Service Medal from Nevada County Sheriff's Office in 2005
- Delivered my daughter in 1979

Building his Dojo

He moved from Reno, Nevada to Grass Valley, California, that night. This was far enough away to not compete with his master's school and yet close enough to make frequent trips for training, healing, enlightenment, tuna sandwiches, and even to be the butt of his teacher's jokes.

The year was 1977. Hikari Do Kan was a carport with moving blankets for a mat, but it had begun. He's never been the type of man to talk about what he was going to do; he'd just do it. I remember once a friend of his, after touring his Dojo said, "this is what I'm going to do when my ship comes in." This has always been the difference – he never waits for his ship to come in; he always swims out to get it.

These modest beginnings shortly broke way to him procuring a building out in the sticks. It was official! Still, this residential building was not under his ownership, which meant his boyhood dream of building a Dojo on his property could not be fulfilled, at least not there anyway.

Years later, this dream almost came to light but was torn asunder when he had to sell everything he owned in a child custody battle for his daughter. Two-hundred-and-fifty-thousand-dollars and ten years total, he was awarded full physical and legal custody of his daughter, and despite losing everything he owned, walking away penniless and ripping the big, beautiful redwood forms for the Dojo down with his bare hands, he never lost his dream, and he never stopped teaching his Martial Arts. It just wasn't the right time or place.

January 1999, the moment had arrived. New town, new home, new property, still teaching! He shot up out of bed and announced, "it's time!" He walked down the hill and began moving rocks and clearing brush for the site. The students arrived (myself included) for their usual 6 am class, wondering what was transpiring, and dove into the project with him. Eight months later, his labor of love was standing. Now called Hikari Ryuza Do Kan: School of the Way of the Light Dragon.

You'd think that with over 60 years of intense Martial Arts training and teaching all around the world, averaging 40 to 60 hours of weekly mat time, this 10th Degree Black Belt wouldn't have had time for much else, but of course, this isn't the case for the man who sleeps about 3 hours a night.

In his "free" time, he also managed to become a journeyman carpet layer, a director for an NBC affiliate, a Doctor of Oriental Medicine, a POST certified instructor for Law Enforcement, and a devoted father. Come to think of it; there isn't anything that Dr. Crimi isn't capable of once he puts his mind to it.

On a personal note, I'll say that for a man who came from an extremely harsh childhood, I've never met a more unconditionally loving, spiritually evolved, and fiercely loyal human being in my life. I'm proud and humbled to be his most devoted Yudansha and to call him my husband.

"Martial Arts is my life..."

JAMES DEBROW III

"Karate has been my life and still is today...Martial Arts is the best thing that ever happened to me!"

I got started in boxing and martial arts at the age of 4 (1959) years old because my father and two uncles were professional boxers and black belts. My first four black belts ranks were from my father and uncles. Additionally, I studied martial arts while in the United States Army in the Republic of Korea (ROK), Okinawa, and Tokyo, Japan. I was promoted under Dr. Al Francis, 10th Dan black belt, Al Francis Karate Organization 5th Dan to 10 Dan black belt in San Antonio, Texas (1985-2020).

- Shinjimasu International Martial Arts Association, Black Belt Advancement Certificate 9th Dan Black Belt Shaolin Goju ID#Nbq 10137 on July 18, 1993, by Soke Charles Dixon 10th Dan, Chairman of the Council and the Shinjimasu Board of Directors, Temple, Texas.

- Shinjimasu International Martial Arts Association, United Federation of International Grand Masters, Letter of Recognition and Inauguration, Recognized as a 10th Dan Black Belt, Professor of Martial Arts, Lifetime Member on June 22, 2019, by Soke Charles Dixon 10th Dan, Chairman of the Council and the Shinjimasu Board of Directors, Temple, Texas.

TRAINING INFORMATION

- Belt Ranks & Martial Arts Styles: Tae Kwon Do 8th to 10th Dan, Goju 6th to 10th Dan, Hapkido 6th Dan, Police and Military Combat Instructor: Physical Fitness & Defensive Tactics Instructor/Coordinator-Texas Department of Public Safety (State Trooper) agency-wide

- Instructors/Influencers: James Debrow, Jr., Herbert Debrow, Johnny Davis, Masters Choi, Kim & Chang, Dr. Abel Villareal, Professor Charles Dixon, Grand Master Richard Dixon, Grand Master Mike Fillmore, Dr. Dan Roberts

- Birthdate: May 23, 1955

- Birthplace/Growing Up: San Antonio, TX

- Yrs. In the Martial Arts: 61 years

- Yrs. Instructing: 53 years

- School Owner, Manager & Instructor at James Debrow Fighting Tiger School, LLC

PROFESSIONAL ORGANIZATIONS

- Al Francis Karate Organization
- Shinjimasu International Martial Arts Association
- Global Tae Kwon Do Association
- Tae Kwon Do, Yong Moo Kwan Federation

PROFESSIONAL ORGANIZATIONS

- The World Moo Duk Kwan Alliance-United States Branch of Tae Kwon Do Association

PERSONAL ACHIEVEMENTS

- Shinjimasu International Martial Arts Association, Temple, Texas: Golden Life Achievement, Karate Achievement and Black Belt Advancement Certificate (Grand Master Levels)

MAJOR ACHIEVEMENTS

- Physical Fitness and Defensive Tactics Coordinator for the Texas Department of Public Safety-State Trooper Training Academy agency-wide 1994-2003, developed and implemented the physical fitness and wellness program and the defensive tactics program for recruit school cadets and agency incumbents, Use-of-Force Expert/policy developer, Court-certified Use-of-Force, assigned to develop, implement and instruct in the new Texas Conceal Handgun Program at the Texas Department of Public Safety as approved by the Texas Legislatures.

- Philadelphia Historic Martial Arts Society, Martial Arts Hall of Fame inductee Class of 2020; United States Martial Arts, Martial Arts Hall of Fame Inductee Class of 2020; and The Universal Martial Arts Hall of Fame Inductee Class of 2020; Texas Amateur Martial Arts Association-Executive Committee Chair; The World Moo Duk Kwan Do Alliance appointed as Central Director of the National Hapkido Association; and International Police Tactical Training Academy of the International Police Tactical Training Unit

- International Police Tactical Training Academy, Appointed International Director of Training of the International Police Tactical Training Unit on June 26, 2020, by President, Grand Master Robert J. Fabrey, 10th Dan Black Belt and President, United States Karate Federation, National Headquarters, St. Portia, Florida. Promoted and registered member of the United States Karate Federation since 1997

- Philadelphia Historic Martial Arts Society, Martial Arts Hall of Fame Inductee Class of 2020.

- United States Martial Arts, Martial Arts Hall of Fame Inductee Class of 2020, and Membership. International Martial Arts Council of America. Hot Springs, Arkansas.

- The Universal Martial Arts Hall of Fame Inductee Class of 2020 and Membership.

Martial arts have added value to my life and gave me the following skills: discipline, respect, motivation, trust, leadership, communication, teamwork, teaching, follower, emotional control, physical fitness, mental fitness, resiliency, character, spirituality, attention span growth, calmness, loyalty, commitment, veracity, tenacity, competitiveness, goal orientation, cognition, and motor performance.

Martial arts helped me to meet all races, both male and female domestic and international. I worked with elementary, junior high school, and high school at-risk students and helped many of them stay in school and graduate. Karate was also a source of income.

Martial arts helped me promote to the rank of sergeant at the Texas Department of Public Safety-State Trooper Training Academy, where I served for over eight years in the state police training bureau. Karate has been my life and still is today. I am currently working on a program to help children with memory, attention span, and concentration skills.

Martial Arts is the best thing that ever happened to me!

LUIS A. DURAND

"I am proud to be the person I am today because of the impact Martial Arts has on my life."

TRAINING INFORMATION

- Belt Ranks & Martial Arts Styles: Okinawa Kempo Karate Do, 9th Degree Black Belt

- Birthdate: August 10, 1962

- Birthplace/Growing Up: Bronx NY / Puerto Rico

- Yrs. In the Martial Arts: 48 years

- Yrs. Instructing: 33 years

- School owner (T.A.K.A), Instructor

PROFESSIONAL ORGANIZATIONS

- Latin American Martial Arts Society

- Universal Black Belt Society

- Okinawan Goshin-Ryu Karate-Do Association

As every child and enthusiast of karate, my interest in the fascinating world of martial arts started at the young age of 10. I enjoyed Chinese karate movies, especially those of Bruce Lee, who I believe was the person who motivated me in this millenary martial art and what first motivated me to practice Shaolin Tsu Kempo in my hometown of San Sebastian, Puerto Rico in 1972. I also practiced boxing and then Okinawa Kempo Karate-Do with my martial arts teachers Miguel Montalvo and Carlos Montalvo, both currently with the title of Hanshi, 9th Dan, and 10th Dan, respectively.

Between 1980 and 1995, I won countless national and international karate tournaments, which led to being ranked among the best in Kata and Kumite competitors in all of Puerto Rico.

In 1982, when I was a brown belt, I accepted an invitation to participate in

PERSONAL & MAJOR ACHIEVEMENTS

- 1987 I received my black belt first Dan diploma from the Puerto Rican Institute of Tae Kwon Do (Tae Kwon Do Olympic) in the city of Guaynabo, Puerto Rico.

- 1997 I received my 2nd Dan black belt in the city of Cidra from the Caribbean Moo Duk Kwan Academy (Tang Soo Do).

- 2006 I received my 6th Dan with the title of Shihan from T.A.K.A. and validated by the Ronin Goju Ryu Kai World Karate Organization.

- 2008 I received my 7th Dan with the title of Kyoshi from Ronin Goju Ryu Kai World Karate Organization.

- 2010 I received my 8th Dan from Grandmaster Carlos Silva Jr. Hanshi, 10th Dan (Bushido Karate Jitsu-Do) and validated from Grandmaster Dr. Juan Otero Hanshi, 10th Dan (Okinawan Goshin Ryu Karate-Do Association).

- 2016 I received my 9th Dan and the title of Hanshi from William Solano Meijin, 10th Dan (Okinawa Shorin Ryu Kokusai Kempo-Karate-Do & Kobudo Federation and Universal Black Belt Society).

- 2009 – Lifetime Triple Diamond Achievement Award from the Southeaster Hall of Fame Martial Arts Brotherhood Association, Orlando, Florida

- 2015 – Grandmaster of the Year from the Latin American Martials Arts Society Hall of Fame, Orlando, Florida

- 2018 – Grandmaster Diamond Awards from the Night of Knights of Bushido Hall of Fame, Tampa, Florida

the Pan-American Tae Kwon Do Games Championship with the Puerto Rico team, where I won a gold medal and proclaimed champion of Puerto Rico in the middle light-weight division. I was the first competitor who practiced Japanese style karate and held a brown belt rank winning an International and exclusive competition for competitors of Tae Kwon Do with the rank of black belts.

I've won so many karate tournaments around Puerto Rico in Kata and Kumite for more than 20 consecutive years. I have visited several countries in my career as an international competitor in the Dominican Republic, Venezuela, Mexico, Canada, Santa Cruz (Virgins Islands), San Thomas (Virgins Islands) and several U.S. States.

I started to practice in the city of Bayamón, Puerto Rico, Korean karate (Tae Kwon Do) at the I.T.F. Young Brothers Academy of the Grandmaster Benny Rivera (R.I.P.) where I obtained my rank of a red belt in the year 1985.

In 1998, married and with two children, I moved to my hometown, San Sebastian where I joined the karate academy of my friend Herrison Torres, Senior Kyoshi, and we founded Torres & Associates Karate Academy (T.A.K.A.) with schools in three cities, San Sebastian, Moca, and Aguadilla.

PERSONAL & MAJOR ACHIEVEMENTS

- 2019- Gold Honor-Traditional Karate Trajectory in Puerto Rico (40 year or more) from the 1st Puerto Rico Martial Arts Diamond Awards Hall of Fame, San Juan, Puerto Rico

- And many other awards and certificates during my career as a martial artist (48 years)

- I continue to teach, compete in Kumite and kata and give seminars of our karate style and methods around all Florida

- Our Organization has more than 35 black belts and more than 300 members between Florida, South Carolina, Kentucky and Puerto Rico

In 2003, our family went through a harrowing family loss when our oldest son, Luis Antonio Durand, only 17 years old, died in a tragic car accident on Road 111 in the city of San Sebastian, Puerto Rico. At the time of his accident, he was a successful competitor of karate, black belt 1st Dan and active player of baseball, where he played for our hometown San Sebastian and the city of Isabela, Puerto Rico.

In 2006, my wife, Vivian Durand and I decided to move to the State of Florida, and try to start a new life with our youngest son, Anthony Durand, who is also a Black Belt 2nd Dan. I contacted my friend, Herrison Torres Kyoshi, who had moved to Florida a few months before. In the last 14 years in Florida, I competed in many Karate tournaments, winning many of them in Kumite and Kata in the Master's Division.

Martial Arts has had a significant impact on my life since I was ten years old. The person that inspired me the most still to this day was the legendary Martial Art and Actor, Bruce Lee. I knew from that point on; I needed a change in my life. Martial Arts allowed me to be passionate about something other than baseball. I remember my first time stepping foot into a karate class taught by Miguel Montalvo Hanshi. Let me say I still, to this day, remember like it was yesterday. He trained with passion. He also taught me self-discipline how his students looked at him with respect, honor, and discipline. The way that he taught each class, I learned to be a better person. Without the life lessons, I wouldn't be the person I am today. Not only have I embraced my passion, learned, self-confidence/self-perception, but I have also been able to pass these lessons on to my children and students. Since growing up with karate as a part of my life, I have had the opportunity to teach and guide adults and children to achieve many goals—the privilege to bond with new people who share the same goals and passion as myself. Throughout my life, Martial Arts have given me a healthier lifestyle for my family and I. I am proud to be the person I am today because of the impact Martial Arts has on my life.

CELINDA ELLSWORTH

"The Martial Arts gave me the confidence to change my life for the better."

I was active in sports in school and studied gymnastics. I was also a cheerleader. I had my first inklings of protecting my fellow students from bullies. I studied as a Physical Education major for two years which made me understand the fundamentals of teaching and the importance of maintaining a healthy lifestyle. When my older brother returned from the Vietnam War, he exposed me to basic karate moves he picked up overseas. I found the movements and applications intriguing and felt I would like to pursue this further but, at that time the opportunity to train did not exist. Years later, I moved to the Eastern Shore of Maryland and found the opportunity to train with instructor, Philip M. Scudieri, who could show me many aspects of the martial arts which I was looking for.

TRAINING INFORMATION

- Belt Ranks & Martial Arts Styles: Kyoshi-8th in Nihon Kenjutsu, Kyoshi 8th in Karate, Kyosei 3rd Dan Kenjutsu- Itto Tenshin Ryu, Il Dan in Tae Kwon Do, Yoriki Edo Machikata Taiho Jutsu, 16 Years Kyudo Miyako Dojo
- Instructors/Influencers: Hanshi-Philip M Scudieri, Arvind Rajguru Sensei, Fredrick Lovret Sensei, Kanjuro Shibata XX, Ken Rawie Sensei, Cha Soo Young -Sa Bum Nim
- Birthdate: April 6, 1954
- Birthplace/Growing Up: Broad Brook, CT
- Yrs. In the Martial Arts: 39 years
- Yrs. Instructing: 38 years
- School Owner, Delaware Budokan, Instructor

PROFESSIONAL ORGANIZATIONS

- All Japan Budo Federation--Kyoto Japan
- Nippon Seibukan Dojo --Kyoto Japan
- Edo Machikata Taiho Jutsu
- American Bikers Aiming to Educate or A.B.A.T.E. of Delaware

PERSONAL ACHIEVEMENTS

- 3 Time Maryland State Tae Kwon Do Poomse Champion
- Member of the US Delegation to Kyoto in 2011 and 2020 for the All Japan Grand Nationals.
- Taught Kenjutsu and Aikijutsu in 4 Cities in Serbia
- Vice President of the Ronin Knights Motorcycle Riding Club since 2000

The martial arts gave me the confidence to change my life for the better. My purpose in teaching today is to do the same for people of all ages and backgrounds. Also, in preserving Budo: The classical martial ways of Japan. I grew up in a small farming community where throughout my early life I was very active working on the family farm or sports in school. I worked hard on gymnastics and cheerleading where I had my first inklings of wanting to protect my fellow students from bullies.

When my brother returned home from the Vietnam War, he exposed me to the basic karate moves of kicks and punches he picked up overseas. After two years as a Physical Education major I learned the fundamentals of teaching and maintaining a healthy lifestyle. I also enjoyed the movies of Bruce Lee and the TV show Kung Fu. I still had the desire and martial arts was still very intriguing for many reasons. The next direction for me was to learn to defend myself, but at that time I knew of no places that taught karate or self-defense in the region.

I moved to the resort town of Ocean City, Maryland and the only thing there was a local gymnasium. This would help to stay in shape, but it was not what I really wanted. So, I did a lot of bike riding and staying in shape on my own while working 2 jobs. One day I saw an ad in the newspaper with a gentleman doing a karate stance on the beach. It said, "Tae Kwon Do Class forming at the Recreation Center." This was a Korean martial art I was not familiar with. I was able to adjust my schedule to get to the building for the class where there was 55 people standing in a line. I was very curious and excited when the instructor Philip Scudieri demonstrated punching drills, kicking techniques and Hyungs or "forms" which are a prearranged set of techniques moving in different directions. Mr. Scudieri explained this was different from karate because it used more kicking techniques than hand techniques. I liked this idea of being able to kick from a distance, plus my legs were strong from riding motorcycles and my horse that I owned for years. The teacher also gave us some interesting philosophy and some background on the tenets of the art like protecting your country, family, and friends. I had wanted this ability from the early years, but now I had access. The part about protecting your family, friends, and country was especially important because my direct descendant Oliver Ellsworth was appointed to the First Supreme Court by George Washington and was 3rd Chief Justice of the United States.

MAJOR ACHIEVEMENTS

- Owner of the Delaware Budokan Nippon Seibukan Honbu Dojo with support of the Imperial House of Japan.

- Have several Dojo Affiliates Worldwide

- Trained 150 Black Belts of all ages and belt levels.

- Currently training future delegates to the Grand Nationals and Kyoto Budosai for 2020 and 2021. The American team was victorious in 2017. The first American team to win in 26 years.

He not only helped write the Constitution, he crossed out the individual states names in the beginning and wrote "We The People." He also held the bible for John Adams swearing in as president and wrote the Federal Judiciary Act. I cannot be prouder as an American to have this heritage. I decided right there the first night that I would do this. The best choice I ever made, except to marry my teacher Philip Scudieri Hanshi. Thirty-nine years later, our dojo, the Delaware Budokan won the 2017 All Japan Grand Nationals in Kyoto, Japan. In the spirit of my ancestors and with the American Flag flying high, we were the first Americans to do this in 26 years.

AL FARRIS

"My philosophy is to Touch Lives, Change Lives and Save Lives!"

TRAINING INFORMATION

- Belt Ranks & Martial Arts Styles: Shaolin Kung Fu, Grandmaster, Modern Warrior System, Mixed Martial Arts, Grandmaster, Soke, Gracie Jujitsu, Law Enforcement Instructor, Aikido, Boxing, Jeet Kune Do, Judo, Karate, Mixed Martial Arts, Wing Chun, Silat, Knife Fighting

- Instructors/Influencers: Grandmaster Paul Newton, Grandmaster Henry Cook, Grandmaster Jim Thomas

- Birthdate: March 3, 1964

- Birthplace/Growing Up: Kentucky

- Yrs. In the Martial Arts: 40 years

- Yrs. Instructing: 39 years

- School owner, (The Modern Warrior System), Instructor

PROFESSIONAL ORGANIZATIONS

- International Congress of Grandmasters, Deputy Director

- Official Affiliate-Alliance Correspondent (U.S.A. Hall of Fame)

Growing up, I lived in a low-income, high crime community. The area I grew up in was plagued with assaults, drugs, and people trying to just make it in life. I watched the police and criminals exchange gunfire at times thinking this was just normal. I was jumped and attacked growing up. I was bullied all through school. I had a very strong motivation to learn the martial arts. Studying the Martial Arts has made such a positive impact on my life.

I had two World Class mentors, Mr. Chuck Norris and Mr. Bruce Lee. They became my inspiration and drive. I began studying their techniques and great words of wisdom. I learned to develop a very strong sense of situational awareness. After a year in training, I realized this was just the beginning of a long journey. After two years, I was seeing very strong significant changes in myself. I was healthier, stronger, more flexible, agile, faster and getting very toned.

PERSONAL ACHIEVEMENTS

- A career in law enforcement
- Achieved my 1st Degree Black Belt
- Graduated college with the following degrees:
- Bachelor of Science, Business and Marketing
- Masters, Philosophy
- Ph.D. Philosophy
- Being in law enforcement is my life, instructing others how to be successful and survive in this career is an honor
- I am the Senior Firearms and Primary Instructor for all firearms training
- I am the Head Defensive Tactics Instructor
- I am a Master Instructor for Use of Force Training
- I am certified to instruct in over seventy areas of Law Enforcement and the Martial Arts

MAJOR ACHIEVEMENTS

- Thirty Five years in Law Enforcement
- Forty Years in the Martial Arts
- Achieved a 10th Degree Black Belt, in Shaolin Kung Fu, and the status of Grandmaster, Shaolin Kung Fu
- Achieved a 10th Black Belt, The Modern Warrior System, Grandmaster - Soke
- I have been blessed to have been awarded the following martial art awards:
- Inducted into the U.S.A. Martial Arts Hall of Fame, "Hall of Heroes"

The benefits were amazing all the way around. My confidence began to rise, and I felt comfortable for the first time in my life protecting myself.

Once I began a career in law enforcement, I could see a tremendous need for various forms of martial art training. As an officer I would run into criminals who seemed to feel no pain and refused arrest. The bad guys do not always listen and do exactly what the law enforcement officer requests. I realized that an officer needs to be very well rounded in this career. For example, when the Ultimate fighting Championship (U.F.C.) first developed, it was unclear how the fights would end. Everyone thought the lifelong martial artist would gain an easy victory. One of the first fights I watched, a high black belt was easily defeated by a street fighter who was extremely aggressive and did not care about how many black belts his competitor was wearing. The same thing goes for law enforcement today. Our adversary only sees us as a hurdle or roadblock to freedom. So, with all respect, it is quite clear for the need to be a complete well-rounded martial artist!

Studying the Martial Arts has made such a positive impact on my life. I had a very strong motivation to learn martial arts because I was bullied and attacked growing up. I had two World Class mentors, Mr. Chuck Norris and Mr. Bruce Lee and they became my inspiration and drive. I began studying their techniques and philosophy. I began developing a very strong sense of situational awareness. I dedicated a significant amount of time training daily. I attended class once a week. That is all that was offered at that time forty years ago. I would then train four hours every day, six days a week. I would wake up and immediately began my morning protocol. I would do one hundred pushups, one hundred sit ups and run two to three miles every morning. That was my morning routine. After a few years, I was able to protect myself from the bullying and assaults. I was in high school at the time.

One day I was jumped at my new high school. I was able to protect myself without hesitation. The word spread very quickly of how I ended the fight with one punch. I became a hero, and everyone looked up to me. My world instantly changed for the better. After class, I would begin my structured blocks of training and cover stretching, breathing exercises, short forms, long forms, weaponry and sparring. I would always spar and train with a higher belt, degree above my rank so I could learn.

MAJOR ACHIEVEMENTS

- Inducted into the U.S. Martial Arts Hall of Fame
- Inducted into the Action Martial Arts Hall of Honors
- Grandmaster of the Year Award
- International Grandmaster of the Year Award
- The Modern Warrior Award
- I have been blessed to have been awarded the following law enforcement awards:
- The Medal of Honor
- The Veteran of Foreign Wars Award
- The Millennium Maker Award
- Officer of the Year Award
- Top Gun Award
- Numerous Exemplary Awards
- Being in law enforcement is my life, instructing others how to be successful and survive in this career is an honor.
- I am the Senior Firearms and Primary Instructor for all firearms training.
- I am a certified Rangemaster
- I am the Head Defensive Tactics Instructor.
- I am a Master Instructor for Use of Force Training
- I am certified to instruct in over seventy areas of Law Enforcement and the Martial Arts

I have always had a very strong passion to learn and improve.

I soon chose a career in law enforcement. As an officer, the martial arts have saved me numerous times. I now train law enforcement, emergency first responders, military and others how to protect themselves. The Martial Arts is a passion and I enjoy helping others achieve their life goals. The Martial Arts is a lifelong journey! Utilizing the martial arts in my life and career has allowed me to save lives. Once I began to see how much of an impact it has had on me and others, I developed a unique system for emergency first responders, law enforcement and military units. I have devoted forty years to studying, analyzing and developing a system that has worked very well without fail. I have incorporated the techniques utilized in self-defense to contain, restrain, submit and allow law enforcement to take violent individuals into custody without injury to the officer or threat the majority of the time. A unique system for a warrior of today. Hence the Modern Warrior System came about and has saved many lives in law enforcement and the community. My philosophy is to Touch Lives, Change Lives and Save Lives! I am beyond thankful for the martial arts and the many blessings it has bestowed upon me!

I would like to thank Grandmaster Chuck Norris for all he has done and accomplished for the world of martial arts. I am very grateful and honored to be a part of the Masters and Pioneers book. This is the Honor of a Lifetime and being in the Who's Who in the Martial Arts Legends!

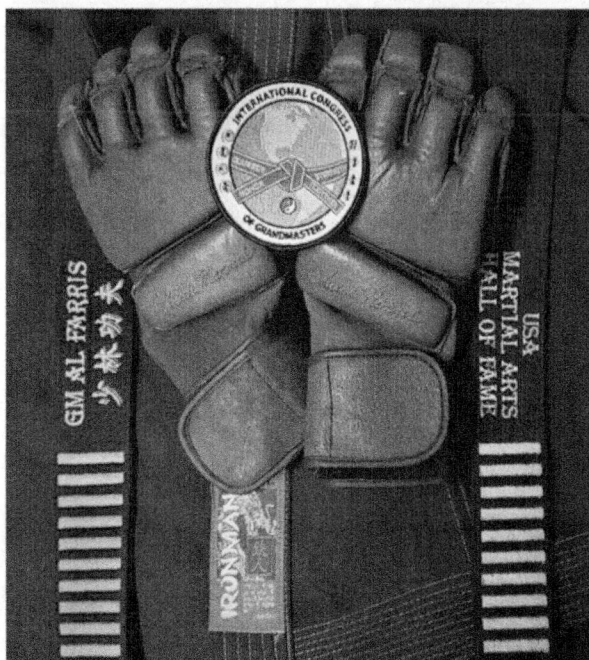

TIM FOX

> "The longer I remain in martial arts, the more of a brotherhood I see."

TRAINING INFORMATION

- Belt Ranks & Martial Arts Styles: Shuri-te (Okinawan), 1st Degree Black Belt, American Tae Kwon Do, 10th Degree Black Belt

- Instructors/Influencers: Grandmaster Billy Smith and Grandmaster Steve Park

- Birthdate: July 16, 1966

- Birthplace/Growing Up: Norman, OK

- Yrs. In the Martial Arts: 40+ years

- Yrs. Instructing: 31 years

- School owner, (TNT school of Martial Arts/ Fox's American Martial Arts), Instructor

PROFESSIONAL ORGANIZATIONS

- Member UMAHoF- History General Sports Karate Museum

Before engaging in the world of martial arts, I believed that I wanted to learn how to fight! Boy did this journey teach me so much more about life. In second grade, as a result of getting targeted by bullies, my parents signed me up with Grand Master Jack Hwang. I trained with him in OK and one of his students' schools in Norman. In high school, I met Tim Bowen, who introduced me to an Okinawan karate style called Shuri-te. I trained with him up to my black belt. At that time, Grandmaster Billy Brammer started teaching me. He and Grandmaster Jim Butin allowed me to train in OK with Grandmaster Butin for a while till I moved closer to Mr. Brammer, whom I learned from till his passing. Not only have I learned how to fight from great men, but they have also taught me so much more about the martial arts lifestyle and the responsibilities of helping and respecting others in the community I live.

PERSONAL ACHIEVEMENTS

- I run the Oklahoma chapter of the Cancer Warrior M.A.P. For children and martial arts affiliated persons with cancer

MAJOR ACHIEVEMENTS

- Won several tournaments in Oklahoma in the 80s and early 90s
- Raised 2 awesome children and somehow remained married for over 31 years

I continue to learn new things every day about martial art history, humility, and what a little kindness can do for others. I now train under Grandmaster Billy Smith and Grandmaster Steve Park, who I am very grateful to for the knowledge and history they share.

I have discovered that the best fight won is the one that never happens. As martial artists, we learn how to read people and to be more conscious as to what is going on around us. Yes, I am still human and sometimes forget to open my eyes, my mind, and am quick to judge others, but I remind myself of the training and lessons I have gained through the years and learn from the mistakes I have made. There are other ways to help and teach people whether it is befriending someone in need or providing corrective guidance. The longer I remain in martial arts, the more of a brotherhood I see. I have made some great friends whom I shall treasure till my deathbed and probably a few enemies along my path. Not only is martial arts about fighting, but it is also a way of life bringing the physical, emotional, and spiritual elements together. I will always be a martial artist.

HANSHI
RICO GUY

Rico Guy, born Corinthians Guy in 1943 in Rahway, NJ with 2 sisters and 5 half siblings. He was raised in Staten Island and began his martial arts training (Combat Judo) in 1954 under Master Billy Davis. After several years, and Master Davis going into the Army, Rico gravitated to Master's Conrad and Chris DeBaise. He and Louis Delgado both changed schools to join Owen Watson at the University of the Streets on 7th Street in Manhattan. Louis and Rico began teaching all new students Goju Kata, weaponry and sparring. Frank Ruiz was a 4th dan from Nisei Judo and came to join the group. It became known as the "one punch knock out" school.

Rico received his 1st and 2nd degree black belt from Nisei Goju School. Then everything changed when Rico met Yoshiteru Otani and joined the Japan Cultural Center in Greenwich Village. Otani-san was the first martial artist to bring Iaido to the East Coast of the US. Rico taught Goju and began learning Iaido, Kendo, Jo, and Shorinji Kempo. He became Otani O'Sensei's top student. He was the first African American in the U.S. to receive black belt dan ranking in Kendo. He opened his U.S. Budo Kai Kan School in 1974, where he began teaching Goju, Iaido, Kendo, Jo, and Go Kempo-Jitsu.

Chief Grandmaster celebrated 45 years teaching at USBKK and had up to 25 classes per week. He and USBKK recently received a PROCLAMATION from Gayle Brewer Manhattan Borough President lauding Rico and his school. It made July 6th Rico Guy Day.

"THE BLACK SAMURAI"
OCTOBER 16, 1943-APRIL 10, 2020

DANIEL HOLLOWAY

"Karate taught me to stand firm while bending at the same time, to flow like water but break the ice like a rock."

TRAINING INFORMATION

- Belt Ranks & Martial Arts Styles: 9th Dan in Isshin Ryu Karate, 5th Dan in Tokushin Kobudo
- Instructors/Influencers: Harold Mitchum Sensei, Kensho Tokomura Sensei
- Birthdate: October 9, 1952
- Birthplace/Growing Up: Tokyo, Japan/Keego Harbor, MI
- Yrs. In the Martial Arts: 52 years
- Yrs. Instructing: 45 years
- School Owner, Manager & Instructor at Holloway's Isshin Ryu Karate

PROFESSIONAL ORGANIZATIONS

- AOPA Pilot's Association
- WUIKA - President
- Isshin Ryu Hall of Fame-BOD

I began my Martial Arts training to understand my heritage better. My Mother's side of the family was Japanese, and I began searching for my roots. I knew I had been raised differently than the other kids and thought Karate would help. When I was 15 in 1968, I had my tail handed to me in a very short street fight; he was a Judoka. I immediately found a karate school (Isshin Ryu) and started studying. About six months later, the kid tried to smack me around again and got his tail handed to him. He then converted to Karate.

Harold Mitchum Sensei was my last promoting instructor. Master Mitchum was a Marine who served two tours in Vietnam and one in Korea. He was trained in Okinawa and was Master Tatsuo Shimabuku's highest-ranking American. He became the 1st President of the AOKA and was the first American promoted in the system to 8th Dan. He was promoted to 9th Dan Hanshi by Matsufumi Suzuki of the All Japan Budo Association in 1988. He later received an acknowledgment as a 10th Dan and Senior student of Isshin Ryu Karate.

PERSONAL ACHIEVEMENTS

Have both an MBA and a Doctorate in Business. Graduate School Adjunct Professor. Inducted into the Isshin Ryu Hall of Fame 2008. Community awards for helping others. Serve as a Captain in the Civil Air Patrol (Air Force Auxiliary).

MAJOR ACHIEVEMENTS

Personally received an earned Doctorate in 2013. Inducted into the Isshin Ryu Hall of Fame 2008. Trained commercial pilot. Instructor / Professor at Northwood University Graduate School of Business.

I was promoted to 10th Dan by my instructor Harold Mitchum Sensei upon his death. I was one of his senior students. I do not wear it yet, as I feel I need a few more years.

Karate taught me to first then persevere, then as in any "Budo," it taught me about family and community. The old Samurai were not just fighters; they took care of each other and their community. It also taught me to see people's potential and see them for what they could become. It helped me understand what a strong work ethic could do. It taught me to stand firm while bending at the same time, to flow like water but break the ice like a rock.

DOUG HANSON

> "You are a Martial Artist and you are held to higher standards than the average person."

TRAINING INFORMATION

- Belt Ranks & Martial Arts Styles: 8th Dan Black Belt in Judokwan Tae Kwon Do, 8th Dan Black Belt in International Tae Kwon Do Association, 5th Dan Black Belt in World Tae Kwon Do Federation, Kukkiwon, 1st Dan Black Belt in Kempo

- Instructors/Influencers: Grand Master Tae Hong Choi, Grand Master Scott M Rohr, Grand Master Ken Olcott, Grand Master Erine Escalante

- Birthdate: April 15, 1959

- Birthplace/Growing Up: Portland, OR

- Yrs. In the Martial Arts: 45 years

- Yrs. Instructing: 34 years

- Instructor at Counter Point Martial Arts, Hubbard, OR

PROFESSIONAL ORGANIZATIONS

- Life time member of the VFW

I have always had a love for the Martial Arts. However, it was not until I was 16 when I started training in Taekwondo at the YMCA Portland Oregon with Grand Master Tae Hong Choi. Grand Master Choi was like a father figure to many of his students. Martial Arts gave me direction on how to live my life and treat others with respect. We trained hard in winter and even harder in the summer, wearing a sweatshirt over our Dobok. Sometimes during the summer, we would train twice a day. After finishing one class and then driving over to the Dojang to train for another two hours, I made many new friends.

I can truly say it has changed my life and made me into the person I am now. In 1980, I enlisted in the United States Air Force. I entered into the Law Enforcement career field. After my training, I was stationed at OSAN Air Force Base South Korea. Many of my friends I worked with in Korea trained in the Martial Arts, not only in Tae Kwon Do. In April of 1981, I tested at the Kukkiwon in Seoul South Korea for my 1st Dan Black Belt. It was not an easy test! I pushed myself hard to do my very best. It will be a test I will always remember. In a few weeks I was told I passed my test and was awarded my 1st Dan Black Belt.

PERSONAL ACHIEVEMENTS

- Retired from the United States Air Force after 20-years (Law Enforcement)
- Retired from the State of Oregon after 14 years
- Director of Security for Special Olympics Alaska from 1992 to June of 2000
- Volunteer of the Year (Angel Award) 1997, Elmendorf AFB Alaska
- Noncommissioned Officer of the Quarter, October - December 1997 Elmendorf AFB (Security Forces)
- Team Leader, Hostage Rescue/ Counter Terrorism, 51st Security Forces Sq. Osan Korea 1989 to 1990

MAJOR ACHIEVEMENTS

- Inducted in the Legends of the Martial Arts, Grand Master of the Year (Jidokwan) Tae Kwon Do (Sept 2019)
- Action Martial Arts Magazine Hall of Honours, Outstanding Achievement of a Grand Master in the Martial Arts (Jan 2020)
- Suisse Hall of Honour. Gold Award, Grand Master of the Year (September 2019)
- Munich Hall of Honours and Spirit Senior Master of the year (April 2019)
- Graduated Central Texas College

Over the years I have trained with many Masters and Grand Masters in the Martial Arts, making many close friends.

The Martial Arts gave me direction in my life, and strength to deal with problems. Not only in life but also in the workplace, learning how to deal with people that do not see things the way you do. Also learning to treat everyone with respect; even people you might not like! The Martial Arts has trained me to push myself hard, not to give up on myself! Keep trying, ask for help when needed, and to believe in myself. Learning you do not always have to fight. Try to avoid a confrontation whenever possible. Understanding that people will look and watch how I treat other people. Understanding that you are a Martial Artist and you are held to higher standards than the average person.

The friendships I have made over the years have lasted the test of time. Just this year I was able to visit and train and be inducted in the Action Martial Arts Hall of Honors with a close friend I had not seen in 29 years. We were inducted side by side that wonderful evening. None of this would have happened if I had not started training when I was a teenager.

JOHN HAWK

"Karate has taught me to stick to what I start until a meaningful conclusion and maintain that professional level as a lifelong endeavor."

TRAINING INFORMATION

- Belt Ranks & Martial Arts Styles: Goshindo Kempo Karate (5th Degree), Wadoryu (9th Degree), Wado Shinzen-Kai Kokusai (10th Degree)

- Instructors/Influencers: Shihan Isaac Henry Jr., Hanshi George Chalian, GM Robert Trias, GM Gary Alexander, Master Michio Nozumi Haramachida-Chi

- Birthdate: January 21, 1942

- Birthplace/Growing Up: Toledo, OH

- Yrs. In the Martial Arts: 55 years

- Yrs. Instructing: 51 years

- Instructor, Founder of Wado Shinzen-Kai Kokusai

PROFESSIONAL ORGANIZATIONS

- The Honorable Order of St. Michael (AVIATION) 2010

- AVIATION: inducted into the Who's Who of Professionals in 2000

I initially looked for a judo school. I had no idea about Karate or that the art even existed. I was active duty in the Army in 1965 and thought the art would better my abilities physically. My judo Sensei John Graham received orders for Vietnam, and I believe he was KIA in Vietnam in 1967. In my last lesson with Sensei Graham, a young fellow named George Chalian was doing a funny dance in the corner of the wrestling room in the Ft Monmouth NJ gym. He approached me and told me he could teach me Karate, I said OK, and a lifelong passion was born.

By following the BKG MOTTO "BEGIN AND PERSEVERE," Karate has taught me to stick to what I start until a meaningful conclusion and maintain that professional level as a lifelong endeavor.

I also follow our WADO SHINZEN-KAI MOTTO "KARATE" KEEP A RESPECTFUL ATTITUDE TOWARD EVERYONE."

PERSONAL ACHIEVEMENTS

- I received the Lifetime Achievement Award from the International Association of Martial Artists in 2007, the Lifetime Achievement award from the Beikoku Karate Do Goyukai (BKG) in 2009, inducted into the World Karate Union Hall of Fame 2014, Ambassador of the Martial Arts at Action Martial Arts Magazine 2014. I also received the Meritorious Service Medallion from the International Armed Forces Judo and Jujitsu Academy in 2015, Medallion #72 out of 100 issued in five countries. Shodai Hawk co-sponsored the 1st USKA European tour in 1971, including GM Robert Trias, Bill" Superfoot" Wallace, Glenn Keeney, Wally Sloki, and Robert Bowles and James Fraser to mention a few. He is listed in the SHURI-RYU KARATE BOOK by GM R.A. Trias "The Pinnacle of Karate" Okinawan Methods of Shuri-ryu circa 1965-69, published 1980 revised 1988 and in Grand Master Gary Alexander's book "Trailblazer 1" in 2014, Action Martial Arts Magazine HALL OF HONORS 2020, page 143, and WORLD'S GREATEST MARTIAL ARTISTS Vol 21.

- Shodai Hawk is a senior member of the Board of Directors of Gary Alexander's International Association of Martial Artists and a member of the Board of Directors of the World Karate Union.

MAJOR ACHIEVEMENTS

Shodai Hawk is a proud retired Army and retired Army Civilian with a combined 47+ years. Federal service. The last 27+ years in Aviation retiring as Flight Simulation Supervisor Aviation Directorate, Ft Hood, TX

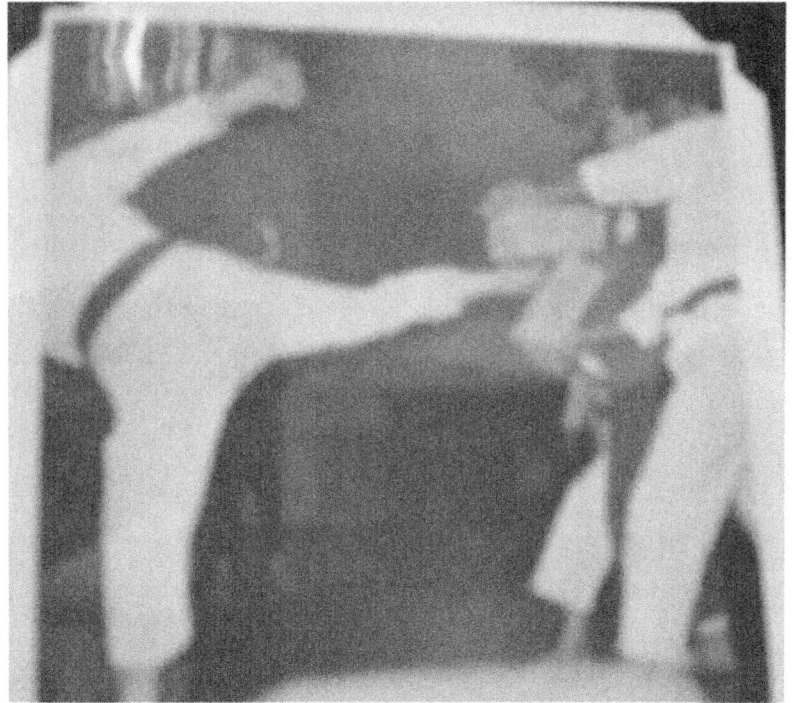

NATHANIAL HOGE

"*Through Martial Arts we learn that the journey is often more important than the destination.*"

TRAINING INFORMATION

- Belt Ranks & Martial Arts Styles: TaiKiJitsu - Sōke/8th Dan

- Instructors/Influencers: Grandmaster Geoffrey Spohn, proprietor of West Michigan Karate Academy, and World Director of Intercontinental Martial Arts Union

- Birthdate: November 15, 1982

- Birthplace/Growing Up: Princeton, WV

- Yrs. In the Martial Arts: 34 years

- Yrs. Instructing: 10 years

- Instructor

PROFESSIONAL ORGANIZATIONS

- Advisory Board member of Intercontinental Martial Arts Union

I first started in the martial arts as a small child at the age of 3. However, I began training much harder around the time I turned 10 years old. The movie Bloodsport had been out for a few years, and when I saw it, it inspired me. Many years of blood and sweat later, I finally met the man himself. Admittedly, the saying that you should never meet your heroes holds true here, but I refuse to not give credit where it was due. As I grew up, I began to truly embrace the principles. The more I learned, the more I needed to know. The thirst for knowledge only grew over the years. Now, here I am all these years later, dying to know more, and enjoying passing what I know to those who will carry it on in the years to come!

Martial arts has had a truly massive impact on my life. It has taught me more about the proper way to live than anything else. When young, all I cared about was being able to handle myself. But as I grew, I came to learn the value of discipline, respect, honor, integrity, passion, and dedication.

PERSONAL ACHIEVEMENTS

- Action Martial Arts Magazine Hall of Honors inductee 2018, 2019, 2020
- Former WV State Director of IMAU

MAJOR ACHIEVEMENTS

- My greatest achievement will be passing my knowledge to anyone who truly thirsts to know more. There can be no higher honor than to fulfill someone's request for knowledge and skill.

Somewhere along the way, I believe we all finally learn that it isn't about what we can get out of the arts, nor truly about what we can put into them. We discover instead that we become the arts. The arts become us. We learn that the journey is often more important than the destination. This journey has brought me so far already. Through it I have had the opportunity to meet some of the most amazing people on the planet. It is truly amazing to be side by side with many of my heroes, my inspirations, my friends. Martial arts has made me a better person, without doubt. I only hope to one day be an inspiration to those who come after me the way those who come before me have inspired me.

DALE KAHOUN

"Primarily though, Martial Arts is not a concept; it's not fighting; it's people."

TRAINING INFORMATION

- Belt Ranks & Martial Arts Styles: 8th Degree Black Belt- Kodenkan Danzan Ryu Jujitsu, 4th Degree Black Belt- Kodokan Judo, 2nd Degree Black Belt- Ken Ju Ryu Kenpo Jujitsu, Assistant Instructor's rank- Inayan Eskrima by Mangisursuro Mike Inay, Brown belt-in Aikido, Kirikami rank- Kashima Shinryu (Japanese sword)

- Instructors/Influencers: Ben Patterson, Mervin Tate, Charles Robinson, Phillip Porter, Russ Rhodes, Richard Pietrelli, Richard Kahoalii, and Dai Shihan Siegfried Kufferath

- Birthdate: August 15, 1950

- Birthplace/Growing Up: Tacoma. WA/Northern, Central, and Bay Area, CA

- Yrs. In the Martial Arts: 51 years

- Yrs. Instructing: 45 years

- Instructor at Mushinkai Dojo

PROFESSIONAL ORGANIZATIONS

- United States Judo Association

- The American Jujitsu Institute

- The American Judo, and Jujitsu Federation

- Kilohana Martial Arts Association

- Founder of Kilohana

- Secretary and Sergeant at Arms

My Martial Arts study started when I began my study of Police Science at a California Community College. The Judo and JuJitsu course was also a Police Defensive Tactics course. I fell in love with Judo, entering my first contest with two weeks of training. I kept Martial Art in my occupation. I was an Intermediate Police Defensive Tactics Instructor for 12 years (ranked to instruct instructors) with three styles of police batons and police defensive tactics. I occasionally served performing 'Executive Protection' of dignitaries and crowd control at protests and disturbances. I was FBI certified as a Firearms Instructor.

Martial Arts changed my life by offering alternatives in my career. Primarily though, Martial Arts is not a concept; it's not fighting; it's people.

I have lifelong friends through Martial Arts and its practice. The understanding goes beyond words. I don't have a clue what my personality would be like without this life-long study. The amazing people who are my Sampai, my Sensei, those who have gone before, many of my

PERSONAL ACHIEVEMENTS

I competed in Judo until I was 37 years. My last two tournaments were the Desert Classic and the World Police and Fire Games; I got second places. I entered another style of competition. In the San Francisco area Battle of the Bay and Golden Bear Martial Arts Tournaments in self-defense demo division in 1993-94, I got seven first places and two-second places. Demonstrating was fun. I enjoyed showing the techniques that had history.

I've received several awards for service to and for teaching Martial Art (including two 'Hall of Fame' awards); above all, I prize the 2015 Kilohana 'Legend' Award, an award from my "Ohana" (Hawaiian for extended Family).

I retired with a Distinguished Service Award after 27 years of police service (patrol).

MAJOR ACHIEVEMENTS

I taught several students that did very well in competition, winning at Judo and BJJ. One is a great promoter and event organizer. All are extended family.

I wrote a 400+ page training manual for Kilohana of the techniques of Kodenkan Jujitsu as related to me by Professor Kufferath (ISBN, Library of Congress)

I investigated a crime that received international attention and was featured on 'Sixty Minutes' and required presidential intervention in Serbia. I initiated an Interpol Warrant and was lucky enough to arrest the suspect when he returned illegally to the USA. I recognized him from photographs ten years after I wrote the original report. The arrest might have saved a life.

casual martial 'contacts' have been my teachers too. They are famous, but not to the whole world. Many of you would know their names because we are in that other-world together. My contemporaries who are at my eye-level. We have an understanding; even if it looks like we are fighting, we mostly are not. Our students, we owe them, we need to deliver as good as we got. What if you have a student that excels you, they do not stand in your shadow, that is the greatest gift. As their teacher, you have just gifted your entire ryu-ha and improved martial art. To be a respected part-of. If you live and practice, you are in-between; in the middle always. Between your teachers and your students, amazing people, and family all around. Not all humans have this; we do.

JAMES KELLER

"I am committed to teaching and sharing my knowledge to children and adults hoping to make a positive impact in their lives."

TRAINING INFORMATION

- Belt Ranks & Martial Arts Styles: Legend Martial Arts-10th Degree Black Belt, Kwon Bop Do-9th Degree Black Belt, Arnis and Pencak Silat, Eagle Star Self Defense-10th Degree Black Belt, Cadena de Mano, Kuntao, Silat, Eskrima-Instructor, Sirat as Sayf-Level 4 Green Belt, Tai Chi

- Instructors/Influencers: GM Richard Lenchus, GM Joe Onopa, GM Billy Bryant, Guru Greg Alland, Soke Najee Hassan, GM Rudy Jones, Sifu Allan Foung and Master Lee

- Birthdate: January 6, 1952

- Birthplace/Growing Up: Queens & Brooklyn, NY

- Yrs. In the Martial Arts: 45+ years

- Yrs. Instructing: 30+ years

- Instructor

PROFESSIONAL ORGANIZATIONS

- International Grandmasters of the Roundtable

- Legend Martial Arts System

- Kwon Bop Do Federation

- Sirat as Sayf

Growing up in Brooklyn and later working in Manhattan, I met Grandmaster Richard Lenchus who was head and founder of Legend Shotokan Karate Association. I started learning karate under him for over 35 years. I have studied with Guru Greg Alland Arnis and Pencak Silat, Grandmaster Joe Onopa Kwon Bop Do to rank of 9th Degree Black Belt, and Guru Billy Bryant Cadena De Mano, eskrima to the rank of instructor. I also have a Grandmaster rank under GM Rudy Jones in Eagle Star Self Defense System who studied under Moses Powell and Prof Vee. Now I'm studying with Soke Najee Hassan and his wife in Sirat as Sayf. I am also studying Tai chi yang style under Sifu Allan Fung and Master Lee.

In 2011, I inherited the Legend Martial Arts Association from GM Lenchus. I was a coach on the USA Martial Arts team from 1996-2000.

I've been inducted into the following Martial Arts Hall of Fames: World Christian Martial Arts and Pastoral United International Kung Fu

PERSONAL ACHIEVEMENTS

- Being married to the same beautiful woman for 47 years.
- Still being in the martial arts for 46 years and still have the thirst to still wanting to learn more.

MAJOR ACHIEVEMENTS

- To still be able to teach students and have a positive impact on their lives.

Federation, World Karate Union HOF, Action Martial Arts Magazine HOF, World Head of Family Soke Council HOF, Masters of Martial Arts Awards HOF.

I have taught kids, adults and women self-defense classes in several centers and schools in Brooklyn and Queens. I am committed to teaching and sharing my knowledge to children and adults hoping to make a positive impact in their lives.

Studying the martial arts has given me the chance to travel nationally and internationally to judge and referee at tournaments events. During these travels, I have met many great people, teachers, and friends. Studying the martial arts has made me a better person, husband, and friend. Also, the martial arts has given me the chance to work with disadvantaged youth in NYC as well as teaching self-defense classes for women. During my travels, I was given the opportunity to do demos and seminars.

I had the chance to study several different martial arts cultures. I have studied Shotokan Karate, Kwon Bop Do, FMA (Arnis, Escrima, Kali, dirty boxing), and Tai Chi.

WADE KIRKPATRICK

"Martial Arts taught me how to respect and interact with people; gave me the opportunity to travel to new places..."

TRAINING INFORMATION

- Belt Ranks & Martial Arts Styles: Zen Do Kai- White belt to 5th degree Black Belt, Hawaiian Kosho Ryu Kenpo Karate 6th, 7th, 8th Degree Black Belt, Muy Thai- 5 years, American Boxing- 20 years, KickStart Instructor for Chuck Norris Kick Drugs Out of America - 12 years

- Instructors/Influencers: Robert Gifford, Gary Lee, Kru Pong

- Birthdate: March 13, 1972

- Birthplace/Growing Up: Houston, TX/Sugar Land, TX

- Yrs. In the Martial Arts: 39 years

- Yrs. Instructing: 33 years

- School owner & Instructor at Fulshear Family Karate

PROFESSIONAL ORGANIZATIONS

- Golden Greek Award Hall of Fame
- USA Martial Arts Hall of Fame

Sensei Wade Kirkpatrick got started in Martial Arts to build his strength and endurance and began to feel the positive impact of helping others in his community as he earned his Brown and Black belts. Being an assistant instructor boosted his self-esteem. It developed leadership opportunities that led to improved grades in school, teaching karate classes consistently, participation in karate tournaments throughout the state of Texas and the United States. He received a scholarship from the University of Houston to attend college in Nanning, China. He trained in a Kung Fu school in Mexico City, Mexico, where He prepared for the NBL competition.

Sensei Wade Kirkpatrick is an 8th degree Black Belt and Master Instructor. Sensei Kirkpatrick has been training in Karate since the age of 9 years. Over three decades of that time has been spent teaching martial arts. He is a direct student of Sensei Robert Gifford, 9th Degree Black Belt and Director of the Zen Do Kai Karate System in the southwestern United States. Master Kirkpatrick became the youngest person to achieve a Black Belt in the history of Zen Do Kai Karate. Sensei Kirkpatrick was employed by the KickStart Foundation for 12 years and has taught Karate in the Galveston, Houston, and Fort Bend Independent school districts. He is now a school administrator in Fort Bend ISD.

PERSONAL ACHIEVEMENTS

- 10 Amateur Organization of Karate State Championship Titles in Kata, Musical Kata

- 4 Texas National Tour State Championship Titles in Kata, Weapons, Musical Kata, Light Heavyweight Sparring

- 37 consecutive first-place victories in a two-year span with 0 losses. 1996-1998

Sensei Kirkpatrick is an eight-time Texas State Champion having won the title in A.O.K, T.N.T, and N.B.L all in the same year to unify the title. State titles were won in weapons, traditional Japanese kata, musical kata, and light heavyweight point sparring. He later went on to win 37 consecutive 1st place victories, a state record, over a year and a half span, culminating with being named Men's Golden Greek Award winner for the best all-around black belt player in 1997.

Sensei Kirkpatrick was named to Texas' Golden Greek Award Hall of Fame that same year and was on two magazine covers and many feature articles related to the events. After competing at the state level for many years, he went on to represent Texas as the number one seed in the National Black Belt Leagues' World Championships in Washington, D.C., placing 6th in the World. His fight was shown on ESPN's "prime sports."

Master Kirkpatrick then got his boxing license in the USA Gulf Coast Association Boxing and fought under Carlos Patina of Galveston, Texas. Muay Thai full contact matches came next under the tutelage of Kru Pong of Thailand.

Master Kirkpatrick served as KickStart's Houston City-Wide Black Belt Demo Team Coach for two seasons. He was responsible for choreographing demonstrations for former President George Bush, President George W. Bush, Representative Sheila Jackson Lee, Chuck Norris, former Mayor Lee Brown, and other individuals. In 1999, Sensei Kirkpatrick's City Wide Team was asked to perform on an episode of Walker, Texas Ranger. Kirkpatrick has been named Zen Do Kai's Instructor of the Year twice, Black Belt of the Year, and won the Bushido Award for bringing recognition to the Zen Do Kai system through tournament competition.

In 1995, He was named Sugar Land's Outstanding Citizen by Sugar Land Mayor Lee Duggan and Police Chief Ernest Taylor. Sensei Kirkpatrick has been an avid competitor since 1984, having competed in Karate tournaments, boxing, and Muay Tai full contact kickboxing events.

Sensei enjoys using these experiences to bring out the best in each of his students, whatever their ambitions in the "Art" may be as well as operating a well-rounded dojo. Martial arts taught him the value of discipline and routine. Martial Arts taught him how to respect and interact with people, gave him the opportunity to travel to new places, meet people he never otherwise would've met, and experienced things he would never have otherwise got to experience.

With a little effort, you can find studies showing martial arts benefiting everything from the exercise capacity and self-efficacy of the elderly to the immune system and autonomic nervous system—an overall increase in mental and physical health, as well as an improved sense of well-being. Consistent training not only conditions the mind and body to have strength and stamina to fight back in a violent situation but also helps the body fight disease, stay flexible, strong and active as people age. Martial arts provides stress relief and ways to release pent up energy.

MAJOR ACHIEVEMENTS

- Golden Greek Award 1997
- NBL Champion 1996
- #1 Hard Traditional Weapons NBL 1996
- Golden Greek Award Hall of Fame 1997
- USA Martial Arts Hall of Fame 2013
- Sport Karate Museum Rocky DiRico International Black Belt Hall of Fame 2019
- Sport Karate Museum Joe Lewis Fighting Award

T. SABU LEWIS

"Master Sabu is not just teaching Martial Arts. He's teaching them discipline. He's teaching them everyday life. And having a little fun with it."

TRAINING INFORMATION

- Belt Ranks & Martial Arts Styles: Tae kwon do - 9th Dan, Karate - 1st degree, Arnis - 2nd degree, Other related styles - intermediate belt level

- Instructors/Influencers: Great Grand Master Ken E. Lee, David Kim, Remy Amador Presas, "The Father of Modern Arnis," Great Grand Master Dr. Moses Powell, Great Grand Master Kurtis Black, Grand Master Aaron Adams

- Birthdate: December 22, 1949

- Birthplace/Growing Up: Brooklyn, NY

- Yrs. In the Martial Arts: 55 years

- Yrs. Instructing: 51 years

- School Owner, Manager & Instructor at The Humble School of Martial Arts, PKA Worldwide Member

PERSONAL ACHIEVEMENTS

I have competed on the National and International Martial Arts circuit and placed top 5 in the National Circuit.

Chief Master Sabu has been a long-standing pillar of excellence in New York City's borough of Brooklyn for decades, and his impact on his community is evident. His love for martial arts began at the age of 16 years old. Not only did he have an uncle in the service, but he was highly influenced by a friend in high school who was a black belt. Those two individuals were the driving force Chief Master Sabu needed to begin his career.

While he studied multiple styles of martial arts, his main focus was Tae Kwon Do. At the height of his career, he managed to obtain national and regional competitive ratings, winning over 700 trophies and becoming a top 5 martial arts instructor in the nation. His success is evident, but he humbly praises Remy Presas, Ken E Lee, Moses Powell, David Kim, Aaron Adams, and Kurtis Black, just a few of the Great Great Grandmasters. He, too, has become a beacon of leadership for others, catapulting the martial arts careers of Aki Williams, Jadi Tention, and Chris Styles, all of which are international, national, and regional master instructors of champions.

Martial arts is no doubt an art form that Chief Master Sabu loves, but what he appreciates the most is that he has been blessed with the power to give back and positively impact neighborhood youth. Under Master Sabu's leadership, Humble School is known for its broad approach to martial arts instruction, including physical, mental, and spiritual development. While parents enroll their children in Humble School for self-defense classes, Chief Master Sabu's guidance also helps children develop the self-confidence and self-discipline needed to excel academically, socially, and mentally. He has a reputation for helping restore one's confidence and self-image and inspire his community to follow their dreams, no matter what obstacles come their way. An article in "The Local" of Clinton Hill quotes the parent of a Humble student: "Master Sabu is not just teaching them [Martial Arts]. He's teaching them discipline. He's teaching them everyday life. And having a little fun with it." It's no surprise that Chief Master Sabu has the reputation he does. He was even featured as the New Yorker of the Week in 2013. He talked about his duty in showing his neighborhood how to be strong (both physically and mentally). His work ethic and the impact he has had on many students are a true testament to his character, his ability to inspire people of all backgrounds. To put it simply, he is invaluable to the people of Brooklyn and anyone he comes in contact.

FERNANDO LIMON

"Martial Arts has opened many doors in my personal and professional life."

TRAINING INFORMATION

- Belt Ranks & Martial Arts Styles: Goshin Jutsu Kyo Jujo Budokan (8th Degree Hachidan Black Belt), Tang Soo Do (7th Degree, Honorary Chil-Dan)
- Instructors/Influencers: Grandmaster Salvador "Sal" Narvaez
- Birthdate: June 14, 1963
- Birthplace/Growing Up: Laredo, TX
- Yrs. In the Martial Arts: 48 years
- Yrs. Instructing: 40 years
- Instructor, Manager

PROFESSIONAL ORGANIZATIONS

- (A.O.K.) Amateur Organization Karate
- (U.M.A) United Martial Arts
- (T.K.O) Texas Karate Organization
- (S.T.K.B.B.A.) South Texas Karate Black Belt Association
- (T.K.A.) Tang Soo Do Karate Association

It was a Monday, February 14, 1972, when my father (Abel Limon Martinez) asked my siblings and I if we wanted to learn karate. I was almost nine years old and was not interested in joining. My dad parks his vehicle on Market and Zapata Highway. We proceeded to go into the building where only adults were being taught. Men and women were being instructed to punch and kick by Johnny Rendon, the black belt instructor. He walked over to talk to my father. My dad said to him, "Here are my sons and daughter, and I want you to teach them karate." Johnny Rendon replies, "I do not teach children only men and women." My father told him, "Well start a children's class and tell me how much to pay you."

We immediately took our shoes off and began to practice; this was the start of my karate journey, and I learned discipline and respect for the arts. This was a historical event in karate for the children of Laredo because it was the first time a class would be offered to younger generations. Bruce Lee and Chuck Norris were two karate idols that I was attached to and attracted to in the world of karate. I began my training under Sensei Johnny Rendon in the style of Goshin Jutsu Kyo Jujo Budokan.

PERSONAL ACHIEVEMENTS

- County Sheriff Peace Officer - Serving my community

MAJOR ACHIEVEMENTS

- World Pugilist Hall of Fame
- United State Hall of Fame
- Karate Sport Museum - History General (all time living legend)

My first karate tournament was in Harlingen, Texas, where I won first place in KATA's. I loved it so much and that was when I decided that karate was for me. As for my five siblings, they did not pursue the Martial Arts. I trained under Sensei Johnny Rendon for the next four years, and unfortunately, he decided to close his academy and pursue another career. I obtained my Green Belt with Shihan Rendon.

I needed a new instructor since I wanted to continue training. I found Salvador "Sal" Narvaez as my new instructor. As I got older, I realized that the Martial Arts was like a big family in which you will be a part of it for life. Karate is a way of life, and you grow with it. The more I practiced, the more I expanded my way of thinking and living. My experience in Martial Arts is like chapters in a book because every time you win tournaments, they are embedded in the book of your life. I went up in the ranks, and I got better and better. When I reached Black Belt, I realized that there was so much more to accomplish. Grand Master Sal Narvaez is my lifetime mentor. Karate has been a part of my personal and professional accomplishments.

Martial Arts has opened many doors in my personal and professional life. In my personal life, it has given me focus on taking life differently and spiritually. In my professional life, all the jobs that I held, including law enforcement, I have gone up in ranks due to my discipline and training in Martial Arts.

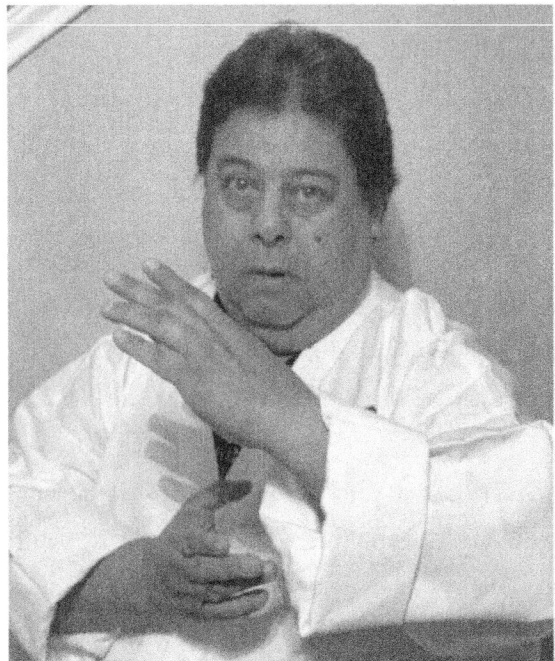

DONALD MATHEWS

"The balance of old and new thinking creates a dynamic learning environment that helps each child be their best."

TRAINING INFORMATION

- Belt Ranks & Martial Arts Styles: Senshi Damashii - 8th Dan, Shindo Jinen Ryu - 4th Dan

- Instructors/Influencers: Sensei Kiyoshi Yamazaki, Sensei Hideharu Igaki, Sensei Fumio Demura, Sensei Bill Wallace, Sensei Joe Lewis, Sensei Remy Presas, Sensei Phil Maldonado, Sensei Don Wilson, Sensei Al Timen, Sensei Moe Stevens, Sensei Greer Golden

- Birthdate: May 22, 1956

- Birthplace/Growing Up: Columbus & Grove City, OH

- Yrs. In the Martial Arts: 37 years

- Yrs. Instructing: 30 years

- School owner (Warrior Spirit Karate, LLC), Instructor

PROFESSIONAL ORGANIZATIONS

- USA-NKF

- Lifetime member of USA Martial Arts Alliance Association

- Unified Kempo Karate System

- AAU

- Ko Sutemi Seiei Kan

I got started in martial arts out of curiosity. A few of my co-workers at the time were attending classes at a local dojo, and they had invited me to watch a demonstration that they were doing. I watched them perform open hand kata, weapons kata, and self-defense techniques. I was mesmerized at everything that they were doing. It didn't take long for me to sign up as soon as I could. And it didn't take long for me to realize that it turned my curiosity into a passion for learning everything. I immersed myself into not just the kata, the weapon kata, the physical aspects of training and the self-defense movements, but to delve into the real physiological aspects of the martial arts. My passion for learning is still as great as ever before, even after all these years. I never forget that though I am an instructor, I am still a student and always will be. I still have that curiosity to seek out the best instructors in the world and learn everything that I can from them. Martial Arts has been my life and will continue to be my life until the day I pass onto the next world.

PERSONAL ACHIEVEMENTS

- Opened my own dojo in October 2011

- Promoted to 8th Dan - August 2016

- Competitor in AAU, USA-NKF, Alliance and Ko Sutemi Seiei Kan organizations

- Taught numerous National and International seminars

- Referee for local, regional and national events

- I've been fortunate to win many trophies and medals in competition over the course of 37 years

MAJOR ACHIEVEMENTS

- 2017 Leading Japanese Martial Arts Master of the Year - USA Martial Arts Hall of Fame

- 2016 Traditional Martial Arts Master of the Year - USA Martial Arts Hall of Fame

- 2016 Diamond Award - Miami Valley Tournament Association

- 2015 Leading International Sensei of the Year - USA Martial Arts Hall of Fame

- 2015 Leading Karate Master of the Year - International Hall of Fame

- 2015 Master Instructor of the Year - United States Martial Arts Hall of Fame

- 2014 Instructor Award - United States Martial Arts Hall of Fame

- 2014 Black Belt Competitor of the Year - USA Martial Arts Hall of Fame

- 2013 Instructor of the Year - United States Martial Arts Hall of Fame

The impact of martial arts in my life was so significant that I opened my dojo, Warrior Spirit Karate, in October 2011 with a handful of students and the vision to become the essence of what the martial arts was historical. With nearly 35 years of experience competing and teaching, I have the passion for passing on that extensive knowledge and expertise to my students. I am accomplished in a variety of martial art techniques, having trained with some of the most accomplished and recognized in the martial arts. My eye is toward maintaining the real traditional history and teachings; I immerse my students with not only the technical instructions but the rich history and philosophy that will serve to enrich the personal growth of them as well. I am focused on youth development, fusing traditional martial arts values with cutting edge child development and parenting skills. My statement, "The balance of old and new thinking creates a dynamic learning environment that helps each child be their best." With values such as focus, discipline, confidence, teamwork, respect, and family, every student learns the life skills necessary to become our leaders of the future.

MAJOR ACHIEVEMENTS

- 2013 Karate Lifetime Achievement Award - USA Martial Arts Hall of Fame

- 2013 Martial Arts Dedication Award - Eastern USA International Black Belt Hall of Fame

- 2012 Karate Lifetime Achievement Award - International Karate and Kickboxing Hall of Fame

RANDAL MCFARLAND

"Being in Martial Arts, my work ethic has improved and I seek to do my best at all things in life."

TRAINING INFORMATION

- Belt Ranks & Martial Arts Styles: Kosho Ryu Kempo Karate - 4th Dan, Ryobu Ryu Karate - 6th Kyu, Korutadori Ryu Karate - 6th Kyu, Aikido - 9th Kyu

- Instructors/Influencers: Professor Gary Lee

- Birthdate: June 4, 1972

- Birthplace/Growing Up: Fort Smith, AR / Stockton, CA

- Yrs. In the Martial Arts: 19 years

- Yrs. Instructing: 10 years

- School owner (Inochi No Ki Ryu), Instructor

PROFESSIONAL ORGANIZATIONS

- American Association of Christian Counselors

- Sport Karate Museum

Honestly, what inspired me to get started in the Martial Arts was Saturday morning Kung Fu Theater. I would sit and just watch them do all the cool moves. Later, it was more about being bullied. I wanted to learn to defend myself and be able to fight if I needed to. I tried for years to get involved with martial arts of all kinds, but my parents wouldn't let me because we moved around a lot. They gave in after I spent all my money on martial arts magazines and videos.

Since studying the martial arts, I have learned to harness my inner strength and take pride in myself. It has helped me become a person that is more trustworthy and reliable to more than just my family. My work ethic has improved and I seek to do my best at all things in life. This has led to my doing well in school and in my career field.

PERSONAL ACHIEVEMENTS

- Bachelor Degree in Christian Studies Graduating Magna Cum Laude

- Ambassador of Sport Karate Museum

MAJOR ACHIEVEMENTS

- Testing and receiving my 4th Dan in front of the board at Living Legends

EDDIE MINYARD

> "I lead my teams with confidence and calm, because of my training in the Martial Arts."

TRAINING INFORMATION

- Belt Ranks & Martial Arts Styles: Traditional Taekwon-Do - 8th Dan, Sun Do Sul - 8th Dan
- Instructors/Influencers: Grandmaster Yong Sung Choi, Grandmaster Yong Duk Choi
- Birthdate: April 19, 1950
- Birthplace/Growing Up: USA
- Yrs. In the Martial Arts: 47 years
- Yrs. Instructing: 44 years
- Instructor

PROFESSIONAL ORGANIZATIONS

- International Jun Tong Federation
- United States KIDO Federation
- International Sun Do Sul Federation
- Chopra Center for Health
- International Association of Emergency Managers

Being a "military brat," we were constantly moving. I was always the "new kid" - and always seemed to be having to prove myself. I began training in Martial Arts in 1965. I started my studies in Judo under the tutelage of my stepfather, a former military instructor. Then began training in Shorei Ryu, in Moline, Il – taking a bus for 45 minutes each way to the school.

While in the US Army in Vietnam, I saw a demonstration of Taekwon-Do (TKD), by the ROK White Horse Division. It became clear that TKD was what I wanted to study. I was informally trained by Master Roger Dorethy, beginning in 1970, and began formal training in 1973, under GM Chung Eun Kim (RIP) (Chang Moo Kwan).

As I began to truly understand the depth of Taekwon-Do, I also began to understand myself - and the importance of using my skills and knowledge to build a better world.

Throughout my life, Martial Arts has been my foundation. I have chosen the life of a warrior in every aspect. As an Infantry (RECONDO) soldier in Vietnam, a competitor in tournaments, and having a career as a First Responder - I always fall back on my martial arts training to help me through my day.

PERSONAL ACHIEVEMENTS

- Day of Honor - City of New Orleans - for aiding the City, immediately following Hurricane Katrina
- Author of "After Disaster: An Insider's Perspective from the Heart of Chaos"
- Recognized for Service during the Gulf Oil Spill
- Commissioned as Sergeant, St. Bernard Sheriff's Office
- Recognized for Service to the People of Haiti, after the 2010 Earthquake

MAJOR ACHIEVEMENTS

- Promotion to Grandmaster, Sun Do Sul
- Promotion to 8th Dan, Traditional Tae Kwon Do
- Certified Meditation Instructor, Chopra Center
- Ordained Minister, Universal Life Church
- Honorable Discharge, United States Army

As a father, the first education I've given to each of my children has been of the Tenets of Taekwon-Do – Courtesy, Integrity, Perseverance, Self-Control, and Indomitable Spirit – these are the foundations of life. Combined with Faith-Based Values and the strength gained from them, Martial Arts are embedded within me. And I do my best to share those values with the world.

In the course of my work, I see the worst of situations – hurricanes, earthquakes, fires, and yes, even pandemics. I know the impact they have on human beings – it's never easy. But, I lead my teams with confidence and calm, because of my training in the Martial Arts. In the worst of situations, I find inner peace. This emanates in ways that are hard to explain but unmistakable. People look to that and gain from it – they readily migrate to a leader who demonstrates these traits. Even when they, themselves, are also feeling the fears on the inside. Again, it's the strength and calm gained through my training that allows me to keep my focus on the mission.

So, how have the Martial Arts impacted my life? By giving me the tools to impact the lives of others in their darkest moments.

JOHNNIE MURPHY

"My martial arts wisdom will live on long after I am gone. When I leave this world, I leave knowing I will not be forgotten."

TRAINING INFORMATION

- Belt Ranks & Martial Arts Styles: Kyokushin Kai/Bushido Kan - Black Belt, Tang Soo Do Soo Bahk Do Moo Duk Kwan - Black Belt/Midnight Blue, Grand Master Bushido Kai Karate Jutsu, Bushido Kai Iai Jutsu, Bushido Kai Aki Jutsu

- Instructors/Influencers: Master Donald Radcliff, Grandmaster James Radcliff II, Master Bill Milberger, Master Wayne Nguyen, Master Norman Roberts

- Birthdate: April 29, 1957

- Birthplace/Growing Up: Wurtzburg, Germany / Colonial Heights, VA

- Yrs. In the Martial Arts: 50 years

- Yrs. Instructing: 35 years

- School owner, Manager & Instructor at Champions Budo, Head of Bushido Kai Karate Jutsu Systems

PROFESSIONAL ORGANIZATIONS

- Texas State licensed HVAC contractor TACLA3134E

- Texas Sport Karate News

Leo Leighton Murphy, my father, was in the US Army and was a decorated combat veteran from Korea and Vietnam. While living on base in the USA, he was assigned as a drill sergeant who taught what he called combat Judo. Combat Judo was a combination of wrestling, boxing, and Jui-Jitsu, and as a child, he would playfully wrestle with my older brother and me. He would try to show us moves and takedowns.

That was my first contact with the martial arts. In 1964 while I was living in Ankara, Turkey, and housed at "Site 23", a US Air Force base.

My father spoke seven different languages and was a top cytologist and a pro golfer, so he always got cool assignments everywhere.

They had a base theater there, and we would watch the latest movies. I always pretended I was the hero doing the cool fight scenes. Instead of playing cowboys and Indians, we played secret agent and would attempt choreographed fight routines that would lead to minor injuries and sprained ankles. I still remember my mom's upset voice and her tears on several occasions. Several years later, in 1967, while living in Oslo, Norway, I watched a James Bond movie and an imported Kung Fu movie and was sold on the Idea of learning Karate. By the time I made it back to the stateside, I was 13 years old. We were stationed at Fort Lee, Virginia, a backwater and not so impressive army base. By then, I had already made

PERSONAL ACHIEVEMENTS

- Being the father of 3 wonderful children
- Learning patience
- Being the best example for all who come to train with me
- Making it to 63 years old
- Being in very good health
- Still able to compete with way younger competitors
- Still winning championships in martial arts
- Being a pro musician – guitar since 1966

MAJOR ACHIEVEMENTS

- Starting an HVAC company and staying in business for 33 years
- Creating and maintaining a top-rated karate school
- Becoming a multiple world champion & winning over 1,000 national titles
- Being friends with world-famous martial artist celebrities
- Finding harmony in my life

my mind that I wanted to learn Karate and become a prestigious black belt one day.

I eventually moved off base, and we settled down in Colonial Heights, Virginia, where at 13, I was introduced to the local school and began to learn Karate.

Training in martial arts has been my challenge and produced lofty life goals. It has given me the strength to face life's greatest challenges. It has been a galvanizing force that carries me through the worst of times, including this current pandemic of 2020 and the hate people express against each other.

It has given me a vision beyond the obvious, and it sparks my creativity.

Martial arts have allowed me to be a champion and successful in all my endeavors and carried me through my worst night. I walk with the confidence that no man is better than me because we are all equal and I believe the creator has a special purpose for me. I will accomplish even more with his help.

My martial arts wisdom will live on long after I am gone. When I leave this world, I leave knowing I will not be forgotten. A thousand years from now, I hope that a person will be sitting under a tree-free from the bondage of technology, reading, and studying the words I have said in a simple book.

WALTER ORTH

"It has been my highest honor to pass along the knowledge I have gleaned to future generations of martial artists."

TRAINING INFORMATION

- Belt Ranks & Martial Arts Styles: Sansai Ryu Kenjutsu - 8th Degree Black Belt (Kiyoshi), Sansai Ryu Karate - First Degree Black Belt

- Instructors/Influencers: Hanshi Philip Scudieri

- Birthdate: April 20, 1966

- Birthplace/Growing Up: Newark, Delaware

- Yrs. In the Martial Arts: 35 years

- Yrs. Instructing: 29 years

- Instructor

PROFESSIONAL ORGANIZATIONS

- All Japan Budo Federation Seibukan Academy - National Budo Governing Body of Japan

- Kenjutsu International Association of Instructors

I was first drawn to the martial arts by the cinema. What they showed in those films seemed utterly phenomenal but quite realistic at the same time. I was a physically active 18-year-old living at the beach for the summer. Ninja films were all the rage in those days, so I was looking for someone to teach me about Japanese swords. Of course, what the films fail to show is the amount of hard work that must be applied to obtain any degree of success in this endeavor. A friend mentioned that he was taking karate lessons from someone who was also introducing swordsmanship to his curricula. One Tuesday night, I decided to give the class a try and became instantly hooked. The workouts were hard, but I would not give up. When I returned to college, I was almost two and a half hours away from the dojo; I did not let that deter me and drove to the weekly class during my college career. Little did I know that my early fascination would lead to a lifelong commitment to the martial arts and the art of the sword.

PERSONAL ACHIEVEMENTS

- BA and MA degrees in Chemistry (University of Delaware)
- Doctor of Veterinary Medicine Degree (University of Pennsylvania)
- Major in the United States Army Reserve
- Veterinary Practice Owner
- Husband and Father of 2 children (both future Sword Masters)

MAJOR ACHIEVEMENTS

- Member of the US Delegation to the Nippon Budo Renmei (2011 & 2017)
- Led US Delegation (2019)

How has the study of martial arts not affected my life? When I first started studying martial arts, I was a college student with a challenging first year of college that resulted in my having the worst grades of my scholastic career. My decision to travel two and a half hours (each way) once a week to attend training at the dojo resulted in my spending the rest of my college career on the dean's list. I learned how to focus on training with a two-and-a-half-foot razor blade. Since those early days, Martial Arts has become a part of who I am. I cannot even imagine what my life would have been like without Kenjutsu to include fulfilling my dream of going to Japan. I have now gone to Japan three times, twice as a member of the US delegation, and the third time as the leader of the delegation. This way of life governs every aspect of my life. It allows me to be the leader I am in civic duties and my military duties. It has been my highest honor to pass along the knowledge I have gleaned to future generations of martial artists. I have been even more blessed that two of my children are amongst those ranks.

ANDRE RICHARDSON

"Martial arts allows me to be an example as a leader and a role model to my students and the karate population of New York City."

TRAINING INFORMATION

- Belt Ranks & Martial Arts Styles: AMERICAN GOJU RYU - 8th Degree Black Belt

- Instructors/Influencers: Kushinda Lamarr Thornton

- Birthdate: December 18, 1962

- Birthplace/Growing Up: New York City, NY

- Yrs. In the Martial Arts: 39 years

- Yrs. Instructing: 35 years

- School owner (Andre Richardson PowerZone Karate Institute), Instructor, Manager

PROFESSIONAL ORGANIZATIONS

- Karate Specialist for the Harlem Children Zone Inc.

I was in my first year of college when the community center across the street was giving free karate classes. I always wanted to learn karate, but I couldn't since my mother had me taking piano lessons from ages 5 to 15 and private piano classes were expensive. The karate class was made for students 5 to 16 years old. I wanted to learn, so I joined the school the summer of 1981.

Martial arts allows me to be an example as a leader and a role model to my students and the karate population of New York City. I became the 1st person out of New York to receive a "World Champion' status from a sanction Sport Karate league. I paved the way for other fighter to become World Champions. Fighter like Jesse Wray, Peter Allende, Jadi Tension, Akin Williams, Ross Levine, Hakim Walker.

PERSONAL ACHIEVEMENTS

- North American Sport Karate Association

- (NASK) Hall of Fame 1988 Men Fighting "Rookie of the Year" (It was a duel award with Pedro Xavier)

MAJOR ACHIEVEMENTS

- Opening up high-end night clubs for mogul Andrew Sasson in New York City, The Hamptons, and Las Vegas

I also had one of the 1st National Sport Karate Team in the NASKA circuit. The Power UP Karate Team. We were sponsored by Power Within Vitamins. I was credited for first introducing some of the top legends in Sport Karate. Donald and Ronald Brady, Kierston "Peaches" Sims, Shon "EA Ski" Adams. We took every # 1 weight class in fighting in Sport Karate leagues NASKA, NBL and PKL.

KYM ROCK

"My life has had a significant impact on changing the way women and girls learn self-defense..."

I started the martial arts in the '80s with now Hanshi Jerry Lemon to learn to defend myself and get away from an abusive young husband. I found out early on that there were not enough women in the martial arts and that the train was more geared to the male body. I even went so far as to tell my Sensei," This karate is stupid and did not work." My partner at the time said, "You are doing it right. It just doesn't work for you." We did not know it at the time, but this was Fight Like a Girl's birth. I would put forth situation after situation to my Sensei, and we would work on it until we came up with a solution to escape. New ways of sparring as well. I found I had a unique gift and made up my mind. I was going to win every tournament I could. Get as many credentials as possible. Then move on with my plan to get women to take personal responsibility for their safety. Also, I wanted martial arts studios to flourish and appeal to women and girls.

So, I created the Fight Like A Girl program to change the statistics of violence in our world and teach women and kids personal violence prevention. Over 2 million women and girls have attended our seminars. A twenty-one proven program of unique techniques and skills developed by Kym Rock and her Sensei teaches women and girls to think smarter and get away from an attacker, abductor, or abuser.

TRAINING INFORMATION

- Belt Ranks & Martial Arts Styles: Okinawan Karate, 7th Degree, Fight Like a Girl, 8th Degree

- Instructors/Influencers: Master Hanshi Gerald L. Lemon, Master Ogawa

- Birthdate: August 13, 1964

- Birthplace/Growing Up: Williamsburg, VA/Deltaville, VA/ Nags Head, NC

- Yrs. In the Martial Arts: 37.5 years

- Yrs. Instructing: 32 years

- School owner, Manager & Instructor at U.S.A. Karate Center

PROFESSIONAL ORGANIZATIONS

- A.A.U.
- U.S.A. Karate-Do Han Japan Association
- U.S.A. Karate Federation, W.K.U.

PERSONAL ACHIEVEMENTS

I think my achievements have a direct relation to my martial arts. One of the best gifts God Blessed me with to share with others and helping them. Helped me so much more than any of my students will ever know. I learned just as much from them as they did from me. Most recent personal is I am back in college after all of these years finishing my Degree during the COVID crisis. My goal is to have my bachelor's, so when this is over, I can create a much larger platform to help as many as I can.

MAJOR ACHIEVEMENTS

A resourceful, creative, hard-working, and self-motivated achiever with a love of organizing and helping people. My goal in life is to stop the senseless violence against women and children by instilling the ability to be motivated not to become victims. Founder and creator of the largest personal violence, sexual assault, domestic abuse, bullying prevention, and school shooting survival program, Fight Like A Girl.

- AAU Karate Sports Director for Colorado

- Fight Like A Girl program, and Kym Rock featured on Fox News national broadcast

- Fight Like a Girl book: Be Scared with a Plan

- Fight Like a Girl mobile app - available on iTunes and Google Play

- Keynote Speaker for Girl Scouts international conference of over 10,000 girls

- Implemented first Girl Scouts statewide program training instructors and hosting seminars in each region. Fight Like A Girl badge earned by Scouts.

Our mission is to make a difference in the horrendous statistics of violence and abuse worldwide by teaching escape techniques and life skills.

The program encompasses seminars and on-going classes that empower women and kids to have greater self-esteem by knowing these physical and mental life skills to grow to their full potential. Fight Like A Girl is fun, always active, and creates a vibrant community of people who can make a difference through personal violence prevention.

Because my life has had a significant impact on changing the way women and girls learn self-defense and what I overcame in her life to be where I am today, my life is being depicted in a Hollywood Feature Film called "Fight Like A Girl!" The true story of a real female karate kid, Meta Hara Productions.

MAJOR ACHIEVEMENTS

- U.S. Department of Justice Meeting with Director on September 19, 2018, to discuss implementing our programs worldwide.

- Training of U.S. Navy Flight Officers in our program skills at Oceana Naval Air Station in Virginia Beach, Virginia.

- "The Life Magazine" Fight Like A Girl Front Cover Feature

- Kym Rock featured on Martial Arts Success Magazine with Bruce Lee, Joe Lewis, Ernie Reyes, and Aaron Ralston. Personal Violence Prevention Specialist Endorser for Yellow Jacket Stun Gun Phone Case

- Hollywood Feature Film is currently in development about her life: Fight Like A Girl

- Positive Power Anti-Bullycide

- Fight Like A Girl. U.S.A. Karate Center.org & Dragon Peak Martial Arts Owner and President. 1997-present.

- Self-defense company instructing women and girls

- Nationwide speaking engagements and interactive seminars concerning travel safety, situational awareness, anger management, rape prevention, child abduction awareness, escape techniques, and basic self-protection

- Conduct full-scale girl scout events, large corporate seminars, school groups, and women's events. I contracted the first statewide initiative in Colorado for the Girl Scout of America Fight Like A Girl Scout Program

- The contract for Fight Like A Girl book series

Martial arts has taught me how to handle things, I think, in a much better light than those who do not know the martial artist's way. Most of all, the best thing is to see how you have impacted the people you have helped and understand how they are doing the same and positively contribute to society. Kindness: please pass it on!

MAJOR ACHIEVEMENTS

- Hollywood Feature Film in Development about her life Called Fight Like a Girl Movie contract with MetaHara Productions.

- Launched the Positive Power Karate Program in Eagle County Schools focusing on bullycide & suicide prevention, self-esteem building, social-emotional education, teaching respect for each other, school shooting survival, rape prevention, abduction prevention, and lastly, learning Japanese Competition Karate with no expense to the kids who need it the most

- Coach and Instructor U.S.A. Karate Center located in Fight Like A Girl Training Center and Dragon Peak Martial Arts 25 Eby Creek Road, Eagle CO

- Has coached and lead 100's of student to regional, national and international championships

- Vail Land Company Partner, Broker, and development strategist 2016 to present

- Awarded Women's Warrior Award in 2008 for distinguished service regarding women's and girls' safety by Vagina Monologues Host Kim Reese

- Featured on the Hallmark Channel "Naomi's New Morning,' Host Naomi Judd

- Key Note Speaker, Deloitte & Touche' Manhattan, New York Education For Youth Conference, Working Mother Media Congress Manhattan

- Outer Banks Karate, Owner and President, 1995 – 2009, Nags Head, NC

- Full Time Instructor, Owner and Operator-Instructed children and adults from ages 5-65

- Coached students to national and world titles

- Trained and graduated 65 black belts

MAJOR ACHIEVEMENTS

- I earned a Master's (7th) Degree in Shorinryu Karate

- Weapons Expert

- Director of operations - scheduled all technicians for yacht installations and repairs, return authorization specialist for faulty equipment, Office Manager

- Author of Fight LIke a Girl BE Scared with a Plan

- Signed Movie Contract for Fight Like a Girl Hollywood Feature Film MetaHara Productions

- Creator Founder of the Largest Personal Violence Program for Women and Girls Life Time Member Corp Combative M.C.M.A.P. Leon Wright

- Shorinryu Japanese Karate 7th Dan Kyoshi

- Hanshi 8th Dan Fight Like a Girl M.M.A.

- 7 Time World Karate Champion

- Presented National Program to Katie Sullivan Office of Violence Against Women 2018 D.O.J. Featured Segment Fight Like a Girl Fox News National

MAJOR ACHIEVEMENTS

- Speaker/Presenter G.I.R.L. 2017 over 10,000 attendees

- T.V. 8 Self Defense Contributor

- Key Note Speaker Working Mother Media

- Awarded Women's Warrior Award in 2008 for distinguished service regarding women's and girls' safety Hallmark Channel segment featuring Fight Like A Girl program.

- 2-time World Karate Hall of Fame

- 5-time U.S.A. Karate Hall of Fame

- U.S.A. Female Martial Arts Instructor of the Year

- U.S.A. Martial Arts Competitor of the Year

- U.S.A. Self Defense Instructor of the Year

- Vice-chair Hotline Domestic Violence Shelters 2006- 2008

HAYME SERRATO

"Martial arts has taught me self-control, respect for others, and a positive perspective to strive for the best in me."

TRAINING INFORMATION

- Belt Ranks & Martial Arts Styles: Shaolin Kung Fu Green Sash, American FreeStyle Green Belt, Tang Soo Do 8th Degree Black Belt, Combat Hapkido 1st Degree Black Belt, Korean Hapkido 2nd Degree Black Belt, Kage Iaijutsu Ryu Sword 1st Degree Black Belt

- Instructors/Influencers: GM David Praim, GM Henry Fuentes, GM James Saffold, Senior GM Koe Woong, GM John Pellegrini, GM Joe Sanders

- Birthdate: July 29, 1953

- Birthplace/Growing Up: Fredericksburg, TX

- Yrs. In the Martial Arts: 47 years

- Yrs. Instructing: 40 years

- School owner & Instructor at Hayme Serrato's Martial Arts

PROFESSIONAL ORGANIZATIONS

- PKA
- PKC
- ISKA
- NASKA
- MSKC

I thought there was a mystery to martial arts at a very young age. In junior high, I used to go to the library to look at karate books and was intrigued by the judo throws and kicks illustrated in the books. Growing up in a small town in the Southwest, martial arts was not popular. I didn't get involved in Shaolin Kung Fu until I moved to Michigan in 1973. This was when my karate career began. After being involved in Shaolin Kung Fu for 1 1/2 yrs, I received a green sash. From here, I moved into the study of American FreeStyle Karate. I then moved onto Tang Soo Do with GM David Praim. I started competitions in 1976, and this is when I truly fell in love with martial arts. From there, I have never looked back.

After receiving my 1st degree black belt in Tang Soo Do in 1979, I opened my school in 1981. After many years of teaching students and furthering my knowledge, I progressed through the black belt ranks and now have an 8th degree-Grand Master in Tang Soo Do under Grand Master

PERSONAL ACHIEVEMENTS

- Receiving my black belts
- Owning my martial arts school
- 40+ years in the martial arts

MAJOR ACHIEVEMENTS

AWARDS & ACCOMPLISHMENTS

- 1980 to 2000 Michigan Karate Circuit top competitor in Weapons, Forms & Sparring
- 1982 to 1984 Karate Institute's competitor of the year
- 1993 Elected by the Michigan Karate Circuit Board of Directors as "Michigan's Most Outstanding Referee" for his honesty (integrity), sportsmanship.
- 1990 to 2000 North American Sport Karate Association (NASKA) Top Ten Competitor's in Senior Sparring National Karate Circuit and fairness (impartiality).

KICKBOXING

- 1982 to 1985 For three years, Mr. Serrato trained under Terry Shipman and Kerry Roop. Full Contact & Kick Boxing, with a record of 3 wins – 1 loss.
- 1984 Awarded Class "A" Official Certification by Don Quine of the Professional Karate Association (PKA)
- 1989 Awarded Class "A" Official Certification by Don Willis of the Professional Karate Commission (PKC)
- 1993 Awarded Class "A" Official Certification by the International Sport Karate Association (ISKA)

James Saffold. Some of my most significant accomplishments have been to teach over 10,000+ students and to promote over 300 Black Belts.

In my teaching endeavors, I have had many students compete statewide, nationally, and worldwide. Several of these students have gone as far as earning gold medals in forms, weapons, and sparring.

I also started promoting my own martial arts tournaments in 1981 to the present. These tournaments are one of the oldest tournaments in Michigan and have given me the chance to further the art and grow as a martial artist.

Over many years of owning and teaching in a martial art school, my philosophy is on the life cycle. What you put into life is what comes back to you. You are only as good as what your efforts are in life.

MAJOR ACHIEVEMENTS

TV SPOTS

- 1983 to 1992 Produced "Martial Arts Today" for Comcast cable television. The show introduced the many Martial Arts styles to the public, educated its audience about Martial Arts' true nature, and dispelled any misconceptions about karate.

HALL OF FAME

- 2004 MSKC – In recognition of being one of the top karate instructors & referees in the open Michigan Sport Karate Circuit

- 2004 Detroit International Class of 2004 Hall Of Fame -in honor of hard work, dedication and support to the martial arts community

- 2006 Huron Valley Karate 25th Anniversary – in recognition of 25 years of excellence in the martial arts

- 2007 United States Martial Artist Association Hall Of Fame – Golden Life Achievement for Tang Soo Do

- 2008 Yellow Tigers Karate Hall Of Fame

- 2008 World Council Of Martial Arts Hall Of Fame

- 2012 Legends of the Martial Arts Hall Of Fame

- 2017 World Tang Soo Do Federation Hall of Fame – Outstanding Tang Soo Do Master

- 2019 American Kwan Tang Soo Do Federation Hall of Fame – Award 40 Plus Years

Before starting karate, I felt lost in my life. I left the only home I knew and traveled 1500 miles to restart my life in Michigan. I was young and lonely and didn't know where to turn. I reached deep inside myself and realized the one thing I wanted to explore was karate. At the age of 20, I began martial arts, and this life choice has been my best choice in life. Martial arts has taught me self-control, respect for others, and a positive perspective to strive for the best in me. I can never repay what I have learned, earned, and respected. The only way I can show my gratitude is to continue to teach and give back to the very thing that has brought me where I am today.

JAMES STEVENS

"Through the philosophies of Karate, I've applied its principles to master other trades."

TRAINING INFORMATION

- Belt Ranks & Martial Arts Styles: Founded Stevens Karate-Do, a combination of Karate, Judo & Aikido

- Instructors/Influencers: Grand Master David Yamens

- Birthdate: December 27, 1948

- Birthplace/Growing Up: Galveston Island, TX/Hitchcock, TX

- Yrs. In the Martial Arts: 55 years

- Yrs. Instructing: 54 years

- School owner & Instructor at Stevens Karate-Do

PROFESSIONAL ORGANIZATIONS

- Universal Black Belt Hall of Fame
- Masters Black Belt Hall of Fame
- Texas Black Belt Hall of Fame

James Stevens, a Native Texan, born on Galveston Island, competed during a time when Martial Arts was exploding on the scenes in America—a time distinguished by its tenacious and legendary fighters. From the late '60s to the early '70s, this era produced World Champions: Chuck Norris, Joe Lewis, Howard Jackson, Skipper Mullins, Jeff Smith, Mike Stone, Bill Wallace and Linda Denley.

During this same phenomenal era, James Stevens won over 60 Championship Awards. Extraordinarily, in over 1/3 of these tournaments, he earned 20 Grand Championship Titles. By 1974, he was ranked as the #1 Fighter in the Southwest by Professional Karate Magazine. These feats are made even more amazing when one considers that James Stevens, as a true lightweight class competitor, defeated opponents who were often 30 to 50 pounds heavier.

Whether known as the "Louisiana Lightning Bolt" or as described by Black Belt Magazine as the Master of the Take Down, James Stevens competed in many memorable bouts against such top competitors as Darnell Garcia (Top Ten), Skipper Mullins (World Champion), Jeff Smith

PERSONAL ACHIEVEMENTS

- Donating time and money to underserved communities

MAJOR ACHIEVEMENTS

- James Stevens won over 60 Championship Awards.
- Earned 20 Grand Championship Titles
- 1974, Ranked as the #1 Fighter in the Southwest by Professional Karate Magazine.
- Appeared in Black Belt Magazine 1972 and 1974
- Official Karate Magazine- Article - King of the Takedowns

(World Champion), Fred Wren (Top Ten), and Jim Butin (Top Ten).

It was Mr. Butin's opinion, in a published interview, that James Stevens was pound for pound the hardest-hitting competitor he ever fought, an opinion shared by many.

James Stevens, the product of the aggressively rugged style of Karate, received his 1st Black Belt in only 15 months under the instruction and guidance of Sensei David Yamens. Mr. Yamens is a Black Belt Instructor under Mr. Robert Moore. He was a direct student of the late Grandmaster Robert Trias, 9th Degree Black Belt and founder of the United States Karate Association and member of the Black Belt Hall of Fame.

During the ensuing years, James Stevens trained with such notable instructors as Master Kim Soo (Tae Kwon Do), Master Pat Burleson, Master Takayuki MiKami (JKA Shotokan), and the legendary Texas Judo-Ka and member of the Black Belt Hall of Fame – Master Kari Geis.

After a year of teaching Martial Arts at the College of the Mainland, James Stevens opened his 1st Karate Institution, The Island Karate School, on Galveston Island in 1966. Via Youth Outreach Programs, Rape Prevention Workshops, Self Defense Seminars, and Defensive Tactics training of Law Enforcement, he has rendered unselfish service to the community.

The Official Karate Magazine noted his humanitarianism when Stevens held a Karate tournament, then gave all the proceeds to the League of Latin Americans Scholarship Fund.

Grand Master James Stevens has trained many top competitors and skilled martial artists including Robert Beverly 9th Ku Dan, Nathaniel Beverly 9th Ku Dan, the late Ronald (Candy) Lewis 8th Dan, Rev. Eugene Pack 8th Dan, Anthony Johnson 8th Dan, Wayne Vallie 7th Dan, Ishmael Robles, Al Frances, Raymond McClan, Jessie Benavidez and Curtis Dunbar. As a tournament official, Grand Master Stevens is a highly respected referee in the South West. He is especially noted for his objective and expeditious officiating within the Amateur Organization of Karate (AOK), National Blackbelt League (NBL), Sport Karate International (SKI).

After 20 years retired from competition, Stevens earned a World Breaking Title (NBL) in 1994 and 1995. He was inducted into the Universal Martial

Arts 2003 and Master Hall of Fame 2006. He was also inducted into the Texas Black Belt Hall of Fame in 2020. Recently, He was appointed Board Member of the Texas Police Association of Tactical Training.

Grand Master Stevens had to reduce his participation in the tournament circuit to care for his loving wife, Rose, who was diagnosed with terminal lung cancer. After the chemotherapy treatments, she became bedridden, where he remained by her side. He cared for her until she passed away ten years later on March 9, 2020.

As an instructor of Grand Master Yamens legacy, he hosts a number of trained black belts that continue to teach Stevens Karate-Do.

Today, Grand Master James Stevens, a noted Karate competitor, instructor, and referee, continues to teach and inspire other aspiring martial artists, both young and old alike.

"Martial Arts totally changed my life in every aspect. Through the philosophies of Karate, I've applied its principles to master other trades. Most importantly, how to treat and respect people from all walks of life. "

TONY GARCIA TABOADA

"In Taekwondo and how all the other martial arts are, the most important is the road, the constant learning, the process of always being better..."

TRAINING INFORMATION

- Belt Ranks & Martial Arts Styles: 8th Dan TAEKWONDO ITF

- Instructors/Influencers: GM Orlando Vega

- Birthdate: November 4, 1959

- Birthplace/Growing Up: Caracas, Venezuela

- Yrs. In the Martial Arts: 44 years

- Yrs. Instructing: 40 years

- School owner & Instructor at GTG VENEZUELA

PROFESSIONAL ORGANIZATIONS

- ITF The Americas
- Taekwondo Hall Of Fame
- Master Hall Of Fame
- ITF HQ
- Sports Glorys Of Carabobo
- Sport Glorys Of Venezuela
- Blacks Belt School Of Venezuela

From a very young age, I had an attraction for Martial Arts and sport. I've always played all the traditional sports like soccer, basketball, baseball, and others. One day, I decided to start in the world of martial arts around the '70s with the GM Chong Koo Lee, which started to teach Venezuela classes. I was one of the first participants and pioneers in my country achieving important triumphs and international representations. Every day it involved more practice of Taekwondo. Because of my staying focused, I developed the most important academy in my country around the 80's. GM Suk Jun Kim and the GM Orlando Vega each played an important role in my career because of their extraordinary capacity to teach the martial arts.

The success in the nationals and international tournaments and championships, personal and professional level of my students and disciples, contributed that my commitment to the Taekwondo and their

PERSONAL ACHIEVEMENTS

- Black belt 8th Dan Taekwondo
- Master International of Taekwondo
- Judge International of Taekwondo
- Member of The Taekwondo Hall of Fame (New York 2017)
- Member of Master Hall of Fame (Los Angeles 2012)
- International represent of ITF Las Americas in Venezuela
- Member of the Committee of Ethic of ITF Las Americas
- Member of the Committee of verification of Danes of ITF Las Americas
- National Director of Venezuela for Taekwondo Hall of Fame
- One of the pioneers of Taekwondo in Venezuela
- Founder Member of The Taekwondo Association of the Carabobo Estate /Venezuela
- Founder Member of The Pro Federation of Taekwondo of Venezuela
- President of The Association Sport Glories of Carabobo Estate
- President of GTG ITFA Venezuela
- Vice-President of Black Belts School of Venezuela
- Official 1st winner of Taekwondo of Venezuela (II Pan-American of W.T.F of Taekwondo Guayaquil, Ecuador 1980)
- National Champion of Taekwondo 1979, 1980 and 1981
- National Sub champion of Taekwondo 1978 and 1982
- Sub champion of the 1st International Championship of Caribbean 1980 (Combat)

personal growth even in the national and international competitions increase every day more and more, even today.

The martial arts had a big impact in my life, because thanks to the multiple achievements that I reached, I got involved more in the world of sports. My university studies were in Mechanic Engineering. I had an orientation for the design and development of physical equipment for the physical conditioning and design of gyms and sports installations, making me develop more than 200 projects in Venezuela.

The sport management and trajectory in this field have contributed to the founding of important sports and sociable associations in my country. This contributes to Taekwondo's development and the sport in general, making a great satisfaction for the kids and young men who change their entire life for good thanks to martial arts and sport.

In Taekwondo and how all the other martial arts are, the most important is the road, the constant learning, the process of always being better and if we would concentrate on the road, all the goals will be achieved and met.

PERSONAL ACHIEVEMENTS

- Champion Shapes of the 1st International Championship of Caribbean (Shapes)

- Champion of the Inter-American Tournament of Martial Arts 1982, 1983 and 1984

- Champion of the Continental Tournament of Martial Arts 1981 and 1982

- Champion of the International Tournament of Full Contact of Caribbean

- Multiple champions in International Tournament of Martial Arts and Taekwondo in Puerto Rico, Dominican Republic, U.S.A, Canada, Ecuador, and Europe

- National Champion for Teams of Taekwondo 1980, 1981, 1982, 1983, 1984, 1985 and 1986

- Coach and Technical Director with more Triumphs in Taekwondo of Venezuela 1980, 1981,N 1982, 1983, 1984, 1985 and 1986

- Coach of the Greatest Athletes and Champions of the nation, an international

- Founder and directive of many sports organizations and associations

- International Sport and Technical adviser

- Public and private security and personal defender adviser and pacification of many organisms

- Mechanic Engineer

PERSONAL ACHIEVEMENTS

- Degrees in Sports Administration and Management, Design of equipment for physical conditioning, Human Resources, Teaching formation for Martial Arts Instructors, Administration and Planning of sports installations, sports phycology, Physic Conditioning for athletes of high capacity and Sport Science

- Technical Director of multiple gyms in Venezuela

- Recognized and decorated by many estate organisms, governmental including The President of The Republic of Venezuela in 1983, 1986 y 2013

- Multiple recognitions of sports associations and clubs from different sport disciplines of the nation

- Different works and publications of Sport, Physical Conditioning, and Martial Arts in journals and specialized magazines.

- Over 200 sports projects and sports installations develop in Venezuela

MAJOR ACHIEVEMENTS

- 8th Dan of Taekwondo

- More than 45 years practicing Taekwondo

- Several times National and International champion

- One of the pioneers and 1st WTF medalist in Venezuela at the II Pan American Taekwondo Championship, Ecuador 1980

- International judge

- Director of ITF the Americas in Venezuela

- Official member of Taekwondo Hall of Fame since 2017

- Official member of Masters Hall of Fame since 2012

- Recognized and decorated by many estate organisms, governmental including The President of The Republic of Venezuela in 1983, 1986 & 2013

STEPHEN THOMPSON

"Martial Arts encouraged me to stay physically fit and mentally strong."

TRAINING INFORMATION

- Belt Ranks & Martial Arts Styles: Taekwondo (Geedokwan) - 1st Degree Black Belt, International Taekwondo - 1st Degree Black Belt, Japanese Shotokan - 10th Degree Black Belt, Kushindaryu - 10th Degree Black Belt Kyokushin

- Instructors/Influencers: Master Lamar Thornton, Master Henry Cho, Master Kwang Duk Chung, Master Errol Bennett

- Birthdate: July 2, 1952

- Birthplace/Growing Up: Bronx, NY

- Yrs. In the Martial Arts: 55 years

- Yrs. Instructing: 15 years

- Instructor

PROFESSIONAL ORGANIZATIONS

- Central Baptist Church

The reason I got into Martial Arts was that I wanted to compete against the best. Martial arts was a way for me to learn discipline and push myself to a higher level. My parents always told me that with my Lord and Savior Jesus Christ, nothing could stop me. One of the many ways that statement became true was through fighting the best in the world. People such as Albert Cheeks, Steve Anderson, Richard Plowden, Terry Cramer, Anthony Price, Andre Richardson, and many more.

Andre Richardson was my sparring partner who introduced me to the new way of fighting and brought me to the national and international circuits. Master Lamar Thornton and Master Errol Bennett were my teachers and trainers; they were both a great inspiration to me. I am grateful for one of the things through competing. I fought people from Japan, Korea, England, Canada, and the United States. I had the opportunity to meet people from different countries and cultures. I also had the chance to mentor young men and women from the inner city and beyond.

PERSONAL ACHIEVEMENTS

- Ordained Pentecostal and Baptist Minister
- Husband and Father
- Military - Army/Marines
- Retired from NYC Department of Corrections
- Retired from Florida Department of Corrections
- College graduate

Martial Arts encouraged me to stay physically fit and mentally strong. It played a big part in me doing well in the military and with the department of corrections. I also must thank my parents and my Lord and Savior, Jesus Christ, for allowing me to be a part of something so inspirational.

BILL VIOLA, SR.

"The more you sweat in here, the less you bleed out there."

TRAINING INFORMATION

- Belt Ranks & Martial Arts Styles: : Shotokan 9th Dan, Co-creator of the sport mixed martial arts in United States Kickboxing

- Instructors/Influencers: Teruyuki Okazaki (JKA) Robert Trias (USKA) and George Anderson (USAKF)

- Birthdate: November 5, 1947

- Birthplace/Growing Up: Brownsville, PA

- Yrs. In the Martial Arts: 60+ years

- Yrs. Instructing: 51 years

- School owner & Instructor, Shihan

PROFESSIONAL ORGANIZATIONS

- USA Karate (USAKF)
- USA National Karate Federation (USANKF)
- United States Karate Association (USKA)
- Police Athletic League (PAL)
- Champions Association
- North American Sport Karate Association (NASKA)
- Sport Karate Museum History General
- World Karate Commission (WKC)
- United States Association of Martial Artists

Viola got his first taste of combat sports in 1955, studying boxing from a family friend, the legendary Marion "Slugger" Klingensmith (later to become the Pennsylvania State Athletic Commissioner, Brownsville Mayor and Police Chief, Fayette County Commissioner, and Congressman). He discovered martial arts in the early 1960s as a teenager in high school. Viola recalls, "My friend Medick Capirano picked up karate at WVU in the ROTC program. I thought I was pretty tough, but he threw me all over the room when we'd work out on the weekends. I was addicted." He continued training throughout college at California State under The All-American Karate Federation, a split-off from the Japanese Karate Association (under Teruyuki Okazaki), and then gaining rank under icons Grandmaster Robert Trias, the father of American Karate, and Grand Master George Anderson, the founder of the Father of Olympic Karate.

Viola Sr., now 73, still teaches his black belt class every Monday evening, a reminder to everyone that karate is a lifelong journey. In fact, Ray Adams, 76, joined the club in 1971 and is still actively training today.

PERSONAL ACHIEVEMENTS

- Allegheny Shotokan Karate (1969-2019) celebrates its 50th anniversary as the gold standard for martial arts in Western PA. The family-owned and operated dojo is blessed with three generations of Violas who carry on the legacy. All five of Viola's children have earned black belts and his eldest, Sensei Bill Viola Jr., now heads the school. Viola Jr.'s daughter Gabby and son Will [William Viola IV] are fixtures at the martial arts studio. Sr.'s other children Joce and Jacque, are Doctors of Pharmacy in North Huntingdon, Addie, a teacher in Bethel Park and Ali, a Lawyer downtown. He's proud that their karate foundation has helped them pave the way for fulfilling careers.

- Owner and founder of Viola Estates (Commercial and Residential) real estate company.

- 2020 recognized as "Illustrious Californian" by California University of Pennsylvania for lifetime achievements.

MAJOR ACHIEVEMENTS

- 1969 Founded Allegheny Shotokan Karate (Pittsburgh, PA)

- 1971-1972 Taught the first accredited marital arts activity course in a high school in the United States (East Allegheny School District).

- Viola has promoted over 200 events in his career, beginning in 1975 with karate and kickboxing competitions, followed by a host of unique productions including; The Crossroads Antique Faire, auctions, baseball card shows, martial arts banquets, seminars, and mixed martial arts fights.

He is the longest-tenured student and says, "I just earned my Master rank and have no plans of slowing down; my next test will be in my 80s." One of Adam's favorite training partners and the dojo's first black belt was Jack Bodell. Known as the "President's Bodyguard" as a member of the United States Secret Service in charge of protecting President Jimmy Carter, Jack explains, "Sensei gave me the skills to succeed in life." Jack Bodell, Ray Adams, Ray Walters, Dave Zezza, and Viola Jr. round out the "Master" ranks at Allegheny Shotokan. Viola Sr., 9th Degree Black Belt, remains the patriarch.

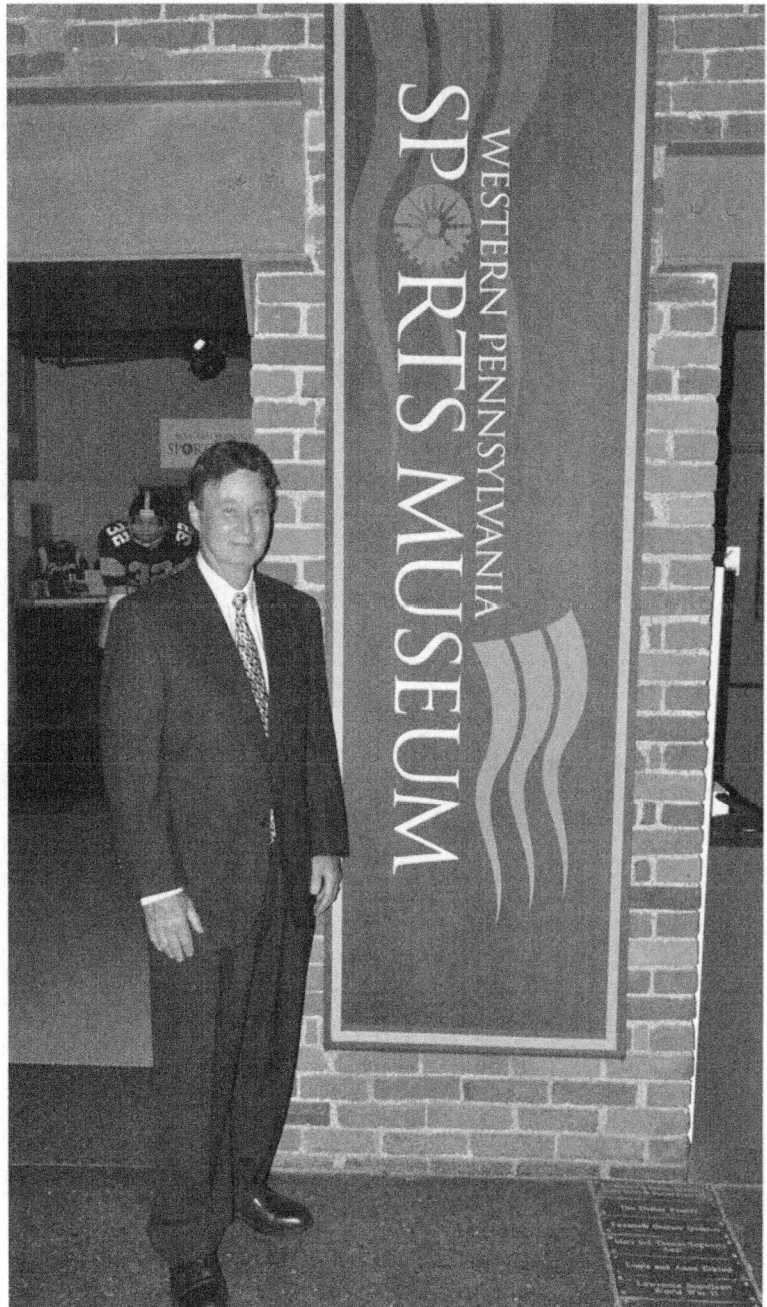

MAJOR ACHIEVEMENTS

- 1979 Co-founded CV Productions Inc., the first mixed martial arts company in America.

- 1979 wrote the first codified set of rules for mainstream MMA competition.

- CV Productions introduced regulated mixed martial arts competition to mainstream America.

- 1983 was subject to the first mixed martial arts law in United States history: The Tough Guy Law (Senate Bill 632).

- Arnold Schwarzenegger recognized Allegheny Shotokan Dojo as the number #1 team in America in 1998.

- Viola was inducted into the prestigious USA Karate Hall of Fame, who named him the Man of Year (2003) for distinguished service and lifetime achievement.

- As karate approaches its first Olympic berth at the 2021 Tokyo Games, Viola was instrumental in the movement as he hosted the USA Karate Jr. Olympics at the University of Pittsburgh's Fitzgerald Field House in 1992 under the auspices of the United States Olympic Committee. Incidentally, Viola Jr. was a triple Gold Medalist, the only athlete to earn that status. In March 2019, USA Karate honored Viola with the "Pioneer of USA Karate" award for his dedication to the Olympic karate movement.

- In 2011, Viola was honored with a permanent exhibit installed at the Western PA Sports Museum and Senator John Heinz History Center in association with Smithsonian institute recognizing him as the co-creator of the sport of Mixed Martial Arts (the display is located next to the Franco Harris "Immaculate Reception").

MAJOR ACHIEVEMENTS

- He was awarded the Champion Associations Willie Stargell M.V.P. Award (2011) for community service, a tribute that includes Michael Jordan and Muhamad Ali as an alum.

- His life was the subject of the books Godfathers of MMA (2014) and Tough Guys (2017), which peaked at #1 on the Amazon charts in the sports category in September 2017. The book was authored by his son Bill Viola Jr. The work, in turn, inspired the SHOWTIME documentary film Tough Guys (2017) produced by an Academy award winning team. Viola and his business partner Frank Caliguri were co-stars of the film, which ran for two years on the Showtime network. Tough Guys documents Pittsburgh, Pennsylvania, as the birthplace of modern MMA in the late 1970s and early 1980s, more than a decade before the creation of the Ultimate Fighting Championship (UFC).

- The dojo is internationally renowned as the most successful sport karate school in the Pittsburgh region, garnering the only dual Pan American Gold Medalists in both traditional karate (WUKO) now WKF and kickboxing (WAKO), as well as countless national, international, and world titles.

- The City of Pittsburgh, Pennsylvania named September 23rd, 2019 as "Sensei Viola Day" in the region to celebrate the 50th anniversary of Allegheny Shotokan Karate

Pioneers
MASTERS

HALEIGH ARNOLD

"I truly believe that God gave me many different talents, but my greatest one is teaching martial arts to so many people."

TRAINING INFORMATION

- Belt Ranks & Martial Arts Styles: 5th Degree Black Belt, Taekwon Do, Krav Maga, Brazilian Jiu Jitsu

- Instructors/Influencers: Rick Arnold

- Birthdate: March 1, 1996

- Birthplace/Growing Up: Sherman, TX

- Yrs. In the Martial Arts: 21 years

- Yrs. Instructing: 11 years

- Manager, Instructor

PROFESSIONAL ORGANIZATIONS

- United Taekwon Do Alliance

"I will never force you to do martial arts, but if you want to, we will do it right." My father, Rick Arnold, is a great martial artist. He has traveled, fought, and built a successful martial arts school, but his greatest achievement was raising four kids. With my dad being who he is, it was evident that at some point in my life, I would at least try martial arts; little did I know that my life would be changed by it.

I was never forced to train or compete; however, I was always taught that I could accomplish anything I put my mind to with hard work and determination. My father laid the stepping stones for me to pursue a career in martial arts. I quickly found out that the passion he had for martial arts became my passion from then on out.

I started martial arts as soon as I can remember and trained alongside my dad ever since. I began competing at age six and fell in love with the competition.

PERSONAL ACHIEVEMENTS

- All About M.A.D., Founder
- Bachelor of Arts Degree in Psychology with a minor in Business
- Head Instructor at Arnold's Martial Arts

MAJOR ACHIEVEMENTS

- Team USA Women's Captain 2014, 2015, 2017
- Instructor of the Year 2017
- International and National Champion

My favorite part of the competition is the people. Every place you go, you meet so many amazing people. On top of that, I got to travel with my family, which is always a plus. I competed all over the country, and then my dad decided it was time to compete internationally.

At the age of 17, I made the Women's USA Team through the United Taekwon Do Alliance and competed in Scotland in 2013. The Women's Team came home with both gold medals in forms and sparring. I had a taste of victory, and I didn't want to stop. From there, I competed against the English Teams in Florida in 2014, traveled to Italy and competed in the ITF competition in 2015, and competed in Scotland once again in 2017.

It has always been a dream of mine to teach alongside my dad. I began teaching for him when I was just 13 years old, assisting in classes. Now, I am his head instructor leading students daily in personal growth and success.

I have found my passion in serving others through martial arts and teaching. I truly believe that God gave me many different talents, but my greatest one is teaching martial arts to so many people. God put me on this path at such a young age because He knew that through the martial arts, I would help bring people to Jesus. I believe that the mat is my ministry. The most significant part of teaching martial arts is that I get to do it with my family. All four Arnold kids teach at the academy under my father; my mother is the glue that holds all of us together. Not to mention, I met my husband through the academy, too, so that is a plus. We have a motto at our academy, "One team, One family," and we show that love and mindset to our students daily.

Because of the skills I have learned through teaching and practicing martial arts, I have now started my non-profit called "Allaboutmad" which is about mad (making a difference) in the lives of different people through the martial arts. It is my goal to influence people in the Godly way to show them that they are not alone in this life, that no matter where they come from, they are loved, and that there is a plan, hope, and future for them (Jeremiah 29:11). I have been able to speak to hundreds of people about their passion and purpose in life. The martial arts have given me the confidence to pursue public speaking and follow my dreams.

I have been blessed with many opportunities to meet so many amazing people in the martial arts world. Men and women who have shaped me into the woman I am today. I have had the chance to travel all over the world, pursuing my passion. God has continuously shown his love for me through this sport and continues to open doors for me through martial arts. I am forever grateful for being born into a martial arts family and finding my calling.

KELVIN BASS

"Giving back to the community, helping kids and adults through my teaching and knowledge is my blessing."

TRAINING INFORMATION

- Belt Ranks & Martial Arts Styles: Tae Kwon Do (5th Degree Black Belt)

- Instructors/Influencers: Master Freddie Mcneil

- Birthdate: June 6, 1973

- Birthplace/Growing Up: Durham, NC

- Yrs. In the Martial Arts: 33 years

- Yrs. Instructing: 31 years

- Instructor

PROFESSIONAL ORGANIZATIONS

- Freddie Mcneil School of Taekwondo and Diversity Martial Arts, Durham, NC

- Hammer Kickboxing, Ft. Lauderdale, FL

- Team JBM JiuJitsu, Wilmington, NC

When I was younger, I used to watch Bruce Lee movies. I saw my first teacher Master Freddie Mcneil doing a demonstration in the mall and that's when I wanted to do martial arts.

Martial Arts has impacted me in a lot of ways with discipline, respect, leadership, family values, morals, self-control, hard work, focusing on a task, and helping people achieve goals! Giving back to the community, helping kids and adults through my teaching and knowledge is my blessing, and I want to help impact someone else's life through Martial Arts as it has helped me in my everyday life and Journey.

PERSONAL ACHIEVEMENTS

- 1988: North Carolina State Games Silver Medal in forms

- Regional karate champion in forms and fighting

- National Champion in fighting and forms and weapons

- 1998: 1st place in Korean forms 2 place in Olympic style taekwondo fighting Internationals Master Joon Lee

- USA Extreme Challenge, Fort Lauderdale FL

- Shiodkan Open in Ft Lauderdale, FL

- Battle Ground 2 and 3 Kickboxing

- 1st place IKF Kickboxing Senior's Division

MAJOR ACHIEVEMENTS

- Receiving my Black Belt Under Master Freddie Mcneil

- Fighting as a Professional fighter Kickboxing /MMA in South Florida

THOMAS BOYAJIAN, JR.

"Martial Arts is life to me. It's my religion, and it has taught me respect and discipline."

TRAINING INFORMATION

- Belt Ranks & Martial Arts Styles: Judo 1st Dan, Tang Soo Do 1st Dan, Goju-Ryu 5th Dan, Shuri-Ryu 5th Dan

- Instructors/Influencers: Grandmaster Victor Moore 10th Dan, Grandmaster Johnny Jelks 10th Dan, Grandmaster Laci Green 10th Dan, Sensei Chang Sun 3rd Dan

- Birthdate: February 4, 1978

- Birthplace/Growing Up: Cincinnati, OH

- Yrs. In the Martial Arts: 35 years

- Yrs. Instructing: 19 years

- Instructor

PROFESSIONAL ORGANIZATIONS

- Traditional World Karate Association

My late Uncle Tom Rizzo got me started into karate. When he came over, he would ask my siblings and me to punch him in the stomach for as long as I could remember. When I was five years old, he would do katas, punching the air and screaming really loud. My siblings and I used to think he was playing games; we used to run around and laugh. I dedicate my karate to him.

Growing up with Dyslexia had its limits. Martial Arts and Karate made me feel better about myself. It allowed me to see that there are no limits to what you can achieve with hard work and determination. Putting my mind to studying Martial Arts has improved my focus. It has taught me that all walks of life can benefit from Martial Arts. I love learning about the history of Martial Arts. Where all the different styles originated and how they have evolved over the years. It is essential to give that knowledge to my students so that they know where their karate comes from and have information about the other styles.

Having this knowledge is necessary because karate is more than fighting. It is more than certificates and trophies. Martial Arts is life to me. It's my

PERSONAL ACHIEVEMENTS

- Having attained the rank of Renshi (5th Dan) in two different styles of Karate: Shuri-Ryu and Goju-Ryu

MAJOR ACHIEVEMENTS

- Having my wonderful son, Tyler and my beautiful understanding wife, Stephanie

religion, and it has taught me respect and discipline. It has taught me to be humble. All the things I feel the world needs right now. It has given me the skills and techniques to be able to protect my friends, my family and loved ones, and myself. Being able to pass on those skills and that knowledge is my way of contributing to making the world a better place.

KELVIN B. CALDWELL

"Through the Martial Arts, I've been able to meet and train with some of my martial arts heroes and even work with them."

TRAINING INFORMATION

- Belt Ranks & Martial Arts Styles: 7th Dan - Integrated Taekwondo Systems, 7th Dan - Shorei Goju Ryu, 5th Dan - Integrated Tae Kwon Do, 2nd Dan - WTF Tae Kwon do, Blue Belt - Brazilian Ju-Jitsu, Instructor - Progressive Fight Systems

- Instructors/Influencers: Grand Master Kim Lee Wyong, Grand Master Preston, Grand Master Otis Baker, Sifu Paul Vunak, Sifu Dion Riccardo, Sifu Ron Balicki

- Birthplace/Growing Up: Chicago, IL

- Yrs. In the Martial Arts: 40 years

- Yrs. Instructing: 25 years

- School owner (Caldwell's Wellness Center), Manager, Instructor

PROFESSIONAL ORGANIZATIONS

- United Martial Arts Association

- Thompson Karate Federation

- International Private Security Federation

- Illinois Police Athletic League (Youth Combat Sports)

- United Mixed Martial Arts Alliance

- Parent Advisory board of (PAACT) Preventing Alcohol Abuse in Chicago

Around 1974, Instructor Kelvin Caldwell's older brother took him to see his first martial arts movies, Five Fingers of Death and Enter the Dragon. During that time, double features was the norm at the theaters. He really couldn't appreciate Five Fingers of Death at that time, especially due to the long death scene at the end of the movie. However, he stomached that movie because he really wanted to see the cool Chinese guy called Kato that kicked butt using his legs and feet on the Green Hornet TV series. to my students so that they know where their karate comes from and have information about the other styles. In the area where Instructor Caldwell grew up, boxing and wrestling were the preferred tools for the streets.

PERSONAL ACHIEVEMENTS

In 2001, Instructor Caldwell offered the first martial arts program for Maggie Daley's After Schools Matters - Sport 37 at the Austin YMCA on Central Ave. This program was featured on the local Chicago cable show "Chicago Works". In 2003, he opened Universal Touch Center which was not just a place where martial arts was being taught but where he served the needs of the inner city and at risk youth between the ages of 6–17 and their families. The goal was to keep the youth off the streets, out of gangs, reduce teen violence, and from doing drugs. In 2014, Instructor Caldwell opened the Sun of Ari-Ka Institute which was an extension and continuation of his first location teaching cultural arts as well as martial arts. Today, he is the founder of Caldwell's Wellness Center located on 5835 West Madison on Chicago's Westside (Austin community) where he offers youth martial arts programs, youth and family consulting, and meditation and mindfulness classes.

MAJOR ACHIEVEMENTS

In March 2014, Instructor Caldwell was acknowledged by the Illinois Martial Arts Hall of Fame as an Official. In March, 2018, he was inducted into the Illinois Martial Arts Hall of Fame. In April 2018, the Chicago Martial Arts Society recognized his 40 years in the Martial Arts Industry. February 2018, Grand Master Stan McKinney and Founder Grand Master Preston Baker promoted Instructor Caldwell to 7th Degree Black belt.

His older brother, who was 7 years older than him and in high school, was very excited about the character Kato and tried to reenact the moves that he saw on the television show. Even though his brother was into weights and wrestling, he wanted to learn martial arts, but just never got around to it. Nobody really took martial arts to learn how to fight, because the kids already knew how. Some of them were pretty good at it and sometimes they were brutal. Instructor Caldwell never wanted to fight, however in his household, running was not an option. If his parents heard that he ran, he would get a butt whipping from them. They had two rules: never fight a female and never run from a fight! If you get whipped, then you get whipped, but you make sure you get your licks in.

Instructor Caldwell's brother later received a job at a magazine distribution warehouse and he was able to get every martial arts magazine. Instructor Caldwell read all that he could about Bruce Lee, Jim Kelly, and the martial arts. When he turned thirteen, he didn't just decide to join the martial arts club, he was kind of forced. A gentleman named Major Adams ran the operation at the boys' club, he saw Instructor Caldwell throwing rocks, probably because he had nothing to do. Major Adams asked him what he was doing. Instructor Caldwell replied, "Nothing". Major Adams then asked if Instructor Caldwell thought he was tough. Instructor Caldwell replied, "Yes, tough enough!" Major Adams then directed him to the martial arts club at the boys' club.

Instructor Caldwell was a little apprehensive, even though he was familiar with some of the students there because he'd seen them around the neighborhood. Some of them went to high school and knew his older siblings. However, during the 70's, there weren't many children his age (12/13 years old) in the class. Most of the students were in high school or college and out of the Armed Service.

In 1978, Instructor Caldwell started his martial arts training in Shorei Goju Ryu Karate while living in the Henry Horner housing projects on Chicago's Westside. Sensei Lorraine and Jerry Norsworthy ran the satellite Karate Program at the Henry Horner Boys Club under the supervision of Baker's Dojo (Masters Preston and Otis Baker). He attended Westinghouse Vocational High school, and later he left Chicago to attend the Job Corp in Joliet, IL. While there, he learned many helpful life and personal development skills and also joined the boxing club.

In 1988, he tried Kickboxing at Super Kicks (owned by the late Kevin McClinton) in Maywood, IL. He later trained in Tae Kwon Do with Grand Master Dr. Duk Gun Kwon in Villa Park, IL. After Master Kwon sold the school to T-USA Martial Arts, he earned his black belt in Tae Kwon Do from Master Min Goo Seo and is registered with Kukkiwon from Seoul, Korea. Instructor Caldwell later continued his training to the rank of 5th degree black belt in Integrated Taekwondo under the late Master Kim Lee Wyung in Seoul Korea. He had the opportunity to obtain instructor ships in other martial arts systems as well.

During his Martial arts career, Instructor Caldwell attended seminars, workshops, and trained with some of the most experienced and renowned martial artists in the country like: Sifu Dion Riccardo, Paul Vunak, Guro Dan Inosanto, Sifu Ron and Diana Balicki, the late Joe Lewis, Bill Wallace, Shonie Carter, Michael Jai White, Frank Shamrock, Mike Lee Kanarek and the African Fighting Systems with Mwalimu John Poole and Ahati Kilindi Iyi, just to name a few.

In 2000, utilizing techniques from his personal training and many years of experience fighting in the martial arts, Instructor Caldwell trained, experimented, tested and documented his many years of experience in the fighting arts and formed Integrated Tae Kwon Do Systems; which is a blend of Traditional and Progressive Martial Arts such as,

Kelvin B. Caldwell, N.D.
Chief Instructor

Instructor Caldwell is a (ABC) Certified and licensed combat sports professional official and events consultant. He works as an official with the Illinois, Indiana, Iowa, Kansas, Wisconsin and Michigan Athletic Commissions, as well as many amateur sanctioning bodies. He has worked as an official for such events as the UFC, WEC, XFO, Strike Force, Bellator Fighting Championships, Glory Kickboxing, ESPN Boxing, Hitz Boxing, and many other Pro and Amateur fight sporting events throughout the United States. He has officiated thousands of bouts in MMA, Boxing, and Kickboxing combined. Instructor Caldwell is a proponent for training and continues to stay updated and current with his combat sports knowledge and its many changes.

Instructor Caldwell wanted to train in martial arts because he heard from a friend that it would help his basketball game due to the stretching and conditioning involved. He was on an elementary basketball team in the 7th and 8th grade and wanted to play in high school, so he thought joining would be a plus. Well, it turned out to be the best thing for his limited basketball career, but more importantly for his life.

Through the Martial Arts, he's been able to meet and train with some of his martial arts heroes and even work with them. Instructor Caldwell remembered when the UFC came out on television for the first time; he was immediately addicted. He never thought that he would have been a part of many of their pay per view and live productions and would have accomplished the things that he did. He has traveled almost the entire region of the United States excluding: Hawaii and Colorado. Most importantly, his martial arts career and programs has always focused on being a "Supplement to his students' Development", following the footsteps of those that provided that for him.

JASON COULTER

"The Martial Arts has taught me how to become a better person in life. It has brought me closer to my religion in Christ."

TRAINING INFORMATION

- Belt Ranks & Martial Arts Styles: Okinawan White Crane Method Karate, 6th degree Black Belt and Title of Shihan

- Instructors/Influencers: Tim Prodyma

- Birthdate: December 27, 1978

- Birthplace/Growing Up: Murphysboro, IL

- Yrs. In the Martial Arts: 25 years

- Yrs. Instructing: 20 years

- Instructor

PROFESSIONAL ORGANIZATIONS

- USA Martial Arts Hall Of Fame Grandmaster and Master Organization

I began training in the Martial Arts to have positive way of expressing myself, to learn how to defend myself, stay out of trouble in the neighborhood and to become a better person in life.

The Martial Arts has taught me how to become a better person in life. It has brought me closer to my religion in Christ. Through the principles of the martial arts has made me a better person at work through the discipline I have learned in the martial arts.

PERSONAL ACHIEVEMENTS

- 6th degree black belt and the title of Shihan
- Twice inducted into the USA Martial Arts Hall Of Fame
- Twenty years of teaching the martial arts

MAJOR ACHIEVEMENTS

- Earning my black belt
- Earning the rank of Rokudan and the title of Shihan
- Teaching my own Martial Arts class for kids and adults

WAYNE DEAN

"Martial arts impacted me in many ways. It taught me confidence in myself, humbleness, and appreciation for life."

TRAINING INFORMATION

- Belt Ranks & Martial Arts Styles: Kyokushinkia-Black Belt 3rd degree, Okinawa Kenpo-Black Belt 7th Degree

- Instructors/Influencers: Master Hulon Willis, Master Michael Morris, Hanshi George Epps, Master George Dillman, Mr. Danny Ray Bolton

- Birthdate: July 6, 1955

- Birthplace/Growing Up: Sutherland, VA/Petersburg, VA

- Yrs. In the Martial Arts: 51 years

- Yrs. Instructing: 48 years

- Instructor at Wayne Dean Dojo

PROFESSIONAL ORGANIZATIONS

- W.S.K.K.F

The Martial arts Journey started when Wayne Dean watched the Green Hornet on television and saw Bruce Lee jumping with a high kick to kick the lights out!!!! Wayne Dean Martial arts adventure started in 1970 While attending High School. Wayne used to sit in the stands at Virginia State at the old gym and watch karate classes taught every day by Master Hulon Willis and Master Mike Morse. One day Master Willis told him to come down and try it. Once he tried it, there was no turning back. Wayne dedicated himself to Karate. In 1973 Wayne started intense training and sparring with Instructor Danny Ray Bolton at the A.P. Hill Community Center. Bolton promoted Wayne up through the ranks until 1975, and he obtained the black belt. Five years of training in Kyokushinkia Karate paid off. After a brief period in Kung Fu, Wayne returned to studying under Danny Ray. In 1978 Wayne received his second degree from Mr. Bolton. 1984 after being Ni-Dan for six years, Master Willis had seen all the

PERSONAL ACHIEVEMENTS

Wayne Dean competed faithfully with his students in statewide tournaments and won several state black belt championships in the Virginia Karate Alliance. Held Statewide grand championships in sparring. Served with the United States Marines, and retired.

MAJOR ACHIEVEMENTS

- Won over 75 grand Championships in Fighting, taught a successful dojo, rated #1 on the east coast in fighting according to Karate Illustrated magazine, a proclamation for Wayne Dean Day in 1999 and 2009 for the city of Petersburg city named Wayne Dean day on October 16, 1999, and October 24, 2009

- Conducted Karate Workshops and demonstrations free of charge for churches, community, and civic organizations striving in Petersburg

progress and accomplishments Wayne has done and bestowed the third degree. After Danny Ray moved from the area and the passing of Master Willis, Wayne trained and studied with Master George Dillman. Dillman promoted Wayne to San-Dan in Okinwan-Te. In 1987 Wayne had a thirst for knowledge, and the thirst led him to George Epps. After meeting and surpassing the requirements for promotion in Okinawa Kenpo, Wayne was promoted to fourth degree. To this day, Wayne and George still train together, which Wayne is now a seventh degree in the Okinawa Kenpo style. Wayne Dean has competed in over 500 tournaments and won over 75 grand championships in the fighting. The Wayne Dean Dojo was established in A.P. Hill Community center during the late '70s. When the center closed, he continued to teach through parks and recreation. He has held his own business in the community, Wayne Dean teaching Okiinawa Kenpo to this day at Prince George Recreation Department in Prince George Virginia, and has another location in Petersburg Virginia.

Studying Martial arts impacted me in many ways. It taught me confidence in myself, humbleness, and appreciation for life. Martial Arts taught me the value of discipline and routine. Martial Arts taught me how to respect and interact with people. Having the opportunity to travel to new places, meet people, and experience things I would never have otherwise got to experience.

DONNIE ELLIXSON, JR.

"The world is still a beautiful place if you know where to look and have the right perspective."

TRAINING INFORMATION

- Belt Ranks & Martial Arts Styles: Okinowan Seibukan Karate, ITF Tae Kwon Do, Jhoon Rhee System, Hapkido, Boxing, Kickboxing, Muay Thai, Sport Karate, 5th Degree Black Belt Tae Kwon Do, Brown Belt in Okinowan Seibukan

- Instructors/Influencers: Grand Master John Chung, Sensei Robert Bobak, Trained with: Bill 'Superfoot' Wallace, Ross Levine, Grandmaster Jhoon Rhee, Grandmaster Moo Yong Lee, Joyce Gracie

- Birthdate: April 6, 1974

- Birthplace/Growing Up: Virginia, VA

- Yrs. In the Martial Arts: 39 years

- Yrs. Instructing: 32 years

- School owner (Ellixson's Tae Kwon Do Academy), Instructor

PROFESSIONAL ORGANIZATIONS

- Ellixson's Tae Kwon Do Academy - President

- Ellixson's Elite National Competition Team - Head Coach

- World Forms & Fighting Champion John Chung Tae Kwon Do Institute - Student

As I started teaching and sharing my experiences and my mistakes, I realized I had a unique ability to inspire others to improve themselves through martial arts. I quickly realized that to be on top of my craft; I had to invest in continuing education. I became a sponge, attending any martial arts or business seminar I could, absorbing as much information as I could. I attended martial arts and business seminars from the likes of Jhoon Rhee, Anthony Robbins, and Tommy Lee. I studied Zig Ziglar's "Yes I Can" program and attended conventions of EFC, IFC, MAIA, and NAPMA. These seminars taught me a lot about systemizing, staff training, networking, and marketing. What I found a hard time connecting with was the high-powered selling that was popular in the 1990s. I quickly realized that the 'sales' end of my business strategy would be to teach good martial arts and turn out good martial artists, period... end of story. So, to do that, I needed to offer my students the best instruction possible, so I sought out Grandmaster John Chung. I asked him if he would take me on as a student, he said yes, and our journey began. For 15 years, I ran my school with a 200-250 student enrollment in a small town of about 5,000.

In May of 2009, I had a great opportunity to buy the property where my martial arts school was located. For a kid who has been on his own since the age of 16, this was a fantastic opportunity. It was the chance of a lifetime and a chance to get ahead. I purchased the property.

PERSONAL ACHIEVEMENTS

- After 39 years in martial arts, I have managed to stay true to myself, instructor, students, and my art

- Inspiring my students to become black belts, instructors, tournament champions, or be the best at whatever they do in life.

- Out of hundreds of sport karate wins and an undefeated kickboxing record, my students are my greatest accomplishment.

- I can see the good in people and Remind them of it.

- To work with, inspire, and light the spark for the next generation of martial artists.

- To work in an industry filled with individuals who are passionately devoted to bettering themselves and the people around them.

- The ability to not take myself too seriously.

- Be involved in martial arts with my beautiful wife, Jana, and my kids Tristan, Charlie, and Piper.

MAJOR ACHIEVEMENTS

- 1981 Okinowan Seidokan under Sensei Robert Bobak, Brown Belt

- 1982-1998 over 300 wins regionally and nationally in Sport Karate, competing forms, sparring, breaking, specialized in breaking

- 1985 Tae Kwon Do under Dan Glutz

- 1986 1st Degree Black Belt

- 1986 Kickboxing & Muay Thai training started

February 10, 2010, Ellixson's Tae Kwon Do Academy collapsed in a snow blizzard. Not a single person was hurt, but the entire building was gone. I decided I wasn't just going to rebuild; I was going to rebuild 'The Taj Mahal' of martial arts schools…. And I did.

My gift is that in my life, I've always managed to take the good out of any situation, especially the bad experiences, that's where you learn the most. I have an open mind and learn from everyone I meet. The world is still a beautiful place if you know where to look and have the right perspective.

Ellixson was involved in The Project Action Foundation, 1995-2001, which provided scholarships for 'at risk' kids in the community. He founded and executed Ellixson's Team Elite Golf Outing 1999-2017, with all proceeds enabling students to compete regionally and nationally. He chaired and executed many fundraisers over the years, such as beef & beer events, poker tournaments, hoagie and pizza drives with all proceeds going to the youth in his local area and enabling them to compete in martial arts tournaments.

For the past 25 years, Ellixson has spoken to the youth of elementary, middle, and high schools in his area about the benefits of setting and accomplishing goals and bullying. Coming from a rough upbringing, allows Ellixson to not just talk about what he read in a book, but to talk with the youth about his own life experiences and how he overcame adversity.

As a motivational speaker, Ellixson shares with the youth that a positive, focused, drug-free mind can accomplish anything. Ellixson leads by example, working 50-80 hour weeks since the age of 19 and speaks that nothing great in life can be achieved without hard work and believing in yourself. Donnie always has a handful of 'at risk' students from the community who he trains for free, mentors them on life, and finds their passion to excel. As a service to the community, he volunteers his time mentoring small business owners on the benefits of systems, consistent marketing, and staff training. Donnie volunteers his time coaching those that have fallen on hard times or succumb to substance abuse. A dozen times a year, he donates his time by going out to youth groups, boys & girl scouts, daycare centers, and various churches to teach martial arts.

MAJOR ACHIEVEMENTS

- 1988 Seoul, Korea during Olympics trained with Grandmaster Jhoon Rhee at Kyung-He University and Yudo College

- 1990 2nd Degree Black Belt

- 1990 - 1996 Full-Contact Kickboxing, 7-0

- 1994 - Present Day, worked as a Judge, Center Judge, Event Coordinator, Commentator or Arbitrator at World Sport Karate Tournaments such as US Open, Diamond Nationals, Compete Nationals, John Chung's World Cup, Boston Internationals, Ocean State Grand Nationals, Amerikick Internationals, Capital Classics, Empire State Nationals, Battle of Atlanta

- 1994 3rd Degree Black Belt under 9th Degree Grandmaster Moo Yong Lee

- 1994, 19 years of age, founded Ellixson's Tae Kwon Do Academy in Boyertown, PA

- 1994 founded a National Sport Karate Team, The Dream Team which transitioned to Team Extreme, then to Ellixson's Elite National Demo Team, presently acting Head Coach

- 1995-Present day training under Grandmaster / World Forms & Fighting Champion John Chung

- 1996 2nd Place Breaking in the Tang Soo World Championships, Atlantic City, NJ

- 1996-1999 founded and executed, The PA Super Championships, National Martial Arts Championships, Boyertown, PA, NASKA BBB Rated

- 2019 Pennsylvania Karate Hall of Fame

- 2010 The Movie, The Last Airbender, worked as a Stunt Fighter

"Special thanks to my teacher in martial arts and my teacher in life, Sabumnim John Chung. Thank you for believing in me, supporting me and always inspiring me to be better"

MAJOR ACHIEVEMENTS

- 2001 NASKA Honorable Mention Judge of the Year

- 2000-2003 founded and executed, The Victory at Valley Forge, National Martial Arts Championships, Valley Forge, PA, NASKA AA Rated event

- 2000 4th Degree Black Belt under Grandmaster John Chung

- 2010 Ellixson's Tae Kwon Do Academy collapses in snow blizzard

- 2012 Amerikick Internationals Hall of Fame Inductee

- 2013 Re-opened a new 12,000 sq. ft. Ellixson's Tae Kwon Do Academy. Master Ellixson designed, and was general contractor of the rebuild

- 2013 5th Degree Black Belt under Grandmaster John Chung

DOUGLAS FLEMING

"As I improve myself, I make the world a better place for myself and the beings whose paths I cross on my journey."

TRAINING INFORMATION

- Belt Ranks & Martial Arts Styles: Goshin Ryu Karate (7th Dan), Taekwondo (Brown Belt), Lung Jow Pai (Dragon Style) Kung Fu - Black Sash Assistant Instructor First Section, San Sei Ryu Kenjutsu - Kyosei

- Instructors/Influencers: Hanshi Phil Scudieri

- Birthdate: July 23, 1960

- Birthplace/Growing Up: NJ / Bangkok, Thailand

- Yrs. In the Martial Arts: 49 years

- Yrs. Instructing: 15 years

- School owner (Eastern Shore Martial Arts), Instructor, Manager

PROFESSIONAL ORGANIZATIONS

- All Japan Budo Federation Goshin Ryu Karate, Kyoto, Japan

- Delaware Budokan San Sei Ryu, Selbyville, DE

When I was nine years old, my father, who worked for the Army, received a temporary duty assignment, and our family relocated to Bangkok Thailand for three years from 1969 till 1971. As an American boy in Thailand during the time that the war in Vietnam was at its worst, I was constantly challenged to fight. They would say "boxing Thailand, boxing Thailand" inviting me to have a go at the unique and brutal style of Thai boxing. Because of this, I persuaded my Mother to let me start taking karate classes. As luck would have it there were no shortage of excellent instructors in the area and I began training Tae Kwon Do with a Korean Master after school. The classes were tough, and the instructor was strict, but I was stubborn and determined to learn. Back in 1969 karate was scary, bare-knuckled and bloody, with none of the nice soft sparring gear we have today. Chuck Norris and Bruce lee were the best of the best and provided inspiration for us all. I quickly gained experience and confidence defending myself against strangers in a foreign land. I began to have some rivalries with other students in the class who egged me on, which only made me train harder at home until I could match them in class. Once you get to the point where, with tears in your eyes, rather than submit, you get back up, put your hands back up and get back into the fight, you are a warrior. Once you cross that threshold, you are never the same. I continued to train during the years I lived in Thailand and eventually

PERSONAL ACHIEVEMENTS

- I have been blessed and have achieved a good measure of success through hard work. I have been married to my beautiful wife for nearly 30 years. We have raised 3 wonderful and successful young men. My youngest son Brandon Robert Fleming was my first black belt promotion and is a 3rd degree black belt and a member of my karate organization. I have 30 years of experience as a Network Engineer and I am a trusted contractor with a Top-Secret clearance supporting the efforts of the US Navy. As a second business I lead the All Japan Budo Federation Goshin Ryu Karate schools in the USA with schools in 3 states.

MAJOR ACHIEVEMENTS

- Over the years I have been fortunate to be able to train in several different Martial Arts disciplines to earn Black Belt in 3 different arts, but my most standout achievement was just a few years ago. In 2017, I was invited to participate in the All Japan Budosai which was held at the Butokuden in Kyoto Japan - the Hombu Dojo for the All Japan Budo Federation. At this time after my performance in front of the governing board of the All Japan Budo Federation the Federation officially recognized my style of Goshin Ryu Karate as a cultural asset and part of the All Japan Budo Federation.

earned the respect of my peers in the dojo. I soon had the self-confidence and self-defense skills I needed to defend myself in unarmed hand-to-hand combat. After a couple of short, spectacularly effective fights, I was no longer challenged by other kids on the streets of Bangkok, Thailand.

Studying Martial Arts has redefined my sense of self and my outlook on life and provided me with a glimpse of reality and my purpose in the universe. Soon after being immersed in the study of martial arts, I began to realize that it was larger than life. The fact that most styles are the result of many lifetimes worth of work from many devoted masters diligently documented, annotated, then structured and presented for my benefit is a treasure that increases with value as time moves forward. I received such a tremendous head start and have been trusted with the hard-learned lessons and the legacy of so many masters – the realization is humbling, and yet, at the same time, it evokes a bold commitment. I recognize then that I must be the best that I can be and to learn all the lessons that have been passed down to me.

The Japanese poet Matsuo Basho said, "Do not seek to walk in the footsteps of the wise, seek what they sought." I have then a tremendous advantage! By studying kata, I walk in the footsteps of the Masters who came before me to understand the path they were on so that I might continue in the direction we're headed. To paraphrase Sir Isaac Newton, "to see further and go further than any others have in the past by standing on the shoulders of the giants that came before me." When studying Martial Arts, there is always room for improvement, but it is the journey, not the destination that counts. As I improve myself, I make the world a better place for myself and the beings whose paths I cross on my journey. Every little bit contributes and helps the greater good.

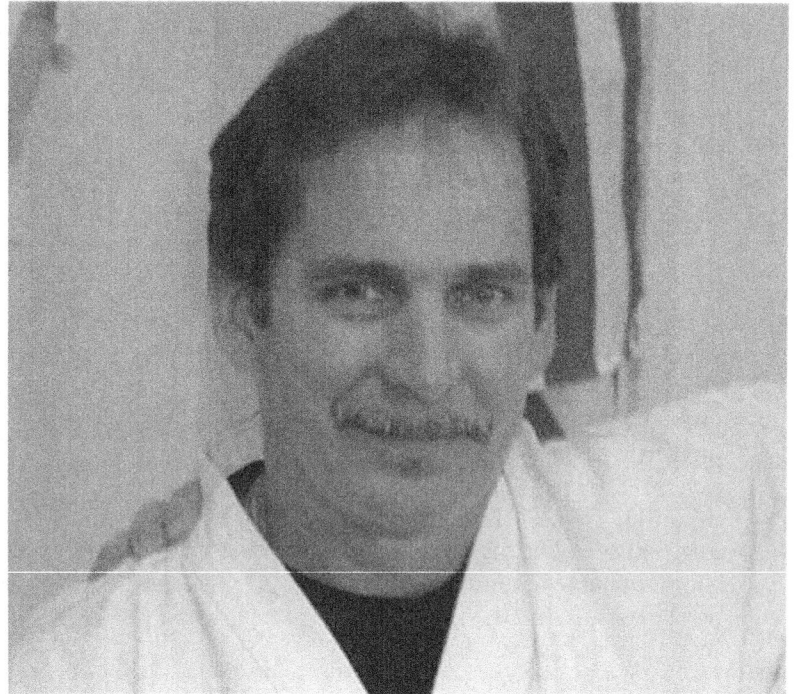

DANIEL GOSSETT

"Martial Arts is not just for the Dojo; it crosses over into all aspects of life in everything you do."

TRAINING INFORMATION

- Belt Ranks & Martial Arts Styles: Shuri - Ryu Go Dan
- Instructors/Influencers: O'Sensei Robert H. Bowles
- Birthdate: January 7, 1955
- Birthplace/Growing Up: Chicago, IL/Ft. Wayne, IN
- Yrs. In the Martial Arts: 43 years
- Yrs. Instructing: 27 years
- Instructor, Manager

PROFESSIONAL ORGANIZATIONS

- International Shuri - Ryu Association Life Member
- Professional Karate Commission
- Martial Arts Masters Association Life Member
- Phi Theta Kappa Life Member

I was the smallest person in the group of friends I ran around with, and I needed to know how to defend myself if something would happen. So, I checked out one of the local Karate schools and took a private lesson and was hooked.

I was always in sports from a young age. Baseball, Track and Cross Country and Karate peaked my competitive spirit, my first tournament I received my first trophy in front of GM Robert A. Trias, the father of Karate in America.

Studying Martial Arts under O'Sensei Bowles, a student of GM Robert A. Trias. I have learned Karate is more than punching and kicking; it is mental as well as physical and a way of life. Martial Arts is not just for the Dojo; it crosses over into all aspects of life in everything you do - the way you move, carry yourself, awareness of your surroundings, and the way you think. I also have friends all over the world; it gave me another Family.

PERSONAL ACHIEVEMENTS

- Husband to Venessa Gossett
- Father to Nicole Rode
- Grandfather to Lauren Reyez and Jackson Rode
- Great Grandfather to Oliver and Theodore Jones
- Graduating Cum Laude from College
- 5th Degree Black Belt

MAJOR ACHIEVEMENTS

- USKA Indiana State Champion
- 2012 2nd USKA World Karate Championships in Forms (with a broken hand)
- 2013 2nd USKA World Karate Championships in Weapons
- 2012 World Champion USKA World Karate Championships in Forms
- National USKA ranked competitor
- Ranked in the top 10 PKC National point from 2013-2018
- 2015-2018 PKC Region 6 points Champion in Weapons and Kata
- In the book World's Greatest Martial Artists the Sensational 600
- 2016 inducted in the Warrior Society Hall of Fame (Vice President)
- Bowles International Budo Society sister society to the Trias International Society
- Dragon Image Fighting Award
- History General US Sport Karate Museum

MAJOR ACHIEVEMENTS

- Di Rico's International Black Belt Hall of Fame
- 1st place Okinawan Division kata Wars
- 8 Certificates of Appreciation

DOUG GRISSOM

"Training has helped me see the positive in everyday life and to do my best to achieve my best in every situation."

TRAINING INFORMATION

- Belt Ranks & Martial Arts Styles: 5th Degree Black Belt TaeKwon Do, Krav Maga Instructor, Color Belts in Aikido, Jujitsu, Kajukembo

- Instructors/Influencers: Chief Master Rick Arnold

- Birthdate: February 20, 1964

- Birthplace/Growing Up: Sherman, TX

- Yrs. In the Martial Arts: 39 years

- Yrs. Instructing: 35 years

- Instructor

PROFESSIONAL ORGANIZATIONS

- Board of Directors Karate for Christ of Arkansas

- City of Greenville Texas Building Inspector

- State of Texas Plumbing Inspector

- International Code Council Building Inspector

Born and raised in Sherman, TX, my Martial Arts career began at the age of seventeen. Looking for self-confidence and self-defense, I studied Kajukembo at the local skating rink after business hours. About a year later, I met Master Rick Arnold who has become my great friend and instructor to this day. Now learning TaeKwon Do, I was one of the original twenty students who joined when Master Arnold opened his first studio in 1984.

After high school, I attended Grayson County College where I graduated in 1984 with an Associate Degree in Science. Then it was on to the University of Texas at Arlington, where I graduated in 1987 with a Bachelor's Degree in General Business.

Progressing through the belts, I received my Black Belt from Master Arnold. Soon after, I injured my knee and had to have major knee surgery. Rehab brought a renewed drive to get back to what I loved doing. After rehab, I discovered Aikido, all the while still studying TaeKwon Do.

PERSONAL ACHIEVEMENTS

- 5th Degree Black Belt
- Arnold's Martial Arts Ring of Honor
- International Gold Medalist
- International Silver Medalist
- 2x International Bronze Medalist
- 5x Karate for Christ of Arkansas Champion
- National Certified TaeKwon Do Instructor
- International Certified TaeKwon Do Instructor
- Krav Maga Association Instructor
- Defensive Tactics for Law Enforcement Instructor
- Active Shooter Response Instructor
- Israeli Knife Fighting Instructor
- V.I.P. Security Specialist/ Bodyguard

MAJOR ACHIEVEMENTS

- University of Texas at Arlington, Bachelor of General Business Studies
- Grayson County College, Associate Degree of Science
- Texas State Board of Plumbing Examiners, Plumbing Inspector-Master Plumber

I have always embraced new challenges and learning experiences. I believe all the Arts have something great to offer.

Many people might not include this part of their lives, but I am doing it in the hope that maybe it will help someone that needs to hear it. All this time, I had been fighting a battle with alcohol. It was as if I was living two different lives. This went on for years, until I finally realized I was not the tough guy I thought I was. My strength gained through the Martial Arts was the only reason I survived, but this dual life was going against all I had been taught. I was living in denial, and I told myself I didn't have a problem. One day I looked in the mirror and didn't like who I saw. Calling on the lessons I had learned about discipline and self-control, I never again indulged in alcohol. That was fifteen years ago.

You can beat addiction and live a much better life. Anyone that needs help, or needs someone to talk to, I am here for you.

In 2004, I married my beautiful wife Leigh, who is also a Black Belt. Two months later, I suffered a stroke. This caused debilitation on the left side of my body, leaving me with no feeling in my left arm and no control of my left leg. The doctors didn't offer much hope of full recovery, so I decided to work with what I was dealt. My wife and I set out on our own rehab program. Working at home for almost a year, I made small steps and improvements until I regained feeling in my arm and full use of my leg. Then, I experienced more setbacks. A ruptured disc in my back and another knee surgery tested my resolve, but I refused to be discouraged. After almost two years of chiropractic rehab on my back, I knew I had to return to what I loved. It was time to resume full training. These experiences gave me a new appreciation for my health and the abilities I had worked so hard to acquire. I was determined to use what I'd been through to make me a better person and martial artist.

Martial Arts 2.0 is how I describe the last five years of my journey. After ten years away from competition, I decided to see if I could still hold my own on the tournament circuit. I started competing again at the age of 51. Achieving my 4th Dan and competing again in tournaments brought me a sense of youth and strength I hadn't felt in years! I was back! I became a member of the United TaeKwon Do Alliance, competed in tournaments and gained many great new friends. I was competing and winning again, better than I ever had before. Age is just a number!

Friendships not just across the country, but all over the world, grew from my involvement in competitions. I was asked by my great friend Mr. Bobby Teague to be on the Board of Directors of Karate for Christ of Arkansas. This is an honor I hold very dear to my heart. My father is a Baptist minister, and through his guidance and teaching, I accepted Christ at the age of 8. My position on the Board of Directors is my way of honoring his influence and giving back to the Arts.

Studying Krav Maga was the next part of my journey. I was intrigued by the realism and effectiveness of this art. After training with some of the very best instructors, I became a certified instructor myself. I now teach Krav Maga at Arnold's Martial Arts every week in addition to my TaeKwon Do classes. Another art means more knowledge!

In 2017, I qualified for the United TaeKwon Do Alliance USA National Team and competed in Scotland, winning four medals. This was my first international competition and I look forward to many more. This experience was the absolute highlight of my Martial Arts career. Representing the United States is an honor like no other.

I tested for and received my 5th Dan from my instructor and great friend, Master Rick Arnold, and Grandmaster Royce Young. This was a milestone the 17-year-old who started Martial Arts so many years ago couldn't imagine reaching! It is my personal mission to spread the benefits of the Martial Arts, and to share the challenges I've been through In hopes to help others better themselves.

Thank you to everyone who had a hand in nominating me for this great honor. Thank you to my friend and instructor Master Rick Arnold and everyone who has touched my life on this great journey! God Bless!

My study of the Martial Arts has had the most positive effect on my life by providing me the tools to overcome life's adversities. Physical setbacks, knee surgeries, back injuries and a stroke were all roadblocks on my journey. The mental toughness gained through my training allowed me to face these adversities with a positive mindset. I know that every step forward, large or small, is positive progress.

My struggle with alcohol was only overcome with the mental fortitude from my training. This training allowed me to put my ego in check and face reality.

I have a great empathy for others that comes from my love of helping others through my teaching. Helping others through training or with everyday situations makes the hard work worthwhile.

Training has helped me see the positive in everyday life and to do my best to achieve my best in every situation. Focus has been a great attribute of the arts that I feel has greatly helped me. To focus on the positive of any given circumstance and fend off the negative has come from my studies. A personal calm from the meditative aspects of martial arts helps me to not overreact when confronted with problems or difficult situations.

Without Martial Arts, I wouldn't be the person I am today. I can face life and the world with a positive attitude and a sense of self-assurance because of my Martial Arts studies.

HOLGER HORN

"I also noticed that Ethics and Morality play a major role in my life and that Integrity must go hand in hand with martial arts."

TRAINING INFORMATION

- Belt Ranks & Martial Arts Styles: Traditional Shotokan Karate-Do, 6th Dan, Traditional Taekwon-Do (original ITF style by General Choi Hong Hi), 5th Dan

- Instructors/Influencers: Bernhard Keller, Huib Ellerkamp, Mike Stone, Hosan Park, Masutatsu Ōyama, General Choi Hong Hi, Hirokazu Kanazawa, Yoon Rhee

- Birthdate: June 13, 1958

- Birthplace/Growing Up: Nordenham, Lower Saxony/N. Germany/Berlin, Asia, Panglao, Bohol, and Q.C., Manila, Philippines.

- Yrs. In the Martial Arts: 45 years

- Yrs. Instructing: 39 years

- School owner, Manager & Instructor, Founder, Pres/CEO at Martial Arts & Sports Academy, President, Chief Examiner & Chief Instructor at IJKA-PH

PROFESSIONAL ORGANIZATIONS

- (Past) DKB, DKV, F.I.M.A.C., and AMA

- IJKA - International Japan Karate Association, HQ Tokyo

- IJKA - International Japan Karate Association, Germany

- IJKA - International Japan Karate Association, Philippines, HQ in Tokyo

My martial arts involvement was inspired by various martial arts movies (Bruce Lee was the main character and driver). From 12 to 16 years of age I trained and competed in track & fields. At the age of 15 a good friend got me to train Shotokan Karate with him in his garage Dojo. After three years of training with him, I met my first JKA Karate instructor Bernhard Keller (8. Dan JKA Shotokan today). I continued studying three different martial arts systems until today with minimal interruptions. But my ultimate goal was studying martial arts in Asia because that (my) mindset of learning, teaching, and fighting in Asia goes back to my childhood. I achieved that goal by traveling to Japan, the Philippines, and Thailand several times between 1984 and 1996 and then moving to Asia permanently in 1997.

Studying and living martial arts quickly became an essential and integral part of my life. Besides every day of training and later on additionally teaching, the weekends were reserved for competitions or special seminars with a number of great martial arts instructors coming into Germany or Europe from around the globe or with instructors we already

PERSONAL ACHIEVEMENTS

Martial arts schools:

After I achieved my 1st Dan 1981 in Shotokan Karate-Do and Taekwon-Do, I opened my first Karate school in Nordenham, Butjadingen, Lower Saxony, Germany. Two more martial arts schools followed, which were close to my hometown (Brake and Burhave).

After I moved to Berlin, I opened my first and only martial arts school in Charlottenburg (Martial Arts Academy Berlin). That school existed until I permanently moved to Asia in 1997.

Presently I own and manage the Martial Arts and Sports Academy Panglao, Philippines, which is under construction and about to be finished.

Competitions:

I competed during most major tournaments and championships on local, national, and international levels in Germany, Europe and Asia from 1979 until 1999. I won championships and tournaments in Fighting, Forms and Special Breaking, landed at second and third places, and lost a few.

One of my greatest achievements, in my eyes, was the Overall Champion (called Grand Champion in the USA) during three consecutive years of international championships. Winning in Fighting (semi contact), Forms and Special Breaking (I still have one newspaper clip, where I jumped over 10 people and broke a 30cm x 30cm x 6cm board with Tobi Yoko Geri Kekomi). During the last championship in 1986, I managed to jump over 12 people. I also won competitions on and around Clark Airbase in Angeles City Pampanga, Philippines, called the Battle of Clark, Full Contact, etc. and during other competitions across Asia. The most remembered full contact fights took place in cockfight arenas around Angeles City.

had in the country. I was taught old teaching methods and traditions that initiated strong positive character changes in others and myself while teaching students, receiving my lessons, or self-studied. And I also noticed that Ethics and Morality play a major role in my life and that Integrity must go hand in hand with martial arts.

In many people and here especially within the youth today, Discipline and Self-Discipline, Focus, Respect, Confidence, Goal Setting, and the Efforts to go through challenging training sequences and the tuning of gross and fine motor skills is minimal or even grossly lacking. Therefore, it was the biggest' pay-off' for me to witness the grand achievements of my students. To also allow potential students to be with the Art by choosing what they want to achieve, I now separate in between Martial Arts, Martial Sports, and Martial Fitness in my Martial Arts & Sports Academy.

The study of Bushido and Zen was, and still is, a very valuable addition to my martial arts education. These virtues of Character forming and Self-control, Loyalty, Honor, Politeness, Honesty and Sincerity, Courage but also Compassion, Humanity, and Justice are still part of my old school martial arts thinking and teachings. Miyamoto Musashi became one of my idols when I started studying Martial Arts in Asia.

Martial Arts helped me build my companies back in Germany and here in Asia, kept me sharp during my military times, and helped me run my security company. The mental and physical preparedness and perseverance, the combined physical and mental strengths, were

PERSONAL ACHIEVEMENTS

First Dojo in the Philippines:

During my stay and work at Clark Air Base, I built my first Dojo in a Japanese style outside the base. Unfortunately, it was destroyed by a major natural calamity (Pinatubo Eruption), which took place on June 15, 1990, and with it, all of my treasured martial arts remembrances were destroyed.

MAJOR ACHIEVEMENTS

- IJKA Tokyo, 6th Dan traditional Shotokan Karate-Do testing and promotion in 2016

- 2017 I became the IJKA Philippines President, Chief Examiner, and Chief Instructor

For the past 2.5 years, I've been building a 3-story, one of a kind martial arts and sports academy in Panglao, Bohol, Philippines. The academy will soon be finished and its programs and amenities are as follows:

Martial Arts (200m2 Dojo/Dojang):

1. Traditional Shotokan Karate-Do

2. Traditional Taekwon-Do

3. Thai/Kickboxing

4. Filipino martial arts such as Arnis/Escrima/Kali

5. Kyokushinkai

6. MMA

7. Krav Maga

8. Realistic Self-Defense

9. Lectures

10. Motivational seminars

Fitness Gym (160m2):

1. HIIT and Tabata training

2. Strengthening training

3. Others

developed throughout my life practicing martial arts and have helped me greatly reach my goals with ease.

When founding, developing, implementing, training and institutionalizing the POI - Program of Instructions for the PNP - Philippine National Police Tourist Police from 2002 until 2010 and starting to work with the Philippine Coast Guard in 1999, without my mental and physical strengths acquired through martial arts, it would have been impossible for me to do so.

It has made enormous sense to incorporate the dogmas of martial arts into my daily life but, at the same time, not making it my main source of income. That decision assured teaching qualities instead of opting for student quantities, which may have degraded my performances, and eventually would have reflected badly onto my students too.

Understanding how our universe is functioning and applying these understandings to my martial arts days, tapped with integrity and spirituality, made me the person I am today. It also made me understand that martial arts will be life-changing and fulfilling if appropriately used. And this is now specifically important when running the IJKA Philippines, the latest and newest arm of IJKA HQ Tokyo, which is in its baby steps here in the Philippines.

The IJKA HQ Philippines is located within the Martial Arts & Sports Academy Panglao, Philippines.

MAJOR ACHIEVEMENTS

Scuba Diving, Freediving and Swimming:

1. Scuba Diving beginner, advanced and professional courses until instructor level, Specialty courses

2. Freediving beginner, advanced and professional courses until instructor level

3. Swimming Lessons

4. In-water resistance training

Amenities:

1. 8 rooms complete and with aircon, hot and cold showers, etc.

2. 6 rooms complete with aircon and very nice common bathrooms

3. 2 common bathrooms with hot and cold showers, sinks, toilets, lockers and changing room

4. Swimming pool for trainings and leisure

5. Bistro bar, Restaurant

6. Diving and martial arts school teaching facility

Future packages offered to the world of martial arts:

1. Martial Arts Training vacation, which incorporates:

Martial Arts training, seminars, testing/promotions

Receiving training, prep. seminars for i.e. the next blackbelt, and black belt

Special courses, practical applications and lectures, incl. motivational seminars.

Instructors can bring their students and have their desired martial arts programs conducted here and function as Sensei's, Sabumnim's, examiners, or co-examiners.

2. Padi Scuba Diving education and/or Fun Diving with Philippine Fun Divers, Inc.

MAJOR ACHIEVEMENTS

Future packages offered (con't):

3. Adventure Trips into Bohol and other areas within the Visayas.

Packages are variable and can be designed by the incoming school too.

CHRISTINA KEBORT

"I am now involved in Martial Arts for my well-being and to improve the well-being of others."

TRAINING INFORMATION

- Belt Ranks & Martial Arts Styles: Shotokan Karate (8th Dan), Kempo Karate (Orange Belt)
- Instructors/Influencers: Hanshi Rick Johnson, Uncle William L. Kebort, Daniel Genovese
- Birthdate: March 15, 1977
- Birthplace/Growing Up: Rochester & Jamestown, NY
- Yrs. In the Martial Arts: 38 years
- Yrs. Instructing: 25 years
- Instructor at YMCA

PROFESSIONAL ORGANIZATIONS

- Johnson's BlackBelt Academy (member)
- World BlackBelt Bureau(member)

I started Martial Arts at the age of 5 with my Uncle William L. Kebort. I continued with Dan Genovese in Kempo and eventually Shotokan with Rick Johnson. I was a child that was bullied along with my little brother because my mother was blind and my dad sustained a brain injury at a young age. My brother had some disabilities himself. My brother and I weren't always well dressed or best looking either. We were to, say the least, easy targets for bullies. My uncle started teaching my brother and I to protect ourselves from the bullies that were tormenting us. Uncle Bill learned Martial Arts during his time in the Military. He taught me the importance of self-discipline & control. I am now involved in Martial Arts for my well-being and to improve the well-being of others.

As a kid and young adult, I had a lot of people looking out for me. I have learned to put others first thanks to his influence, the influence of Bob Servis, my own family, foster family and friends . On March 13th, 2018, I donated my kidney to a complete stranger in honor of my brother.

PERSONAL ACHIEVEMENTS

- I hold an 8th Dan Black Belt in Shotokan Karate becoming the only female to earn that rank at my instructors Dojo.

MAJOR ACHIEVEMENTS

- I have won in Black Belt Divisions, 9 World Championships (5 Kata & 4 Sparring); 2 US Open Championships (1 Kata / 1 Sparring), a National Championship in Self-Defense and a Grand National Championship in Continuous Sparring! On November 10th, 2018, I received the Who's Who In The Martial Arts Elite The Women's Budo Warrior Award from Ni-Dai Soke Michael DePasquale Jr. On November 16, 2019, I received the Martial Arts University Women's Warrior Hall Of Honor Award also from Soke Michael DePasquale, Jr. On March 6, 2020, I received the 2020 Bruce Lee & Arnold Legend Of Martial Arts Hall Of Honor Arnold Legend Master Instructor Dedication Award.

Bill would have turned 40 that day. I didn't want another family to go through what I did nor another person suffer from what my brother did. The recipient of my healthy kidney is doing well & loving life.

CLIFF KINCHEN

"It may sound cliche, but Martial Arts saved my life...I could have quickly become a statistic."

TRAINING INFORMATION

- Belt Ranks & Martial Arts Styles: American Open Karatedo/7th Degree Black Belt/Shihan, TaeKwonDo/5th Degree Black Belt/Master

- Instructors/Influencers: Oliver Miller, Gordon Dixon, Keith Worshaim, Gary Ducote, Carson Hines, Jerry Smith, Carlos Machado, Pat Tray, Frank Cucci, Roger Dahney, Jerry Piddington, and Jim West

- Birthdate: August 19, 1970

- Birthplace/Growing Up: Detroit, MI

- Yrs. In the Martial Arts: 39 years

- Yrs. Instructing: 27 years

- School owner, Manager & Instructor at Kinchen Martial Arts, LLC

PROFESSIONAL ORGANIZATIONS

- American Karate Academies National Association

I began studying martial arts with friends as a young boy in Detroit. It was an escape from unchecked violence that took over Detroit during my childhood. I didn't understand, but I identified intensely with what being a Martial Artist represented. Things like strength, honor, courage, and discipline all resonated with me. Once I joined the Air Force at 18, I traveled and had the opportunity to study many martial arts styles. Each new duty station allowed me to learn new techniques and hone the skills I had previously known. This also presented a challenge, especially after reaching Black Belt, because not many instructors were willing to allow me to train at their schools. I was lucky to have found a few open-minded instructors who were welcoming and allowed me to continue my studies with them.

PERSONAL ACHIEVEMENTS

- 20 Year Retired U.S. Air Force Veteran

- MBA, with a concentration in Strategic Leadership

MAJOR ACHIEVEMENTS

- 2003 U.S. Light Heavyweight Kickboxing Champion, Joe Lewis Fighting Systems

- 2001 North American Super Middleweight Kickboxing Champion, International Fighters Association

- 2000 Inducted into World Wide Martial Arts Hall of Fame, Instructor of the Year

- 1999 Inducted into World Karate Union Hall of Fame, Instructor of the Year

- 1998 Grand Champion, World Wide Tae Kwon Do Association Championships

- 1998 Member, U.S. Air Force Tae Kwon Do Team

- 1998 Welterweight Tae Kwon Do Champion, U.S. Air Force

- 1995 World Top Ten (Welterweight), Karate International Council of Kickboxing

- 1994 Boxing-Judo-Tae Kwon Do, Gold and Silver Medalist, International Law Enforcement Games

- 1994 Judo Gold and Silver Medalist, Mississippi State Games

- 1994 Amateur World Kickboxing Champion, World Council of Championship Kickboxing

It may sound cliche, but Martial Arts saved my life. Growing up in Detroit in a family with no positive role models, I could have quickly become a statistic. However, I found martial arts at a young age, and I clung to it as if my life depended on it. Martial Arts taught me discipline, which allowed me to work hard as a military member, and my achievements are a reflection of that discipline. Martial Arts taught me tolerance, something in short supply where I grew up. Martial Arts allowed me to make lifelong friends from different backgrounds and cultures. I learned so much from those individuals, enriching my life in so many wonderful ways. Martial Arts has allowed me to touch others' lives and share with them all the great things martial arts has to offer. Martial Arts allowed me to train with some of the best martial artists globally and compete on Regional, National, and International levels. Martial Arts has given me the strength to fight for those who cannot fight for themselves.

NELSON LEBRON

"If not for Martial Arts, I would not have survived in the South Bronx or Combat."

TRAINING INFORMATION

- Belt Ranks & Martial Arts Styles: Tae Kwon Do 1st, Tang Su Do 1st, Kyokushin 1st, Sho rin Ryu 1st, Bill Superfoot Wallace 1st, Craig Smith America Karate/Kickboxing 3rd, MCMAP 3 red tab, Roger Greene Chinese Kenpo 5th Degree, Joe Lewis Fighting Systems 5th Degree, Boxer, Nak Muay, American Kickboxer, Brazilian Jiu-jitsu student

- Instructors/Influencers: Joe Lewis, Alex Humen, Craig Smith, Tom "the Phenom" Poey, Roger Greene, Heather "the tiger" Stevens, Bill Wallace, William Martinez, Kenji Amano, Roger Belch, Dennis Aguirre

- Birthdate: January 24, 1975

- Birthplace/Growing Up: South Bronx, NYC

- Yrs. In the Martial Arts: 40 years

- Yrs. Instructing: 25 years

- Instructor

PROFESSIONAL ORGANIZATIONS

- UFC Gym

Nelson "the Tyrant " Lebron began his Martial Art journey in 1980 in the South Bronx under William Martinez. Black belt in 9 Disciplines to include 5th Degree under the late Joe Lewis, 5th Degree under the late Roger Greene, 3rd Degree under Kickboxing sensation Tom "the Phenom" Poey, 1st Degree under Bill "Superfoot" Wallace, and Black Belt Instructor trainer in the Marine Corps Martial arts. These do not include his Disciplines of Muay Thai, American Kickboxing, and Western boxing. He's a 21-year retired combat veteran of 9 combat tours to include Kosvo, Iraq, Afghanistan, evacuation Operations in Bierut, Lebanon, Syrian Border Operations, Counter-Terrorism, and drug Operations in Africa

PERSONAL ACHIEVEMENTS

- 5x World Champion

MAJOR ACHIEVEMENTS

- Father to an amazing little girl
- Retired Combat Veteran of 9 Combat tours

and Latin America. Nelson is a professional bodyguard, bouncer, Combatives instructor, actor, photographer, fighter, and coach.

With a combined fight record of 188 wins - 36 losses, and 6 draws (Boxing, Kickboxing, MMA).

Nelson prides himself on the fact that he has competed in most rule styles of fighting. As a bouncer of 24 years and Combat Veteran of 9 tours, he has survived and been involved in over 1000 street conflicts. He's a former NYC silver gloves champion, 6x Virginia Golden gloves champion, former WAKO, IKF, WKA, WKKO, IFA, ISKA, KICK, Kickboxing champion, Okinawa Armed Forces Champion, Founder of Tyrant Modern Martial arts, recipient of Fight Gallantry award, and 2x Fighter of the year recipient for the Joe Lewis Fighting Systems. Nelson currently teaches at the UFC gym in Norfolk, Virginia, travels the world as a government contractor, teaches Active shooter survival for Sentinel Security group, and is a full-time Single dad to his beautiful daughter Adryanna Lebron.

"If not for Martial Arts, I would not have survived in the South Bronx or Combat. "

PAUL LEPKOWSKI

"The martial arts have impacted me, whereby I prefer to teach others as a focus rather than grow my own aspirations."

TRAINING INFORMATION

- Belt Ranks & Martial Arts Styles: 7th Degree Black Belt Karate and Bujutsu, 6th Degree Black Belt Jujitsu, 6th Degree Black Belt Tae Kwon Do, 4th Degree Black Belt Hapkido

- Instructors/Influencers: Fred Murphy, John Enger, Phil Porter, Neal Schiesske, Hidy Ochiai, Anthony Antoniades

- Birthdate: September 8, 1970

- Birthplace/Growing Up: Elmira NY/Corning NY

- Yrs. In the Martial Arts: 36 years

- Yrs. Instructing: 19 years

- School owner, Manager & Instructor at Everlasting Life Martial Arts

PROFESSIONAL ORGANIZATIONS

- Shinja Martial Arts University

I got started in martial arts as a young teenager because I wanted to be able to defend myself and gain confidence. I was always interested in the martial arts, and it had a strong appeal to me, especially with self-defense. I saw an ad in the newspaper for a local karate school. I then asked my dad if I could attend, and he said, "How are you going to pay for it?" I then decided to get a newspaper route, which is how I ended up being able to afford lessons as a teenager.

At first, I became very interested in sparring and kata. Over the years, I have shifted towards focusing on the self-defense aspects of the martial arts. Overall, it's been an incredibly rewarding experience and journey.

PERSONAL ACHIEVEMENTS

I have taught several hundred students over the years on a volunteer basis. I've promoted 13 students to black belt ranks in a very rigorous program. I have also taught over 100 students in various self-defense seminars.

MAJOR ACHIEVEMENTS

- 2018 Inductee into the Philadelphia Historic Martial Arts Society Hall of Fame

Studying martial arts has had a tremendous impact on my life. I've met many wonderful people over the years. I've learned self-defense and self-discipline. I've gained confidence in myself. Teaching others has been an incredibly rewarding experience. Instilling values and proper conduct into the students and watching the students continue to grow is amazing.

Being able to teach others how to defend themselves, especially in utilizing the least amount of force necessary, is really important in today's world. Teaching students how to avoid being in a physical altercation and also how to escape from a physical altercation are critically important. Teaching young children has been very rewarding in watching their confidence and self-control continue to grow and grow.

The martial arts have impacted me, whereby I prefer to teach others as a focus rather than grow my own aspirations. I find that teaching is something I look forward to especially watching students advance from belt to belt as their skills and proficiency grows.

Through the teaching of the martial arts, we have started to build more schools with more instructors and more students. That shows the value of martial arts and also demonstrates to others the rewarding journey ahead for those dedicated to the martial arts as a way of life.

MICHAEL J. MARTIN

"Martial Arts it has given me the skills and desire to do better in all aspects of my life...and to share this gift with others."

Like many who started martial arts, I started because I was bullied as a child and I didn't have the skills or confidence to stand up for myself. I started training in Shotokan Karate under Shihan F.V. Ramano. I found that I really enjoyed the training and it was an athletic endeavor that I was good at. I found that as my skills grew, so did my confidence. I no longer worried about having to defend myself, as I was no longer a target for bullies. This, to me, is one of the many great gifts of martial arts training...confidence. This confidence was not only for the dojo or fighting but for everyday life as well. I would not have done half the things in my life that I have done if it were not for the confidence that I gained through training. Another reason that I continued to train was Shihan Ramano. To me, he embodied the spirit of Bushido.

TRAINING INFORMATION

- Belt Ranks & Martial Arts Styles: 7th degree Black Sash Tien Hu Ba Gua Zhang, 5th degree Black Sash Ba Men Tai Chi Chuan fa, 3rd Dan Shotokan Karate Do, 1st degree Black Sash Shaolin Tiger Kung Fu

- Instructors/Influencers: F.V. Ramano, Sheng Yui Ho, Tim Norman, Clement Riedner, Bok Nam Park, Wilson Pitts

- Birthdate: September 28, 1965

- Birthplace/Growing Up: Gettysburg, PA/Taneytown, MD

- Yrs. In the Martial Arts: 38 years

- Yrs. Instructing: 34 years

- School Owner, Living Waters Martial Arts, Instructor, Manager

PROFESSIONAL ORGANIZATIONS

- Christian Black Belt Association

PERSONAL ACHIEVEMENTS

- Honor Graduate from Air Force Basic Training

- Promoted to Senior Airman Below the Zone

- Graduated 2nd in my class from the Police Academy

- Sifu Tim Norman's first Black Sash

- Graduating from Koinonia College of Arts and Science with Bachelor's degree in Martial Arts Ministry

- Fought in the Sabaki Challenge--a full contact bare knuckle tournament in Denver, CO

- Mentioned in an article about the tournament in Black Belt Magazine

- In 1995 I was able to train at the Shaolin Temple for a short time, and trained several students who have gone on to become quality instructors.

He was retired from the Army with a tour in Korea and two tours in Vietnam. He was an 8th dan in Shotokan. I can't begin to describe the influence he has had on me. I joined the Air Force because of his influence. I became a police officer because of his influence. I still train to this day because of him.

How has Martial Arts impacted my life? Wow, that is a good question. Martial Arts has impacted everything I have done over the last 40 years from where I live to the jobs I have taken. I want to share a story here: I was having a seminar on Ba Men Tai Chi and Dr. Clement Riedner, head of the system, came and he brought his wife, Sandy, with him. My wife Donna and Sandy were sitting and talking, comparing notes on what it is like to be a martial arts widow. Sandy told my wife something that I knew but I didn't realize others saw it as well. She told my wife, "Martial artist are not wired like everybody else. They don't do things for money or prestige. Their goal is to live a life dedicated to making themselves and people better and share their skills and knowledge with others." The impact martial arts have had on my life, it has given me the skills and desire to do better in all aspects of my life, and the desire to share this gift with others. As I have gotten, older my goals in the arts have changed slightly. I am now focused on sharing and passing along this gift I was given to the next generation in hopes that they will find the value that I found in studying the martial arts.

MAJOR ACHIEVEMENTS

- Being named the inheritor to Ba Men Tai Chi Chuan fa in 2017

- Being made Director of the Chinese Division of the Christian Black Belt Association in 2017

- Being asked to serve as a Board member of the Christian Black Belt Association in 2018

SAÚL GARCÍA MUÑIZ

"Thanks to the practice and excellent teacher that I've had, I have been able to be a better human being for the benefit of society."

TRAINING INFORMATION

- Belt Ranks & Martial Arts Styles: Black Belt in Kung Fu, 1st Dan in Niho Koden Shindo Ryu (Karate-Do), Seventh Dan (Master) in Taekwon-Do (ITF)

- Instructors/Influencers: Sense Hector Mendez, Bosabonim Irving Caraballo (Vincy), Sense Miguel Alicea, Great Master Orlando Vega, Great Master Benny Rivera

- Birthdate: May 18, 1960

- Birthplace/Growing Up: Philadelphia, PA / Yauco, PR

- Yrs. In the Martial Arts: 46 years

- Yrs. Instructing: 42 years

- School owner (Life & Heart Taekwon-Do Yauco), Instructor

PROFESSIONAL ORGANIZATIONS

- Associate Degree of Physical Therapy Assistant (RPTA)

- Bachelor Degree in Social Sciences (Criminal Justice)

- Treasure of the Puerto Rico ITF National Taekwon-Do Federation

- Secretary General of Puerto Rico ITF National Taekwon-Do Federation

- Vice-President of the Puerto Rico ITF National Taekwon-Do Federation

I started practicing martial arts due to several confrontations I had, in addition to looking for a way to channel all the energy I had. Also, after this time that I started, there was a lot of promotion.

Thanks to the practice and excellent teacher that I've had, I have been able to be a better human being for the benefit of society. I have also been able to help other people in their physical and emotional development by transmitting the knowledge of martial arts.

PROFESSIONAL ORGANIZATIONS

Founder and Instructor of Taekwon-Do in:

- University of Mayaguez (CAAM) (Continuing Education)
- Guayanilla ITF Taekwon-Do
- Sabana Grande Taekwon-Do ITF
- Catholic University of Ponce (Sports Complex)

PERSONAL ACHIEVEMENTS

On October 6, 1973, he began practicing Karate-Do at the Holy Rosary School with Sense Hector Méndez. At the end of 1974, he continued practicing Shaolin Kempo with Sifu Miguel Alicea. In 1975, he practiced Taekwondo with Mr. Irving Caraballo "Vincy". In 1978, he returned to practice Kung Fu with Sifu Alicea and obtained his degree of black belt.

From 1982 to 1984 he began practicing Nihon Koden Shindo Ryu Karate Do with Sense Miguel Alicea and obtained his re-evaluation for the 1 Dan Degree with teacher Felton Messina Javierre. During this period, he taught Karate in the city of Mayaguez at the University College (CAAM). He participated in National and International competitions obtaining awards. In the Dominic Republic, he obtained individual gold and silver (forms and fighting) and team bronze.

In 1985, he continued the practice of Taekwon-Do with the current Great Master Orlando Vega in Ponce, Puerto Rico and re-valued him as 1 Dan of Taekwon-Do. Because the GM Orlando Vega left for the United State, he continues practice with Great Master Benny Rivera (RIP).

VIII JUEGOS PANAMERICANOS DE TAEKWONDO I.T.F.
Tarija - Bolivia   Octubre 2007

PERSONAL ACHIEVEMENTS

In 1989, he founded, along with Mr. Miguel Feliciano Ramirez, the Guayanilla Academy ITF Taekwon-Do. That same year, he joined the National Team of Puerto Rico, also continuing to participate in different tournaments. That same year, he obtained the title of National Champion of the "Fajas Boricuas". In 1990, he represented Puerto Rico in the 7 Taekwon-Do World Championship held in Montreal Canada.

From 1991 to 1994, he taught Taekwon-Do in Sabana Grande and at the Sports Complex of the Catholic University of Ponce. He joined the National Team again, participating in the 9 ITF World Taekwon-Do Championship held in Malaysia.

MAJOR ACHIEVEMENTS

- Acknowledgments by Municipal Legislature of Yauco

- Chambers of the Representative Senate of Puerto Rico

- Exalted to the Hall of the Immortals of the Yauco Sports

- Recognized as adopted son of the City of Yauco in 2014

- Recognition at the Taekwon-Do Hall of Fame in New Jersey in 2009

- He took his exam for the Master's Degree (VII-Dan) with GM Kim Ung Choi. In August 2019

JEFF OWEN

"Martial Arts showed a kid that was bullied how to overcome emotions, to do the right thing, and not use excuses."

TRAINING INFORMATION

- Belt Ranks & Martial Arts Styles: 5th Degree in Shotokan, 2nd Degree in Aikido, 2nd Degree in BJJ

- Instructors/Influencers: Barry Holcomb, Travis Lutter

- Birthdate: July 30, 1972

- Birthplace/Growing Up: Dallas & Granbury, TX

- Yrs. In the Martial Arts: 37 years

- Yrs. Instructing: 28 years

- Instructor, Student who still loves learning

PROFESSIONAL ORGANIZATIONS

- Team Lutter BJJ

At 5 years old, it was all about Bruce Lee. I wanted to be like what I saw on TV. I had problems in school. I was bullied badly for my physical problems and my reading problems. TV was my only outlet. At 12, we moved to Granbury. I found a school where I could be who I wanted to be. I started the work. But as I was learning my body, I realized that I could only kick with one leg. How could I do this? My instructor told me about Superfoot, so I watched him and tried to do what he did. With much practice, I became 5-0 in amateur kickboxing.

At 29, I met Travis Lutter and I learned what true fighting was. I was playing catch up. I wanted to be an MMA fighter, just didn't pan out because of life and hard times. Travis Lutter saved my life. I owe everything to him. I can't write enough to tell the story. Thank you, coach!

PERSONAL ACHIEVEMENTS

- I love helping and giving back to the community.
- I have helped police officers all over for the past 10 years. This is how I give back to my community. I saw a problem, so I wanted to help. I wanted to be a cop, but my reading and writing stopped me from becoming one. And the army would not take me. So instead of using excuses, I found a way to help.

MAJOR ACHIEVEMENTS

- Blue belt Pan AM 2004 2nd place
- Blue belt Pan AM 2005 3rd place
- Purple belt Pan AM 2006 1st Division and 1st in open
- Purple belt Master Senior 2006 1st Division
- Brown belt Master Senior 2011 1st Division 1st in open
- Black belt Master Worlds 2014 3rd Division 3rd open
- 2012 Masters Hall of Fame
- 2019 USA Martial Arts Hall of Fame

Martial Arts showed a kid that was bullied how to overcome emotions, to do the right thing, and not use excuses.

In 2006, Travis Lutter, my coach, asked me to train for the Pan AM BJJ games. I also received help from Brad Rehor. They talked me into going. Long story short, I won my division and the open as a Purple Belt.

So, when we got back home, Brad wanted me to go to Brazil with him to compete. He won the Master Senior BJJ tournament for many years in his division.

We left on a Wednesday. I was 34 and had never been to Brazil. We arrived on Thursday. We went to train at Gracie Barra. Brad did amazing rolling. I did well, too. We went to eat and got back to the hotel for the night. He woke up complaining about heartburn. He told me to leave and go eat and that he would be ok. Just give him some time. I came back to our room after eating, but he was not there. So, I went down to the lobby and his driver ran to me and said he had a heart attack and took him to hospital. I immediately went to check on him. Long story short, they put a stent in. He told me to compete in the morning and to go back to the room to rest. I said that I wasn't leaving. The next day, I competed and won my division. I am a World Champion (there's more to the story). Afterwards, I went to the ICU to see him. We both cried and laughed. I said, "We are going home tomorrow. See you in the AM my friend." I got a call at 3 AM saying Brad passed away. So, I called my coach, Travis. Now you know why I say Travis saved my life (there's more to the story).

CAROL PARENTI

"You can do ANYTHING if you put your mind to it. Never give up, and push yourself beyond what you think you can do or achieve."

TRAINING INFORMATION

- Belt Ranks & Martial Arts Styles: Bushido Kai Karate Jutsu (6th Degree Black Belt), UFAF (2 Black Belts), Training in Aikido

- Instructors/Influencers: GM Matt Durant, Rick Prieto, Johnnie Murphy

- Birthdate: January 16, 1959

- Birthplace/Growing Up: Baton Rouge, LA/CA, TX

- Yrs. In the Martial Arts: 22 years

- Yrs. Instructing: 15+ years

- School owner, Manager & Instructor at Champions Bushido Karate School (Partner)

PROFESSIONAL ORGANIZATIONS

- UFAF Chuck Norris organization (United Fighting Arts Federation)

I always wanted to be in the Martial Arts from a young age, but there weren't many opportunities in the Martial Arts back then. I have always been one who loves a challenge, so I began my training at the age of 39, back in 1999. A friend, who I hadn't seen in a couple of years, walked into the place where I worked one day, and I was amazed at how good she looked. I asked her what she had been doing to look so wonderful, and she told me that she had gotten a new job and had been taking Martial Arts lessons for the last two years. She was a Brown Belt at the time and invited me to come and try a class at her Dojo. I was so excited because I had always wanted to train in the Martial Arts, but time just slipped by, and I thought it was too late for me. I was hooked on the FIRST day! That was almost 22 years ago! I am excited to say that I am a 6th Degree Master Ranked Black Belt now, and have earned 3 World Titles, Several State Championships, a few Grand Championships, and many 1st, 2nd, and 3rd places in hundreds of tournaments and I am still competing to this day.

I am a partner with GM Johnnie Murphy in a great school in Spring, TX,

PERSONAL ACHIEVEMENTS

- Business Owner of Millennium Shutters and Blinds also since 1999

- Business Partner and Instructor at Champions Bushido Karate School from 2009-Present

- I have a Business Degree from the University of Nebraska. I also have a degree from the International Institute of Holistic Iridology.

- I am a mother of 3 incredible children (Cheree, Nick, and Scottie)

MAJOR ACHIEVEMENTS

- While Working for Southwest Airlines as a Flight Attendant, I was selected out of 4000 Flight Attendants to walk Bob Hope and Chuck Yeager on Stage and present them with awards at a Gala Dinner sponsored by the airlines.

- Martial Arts Accomplishments: 3 World Titles, Multiple State Championships, a few Grand Championships, along with

- Many other 1st, 2nd, & 3rd place wins throughout my 22 years in Martial Arts.

- I was asked by Chuck Norris to perform a half time show at one of Chuck's WCL (World Combat League) events

- One of Chuck Norris's Black Belts # 2910

called Champions Bushido Karate School. It is so rewarding to watch each and every one of our students excel in the Martial Arts. What an incredible way to learn self-defense, confidence, discipline, and good ole fashion hard work and perseverance!

I am so grateful for all of the opportunities that it has brought to me, including meeting and training with Mr. Chuck Norris, Mr. Aaron Norris, and all of the UFAF (United Fighting Arts Federation) organization. Now I train with World Champion GM Johnnie Murphy and have a school with him. I will continue to train, compete, and teach karate as long as I can.

Thank you to the Martial Arts and to all of my Martial Arts friends that I have met over the last 22 years. I cherish all of these times.

Studying Martial Arts has impacted my life in so many ways. It has allowed me to meet so many other incredible Martial Artists and their families from all over the world. There is so much camaraderie that I consider all of my Martial Arts friends as a family! As a female, it gives me great confidence to know that I can protect myself with all of the excellent skills that I have learned over the years. Being able to pass those skills on to my students, especially my female students, is enriching. That is why I put on Self Defense seminars for women a few times a year. Just knowing that you can help other women with some simple self-defense techniques is so gratifying. It's sad how little most people know about defending themselves, especially women. It gives me such joy teaching our students and watching them excel. We have had many students start at a very young age, and they are still with us—some for over 10, 11, 12 years. I have exceeded my goals in the Martial Arts. It has impacted my life because I have accomplished things that I have set out to accomplish, mostly because I started Martial Arts as an adult. So when people tell me, "I'm too old, or it's too late for me, I am a great example of, "You can do ANYTHING if you put your mind to it." Never give up, and push yourself beyond what you think you can do or achieve. Accomplishing what I have in the last 22 years is something that I will always be proud of.

CREED POTTER

"I have found that pursuing martial arts has really been a personal growth journey, and sharing that opportunity with others."

TRAINING INFORMATION

- Belt Ranks & Martial Arts Styles: 6th Degree Texas Karate, 5th Degree American Fitness and Martial Arts, 3rd Degree Bushi Ban, 2nd Degree Kenwayoshin Ryu Bujutsu

- Instructors/Influencers: Professor Gary Lee, Grand Master Eric Loveless, Zulfi Ahmed, Dr. Mong Gi

- Birthdate: February 25, 1966

- Birthplace/Growing Up: Houston, TX

- Yrs. In the Martial Arts: 26 years

- Yrs. Instructing: 18 years

- School owner & Instructor at American Fitness and Martial Arts Almeda

PROFESSIONAL ORGANIZATIONS

- Sport Karate Museum
- Texas Sport Karate
- Gulf Coast Martial Arts

I started training in Martial Arts as a child at Powell Gymnasium in Pasadena, Texas. I was fascinated with karate from watching Kung Fu theater on Saturday mornings. I trained with my uncle in karate, who learned while serving in Japan as a member of the US Air Force. My Dad and others taught me to wrestle, box, and how to defend myself. This training was not very formal, but it was very effective. All of my training was sporadic until my kids enrolled in Bushi Ban in Deer Park, Texas. Sitting there, watching my kids' train rekindled the fire in me, and I enrolled in 1994.

It has been a family affair ever since. I have continuously trained and taught for the last twenty-six years. I had the good fortune to meet many amazing people along the way. Grand Master Zulfi Ahmed has been an inspiration to me and taught me a great deal about Martial Arts. He introduced me to breaking, which has led me to where I am today. I spent some time competing, refereeing, and judging karate. One of the tournaments was the internationally renowned tournament in Texas, called the Dungal. One of my five daughters got involved in kickboxing

PERSONAL ACHIEVEMENTS

- Performed at many venues, including Toyota Center for the Houston Aeros, San Jacinto College, College of the Mainland, and many other places.

- Coached and cornered MMA fighters, some of who became champions for organizations including Extreme Fighting Championship, Strike Force, Young Guns, Legacy Fighting Championships, Renegades, Superior Combat and the World Combat League.

- Coached numerous competitors/ champions in TKO, NAGA, New Breed, Gulf Coast Regional, and numerous other tournament circuits.

MAJOR ACHIEVEMENTS

- USA Martial Arts Hall of Fame 2013 Kickboxing Instructor of the Year

- USA Martial Arts Hall of Fame 2014 Master Breaker of the Year

- Sport Karate Museum Inductee 2015

and became a 16-year-old silver medalist and the 17-year-old gold medalist in kickboxing at the Bando Nationals. In 2001 I met Grand Master Eric Loveless, and we became good friends. I trained, traveled, and sparred with him for years.

It is difficult for me to list the many impacts martial arts has had on my life. I believe the most significant change has been the pursuit of self-mastery. This is an ever-elusive goal for me. How do I become the best "me" in each aspect of my life? Many people will speak of self-defense, respect, and confidence when it comes to speaking of karate. This seems to be a selling point in any given conversation when someone is looking to join a dojo. However, I have found that pursuing martial arts has really been a personal growth journey, and sharing that opportunity with others. At some point, karate moved from a hobby to a way of life. I had excellent guides on my journey. People like my good friend Professor Gary Lee and Grand Master J Pat Burleson. In any contest I have ever had with another martial artist has been less about being a winner and more about me bringing the best version of myself to the challenge. It is not what another person is capable of. It is about, can I overcome adversity? Can I overcome my weaknesses? Can I overcome my fears and doubts? I do not believe that I can find any other "sport" that teaches me these lessons. Karate has been a great part of my journey in life. I have had the good fortune to train all of my children in martial arts and I am now training some of my grandchildren. One person may find their interest is in fighting, another self-defense, and another may focus on kata's beauty. There is something in martial arts for everyone.

DAVID SHEPHERD

"I feel like being a martial artist is not only my profession, it is who I am."

I started my studies in the Arts in 1974. I was initially intrigued by the martial arts in the early '70s due to the Bruce Lee movies. However, it wasn't until Master Chuck Norris visited my High School in 1974 conducting Tang Soo Do demonstrations, with some of his students and Sensei Mike Stone, that truly sparked my interest in the arts.

My first steps in the martial arts were in the "Tang Soo Do" Chuck Norris studios in California. After my family moved from Los Angeles to Orange County, I continued learning American Kenpo under Master Bob Perry, one of Grandmasters Bob White's top students. It was during my studies in Orange County that I decided to teach youth.

TRAINING INFORMATION

- Belt Ranks & Martial Arts Styles: Kenpo 4th, Okinawa Shorin Ryu 4th degree, Tang Soo Do 5th degree, THKDO 6th degree, Aiki Jujutsu 5th degree
- Instructors/Influencers: GM Bob Perry, GM Tony Sandoval, Sifu Taky Kimura, GM Dr. John Hunt
- Birthdate: December 8, 1959
- Birthplace/Growing Up: San Diego, CA
- Yrs. In the Martial Arts: 46 years
- Yrs. Instructing: 36years
- Instructor, Owner of an Outreach Martial Art Program

PROFESSIONAL ORGANIZATIONS

- ALL JAPAN JU-JITSU INTERNATIONAL FEDERATION
- World Registry of Black Belts Martial Arts Organizations, Federation & Associations
- International Tang Soo Do Moo Duk Kwan Association
- THKDO of Australia under Grand Master Dr. John Hunt
- World Registry of Black Belts
- Shobu Ryu Aiki Torite Jujutsu/ Kobujutsu
- Sandoval Karate Kobudo Federation
- Modern Warrior Arts Union
- Italian Chin Woo Athletic Association
- Federation of Israeli Martial Arts (FIMA)

Not only the arts but also self-respect, self-control, positive thinking, patience, responsibility, and stress relief. All badly needed in such an impressionable age.

In 1984 I started teaching through the Parks and Rec. Dept, YMCA, YWCA, Boys and Girls Clubs, and Community Schools in the Orange County and L.A area. That was a hectic yet successful time. I had an opportunity to work with some great instructors and teach hundreds of students.

In 1988, I moved to Seattle, Washington, and opened up Young American Self- Defense, A "Youth Self-Defense, Safety Awareness Education Classes.

As an instructor, it was a hectic but successful period. As a student, it was an exceptional time because I got to meet one of Bruce Lee's top students - Mr. Taky Kumara, and for 2.5 years, learn from him the (classical) style of Wing Chun. Mr. Kumara is a humble teacher and a great spirited man; he taught me so much.

In 1990 I moved back to California and started teaching in San Francisco, San Jose, and Santa Cruz area. During that period, I had the pleasure of studying under my Grandmaster Tony Sandoval, the Founder America's Hakutsuru "The Father of America's Hakutsuru" & Sandoval Karate Kobudo Federation. GM Sandoval was a retired marine who studied many years in Okinawa. His wisdom still leads me through my studies. Tony also introduced me to Grandmaster – Soke Robert Bugh, the creator of the Shobu Ryu Aiki Torite Jujutsu/Kobujutsu Bugh Ha. I trained with him also for many years. Both - great men, and I am honored to have them as my teachers, mentors, and friends.

During that time, martial arts was very popular, and we had close to 1,500 students. Thanks to that popularity, I had the pleasure to hire and work with close to 20 instructors from various arts: Black belts, Michael Zapien (Cuong Nhu) "Razor" Riz Angel (Kenpo & Tae Kwon do), Mike Dowd (Shotokan) and many others. I also had the privilege to meet lifetime friends in the Arts including Mr. Ernie Reyes Senior & Jr, Larry Lam, Don Wilson Dragon, Benny the "Jet," Sifu GM Lung Ting.

I knew I was going to keep teaching where ever I lived. We had the opportunity to work with the Dare program with the San Jose Police

PERSONAL ACHIEVEMENTS

- Inducted into the Legends of the Martial Arts Hall of Fame 2011
- Inducted into the Action Martial Arts Magazine Hall of Fame 2013
- World Karate Union Hall of Fame 2012
- Inducted into the Masters Hall of Fame 2012
- Inducted into the Legends Hall of Fame 2016 with 2 awards, one of them is the first prestigious Cynthia Rothrock Award
- Inducted into the All Pro Tea Kwon Do HOF 2018
- Inducted into the Argentina Hall of Fame 2016
- Inducted into the Action Magazine Hall of Honors 2020
- 2012 Legends Alumni Association
- A member of ALL JAPAN JU-JITSU INTERNATIONAL FEDERATION
- A member of World Registry of Black Belts Martial Arts Organizations, Federation & Associations
- A Member of International Tang Soo Do Moo Duk Kwan Association
- A member of THKDO of Australia under Grand Master Dr. John Hunt
- A member of World Registry of Black Belts
- A member of Shobu Ryu Aiki Torite Jujutsu/Kobujutsu
- A member of Sandoval Karate Kobudo Federation
- A member of Modern Warrior Arts Union
- A Member of Italian Chin Woo Athletic Association
- Founder of Young American Self-Defense "1990"

Department for three years; this fits with what we believed in - Kick against Drugs.

I moved to Boston, Massachusetts, in 1995, where I opened Champion Youth Self – Defense teaching in many locations across Massachusetts with a great practitioner of the Arts, friend, and black belt (Kenpo & Aiki Jujutsu) - Sensei Shawn Thompson. Sensei Shawn Thompson and I founded Kenjitsudo USA and are still teaching in our 25th year together... Since moving to New England, I have traveled all over Europe (Sweden, Norway, Poland, Ukraine, Austria, Hungary, Czech Republic, Greece, France, Italy), and Africa to name a few. The many years of teaching and meeting many black belt practitioners, Masters, and Grandmasters from all over the world, this gave me a broader spectrum of the Arts and a sense that there is a lifetime of continuous learning. On that journey - if you will - to finding my Zen in the Arts... I met Grandmaster John Hunt from Australia, creator of (THKDO) Muay Thai & Kickboxing, and had the privilege of learning the arts and gain the 6th degree in.

Meeting practitioners of different arts from all over the world, helped me gain an even greater appreciation for the various styles. There is no such thing as the best Art or the best style of the Arts. As the late and great Bruce Lee would say, "Bound by none, utilize all ways" this is what I believe in expanding your horizons in the arts "Why learn one way when you can learn many ways." Years ago, I asked one of my Grandmasters (in the Okinawan Arts) - Tony Sandoval: If I should learn one art or style and go as far as I can in that art or instead learn multiple styles. He said it is best to learn one Art and then learn another style, and keep going. My goal is to learn as much of the arts from many practitioners as I can and to share my learnings with as many people as I can.

I am a constant learner of the arts. Not just an instructor, a mentor, but also a student. As encouraged by my grandmasters and students alike, in 2012, I established my own style: Kenjitsudo USA, because I firmly believe and have applied for years Bruce Lee's wisdom: "Adapt what is useful, reject what is useless, and add what is specifically your own."

Since teaching the Arts from 1984 to 2020, I have taught over 6000 students providing very affordable classes for the Youth. Safety awareness is the best deterrence for the growing problem and is a vital part of every

MAJOR ACHIEVEMENTS

- Founder of KenJitsuDo USA 2012

- Honorable Discharge from the United States Navy

- Stuntman for "United Artist" in the 80's for 2.5 years

child's education. As teachers, parents, adults, it is our job to help kids, and students become more aware and more capable of coping with their environment and, at the same time, promoting mental, physical well-being. This is why I teach the Arts being able to share knowledge and providing safety education to thousands of youth.

I feel like being a martial artist is not only my profession but – who I am. I believe in its values and do my very best to 'do' what I 'preach.' Though my upbringing was rough, I have gained confidence and the ability to attain and pursue long term goals. I have learned not to be intimidated by what I want to achieve and keep going. It allowed me to appreciate different cultures, people with various experiences, and what they have to offer and how they enrich us. It taught me patience, how to work with others, and opened the world of possibilities by creating meaningful relationships with amazing practitioners, friends in the arts from all over the world.

JERRY SILVA

"My grandmother, my mother, and my wife Maria are the driving force for my passion for the martial arts."

TRAINING INFORMATION

- Belt Ranks & Martial Arts Styles: Tae Kwon Do (1st Dan), 7th Duan Kung Fu/Wushu, Master Blackbelt Instructor, Elite Athlete

- Instructors/Influencers: Sifu Peter Morales, Coach Ming Liu "Qiu Ming," Master Zhuang Hui, Master Jin Heng Li, Bobby Czibok, Robert Heckman, Bing Tran

- Birthdate: February 28, 1972

- Birthplace/Growing Up: Denver, CO/San Jose, CA

- Yrs. In the Martial Arts: 39 years

- Yrs. Instructing: 20 years

- School owner (National Martial Arts Academy LLC), Instructor, Manager

PROFESSIONAL ORGANIZATIONS

- United States Kung Fu Wushu Federation

My grandmother started me out in martial arts at the young age of four years old. She knew how hard life would be and wanted me to grow up and be a strong man. We didn't live in the best neighborhood and learning self-defense and how to take care of myself was a must. I didn't have a father growing up; all I had was my mother and grandmother. My grandmother had taken me to my first martial arts class held at a church in our neighborhood, where I learned to understand and appreciate the martial arts. I fell in love after the first class. I continued my training through high school but didn't truly understand what martial arts meant to me or what it would do for me in the future. I was having fun. I always wanted to keep training because, at that time, I wanted to be like some of the hero's in martial arts movies that I would watch every Sunday at the local cinema. Such hero's like; Jet Li, Samo Hung, Jackie Chan, Bruce Lee, Gordon Liu, etc. They always had the coolest moves and most ridiculous levels of flexibility and fighting styles. As I got older, I decided to take my training more seriously and started to compete in local martial arts tournaments. I did pretty well, but I wanted more out of competition, so I began to look for more opportunities.

PERSONAL ACHIEVEMENTS

- Undergraduate degree in Criminal Justice 2001
- Master's Degree in Business Administration "MBA" 2005
- 2018 IWUF/PAF Certified Wushu Judge

MAJOR ACHIEVEMENTS

- 1995 US Olympic Demonstration Team Member
- NBL World Champion 1997
- Naska Champion 1998-2000
- 2011 US Team Member
- 2011 US Team Member toured; Russia, Ukraine and Amsterdam
- 2016 Team USA Wushu Coach Pan American Games
- 2017 Silver Medalist, 7th World Kung Fu Championships, Emeishan, Sichuan Province China
- 2017 Bronze Medalist, 7th World Kung Fu Championships, Emeishan, Sichuan Province, China
- 2019 Team USA Wushu Coach for the Pan American Games

In 1993 I talked with my Shifu's Bobby Czibok and Robert Heckman about wanting to change martial arts styles to try something different. I left my fighting system to learn how to perform with martial arts. They gave me their blessings and I started to train with Sensei Bing Tran. He and his children were competing and performing all over Colorado and doing very well. I liked what they were doing, so I decided to train with them at their school. There I started to train in TaeKwonDo; it was something very new and different for me. As I moved up the ranks, there was a unique opportunity that got dropped in my lap.

The United States Olympic Center based in Colorado Springs, Colorado, was looking for performers for the 1995 U.S. Olympic Festival to be held that summer. They started drafting students from the school I was training for this performance. I ended up the last one to be added to the team. I was excited since this was the most significant platform I would be able to showcase my skills. After the Olympic Festival, I kept the momentum and decided to compete in the National Black Belt League, where I won 2 world titles in 1997 in the soft style division "Wushu" and the Rookie of the Year title. I traveled all over the country and to other countries such as Mexico, Ireland, Guatemala, to perform and compete. I continued training and building my skills, and in 1998 I began competing on the NASKA circuit. I was able to win several national championship titles as well.

In 2000 I started training for the film industry and was able to work on a few low and medium budget films trying to get my big break. During that year, I had a significant injury that put my film and competition career on indefinite hold. Once healed, I started teaching martial arts classes privately, and it later turned into a career with a great future.

I believe without a doubt that martial arts saved my life. Without learning the fundamental principles of martial arts, I would not be able to make the proper decisions in my life and my future. I am the only person in my family to ever go to college. Going to college wasn't an option for us growing up; we needed to get a job right away and leave college for other people. However, with the guidance of my grandmother and the tenets I learned through martial arts, I knew there was a different life and future for me. There was no path; I had to push my way through the obstacles in my way and create a path for myself and others to follow. As a young man, I was timid and shy, not speaking up or advocating for myself. Martial arts helped me to become the man I am today. The tournament circuit allowed me to voice myself and speak to everyone through my movements and forms on the "big stage," this process taught me how to stand alone and be confident in who I was and how I will become. In 2002 I decided to enter graduate school because I believed if I could finish and complete this level of education, I could separate myself from everyone around me and create a strong force to be reckoned with changing my future and the future of my family.

You see, I could never have accomplished what I have if I never was taken to my first martial arts class in my small neighborhood church. My grandmother, my mother, and my wife Maria are the driving force for my passion for the martial arts.

VICTOR TERAN

"Thanks to martial arts and its discipline. Discipline is a must in our lives. It's what gives us structure and reason to do what we do."

TRAINING INFORMATION

- Belt Ranks & Martial Arts Styles: International Taekwon-Do Federation - 7th Dan

- Instructors/Influencers: Great Grandmaster Kwang Duk Chung

- Birthdate: June 6, 1977

- Birthplace/Growing Up: New York

- Yrs. In the Martial Arts: 38 years

- Yrs. Instructing: 30 years

- School owner, Manager & Instructor at International Taekwon-Do Academy

PROFESSIONAL ORGANIZATIONS

- All International Taekwon-Do Federation

- International Taekwon-Do Federation

Master Teran is an award-winning published author, inducted in the Master's Hall of Fame for class 2019 and the United States Hall of Fame for class 2020. Served and defended our great nation from late 1996 until August 2013. He is a 7th Degree Master Instructor Trainer. U.S Marine Corps Combat Veteran. Sergeant in the United States Marine Corps. Diplomatic security for Blackwater and Triple Canopy. (Security Protective Specialist) Agent-in-Charge direct hire for the U.S. Department of State in the Diplomatic Security Service. Ambassador for the American Military University.

Mr. Teran was first introduced to Taekwon-Do in New York City at the age of 5. He is presently training under his Great Grandmaster Kwang Duk Chung in New York. Mr. Teran became a Black belt at age 13. He first started his initial training as an assistant instructor teaching children ages 8-12 and assisting the adult classes under his instructor's supervision.

At the age of 15, Mr. Teran could compete at the Tri-State Championship in Virginia, taking Gold in Sparring and silver in the Grand Master Championship. Mr. Teran was a Silver medalist for the All-American Grand National Championship in New Jersey. In 2015, he competed once again at the 10th Metro Championship in New Jersey, bringing home a Gold. In between his martial arts years, Mr. Teran competed in numerous

PERSONAL ACHIEVEMENTS

- Personal Security Specialist
- Tactical commander
- Quick reaction force commander
- Advance/reconnaissance commander
- Air reconnaissance and reaction force
- Shift Leader
- Detail Leader and finally Agent-in-Charge (Security Protection Specialist) for the U.S. Ambassador /Consul General protective detail in Iraq and any other high-level Diplomatic Advisors under the U.S. Department of State and the U.S. - Foreign government relation
- In 2011, Mr. Teran became the Chief Instructor for the Baghdad Taekwon-Do Club, where he trained the Iraqi Olympic Committee in Baghdad Iraq under a U.S. – Iraqi Diplomatic program. Shortly after, Mr. Teran reported back to Washington, DC, for six months of intensive training. Upon graduation, he gained the title of Security Protective Specialist (Agent-in-Charge), returning to Iraq as his first post as direct hire with the U.S. Department of State.

MAJOR ACHIEVEMENTS

- International Taekwon-Do Academy has been awarded the "Best of Jersey City" in the Martial Arts category for six consecutive years (2015-2020)
- Business Hall of Fame for six consecutive years (2015 & 2020)
- Awarded "Best School" in Championships six consecutive years. (2014-2019)

championships placing Gold and Silver in Sparring.

His hard work, dedication, and determination have helped him learn and appreciate Taekwon-Do as an art and has allowed him to travel to Seoul, Korea, to train with the Korean Olympic Team.

Upon his return to the United States, Mr. Teran was offered six more months to train in Seoul with the Olympic committee and an opportunity to travel to Colorado Springs for the United States Olympic team trials. Throughout the years, Taekwon-Do has given him the tools and discipline to take on any challenge life would throw at him. Mr. Teran joined the Marine Corps at age 18, attending Marine Corps Boot camp in Parris Island, SC.

Upon graduation, Mr. Teran was stationed in Camp Lejeune, NC, taking on a new challenge as an Infantryman. In early 1999, he came across a Taekwon-Do club where he continued his training, and within a few weeks, Mr. Teran became the Chief Instructor for the Marine Corps Taekwon-Do team. Mr. Teran's focus was on "fighting" drills while waiting for approval to participate in the Pan American Games in late 1999.

In 2002, Mr. Teran attended the Marine Corps Martial Arts program. Through hard work, blood, and sweat, he moved up the ranks and graduated as a Marine Corps Martial Arts/Close Combat Instructor trainer. Mr. Teran continued his service in the military for eight years. He then left the Marine Corps to pursue other challenges in life.

MAJOR ACHIEVEMENTS

- Received the 2017, 2018, 2019 and 2020 Martial Arts Excellence Award

- Ranked Top ten "Best Master Instructor" in New Jersey for three consecutive years (2017-2019)

- Best of 2018 Garden State Cup Taekwon-Do Championship

- Five-time New Jersey Metro Taekwon-Do Champion (2015-2019)

- Four-time New Jersey State Champion (2016-2019)

- United States National Taekwon-Do Champion (2019

Mr. Teran became a close combat instructor (Hand-to-Hand) and a Military Operation in Urban Terrain instructor (House to House clearing), Enemy Prisoner of War instructor, and an attending advance sniping and counter sniping instructor course. Mr. Teran attended many other tactical courses to include intensive weapons training, tactical operations, medical training (Johns Hopkins hospital and field related), and multiple high threat evasive driving courses, to name a few.

In 2003, Mr. Teran deployed to Iraq, fighting the war on terror. In March 2004, he decided to leave the Marine Corps to join the U.S. State Department as a Private Security Contractor stationed in Iraq, conducting high threat personal protection for High-level dignitaries. During this time, Mr. Teran would train his teammates in both martial arts and Close Combat.

Mr. Teran promotions/titles are as follow:

- Personal Security Specialist

- Tactical commander

- Quick reaction force commander

- Advance/reconnaissance commander

- Air reconnaissance and reaction force

- Shift Leader

- Detail Leader and finally Agent-in-Charge (Security Protection Specialist) for the U.S. Ambassador /Consul General protective detail in Iraq and any other high-level Diplomatic Advisors under the U.S. Department of State and the U.S. - Foreign government relation

In 2011, Mr. Teran became the Chief Instructor for the Baghdad Taekwon -Do Club, where he trained the Iraqi Olympic Committee in Baghdad Iraq under a U.S. – Iraqi Diplomatic program. Shortly after, Mr. Teran reported back to Washington, DC, for six months of intensive training. Upon graduation, he gained the title of Security Protective Specialist (Agent-in-Charge), returning to Iraq as his first post as direct hire with the U.S. Department of State.

After ten and a half years operating in Iraq, Mr. Teran decided to resign his Federal government's position to continue his teachings and training in the art that first taught him the fundamentals.

"Taekwon-Do is a way of life; by following the tenets of Taekwon-Do it can only lead to success. What I have learned over all these years is not just kicking, punching, or doing the exercises, but understanding the importance of these fundamentals and guidelines, we must abide by. These guidelines are what made me successful in life and kept me alive".

Mr. Teran's understanding of the tenets of Taekwon-Do and the Marine Corps' core values is what he plans to bring forth into his school – courtesy, integrity, perseverance, self-control, indomitable spirit, honor, courage, and commitment. In addition, Mr. Teran is also looking forward to teaching the next generation of students and see them grow and learn the art of Taekwon-Do.

"One of the most rewarding things as a teacher is passing my knowledge and the love for the art. The greatest gift that I can receive is having those who want to put that extra effort to learn…"

Mr. Teran has received many awards and letters of recommendations from American Ambassadors in Iraq, Secretary of State Condoleezza Rice, and Consul General in Basra Iraq. He received a Certificate of Appreciation from the Baghdad Taekwon-Do Club and many other Diplomatic figures/Prime minister(s) who were stationed in High Threat.

The International Taekwon-Do Academy has received a 'Letter of Proclamation' from the Jersey City Mayor's office. Letter from Governor Chris Christie from New Jersey and two Outstanding Leadership Awards signed by Mayor McCormac from Woodbridge, New Jersey.

Mr. Teran not only teaches martial arts and teamwork to the youth in our community, but he is also an Ambassador for the Student Veterans of America Chapter for the American Military University. His focus is to work with veterans' outreach programs, partnering with other organizations like the Wounded Warrior Project to provide mentorship and training for the wounded veterans who suffer from post-traumatic stress syndrome, chronic traumatic encephalopathy, and traumatic brain injury.

Mr. Teran also partners with the Play4Autism Foundation to provide training to children with Autism spectrum disorder.

This is a special project simply because it's all about giving back to our community in the belief that the opportunity to learn martial arts should be available to everyone, no matter their condition, setbacks, or limitations.

Mr. Teran is specialized not only in personal protection (Diplomatic Protection in high threat), but he has also been in the fitness industry for many years. His passion is to teach self-defense and fitness. This passion has earned him the opportunity to partner with a bodybuilding supplement and fitness company, to one day reach the goal of becoming a "Sponsored Athlete" and "Elite Trainer".

Mr. Teran has also been accepted and is part of the Men's Health Fitness Council, where he will share fitness strategies/exercises, meals plan, etc. and be featured in future fitness articles. Mr. Teran was also offered a position to become a "Sponsored Fitness Apparel" Ambassador.

Mr. Teran is always seeking self-improvement, and whoever is part of his team will ensure to do the same for them. "Our training is reality-based, as well as the art of Taekwon-Do. I don't just teach kicking and punching, but also share my experiences with my students that have helped me become a better person in life. I teach the D.O. in Taekwon-do. We do this as a way of life, not as a sport but as a Martial Artist, elevating our Martial Spirit in every training session. For my students to progress and learn about the D.O., I must train and learn from my Great Grandmaster KWANG DUK CHUNG. I must always set that example for students/disciples to follow. If not, then what kind of Master will I be?"

International Taekwon-Do Academy has been awarded:

- The "Best of Jersey City" in the Martial Arts category for six consecutive years (2015-2020).

- Business Hall of Fame for six consecutive years (2015 & 2020)

- Awarded "Best School" in Championships six consecutive years. (2014-2019).

- Received 2017, 2018, 2019, and 2020 Martial Arts Excellence Award

- Ranked Top ten "Best Master Instructor" in New Jersey for three consecutive years (2017-2019)

- Best of 2018 Garden State Cup Taekwon-Do Championship.

- Five-time New Jersey Metro Taekwon-Do Champion (2015-2019).

- Four-time New Jersey State Champion (2016-2019)

- United States National Taekwon-Do Champion (2019).

"We are looking forward to continuing our service in the community and making a difference one student at a time…"

Martial arts have allowed me to grow physically, mentally, and spiritually. It has helped me overcome many insecurities and assist me in my personal growth as an individual and team player. Martial arts have also allowed me to be pro-active with the "I can attitude."

The fact that it allows you to grow and become a better version of yourself is a great advantage. I grew up training like it was the military. Hence, the reason why I joined the United States Marine Corps and excelling in everything I came across.

Martial arts has been the best thing I have done in my life. It has given me the confidence to try something I never thought possible. While in the Corps, I always volunteered for every instructor course, either sniping, counter sniping, urban warfare, martial arts, etc. It did not matter what instructor course it was; I took it for the sole purpose of being ahead of my peers and seeking self-improvement. The "taking on the challenge," always "competitive," and staying "pro-active" is all thanks to martial arts and its discipline. Discipline is a must in our lives. It's what gives us structure and reason to do what we do.

THEODORE VICK

"Martial Arts have impacted my life in various ways, such as increased knowledge of dealing with people inside and outside the arts."

TRAINING INFORMATION

- Belt Ranks & Martial Arts Styles: Eclectic Karate - Black Belt, Five Animal Style Kung Fu - Black Sash, Sho Tai Flow Combat - Seventh Dan, Shotokan Karate Do - Seventh Dan, Mind Body and Shen - Black Belt/Sixth Level

- Instructors/Influencers: Sensei William Mason, Sifu Pearl, Grandmaster Jay-Bee LaPuppet, Grandmaster Matthew Trimmer, Grandmaster Derrick Trent

- Birthdate: September 1, 1956

- Birthplace/Growing Up: New York City, NY

- Yrs. In the Martial Arts: 51 years

- Yrs. Instructing: 51 years

- Instructor and Co-founder of Mind Body and Shen School

PROFESSIONAL ORGANIZATIONS

- Mind Body and Shen
- Shotokan Karate Do
- United Nations of Martial Arts
- United Warriors Association

My name is Grandmaster Theodore Vick, and I have over 50 years of experience in martial arts. My father and mother kept me in Fordham University Sports Program as a youth. My father brought home a book called defend yourself with Ketsugo. The book contained various martial arts styles. I practiced the exercises and techniques every day. One day, a new kid moved to into my neighborhood, and he was a martial artist. He started teaching me when I was 13 years old. I was interested in other sports and taught him basketball in return for his martial arts skills. What made me start taking martial arts seriously is when I started protecting the younger kids from the older ones. I started teaching many kids what I had learned. I believe I got started in martial arts to help people and show them a better way to live mentally and physically. I studied eclectic karate under Sensei William Mason and various styles of Kung Fu under Sifu Pearl.

PERSONAL ACHIEVEMENTS

- B.A. in Liberal Arts from College of New Rochelle

- Participated in the NBA Pro-Am/ Basketball League

- Invitation for United States Basketball Tryouts (Staten Island Stallions)

MAJOR ACHIEVEMENTS

- National Youth Sports Program Appreciation Award (2002)

- Lifetime Appreciation Award from Mind Body and Shen (2005 & 2007)

- Tai Chi Hall of Fame Certificate of Martial Arts Dedication (2007)

- The American Shotokan Appreciation Award (2008)

- Induction into the Action Martial Arts Hall of Honors (2009)

- Action Martial Arts Magazine Award for Exemplary Dedication to The Martial Arts for 35+ Years (2009)

- Exemplary Contributions as an Ambassador to The Martial Arts (2010)

- Goodwill Ambassador to The Martial Arts (2013)

- Platinum Contribution to The Martial Arts (2015)

- Esteem Martial Artist Award (2019)

- 50 years Dedication to The Martial Arts (2020)

In 1989, I was certified by the Dallas Texas Institute of Aerobic Technology. I competed in various martial arts tournaments and taught martial arts in various locations such as Grambling State University, Lincoln University (PA), and Bronx Public School #151. One of my greatest accomplishments is co-founding The Mind Body and Shen Organization. Martial Arts has impacted my life in various ways, such as increased knowledge of dealing with people of all walks of life. My thought process is philosophical and open and has put me in the position to be recognized in books and magazines; I even wrote an article for Action Martial Arts Magazine in 2008. I've also received many awards and recognitions from my peers:

- National Youth Sports Program Appreciation Award (2002)

- Lifetime Appreciation Award from Mind Body and Shen (2005 & 2007)

- Tai Chi Hall of Fame Certificate of Martial Arts Dedication (2007)

- The American Shotokan Appreciation Award (2008)

- Induction into the Action Martial Arts Hall of Honors (2009)

- Action Martial Arts Magazine Award for Exemplary Dedication to The Martial Arts for 35+ Years (2009)

- Exemplary Contributions as an Ambassador to The Martial Arts (2010)

- Goodwill Ambassador to The Martial Arts (2013)

- Platinum Contribution to The Martial Arts (2015)

- Esteem Martial Artist Award (2019)

- 50 years Dedication to The Martial Arts (2020)

Martial Arts have impacted my life in various ways, such as increased knowledge of dealing with people inside and outside the arts. I started sharing what I had learned with many kids. I believe I got started in martial arts to enhance myself and others to a better way of thinking. My thought process is systematic and open and has put me in the position to be recognized in books and magazines; I also was pictured on the cover of Action Martial Arts Magazine Hall of Honors World History Book in 2020.

I've also received many awards and recognitions from my peers. My greatest achievement was receiving the 50 years of Dedication Award from Action Martial Arts Magazine in 2020. I received this award in front of a huge audience with my family and close friends present. This award truly signifies the impact I have made to the Martial Arts and its impact on me. Martial Arts has allowed me to travel to numerous places such as Grambling (Ruston) LA, Longview TX, and Memphis, TN. I met different people from all walks of life and a few celebrities Grandmaster Cynthia Rothrock, Grandmaster Ronald Duncan, Grandmaster Ron Van Clief, and Michael Jai White.

Pioneers
BLACK BELTS

ROBERTO ARREDONDO

"I owe the Martial Arts community a great deal of gratitude! Without this knowledge, I wouldn't have served as I have for the last 45 years of my life..."

TRAINING INFORMATION

- Belt Ranks & Martial Arts Styles: Judo - Green belt, Karate Shotokan - 1st Dan, Wrestling, Boxing, Taekwondo Kukkiwon- 1st Dan, Shijou Ryu Aiki Jiu-jitsu - Brown belt

- Instructors/Influencers: Coach Larry Godin, Joe Gomez, Reyno Arredondo, GM Chang Lee, Master Stephanie Johnson, Sensei James Karin, Sensei Ken Rebstock, GM Guy James, Master Mack Gore, Sifu/Sensei Jermaine Garcia

- Birthdate: October 27, 1963

- Birthplace/Growing Up: Dallas, TX

- Yrs. In the Martial Arts: 45 years

- Yrs. Instructing: 38 years

- School owner, Manager & Instructor, Partner in Chang Lee's Taekwondo, Manage & Coach of Dallas Park Dept., Forest Audelia Boxing Gym

PROFESSIONAL ORGANIZATIONS

- The Alliance of Guardian Angels since 1982 – Dir. of Operation

- International Chinese Boxing Association

- USA Archery Instructor Level ll

- USA Boxing Coach

I was introduced to Martial Arts at the age of eight. My father wanted to make sure I could defend myself and my siblings. We lived in a rough neighborhood of West Dallas and were constantly challenged.

Dad's friends were coming home from Vietnam so, I learned early and hard. The stories for survival and philosophy of fighting (Martial Arts) changed my perspective on the matter. It was just a matter of time before I would have to endure my first fight and how I thought about the entire situation. "It was no longer something which just takes place in the schoolyard." The decision to gain the knowledge and tools to give me the upper hand in a hostile altercation was made. Having family and friends interested in Boxing, Karate, and other Arts just made it easier to do. I was learning from any and every one possible.

The movies made it the combative arts enticing, watching Chuck Norris and Bruce Lee, TV show Kung Fu with David Carradine (Carradine befriended my father after making a movie [On the Line]) and Boxing

PROFESSIONAL ORGANIZATIONS

- International Mountain Bike Instructor
- USA Taekwondo and USA wrestling Pending approval
- NOLS Wilderness training

PERSONAL ACHIEVEMENTS

- Lettered in both Football and Wrestling in High School and most improved Wrestler of the year
- I earned my first black belt in Karate at 13 years old.
- Boxed while serving in the United States Army, Ft. Leonard Wood MO.
- I joined and remained in a leadership role in the Alliance of Guardian Angels and served my community. Since June of 1982.
- USA Boxing and Archery Instructor level ll, International Mountain Bike Instructor, Earned my 1st Dan in Taekwondo after two knee replacements.
- Selected to escort to Congressional Medal of Honor winner MSGT. Roy Benavidez 1984

MAJOR ACHIEVEMENTS

- Joined the United States Army, served from June 83 to May of 89. 12-B/62-J Combat Engineer and earned the rank of Sgt. E-5

Champion Greatest of All times, Muhammad Ali! This was early in my childhood life, but it set in and didn't stop. I continue to learn from whoever I can. It's created a balance. My physical, mental, and spiritual life are complete.

Martial Arts has given me the ability and confidence to serve my community, even in its worse environment. And as a Guardian Angel patrolling the streets of Dallas without a weapon, putting boots on the ground, standing toe to toe, eye to eye in communities desperately needing help. Deterring would-be criminals, safeguarding the streets and other public areas, and empowering others to clean up their neighborhoods, take ownership, and move forward on their initiative. To lead by example and teach with humility.

Studies of the arts have inspired us to teach others, not just in hand to hand but in community service and quality of life issues in our backyard.

Also, managing a boxing gym for the City of Dallas since August 2017 allows for coaching, advice, and training knowledge to be used. Hundreds of participants have passed through the program, learning how to box and learning good sportsmanship, camaraderie, overcoming adversity, and being self-reflective. And having several Golden Gloves, State and a National Champion feel pretty good too!

MAJOR ACHIEVEMENTS

- Employed by the City of Dallas, Park & Recreation for Since 1991. Working with at Risk youth my entire career as a Gang Intervention/Prevention working supervisor and outreach specialist for nine years, managing After School Programs with the Dallas Independent School District for 16 years and the Forest Audelia Youth Boxing Gym since September of 2017 and reaching thousands of adolescents to impact their lives positively. It offers hundreds of programs over 29 years, ranging from cultural arts, sports programs, fitness, health and wellness, personal development, mentoring, leadership, and business development. Also included were entrepreneurial training, GED/ High school diploma, drug rehabilitation and runaway recovery/extraction, and outdoor adventures, to name a few.

- National Geographic featured me working with at Risk Youth on a cultural art project called Save Outdoor Sculptures in collaboration with the Office of Cultural Affairs, City of Dallas.

- Created an Entrepreneurial program, a teen-only operation, making art frames for sale,

- "Cliff Hangers" in Oak Cliff, Dallas, Texas.

- Played a role on "Dallas" as the House boy during the 80's

- Owned and coached Semi-Pro Football from 1989 to 1999, Dallas Express, Texas Rampage, and the Dallas Diesel. Butch Johnson of the Dallas Cowboys was our commissioner for the North American Football League, and we had Tex Shramm, former owner of the Dallas coin tossed our games and air on television.

Holding self-defense/anti-rape classes gratis, training neighborhood watch groups, and recently training Dallas Police Department as well as other departments around the Dallas/Ft. Worth Metroplex in non-lethal arrest techniques, demonstrating ways to restrain and subdue an assailant without kneeling on the neck or even mounting the torso.

I owe the Martial Arts community a great deal of gratitude! Without this knowledge, I wouldn't have served as I have for the last 45 years of my life and hopefully continue to do so by God's grace.

MAJOR ACHIEVEMENTS

- Welcome the Attorney General of United States, William Barr, to our boxing as part of Project Safe Neighborhood
- Senior Vice president of T3RUST Consulting LLC

THOMAS CATER

"Martial Arts has allowed me to help and encourage individuals of all ages to achieve things they thought were not possible."

I have always had the desire to help people. As a kid my friends and I used to go to Chinatown to watch martial arts movies. I got started in the martial arts because I met Master Bow Sim Mark after a demonstration of drunken sword and started training with a friend in Hung Gar. Shortly afterward, I saw Sun Dragon and wanted to be like Carl Scott. The study of martial arts has helped me in every aspect of my life. It has allowed me to help and encourage individuals of all ages to achieve things they thought were not possible.

Thomas Cater born in Boston Massachusetts to Carol and Sam, has been involved in the martial arts for over 35 years and has been competing and teaching for well over 25 years. He was interested in martial arts as a kid partly due to his legendary

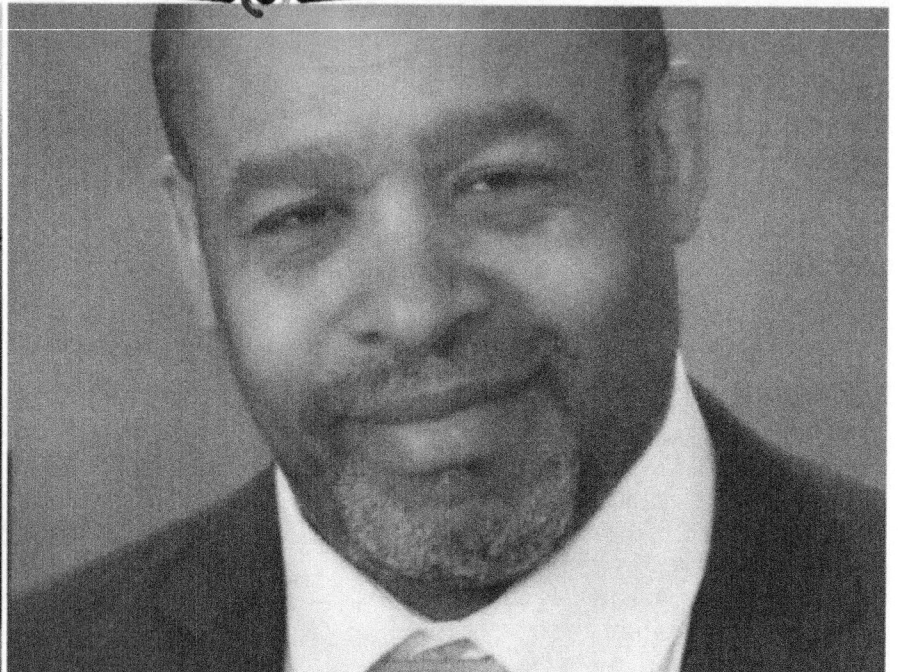

TRAINING INFORMATION

- Belt Ranks & Martial Arts Styles: 4th degree black belt in Pai Lum, Black belt in Clawfist Gung fu, Black Sash in White Crane Kung Fu, Brown Sash in Chinese Boxing

- Instructors/Influencers: Sigung Clarence Cooper, Sijo Stephen Key, Sifu Woo Chin, Master Frankie Dow

- Birthdate: September 5, 1965

- Birthplace/Growing Up: Boston, MA

- Yrs. In the Martial Arts: 36years

- Yrs. Instructing: 34 years

- School Owner, Roslindale Martial Arts Program & Inner Strength Self Defense Martial Arts Academy, Instructor

PROFESSIONAL ORGANIZATIONS

- United States Martial Arts Hall of Fame

- Krane International Inc.

- United States Martial Artist Hall of Fame

PERSONAL ACHIEVEMENTS

- United States Martial Arts Hall of Fame Inductee Master's Degree in Conflict Resolution

- United States Martial Artist Hall of Fame Inductee City of Boston Citation for community service City of New Bedford Citation

Uncle Abraham Madre, founder of Boston Inner-city Taekwondo, located in Grove Hall, Massachusetts . He fell in love with Kung Fu after going to the public theater in Chinatown and seeing Carl Scott and Soul Brothers of Kung Fu in 1977. Cater is a social justice and community activist, with strong roots in the community. He's known for working with, encouraging, and mentoring young people of all ages and diversities.

MAJOR ACHIEVEMENTS

- Founder and Chief Instructor of Roslindale Martial Arts Academy and Inner Strength Self Defense Kung Fu School

- Assistant Instructor at Fitness Essentials Northeast Dragons

- Social Justice coordinator at Massachusetts Church of Our Lord Jesus Christ (COOLJC)

- Supervisor for COOLJC National Security Team

- Boston Citizen Schools after school martial arts Instructor

- Shelburne Community Center seniors Tai Chi Program Instructor

- Citation from the cities of Boston and New Bedford, Massachusetts

- 4th Higher level (4th degree black sash) Pai Lum (White Dragon Fist Kung Fu)/ (Clarence Cooper and Malcolm Lucas)

- Black belt Clawfist Gung Fu (Steven key)

- Instructor White Crane Kung Fu (Woo Chin)

- Advanced rank Chinese Boxing (Frankie Dow)

- Studied Jeet June Do (Exlus Bennet)

- Shao Lin Kung Fu (Master Lee and David Bowden)

- Former Martial Arts Instructor for the Boston Area Health and Hospitals Education Center (BEHEC)

- Massachusetts State and National Championships

- NASAK (North American * Sports Karate Association)

- United States Martial Arts Hall of Fame

- International Martial Arts Council of America

- Christian Martial Arts Council

- NBL/SKIL (National Blackbelt League/ Sports Karate International League

- United States Martial Arts Hall of Fame Inductee

- 2018 United States Martial Artist Hall of Fame Inductee

- 2017 Krane National Champion Krane Overall Grand Champion

ISAAC "IKE" DAVIS

"Studying martial arts/boxing has blessed me and strengthened me in mind, body, and spirit."

TRAINING INFORMATION

- Belt Ranks & Martial Arts Styles: Chinese Boxing/Shotokon Karate (Green Belt), WuzuQuan Kungfu, Chen style Tai Chi (Red Sash), Wing Chun (Black Belt)

- Instructors/Influencers: Isaac "Ike" Davis (Father), Grandmaster Gary Baker, Grandmaster Kam Po Lee, Grandmaster Anthony Arnett

- Birthdate: September 28, 1962

- Birthplace/Growing Up: Jacksonville, FL

- Yrs. In the Martial Arts: 38 years

- Yrs. Instructing: 20 years

- School owner (Ike Davis Box-Fit LLC), Instructor

PROFESSIONAL ORGANIZATIONS

- Guns n Hoses Boxing Committee
- The Global Traditional Wing Chun Kungfu Association.

My father was a boxing enthusiast. It was my father that introduced me to fight training of any kind. Boxing is my first love. I got interested in martial arts by seeing martial arts on television via shows like The Green Hornet with Bruce Lee as Kato. I also watched "Black Belt Theater" on Saturday nights. Once I got older, my friends and I would go to the theater to see martial arts movies on the big screen. We were too poor to afford lessons back then, so we would leave the theater and remember as many techniques and training from the film as possible and practice that. I fell in love with the arts and have been training ever since.

PERSONAL ACHIEVEMENTS

- I became head coach and lead trainer of the Jacksonville Fire Department Boxing Team in 2004 and still hold that position today. I have the most wins among all other coaches to this date. I became lead Kung Fu Sanda instructor for Master Kam Lee at Tai Chi Kungfu Academy in 2005. I still teach there. I am a junior instructor at Arnett's Wing Chun Training Center. I started my business, Ike Davis Box-Fit LLC in July of 2019.

MAJOR ACHIEVEMENTS

- 2003 Guns n Hoses trainer of the year. In 2014, we helped coach a student to a world Sanda title in the ICMAC Orlando. Also, in 2014, I was inducted into the Guns n Hoses Boxing Hall of Fame. In 2018, the Fire Department Connection wrote an article on my coaching: *Coach Ike's Camp Packs a Punch and Much More*

Studying martial arts/boxing has blessed me and strengthened me in mind, body, and spirit. It has aided me and inspired me to become the teacher, coach, and mentor that I am today. My greatest achievements come not from winning tournaments or trophies. The greatest success and sense of well-being, along with personal gratification for me, comes from the fact that the martial arts prepares one for the ultimate fight. That fight is life itself. I've learned, and I teach my students that the fight is to do the right thing. It is to live life to the fullest, to encourage and help our fellow man. In essence, fight to consistently do the right thing by ourselves and others no matter the circumstances.

CURTIS DIAZ

"Martial Arts has been a relationship that taught me focus and discipline, regardless of where I was in life."

TRAINING INFORMATION

- Belt Ranks & Martial Arts Styles: Shotokan Karate: Purple Belt, Kali Escrima, Jun fan Jeet Kune Do, Muay Thai, Wrestling/Freestyle & Greco Roman/Shuai Jiao, Southern Shaolin Five Animal Five Family Kung Fu: Black Sash/Sifu, Shaolin Hung Gar: Black Sash/Sifu, San Shou/San Da/Coach/Instructor, Xing Yi Quan

- Instructors/Influencers: Sensei Katsuya Kisaka, Sifu Rick Tucci, Sifu Louis Diaz, Sigung Jamal Rashad El

- Birthdate: October 2, 1981

- Birthplace/Growing Up: Trenton, NJ

- Yrs. In the Martial Arts: 34 years

- Yrs. Instructing: 21 years

- School owner (Shaolin 3 Warriors San Da), Instructor, Manager

PROFESSIONAL ORGANIZATIONS

- United States Head of Family Martial Arts Association

- Philadelphia Historic Martial Arts Society

- United States Black Belt Federation

- Puerto Rico Martial Arts Society

- Hung Gar Family Worldwide

- WEKAF (World Escrima Kali Arnis Federation)

I was motivated by my Uncle Carlos Diaz. He was a marine who trained in Isshin-ryu while stationed in Japan. He inspired me and I wanted to train with him, but I couldn't train with him because he lived too far. So, on my fourth birthday I was introduced to Sensei Katsuya Kisaka. I was also very inspired by watching martial artists on Black Belt Theater and Bruce Lee. Watching them was like watching superheroes. They were warriors and pushed their bodies above and beyond. They embodied all the characteristics that I wanted to have: loyalty, honor, integrity, courage, and discipline. A native of Trenton, NJ, I started martial arts training in the styles of Shotokan Karate under Master Kisaka. I then went on to train under Sifu Rick Tucci, where I trained in the styles of Jeet Kune Do (Jun Fan Gung Fu), Muay Thai (Thai Boxing), and Kali Eskrima (Filipino Martial arts). While training under the tutelage of Sifu Rick Tucci, I also had the privilege to train annually and receive certification under Guru Dan Inosanto and Ajarn Chai. I began studying more traditional styles of Kung Fu. I met Sifu Louis Diaz, who for the past 22 years has been training me in the arts of the Five Animal, Five Family Kung Fu, Hung Gar, and full contact San Da (San Shou).

PERSONAL ACHIEVEMENTS

- Completion of the State of NJ Department of Law and Public Safety Division of Criminal Justice Police Training Commission (Police Academy)

- The NRA Police Marksman

- DOC (Department of Corrections) Use of Force Specialist (Laddes of Force Training) Force System

- DOC Use of Force Specialist (Emergency Response Belt)

- DOC Argumentative and Physical Stage 2 Control and Restraint Techniques

- Weapons Retention Tactical Training

- DOC Disturbance and Riot Control, Hostage Rescue (Hostage Team Elements, Planning and Tactics)

- US Department of Homeland Security Community Emergency Response Team (Team Training Search and Rescue)

- DOC Less Lethal-Specialty Impact Munitions and Pepper Ball

- Less Lethal Net/Operator/FNH USA Less Lethal Certification

- Chris Cerino Training (Tactical Pistol and Pump Shotgun)

- Chris Cerino Training Group (Tactical Team Operations)

- DOC DNA Collections,

- DOC Use of Oleoresin Capsicum

- Straight Baton PR-24

I had the honor of being a Yup Sut Dai Gee (Inner chamber disciple) under Sifu Louis Diaz. I was also the first student under Sifu Louis Diaz to become a Sifu in Southern styles of Kung Fu and San Da.

Martial arts has been an integral part of my life at every juncture. It has been a relationship that taught me focus and discipline, regardless of where I was in life. It wasn't about being better than someone else, it was about being a better version of myself and earning that at every stage. I married martial arts and I am committed to it. It never gets old. There's always something to learn. As my life continues to change and evolve, so does my martial arts. I have developed a relationship with Sigung Jamal through which I have gained spiritual guidance, knowledge, a friend, and a father figure. Under the wing of Sigung Jamal I have not only learned what it takes to become a better fighter, but also a better instructor. I feel blessed to have witnessed the inspiring legacy and quintessential leadership of Sigung Jamal. I aim to train martial artists striving to achieve their goals and find an appreciation for martial arts. My goal is for all my martial artists is to build and master the physical, mental, and spiritual self in order to find and create balance within themselves.

MAJOR ACHIEVEMENTS

- 1996- WEKAF National Stick Fighting Champion
- 2017-Philadelphia Historic Martial Arts Society Hall of Fame
- 2018-Masters of Martial Arts Hall of Honors
- 2018-Action Martial Arts Magazine Hall of Honors Outstanding Achievements
- 2019-United States Head of Family Martial Arts Hall of Honors
- 2019-Action Martial Arts Magazine Hall of Honors Esteemed Martial Arts Award
- 2019-Legends of Martial Arts Hall of Fame

DAVID FISCUS

"I have the energy and stamina to do anything I choose to undertake!"

TRAINING INFORMATION

- Belt Ranks & Martial Arts Styles: Hawaii Koshoryu Kenpo Karate (3rd Dan)

- Instructors/Influencers: John Morris

- Birthdate: August 15, 1956

- Birthplace/Growing Up: Pontiac, MI

- Yrs. In the Martial Arts: 13 years

- I share knowledge that I've gained from these great masters I've known over the years with individuals to run their own schools

I was 51 years old and weighed almost 400 pounds. I married a lovely Brazilian woman who is 25 years younger than me. I felt for me to be the type of husband and hopefully father that I would like to be, I had to do something about my weight. I am diabetic; I have a 22-caliber projectile from an air gun in between the vertebrae in my neck. That same gun accident caused my left carotid artery to get atrophy to the point where no blood flows through it. I was a time bomb waiting to go off.

At my health club, I noticed there were some individuals wearing karate uniforms. As it turned out, my wife knew one of them. I found out that the health club was offering taekwondo classes. I was a strong man, but I had no cardio whatsoever. But I decided to take a chance to enjoy the taekwondo class. My youngest brother had started taekwondo year before, and I've been sharing with me the benefits that went far beyond self-defense.

So, I decided to start training—those first weeks with the most challenging thing I've ever done in my life. But I was determined not to stop. I eventually started peeling off weight and started getting into shape. The master was younger than I was, it was extremely patient, and he convinced me to participate in a power breaking contest. Much to my surprise, I won the grand championship by breaking 20 boards with one elbow strike.

PERSONAL ACHIEVEMENTS

- 3-time Texas Open Power Breaking Grand Champion
- Ambassador to the national sport karate museum
- Gi on display in the national sport karate museum
- 2016 inductee to the USA Martial Arts Hall of Fame

MAJOR ACHIEVEMENTS

- 3-time Texas Open Breaking Grand Champion

I've lost 100 pounds and have the heart of a 20-year-old man, according to my cardiologist. I've become a father, and I am an active father with my little four-year-old boy George. I have the energy and stamina to do anything I choose to undertake. I've cross-trained with Will champion We Can Kickboxers, Jujitsu Black Belt, Kenpo karate grandmasters, and cane fighting masters. I'm a member of the Houston stick fighting so station at the age of 63 I engage in full contact contests quarterly.

JEFFREY HAWKINS

"I enjoy teaching. I tell my white belts when you start, and I start, we make the journey together."

TRAINING INFORMATION

- Belt Ranks & Martial Arts Styles: Taekwondo Master 4th degree Black Belt
- Instructors/Influencers: Grandmaster Chang Lee, Master Myoung Choi
- Birthdate: August 31, 1961
- Birthplace/Growing Up: Dallas, TX
- Yrs. In the Martial Arts: 50 years
- Yrs. Instructing: 30 years
- Instructor

PROFESSIONAL ORGANIZATIONS

- Alpha Phi Alpha Fraternity Incorporated
- Prince Hall Mason, Texas Jurisdiction
- Dallas Police Department Volunteer Patrol
- Member of the Black Belt Federation

I started Martial Arts at the age of 9 at the Boys Club because of my size and watching various martial arts movies. I told my mother that I needed something to defend myself. I was not tall enough nor big enough to play football or basketball. Watching kung fu movies sparked my interest as my rank grew, so did my confidence. My training required my attention physically and mentally. Even before the blackbelt rank, martial arts became a way of life simply because of its commitment. I had grown into an extended family. Not to mention that I was usually training at least four days a week. One thing about training is that you will become an

PERSONAL ACHIEVEMENTS

- College Degree B.B.A. in Management, East Texas State University

MAJOR ACHIEVEMENTS

- Taekwondo Gold Medalist

- USA Martial Arts Hall of Fame inductee 2018

- USA Martial Arts Hall of Fame 2019

- Taekwondo Blackbelt of the year

- Bio featured in the book "The World's Greatest" Volume 24 (Martial Arts Masters Hall of Fame) - Currently released on Amazon, September 2020

assistant instructor or say helper with other students. At some point, you will compete in tournaments, competitions, etc. So now, my life is consumed with winning, whether good days or bad days. It has taught me that you may or may not be the better guy on any day, or you got outcoached. One's journey in martial arts, in my viewpoint, begins with being all about yourself. But as you mature to the Masters level or simply instructor, you begin to understand your training's wisdom because you transfer your knowledge to your students. It consumes you. I enjoy teaching. I tell my white belts when you start, and I start, we make the journey together.

MADISON HOBBS

"My genuine love for Martial Arts is how much it helps other people change their lives."

TRAINING INFORMATION

- Belt Ranks & Martial Arts Styles: American Open MMA (3rd degree Black Belt), AKANA (2nd Degree Black Belt), Renzo Gracie (Blue Belt)

- Instructors/Influencers: Ricky Smith, Randy Smith, Mike Winkeljohn, Greg Jackson

- Birthdate: February 18, 1992

- Birthplace/Growing Up: China Grove

- Yrs. In the Martial Arts: 23 years

- Yrs. Instructing: 10 years

- School owner (Hobbs JW MMA), Instructor

PROFESSIONAL ORGANIZATIONS

- AKANA
- JacksonWink

I started because of the ninja turtles and power rangers (haha). However, as I continued growing older, I started to see how the martial arts world does so much for those in it. The people I was engaging with were so confident in everything they do, yet still so humble and willing to listen to others' input. I knew that my calling was to bring this type of knowledge and understanding of oneself to the world to the best of my ability. As I continue getting better, those around me get better, and that's all I've ever wanted.

Not to sound cliché, but my genuine love for martial arts is how much it helps other people change their lives. I've seen families who were

PERSONAL ACHIEVEMENTS

- I've competed in over 80 competitions
- 17-time local champion
- 2 state Champion
- Southern national champ

MAJOR ACHIEVEMENTS

- Head striking coach for Belator pro Aj Siscoe.
- My students have won countless state championships, national championships, and placed 2nd in the IKF World Championship Tournament

struggling, come together through our gym. Men and women suffering from things such as depression, social anxiety and PTSD have also changed their lives through being able to come in and interact with our team and becoming part of a system that they know will always have their back.

MINDY JAQUES

"I can sum up my life philosophy in one word, MOVE. This is the essence of the Martial Arts..."

TRAINING INFORMATION

- Belt Ranks & Martial Arts Styles: Moo Duk Kwan Taekwondo, 1st Degree/Cho Dan, Chen stye Taijiquan, Third level, Medical Qigong, Physician level instructor, and practitioner, Various and continuing side studies with diverse instructors in Jo Do, Fencing, Judo, Hap Ki Do, Aikido

- Instructors/Influencers: Jason Paul Hughes, Master Kam Po Lee, Grandmaster Zhu Tian Cai

- Birthdate: September 12, 1968

- Birthplace/Growing Up: Jacksonville, FL

- Yrs. In the Martial Arts: 40 years

- Yrs. Instructing: 6 years

- Manager & Instructor, Doctor of Oriental Medicine and Medical Qigong, Junior partner in Kam Lee Center and Taiji Kung Fu

PROFESSIONAL ORGANIZATIONS

- National Certification Commission for Acupuncture and Oriental Medicine (NCCAOM)

- International Tian Cai Chenjiagou Taijiquan Federation

- Florida State Oriental Medicine Association (FSOMA)

- American Heart Association (AHA)

- National Qigong Association (NQA)

At age 12, I attended a summer camp in Jacksonville, Florida, for gifted students. We were allowed to pick our course of study. I was a small girl, always upset to see bullying at school, and always standing up for the underdog. I always used my intellect to help stop bullying, now came an opportunity to have an ace up my sleeve. When and if push came to shove, so to speak, for when the time for words was past. So, I selected a Taekwondo Bootcamp with Grandmaster John Chung. It was grueling. He gave no quarter. Many fell by the wayside during the summer course, but I was determined not to give up and to make Grandmaster Chung, if not proud, then at least not disgusted! Thus began my love of Taekwondo and the martial arts. My parents decided at one point that Taekwondo was not an appropriate course of study for me for various reasons and pulled me from the class with Grandmaster Chung. But I held on to my intention to learn and years later, as an adult in my 20s, found a brilliant and dedicated new Taekwondo teacher in Athens, Georgia; Jason Paul Hughes.

PERSONAL ACHIEVEMENTS

- Gold medal push hands, Jacksonville, FL 2012

- Silver medal 72 postures 2011, China

- Certificate of Achievement from Grandmaster Zhu Tian Cai, 2011, China

MAJOR ACHIEVEMENTS

- Graduated from Dragon Rises College of Oriental Medicine 2015, Florida licensed acupuncture physician, doctor of Oriental Medicine and Medical Qigong

- Design curriculum and teach Medical Qigong Classes for Kam Lee Center

- Design curriculum and teach self-defense classes in partnership with Sifu Isaac Davis; these classes focus on both de-escalating potential conflict and effective practical applications

I can sum up my life philosophy in one word, MOVE. This is the essence of the martial arts and the essence of Oriental medicine. It is also the essence of true health; mental, physical, and emotional. Without movement, there is stagnation, the mother of all disease. My study of the martial arts ultimately placed my feet on the path of becoming a doctor of Oriental medicine. My immersion in the martial arts helped me develop the dedication, consistency, discipline, and compassion (yes, compassion!) needed to become a healer, a physician, and a teacher. Before studying Oriental medicine, I became a paramedic (still licensed in Florida), a very physically demanding career, requiring courage, fortitude, and the ability to think quickly on your feet, changing plans on the fly, minute by minute. Again, my years of training in the martial arts prepared me for this career and helped me excel in the challenging atmosphere of EMS. During my EMS career, I was an instructor for the American Heart Association (AHA), teaching cardiopulmonary resuscitation and other advanced classes. Again, the martial arts helped me with my understanding of anatomy, circulation, and body mechanics. So, then what have the martial arts done for me? Simply everything.

BRIAN V. JOHNSON

"It's obviously clear that Wing Chun and Martial Arts has been the main factor for all the positive areas in my life.**"**

My parents enrolled me in martial arts as a form of therapy. I was the smallest of 8, and in my neighborhood, they knew that I might be a victim of bullying. And being my father's only son, he saw the need that I learn to protect myself. He also knew that it would be a form of release and discipline that would help me later on in life. Once I was exposed to martial arts, it became my most favorite thing to do. From boxing to wrestling, etc., Martial Arts is and was my life, and therefore I became committed to it.

Martial Arts has given me a very optimistic outlook, a passion to never quit and an unbelievable drive to focus and complete goals I've had in place or set new goals. Wing Chun in particular, through the teachings from the Nun Ng Mui down to Grandmaster William Cheung, who taught my instructor Sifu Anthony Arnett. I met Sifu Arnett in late 1997. As a whole, this system has improved all aspects of my martial arts journey, from boxing, wrestling, judo, Tang Soo Do, JKD, and finally I made wing chun my home. I have learned an array of different ways to govern myself and wing chun showed me how not only to apply science in fighting, but how to teach, speak, conduct myself to motivate others, and show others how to be powerful by using scientific mental ways to

TRAINING INFORMATION

- Belt Ranks & Martial Arts Styles: Japan Judo, Karate and Aikido (4th Degree Brown), Tang Soo Do (1st Dan), Self Defense (Blue Belt), Jeet Kune Do, Wing Chun (Level 8 Black Sash & Provisional Master Certification)

- Instructors/Influencers: Sa Bom Nim Joseph DeVita, Sifu Anthony Arnett

- Birthdate: April 5, 1971

- Birthplace/Growing Up: Stamford, CT

- Yrs. In the Martial Arts: 40 years

- Yrs. Instructing: 20 years

- School owner (Urban Combat Wing Chun Training), Instructor, Head Director and Co-Founder of Non-Profit Domestic Violence Prevention Awareness Program

PROFESSIONAL ORGANIZATIONS

- CT Wing Chun Against Domestic Violence

- Ct Wing Chun Against Bullying Representative

- Arnett Sport Kung Fu Association

- Arnett Wing Chun Training Association

PERSONAL ACHIEVEMENTS

- Being appointed Sifu Arnett's representative for his system
- Being nominated at the Kung Fu Expo in New Jersey 4 times

MAJOR ACHIEVEMENTS

- Being nominated for AMAA award
- Being nominated and appointed as domestic violence prevention leader for the Greater New Haven area

overcome or push through obstacles in their life. I've had a lot of bumps and bruises, lessons learned, losses, and gains, just as anyone else. However, Sifu Anthony Arnett has been gracious enough to accept me and continues to guide me.

It's obviously clear that Wing Chun and Martial Arts has been the main factor for all the positive areas in my life and serves me when bad times come. Martial arts brings peaceful meditation in my times of a situation when things get out of hand in my life. It's shown me how to have patience when I lose patience, it's shown me how to focus when life's out of focus. I've learned how to see through the 9 gates of vision taught to me by Sifu Arnett, how to get out of the way of irrational actions that might harm me and others, and how to step off from things that really don't matter. It helps me in so many ways and from Sa Bom Nim Joseph DeVita (T.S.D. M.D.K- M.G.K) to Sifu Anthony Arnett, these men have truly taught me the meaning of true martial arts and life lessons that will last a lifetime. I'm merely an instrument to their lessons. They are two men I can never thank enough and this is what I teach to those who want to learn.

DEREK JOHNSON

"From evolving as a shy kid to an outgoing adult, the martial arts have given me the confidence, attitude, and discipline I needed..."

TRAINING INFORMATION

- Belt Ranks & Martial Arts Styles: American Karate - 3rd Level Black Belt (Sandan), Kickboxing, Boxing, Full Contact Karate and Sport Karate, Experience in Ground Fighting, Weapons, Taekwondo and MMA

- Instructors/Influencers: Mr. Robert La Mont - (Kyoshi)

- Birthdate: February 23, 1983

- Birthplace/Growing Up: Carthage, TX

- Yrs. In the Martial Arts: 23 years

- Yrs. Instructing: 19 years

- Instructor

PROFESSIONAL ORGANIZATIONS

- East Texas American Society of Karate (E.T.A.S.K.)

- American Society of Karate (A.S.K.)

- Superfoot System

As a child, I absorbed martial arts movies and had a profound interest in studying martial arts, as well as having a knack for fighting. I never started a fight but being as small as I was, I made an easy target for bullies. Never backing down and never losing a scuffle, I could tell early on that I was good at fighting but hated having to get into trouble as I was a goodhearted kid that reacted physically only after I had had enough.

Growing up in a small town in East Texas there were not many options for formal martial arts training. My dad showed me how to defend myself and he pushed my brothers and I to give our best in team sports and the outdoors, but something was missing for me from regular sports and activities. I wanted to express myself as an athlete in a different way and I felt a spiritual connection to the martial arts. I began reading martial arts books at my local library and practicing the moves in the photographs, as well as mimicking Bruce Lee, Jean Claude Van Damme, Chuck Norris and The Karate Kid over and over again in front of the TV.

PERSONAL ACHIEVEMENTS

- Earning my Black Belt
- Undefeated empty hand, musical and weapons Kata Champion (including a rare perfect score)
- Numerous Point Fighting Grand Championships (including a Best of the Best State Tournament win)
- Undefeated in Amateur Boxing (including a 1st round TKO by RSC in my first ever bout)
- Graduating from film school at Stephen F. Austin State University

MAJOR ACHIEVEMENTS

- Becoming an Award-Winning Filmmaker
- Commendation by the City of Los Angeles
- Working with Sylvester Stallone, Arnold Schwarzenegger, Ralph Macchio and many other childhood heroes on my films and documentaries
- Being a good family man and friend

One day when I was 13 years-old I caught a flier at school promoting a new martial arts program that was starting up at the local college. This was huge news to me and I couldn't wait to get home to tell my parents. My father was reluctant for me to join, as he feared I would get my nose busted, but my mother knew how passionate I was and signed me up for American Karate. I immediately knew this was the place for me. Over time, I watched how my body transformed from scrawny to muscular and my personality from shy to extroverted. I was finding myself through the martial arts.

Karate came naturally for me, and I trained every day after school for hours at a time. Pretty soon I was on my way to becoming an undefeated kata champion and a prolific point fighter. I excelled in the art, sport, and self-defense aspects of karate. I was inventive and creative, all the while staying practical and logical in my approach to mastering and executing techniques. At age 16 I authored my own martial arts exercise, stretching and workout program that I still practice to this day when training. I lived and breathed the martial arts and never again had trouble with bullies as word got around school that I was a serious and respected fighter.

After four and a half years of intense focus and steady diligence, I earned my 1st Level Black Belt a week before graduating high school. From there, I continued training, competing and teaching throughout college. While in film school at Stephen F. Austin State University, I taught private karate

lessons, studied a variety of martial arts styles and participated in different activities like Taekwondo and boxing. I won my first amateur boxing match within 30 seconds of the first round with a TKO by RSC (referee stops the contest). Incidentally, my opponent was a Brown Belt in karate and I was a Black Belt in karate, but the poor kid never had a chance. Full contact was exhilarating, humbling, and much different than the previous point matches I was used to, and I knew that there was a big difference in controlled fighting and knocking your opponent's head off. To this day, I believe in the power of both concepts. Anyone can hit someone, but not everyone can come within a quarter of an inch at full speed and not hit their target by choice.

After college I became more and more focused on my filmmaking career: directing, writing, producing and editing feature films and documentaries. I taught private karate lessons and fight choreography seminars on the side but decided to not make the martial arts a full-time job, but rather a full-time passion when I'm not making movies. Upon moving to Los Angeles in 2014, I joined a UFC Gym and the Hollywood Boxing Gym where I continue my intensive training and heavy workouts and practice American Karate in my home gym. When visiting back home in Texas, I train in my original karate school as well as teach and compete.

Recently, my instructor of 23 years, Mr. Robert La Mont, director of the East Texas American Society of Karate, promoted me to 3rd Level Black Belt in American Karate as part of the Superfoot System. I plan to continue my lifelong journey as a martial artist in all aspects such as lifestyle, training, competing and teaching and hope to give back to the martial arts as much as it has given me.

Studying martial arts has impacted every aspect of my life since I was a child. From evolving as a shy kid to an outgoing adult, the martial arts have given me the confidence, attitude, and discipline I needed to achieve my life's goals. Not a day goes by that I don't think of my early life when I began training and how impactful those lessons and experiences were, and how they translate into my life today. As I grow older, I try and push myself further and further to the limit and strive to be the best human being I can be. From some of the worst tragedies in my life to some of the happiest triumphs, the tools I learned from karate helped guide me from darkness to light.

MICHAEL JOHNSON

"Through studying the martial arts, I've learned who I am as a person, but more importantly, that it is who I choose to be."

TRAINING INFORMATION

- Belt Ranks & Martial Arts Styles: 4th Duan - Five Family Fist Shaolin Kung Fu, 4th Duan - Emperor's Long Fist Kung Fu (Tai Tsu Chang chuan), 4th Duan – TaijiQuan, 4th Duan - Chinese Chin Na, 4th Duan - Natural Fist Kung Fu, 1st Degree Black Belt - Modern Arnis, Certified Instructor: Massage & Bodywork Therapies National Board Certified: Massage & Bodywork Therapy Neuromuscular Medical Massage

- Instructors/Influencers: GM David Kash, GM Rick Ward, GM Chris Laing, Hanshi Larry Isaacs, Hanshi Bruce Juchnick, GM Rondy McKee, Master Bob Reynolds, Master John Card, GM Steve McGowan, Master Matthew Staley

- Birthdate: April 13, 1978

- Birthplace/Growing Up: Mountain City, TN

- Yrs. In the Martial Arts: 27 years

- Yrs. Instructing: 9 years

- School owner (Cloud Forest Chin Woo College of Martial Arts), Manager, Instructor

It's been 27 years since I first stepped into a Kung Fu School and shook hands with my first teacher.

Why did I get started? That's not very interesting, as I had just heard from my best friend, Ethan, that he had started the day before and I wanted to also participate. No, the real story is why I stayed. For the first decade, I studied with Blue Ridge Kung Fu & Arnis Academy under Grandmasters Chris Laing and Rick Ward. Under their tutelage, I learned hard lessons in combat training. We trained traditional Sil Lum Kung Fu, Modern Arnis, Chinese Chin Na, Emperor's Long-Fist, and Natural Fist Kung Fu. My teachers taught me that in order to be a Master of Kung Fu, one must never stop being a student. This is why I pursued so many other systems under different Masters. There's too much for one person to learn, but that doesn't mean we can't try.

PROFESSIONAL ORGANIZATIONS

- American Massage Therapy Association (AMTA), NC Chapter Member
- World Wide Martial Arts Association (WWMAA) - Lifetime Member
- United States Kuo Shu Federation (USKSF) -Level A Judge
- Sei Kosho Shorei Kai - NC Representative
- Kosho Ryu Okuden - Founding Member
- International Martial Arts Kung Fu Federation - International Judge & Referee
- Cloud Forest Chin Woo Association - President
- Golden Lion Kuo Shu - President
- Wei Family Style Tai Chi Association - Lifetime Member
- Indonesian Pentjak-Silat Association -Lifetime Member
- International Shaolin Wu Su General Committee - Lifetime Member
- Wah Chiao Guo Ji Hui (Overseas Chinese Martial Arts Association) - Lifetime Member
- International Cupping Therapy Association - Member

PERSONAL ACHIEVEMENTS

- My biggest achievement on a personal level is to be loyal, kind, fair & honest in all of my dealings

At first, martial arts was just something for me to do after school. It was just physically challenging, and I liked how the exercise made my body feel. Then there came the friends that I made, and the community that built around my kung fu school. These were the main reasons that I stayed involved. When I entered college, training became more difficult as my responsibilities were getting heavier, but I kept training. As I would quickly discover though, the world is a real place, and bad things can happen and will happen. At the time, my study partner was a young kid named James. He was a nervous-looking freshman who always tried to do the right thing. James was a good kid, if a bit quirky, but was fascinated that I could teach him Kung Fu. One day, James came to me asking me if I would train him to defend himself. "Absolutely, maybe next week" I said. But I didn't train him. After a week went by, James approached me again asking, and I responded "Yes, of course, but not right now, I'm busy". Then after a few days more, James came in looking out of sorts and nervous, telling me that he may really need to know how to defend himself. I remember telling him "Soon, I'm just busy. Let's start next week".

The next day, James didn't show for classes. A week later, his body was found floating in a river. James was beaten by two of his 'friends'. They planned it for weeks according to the police.

Instantly I felt my mistake as my heart felt it was going to explode. I could not believe he was dead. But he was, and I was responsible. I didn't believe I was directly responsible for his death, but I felt like so in my heart. Perhaps I could have drilled some escape techniques or taught him to understand when people have intentions to harm you. Losing James taught me that as a martial artist, there is a responsibility that comes with it.

Now at the age of 42, I am the President of the Cloud Forest Chin Woo Martial Arts Association. ChinWoo is a Worldwide Martial Arts Association with headquarters located in all continents of the world. It was first founded by Huo Yuan Jia in 1909, in Shanghai China (See Jet Li, "Fearless"). ChinWoo saved martial arts. After the Chinese Boxer Rebellion, the public hated martial arts. ChinWoo Athletic Association changed the public's opinion by promoting martial arts as a form of positive exercise and community building. ChinWoo was the first Kung Fu school to allow women to teach classes as equals and supported equality among the arts.

MAJOR ACHIEVEMENTS

- Cloud Forest Chin Woo Association - President
- Golden Lion Kuo Shu - President
- National Board Certified Massage & Bodywork Therapist
- Founded Artists in Motion Massage Therapy
- Founded Behind the Cross Performing Arts Ministries

Cloud Forest Chin Woo is one of three headquarters located in the USA. Created in 1979, the Republic of China's Tai Chi Chuan Association appointed Grandmaster Chao Yuh Feng as branch director for Yun Lin (Cloud Forest) County Chin Woo Association, which was later moved to the United States when GM Feng moved to be with his daughter. In 1996, Cloud Forest was inherited by Grandmaster David Kash, and was kept under his watchful eye until 2019, when he retired and elected me as his Inheritor & President/CEO of the Association and College. I took the resources from my current school and joined the two schools, teaching both the traditional arts and the more modern-day arts.

Chin Woo embodies the spirit that I believe saves lives. This is why I push to open our doors to different styles, so that different kinds of people can come and find a martial arts home with us. Our school teaches 20 different systems, hoping to find a home for all people who need self-defense, or just the exercise. I donate time to teach at colleges & public schools, helping to empower others.

Through studying the martial arts, I've learned who I am as a person, but more importantly, that it is who I choose to be. So many people feel they are victims of circumstance, and maybe they are, but for me, I've learned that I have a big say in the fray and I get to choose my identity. By studying the martial arts, I have the chance to reflect on the historical context of many of life's biggest physical moral questions, the nature of violence, of right and wrong, of self-worth. I am a product of a lifetime of martial study. Even deeper than those questions, is the undying recognition that while there is much that can be accomplished through one's hard work and self-discipline, there are many other things that cannot be handled without great support in your life. A heartfelt thanks goes out to Erin, for always believing in me; to Marjory for traveling internationally to be part of this; to Corey for helping me build a dream, and to my core students: Michael & Nancy Bucknall, Phil Hudson & Diana Halsey, Catherine Priestley, Jayden Griffith, Katia Clements, Sifu John Card & Sifu Brandon Spencer.

WILLIAM MAYHAN

"Martial arts has made me the man I am today. It taught me Honor, Respect and Patience..."

TRAINING INFORMATION

- Belt Ranks & Martial Arts Styles: Isshin-ryu Karate, Yondan (4th Degree Black Belt)

- Instructors/Influencers: Sensei Doug King of King's Isshin-ryu Karate Club

- Birthdate: March 27, 1976

- Birthplace/Growing Up: Sussex County, NJ

- Yrs. In the Martial Arts: 30 years

- Yrs. Instructing: 10 years

- Instructor

PROFESSIONAL ORGANIZATIONS

- Member of Elks Lodge 2288

- Loyal Order of Moose

- New Jersey Chapter 13 of the Red Knights

- Volunteer Fireman

- Appalachian Bowman of New Jersey – Past President

- Competition Archery Shooter for PSE, Martin Archery and Matthews Archery

When I was barely a teenager, I found myself becoming infatuated with tv shows and movies like the old Kung fu theater movies and Bruce Lee and Chuck Norris movies; admiring the skill and discipline they showed as martial artists. I would mimic their movements on my own until the day I met my first instructor at the age of 13 - Sensei Doug King. He would become my first and only Sensei as I am still training under him 30 years later.

Not only has martial arts impacted/changed my life but most of it is due to my instructor Sensei Doug King who showed me the way of the Bushido.

Martial arts has made me the man I am today. It taught me honor; honor my teacher, the ones who came before me and the path that they have paved for us to follow.

PERSONAL ACHIEVEMENTS

- Starting my own business
- Being a professional archery competition shooter, a volunteer fireman
- Volunteering to help veterans
- Having a wonderful family and circle of friends

MAJOR ACHIEVEMENTS

- At 16 years old starting the first self-defense club at Wallkill Valley Highschool, Wallkill, NJ
- Winning Mt. Arlington F.O.P. International Karate Kung Fu Karate Grand Championship and has competed at many other tournaments.
- Lifetime Member American Isshin-ryu
- World Karate Union Inductee June 2015 for Competitor of the Year
- Action Martial Arts Magazine Hall of Honors 2018 Outstanding Achievements in the Martial Arts
- Action Martial Arts Magazine Hall of Honors 2020 Esteemed Martial Artist

Respect. Respect the ones you train with, your dojo, the history and legacy of your style.

Patience. Patience to know that life is a journey, that everything begins with the first step and that all things come with hard work and perseverance.

DAVID MORGAN

"As a martial artist, I must be a gentleman, I am not at liberty to be anything less."

I've had three starts in my martial arts career. The first was when my mother put me in TaeKwonDo in 1984 under now Grand Master Buddy Hudson in Pine Bluff, AR. As many parents do, it was an opportunity to involve me in a sport, especially for a kid that loved to play rough. I decided it was not for me in 1986 and left after earning a green belt. The second start was under now Grand Master Ron Turchi in Pine Bluff, AR, through the ATA, in 1990. I earned my 1st dan in TaeKwonDo in 1994. My third start was under Liam Jackson, 7th dan Goju-Ryu, in 2010, where I still train today as one of his assistant instructors and one of his five 2nd degree black belts. In 2010, I started my journey with Mr. Jackson when my ex-wife and I enrolled our daughter at his dojo. When he mentioned to me that his students had competed in eleven tournaments the year before, I had to give serious thought to returning to martial arts, although I was a fulltime college student with a fulltime job. My daughter decided it was not for her, but I was having too much fun. I realized that martial arts was a calling for me and that is where I belonged. I also began a journey with the Kobukan Karate Federation and earned a second dan under Kyoshi Mark Vellucci to enhance my Okinawan Karate journey.

Martial Arts has taught me several things. Numerous people over the years have had enough patience to teach me, and to stick with me enough to make me what I am today. I must do the same with the white belt in class. It taught me that the cream rises to the top. When I have a bad tournament performance, I go back to the drawing board to attempt to correct and improve, because blaming others will not help me.

TRAINING INFORMATION

- Belt Ranks & Martial Arts Styles: 2nd Dan Goju-Ryu 2nd Dan Shorin-Ryu 1st Dan TaeKwonDo

- Instructors/Influencers: Liam Jackson

- Birthdate: August 14, 1978

- Birthplace/Growing Up: Pine Bluff, AR/Star City, AR

- Yrs. In the Martial Arts: 15years

- Yrs. Instructing: 6 years

- Instructor

PERSONAL ACHIEVEMENTS

- MBA degree, Southern Arkansas University, 2012

- BBA degree, University of Arkansas at Little Rock, 2011

- AAS degree, Southeast Arkansas College, 2007

MAJOR ACHIEVEMENTS

- 2013 United States Martial Arts Hall of Fame Inductee as Competitor of the Year 2015

- Action Martial Arts Magazine Hall of honors Inductee 2018

- MMASC Karate Tournament Circuit Hall of Fame Inductee 2018

- MMASC King of the Midwest Competed in 81 Karate tournaments across 14 states, as of 09/16/19 3

- USKA World Championships 11 MMASC National Championships 30 Grand Championships, as of 09/16/19

- 140 1st place finishes in karate tournaments, as of 09/16/19

It has placed many great people in my lives across the nation that otherwise would not be in my life. Competition rivals have turned into great friends. Usually handshakes turn into hugs, the more I see someone. I strive to be the guy that quietly accepts first place, but when I do not place first, I want to be the man that cheers the loudest for who placed ahead of me. Respect and class should always be the first qualities of a martial artist. My daddy has told me several times over the years, "be a gentleman, even if it kills you". As a martial artist, I must be a gentleman, I am not at liberty to be anything less. Martial arts is also a cycle. Many great people have paved the way for me. I must carry on what they have done for me and help the next generation on this path.

MARK MYERS

"Respect, Loyalty, and Commitment are words I have lived by since starting Karate."

TRAINING INFORMATION

- Belt Ranks & Martial Arts Styles: Tang Soo Do - 3rd Black, Tae Kwon Do - 1st Black, UFAF - 2nd Black

- Instructors/Influencers: Ed Saenz, Rick Prieto

- Birthdate: February 26, 1965

- Birthplace/Growing Up: Norfolk, VA

- Yrs. In the Martial Arts: 42 years

- Yrs. Instructing: 35 years

- School owner (Ocean Martial Arts), Manager, Instructor

PROFESSIONAL ORGANIZATIONS

- World Head of Family Sokeship Council

- North American Sport Karate Association (NASKA)

- Ohana 8

The year was 1978. When I was growing up, the world was totally different. People had manners and parents actually held their kids accountable for their actions. There were no home video games and children actually played outside, rode bicycles and such.

I used to play with this girl, her name was Jennifer Little (name changed for her privacy). We had been friends since we were five years old. I also played little league baseball. One day while coming home from junior high school, we were getting off the school bus together. Jennifer was mad at me because she wanted me to be her boyfriend and I told her "No" because we are like brother and sister. She did not like that answer and told four boys to get me. Well, they proceeded to beat me up really bad. I was embarrassed and ashamed. I went home, and my dad was mad that the boys had done this. Next thing you know, I had a weight set in the garage. At twelve years old, I was a tall, skinny, and boney kid. I had no confidence or self-esteem.

PERSONAL ACHIEVEMENTS

- Father of Three Great Children: Amber, Breanna and Bryan.
- Grand Father of One: Alyssa
- Received Black Belt in the fall of 1989 - Tae Kwon Do & Tang Soo Do
- Passed my Electrical Apprenticeship in 1998
- Received my 3rd Degree in 2016

MAJOR ACHIEVEMENTS

- Main evented as a pro wrestler in the Norfolk Scope against WWE Legend "Rakeshi"
- 2016 & 2017- No. 2 in the World in Fighting, Forms and Weapons (NASKA)
- 2017- Inducted into the World Head of Family Council Hall of Fame
- 2018- Opened Ocean Martial Arts in Va. Beach
- 2019- Became Forms World Champion at the ITC Chuck Norris World Championships
- 2019- No. 5 in the World - Weapons Competitor (NASKA)
- 2020- Received my 2nd Degree in the United Fighting Arts Federation

I started working out with those weights with the garage door open so that everyone passing the house could see. I lived across from the local Seven Eleven where the boys that jumped me would frequent quite often. I remember telling the boys that one day I was gonna get them back.

The following Saturday came and it was time to go play baseball. When we got to the fields, there was something going on. It was some kind of carnival day at the fields. There were booths, ride attractions, and of course baseball. After my game, my parents and I walked around and there it was. The Chuck Norris Karate booth where you could sign up for free lessons and get a free cool button. My father put my name and my little brother's name in the box. Two days later, the house phone rang. It was the karate school calling to set up our free lessons. My brother was six and I was twelve, we were both so nervous. After three classes, my dad signed us up and I never played baseball ever again. I was hooked like a fish.

I would always lift weights and practice karate at home. Yes, in the driveway so that everyone could see. After a while, I was not so skinny anymore and my karate was getting so much better. I would purposely do jump spinning outside crescent kicks in our front yard knocking pine cones off the tree while those boys would walk to and from the store. . I think in my mind that the boys didn't want any parts of me. In fact some years later, one of them approached me and I started to shake.

Not in fear for what he might do, but instead in fear for what I was going to do. The guy stuck out his hand and said we were wrong and apologized. As a man, I shook his hand. I told him that he had said his piece and to go on about his business. This is my story of why I started karate. I guess this all came about because I told a girl "No".

Martial Arts has impacted my life in so many ways. As a young adult, I learned how to treat people with respect and kindness. I have learned to feel for other people. In other words, how would I feel if I were being picked on or messed with?

Martial arts taught me how to be strong and independent at the time in which my parents passed away. Knowing that I would have to provide for myself or my family. As a father and a husband, my children were raised with the same values that were bestowed upon me by my instructors. I believe that these values have made them the great young adults that they are today.

As a school owner now myself, I am giving back to the new generation. Teaching the basics such as blocks, kicks, punches and stances along with the importance of how to do each one properly with timing and focus. But karate goes far beyond the physical aspect of the art. We must teach life skills everyday such as ethics, courtesy and teamwork. So that the youth of today can grow up to be the leaders of tomorrow. Respect, Loyalty, and Commitment are words I have lived by since starting karate. I hope I have impacted others the way my teachers impacted me.

RONALD PETTIE

"Martial arts have served my life well. I have met and maintained relationships with some of the most amazing people this world offers."

TRAINING INFORMATION

- Belt Ranks & Martial Arts Styles: Tang Soo Do. 1st Degree, Tae Kwon Do. 4th Degree, American Freestyle Hapkido. 4th Degree, U.S. Hapkido. 4th Degree

- Instructors/Influencers: G.M. Dr. Buzz Mingin, Master Kenneth Hill, GM David Brodecki

- Birthdate: October 22, 1975

- Birthplace/Growing Up: Philadelphia, PA/NJ

- Yrs. In the Martial Arts: 30 years

- Yrs. Instructing: 14 years

- Instructor

PROFESSIONAL ORGANIZATIONS

- World Karate Union HOF Inductee

- World Hapkido Alliance Inc

- American Freestyle Hapkido HQ Instructor

I was first drawn to martial arts for the physical outlet after going through some tough times. I quickly discovered that there was so much more than just the physical. The arts became a pillar of my life and crucial in my drive to help others. The more I could learn, the more I could teach. I could work with those in need and those who simply wanted to learn, as I did. I sought out training in various martial arts from around the world in order to research the roots of this tradition. These experiences in Japan, Thailand, and Brazil helped shape my style and my character. The lessons from these masters, teachers, and certainly my students will carry me in life.

PERSONAL ACHIEVEMENTS

- Trained Karate in Japan
- Trained Caporeira and BJJ in brazil
- Trained Muay Thai in Thailand

MAJOR ACHIEVEMENTS

- 2006 Instructor Award NAFMA
- 2011 certificate of Distinction from Rising Dragon Wushu
- 2012 World Karate Union HOF Hapkido Master of the Year

Martial arts have served my life well. I have met and maintained relationships with some of the most amazing people this world offers. Some were masters of small, quiet systems passed down through small close-knit groups, while others ran training camps or martial conferences. Each of them brought me into their world to share their knowledge, traditions and allowed me to be part of their martial family.

With both of my parents being deceased by the time I was 20 years old, I never thought that I would have been able to travel the world to study martial arts. With study, focus, and discipline, so many dreams I thought would have passed me by were realized. Martial Arts stands as a crucial pillar in my life.

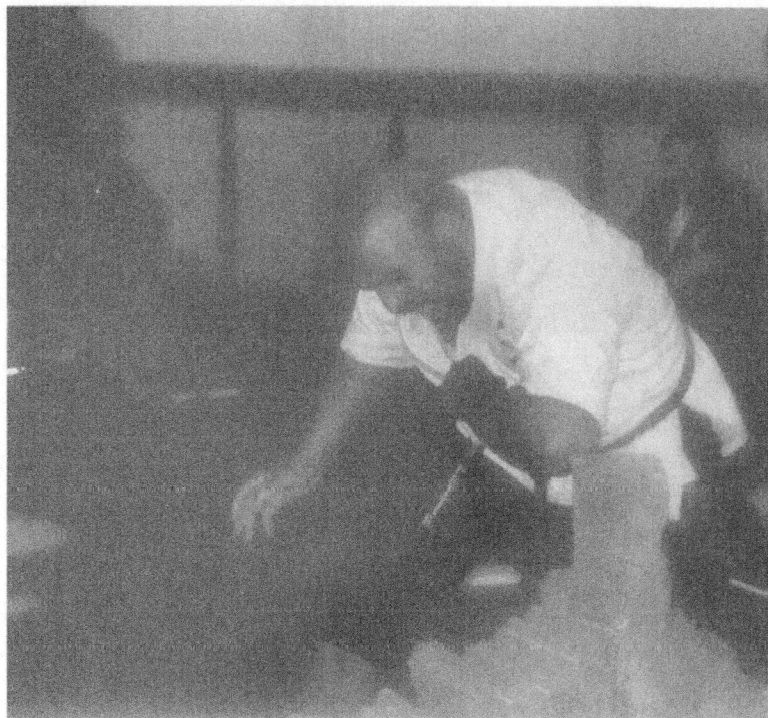

ELAINE YAMANO

"I've been able to deal with life much better than if I weren't in the Martial Arts."

TRAINING INFORMATION

- Belt Ranks & Martial Arts Styles: Isshin-ryu Karate, Yondan (4th Degree Black Belt)

- Instructors/Influencers: Sensei Joe Pagliuso

- Birthdate: February 8, 1960

- Birthplace/Growing Up: Corona & Riverside, CA

- Yrs. In the Martial Arts: 27 years

- Yrs. Instructing: 27 years

- School owner (Yamano's Shorin-Ryu Karate), Manager, Instructor

PROFESSIONAL ORGANIZATIONS

- United States Karate Organization
- Sons of the Pacific

Believe it or not, I got into the arts because of a man. He was into karate, a brown belt at the time, and we started dating. I wanted to take an interest in what he was passionate about, went up in the ranks loving the art and what it represents. I learned quite a bit about people and myself on how weak-minded we all are. As we grow, we can choose to stay on a path that is damaging to others and yourself or flourish, gaining knowledge in areas you never dreamed of.

I started karate around 1993. Because I was in the dojo every day, I made sure that I worked hard to be the best that I could be. I received my Shodan-1st Dan about 1996-1997 and I haven't stopped yet. I'm teaching karate and working full-time, so that leaves me little time to train for myself. But I've come to a point where I love to teach what I have learned and hope that my students will get what I have in life.

Martial Arts has taught me to to be calm in situations that the average person would get angry or enraged. I've been able to deal with life much better than if I weren't in the arts. And I have met some incredible people whom I can call "Ohana."

PERSONAL ACHIEVEMENTS

- Many 1st place titles in various tournaments, Female Competitor of the Year, Martial Arts Hall of Fame-twice, Own my own dojo, brought up several students to black belt, gained dear friends through the tournament circuit, learned how to detect individuals that claim they've trained w/a specific Grand Master/Sensei/Sifu. But I try to stay away from negativity. Life is too short to be around people that feels that a "title" deserves all this respect and acknowledgement. I believe that most people that have earned their black belts in the proper manner, deserve respect but it all boils down to: We are all equal and should respect all.

MAJOR ACHIEVEMENTS

- The most important achievement that I have and still am accomplishing is being a good person, a wonderful parent and grandparent.

ARSENIY ZHUKOV

"Not only as an instructor, but also as a student, you get a sense of joy coming to class..."

TRAINING INFORMATION

- Belt Ranks & Martial Arts Styles: 1st Degree Black Belt

- Instructors/Influencers: Sifu Anthony Arnett, Sifu Kevin Alford, Sifu Isaac Davis

- Birthdate: July 24, 1996

- Birthplace/Growing Up: Ukraine, Odessa / Jacksonville, Florida

- Yrs. In the Martial Arts: 10 years

- Yrs. Instructing: 3 years

- Instructor

PROFESSIONAL ORGANIZATIONS

- The Global Traditional Wing Chun Kung Fu Association

Sifu Arsen Zhukov began his martial arts journey at a young age, learning boxing with a close family friend. What started as a simple means of self-defense would later cultivate a new lifestyle.

Sifu Arsen stopped training in his youth, then in his teenage years, joined Arnett Sports Kung Fu Academy. Originally, Sifu Arsen only joined to learn the history behind the art and had no real vision of what this decision would entail. In the first couple of months, Sifu Arsen stuck to his original path to learning Wing Chun, but he would soon begin to get engulfed in the school's energetic pathway to sparring and training. Sifu Arsen started to train privately with GrandMaster Anthony Arnett, where he put his focus on continuing to learn the art but also training as a fighter.

Throughout the following years, Sifu Arsen competed in various martial arts circuits, participated in seminars, and became an instructor. Sifu Arsen dedicates his success to his martial arts instructors. Under Grandmaster Anthony Arnett, Sifu Arsen got a chance to push past his

PERSONAL ACHIEVEMENTS

- Democracy, Stability Are Threatened in Honduras, April 19, 2017, The Florida Times Union
- Showcase of Osprey Advancements in Research and Scholarship - University of North Florida, Jacksonville, FL International Studies
- Mixed Martial Arts Versus The Medical World: Mixed Martial Arts has rapidly grown as a contact sport and gained scrutiny from medical associations around the globe, petitioning for its ban due to the dangers the sport held and lack of safety. My argument is against the MMA being banned for its dangers and risk to the competitors.
- University of North Florida, Jacksonville, Fl
- Bachelors in Arts - Political Science
- Bachelors in Arts - International Studies
- Minor in Public Administration

MAJOR ACHIEVEMENTS

2017

- National Karate & Kung-Fu Union - U.S. - N.K.K.U, Savannah, GA: 1st Place Under belt Division Weapons, 3rd Place Under belt Division Forms, 4th Place Under belt Division Sparring
- Gainesville Challenge, Gainesville FL: 2nd Place Under belt Division Weapons, 2nd Place Under belt Division Forms, 3rd Place Under belt Division Sparring

limits, explore new approaches, and channel a new passion he had not yet discovered. Sifu Arsen remembers his first tournament with Grandmaster Arnett The thrill of the moment and the exchange of movements were beyond captivating. It was at that point that Sifu Arsen knew he wanted to become an instructor and pass on the knowledge which had been passed onto him. Sifu Arsen trained continuously with Grandmaster Arnett until 2018, when he was sent to another Kung Fu school in order to broaden his horizons, assisting him as an instructor. From 2018 to 2019, Sifu Arsen trained under Sifu Kevin Alford, where he got to train in Sanda and full contact fighting.

After completing his time with Sifu Kevin Alford, Sifu Arsen returned to training as an instructor with Grandmaster Arnett, who mentors him to this day. Sifu Arsen also continued his full contact training with Sifu Isaac Davis, who is currently preparing him for full contact. Sifu Isaac, who practices Wing Chun, among other styles, provides an equal balance of Wing Chun and boxing. Sifu Arsen combines his styles and different training methods to create a unique training program for his students, showcasing a part of each instructor in every class. Sifu Arsen currently teaches as an instructor part-time and continues his education as a student. In Sifu Arsen Zhukov's own perspective, "You have 1440 Minutes in a day, and every minute you spend thinking of what you want to do is every minute you waste not doing it." Make the most out of your day. You are in charge of your ambitions, and the only one who will get in your way is yourself. Step to the right and keep moving forward.

MAJOR ACHIEVEMENTS

2018

- BLITZ Martial Arts Tour, Orlando, FL: 1st Place Black Belt Division Forms, 1st Place Black Belt Division Weapons, 1st Place Black Belt Division Continuous Sparring, 3rd Place Black Belt Division Point Sparring

- International Chinese Martial Arts Championship, Orlando, FL: 2nd Place Advanced Division Forms, 2nd Place Advanced Division Weapons, 2nd Place Advanced Division Continuous Sparring

- National Karate & Kung-Fu Union - U.S. - N.K.K.U, Savannah, GA: 1st Place Black Belt Division Forms, 2nd Place Black Belt Division Sparring, 3rd Place Black Belt Division Weapons

- Legacy Kung Fu Tournament and Interactive Health Expo, Coral Springs, FL: 1st Place Advanced Division Weapons, 1st Place Advanced Division Sparring, 3rd Place Advanced Division Forms

2019

- National Karate & Kung-Fu Union - U.S. - N.K.K.U, Savannah, GA: 1st Place Black Belt Division Forms, 2nd Place Black Belt Division Weapons, 1st Place Black Belt Division Sparring, Runner Up for Grand-Champion Black Belt Division Sparring

Sifu Arsen Zhukov owes a lot to his martial arts styles and instructors. What was originally a hobby, quickly became a lifestyle. Learning under his instructors, Sifu Arsen Zhukov was able to cultivate values that he now passes along to his students. Sifu Arsen instills his students with a willingness to change their lives. Most or all who walk through the school's doors come with little to no experience but wish to be a part of something more than just a gym. Each student comes in with a mindset focused on gaining more discipline, getting into shape, eating healthy, and, most importantly, being able to protect oneself in a high-risk situation. Sifu Arsen Zhukov structures his classes by combining boxer workouts with traditional Wing Chun to provide a balanced class for the body and mind. While the classes are physically intense, each class has a portion dedicated to situational awareness and exercising the mind's ability to recognize different situations. In today's technological era, more and more people are less focused on their surroundings than what is on their handheld device. By providing situational awareness exercises, students can get a grasp on how truly unaware they are.

Sifu Arsen Zhukov never saw himself as an instructor, nor as someone who would have martial arts so deeply embedded into his lifestyle. Not only as an instructor, but also as a student, you get a sense of joy coming to class, practicing an art you love, interacting with your fellow brothers, and seeing them progress alongside you. Since he began training, Sifu Arsen Zhukov has been an advocate for Martial Arts competitions, in particular, sparring. So many practitioners reach high ranks in their respective style without ever testing the practicality of what they are practicing or have minimal experience doing so. Furthermore, people who do spar only spar against their respective styles and do not get to experience sparring with other styles and seeing how they can apply what they have learned against a style they have never fought. By going to competitions, Sifu Arsen got to experience and learn from other styles and build up his arsenal with techniques foreign to his own. These days, Sifu Arsen Zhukov continues teaching and actively competing in various martial arts circuits. Sifu Arsen plans to open up his own studio to continue the growth of his students, as well as his own growth.

THE AMERICAN MARTIAL ARTS ALLIANCE

MARTIAL ARTS
MASTERS & PIONEERS

HALL OF HONORS

Honor Roll

MARTIAL ARTS MASTERS & PIONEERS

Abisu Nanji	Don DeVries	Jose Dimacali	Peter Porter
Adrian Turpin	Donald Plummer	Joseph Gutowski	Rahni "Nikki" Jenkins
AJ Perry	Donald W. Barlow	Joseph Preira	Ralph Hernandez
Al Dacascos	Dongju Lee	Josh Allen	Rebecca Novak
Alex Zwak	Donna Cancila Keating	Juan Harnett	Richard Jenkins
Alfie Lewis	Dr. Len Brassard	Justin McDaniel	Richard Mcclain
Amy Hawkins	Dr. Mark McCumber	Karen Ware	Richard Morris
Andrea McKey	Dr. William A. Rankin, PhD.	Keith Elkins	Richard Norton
Andrew Linick	Dwight Romeo Cross	Keith Graham	Riley Hawkins
Anthony Letourneu	Eddie Thomas	Keith Rosary	Rita Hundley Harris
Anthony Lingo	Eric Caldeira	Keith Zielke	Robert "Teddy" Jordan
Anthony Linson	Erik Harris	Kevin Schultz	Robert Leclerc
Apolo Ladra	Francis Pineda	Khalid Raheem	Robert Maxwell
Arnold "Zip" White	Freddie Relevante	Kirby Roy III	Rod Hillegass
Barbara Duffy	George Reynolds	Krishna Balal	Ron Jenkins
Barry A. Broughton	Glen Murray	Kurt Shyrock	Ron Lee
Bernard Kerik	Glenn Keeney	Len Brassard	Ruben Rodriguez
Bill Viola	Greg Macy	LiL John Smith	Rudy Timmerman
Bob Leiker	Gregory Duncan	Lloyd Thompson	Russell Willey
Bob Martin	Guy James	Louis Markstrom	Rusty Burke
Bryan Otto	Harold Evans	M. Karim Ratcliff	Samuel Scott
Bryant Harrell	Harry Lawson	Mark Glazier	Scott Hartsell
C. Matthew White	Herbert Thompson	Mark Johnson	Scott Yingling
Carl Piper	Huda Saffar Smith	Maurice Elmalem	Sean Smith
Carmichael Simon	Hung Cao	Michael DePasquale, Jr.	Sergio Von Schmeling
Charles "Buddy" Watson	Ishmael Robles	Michael Matsuda	Shar Stephens Courtney
Charlie Anderson	Jack Ballard	Michele Kennedy	Shawn Doyle
Christopher Hovey	Jack Shamburger	Mike O'Brien	Sherri Arthur
CJ Mayo	James O Cannon	Mike Shintaku	Stacy Burke
Clarence Smith	James Robinson	Mike Stone	Stanley Tippings Sr.
Constance Funderburk	James Theros	Mitchell Bobrow	Steve Magill
Dan Hausel	Jarrett Leiker	Morris Pollio	Tayari Casel
Dana Stamos	Jason Sterling	Mwanzo Mwalimu Umeme Mpingo	Terri Smith
Dane S. Harden	Jay Bell	Nada Conway	Thomas Cleary
Daniel Jolly	Jean Phoenix Le Grand	Neil Ripski	Thomas Wright
Daniel Nyce	Jeff Thompson	Odette Russell	Tim Henton
Danny Boccagno	Jefferson Davis	Otis Hooper	Tye Botting
Danny Lane	Jens Finck	Paka Khan	Ujjwal Thakuri
Darius Ross	Jerome Johnson	Pat E. Johnson	Victor Theriault
Darren Smith	Jerry Fontanez	Patrick Matthews	Walt Sapronov
David Nyce	Jim Thomas	Patrick Wrenn	Walter Anderson
Dean Conway	John Bussard	Paul Calligan	Warren McKay
Dean Pyles	John Crudup	Paul Dyer	Wesley C. Jenkins
Dennis Brewer	John Smith, Jr.	Paul Prendergast	William Roy
Dennis Warren	Johnny K. Thompson		William Shelton

Printed in Great Britain
by Amazon

41742582R00328